D1636316

LENIN:
THE COMPULSIVE REVOLUTIONARY

"For they filled the endarkened places
of the earth with habitations of cruelty."

(Psalms, 74:20)

LENIN:
THE COMPULSIVE REVOLUTIONARY

by Stefan T. Possony

HENRY REGNERY COMPANY
CHICAGO

THE HOOVER INSTITUTION SERIES

Copyright © Henry Regnery Company, 1964
Manufactured in the United States of America
Library of Congress Catalog Card No. 64-12887

to the memory of

MICHAEL GOLBINDER

and

ERNST POSSONY

PREFACE

The reign of Lenin, the first revolutionary tsar of Russia, lasted from November, 1917, to January, 1924. During these seventy-five months he was incapacitated for almost twenty of them, and he operated at reduced efficiency for about ten more. In all, his effective rule lasted less than four years; yet in this short span of time he influenced the course of world history more profoundly than any other ruler of the twentieth century.

Lenin was a thinker, a political boss and a strategist. As a thinker, he combined Marx with the Russian revolutionary tradition and integrated the new amalgam with Machiavelli and Clausewitz. As a political boss, Lenin invented new political techniques and organizations and put in motion a world-wide totalitarian movement. As a strategist, he introduced novel combinations of violent and non-violent combat, conquered a great empire, and conceived the multi-dimensional war of the modern age.

Lenin started communism—or Russia—on the road to world domination. He begot the victories which Stalin, his successor, won twenty years after his death. By way of historical parallel, Lenin may well be compared to Philip of Macedon, who prepared for the victories of Alexander the Great; but Lenin's role also resembled that of Aristotle, who functioned as Alexander's intellectual guide.

The great world struggle between freedom and totalitarianism which Lenin initiated has lasted for more than four decades. Presumably it will continue for several more generations, and it may terminate in nuclear war. The outcome of the conflict which Lenin bequeathed to mankind will probably for several centuries determine the fate of the human race.

The type of man Lenin was, the intellectual contributions he made, and the causes of his success are still difficult to ascertain four decades after his death. Many details of his life have remained undisclosed and there is little information available about his family background. The propagandists of Moscow are still drawing the curtain of prudishness over his emotional life. Not all of his writings, and only few of his letters, have been published, and much of this output has undergone considerable "editing."

Lenin's court biographers affect the style of Scheherazade or Carlylian hero-worshippers, and his opponents labor the devil theory of history. But saint or devil, Lenin was a man of remarkable intellect and strong will. His thinking was ideological and dogmatic, but his actions were pragmatic and effective. His roots were in nineteenth century Russia, but his immense urge to act for the sake of action was typical of the rootless and irrational Europe of the twentieth century. As a leader of men he intended to emulate Chernishevsky's "new man": "like theine in tea, like the bouquet in fine wine . . . the prime source of energy. . . the salt of the salt of the earth." He dreamt of a new life and, like Nietzsche, he saw himself as the redeemer of mankind. Lenin flew high but, unfortunately, in the wrong direction.

During the last months of his consciousness Lenin surveyed his life, and he recognized that destruction had been his outstanding achievement. Tsarism and capitalism were gone. He regretted nothing, but he knew that his constructive efforts had failed: the socialism of his dreams had not yet materialized. Physically paralyzed but still lucid, he clung to the belief that socialism was inevitable.

Lenin died a keenly disappointed man. At the moment of his death, true to the Hegelian scheme, the negation, which had been his revolution, was itself negated by counter-revolution. He was spared of learning that this counter-revolution was carried out in his name—with the tools he had fashioned, and for the purposes of that totalitarianism which (as in the fable of the sorcerer's apprentice) he had intended to invoke as a means, but found them to have become an end in themselves.

Lenin's life had been devoted to practicing the maxims of expediency. His failure proved the incompatibility of immoral methods with "noble" results. Lenin's heirs were faithful to the means, lost sight of original purposes, and ended by worshipping dictatorship for its own sake. The pattern of history was repeated once again. It is a pity that Lenin never studied the dialectics of ethics and political morality. If he had done so, this born leader might have prodded mankind forward on the road to progress.

Acknowledgements

My thanks go to the National Archives and the Army Library, Washington, D.C.; the Library of the British Foreign Office and the Public Records Office, London; Oesterreichichisches Haus-, Hof- und Staatsarchiv, Vienna; Schweizerisches Sozialarchiv, Zuerich; Internationaal Instituut voor sociale Geschiedenis, Amsterdam; War Documents Section, Defense Agency, Tokyo; the Danish Embassy, Washington D.C., for allowing use of their materials; to Albert P. Hinckley, Washington, D.C. who made it possible for me to start the project; to the Editors of *Life-Time-Fortune* who supported my early researches in connection with the series of articles which Alan Moorehead wrote on the fortieth anniversary of the Russian revolution; to the Foreign Policy Research Institute, University of Pennsylvania, and its directors, Robert Strausz-Hupé and William R. Kintner, who enabled me to carry on; to my patient friends and *quondam* assistants, Julius Epstein, now at Hoover; Helga Grebing, Munich; Ruth Harman, London; Stephen H. Johnsson, formerly of Washington, D.C., now at Hoover; Ernst Kux, Zuerich; Herma Landau, London; Hiroshi Sano, Tokyo; and Edward E. Smith, Palo Alto, California; and to the members of the Hoover Institution, Xenia J. Eudin, Irene Hoggan, Karol Maichel, Agnes F. Peterson, Tamotsu Takase, and Marina Tinkoff.

My special thanks go to Franz G. Lassner, formerly of Washington, D.C., now at the Hoover Institution, for his enormous help in research and reproduction logistics, for his unearthing of valuable German documents and especially for ferreting out the ways of using the enormous collection of German Foreign Office microfilms to best advantage.

I owe a particular obligation to my various girls-Friday who were struggling valiantly, and through endless hours, against my bad handwriting, and who feared, as I did, that the rewriting would never end—Florence S. McCall, Shirley Musselman, Eva Ermeler, Roberta

ix

M. Nasra, and especially Sylviane Lunn, without whose organizational talent and limitless patience the assembly line would have broken down.

I benefitted from the good counsel of such experts as Isaac Don Levine, Richard Wraga, Wlodzimierz Baczkowski and Wolfgang Leonhard, and from the pioneering labors of my predecessors, David Shub and Bertram D. Wolfe, as well as Leonard B. Schapiro.

The sound advice of Professor Witold S. Sworakowski, Assistant Director of the Hoover Institution, and his profound knowledge of the Institution's enormous holdings, enabled me to take full advantage of the untold and unique treasures painstakingly collected in the Hoover Tower.

The generosity and forbearance of W. Glenn Campbell, the vigorous Director of the Hoover Institution, made it possible for me to complete this arduous task. Dr. Campbell not only provided me with ample administrative support but also had the wisdom to listen knowingly and smilingly to about twelve monthly reports announcing that the manuscript was "about ready."

I want to thank Jameson G. Campaigne, Jr., my dependable and skillful editor, and Henry Regnery, my cooperative publisher, to whom I also owe gratitude for the success of a previous book.

Regina Possony, my chief linguist, principal assistant, and loving wife, shared with me the main burdens of research. Without her skill in reading handwritten documents in various languages, her persistence in wading through reams of barely digestible Communist memoirs, her psychological feel for the personality types that appear in this story, and her overall stimulation and intuition, I would have missed many important facts and insights into human relationships.

Five bookkeeping items: I transliterated toward accuracy, simplicity and custom. Documents are identified by collection and date. Unless otherwise indicated, all dates are in the Western calendar. Persons are called by their best known appellations, e.g., V. I. Ulyanov is referred to as Lenin, and his wife appears under her maiden name of Krupskaya. Gorki, the site of Lenin's retreat and death, is spelled with an "i" throughout; this spelling is meant to differentiate it from the name Gorky.

Stefan T. Possony

Stanford, Calif.

January 1, 1964

TABLE OF CONTENTS

INTRODUCTION

Lenin once predicted his own fate when he noted that great revolutionaries, after their death, are often transformed into "harmless icons." The "sanctification" of Lenin's name, which Stalin instituted for personal political reasons, was carried to such extremes that it disgusted even Lenin's widow. "To invent what did not take place, what in no way corresponds to reality, to put into Ilyich's mouth words he never uttered . . . is inadmissible," she once complained.[1] But it was only in the dusk of her life, when most of the followers of Lenin had been eliminated, that she dimly sensed that genuine Communists, like other human beings, are better served by historical truth than by fraud.

The historian dedicated to reconstructing the lives of persons and the course of events as they really were must pierce through many layers of *beatific* fables; in some cases, he also must fight political distortion and outright falsification.

The task is rendered triply difficult in the presentation of Lenin's life. First, Stalin deliberately and skillfully fashioned a legend about Lenin which he used for thirty years to manipulate and purge certain pieces of evidence. Secondly, many of Lenin's operations were of an ultra-secret and conspiratorial nature. Even if documentary traces were left in existence, which is not always the case, the Soviet government has not been anxious to release this sort of data. In fact, it has often employed deception to disorient research. Thirdly, during the past five years or so, some useful biographical information has been trickling out of the Soviet Union, but it has become apparent that the documentation at Moscow is by no means complete. There remain surprising gaps, on both the very early and the later years of Lenin's

[1] N. K. Krupskaya, April, 1937, about a film script on Lenin. *Istoricheskii Arkhiv,* (1958), No. 4, p. 73.

life.[2] It is only since the Twentieth Party Congress in 1956 that the Party has reconsidered (to a limited extent) the value of historiography. The long neglect of historical research still causes the Party historians themselves to not always be certain of their basic information on events, personalities, and dates. Such neglect has been disclosed in some reasonably frank discussions in Russian journals.[3]

The great movement to "debunk" a history of kings and statesmen, empires and nations, capitalism, democracy and freedom—a necessary and useful movement which owes much to the crusading spirit of idealists eager to build a "classless society"—has stopped short of delving into many of the disturbing facets of revolutionary history. Naturally, historical materials can be woven into fairy tales to be told to children and naive believers. The stories concern the dignified bearded socialists who advocated and initiated revolution because they were inveterate seekers of justice and truth; those who, out of sheer altruism, sought to save mankind from the dire tragedies of inequality and conflict; those who acted as the legitimate leaders of morally pure masses because they alone understood the laws of social development; those who were honest and humane, but also hard and forceful—these are the tales "full of sound and fury, but signifying nothing."

A mystical or chiliastic movement must have its heroes, legends, apostles, saints, and even gods, but if the modern world is to evaluate seriously such a movement's worth, its epoch desperately needs solid historical information. What mistakes were committed? How and why? Where did judgments go astray? Were the best leaders selected? Was the selection procedure an appropriate one? Did the theory stand the test of reality? Has the validity of the objective been confirmed?

For obvious reasons, the Communists, almost from the inception of their rule, terminated serious work on their own history. Its transformation into myth may have pleased Vilfredo Pareto and Georges Sorel, the intellectual ancestors of fascism, but Marx would have regarded Soviet political mythology as a dangerous "opiate for the people." Lacking the vigor of truth, the Communist creed has stagnated and degenerated into an apologia for the personal power of a bureaucratic tyranny. But there are signs that the more responsible and ideologically honest Party leaders are beginning to realize that they can no longer rely on fiction if they are to be effective in their future decisions.

I suspect, therefore, that though this book will be greeted with hisses and howls, the Communists actually will study it with great care.

[2]It would seem as though not even all *Russian* archives have been searched thoroughly for documents related to Lenin, his family, and friends. See *Istoricheskii Arkhiv* (1958), No. 3, p. 230.

[3]See, for example, M. V. Fofanova, "Posledneye podpolye. V. I. Lenina," *Istoricheskii Arkhir*, No. 4, Moscow, July-August 1956, pp. 166-172.

(This has been the fate of some of my previous writings.) But many non-Communist utopians will instinctively be critical of my iconoclastic interpretations: even the repeated discovery that the most loudly self-proclaimed promoters of terrestrial paradise were, in reality, power-politicians, elitists, cynics, haters, cheats, liars and murderers may be experienced as a great emotional shock. As Shakespeare put it, "Lilies that fester smell far worse than weeds."

Some readers will accurately observe that Lenin's behavior pattern was not basically different from that of innumerable political precedents. An argument dealing with whether his actions were somewhat worse or somewhat better than the performance of other power practioners is quite futile. The point is that, intellectually, Lenin was a counterpart of Cesare Borgia—not of Moses, Buddha, Mohammed, or Jesus. Lenin was more successful and far less ephemeral than Borgia because his political acumen was greater; because his know-how exceeded that expostulated by Niccolò Machiavelli on the basis of Borgia's model operations; and because the spectrum of resources and techniques at his disposal was far broader than that available to the Renaissance prince. But Lenin's bones were the bones of a conqueror and his flesh the flesh of a voluptuary of power.

The sociologist Karl Mannheim once asked, "Who is going to plan the planners?" Not wishing to disprove the feasibility of a dream society, Mannheim left his own question unanswered. Lenin's life suggests that those who pursue the shadows of utopia are forced far deeper into Machiavellianism than politicians who aim modestly at improving society by patchwork or by overcoming specific defects and crises. Biography, according to Disraeli, is "life without theory": it shows man as what he is, namely, a human hobbled with disabilities. Lenin's biography convincingly refutes the notion that utopia is feasible without the existence of supermen. Lenin himself realized in the end that the perfect society—which, incidentally, he was unable to visualize with any clarity—cannot be constructed, even by the most ruthless of mortals.

I do not feel that I have done any disservice to Lenin. The dexterity of his strategy, the skill and flexibility of his tactics, the virtuosity in his orchestration of simultaneous complex operations, the expertness of his conspiracy, the impact of his leadership, his endurance against adversity, the acuity of his intellect, and the tragedy in his downfall—all appear in bold relief. His immorality and even criminality are starkly etched, but so is his political genius. For me, the Lenin portrayed in this book is an impressive and formidable opponent. Moreover, irrespective of whether Lenin is regarded as a savior or a scourge, his was a unique life. Enthusiasts and detractors alike will benefit from a fuller insight into the real man. The true drama of his life serves his memory better than the self-serving manipulations of his alleged followers; and perhaps the time has come to save him from adulation as well as from incomprehension. As Carlyle said of Sir Walter Scott, "When he departed, he took a man's life along with him."

The holdings of the German, Austrian, and, to a far lesser extent, Japanese foreign offices, combined with the vast resources of the Hoover Institution (including the Paris branch's invaluable archive of the Tsar's political police) and the more detailed data recently published in the Soviet Union, have enabled me to construct a more complete and a more fully documented story than was heretofore possible. Yet I have not the delusion that all of my interpretations and reconstructions will stand the test of time. I have used the available evidence as massively as I could and interpreted it on the basis of logic, as well as knowledge of, and experience in, revolutionary operations. The full opening of Russian archives and the discovery of new significant documentation within the free world undoubtedly will necessitate corrections, and critics will not fail to suggest alternate interpretations. The leftist ideologue will resent my realism and lack of reverence. The rightist partisan will deplore the demise of many clichés and simplifications. Pierre Bayle was correct when he said, *"La perfection d'une histoire est d'être desagréable à toutes les sectes."* In this spirit, I am planning, hopefully, to take emotional reactions in my stride.

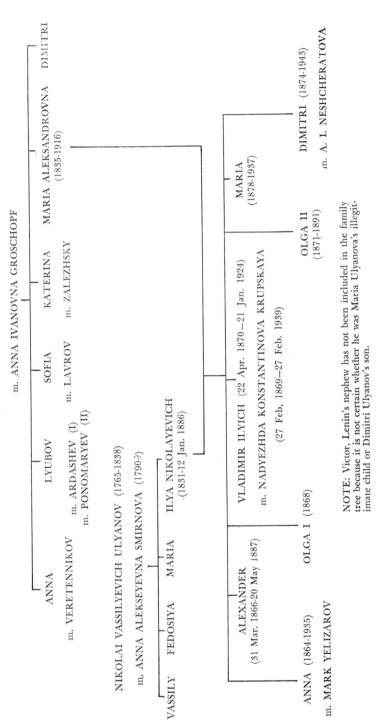

ALEXANDER DIMITREVICH BLANK (1802-1873)

m. ANNA IVANOVNA GROSCHOPF

ANNA
m. VERETENNIKOV

LYUBOV
m. ARDASHEV (I)
m. PONOMARYEV (II)

SOFIA
m. LAVROV

KATERINA
m. ZALEZHSKY

MARIA ALEKSANDROVNA
(1835-1916)

DIMITRI

NIKOLAI VASSILYEVICH ULYANOV (1765-1838)

m. ANNA ALEKSEYEVNA SMIRNOVA (1790-?)

VASSILY   FEDOSIYA   MARIA

ILYA NIKOLAYEVICH
(1831-12 Jan. 1886)

VLADIMIR ILYICH (22 Apr. 1870—21 Jan. 1924)
m. NADYEZHDA KONSTANTINOVA KRUPSKAYA
(27 Feb. 1869—27 Feb. 1939)

MARIA
(1878-1937)

ALEXANDER
(31 Mar. 1866-20 May 1887)

OLGA I (1868)

OLGA II
(1871-1891)

DIMITRI (1874-1943)
m. A. I. NESHCHERATOVA

ANNA (1864-1935)
m. MARK YELIZAROV

NOTE: Victor, Lenin's nephew has not been included in the family tree because it is not certain whether he was Maria Ulyanova's illegitimate child or Dimitri Ulyanov's son.

LENIN:

THE COMPULSIVE REVOLUTIONARY

Family Background

Lenin's real name was Vladimir Ilyich Ulyanov. He was born on April 22, 1870, at Simbirsk, a small, sleepy town on the Volga river, now named Ulyanovsk in his honor. His father, Ilya Nikolayevich Ulyanov (1831-1886), a graduate of Kazan University, climbed the bureaucratic ladder steadily and diligently. Ilya began his career, in 1855, teaching mathematics and physics at the Institute of Nobility in Pensa. In addition to his teaching job, he served as a meteorologist, having been appointed to both positions by the celebrated mathematician N. I. Lobachevsky.[1] It is said that some of Ilya's observations were published in a French scientific publication. Between 1863 and 1869 he taught at the gymnasium in Nizhni-Novgorod. After a period as regional school inspector in Simbirsk (1869-1874), Ilya was promoted to the position of director of schools in Simbirsk *gubernia*. He thus reached the upper ranks of the medium civil service, the promotion being accompanied by a patent of hereditary nobility. After years of modest circumstances Ilya had become well-to-do, and he moved his family into a spacious middle-class house, where the Ulyanovs stayed until after Ilya died of a stroke[2], or more probably a heart attack, in 1886, at the age of 55.

Nikolai Vassilyevich Ulyanov (1765-1838), Lenin's paternal grandfather, began life as a painter. He became a successful self-made merchant, a "capitalist" of sorts in the active trading city of Astrakhan. Records indicate that shortly before his death he acquired a "one-and-

[1]*Istoricheskii Arkhiv* (1958), No. 2, p. 31ff.

[2]This is Anna Ulyanova's version, "Souvenirs sur Ilitch," *Lénine tel qu'il fut, Souvenirs de Contemporains*, Vol. I, Moscow, Editions en Langues Etrangères, 1958, p. 13.

a-half story house."[3] Very little is known about his wife, Anna Alekseyevna Smirnova (1790-?), except that she was of Kalmyk ancestry
and twenty-five years younger than her husband. At the age of sixty-six,
Nikolai fathered his second son, Ilya. There were two older sisters,
Fedosiya and Maria, and the eldest child, Vassily. Maria married a
certain Gorshov, a middle-class merchant.

After his father's death, Ilya was brought up by his brother, Vassily, who is generally believed to have been very poor, although it is
said that he gave money to Ilya on two occasions: during the first
months of Ilya's marriage and shortly before his, Vissily's, death in
1878. It is also reported that a priest helped the family after old
Ulyanov's death. Whether or not the priest was a relative—or even if
the family was religious—is open to speculation.

Ilya knew nothing about the history of his family, and remembered
his father only vaguely. The family name was uncertain and was
listed variously as "Ulyaninov" or "Ulyanin." Ilya adopted "Ulyanov."
Despite his alleged plebeian background, Ilya was educated in a school
for children of officials and aristocrats. (Soviet historiography has per-
sistently endeavored to prove Lenin's proletarian origin.) Whatever
his background, Actual State Councillor His Excellency Ilya Nikolayevich Ulyanov was not an opponent of tsarism. His daughter Anna, in
fact, stated bluntly: "Father never was a revolutionary."[4] Ilya never
made any utterances regarding "social ideals," certainly not in the
presence of his children and pupils. He had grown up under Nikolai
I, and the regime of Alexander II, especially at its beginning, appeared to him to be an enlightened era. The assassination of Alexander II upset and saddened him, for he strongly disapproved of terrorism.

Communist historians suggest that Ilya was a revolutionary, running a sort of party headquarters in his home, where his two sons made
fiery speeches. This hardly concurs with his function as inspector and
regional school director. The schools, were run by the Zemstvos, local
and often liberal self-governing organs, and the Ministry of Education saw to it that the schools were kept in line. As one of the Ministry's field officers, Ulyanov checked to determine that the instructors
were not teaching in a manner contrary to the Tsar's desires. Persons
whose opinions were suspect hardly became prominent in the in-
spectorate of the Tsar's educational bureaucracy.

There exists no record of Ilya ever protecting students accused of
radical activities. He seemed to have been religious, and he reported
to his superiors village priests who lacked zeal in catechism instruc-

---

[3]Many data on Lenin's ancestry are found in *Molodiye Gody V. I. Lenina, po
vospominaniyam sovremennikov i dokumentam*, ed. A. I. Ivansky, (2nd edition;
Moscow: Molodaya Gvardiya, 1958). The reference to the house appears on p. 7f.
[4]*Ibid.*, p. 37.

tion. A firm disciplinarian, he never was questioned on his political beliefs, and was given bonuses and awarded the Order of St. Vladimir. Clearly, though he probably was no zealot, he was a thought-control expert and a faithful servant of the Tsar.

Lenin's mother, Maria Aleksandrovna Blank (1835-1916), was an attractive and cultured lady. Although she did not attend the gymnasium, she was certified as a private tutor at the age of twenty-eight. She proved to be a capable manager of the family under trying conditions, and was a highly devoted mother to all of her children.

Because Maria's mother, Anna Ivanovna Groschopf, died very young, Maria was brought up by her mother's sister, Katarina Ivanovna Essen. According to some sources, Lenin's maternal grandmother was of mixed German-Swedish origin; like Katarina Essen, she presumably used German as her customary tongue. The maternal great-grandmother, Anna Karlovna Oestedt, probably was Swedish; she married a German, most likely a Balt. The brothers of Lenin's maternal grandmother held prominent governmental positions: Karl Ivanovich Groschopf was vice-director of customs in Riga, the owner of a fashionable house in one of the best quarters in St. Petersburg, an accomplished musician, and a collector of violins. The family clearly belonged to the "upper bourgeoisie."

Lenin's maternal grandfather, Alexander Dimitrevich Blank, was born in 1802, allegedly in Odessa and of Ukrainian origin. Blank, of course, is not a Ukrainian name. Since it is known that he spoke Russian poorly and preferred German, the theory of his Ukrainian origin is best discarded. Evidence indicates that Blank was born a Jew, and that he served as a *feldsher* (medical technician) in the army.[5] After he was converted to Christianity, probably to Lutheran protestantism, he was allowed to study medicine at the University of St. Petersburg. Subsequently, he worked as a physician in Smolensk *gubernia;* then for seven years he served as a police physician in the capital. After a one-year vacation, he was appointed chief of department in a hospital financed by Duke Maximilian von Leuchtenberg, a member of the Tsar's family. Later he moved to the Urals and served as hospital inspector in Zlatoust and Perm.

Blank was described as quarrelsome and headstrong. In 1847 he retired to Kokushkino near Kazan where he bought an estate, lived as a country squire, and became a member of the nobility. The purchase of this estate, of course, transformed Blank into the owner of the serfs

[5]David Shub, "Po povodu stati N. Valentinova i pisma v redaktsiyu 'Istorika,'" *Novyi Zhurnal* (New York, 1961), No. 63, pp. 288-291. Shub's article is in answer to N. Valentinov, "O predkakh i yego biografkyakh," *Novyi Zhurnal* (New York, 1960), No. 61, pp. 217-236. *See also:* David Shub, "O predkakh Lenina," *Novoye Russkoye Slovo* (New York, April 23, 1961), p. 3. Valentinov's arguments why Blank could not have been of Jewish origin are entirely unconvincing.

that were attached to his land.6 While in retirement he wrote a
medical book in which he expounded the virtues of a German water-
cure treatment; he was said also to have been interested in diet as a
factor of health.

At Kokushkino, Blank lived with a son, Dimitri, and five daughters—Anna, Lyubov, Sofia, Katerina and Maria. The household was
managed by Katarina Essen, his sister-in-law. Blank died, quite well-
to-do, when he was seventy-one.

Maria, the second youngest, was brought up in the stern German
tradition. Her aunt inculcated discipline, love of work and reading,
and three languages. A quiet and serious-minded girl, she was her
father's favorite.

The Blank girls' family life was not soft, and except for Maria, they
all married at early ages. Anna, the eldest, who was neurasthenic and
as cranky as her father, and who liked to surround herself with artists
and writers, married a man named Veretennikov, a teacher who became a school inspector and a colleague of Ilya Ulyanov. The next
daughter, Lyubov, first married a certain Ardashev by whom she had
nine children. After his death she remarried, this time to a retired person by the name of Ponomaryev. Sofia is known to have married Lavrov, a rich landowner who had a large estate near Stavropol on the
Volga; after her marriage she terminated all communication with her
family. Of Katerina, it is recorded that her husband was a teacher by
the name of Zalezhsky.7

This large family should have presented Lenin with a considerable
number of cousins, but barely anything is known about these relatives.
It seems that, with perhaps one exception, they did not choose to become Communists.

6Valentinov, *op. cit.*, p. 221.
7Valentinov, *op. cit.*, p. 219f.

Parental Courtship

Ilya Ulyanov met Maria Blank at Pensa in 1860 at her sister Anna's
house. Ulyanov was rooming with V. I. Zakharov, a language instructor
at the Institute of Nobility. The two young men were both acquainted
with Maria and were equally drawn to her; the courtship competition
appears to have been a stormy one. Zakharov was a revolutionary who
assigned his pupils articles by Chernishevsky, the foremost radical of
his time, and who taught the young noblemen that aristocrats were
not worthy of being called humans. He maintained that Ulyanov,
because he was too religious and peaceful and worked too much,
would not change the world. Maria apparently was attracted to him,

but when Zakharov was dismissed from the school and left town, she married Ulyanov in 1863. The couple then moved to Nizhni-Novgorod.

Maria soon regretted her choice, for Ilya, who was busy with several jobs including one in the local Institute of Nobility, was rarely at home. He had difficulties with some of his pupils, displayed moodiness, and found himself bored with his wife. Replying to Maria's complaints, sister Anna criticized Ilya's negligence and his lack of interest in "togetherness," but Maria realized that it was the fate of many wives to be lonely. She made an effort to control her nerves and not to cry in bed, because she knew that "if she were to leave him, it would be as though a light would go out in his life." The marriage was on trial, but in 1864, a daughter, Anna, was born.

Nevertheless, Ilya's absences continued to burden his wife. Maria was a number of times jealous without reason and she became ever more irritable and moody. She abandoned music, stayed in bed late, and neglected her household chores. From the time they moved to Novgorod, the Ulyanov couple did not share a bedroom, Ilya sleeping in his study and Maria in the bedroom with her child. Perhaps Maria found her husband repulsive to her, for it is reported that when she helped him dress she felt that he was smaller than she was, that she thought him to be weak, and that she greatly disliked the smell of his clothes after his daily work. But she also pitied him: when once she tenderly greeted her returning husband, he perplexedly asked, "What is the matter? You are so nice to me tonight."[1]

Zakharov also was living at Nizhni-Novgorod. Not surprisingly, Maria met him again. Zakharov told her that an "educator" (the position her husband held at the Institute of Nobility) was a spy, obliged to report on his pupils. This upset her so much that she pleaded with Ilya to leave his job. The children, she said, would never trust him. Ilya asked her for the source of this nonsense and she replied, "Zakharov." "Aha, Zakharov," said Ulyanov. Maria mimicked the "Aha," blushed, and walked away. The marriage had reached a point of crisis, but Ilya ignored the outburst and Maria, pregnant again, did not leave him. A deep change, however, had taken place. Henceforth Maria was glad when her husband left the house.

The tense domestic atmosphere affected the baby, who was very restless and fearful. Maria later attributed the blame for her daughter Anna's nervousness on these marital difficulties, but she gradually learned to live her own life.

On March 31, 1866, a son, Alexander, was born. On April 4, while Maria was still convalescing in bed, she was called to the door and informed by a visitor that an unsuccessful attempt had just been made

[1] On many of these details *see* Marietta Schaginjan, *Die Familie Uljanow* (Berlin: Kultur und Fortschritt, 1959).

against the Tsar's life. Horrified, she almost dropped her child in her excitement, for the Tsar, she was told, had been assaulted by the incurably sick D. V. Karakozov and N. A. Ishutin, both former students at Pensa—both pupils of Zakharov. It is not known if Zakharov had sent the messenger, but the pathetic teacher-revolutionary disappeared: he evidently averted arrest through suicide.[2]

No harm came to Ilya, although he, too, had taught the "assassins" and roomed with their mentor. The blame for the attempt was placed on the school system and Count Ilya Tolstoi, a reactionary, was appointed Minister of Education, with orders to dismiss radical teachers. It was during Tolstoi's ministry that Ilya Ulyanov's career blossomed.

[2]The plot was supported by nobles from Pensa, including P. D. Yermolov, who financed the operation.

The Siblings

Lenin is usually described as the third child. This is not accurate, for after Anna and Alexander, there was a baby girl, Olga, who must have been born defective or sick. Almost immediately after her birth it was believed that she would not live long, and she died after a few months, late in 1868. The mother was heartbroken. But Ilya had additional troubles. He lacked energy and felt tired: at thirty-six or thirty-seven, his brain no longer "was supplied with blood," and his teachings had become dull.[1] He sent his wife and the two children to visit his family in Astrakhan, and in their absence he recovered. When Maria returned to Nizhni-Novgorod, the two "found each other in a real sense." Ilya was appointed inspector of public schools at Simbirsk (1869) and on April 22, 1870, Maria gave birth to her fourth child, a boy, who in the orthodox and tsarist tradition was christened Vladimir—literally translated: "Rule the world."

In 1871, another girl, again named Olga, was born, but she lived only to twenty years of age. Dimitri (1874-1943) was the next born. After some desultory political activity, he became a physician and found his way to what was probably to be the most enviable position the future Soviet government had to offer: Director of Recreation and Rest Homes. Finally, there was Maria, the youngest sister (1878-1937), who studied in Russia, Belgium and France. Intelligent and alert, she knew several languages, and during 1917-1929 served on the editorial board of *Pravda*, was a member of the Central Control Commission on the Fourteenth Party Congress, and in 1935 held membership in the Central Executive Committee of the USSR. During Lenin's prolonged illness, his youngest sister served as his nurse.

[1]Schaginjan, p. 184.

Like Maria, the eldest sister Anna also was very close to Lenin, and was at his side the many times he needed her. She was a gifted girl who had inherited her father's mathematical talents. Having finished her gymnasium studies at sixteen with a gold medal, she was an active revolutionary long before Lenin, and held party positions from 1898 onward. Anna apparently disliked Lenin's wife and often left her own husband, Mark Yelizarov, to follow Lenin abroad, though she invariably returned to her own home. Anna worked and wrote for almost all of the papers and magazines which Lenin controlled, and after 1917, acted as secretary of the editorial board of *Pravda*. During 1918 and 1921, she worked with the Department for Education and concluded her career working in the Marx-Engels-Lenin Institute.

Throughout his life, Lenin relied upon the help of the women of his family. These women—his mother and his two sisters, and later his wife and his mistress—were devoted admirers, eager to advance his career. Lenin composed endless lists of things "to be done," and in following his instructions his women often made considerable sacrifices while assuming great risks.

All the Ulyanov siblings, in varying degrees, had rebellion in their blood.

Childhood

At the time of Lenin's birth the Ulyanovs hired a *nanya*, Varvara Grigorevna Sarabatova, a peasant woman from the Pensa area, who nursed young Vladimir. He became attached to her and Varvara stayed with the family, dying in 1890 at the Ulyanov house in Samara.

Vladimir did not walk until he was almost three years of age; it is reported that he at first fell frequently and often hurt his disproportionately large head. After he had learned how to use his feet, however, he moved about incessantly, often as though in a rage. He was a wild, unruly child who liked to destroy his toys as well as those of his playmates. He invented strange games whose rules could be varied according to his moods and successes. Both his urge to lead and his ability to impose his will—by violence if necessary—manifested themselves early. Vladimir was also highly intelligent and alert, learning to read at the age of five—one year later than his even more precocious brother Alexander.

At eight, Vladimir started to play chess. When he reached puberty he became something of a prankster and indulged in a good deal of physical exercise—fishing, swimming, skating, hiking and, later, hunting. He spent his summer vacations at the Kokushkino estate, which at the time of Maria's marriage had been divided equally among old Blank's five children.

It is said that the Ulyanov children never witnessed a quarrel between their parents: apparently Ilya and Maria had reached a tacit understanding. The father was constantly on inspection trips and was often absent for weeks. Yet Ilya was able to instill in his children a high sense of devotion to duty, a great diligence, and a respect for status. He does not seem to have been harsh, although he undoubtedly was distant and without warmth. The mother took a close interest in her children, tutored them, and reportedly tried to teach Vladimir to play the piano, although he never mastered this art.

According to sister Maria, Lenin's character resembled that of their mother. His physique, stature and features—the Mongolic cut of the eyes and the form of his skull—were inherited from his father, from whom he was also endowed with his logical mind, love for work, drive, energy, vivacity and quick temper.

The Ulyanov children were outstanding students. In August of 1879, at the age of little more than nine years, Vladimir entered the gymnasium at Simbirsk. With his extraordinary memory—a most important resource of a political leader—he proved himself to be a brilliant pupil who consistently won high grades. A report card of his last year in the gymnasium shows that his grade in religion was better than in logic. This is of special interest, because it is alleged that shortly before his father's death (when Vladimir was fifteen), having been angry at his father's insistence on religious observances, he tore off his cross, threw it on the floor and spat on it. Had he done this his father would have reprimanded him sternly—but Vladimir scored a high grade in religion about one year and a half *after* his father died. Thus the early religious rebellion of Vladimir is dubious.

The death of father Ilya on January 12, 1886, was unexpected, occurring within minutes after he had made a strange appearance at the dinner table, as though to say good-bye.[1] The survivors were only mildly affected, since Ilya's death brought about no significant changes in the life of his family. For a while, before the pension for the Actual State Councillor's widow and children had arrived, finances were a bit strained. But matters soon straightened out, and the children continued to establish impressive records at school.

[1] For more details on Ilya's death *see* V. Kanivets, *Alexander Ulyanov*, Moscow, Molodaya Gvardiya, 1961, p. 104f. Ilya felt unwell on January 11, when his illness was diagnosed as an upset stomach.

Alexander

Within a year, tragedy struck again: brother Alexander, a biology student at the University of St. Petersburg, was involved in an attempt on the Tsar's life. Alexander was arrested on March 13, 1887, tried, and on May 20, 1887, was executed by hanging.

Alexander had been studying the natural sciences, especially chemistry and biology, since 1883. An outstanding student, he earned an academic award for a paper on worms. Sister Anna also was a student at Petersburg University. Each was living on a comfortable monthly allowance of forty rubles. Alexander was concentrating on his scientific studies, allegedly because he felt that scientific knowledge pointed the way to the solution of social problems, but shocked by his father's death and the unnecessarily harsh police measures against a student demonstration, he suddenly displayed an interest in politics.[1] His father's death apparently aroused guilt feelings which were exacerbated when he participated in a protest demonstration and, unlike the other students, was not arrested by the police. He began to study revolutionary literature and considered publishing a socialist library; allegedly he actually did translate a few philosophical passages from Marx. Soon he was surrounded by a few kindred souls. The political orientation of these youngsters was not uniform, for some of his friends were Poles who wanted national freedom, while his Russian comrades wanted to destroy despotism. Most of the "Russians" were Cossacks and Ukrainians; there apparently was a tenuous link with the old Ishutin group.

Alexander envisioned himself as a "populist," which might be described, though somewhat inaccurately, as an agrarian socialist. The group, so it was said later, included several Marxists (i.e., proletarian socialists), yet according to contemporary police findings, it was entirely oriented towards the populist *Will of the People* tradition. The customary version is that the group's program constituted a transition between populism and Marxism, but this is not borne out by police evidence.[2] The youngsters actually did adopt the old *Will of the People* program, but Ulyanov wrote an additional set of principles—specifically for the group—which was imbued with the ideas of political liberty.

Ideological distinctions were not yet significant and the group agreed that protest and propaganda were impractical and that words and deeds did not coincide among Social Democrats. By contrast, *they* would succeed by terror, by killing Tsar Alexander III. By 1887, there was little revolutionary enthusiasm in Russia: the number of active

[1] *A. I. Ulyanov i delo 1-go marta 1887 g.*, Moscow, 1927, as quoted in Peter Scheibert, "Über Lenins Anfänge," *Historische Zeitschrift* (1956), Vol. 182, p. 559.

[2] Major sources include General Alexandre Spiridovich, *Histoire du Terrorisme Russe 1886-1917* (Paris: Payot, 1930), p. 14ff, and especially Lt. General Schébéko, *Chronique du Mouvement Socialiste en Russie, 1878-1887*, "confidentiel et exclusivement personnel," (St. Petersburg: Ministry of the Interior, 1890), pp. 622-640.

revolutionaries was small, the number of those who were considering methods of terror was still smaller, and the number of those who actually plotted terroristic acts came to less than a dozen. Ulyanov was the most outspoken proponent of "armed struggle."

The group called itself *Terror Section of the Will of the People* and Ulyanov was its first leader. The Polish members procured chemicals sufficient for more than six bombs and Ulyanov prepared the dynamite outside the capital in the house of a midwife, mother of a girlfriend of one of the terrorists. He constructed three bombs, stuffing them with strychnine, while the terrorists practiced bomb-throwing and carefully reconnoitered the road on which the Tsar was expected to travel. The bomb was to be hurled by a certain Ossipanov, formerly a student of Kazan University. Ulyanov briefed him carefully, hoping that Ossipanov would have an opportunity to explain the program of the revolutionaries in court. Apparently, Ulyanov did not expect to be brought to trial himself.

The police, however, had been alerted by an intercepted letter and they patrolled the streets, noticing on successive days the same young men walking on Nevski Prospect, St. Petersburg's main street, with heavy packages. They investigated and found the bomb in a hollowed-out book carried by one of the strollers.

Ulyanov was supervising the operation from a distance. On the days preceding the attempt he allegedly continued his studies of sea spiders; but he also concerned himself with the chemistry of explosives. For good measure we are assured that he also leafed through Marx's *Das Kapital*;[3] but if this happened, it escaped the attention of the police, who had already been informed of the planned assassination. Anna was arrested in her brother's room, while Alexander, in turn, was found hiding in the apartment of a friend. Incidentally, Bronislav Pilsudski, in whose room the program had been multigraphed and who together with his brother Joseph, the later Marshal of Poland, had procured the chemicals, also was indicted and convicted. Joseph was forced to testify.

Mother Maria Ulyanov received a letter informing her of Alexander's imprisonment. Vladimir read it first and commented: "This is a serious matter, this can end badly for Sasha."[4] The family was ostracized and Lenin experienced bitter disappointment when he tried to secure a carriage to drive his mother to the station. Maria was permitted twice to visit Alexander in prison. He asked his mother to pay his debts and to forgive him: one has duties toward the people as well as toward the family.

On April 19, 1887, the trial was held. Alexander addressed the

[3]Kanivets, p. 95.

[4]*Ibid.*, p. 221; *Molodiye Gody*, p. 233.

court and criticized the government: terror was needed as a riposte to the "violence of the state," and neither he nor his comrades were afraid to die. They would be followed by other fighters: despotism would be overthrown in the end. The plotters were not advocating a particular policy but had united to prevent the government from instituting further reactionary measures. They wanted "to force the despotic regime to grant political freedom to the people." Alexander added that he had not run away because he preferred to die for his country. Time and again he accepted the blame, but even the judge did not believe the accusations he heaped upon himself. Alexander was sentenced to death, but had he asked for clemency his sentence undoubtedly would have been commuted: the Tsar preferred repentance to execution.[5] Yet Alexander refused to beg for mercy, and thereby rendered his own execution inevitable. Anna was banished to Kokushkino.

When the news of Alexander's execution reached Vladimir, he heard it with astonishing calm: "Another way is necessary"; a significant, though apocryphal, comment. The statement hardly indicates that in the youngster's mind "Leninism" already was preformed. But Lenin *was* a master in finding "other ways"—this dictum could serve as a motto for his life.

[5]To the transcript of self-accusation, the Tsar appended a marginal note: "This frankness is touching." *(Molodiye Gody,* p. 227). On the Tsar's inclination to clemency, see also Kanivets, p. 198.

Two Brothers

Legend has it that Lenin vowed to avenge his brother's death. Systematically, it is said, he interrogated I. N. Chebotaryev, a friend of Alexander's, to learn the nature of the plot and the causes of its failure. But Lenin was not the romantic type; he had little patience with heroics. He never became involved in a plot to kill the Tsar or other high officials. Although he instigated violent acts when later he was in power, terrorism was not the revolutionary way of life he chose for himself at this time.[1]

Vladimir displayed considerable detachment from his brother's troubles even though the hours following Alexander's arrest, his trial, and execution constituted a period of extreme anguish for the Ulyanov family. Lenin remained very close to his mother, who was suffering

[1]Lenin's early rejection of terrorism may have been less firm than is generally asserted. Apparently he preserved enthusiasm for the traditional forms of terrorism until 1893. (See Richard Pipes, *Social Democracy and the St. Petersburg Labor Movement, 1885-1897* [Cambridge, Mass.: Harvard University Press, 1963], p. 48.)

greatly under the ordeal. The family was shunned by its neighbors—yet Vladimir, while Alexander was surrendering his life, registered for final examinations, quietly passed a series of rigorous tests and finished school, earning a gold medal.

Alexander's psychology differed markedly from Vladimir's. Lenin early admired and imitated his older brother, but their bonds loosened after their father's death. Alexander was given to tears and silent suffering; Lenin was harsh and loud. Alexander, unable to lie, detested mendacity and cowardice, while Vladimir was often untruthful and lacking in physical courage. Alexander was morbid, sentimental, humble and compassionate; all of these qualities Lenin lacked. It is recorded that Alexander courted a distant cousin and planned to marry her. Lenin in his early years showed no interest in girls. Alexander had numerous friends; Vladimir was not given to friendship. When Alexander became the head of the family, he frequently rebutted Vladimir for rudeness to their mother. Lenin continued in his precocious ways.

Alexander's interests were channeled toward the natural sciences, while Lenin was attracted by social studies, and directed arrogance and sarcasm against his brother whose interest in the sex life of worms he mocked. Alexander told his sister, when both were students in St. Petersburg, that though Vladimir was very capable, "we will never become close friends, as a matter of fact, not at all."[2]

It has been suggested that there were political differences between the two brothers, Alexander being a populist, while the young Lenin showed an early interest in Marxism. This interpretation is almost certainly false: Lenin probably did not even know that Alexander was involved in politics. Lenin learned of the plot with complete surprise. The primary difference in their personalities was revealed through Alexander's participation in the plot, his behavior in court, and above all, his refusal to ask for mercy. Lenin rarely was inclined to take risks. He avoided assuming responsibility for the deeds of others and even for his own, usually being the first to disappear from dangerous scenes. Alexander suffered from guilt feelings; Lenin apparently was singularly free of this problem. Lenin disliked Dostoyevsky, Alexander's favorite author. Alexander, in fact, closely resembled Dostoyevsky's Raskolnikov. Alexander's actions imply that he was driven by strong suicidal impulses.

The circumstances of his upbringing would seem to be conducive to a placid career in science or government for Alexander. He scarcely witnessed revolting scenes of cruelty and exploitation. The causes which propelled Alexander to terrorism presumably were deeply rooted in his nature.

[2]Leopold H. Haimson, *The Russian Marxists and the Origins of Bolshevism* (Cambridge, Mass.: Harvard, 1955), p. 95.

It is of interest to investigate the Ulyanovs's familial behavior. Perhaps there existed a state of general rebellion against a stern, rejecting father: we do have indirect evidence that sister Anna rebelled against the old man, as did Alexander in his refusal to attend church. But the mother, who had grown up under an extremely tyrannical father, and who appears to have been mildly manic-depressive, was probably the conditioning factor. She apparently never rebelled openly against her father, but she did rebel against her husband in identifying herself with the revolutionary activities of her children. It is not known whether, even after the death of her eldest son, she ever admonished her surviving children to desist. She did become morose, and Anna took great pains to avoid discussion of "conspiratorial" matters in her presence.

Student

With his brother dead, seventeen-year-old Lenin established himself as head of the family. The school principal, father of Alexander Kerensky, whom Lenin was to overthrow in 1917, protected him from possible expulsion due to his brother's actions, but the gold medal which Lenin had earned upon completion of his school work was denied him. He applied for admission to the law school at Kazan University; upon acceptance he and his family moved to Kazan.

Lenin immersed himself in his law studies, avoiding the revolutionary plots planned to avenge his brother. On December 4, 1887, he happened to participate in a student meeting, which presumably was protesting against a lack of academic freedom. Lenin played no leading role but upon leaving the meeting was asked, like more than one hundred other students, to identify himself. After two days in jail he was excluded from the university. Customarily such a penalty was applied against notorious rabble-rousers. In this case, the penalty clearly was undeserved—undoubtedly meted out because of his kinship to Alexander.

Lenin moved to Kokushkino, situated about twenty miles from Kazan. His sister Anna was there already, and for some time Valdimir and Anna were by themselves, making full use of the excellent library that their grandfather Blank and their late uncle Dimitri had collected. Shortly afterwards, the remainder of the family joined the exiles, living comfortably as country squires. Their mother[1] received a pension of 1,200 rubles annually, or about fifty dollars a month—approximately the equivalent of 300 to 400 dollars with the purchasing power of 1962.

[1]*Molodiye Gody,* p. 305.

Kokushkino provided free quarters and free food, and there may have been an income from farming.

At that time, 100 rubles a month was a very comfortable middle-class income in any Russian city, but the financial situation of the Ulyanov family was even better: Uncle Vassily had left to Ilya a legacy with which, perhaps, the Ulyanovs bought their house. In any event, Ilya, though he had not accumulated a large fortune, left behind enough for the establishment of a "family fund," which was skillfully administered by his widow. The Simbirsk house was sold at a profit, and there was later an inheritance from the Blank side. As we shall see, Mother Ulyanov bought an estate for 7,500 rubles, and sold it again without gain or loss, although it probably yielded an income for a time. There was sufficient money for Lenin not to need to earn any before he was twenty-seven, and Dimitri before he was twenty-eight. Maria, who had chosen no profession, made five trips to Europe, and attended courses in Belgium, France and Switzerland for several years. Her mother sent money whenever Maria requested it, this outlay causing no strain on the family's finances. Mother Ulyanov also made two or three European trips,[2] traveling first class.[3] Sister Anna married a good provider. Lenin frequently obtained money from his mother; all the brothers and sisters were assisted by the old lady when they were removed from her, in jail or in exile. In brief, the Ulyanov family was wealthy enough to allow its offspring to become professional revolutionaries.

Concentrating on his law studies, Lenin determined to discipline himself further. He smoked for a while but then gave it up, according to one version, because his mother told him it cost too much, and according to another, because his mother was very worried about his health. It is said that he stopped playing chess because it required too much of his time, but this renouncement occurred much later.

The police reported favorably on Vladimir's activities in Kokushkino. Still, his application for readmission to the University was rejected. In the fall of 1888, Lenin was permitted to return to Kazan. The family moved back with him, except Anna, who was allowed to follow only later. He twice requested permission to go abroad, once for study and another time for medical purposes, but was refused. His sister Anna related that Lenin entered a Marxist circle, which Nikolai E. Fedosseyev had organized, and sought to master the theories of Marxism. No witness of this effort has ever come forward; Fedosseyev had a "circle" at Kazan, but Lenin was not acquainted with him, as Anna herself admitted.[4] According to the police, Lenin associated at

2Valentinov, *Novyi Zhurnal, op. cit.*, p. 225.

3*Istoricheskii Arkhiv* (1958), No. 2, p. 13.

4*Molodiye Gody*, p. 295ff and 300.

Kazan with Lazar M. Bogoraz, described as a "notorious revolution-ary."[5] The tie with Fedosseyev is unsubstantiated, as is Anna's assertion that during that period Lenin studied *Das Kapital*.[6] Anna was an eager contributor to Lenin mythology; her testimony is particularly suspect.

In the spring of 1889, Ulyanov moved to Alakayevka, a village near Samara, and soon the entire family joined him. This was a purely professional maneuver: fearful that Lenin's schooling was blocked per-manently and that he would be unable to practice law, his mother decided to establish him as a farmer.[7] She sold the Simbirsk house, and perhaps her share in the Kokushkino estate, and for 7,500 rubles purchased a 225-acre farm, which included a mill and a manor house. The Alakayevka farm was operated by hired labor and managed by Lenin, an episode of capitalist indulgence which has been kept in the dark. Although he gained some practical knowledge, after a half-year stint Lenin moved to Samara. He went to Alakayevka again for five summer seasons, spending there three or four months a year;[8] the property was sold in 1897.

In November, 1889, Lenin petitioned the educational authorities for permission to take examinations as an external student.[9] The police rejected the application but a second petition was approved in May, 1890. Lenin, who never was readmitted as a regular student, passed his examinations at the law school of St. Petersburg University. In May, 1891, his sister Olga, while a student at St. Petersburg, died of typhus complicated by a skin disease; she apparently had been in poor health for some time. On a later date (October 17, 1895) Lenin reported to his mother that Olga's grave was in order, including "the cross and the wreath." In November of 1891 Lenin was awarded his law degree. He received the certificate of loyalty and good character necessary for admission to the bar, returned to Samara and joined the law firm of A. N. Khardin, who was described as a "liberal." In August, 1892, Lenin was admitted to the lower courts and in Septem-ber, 1893, moved to St. Petersburg, where he joined the law firm of M. F. Wolkenstein, another "liberal." It is reported that he lost all but one of the suits which he handled for the firm.

[5]Letter of September 7, 1910, by the Director of Police Department to Foreign Bureau, Paris. The political affiliation of Bogoraz is not known. (Document in Hoover Institution.) *See also* police report of April 3, 1888 (Old Style) in *Molodiye Gody*, p. 265f.

[6]*Lénine tel qu'il fut*, Vol. I, p. 25.

[7]*Molodiye Gody*, p. 321.

[8]*Ibid.*, p. 459. According to brother Dimitri, Lenin read at Alakayevka, during an unstated time, Ricardo with the help of a dictionary (*Ibid.*, p. 314). He is also said to have been singing there lyrical songs and was accompanied by his sister Olga (*Ibid.*, p. 317f).

[9]A student who did not attend classes but was allowed to take examinations.

When Did Lenin Become a Marxist?

Several versions of Lenin's intellectual development have been advanced. Communist historians assert that Lenin was a full-fledged Marxist by 1887: at seventeen he supposedly was an expert reader of *Das Kapital* and an organizer of Social Democratic cells. It is also said that he inherited Alexander's copy of *Das Kapital* and began its study immediately, so that by the time of his first arrest he already was a learned revolutionary. Yet Lenin said that he read *Das Kapital* first in January, 1889, about a year after his arrest. He had then been in Kokushkino where, almost two years earlier, Anna may have transported Alexander's copy.[1] It is possible that Lenin read *Das Kapital* in January, 1889 at Kazan. But a real study of this work requires months and even years. In any event, this first study hardly transformed him into a "Marxist" as the term is understood today. It is said that he translated the *Communist Manifesto*[2] while in Samara, and that he distributed the translation which, it is claimed, has not been preserved. Undoubtedly, Lenin was anxious to learn German, so it is highly probable that he then became familiar with the *Manifesto*; but from what is known of the development of his facility with the German language, we must doubt that at nineteen or twenty he was as yet able to translate this text. If the story has any factual basis, he may have rewritten or corrected an existing translation, but it is most unlikely that his handiwork was circulated among "illegal" circles, for he did not have any reproduction equipment.

Marx was respected by Russian revolutionaries of all shades. The *Communist Manifesto* was considered by Nechayev to be a key text; Bakunin was its first translator. *Das Kapital* was translated by Danielson, a populist, and published in Russia during 1872;[3] the second volume was issued in German in 1885. Marx and Engels had few contacts with Russian "Marxists" but supported the populists, in the hope that perhaps Russia could achieve socialism without first passing through capitalism. The leading populists considered themselves to be pupils of Marx. The lines between the various revolutionary groups were not yet sharply drawn.

Lenin first embarked on the road to revolution by becoming "irreligious." He had superficially read Chernishevsky's *What Is To*

[1] N. Valentinov, "Vstrecha Lenina s Markizmom," *Novyi Zhurnal* (New York, 1958), No. 53, pp. 189-208. Interesting data on Lenin's intellectual development are supplied.

[2] *Lénine tel qu'il fut*, Vol. I, p. 80.

[3] In her letter to Marx of February 16, 1881, Vera Zasulich stated that the book was confiscated but that the few copies which were saved were being read avidly by "*la masse des gens plus ou moins instruits de notre pays.*" The book, she added, enjoyed great popularity in Russia. *See Marx-Engels Archiv.* ed. D. Ryazanov (Frankfurt, 1926), I. 316.

Be Done? when he was fourteen, but after Alexander's execution he carefully reread it. It is therefore probable that Lenin actually became "irreligious" at seventeen (and not at fifteen as his widow asserted). His high school grades in religion might be explained by a critical interest which arose from his experience with his brother's execution and from his attentive reading of Chernishevsky. He returned to Chernishevsky's book for several weeks in the summer of 1888; presumably he continued to study the remainder of Chernishevsky's works,[4] writings which Lenin believed had influenced Alexander. Indeed, hundreds of Russians became revolutionaries because of the teachings of Chernishevsky.

N. G. Chernishevsky came from a family of priests. He was born in 1828 at Saratov, began writing in 1853, was imprisoned in 1861, exiled to Siberia in 1863, allowed to settle in Astrakhan in 1883, and in 1889 returned to Saratov where he died a few months later. His death deeply disturbed Lenin. Chernishevsky was a materialist similar to Ludwig Feuerbach, a positivist like Auguste Comte, and a determinist, emphasizing the "complete human being." He was a socialist who insisted upon a communist interpretation of the equality of rights. One of his heroes says: "My linen, your linen; my pipestem, your pipestem; my wife, your wife." His models of socialist institutions and private cooperative organizations were patterned after Fourier, Owen, and Louis Blanc. Opposed to "erotic problems," he vowed, "I will love but once in all my life." The ideal men are those able to "realize the correct principles." "Such persons are few in number but through them the general life blossoms and without them, it would be choked. They are few in number but they enable all other men to breathe, for without them, those would be stifled. Honest and good men exist aplenty, but those of whom I am thinking are rare specimens." In Thomas G. Masaryk's words: "what the monk had been for the Church," the ideal man "was to be for the new society."

In a postscript to the second edition of *Das Kapital,* Marx termed Chernishevsky a "great Russian savant and critic." It is not quite clear whether Marx actually read Chernishevsky, who was profoundly influenced by John Stuart Mill, a writer whom Marx detested. Presumably Marx referred to Chernishevsky because he wanted to show his interest in Russia. Yet Chernishevsky was anything but a Marxist. He wanted to base socialism on ethics, and the new order upon a new set of moral

---

4"Thanks to Chernishevsky," Lenin reportedly stated, "I became first acquainted with philosophical materialism. It was he, too, who first showed me the significance of Hegel. . . . From him derives my understanding of the dialectical method, after which it became much easier to grasp the dialectic of Marx....I read Chernishevsky 'with a pencil' in my hand, making long extracts and drafts. These notes I kept for many years. . . . I even wrote a letter to him and was very upset when I did not receive an answer." (Report by V. V. Vorovsky on a conversation with Lenin, *Voprosy Literatury,* 1957, No. 8, p. 133, quoted in *Molodiye Gody,* p. 285f.)

values, most notably, a novel relationship between man and wife; he was opposed to the class struggle. He asserted that knowledge provides essential energy to politics, industry (including the methods of production) and human life. Chernishevsky was logical and rationalistic, but nondialectical and historical. In 1872 a copy of _Das Kapital_ was dispatched to his Siberian exile, but Chernishevsky, although he frequently commented on major works sent to him, never made mention of the book. Highly interested in the British economist David Ricardo, he should have looked at the work of Ricardo's successor, Marx. But apparently he did not take the time to study the weighty tome.

Chernishevsky's plans were vague and his reform proposals timid. He was a shallow thinker and an indifferent writer. His intellectual development was arrested after he reached Siberia and, although he wanted to compile a world encyclopedia, he did not read a single work on natural science after the age of twenty-two. Thus, intellectually, Chernishevsky merely was a cypher. Lenin learned from him that a "thinking and decent person must be a revolutionary"; in the hero of _What Is To Be Done?_ he found the human model towards which he was forming himself.[5]

Lenin pursued his reading with D. I. Pisarev, the nihilist writer, and A. N. Dobrolyubov, Chernishevsky's student. (Lenin's father possessed a collection of issues of the magazine _Sovremennik,_ which published much of Dobrolyubov's writings.) Dobrolyubov averred that "if platonic love of woman is ridiculous, a thousand times more ridiculous is platonic love of country, people, justice . . . . The idyll, that is the enemy." Those who protest but do not act and those who act ineffectually because they shrink from realistic and forceful action,

---

[5]Dietrich Geyer, _Lenin in der russischen Sozialdemokratie_ (Köln: Böhlau, 1962), p. 40. Geyer thinks that Valentinov exaggerated Chernishevsky's influence on Lenin. The exact measure of intellectual influences is not easy to take. N. K. Krupskaya, _Reminiscences of Lenin_ (Moscow: Foreign Languages Publishing House, 1959), p. 503. Krupskaya relates that in Siberia Lenin had an album with pictures of political convicts, and she stressed that there was a picture of Chernishevsky and also a picture of Emile Zola because of his stand in the Dreyfus affair. Moreover, it is noteworthy that the first journal _Iskra_ (1859-1873) stood under Chernishevsky's ideological guidance and was avidly read by the Ulyanov family (Krupskaya, p. 521) . See _also_ Haimson, _op. cit._, p. 97ff, where Lenin's interest is documented. Chernishevsky and Dobrolyubov were described as Alexander Ulyanov's _livres de chevet_. In 1908, Lenin was planning to contribute an analysis of Chernishevsky's philosophy to a collective work about him. Between 1909 and 1911, he reread Chernishevsky and made notes on books written on that author by Plekhanov and Y. M. Steklov. See V. Y. Zevin and A. G. Khomento, "Pomyetki V. I. Lenina na Knige Y. M. Steklova 'N. G. Chernishevsky, yego zhizn i dyeyatelnost (1909)'," _Literaturnoye Nasledstvo, Revolutsionniye Demokraty, Novyye Materialy_ (Moscow: Akademiya Nauk, 1959), pp. 9-78. Vorovsky also quoted Lenin as saying that Chernishevsky was his "favorite author." _(Molodiye Gody,_ p. 285f). See also Nadezhda K. Krupskaya, "Lenin and Chernyshevsky," Appendix III in _Memoirs of Lenin (1893-1917),_ London, Lawrence and Wishart, 1942.

lying instead on their beds "planning"—those phony revolutionaries must be despised. Following a novel by Goncharov, those ineffectual, typically Russian personalities were called "Oblomovs." Throughout his life, Lenin applied this expression to liberal, democratic, and ethical socialists.

In Kokushkino, Lenin had access to much of the informative "legal" revolutionary literature which had been published in Russia since the 1850's.[6] We do not know whether he took key books from Kokushkino to Kazan and then to Samara. Even if he could have done this, he was too busy with his formal studies to devote much time to such extra activities.[7] Lenin presumably knew from his mother about Ishutin and his organizational ideas, and it is likely that there existed at Kokushkino full documentation on the case. Whether Lenin learned anything about Sergei G. Nechayev, founder of the Society of the Ax, is conjectural, but the Nechayev story was well covered in magazines to which Lenin had access. The foremost socialist thinker of the period, N. K. Mikhailovsky, had in his writings analyzed the ideas of Nechayev, and Dostoyevsky and Goncharov had presented the story in fictionalized versions. Mikhail A. Bakunin, in turn, was portrayed in a famous novel by Turgenev. Lenin undoubtedly was familiar with this literature, at the very least through hearsay. Upon his mind were impressed Nechayev's slogans: "Everything for the revolution. The end justifies the means."

It is likely that late in 1888 Lenin read George Plekhanov, the first prominent Russian Marxist writer, who had originally been a populist. The study of Plekhanov may have induced Lenin to look at *Das Kapital.* Plekhanov's *Our Disputes,* essentially a criticism of conspiracy and secret organizations, acquainted Lenin with the ideas of the Russian revolutionary tradition and of Auguste Blanqui, the French preacher of direct action. Plekhanov discussed M. A. Bakunin (and Chernishevsky), opposed the terrorism of the *Will of the People,* criticized the Jacobinism and Blanquism of P. N. Tkachev, and favored the new approach of Karl Marx.

Thus, through primary and secondary sources, Lenin familiarized himself with Russian revolutionary thinking, learning about conspiratorial and organizational techniques before he began reading and understanding the writings of Marx. Perhaps it is true, as Lenin said

[6]"I read articles which had been printed in journals like *Sovremennik, Otechestvenniye Zapiski, Vestnik Yevropy.* Those magazines contained the most interesting and best articles which had been printed during the past decade on sociological and political problems." As to fiction writers, Lenin was very much interested in Nekrassov. He commented about his stay in Kokushkino (December 1887 to fall 1888): "Never again in my life, not even during imprisonment in Petersburg and in Siberia did I read so much as during the year after my expulsion from Kazan." *(Molodiye Gody,* p. 285.)

[7]*Ibid.,* p. 285.

later, that he became a "Marxist" in the fall of 1889; but it was the Russian literature which prepared him for becoming a revolutionary. Although he knew about Marx from Plekhanov and may have read the *Communist Manifesto* very early in life, during the 1886-1892 period he was primarily absorbing the experiences of Russian revolutionaries.

In 1883, Plekhanov, together with Vera Zasulich, L. G. Deutsch, and P. B. Axelrod, founded abroad the first purely Social Democratic group, *Liberation of Labor*.[8] (The three founders originally had adhered to populism and terrorism.) In Russia that year the first Social Democratic group was founded by Blagoyev, a Bulgarian, and by Vassili Kharitonov. Social Democratic cells were formed in Minsk, Vilna, and Kiev in 1883 and 1884. In 1885, the Blagoyev group, whose membership was scattered in the wake of Alexander Ulyanov's *attentat* in 1887, published a magazine, *Rabochy*. The first Social Democratic group in St. Petersburg was formed in 1885 by N. V. Vodovozov. Through the late 1880's Social Democratic organizations existed at Moscow, Odessa, Tula, Saratov, Kazan and Samara. Although prior to 1891 none of these were of any significance, Lenin had ample opportunity to "get organized" if he chose to do so.

[8]How much were these people really committed to Marxism? Plekhanov made contact with Engels only in 1890. The lateness and superficiality of this contact between the first Russian and the first European Marxist are difficult to explain.

What Is Russian Marxism?

The early Russian Marxists experienced considerable intellectual travail: the prophet himself was quite uncertain as to the degree of applicability of his oracular theory to Russia. Vera Zasulich, in 1881, asked him to reveal to his Russian disciples what he thought about the future of the agrarian commune—one of the crucial questions separating the "Marxists" from the "populists." The "Marxists," she wrote to London, allege that the commune is bound to perish. Though Marx did not consider this question in *Das Kapital,* his followers assert that he would have affirmed the commune's doom if he had concerned himself with Russia. Zasulich wanted to know exactly what Marx was thinking about the future of the commune. Was Russia forced to pass through *all* phases of capitalism before it could attain socialism? How long would it be before Russian capitalism would reach the stage of European capitalism? If citizen Marx was unable to write a detailed dissertation on the subject, could he at least render to the Russian socialists the service of writing a letter which Zasulich would translate and publish in Russia?[1]

[1]*Marx-Engels Archiv, op. cit.,* p. 317.

Marx, who was on friendly terms with the populist Peter Lavrov and who had a set of the latter's paper *Vperyed* (1875-76) in his library, found it difficult to reply. He wrote four drafts totalling about 10,000 words, finally penning a short apologetic letter stating that he could not produce an answer suitable for publication. He was ill and already was reneging on a promise, made several months earlier, to clarify the matter. This promise, incidentally, had been given to the St. Petersburg executive committee of the *Narodnaya Volya* which was then preparing the assassination of Alexander II.

Marx told Zasulich that the "fatalité historique," which he had discovered, applied only to Western Europe. In a letter to a Russian editor he had argued the identical point in 1877, but the letter had never been dispatched. *Das Kapital*, he added, contained no statement for or against the "vitality" of the rural commune. (He probably meant "viability.") Still, he was convinced that the commune could serve as the base of social regeneration in Russia, *provided* it were allowed to function properly and develop normally.[2] Naturally, both he and the recipient realized that this qualifying clause negated the point.

Already in 1875 Friedrich Engels had written in a polemic against P. N. Tkachev that the commune was apparently moving to its dissolution but that it might be saved in a higher form, *provided* there were a proletarian revolution in Western Europe. Engels specifically denied that the Russian peasants were closer to socialism than were the European workers. This implied that Engels did not consider the commune to be an easy bridge for Russia's passage to socialism. Actually, he even argued that the *mir* (commune) was the foundation of "oriental despotism."[3]

In his drafts of the letter to Zasulich Marx showed himself to be increasingly undecided or confused. He apparently wanted to say that in Russia the stages of capitalism could be passed through quickly, that the archaic commune could be reconstituted in a more advanced form. Such a belief implied that the commune as it existed would have to be dissolved; the argument was omitted from the letter. Marx also indicated that he did not know the "Marxists" about whom Zasulich was speaking: the Russians *he* knew held opposite views. This statement probably signified that Marx's Russian contacts did not consider the commune to be doomed. This remark he also dropped. Eduard Bernstein later disclosed that Marx and Engels were in fact quite skeptical about the commune but were unwilling to impart their doubts to the populists, whom they believed to be genuine revolutionaries. In fact, after Plekhanov left the populists to go abroad,

[2]*Marx-Engels Archiv, op. cit.*, p. 341f.

[3]Karl Marx and Friedrich Engels, *Werke*, Vol. 18 (Berlin: Dietz, 1962), p. 563.

Marx criticized the gentlemen who opposed revolutionary activity and aimed to achieve the millenium "by means of the dullest of dull doctrinaire views." This was certainly not bestowing the blessing of apostolic succession on Marxism in Russia.[4]

The interesting point is that Zasulich, Plekhanov, Axelrod and Deutsch literally forgot that Marx had replied to the query posed by Zasulich. They did not even recall his answer when, years later, David Ryazanov asked them about Marx's response and they denied that Marx had ever commented. This incident characterizes the authenticity of Russian Marxism, though, admittedly, Marx offered no sensible message to his admirers.

By 1883, Zasulich had begun to consider the gradual dissolution of the commune as "inevitable," though she felt that some "remnants" might continue to be useful. During the nineties, the Marxist group under Plekhanov's leadership was outspokenly critical of the commune, rejecting the romantic notion that this decrepit institution could possibly act as a forerunner to socialism.

A second cleavage between Marx and the Russian revolutionaries concerned political-revolutionary action. Marx cooperated with Bakunin within the First International but broke with him after the collapse of the Paris Commune in 1871. The breach, though due partly to personal reasons, occurred primarily because of a topical disagreement: Marx opposed revolution through conspiracy. The contemporary evaluation of this dispute, as generally accepted by European socialists, held that Bakunin was a "conspirator by profession" who longed "to make revolution" and who believed that the revolution could be achieved entirely by the thought and will of "revolutionary man." This doctrine would play into the hands of reaction. Marx, by contrast, was intent upon identifying "the laws of the organic development of all historical phenomena." He was anything but a conspirator, and already before 1848 opposed the initiating of revolution by a "ferocious devotee of fulminating mercury" (*Knallsilber-Wuetrich*). Marx disliked the pretentious "Rinaldo Rinaldini concept of politics" which characterized Bakunin.[5]

This interpretation would seem to eliminate "professional revolutionaries" from the Marxist fold. But Marx was inconsistent. The Russian writer Paul Annenkov assisted in 1847 at a debate between Marx and Wilhelm Weitling, a German "maker of revolution." Marx asked Weitling: "Tell us, you made so much noise with your Communist propaganda . . . and attracted so many workers, depriving them of their jobs and bread; with what arguments do you

[4]*See also ibid.*, Vol. 19, pp. 107-112, 407-424.

[5]"Karl Marx," *Die Neue Zeit* (1883), I, 447. The article presumably was written by Karl Kautsky.

defend your social revolutionary agitation and on what basis do you want to place this agitation in the future?" Weitling replied that he was using those theories which were most likely to open the workers' eyes and transform them into self-reliant activists.

Furious, Marx argued that it was fraudulent to incite the people without first producing a firm basis for revolutionary action. Arousing unattainable hopes would never lead to the salvation of the sufferers, Marx believed, but would instead entail their perdition: empty propaganda presupposes both an enthusiastic apostle and idiots listening to him with their mouths open. Marx added wistfully that Weitling's tactics perhaps were applicable to Russia, where conspiracies (*Vereinigungen*) were feasible and did in fact exist among "absurd apostles and absurd disciples."[6]

It is impossible to determine whether those Russians who called themselves Marxists actually were Marxists or even whether Marx, had he been a Russian, would have become and remained a Marxist. Almost every Russian revolutionary was indebted to Marx, but practically none could be genuine followers because of conditions existing in Russia to which his doctrines were irrelevant. Lenin was an authentic Marxist in that he extracted from Marx's philosophy the basic concepts pertinent to his operations in a country in which constitutionalism and democracy appeared infeasible.

The insistence on the Marxian figleaf also was due to cultural reasons: to be really acceptable to progressive Russian intellectuals, a political doctrine had to be "scientific" and "Western." The dogmatism of the Russian revolutionaries precluded the cynical use of ideologies as mere façades. Instead, these men argued as true believers. But, while most revolutionaries lived in a realm of fiction, Lenin was a genuine revolutionary in that he was able, and forever ready, to use ideas functionally, in order to respond to the exigencies of concrete situations. He tailored interpretations to realities which he viewed through the eyes of an activist. He used Marxism in the way a military commander uses maps.

[6]"Eine russische Stimme über Karl Marx," *Die Neue Zeit*, I, 238f.

Fedosseyev

The allegation that Lenin joined at Kazan the Social Democratic circle headed by Nikolai Efgrafovich Fedosseyev (1871-1898) has been previously mentioned.[1] Between 1886 and 1887, Fedosseyev, a

[1]N. E. Fedosseyev, *Stati i pisma*, Moscow, 1958; Ts. K.R.K.P. Komissiya po istorii Oktyabrskoi revolyutsii i R.K.P. (b), *Fedosseyev Nikolai Evgrafovich, Odin iz pionerov revolyutsionnogo Marksizma v Rossii (Sbornik vospominanii)*, Moscow, 1923; and S. V. Shcheprov, *Vydayushchiisya revolyutsioner N. E. Fedosseyev*, Moscow, 1958.

pupil of the Kazan gymnasium (from which he later was expelled), participated in a populist self-education circle. It was not until 1888 that he founded a Marxist student group, but by then Lenin had left Kazan, so that Lenin and Fedosseyev did not meet.

According to another version, Lenin joined a Marxist circle headed by L. M. Bogoraz and supervised by N. A. Motovilov. This story is supported by police records which, however, do not mention Motovilov. Among the members of the Bogoraz circle was A. M. Peshkov, later known as Maxim Gorky. Motovilov was exiled from Kazan in 1887, and Gorky and Lenin did not meet. Nor did Lenin meet P. N. Skvortsov, the local Marxist theoretician who was publishing widely and who introduced Fedosseyev to Marxism. It is entirely likely that Lenin occasionally met Bogoraz or other revolutionary students. Police records state vaguely that he continued to be in contact with "unreliable persons,"[2] but no recorded details exist for the period prior to the summer of 1895. In any event, these contacts did not induce him to become an organized member of a circle, certainly not of a Marxist cell at a time when the Marxists had barely begun to differentiate themselves from the populists. Lenin himself discounted stories about his early revolutionary activity.

Lenin's sister stated that her brother was aware of the existence of Fedosseyev's circle, and knew some of the participants, but she specifically denied Lenin's membership in this group; she did not mention any other cell.[3] Lenin, wishing either to be readmitted to the university, or to obtain permission to go abroad, had to be discreet about his connections with revolutionary study groups. Or perhaps he simply was not interested.

At that time, revolutionary self-education was the fashion and, as an aid to individual study, reading lists or revolutionary bibliographies were compiled for distribution among students. Impressed by what may be termed "literary logistics," Fedosseyev went one step further, collecting Russian press clippings concerning Marx and Marxism, putting the data (which went back to 1860) into systematic order, and thus providing an index to Marxism. He established facilities for the reproduction of forbidden or hard-to-obtain books, and distributed bibliographies, synopses, and reviews of books and articles, including a list of the works by Marx and Engels.

Gorky regarded the Fedosseyev catalogue as outstanding, calling it the "font of wisdom." There is little doubt that Lenin's early Marxist knowledge was derived in great part from Fedosseyev's work. Many years later Lenin told Gorky that the "catalogue" had been in

[2]*Molodiye Gody*, p. 303. Concerning the fact that Lenin did not meet Fedosseyev at Kazan, *see* A. Ulyanova-Yelizarova, *V. I. Ulyanov (N. Lenin)*, Moscow, 1934, p. 24.

[3]*Molodiye Gody*, p. 300.

his hands in 1889, adding that "no one could have put together a better guide."[4]

Intelligent, well-read and linguistically as capable as he was, Fedosseyev would, nonetheless, have been unable to compile this documentation alone. He probably received the material from Skvortsov or Motovilov,[5] the leading socialist intellectuals of Kazan. These men, in turn, may have received aid from Professor N. I. Zieber, whose dissertation was devoted to *Das Kapital* and who became the first Russian academician to lecture on Marx. Forced to leave Kiev University in 1875, Zieber died in 1883 after suffering from mental sickness. It is more than likely that the catalogue, for the most part, consisted of materials given to Fedosseyev by Skvortsov and that the summaries of German texts were originally assembled by Zieber.

In 1888, Fedosseyev, at the age of seventeen, was highly active in organizational work. A prodigious worker who read voluminously, he utilized most of his time setting up revolutionary groups and circulating propaganda, expending great energy on the development of a Social Democratic program. Fedosseyev rejected terror and, contrary to other Marxists, called for an alliance between workers and peasants.[6] When interrogated about the program, he stated that it consisted of a theoretical and a technical part, and a third section dealing with the use of propaganda.[7] The first parts were not found, but the last section was uncovered. It divided audiences, for purposes of propaganda, into cultured classes, peasants, workers, soldiers, and "the people." It also asserted the necessity of organizing both for propaganda and combat, stressing the need to spread ideas by print. In prison, Fedosseyev commented that, in his judgment, propaganda was to be directed above all to the workers. He added that legal as well as illegal means were required, and that he was about to work out a scheme for the party's "inner organization." "Leninism," then, was in the making before Lenin.

In the fall of 1889 Lenin was alleged to have joined a Marxist student circle in Samara. This claim is probably false, for Lenin was devoting most of his time to the study of law as well as the business

[4]N. Valentinov, "Vstrecha Lenina s Marksizmom", *Novyi Zhurnal*, Vol. 53, New York, 1958, p. 206.

[5]Fedosseyev, *Stati i pisma*, pp. 32 and 35. Fedosseyev also received Marxist literature from Pavel Levashov who was living abroad. (Shcheprov, p. 19.)

[6]Plekhanov began opposing terrorism during 1879-1881, notably the notion that tsarism could be overthrown by assassinating the Tsar, because it prevented the revolutionaries from accomplishing their real mission of agitation. He did not want a "staff without army," nor a party without foundations and influence among the people. *Cf.* Leopold H. Haimson, *op. cit.*, p. 37f.

[7]Shcheprov, p. 25.

of farming. He was not even in Samara, but on the farm. Unquestionably, he was reading a great deal. Perhaps he met one or another "Marxist," but he probably avoided revolutionaries in order not to jeopardize his readmission to the university.

Sister Anna related that in Samara Lenin was familiarizing himself with the operations and conspiratorial techniques of the old *Will of the People* group. Samara was full of former Siberian exiles who could have served as instructors. A. I. Livanov was identified as one person who taught Lenin. Another was N. S. Dolgov, a former member of Nechayev's group and a student of N. P. Ogarev's writings. (Ogarev, a close friend of Alexander Herzen, was one of the originators of the combat party concept.) The sister disclosed that Lenin studied the trials of the old revolutionaries; thus, he may then have become familiar with the Nechayev case.[8]

In 1891, at Samara, Lenin met Maria Petrovna Yasneva, a revolutionary school teacher who was nine years his senior. It is stated that Lenin was presented to her as an "outstanding democrat."[9] After their first meeting, Lenin walked Maria home—the first time that a romantic interest is reported in his life. (Maria later married V. S. Golubev, a former populist, a compiler of revolutionary bibliographies, and conductor of the populist self-education circle where Fedosseyev began his career.) Maria continued relations with Lenin for some time and in 1893 introduced him to a revolutionary group in St. Petersburg. She finally became a terrorist "judge" in the Bolshevik police. In 1891, Maria was still an ardent populist: she was a pupil of P. G. Zaichnevsky, a leader of *Land and Liberty* and intellectually akin to Tkachev. Zaichnevsky, considering reforms to be mere palliatives, advocated violent revolution made by a dictatorially run centralized party: "We shall cry 'to the axes' and we will strike the imperial family without sparing the blows." He uttered one line which must have appealed to Lenin throughout his life: "Who is not with us, is against us." Maria reported that she talked to Lenin about "seizure of power."[10] Lenin did not dispute her position but asked *who* was to seize power. The people, he argued, were not homogeneous, but rather consisted of different classes. Lenin's points were quite conventional: his argumentation did not disclose that he had become a full-fledged "revolutionary Marxist."

When did this conversation take place? Lenin went to St. Petersburg in March, 1891. It is likely that he met Maria in November, 1891, after his return to Samara. He had passed his examinations

---

[8]*Lénine tel qu'il fut*, Vol. I, p. 30.

[9]*Ibid.*, p. 137.

[10]*Ibid.*, p. 139.

and was petitioning for admittance to the Samara bar. He began working in a law firm only in the spring of 1892 and thus had time for romantic evening walks during this period.

It follows that Lenin's so-called Marxist activities have been predated and exaggerated: Lenin's *serious* study of the Russian economy and of Marx's teachings hardly began before the summer or fall of 1892.

Lenin Becomes Active

There was good reason for the sudden upsurge in Lenin's political interests. The harvest of 1891 had been poor and conditions became worse, so that before the 1892 crop was gathered, a severe famine hit Samara province. About fourteen million people in the Volga area were affected; typhus and cholera were rampant. Government mismanagement was as widespread as hunger and disease: barely one-twentieth of the sum required for relief was made available. But an order forbidding the exportation of grain was generally disregarded, probably because the shipments were indispensable to the financial stability of the Russian government.[1]

Lenin was traveling about on legal business. He observed that, as the peasants fled the villages and went to the cities, they transformed themselves into industrial workers or proletarians. In his preoccupation with the peasant problem, Lenin was still following the main stream of Russian revolutionary thinking. But gradually, as he came to recognize the faults of the populists, he broke his ties with the non-Marxists. It is reported that in the fall of 1892 he began to write about the famine, supposedly arguing that "famine performs a progressive function." "Talk of feeding the starving is nothing but an expression of the saccharine sweet sentimentality so characteristic of our intelligentsia." He apparently discouraged his friends from assisting in the relief actions which might have stabilized the bourgeois order. According to Lenin, the impulse to help the victims arose from bourgeois class interest.[2]

What was bad for the government was good for the revolution—this was the primitive logic which Lenin was learning. If the starving were not fed, the peasants would lose their faith in the Tsar, and the revolution would be hastened. He was beginning to comprehend the importance of the overall social order; this, un-

[1]Haimson commented: "In this respect, the famine of 1891 offers a striking parallel to the famine of 1932-33." There also were striking parallels with the famines which occurred under Lenin's rule. Haimson, *op. cit.*, p. 49.

[2]Scheibert, *Historische Zeitschrift, op. cit.*, p. 561f.

doubtedly, was a reflection of Marxian thought. But his callousness about the famine shows that the traditions of conspiracy were quite alive in him. Plekhanov, by contrast, advocated that the guilt of the government be exposed and a constitutional movement uniting liberals and democrats be created to agitate for a constituent assembly. Such moderation, however, dit not fit Lenin's psychology.

Lenin's early manuscripts, most of which have not been preserved, probably illustrated a confrontation between Marxism and populism. One paper, in fact, is said to have been a dialogue between a populist and a Social Democrat, a likely theme for a person in intellectual transition and travail. Lenin's firm commitment to Marxism indeed presupposed insight into the populist ideology which he had rejected. The confrontations did not take place exclusively in his mind: in his efforts to understand Marxism, he was assisted by others who had already penetrated the mysteries of Marx. Notably fruitful was his association with Isaac Christoforovich Lalayants who, during 1888-1889, had participated in Fedosseyev's group at Kazan. Together with fifty persons, Lalayants was arrested in Kazan on December 31, 1892. After being detained for two months, he was allowed, pending sentence, to choose a place of exile, and he selected Samara. Upon arrival, he contacted an old populist revolutionary, Dolgov, who years earlier had been a defendant in a show trial.

Lalayants met Lenin at Dolgov's home, presumably in March, 1893, where Lenin impressed him as a young man with an "extraordinarily intelligent face."[3] Their conversation "naturally" centered on "the populists and Marxists."[4] They walked and conversed for a long time, agreeing to meet the next evening. Lenin introduced Lalayants to Alexei V. Popov, also known as A. P. Sklyarenko or "Balbutsinovsky." (This person was using several names, not for reasons of conspiracy, but because, an illegitimate child, his real name was uncertain.) Sklyarenko lived on the outskirts of Kazan with his girl friend, Lebedeyeva, a student nurse.

Lalayants described Sklyarenko as a practical Marxist who had served a prison term. Unlike Lenin, who worked best as a "theoretician," Sklyarenko was an active agitator. He analyzed the social conditions at Samara, discussed the "circles" he had formed, and described to Lalayants the arguments he and Lenin had had with the populists. It is useful to remember that Lalayants was under police surveillance and awaiting sentence: he hardly would have

---

[3]*Lénine, tel qu'il fut,* 1958, Vol. II, p. 934. Footnotes by the Institute of Marxism-Leninism state that Lalayants *"envoyé à Samara début 1893, il y fit la connaissance de Lénine."* Since Lalayants was practically the first proven Marxist whom Lenin met, the date is of importance.

[4]*Lénine tel qu'il fut,* Vol. I, p. 144f.

dared to meet persons who were regarded by the police as prominent revolutionaries; yet Lalayants became a frequent guest at the Ulyanov house.

Sklyarenko had complained about the scarcity of illegal literature, but at Samara he discovered many works which Lalayants had not found at Kazan, including German editions of Marx's *The Misery of Philosophy;* Engels' *Anti-Duehring; The Condition of the Working Classes in England;* the *Communist Manifesto;* and issues of the theoretical organ, *Die Neue Zeit.* There was also a very complete "semi-legal" library.

Lenin, Lalayants, and Sklyarenko were called "the trio," and they were often together, meeting at the Ulyanov home, on the banks of the Volga, or in beer gardens. During the summer months, Lalayants disclosed, "the trio consisted only of two, since Lenin went with his family . . . to their farm in Alakayevka."[5] The three were sometimes referred to as "the circle," but, as Lalayants explained, not in "the organizational sense" of a revolutionary cell. There were no regular meetings, no lectures, no reading courses, no tasks and no activities, except random discussions. At a time when the younger generation, still influenced by populism, did not know too clearly what "Marxism" meant, "the circle" discussed the peasant problem, the economic development of Europe and Russia, and the "philosophy of Marx and Engels." Lalayants added, "This was simply a group of friends who had similar ideas and who, in an ocean of different opinions, were drawn together." Lalayants' report shows that Lenin, at twenty-three, was interested in Marxism and preoccupied with social problems, but he was no *Wunderkind* of revolution. That honor belongs to Fedosseyev, who initiated revolutionary activities as well as Marxist study in the gymnasium when he was sixteen.

Fedosseyev, released from prison in January, 1892, was living in semi-exile at Vladimir, a little town not far from Moscow. The local library held an unexpected treasure of revolutionary literature, and Fedosseyev made full use of these documents before he was in September again arrested. He initiated a translation of Karl Kautsky's *The Economic Teachings of Karl Marx* and constructed a program of action for industrial workers. This program, opposed to isolated revolutionary deeds, called for organized, concerted and sustained actions; it asserted that "the economic liberation of the working class can be achieved only through violence and the seizure of state power and the means of production."[6] To achieve political freedom—including a free press and freedom of assembly—the program advocated

5*Ibid.,* p. 148.

6Fedosseyev, *Stati i pisma,* p. 269f.

the unification and organization of the Russian proletariat. Fedosseyev anticipated that the battle for economic justice would be fought only after an effective political organization had been created, that the economic struggle would lead to the strengthening of the proletarian organizations. He stressed that the Russian workers must join forces with the European proletariat and expressed the conviction that the Russian proletariat had a "historical mission" to fulfill. This mission, he implied, was to activate the world revolution. Fedosseyev told the police that he wrote this program at the request of a person he did not desire to name. By 1893, Fedosseyev thought the time had come for Russian Marxists to transform themselves into an organization of Social Democrats.[7]

Fedosseyev did not invent a new doctrine, even though, having taken some of his clues from Plekhanov, he went far beyond the "first Russian Marxist." In 1883, the twenty-six year old Plekhanov had already written a preface to the Russian edition of the *Communist Manifesto* and had completed *Socialism and Political Struggle*. He maintained that the oppressed social class was not class-conscious and emphasized the need for Marxists to become politically active. Though the proletariat does not necessarily understand its political position, he wrote, it could reach political influence and ultimately seize state power, provided the peasant would support the socialist movement.

His brochure was very widely read. The following year, in *Our Disputes*, Plekhanov set out to prove that Russia was proceeding towards capitalism. Industry was rapidly developing and the number of industrial workers increasing. Socialists, he argued, must propagate and organize among the industrial workers and the intelligentsia. His main point was that since Russia had entered the capitalistic phase, the premise of the populist doctrine—namely that capitalism could be avoided—had collapsed. While Plekhanov criticized the belief that conspiracy was the way to seize power, he recognized the need not only for secret conspiratorial organization but for terrorist actions to disorient the government. Although the country must go through all the historical phases of capitalism, he believed, these phases could be very brief sometimes, with some lasting "zero time." "Social development" was the essential factor.

Fedosseyev demonstrated the relevance of these points to current conditions, and showed an original interest in the world revolution. During 1892, Lenin had not yet assumed Fedosseyev's position. In January, 1893, Fedosseyev wrote letters from prison to Samara, and during February and March sent three packages which probably contained manuscripts. The partner in Fedosseyev's correspondence is not known, but probably was not Lenin, although it is known that

[7]Geyer, p. 16.

Lenin wrote to Fedosseyev after Lalayants' arrival at Samara. Together with Lalayants and three other students, Lenin was studying the development of capitalism in Russia and preoccupying himself with the economic position of the peasantry. He was learning the rudiments of economics and was trying, in particular, to grasp the salient features of the Russian economy. In his memoirs, Dimitri Ulyanov recalls that in 1893, when he was living in Samara, he had seen a long article (about thirty-five pages) by Fedosseyev, "The Causes of the Abolition of Slavery in Russia," which had circulated among Samara "Marxists." In this piece, Fedosseyev pointed to the possibility of the ruling classes instituting a "reform from above," one which would be more advantageous than a "reform from below." Lalayants wrote that this was the first article which stressed development precisely from a Marxian point of view.[8]

Thus, Lenin, by the spring of 1893, was a member of a Marxist study group. He himself stated that he joined the Social Democratic party in 1893, and it appears that he was referring to his affiliation with the Lalayants circle.[9] Although Lenin still had merely a superficial familiarity with Marx, he now was thoroughly acquainted with the Social Democratic doctrine. In that period, Social Democratic study circles, concerned with economics and the natural sciences, did not engage in mass agitation or organization. Lenin studied the doctrine primarily through Fedosseyev's works: his catalogue, his writings on the Russian economy and presumably his program. Fedosseyev, from his prison cell, acted as Lenin's intellectual mentor and Lenin made every effort to obtain guidance from him.

Fedosseyev, a year younger than Lenin, had been organizing groups since 1887, and had become a confirmed and informed Marxist in 1888. It was he who organized the Social Democratic party in the Volga area. The attempts to ascribe Fedosseyev's contributions to Lenin should invite only contempt: to suggest that Lenin led the Samara revolutionaries to Marxism is to proceed far beyond the evidence. The Samara populists indoctrinated Lenin on the problems of power seizure; as he gradually veered toward Marxism he adopted this key element of populism.[10] The crucial point is that

---

[8]Quoted in Shcheprov, p. 64.

[9]After completing the above time reconstruction, I read in Haimson: "We know that Lenin's conversion took place between 1892 and 1893." He adds that in that period Lenin was reading Plekhanov's polemical writings and the second volume of *Das Kapital*. The evidence which will be adduced below seems to show that he read *Das Kapital*, including the second volume, in a careful manner, rather between 1893 and 1894.

[10]Krupskaya confirmed that Lenin, like many other socialists, began his career as an adherent of *Narodnaya Volya* and found it difficult to break from this tradition. *See* N. K. Krupskaya, *Reminiscences of Lenin* (Moscow: Foreign Languages Publishing House, 1959), p. 47f.

Lenin still was a student. His initial indoctrination completed, he was not yet a teacher and he certainly was neither an organizer nor a leader.[11]

[11]Haimson, *op. cit.*, p. 103.

Lenin, the Writer

Lenin's literary career began in the spring or summer of 1893 at which time he wrote a book review criticizing a populist agricultural writer. The review had been pieced together from lecture notes into a brochure. The manuscript was rejected by the magazine to which it was sent. Seized by the police late in 1893, it was rediscovered in 1923. In this work Lenin, while reflecting Marxist thinking, did not quote Marx—a remarkable omission for a budding Marxist.

In his Marxist study circle the young recruit first only listened, but once he had mastered the basic teachings, he was allowed to act as a lecturer. The debut of Lenin's speaking career can be dated quite accurately—he gave his first lectures in the summer of 1893.

Thus, Lenin graduated to the position of teacher and agitator during the second half of 1893, when he was a little over twenty-three years of age. This is standard and certainly does not indicate that Lenin's was a tardy development.

Now that Lenin had become a full-fledged revolutionary, he decided that Samara was not the best place for his work and resolved to go to the capital. Passing through Nizhni-Novgorod, he lectured to the local Marxists. In his two-week stay he procured letters of recommendation to local students who had left for the capital and had there joined a Marxist group at the Technological Institute.[1] Lenin arrived in St. Petersburg on September 12 or 13, and on September 15 he joined the Wolkenstein law firm.

Early in October Lenin traveled to Vladimir to establish contact with his imprisoned mentor through Fedosseyev's girl friend. He did not see Fedosseyev but received a manuscript from him which allegedly dealt with the history of serfdom and the emancipation of serfs. Fedosseyev, who had been intensely interested in this subject, continued this work while in prison. One erudite socialist, who read parts of the work in 1897, acclaimed Fedosseyev's knowledge, his analytical talent, and literary gifts. The manuscript supposedly given to Lenin, however, has not been found, though in 1895 Lenin engaged in research on the subject in Berlin.

It is said that immediately after his arrival in St. Petersburg,

[1]Pipes, p. 46.

Lenin was in great demand as a speaker. This is not correct; in fact Lenin, at that time, was skeptical about oratory.[2] However, we know that he lectured once on market theory, about one year *after* his arrival. This lecture, initially an off-the-cuff polemic against another Marxist, gradually developed into a manuscript of seventy-five hand-written pages. Here, for the first time, quotations from *Das Kapital* abound. Even more characteristically, Lenin—like the typical novice who wants to employ what he has just learned—tried to apply Marx's unworkable and purely theoretical algebraic formulae to his current statistical problem. By internal evidence, we can therefore date Lenin's first *serious* study of *Das Kapital:* it took place a good while *after* Lenin's arrival in St. Petersburg. Perhaps it commenced late in 1893; he definitely studied Marx's book in summer of 1894, and continued, in a thorough manner, as he enlarged the lecture into a brochure.

Lenin quoted from the German editions of the first and second volumes of this huge work; it is asserted that he made his own transla-German. And, although he probably managed as best he could, it is that he established himself as an erudite Marxist. To repeat: this was late in 1894.

In December, 1893, Lenin went to Moscow to spend Christmas with his family. It is reported that he attended a populist meeting, where he heckled the speaker until he himself was able to take the floor. Lenin now was ready to engage in his first battle, not against capitalism or aristocracy, but against his fellow socialists.

The Marxist, or rather Plekhanovist, attitude towards the famine had aroused the ire of other radicals. Under the leadership of the venerated N. K. Mikhailovsky, who as late as 1888 had been referred to as "the most hateful of our Marxists," several socialists (among them Danielson, translator of the first volume of *Das Kapital*) attacked the Social Democratic indifference—even glee—concerning the famine. In January, 1894, Mikhailovsky, sensing that the moral socialism of the populists was being perverted into the authoritarian "socialism of revenge" of which Alexander Herzen had spoken, began to oppose the Marxist callousness.

After Mikhailovsky's attack, Lenin and Fedosseyev corresponded. This correspondence is lost, but it is known that, on March 19, 1894, Fedosseyev wrote directly to Mikhailovsky, signing the letter with his full name.[3] He argued for violent revolution and proletarian dictatorship, as well as the unification of the world proletariat. We can merely conjecture that, upon being left without an answer from Mikhailovsky, Fedosseyev asked Lenin to write against the populists. It is reported that Fedosseyev initiated the Social Democratic fight against

[2]*Ibid.,* p. 53.

[3]Fedosseyev, *Stati i pisma,* pp. 101-154.

Mikhailovsky and his group. Indeed, Mikhailovsky's position constituted an enormous threat to the Social Democratic movement
just getting underway.[4]

Lenin's sister Anna reported that in 1894 Lenin studied Marx
seriously, together with Russian statistics, preparing to refute
Mikhailovsky and his friends. Her statement is corroborated by evidence, except for the place, which she claimed was Samara, but
actually was both Moscow and St. Petersburg. In any event, during
January, again at Nizhni-Novgorod, Lenin lectured on the populists
and on the development of Russian capitalism. Between March and
June, 1894, Lenin wrote his first book, entitled, *Who Are the Friends
of the People and How Do They Fight Against the Social Democrats?*
Within three months, the manuscript went through three rewrites
and several hectograph editions; altogether perhaps 250 or 300
copies were produced. The hectographing was done by a village priest,
near Vladimir, in an area where Fedosseyev controlled the organization. The brochure showed no by-line, although one or two editions carried the notation: "Published by a provincial group of Social
Democrats."

There is uncertainty, however, as to the actual author of the
book. In 1907, Lenin published a volume which comprised his major
writings. Entitled *During Twelve Years*, it implied that Lenin's
literary activity began in 1895. *Who Are the Friends . . .* was not
included, nor was it scheduled to be published in the two additional
volumes planned in this series. It is most likely that Fedosseyev, with
whom Lenin, as the latter himself stated in 1922, had been corre-
sponding about the Mikhailovsky controversy, had given him
materials concerning the case. Perhaps the manuscript which Lenin
had picked up in Vladimir had contained more materials of more
timely relevance than the disquisitions on the liberation of the serfs.
One interpretation would be that this book represented a joint effort
by Fedosseyev and Lenin, that Fedosseyev's original work was simply
rewritten and expanded by Lenin. It is plausible to assume that
Lenin utilized Fedosseyev's script. Lenin, of course, may have been
the authentic author. It remains questionable whether this work can
be ascribed to Lenin *exclusively*.

The book contains numerous quotations from several works by
Marx and Engels. If those are attributed to Lenin, his progress as
a Marxist scholar is plainly evident. Mastery of the sources had
improved, and arguments had become more assured. Long and
technical, this brochure was an excellent Marxist tract. Yet Machiavelli
was not forgotten. Lenin, for example, objected to Mikhailovsky's
praise of the purity of the intelligentsia's ideas—and here we *can* be

[4]Shcheprov, p. 73.

sure that Lenin wrote these words: "This is exactly why . . . the intelligentsia always has been impotent." Lenin also penned this remarkable sentence: "The direct purpose of science is to provide a true slogan for the struggle."[5] Lenin, at long last, had become a "Leninist."

[5] V. I. Lenin, *Werke*, Vol. I, (Berlin: Dietz, 1961), p. 334.

Lenin, a Professional Revolutionary

The letters of recommendation which he had secured in Nizhni-Novgorod put Lenin through M. A. Silvin in touch with a Marxist circle led by Stepan Ivanovich Radchenko. Around 1890, this capable propagandist had joined a Social Democratic circle that was run by R. E. Klasson. During 1892, or perhaps early in 1893, he organized a group of his own. Radchenko placed great emphasis on secrecy and conspiracy, rejected the idea that the workers should be the leading element in the movement, and instead called for a "small highly conspiratorial party of revolutionaries recruited exclusively from the intelligentsia." Organizationally speaking, Radchenko's social democratic group was set up according to the principles that had characterized the *Narodnaya Volya*.[1] Radchenko[2] ran his organization through a "central group" of which one member—most of the time, presumably, Radchenko himself—busied himself exclusively with conspiratorial work. Actually, the whole outfit was so small that this division into high command and troops appears ludicrous.

To establish the new venture, Radchenko contacted Herman Krassin, who had preceded Silvin from Nizhni-Novgorod. Krassin became the group's chief theoretician, while Radchenko functioned as organizer. V. V. Starkov, G. M. Krzhizhanovsky and P. K. Zaporozhets, students from the Technological Institute, became the main recruits, together with four women who were teaching at so-called Sunday schools. One of these women was to marry Radchenko, another married

[1] Pipes, p. 43f.

[2] Radchenko (1869-1911) was of Cossack origin, the son of a lumber merchant. He had been educated at Rostov and Kiev. With the exception of a three-month term of imprisonment late in 1893, he was politically highly active for twelve years, between 1890 and 1902, and yet "had an uncanny knack for staying out of the hands of the police." (Pipes, p. 43.) He even escaped arrest after the first party congress in 1898 when practically every one of the delegates was caught. Apparently he kept himself hidden and directed the work of others. (Krupskaya, 1942, p. 16.) Ultimately he was arrested and released after the amnesty of 1905, whereupon he abandoned revolutionary activity. (Pipes, p. 140.) Such a charmed life, especially if it took place in the Russian capital, arouses the suspicion that there might have been some collaboration with the police.

a future member, K. M. Takhtarev. Z. P. Nevzorova perhaps played a fleeting role in Lenin's life and later married Krzhizhanovsky, and N. K. Krupskaya became the wife of Lenin—this was almost a marriage club.

The group was moderately active but had practically no contacts with the proletariat.3 Leonid Krassin, Herman's brother, described these intellectuals as far less educated, almost ignorant, in comparison with Marxist students at St. Petersburg University, who included the learned P. B. Struve, N. D. Sokolov (who was to play a great role early in 1917), and the brothers Gerd. According to Krassin, these men "knew foreign languages and read in the original books."

When Lenin arrived in St. Petersburg, the Radchenko circle had been in existence for about two years. Lenin, Starkov related, was still a passionate advocate of terrorism and apparently was not well received; according to Gleb Krzhizhanovsky, later his close collaborator, Lenin "was temperamentally too 'red'."4

At a Party gathering in February, 1894, Lenin, ostensibly working as a lawyer, met his future wife, Nadyezhda Konstantinovna Krupskaya, an employee of the railway administration. Born on February 27, 1869, she was one year his senior. Quite active in Radchenko's group, she was a member of the Committee for Literacy. At that time, as we know from police reports, Lenin was a member of a "central group" of socialist organizers; this simply meant that he worked in Radchenko's outfit. Vassily Starkov and Pyotr Zaporozhets were described as his close comrades.

Krupskaya's father, Konstantin Ignotyevich Krupski, was a graduate of the Konstantinovsky cadet school. A professional soldier, he served in Smolensk, Poland and his native Kazan. Apparently because of ill health, he resigned from the army and became a civil servant. He was sent again to Poland but was suspended from office. While his case was pending, he earned his living as an insurance agent, clerk, and factory inspector. After ten years the charges against him were dropped and he presently died. The government paid his widow a modest pension which she supplemented by teaching, copying work, and renting rooms. A gifted and fanatical girl, Krupskaya started her revolutionary career in a surviving *Will of the People* cell. She joined Marxist circles in St. Petersburg two years before Lenin arrived.

By fall, 1894, Lenin was in the midst of organizational work. He lectured on the impact of Marxism on bourgeois literature and in December participated in leaflet campaigns. It is at this time that his professional career, began in earnest; there is no doubt that he

3Pipes, p. 53.

4*Ibid.,* pp. 70 and 48.

stimulated group activity and led serious theoretical debates.[5]

Soon Lenin was meeting such leading Social Democrats as Peter Struve and A. N. Potresov. Struve was the well-to-do son of a former governor of Astrakhan and Perm, and the grandson of a famed German astronomer; his wife, Nina Gerd, was a close friend of Krupskaya's. Potresov, son of a cavalry colonel, was wealthy from his mother's side.

Lenin's combativeness was already being displayed: though he was still a novice, he crossed swords with Struve, whom he accused of deviating from Marxism. (It is true that Struve was most impressed by the need to increase economic productivity.) Struve later wrote that Lenin's doctrines "aiming at the final destruction and extermination of the enemy" corresponded to the revolutionary's emotional attitudes. Lenin despised the Tsar, the bureaucracy, and the police, as well as their "antipodes," the liberals and the bourgeoisie. "That hatred had something terrible and repulsive in it." It was at the same time a matter of concrete "animal emotions and repulsions . . . abstract and cold, like Lenin's whole being."[6]

Struve and Potresov were eager to publish their materials in Russia, and to this effect wanted to couch their radical message in "Aesopian" language to render it acceptable to the censor. In 1894, Potresov, visiting Plekhanov in London (where Engels was still living), brought back a manuscript on the unlikely subject of the monistic interpretation of history. The book was published in 1895 in Russia as the product of "N. Beltov." It sold well, solving Plekhanov's financial difficulties.[7]

Encouraged by the potentialities of literary work, the "legal Marxists" decided to publish a volume of articles directed against the populists, and invited Lenin to contribute. Lenin wanted to exploit the opportunity to push the legal Marxists, especially Struve, to the left.

In September, 1894, Struve published the first legal Marxist book. Lenin proposed to write a critique of Struve's product, that was to be included in the collective work against the populists. It did not make too much tactical sense to undermine Struve's effort. Struve's book sold out within the month and marked the appearance of Marxism before the public eye. Yet Lenin was unresponsive to the requirements of literary tactics and in a cell meeting suggested that the political revolution culminating in the overthrow of tsarism might coincide with the social revolution and the fall of the bourgeoisie. He asserted that Struve's criticism of populism was too weak. Struve and

[5]*Ibid.*, p. 54.

[6]*Slavonic and East European Review*, XII, 593.

[7]Geyer, p. 54.

Potresov protested Lenin's forcefulness, arguing for moderation in the tone of his contribution. Lenin produced a draft which proved unsuitable for insertion in a "legal" publication. Only when Fedosseyev (who was then in exile at Solvychegodsk[8]) wrote Lenin, advising moderation and pointing out objectionable portions of the text, did Lenin consent to eliminate the offensive passages.

The article, "The Economic Content of Populism and Its Critique in Struve's Book," was signed by "N. Tulin." The book was printed in May, 1895, but permission was not granted for its distribution. About one hundred copies were given to key revolutionaries. This was Lenin's first printed work, and the first of which Lenin was the authentic and exclusive author. The article was of rather high quality and it established "Tulin" as a promising theoretician. Lenin was gaining a solid reputation for himself. At twenty-five years of age—and almost completely bald—he was emerging as an important leader. His organizational inventiveness was already evident—his group sent out questionnaires to factory workers to acquire first-hand information on social and work conditions. He also stood out as a teacher: while other instructors of Marxism lectured mostly on the more popular philosophical works of Engels, Lenin discussed *Das Kapital,* making every effort to relate the theory to the conditions of contemporary life.

Early in 1895, Petersburg Marxists, sensing the need for better contacts with their comrades abroad, decided to send Lenin as their liaison man. Lenin applied for a passport on grounds of poor health. His sickness was not merely a pretext. His mother had been worrying constantly about his health and at that time felt compelled to nurse him and control his diet. He complained of a "tiresome stomach trouble," probably a nervous stomach or gastritis. (According to a less likely report, he suffered from mucuous colitis.) In March, 1895, he contracted severe pneumonia, which quickly brought his mother and sister Anna to his sickbed.[9] His mother probably insisted that he consult qualified specialists. At that time, well-to-do Russians usually went to doctors in Germany, Switzerland, and France. Lenin, believing it advisable to do the same, convinced his friends that it might be useful if he combined medical treatment with revolutionary contacts. The police granted the passport without difficulties on March 28 (New Style). Because of sudden additional illness, probably

---

[8]This location in the Arkhangel area also served as a place of exile for Stalin, 1908-1911.

[9]There is a vague hint of a possibly amorous interest. When he fell sick, he was taken care of by the sisters Zinaida P. and Sofia P. Nevzorov, yet Lenin himself had been nursing Sofia when she was sick during January, 1895, i.e., after he met Krupskaya. *See* V. Y. Mushtukov and P. Y. Nikitin, *Zdes zhil i rabotal Lenin* (Leningrad: Lenizdat, 1961), p. 34f. Zinaida later married Lenin's friend Krzhizhanovsky.

bronchitis or, less likely, pneumonia, Lenin left only after some delay and arrived in Switzerland in May.

As of January 1, 1895, the Ulyanov file contained no reference to suspect activities. However, on June 19, the Director of Police Department wrote to His Excellency, P. I. Rachkovsky, chief of the Okhrana's foreign department. Rachkovsky's office was in Paris but he was in charge of surveying Russian revolutionaries throughout Europe. The letter, which was classified as secret, read:

> Vladimir Ilyich Ulyanov, Assistant Barrister in Petersburg Okrug and son of a State Councillor, left for abroad on April 25 of this year.[10] He is under police surveillance and is traveling with passport No. 720 issued by the Petersburg authorities on March 15, 1895.
>
> According to information available to the Police Department, above-mentioned Ulyanov occupies himself with Social Democratic propaganda among Petersburg workers. The objective of his trip is to find ways of bringing into the empire revolutionary literature as well as to establish contacts between revolutionary circles and emigrants living abroad. I am informing you about this with the request to establish surveillance [of Ulyanov's] activities and contacts and to report about them.[11]

The slow action of the Okhrana—they wrote five weeks after Lenin had left Russia—was rather typical of their way of operating. But the communiqué makes it clear that the officials knew precisely what Lenin was doing and found it unnecessary to stop him.

Lenin met Plekhanov in Geneva, P. B. Axelrod in Zurich, Paul Lafargue, Marx's son-in-law, in Paris, and Karl Kautsky in Berlin. Kautsky was now considered the leading theoretician of world Marxism, after Friedrich Engels' death. Lenin is said to have discussed with Plekhanov and Axelrod the need to publish a Social Democratic newspaper abroad, but it seems that the final agreement was to increase legal publishing and to prepare a number of *sborniks* (books containing contributions by several authors). Lenin had brought his "Tulin" article (not by any means a copy of *Who Are the Friends of the People*) and Axelrod liked it. But Plekhanov was not enthusiastic about the idea.

Lenin impressed Axelrod as a talented person; the latter wrote to Plekhanov expressing satisfaction in sensing the possibility of new activity. Following Lenin's visit Axelrod also wrote to Kautsky that "our revolution will take a long time, and be characterized by very little poetry."[12]

Yet Axelrod was the movement's foremost organization expert,

10This was May 8 New Style.

11Document in the Hoover Institution.

12Geyer, *op. cit.*, p. 59.

and it is most likely that Lenin was listening to him as a student would to a highly respected professor. The organizational problem was indeed pressing: there existed a sufficient number of Marxist circles in many cities but each "circle" was independent. Lenin's circle now consisted of more than a dozen persons. But Lenin kept his group—or Radchenko's—isolated in order to ground them firmly in Marxist theory. Either because he felt the time had come for a different approach or because Axelrod had suggested a broader perspective, Lenin, after returning to Russia, threw himself wholeheartedly into the task of unifying the Marxist groups in St. Petersburg.

Axelrod may have raised another subject. During the 1870's, he had engaged in polemics with Tkachev on the role of the people in the revolution. Axelrod then considered the widest possible autonomy of each section to be a guarantee of revolutionary consciousness and activism. The problem now was to go beyond this stage. In discussing the next step, it is likely that Axelrod put Lenin on guard against adopting some of Tkachev's theories. Tkachev preached violent struggle through centralization, discipline, decisiveness, unity of command, and combining seizure of power with popular rebellion. Extolling the role of the revolutionary minority endowed with force, power, and authority, he argued the need to force consciousness upon the working class, the possibility of *creating* a revolution, and the necessity of an action party.[13] Axelrod remained skeptical of this approach and placed more emphasis on mass action and agitation. It is evident that Tkachev's ideas impressed Lenin; he later required his followers to read Tkachev carefully.[14] We do not know at what time Lenin himself studied Tkachev, but he may have done so while in Switzerland. When he returned to Russia, he possessed a clearer vision of the tasks ahead.

[13]P. N. Tkachev, *Izbranniye sochineniya* (Moscow 1933), III, 225f, 228f, 264f; *see also* Michael Karpovich, "A Forerunner of Lenin: P. N. Tkachev," *The Review of Politics,* July, 1944, and Haimson *op. cit.*, 16f and 36.

[14]Leonard Schapiro, *The Communist Party of the Soviet Union* (New York: Random House, 1959), p. 4.

First Steps Toward the Action Party

On his way to Switzerland, Lenin had stopped for two days in Berlin. There he had contacted I. L. Eisenstadt-Yudin, a representative of the Vilno Social Democratic organization. On his return trip, Lenin spent seven weeks, through August and most of September, in Berlin.

On August 3, 1895, a day after his arrival, Lenin attended a socialist meeting in Berlin. He was accompanied by Wilhelm Buchholz, the Russian correspondent of *Vorwaerts,* the foremost German Social Democratic paper. Buchholz, a Prussian citizen, had known Lenin in Samara from 1889 to 1891, the period during which he had lived under police surveillance.[1] Buchholz related that the August 3 meeting was devoted to the study of the agrarian question, implying that the discussion had impressed upon Lenin the urgent need for a Social Democratic agrarian program.

On September 15, 1895, *Vorwärts* disclosed a secret letter by the Russian Minister of Interior, I. N. Durnovo, to the Procurator of the Holy Synod, Pobedonostsev. Recently, Communist historians have asserted that Lenin had come into possession of this letter and because of his connection with Buchholz and the content and style of the article, they have argued that "one can assume with certainty that Lenin was the author of this article." It would be of interest to learn how Lenin achieved possession of a classified letter. If this unlikely story were true, it would have to be assumed that Lenin was on good relations with the Ministry of the Interior, which ran the police, and that someone in the Ministry leaked this letter to him.

Between September and November, 1895, *Vorwärts* published several articles dealing with the class struggle in Russia. The arguments are said to resemble those expressed by Lenin in articles published in *Rabochoye Delo.* After Lenin's arrest in December, 1895, these articles ceased. German Communist historians, eager to establish some sort of apostolic succession, intimate that Lenin acted as a *Vorwärts* correspondent. Actually Lenin wrote his three *Rabochoye Delo* articles late in November, only after his return. The paper came out in December—so perhaps it was the *Vorwärts* articles which, in fact, inspired Lenin.

Lenin used his time in Berlin visiting the library and reading additional revolutionary literature. He studied about a dozen large books, including works by Engels and Herzen, a standard history of the Russian revolutionary movement by Alfons Thun, and a three-volume history of serfdom. Most of this literature was printed in German, and on August 29, 1895, he wrote to his mother that he still understood German very poorly.[2] He added that he was doing little sight-seeing, but was enjoying the more popular types of amusement—he probably went to a fair or an amusement park.

---

[1]Buchholz was born in 1866, apparently in Samara. He attended the Samara gymnasium and in 1887 was ejected from St. Petersburg University. Exiled to Orenburg in 1888, he then returned to Samara, and after 1891 completed his studies in Zurich and Bern. He came to Berlin in 1895 and for many years thereafter performed liaison duties for Lenin.

[2]Elizabeth Hill and Doris Mudie (translators and editors), *The Letters of Lenin,* (London: Chapman and Hall, 1937), p. 7.

On September 14, 1895, Plekhanov wrote to Wilhelm Liebknecht, the German socialist leader, recommending Lenin as "one of our best Russian friends." Plekhanov cautioned Liebknecht that Lenin was "on his way back to Russia, therefore nobody is supposed to learn about his visit to Charlottenburg." This letter was sent remarkably late. Lenin, who left shortly after September 21, might still have met Liebknecht, but there is no evidence that this meeting took place.

After his return to Russia, Lenin visited both Moscow and St. Petersburg. He wrote and sent to Switzerland a biographical article on Friedrich Engels, who had died a few months earlier. He launched extensive preparations for the founding of a newspaper. In October he met Y. O. Zederbaum, better known as "Martov," who had just arrived from Minsk. Partly influenced by the physician M. Lyakhovsky, a friend of Fedosseyev, Martov was also interested in advancing the concept of a unified party.

Martov was an old acquaintance of Radchenko. The first meeting of Lenin and Martov which was somewhat of a historic occasion, took place on Martov's initiative. Lenin was accompanied by Starkov and Krzhizhanovsky (the editorial group which was preparing the newspaper), and Martov appeared with Lyakhovsky. Martov criticized the indifference of the Radchenko set-up with respect to spontaneous strikes but proposed the merging of the two groups. It was agreed to initiate a broadly conceived and boldly executed agitational effort. This was a turning away from literature to activism.[3] This joint cell of 22 members became known as the *Group of Social Democrats* or as the *stariki* (the old ones).

Under the name of Fedor Petrovich, Lenin had advanced to the handling of funds: in November he transmitted money from unknown sources to strikers. The five Marxist groups in Petersburg were brought under control of a "central group," divided into a subgroup in charge of workers' activities (which plunged into preparations for a massive strike in the textile industry) and a "literary" sub-group in charge of intelligence and secret operations. Lenin was the most energetic member of the central group. He wrote his first leaflet which was addressed to the strikers at the Thornton textile factory, stressing economic problems, avoiding references to politics, and being careful not to incite to rebellion.[4] The strike failed, and Lenin, together with Krzhizhanovsky, concentrated on preparing the first issue of *Rabochoye Delo*. Silvin related that Lenin informed the contributors that he interpreted his editorial obligations "autocratically."[5] However, early in December, 1895, his efforts were cut

[3]Pipes, p. 82f.
[4]*Ibid.*, p. 92.
[5]*Ibid.*, p. 94.

short. The police apparently felt the need to decapitate an emergent energetic strike leadership and to prevent publication of the new paper. Also, from European agents, they had received disquieting reports about Lenin's activities abroad. Apparently they decided that young Ulyanov was overstepping his bounds.

After a search was made of his home, Lenin was arrested. He had been watched by a police agent, a dentist with whom he was very friendly.[6] But the infiltration was not one-sided. Krupskaya's cousin, who worked in the police address bureau, had warned Lenin of his impending arrest.[7] For some reason Lenin did not go into hiding; this was the last time that he failed to take action after receiving such a warning. The experience taught him the wisdom of organizing in secret and developing a party that was capable of defending itself against the police.

After Lenin was tucked away in jail, the St. Petersburg Union for the Struggle for the Liberation of the Working Class came into being on December 15, 1895. This party was the action or combat party unifying the Marxists in the Russian capital. The name and probably the concept had been suggested to Lenin by Axelrod. However, the organization was given its name only after Lenin was already in prison. It acquired considerable fame, and confusion has been fostered to intimate that Lenin was a prominent member, if not the leader of the Union. Lenin himself initiated the deception in 1902. The fact is that while he belonged to the *stariki,* which formed the parent body of the Union, he played no role in this first *potent* Marxist organization in Russia.[8]

[6]This same agent, Mikhailov, previously had betrayed the main populist group in the capital.

[7]Krupskaya, 1959, p. 23.

[8]Pipes, pp. 68, 84.

Siberia

Political prisoners were not pampered in tsarist prisons, but they were nonetheless treated well and permitted to read and write. When Lenin was arrested, he was suffering from a nervous condition and stomach trouble. In the house of detention, he slept for nine hours every night and practiced callisthenics daily. His own dentist, probably the informer, who, incidentally, was soon to die an unexplained and violent death, treated his toothaches. For the first time, he was able to follow the diet prescribed by a Swiss physician; the prison authorities permitted him to drink mineral water.

During 1896, he was interrogated four times. Only slight information has been disclosed concerning these interrogations. According to one police report, he denied being a Social Democrat, stating that he never participated in the workers' movement, and he refused to offer explanations of his relations with the prisoners arrested together with him. He justified his trip by stating that he needed to have access to certain books! The interrogator reported that manuscripts in Lenin's possession dealt with industrial strikes.[1]

Lenin actually found a way to supply strikers with leaflets which he wrote in prison under the inattentive guard of his jailers. He even produced an entire pamphlet, *On Fines*, which became quite popular.[2] Control over his correspondence was extremely lax. He used double-talk language with milk serving as invisible ink, but such tricks were not unknown to the police. Though he wrote conspiratorial instructions, the jailers did not disturb him. Perhaps the police were content with his writings and watched his messages for purposes of intelligence.

After a while Lenin's health improved. He began work on an ambitious book, *The Development of Capitalism in Russia*. The enormous documentation for this tome was obtained while he was in custody. The prison officials cooperated, checking out entire libraries and carrying the books to his cell. The lengthy work was written entirely while he was imprisoned and in Siberia under police supervision. It was Lenin's most scholarly work, a treatise devoted to economic history and Russian industrialization.

Lenin had committed no overt criminal act, yet early in 1897 he was convicted by administrative decision, without trial, to live in Siberia for three years under surveillance. His mother used her influence to obtain a promise that he would be exiled to a climatically suitable location. She also received permission for him to travel to Siberia at his own expense, in a passenger express instead of a cattle car. He was released from detention in February, 1897, spent a few days in Petersburg, where he had a reunion with his revolutionary comrades, visited his family at Moscow for about a week, and then traveled to Krasnoyarsk, where he remained for some time, studying in the library and petitioning for another place of exile.

In April, 1897, he first met Fedosseyev. (In his later life, when his memory was declining, Lenin denied ever meeting Fedosseyev.) Julius Martov later wrote that Lenin was living in a comfortable room of his own, was very well dressed, and wore an impressive fur coat. Fedosseyev, who was supposed to be released in October, 1895, was

[1]*Krasnaya Letopis*, No. 2-3, 1922, p. 308.

[2]According to other information, this book was published at Kherson, in 1895, which would mean he wrote it before his arrest.

kept in jail because of the activities he had conducted from his cell. In October, 1896, he was condemned to five years of exile in eastern Siberia. Martov, Fedosseyev, and a dozen or so other Social Democrats had been traveling in a prison transport and were lodged in Krasnoyarsk prison. Some of them were permitted to go to town; it thus happened that Lenin was smuggled into the jail where he had a lengthy discussion with Fedosseyev.[3] We do not know what they discussed, nor can we assess Fedosseyev's impression of Lenin. We know that Lenin was much taken by the man, and thereafter wrote frequently to Fedosseyev who did not reply very diligently. Fedosseyev was on more intimate terms with his travel companion, Gleb Krzhizhanovsky, who was also a friend and comrade of Lenin.

Finally, Lenin had to leave Krasnoyarsk. Almost three months after his release from jail, on May 20, 1896, Lenin arrived in the village of Shushenskoye, his assigned residence. There he found quarters with A. Ziryanov, one of the more wealthy peasants; the government paid them eight rubles for room, board and laundry.[4] At first Lenin slept in the family room, but he soon obtained a room of his own with three windows.[5] His diet contained a lot of milk, which improved his health. Soon forsaking his mineral water, Lenin hiked, hunted, swam and played chess. Whatever else he needed— and that was modest because of his frugal habits—was sent him by his mother. The locale reminded him of Switzerland. "I have probably fixed myself up here hardly any worse than in Spiez," he wrote to his mother, who was then recovering in the Swiss mountains from an unspecified illness. Against several suggestions by his mother that she request his transfer, he repeatedly objected: apparently he was happy where he was.

Lenin corresponded regularly with his friends at home, with fellow exiles in Siberia, and with revolutionaries abroad. He undertook at least six trips, including three or four to the town of Minussinsk, and one boat trip to Krasnoyarsk where he visited his dentist and the library.[6] In turn, he was often visited by his friends, especially by Krzhizhanovsky. Otherwise he worked on his book and contributed to "legal" publications.

Lenin was now twenty-eight and apparently a confirmed bachelor.

[3]Yu. Martov, "Iz zapisok sotsialdemokrata," in *Fedosseyev Nikolai Evgrafovich, op. cit.,* p. 113ff.

[4]Krupskaya took pains to point out that eight rubles was not at all a negligible income—a pound of meat cost two kopeks. Lenin, of course, had supplementary income. "In Shushenskoye, Vladimir Ilyich never experienced any need." *Istoricheskii Arkhiv* (1957), No. 2, p. 37.

[5]A. G. Ivankov, *Lenin v Sibirskoi Ssilke (1897-1900),* (Moscow, 1962), p. 133.

[6]Much has been made of his work at the famed Yudin Library at Krasnoyarsk; but though he had a pass for a whole week, he stayed only four days.

There is no evidence that he had ever fallen in love. In 1894, he had met Krupskaya, with whom, it is reported, he had become "friends." Lenin had corresponded with her while in prison, asking her to do errands and perform chores for him. Presumably Krupskaya had become attached to him, but there is no evidence that he regarded her as more than an aide. Rather tall and gaunt, with a narrow pale face surrounded by carrot-red hair, she was devoid of charm, taciturn, and had no sex appeal even when young. Though she greatly liked hats and various hair styles, she was a devout revolutionary, and Lenin cherished her as a comrade-in-arms. But Krupskaya also became involved with the police and was arrested. When a political prisoner, Vetrova, burned herself in her bed in Peter-Paul Fortress as an act of protest,[7] Krupskaya and other women revolutionaries were released from jail. Krupskaya was exiled to the northern provinces. She asked to be sent to Shushenskoye instead, on the pretext that she was engaged to be married to Lenin.

Though there is little doubt that she took the initiative in the marriage, according to legend Lenin wrote her from prison a love letter in milk. It is also said that he replied to her announcement that she would join him by telling her to come as his wife. She allegedly answered: "Well, so I come as a wife." Verification was required for the police. On January 8, 1898, Lenin is supposed to have telegraphed the police requesting permission for his fiancée to join him, and the next day Krupskaya made a similar request to the Ministry of the Interior. The alleged time sequence is suspect; the cable has remained unrecovered.[8] We do know that Lenin wrote to his mother: "I seem to remember having written to you that Nadyezhda Konstantinovna is thinking of asking to be sent here." He did not say that he was happy about this but simply added: "If this plan is realized, it will be a good opportunity to send books, notes and anything else by her"[9]—hardly a passage fit for an anthology of love letters. His libido did not make it difficult for him to live according to Nechayev's notion that sex weakens energetic men and that revolutionaries should not live for their desires but should concentrate on solving social problems.

When Krupskaya arrived, she was duly chaperoned by her mother, Yelizaveta Vasilyevna. Mme. Ulyanova was informed by her future daughter-in-law that Lenin had become much healthier, that he was looking fine, and that his mood had improved. The couple got married—in church, it seems—on July 22, 1898. Lenin promptly began to quarrel with his mother-in-law about religion. He argued good-

---

[7]Krupskaya, 1959, p. 29.
[8]Ivankov, *op. cit.*, p. 128.
[9]*The Letters of Lenin*, p. 49.

naturedly, and "not without humor," it is reported. The arguments occurred daily, lasting through the lifetime of his *ménage* with his mother-in-law. Mme. Krupskaya the elder was the only person in his entourage who dared rebuke him and assert her own personality.

Very soon the family left its old lodgings; the landlord drank too much and it was noisy. They rented a duplex with plenty of ovens and a garden, and hired a sixteen-year-old servant girl, Pasha Yashchenko, to perform the menial household chores. In later years, Krupskaya felt impelled to deny that their life was devoid of poetry and passion.[10] Maybe some form of love existed between them, but it seemed to Lenin more important that Krupskaya establish herself as his research assistant and secretary. Her assistance helped Lenin to increase his output. He finished his book on capitalism and also wrote and published two brochures, twenty-five articles, and nine book reviews—all within the three years of his Siberian exile.

In addition to the significant income that his literary activity returned, both he and Krupskaya received, albeit irregularly, a government "salary." Lenin translated, probably mostly from German, Sidney and Beatrice Webb's *Industrial Democracy*, a job which had been procured for him by his opponent, Peter Struve; later Lenin regretted this assistance to Fabian socialism and made some desultory attempts to conceal his contribution.

In the meantime, on June 21, 1898, Fedosseyev had committed suicide. (Upon hearing the news, Fedosseyev's fiancée also took her life.) He had been accused of counter-revolutionary attitudes and was unable to overcome these unfounded accusations. Actually, a "court" of party comrades had cleared him in September, 1897. He allegedly sent word to Lenin that his faith was unshaken, but since he sent his manuscript to Krzhizhanovsky and failed to answer Lenin's letters, it is unlikely that he chose Lenin as the recipient of his last thoughts. As a faithful Marxist, Fedosseyev probably persisted in his belief that the revolution was inevitable; his faith in revolutionaries as the preservers of the cultural heritage was, however, undoubtedly shaken. Lenin, in a letter[11] to his sister, said that Fedosseyev died "in full belief in life and not in despair"—which could have meant anything. Actually, Fedosseyev was undergoing a spiritual crisis. He wrote three touching letters to Tolstoi.[12] The extremely cordial reply arrived after Fedosseyev was dead. It is open to speculation whether Fedosseyev would have written to Tolstoi if he were staying within the intellectual boundaries set by the Social Democratic party, let alone that he would have shown, as he did, interest in the fate of people exiled for religious reasons.

[10]Geyer, p. 169.
[11]Lenin's letter of July 15, 1898, appears in Fedosseyev, *Stati i pisma*, p. 26.
[12]*Ibid.*, pp. 258-264.

Lenin received the news with complacency: Fedosseyev, as a seasoned revolutionary, should have displayed more inner strength, not taking "exile stories" to heart. But Lenin should have perceived the tragedy of the honest and pure revolutionary who suddenly realized that the ideal was being destroyed by the limitations of real men. Lenin was to find his own calvary twenty-four years later.

Portions of Lenin's book were published in March, 1899, in the legal organ, *Nachalo*. "Ilyin" was the pen name which he came to use often. The police easily identified the conspiratorial author through a certain Gurovich who was acting as the financial supporter of the magazine. Strange revolutionary literature—that the police of an autocracy ensure its publication and circulation! Strange, too, that when the police searched Lenin's home in Shushenskoye, allegedly because they had intercepted correspondence Lenin received about Fedosseyev's tombstone, they found not a particle of evidence that he was continuing revolutionary activity. The incriminating material, Krupskaya related,[13] was lying in the lower shelf but the searching gendarmes grew tired before they got to it. Perhaps there was not much incriminating material to be found. In any event, Lenin's term was not increased.

Lenin's book was published a few weeks later—1200 copies were sold out within a year or two. Since Lenin had more free time after his book was completed, he engaged in polemics with socialists who did not share his opinions, including Kautsky, and corresponded on the need of establishing a truly proletarian party. He organized a meeting of seventeen similarly minded revolutionaries, in September, 1899, at Yermakovsk, about twenty miles from Shushenskoye. The purpose of the gathering was to prepare a protest against the "economists"—Marxists who viewed the struggle in largely economic terms.

To prepare himself better as an international revolutionary, Lenin began to study German systematically. Procuring dictionaries and German translations of Turgenev,[14] he read a great deal in German, including philosophical works. He also dabbled in English and possibly in French. Moreover, he familiarized himself with European socialist writings.

As the end of his exile was approaching, Lenin lost weight rapidly and suffered from insomnia. He left Shushenskoye on January 29, 1900, the very day his term ended, and traveled by steamer

[13]Krupskaya, 1959, p. 45f.

[14]For translation exercises Lenin chose special passages which seemed important to him, e.g., a speech by a figure in Turgenev's drama *Dym* (Smoke), where it is asserted that Russia had not made any contribution to world civilization or world culture. This work of Turgenev's, incidentally, for many years was out of print in the Soviet Union.

to Krasnoyarsk. From there he journeyed by railroad to Ufa, where he left Krupskaya and her mother, finally reaching Russia. Not permitted to enter the capital, he settled in Pskov. He arrived in March, after passing through Moscow, Yekaterinoslav, and St. Petersburg where he met Vera Zasulich, who had come secretly from Switzerland.

Lenin's young wife, whom he had married a year and a half earlier, stayed behind. Lenin's drive for political power obviously was his motivating factor. But Krupskaya found this state of affairs entirely normal, for her instincts were those of a teacher, a revolutionary, and a prematurely withered old maid. They definitely were not those of a healthy young woman interested in sharing her husband's activities. She probably would have been amazed if someone had suggested that perhaps Lenin could have remained with her for the remainder of her exile, which was to expire on March 11, 1901.

Iskra

While Lenin had been in Siberia, the Social Democratic organizations had convened a congress in Minsk (March, 1898), for the purpose of establishing a single, unified party. The initiative for holding this congress was taken by Social Democrats from Kiev and the Jewish Bund, a Marxist organization of Jewish workers and intellectuals founded in 1897. The congress failed to achieve its objective of unifying the socialists, who were divided into two great camps: that of "spontaneity," with primary emphasis on the economic struggle, and that of "consciousness," with emphasis on organization. Despite the stress on "indivisibility" (this concept was an integral part of the tsarist empire's political formula), the Bund preserved its autonomy in dealing with questions affecting the Jewish proletariat. The congress did succeed in establishing a party structure. Along with a Central Committee on which Lenin's friend Radchenko was serving as one of three members, there was planned a party paper, *Rabochaya Gazeta*. Lenin was appointed editor of booklet publications. The leading émigrés in Switzerland bestowed their blessings on the organization.

Lenin had written a first draft of a program, but it was lost. The congress did not have time to develop a program while in session; a few days later most of the participants were arrested. Upon the request of Radchenko and the Central Committee, the manifesto of the new party was written by Struve after the congress had met. The stated goal was political freedom: "The Russian proletariat needs complete liberty like clean air for healthy breathing. This is the prerequisite for a free and successful development of the struggle for improvements and final liberation."[1] Lenin commented that "having made the overthrow of absolutism its immediate task, social democracy must come out as the vanguard in the fight for democracy." He subscribed to the notion that once autocracy had been overthrown, the struggle must be continued "against capital and the bourgeoisie for the complete victory of socialism."[2]

Lenin thus accepted the manifesto. Struve, in fact, had not posited his own ideas in the text, but had simply acted as *rapporteur*. The text, he stated later, was approved by Plekhanov's group and by Lenin, but was disliked by the "economists."[3] Still, Lenin was unhappy with the propensity of some comrades to seek alliances with radical bourgeois and liberal groups. He was particularly dissatisfied with Struve who, in the footsteps of European "revisionists," was pointing out flaws in Marx's predictions on the inevitability of capitalist collapse. Lenin opposed the notion that socialists should adopt democratic and economic methods of struggle instead of relying upon conspiracy and revolution.[4] Lenin was personally obligated to Struve for many services rendered while he was in prison and exile. But Lenin's political instincts were right: Struve was detaching himself from the radical revolutionaries. Struve soon was to advance his belief that socialism would materialize only through the gradual socialization of capitalism (1900).

During 1899, Lenin conceived the idea of founding a newspaper to be used to combat divergent views and to build up an organization suitable for the revolutionary struggle. The paper was to be a forum of political debate and instruction, intended to bring about the ideological consolidation of the movement; simultaneously, it was to serve as a means of unifying the Marxist groups into a centralized structure suitable for concerted revolutionary action. It did not occur to Lenin to join forces with an existing party organ; he was probably correct in maintaining that the paper be published abroad. This idea was discussed with Krzhizhanovsky, and cryptic correspondence with Potresov and Martov was devoted to the

---

[1]Geyer, pp. 106-110. About Radchenko's alleged dissatisfaction with Struve's product, see Krupskaya, 1942, p. 17.

[2]Geyer, chapters III and IV. "In those days Struve was unquestionably on good terms with Vladimir Ilyich." (Krupskaya, 1942, p. 16.)

[3]Haimson, *op. cit.*, p. 81.

[4]On Lenin's stand, and notably on his opposition to the *Credo* written by revisionist adherents of the economic struggle, *see* Geyer, p. 180f. The whole complex, including the divergences with Struve, is discussed lucidly in Donald W. Treadgold, *Lenin and his Rivals, The Struggle for Russia's Future, 1898-1906* (New York: Praeger, 1955), **chapter V.**

feasibility of the publishing venture. Lenin proposed that Potresov and Martov join forces and seek cooperation with Plekhanov and Axelrod.

Lenin's position in the party had reached a degree of prominence so that, after Martov's return from Siberia, the leading Social Democrats—including Struve—visited him in Pskov to discuss strategy. Lenin's program now included a bi-monthly journal in addition to a bi-weekly paper. His plan received general approval, even from Struve whom Lenin was carefully placating.

Thanks to Struve's cooperation, money was raised. Part of it came from Prince Obolensky, a local aristocrat; another contribution was forwarded by Nikolai F. Lopatin, the director of the regional Bureau of Statistics. Alexandra M. Kalmykova, a "patroness" of Struve, Potresov, and Lenin, and the wealthy wife of a senator and financial supporter of many revolutionary undertakings, contributed 2,000 rubles. A Marxist sympathizer and translator of Kant, D. Zhukovsky, offered 1,000 rubles and the well-to-do Potresov himself made 2,000 rubles available. Thus, the initial undertaking was adequately financed.[5]

Lenin, Martov, and Potresov planned to go to Europe. Lenin applied for a passport, obtaining it without difficulty from a sympathetic police official. The passport was issued at Pskov under No. 34 on May 18, 1900 (New Style). Lenin traveled with Martov via Tsarskoye Selo, where they did some sightseeing, to Petersburg. In the capital he was arrested because of his illegal presence, but was released ten days later, without the loss of his passport. Permitted to proceed to Podolsk, he spent a few days with his mother, then made a short trip to Ufa to visit Krupskaya, returned to Podolsk, and on July 16, 1900, went abroad. On September 20, 1900 (New Style), Circular No. 2104 informed the Russian police organs abroad of his departure. A description was appended to the circular: a man of medium height, reddish hair, eyebrows and beard, roundish head, high forehead, normal nose, round face, medium-sized mouth . . . makes good impression. The revolutionaries, the police were warned, considered Lenin to be a serious and energetic person whom they were sending abroad to head the new organization of *Rabochoye Delo*.

The police had known of Lenin's plans since his return from Siberia, when he had stayed in the house of a female police agent in Moscow; they had also placed an informer at the Pskov conference. They had shadowed Lenin and Martov at Tsarskoye Selo and St.

---

[5]Krupskaya wrote that Kalmykova "financed the old *Iskra* right up to the time of the Second Congress." The 1942 edition of Krupskaya's book used the term "subsidized" (p. 10). Krupskaya, *Reminiscences*, 1959, p. 22. Kalmykova arranged for Zasulich's illegal trip to Russia in 1899. Geyer, *op. cit.*, p. 202.

Petersburg, debating whether they should allow Lenin to go abroad or send him back to Siberia. Apparently unable to decide upon a course of action, police arrested Lenin and Martov to obtain more information. After the police discovered 1,400 rubles sewn into Lenin's suit and 500 rubles on Martov, Lenin fruitlessly attempted to explain that he was earning 1,500 rubles yearly as a writer. The police had no doubts as to the proposed use of the money, and believed that it probably came from Nikolai Lopatin. Although the police knew that Lenin intended to establish a paper, they decided to let him travel abroad. We can only surmise that they assumed Lenin would draw strength away from those revolutionary groups which they most feared.

Lenin's case was handled by Colonel Vladimir Piramidov, who served as the interrogator.[6] Piramidov was in charge of controlling the Social Democratic revolutionaries. His activities were described by Fedosseyev in an article published in 1898. According to the account, Piramidov was at times cruel. Enlisting revolutionaries as police collaborators, he was lenient only with those who consciously or unwittingly cooperated with him. When he died of an accident in 1901, Lenin published an obituary in his paper.

Lenin met Axelrod in Zurich. Then, with Axelrod and Potresov, he joined Zasulich and Plekhanov at Corsier, near Geneva. He immediately quarrelled with Plekhanov, who initially did not want to become editor but nevertheless asked for full control. One point at issue was Lenin's outwardly tolerant attitude toward Struve and his tendency to compromise with the economists. Desirous of pulling the Marxists together, he was willing to pay the price for this goal; Plekhanov, a theoretician by nature, took an unbending, doctrinaire attitude, displaying suspicion, even hostility, toward Lenin. Lenin was extremely disappointed and wrote: "It was so unbearably difficult that at times I thought I would burst into tears."[7] But Plekhanov walked away with two votes, giving him potential control of the editorial board. He was never able to actualize his powers.

Lenin solidified his plans during August and, through Plekhanov, established contact with the German Social Democratic party, notably with Adolf Braun and Clara Zetkin, who also was visited by Potresov. The German comrades promised "technical and organizational support" for the printing and distribution of the newspaper. The "support" the Germans gave presumably did not involve money, but rather physical facilities and the availability of the German party apparatus; also utilized were the vast experiences which the German party had gained in the illegal transport and distribution of

6Details on the interrogation in Gérard Walter, *Lénine* (Paris: Julliard, 1950), p. 82.
7On these disputes, see Geyer, p. 204f; for more detail, see Walter, p. 86f.

publications. Without this assistance, the paper would never have seen the light of day.

In September, Lenin, Zasulich, and Potresov settled in Munich. The editorial secretary was I. G. Smidovich, a Russian revolutionary well connected in the subversive world and married to a local socialist physician, Dr. Karl Lehmann. Dr. Lehmann, whom Lenin had met through a Polish revolutionary, Julian Marchlewski, was a close collaborator of Alexander Helphand, better known as Parvus, a native of the Ukraine, who was now a German publicist and a brilliant international Marxist writer.[8] Parvus and Lehmann had secretly visited Russia to study famine conditions on the Volga. Though Lenin usually avoided contacts, he saw Parvus frequently, received help from him in his literary activities, and through him met Rosa Luxemburg, a Polish-German socialist and outstanding theoretician. The 4,000 rubles a year, which Maxim Gorky, upon the suggestion of Parvus (then Gorky's publisher), is said to have been giving to *Iskra* and which Lenin administered, were most helpful in strengthening this ambitious effort.[9]

In November, Lenin went to Leipzig to deal with the printer. No less than 8,000 copies[10] of the first issue of the paper—which bore the programmatic title, *Iskra*[11] or "Spark"—were published, most unfittingly, for an atheistic group, on Christmas Eve. Lenin's article stressed the need to instill political consciousness and socialist ideas into the masses and to put forward political leaders "capable of directing and organizing the movement." These men must dedicate to the revolution "not a free evening but the whole of their lives." But there was a significant concession to the other camp: the revolutionary party was to be tied to the "spontaneous labor movement."

Iskra No. 10 was reprinted in Kishinev, and No. 11 in Baku; it was hoped that a vast reprinting operation could be gotten underway, but publication in Russia remained impractical. The *Iskra* editorial board also published a theoretical organ, *Zarya* ("Dawn"). It was printed in Stuttgart, three issues appearing altogether. The first number was printed on March 23, 1901, with an article by

---

8A police report to Paris of January 2, 1887 announced the departure on October 20, 1886 (Old Style) of Israel Lazarevich Gelfand from Odessa on passport 5787 issued on October 13, 1886. He took with him 300 rubles and 200 rubles were mailed to him for organizational tasks. It was indicated that he had connections at Leipzig, Germany.

9This amount probably was paid once, perhaps twice. If continued, Lenin would not have controlled it after 1903.

10Rumor, perhaps planted, had it that the printing was 100,000.

11The name was allegedly proposed by Potresov, but I would be inclined to think it was Lenin's suggestion: he adopted the title of Chernichevsky's old paper. By contrast, it is plausible that Potresov suggested the motto taken from Pushkin: "The spark will kindle the fire."

Parvus writing as "P. Molotov." The second issue, of December, 1901, was a double number; there our hero used the pseudonym "Lenin" for the first time. The last issue was published in August, 1902.

Iskra was a great success, yet Lenin was unhappy. His health having again deteriorated, he was considering a "water cure" and "more regular treatment." During the Christmas holidays he wrote to his mother that he was "fairly lonely" and that his life was "pretty senseless." He hoped to study more systematically, "but somehow I cannot manage it."[12]

No doubt the strange city, the foreign language, the damp climate, and homesickness were partially responsible for Lenin's unhappiness. Although his sister Anna, who participated in the smuggling of *Iskra* to Russia, had arrived in Germany by early 1901 and saw Lenin often, he remained lonely. The unique life of a revolutionary, who possessed not even his own name—he was using the pseudonyms Frey, Meyer and Petrov—was difficult to live. Lenin was upset by the many disagreements between himself and his co-editors. By publishing the paper in Germany—between December, 1900, and May, 1901, four eight-page issues were printed—he had managed to remove it from the direct control of Plekhanov. But more than personalities were involved: two basically different revolutionary conceptions were in conflict.

According to Marx, the emancipation of the proletariat was to be the task of the proletariat itself. But Nechayev maintained that the people were to be commanded by a supreme committee, while Tkachev said that the people were unable to act and that the revolution would have to be accomplished by revolutionary intellectuals. Just as Axelrod had in 1879 tried to combine the terrorist-conspiratorial struggle with propaganda, agitation and organizational activities among the people,[13] so Lenin pulled the divergent revolutionary theories of his time together. He argued that professional revolutionaries, or intellectuals, should be organized in a committee to lead the proletariat and to imbue it with class and revolutionary consciousness. *Iskra* was to be the instrument through which the leadership was to be forged and the cadres established and indoctrinated. The persons who were smuggling the paper into Russia were to form the cadre. The smugglers, together with the distributors and those who reprinted the journal inside Russia, were to be organized as the kernel of a secret conspiratorial group which, in turn, was to create and lead a mass organization. The entire operation was to be commanded by the *Iskra* board, which was

[12]*Letters of Lenin*, pp. 116, 127.

[13]Haimson, *op. cit.*, p. 39.

keeping informed of events in Russia by a steady stream of correspondence from the smuggling distributors. The approach was the old plan of Ishutin and others, but the use of a newspaper as a connecting link between conspiracy and mass organization was a novel and highly practical idea.

Lenin's colleagues agreed upon this concept, but, as experienced conspirators, they were skeptical of overemphasis on clandestine forms of struggle. Many of Lenin's coeditors were suspicious of this latter-day Nechayev who believed in the supreme wisdom of a directory, with himself as director and dogmatist. The cleavage was considerable, but the disputes with the other camps in the Social Democratic movement kept the *Iskra* group together.

In addition to difficulties of an organizational and tactical sort, there was the problem of relations with unorthodox theorists. Struve, for example, controlled the printshop which published *Zarya,* but Lenin had decided that he no longer was able to cooperate with him. The decision was completely unrealistic, for *Iskra* still needed Struve's support. In a reversal of previous arguments, the board decided to continue the connection with Struve. Lenin found it advisable to conform, but aided by German socialists and a few radical Russians living in Germany, he attempted to infiltrate Struve's own smuggling apparatus. This attempt of seizure from below was unsuccessful: Lenin did not yet have an effective organization of his own. In March, 1901, Struve was arrested in Russia.

In May, 1901, Lenin was joined by Krupskaya.[14] The Lenins had acquired a false Bulgarian passport, on which they were listed as "Bulgarian Doctor of Law, Jordan K. Jordanoff, and his wife, Marika." They moved into a better apartment and began printing the newspaper in Munich.

In the columns of *Iskra* Lenin attacked the competitive papers *Rabochaya Mysl* and especially *Rabochoye Delo,* an important party organ. Unable to counter Lenin's polemics, these papers were put on the defensive, gradually losing their readers. Both ceased publication in 1902. Simultaneously, the *Iskra* group tried, with moderate success, to draw more and more Social Democratic groups to their side.

Things were going smoothly and Lenin devoted more time to writing. His co-editors were rather lazy, so that Lenin dominated the paper by simply working harder and producing more copy. He preoccupied himself with the agrarian question in which the others showed only slight interest. He was intensely involved with the theory of party organization and tactics. In a running debate with Plekhanov about the party program, he exchanged drafts, criticisms

[14]On March 12, 1901, Krupskaya received passport No. 27 at Ufa.

and counterdrafts. Differences arose frequently, and at one point (summer, 1902) a break with Plekhanov was averted only at the last minute. Plekhanov conceded, but Lenin was so much affected by the dispute that he fell ill.

Literary Success

Late in 1901, Lenin began the writing of *What Is To Be Done?* In many respects, this book represents the first clear expression of "Leninism." A blend of Russian revolutionary history and Marxist economics and sociology, the work constituted an original contribution to revolutionary strategy, organization and tactics. Discarding the democratic theory of the socialist revolution, Lenin advocated an elitist party, composed of "professional revolutionaries." *What Is To Be Done?* was a rewritten, improved version—in attenuated form and with some Aesopian camouflage—of Nechayev's *Revolutionary Catechism*. Representing a modernization of Tkachev's[1] notion that socialism would remain utopian so long as it was not supported by force, and if political power was not seized forcefully, the book called for an integration of organizational and combat factors with Marxist economics and sociology—in brief, Marxist Nechayevism.[2]

What Is To Be Done? made Lenin famous among socialists. There was general acceptance of its value as a guide to organizational and political work, while little criticism of its anti-democratic features was voiced. Many Russian Marxists discovered the value of democracy only years later; Masaryk once said, "Secret societies are an incorporation of the aristocratic spirit with its illusion of great deeds and its contempt for the petty details of work—its shyness of work in general." The Russian Social Democrats, certain that they possessed the truth, saw nothing wrong in organizing autocratically or aristocratically. Their bearings disoriented in the power struggle, only a few sensed that in the absence of absolute truth in politics, open debate and democracy are better instruments than the rule-by-quarrel of a few wise men, each of whom thinks he is infallible.

Lenin's book was published in March, 1902, through an outlet controlled by the tolerant and democratic Struve. By December 29,

[1]Lenin's book aroused renewed interest in Tkachev, who was republished in 1904 at Geneva.

[2]On May 22, 1904, Axelrod in a letter to Kautsky characterized Lenin's policy as "bonapartistic-nechayevistiv" (Kautsky, *Archiv DII*, 311, quoted from Geyer, *op. cit.*, p. 412). Incidentally, Marx, who was the First International's Secretary for Russia, opposed Nechayev strongly; he considered him to be a liar and crook who exploited the name of the International in his own interest. (*Werke*, Vol. 17, p. 435.)

1900, Lenin had broken with Struve as a friend and political collaborator. He specifically rejected Struve's offer of assistance, adding that one period of his life was coming to a close. Still, he was "utilizing" the erstwhile friend, who had returned from Russia with sufficient funds to publish a liberal paper. And why not? Lenin always believed in "utilizing" liberals, in fact *anyone* to achieve his purposes. Bakunin described Nechayevism as "violence for the body and falsehood for the soul." Lenin was not adverse to making the formula his own.

At that time the German Social Democratic magazine *Die Neue Zeit* was the main political forum of international socialism. Edited by Karl Kautsky, it included among its prominent contributors August Bebel, Paul Lafargue and F. A. Sorge (grandfather of Richard Sorge of World War II fame). The issues were read avidly even among Siberian exiles and quite regularly by literate émigrés, some of whom contributed to its columns. *Die Neue Zeit's* writers constituted a sort of apostolic succession reaching back to Engels.[3] Kautsky was eager to publish theoretical articles and reports on Russia by *Iskra* editors, notably Plekhanov, Axelrod, and Zasulich. Had these three not been so lazy, their contributions would have appeared frequently. Lenin had not yet been invited to collaborate, but late in 1902, Vera Zasulich wrote an article describing the Russian socialist movement and paying handsome tribute to the comrades who had now returned after an exile of several years to the battlefield, where they had been "longingly" awaited. Without mentioning specific names, she identified for the *cognoscenti* Martov, Potresov and Lenin.

Lenin was a careful reader of *Die Neue Zeit*. To obtain current information on socialist problems and world affairs, he could not have chosen a better magazine. *Die Neue Zeit* was the most suitable source in either Russian or German and was accessible both in the libraries of Central Europe and by inexpensive subscription. Lenin had been reading Kautsky's magazine in Siberia; he received the copies from Potresov, who apparently was a subscriber.

From *Die Neue Zeit* Lenin became familiar with a large range of ideas, many of which later formed the subject of some of his major writings.[4] Several articles, for example, were published on nationality problems in Austria—unquestionably among Lenin's first exposures to the thorny national question. At that time, also, the British were waging war against the Boers in South Africa, and

[3]Marx died when the fourth issue was in print. In its necrology the magazine stated that Marx passed away after achieving, like Charles Darwin and Richard Wagner, the unstinted praise of friend and foe. *Die Neue Zeit* I, 197.

[4]We are discussing issues that appeared while Lenin was working on *What Is To Be Done?*

many contributions in *Die Neue Zeit* were devoted to an analysis of "imperialism." Among the authors dealing with the subject were Kautsky, Heinrich Cunow, E. Belfort-Bax, Max Beer, Theodore Rothstein, and Parvus. These writers proposed many of the ideas which Lenin, in future years, set forth in his book on imperialism. *Die Neue Zeit* contributors occasionally quoted J. A. Hobson, an author whom Lenin later acknowledged. Contemporary comments in *Die Neue Zeit* made it clear that Hobson himself was expostulating a theory of imperialism upon which the socialist movement already had elaborated and which, strangely enough, was a replica of much of the thinking by Cecil Rhodes and the Imperial League.[5]

Lenin also familiarized himself with problems of the Jewish workers' movement and the question of whether or not the Jews constituted a nation. The obstacles posed by the Jewish Bund to the unity of the proletarian movement within Russia were well known to him from his practical politics, but *Die Neue Zeit* supplied much useful background information.

In an article by Kautsky written shortly before Lenin arrived in Germany, Lenin could have read Marx's and Engels' opinion concerning the necessity of a war against tsarism.[6] Marx's enmity towards the "English apostles of peace from Cobden to Gladstone" was due to their preaching a policy of friendliness with Russia. (Kautsky used an expression akin to "peaceful coexistence.") The socialist apostles criticized these men of peace as "democrats only for Britain." Kautsky added that it would be unwise for Social Democrats to provoke the liberation of Russia by means of war. Instead, he suggested that the "inner movement" within Russia, though not yet strong enough to alter the domestic politics of tsarism, was capable of influencing moderation in Russia's foreign policy. Kautsky implied that the time was nearing whem tsarism could be overthrown by internal revolution. This proved to be a bit optimistic. Subsequently another author asserted that Asia must be liberated from Russian imperialism, for which purpose Japan, as well as the

---

[5]Hobson, a partial Marxist, was in his economic theorizing close to Sidney Webb. He firmly believed that imperialism was a conspiracy of finance capital. See the informative article by Max Beer, *Die Neue Zeit*, XX/1 431f. The evolution of Marxist thought on imperialism began with two articles by Kautsky in 1883 where he opposed settlement colonies, on the grounds that the settlers could be used better at home, and "exploitation colonies" because adventurers who run them enrich themselves instead of making their profits available to the working population in the metropolitan country. Because of the enrichment of the most dubious types of entrepreneurs, the exploitation of free labor would become worse (*Die Neue Zeit*, I, 370, 404). Subsequently, imperialism was deemed by socialists to have given capitalism a lease on life precisely because it had "temporarily" improved the living standards of the proletariat in the mother country.

[6]*Die Neue Zeit*, XXVIII/1, 773.

opposition within Russia, would have to be strengthened.[7]

In *Die Neue Zeit*, Lenin could have found a discussion on Engels' ultimate views on armed uprising, a subject on which there was considerable disagreement. Lenin probably read a related excellent analysis of Blanqui and Blanquism: Tkachev had collaborated with the French firebrand. This was a topic about which Russian revolutionaries argued a great deal. Presumably, the article convinced Lenin that, while it was unrealistic to expect a revolution to be fully accomplished by 500 men, carefully developed insurrectional tactics were indispensable. Lenin surely was a Blanquist in that he appreciated the role played by 500 men; but he never overlooked the importance of the masses, realizing that an uprising could succeed only in an essentially revolutionary situation.

Die Neue Zeit occasionally contained hints on how revolutionaries could deal with governments they wished to overthrow. After the assassination of Alexander II, for example, the tsarist court sent an emissary to Peter Lavrov, chief Russian revolutionary leader in Paris.[8] The court offered the liberation of Chernishevsky, amnesty for political prisoners, some reform, and payment to the party of one million rubles, on condition that no further attempts on the Tsar's life would be made. Apparently Lavrov found the offer agreeable, but the government withdrew after it succeeded in arresting most of the dangerous terrorists. Also discussed in *Die Neue Zeit* for the benefit of revolutionary readers was the use of police agents by the Belgium government.

In the 1920's Lenin took a great interest in the electrification of Russia. The potential significance of electric power with respect to agriculture had been forseen by Kautsky about twenty years earlier.[9] Parvus expected electrification to bring about a "fundamental revolution of all industrial production."[10]

A number of articles discussed, in terms of socialist tactics, parliamentarism, its dangers and potentialities. Some of these were written by Emil Vandervelde, the Belgian socialist, others by Kurt Eisner, the unorthodox radical Prime Minister of Bavaria in 1919. These discussions presaged Lenin's arguments in *Left Radicalism, an Infantile Disease.*

Die Neue Zeit gave full coverage to the debates concerning tactics, arguments which were then dividing, and sometimes splitting, socialist parties throughout Europe. These debates had been precipitated by Eduard Bernstein's "revisions" of the Marxian

---

[7]*Die Neue Zeit*, XIX/2, 237 ff.

[8]*Die Neue Zeit*, XVIII/1, 845. Lavrov was a friend of Marx.

[9]*Die Neue Zeit*, XIX/1, 565-572.

[10]*Die Neue Zeit*, XIX/2, 614ff.

theory, as well as by the entry of socialist Alexandre Millerand into the French Cabinet. On the one side stood the pragmatic socialists, interested mainly in day-to-day politics, and whose aim was economic and social improvement of the working class; these figures espoused the notion that the proletariat must come to power by parliamentary means. On the other side stood the orthodox revolutionaries, who wanted to go beyond such limited tasks and intended to restructure the whole of society; these individuals anticipated violent revolutions.

Die Neue Zeit published articles by both groups, but the orthodox line, represented by the most able theoreticians of the movement— Parvus, Rosa Luxemburg and Kautsky himself—predominated. All recognized the existence of the "two methods"—the French socialist Jean Jaurès had published a brochure by this title—and opposed "*ministerialismo*," a term coined by the Italian socialist Arturo Labriola. They all contended that *ministerialismo* weakened consciousness of the class struggle, rendered reforms more difficult, and reduced the psychological effectiveness of the "vision of the ultimate goal." Instead these writers resolutely supported inculcation in the proletariat of a full consciousness of its historic mission. They upheld the Marxian doctrine, criticizing "opportunism" as a policy of limping behind events and restricting goals only to the "immediately attainable."[11]

Kautsky declared that the Social Democratic party was of a special type. He, as well as Clara Zetkin, emphasized the need to carry the class struggle to the masses and to imbue them with socialist concepts and consciousness. The two asserted that radical arguments anchored firmly on socialist principles promised the best results.[12] Vandervelde, whom Lenin later disliked, discussed the "army of the proletariat" with its need of specialists. He underscored the point that tactics which might be successful in democratic countries were not always applicable to "absolutist Russia."[13]

Lenin, while studying the writings of advocates of the "other method," familiarized himself with Kautsky's criticisms of Bernstein. Kautsky argued that, because the political struggle primes all other forms of the class war, the Social Democratic party should exist as a "class party of the fighting proletariat." The party could not function without intellectuals of bourgeois origin, he argued, but it required only those intellectuals who burnt their bridges and were relentlessly fighting bourgeois society.

[11]*Die Neue Zeit*, XX/1, 428. It should be noted that after 1872 Marx and Engels increasingly tended to the pragmatic side of this argument and supported democratic means of struggle.

[12]*Die Neue Zeit*, XVIII/2, 792; XIX/1, 659-661.

[13]*Die Neue Zeit*, XIX/1, 393.

Lenin had early fought against those socialists who opposed the participation of intellectuals in the revolutionary struggle.[14] In *What Is To Be Done?* he quoted from *Die Neue Zeit* Kautsky's article which insisted that "socialist consciousness is something introduced into the proletarian class struggle from without and not something that arose within it spontaneously."[15]

Kautsky exclaimed that the socialists must aim at victory, the conditions for which were to be created by the development of industrial production and the strengthening of the proletariat. The socio-political process was to be accelerated by challenging the proletariat to do its utmost and guiding it to the actualization of its highest potentialities. The tasks of the party, in addition to its daily chores, should include organizing the masses, enlarging the political perspectives of the working class, proposing to it ambitious objectives, and creating a proletarian consciousness of vast historical scope.

In 1902, Kautsky discussed the problem of revolution in a little book which he typically entitled *Social Revolution.* He conceived of revolution as a socio-political process that was to bring about changes in the respective positions of the various classes. Since society would not naturally grow into socialism, the proletariat would have to seize power. This would occur not because the proletariat was becoming increasingly downtrodden, but because it was steadily accumulating material strength. (Without acknowledging the fact, Kautsky thus *did* accept Bernstein's criticism of Marx's essential theorem.) As a result of the proletariat's growing might, Kautsky predicted, the class struggle would become ever more acute. Revolution was simply a protracted civil war, fought, not necessarily with barricades and weapons, but through such democratic means as mass strikes. Political democracy was training the proletariat. Though Kautsky opposed "forcing the revolution," he stated that war would act as an accelerator of the revolutionary development.[16] Intelligence, discipline and organization were the prerequisites of the social revolution, but the specifics of power seizure could not be predicted.

Lenin had debated passionately with those socialists who, expecting progress to come almost exclusively from the economic struggle and unionism, conceived of overall political activity merely as the sum of all local undertakings. While Lenin was still in Siberia, at the end of 1897, P. B. Axelrod argued against these tendencies.

[14]Geyer, *op. cit.,* p. 91.

[15]*Die Neue Zeit,* XX/1, 79.

[16]In June, 1905, Kautsky was to state more explicitly that *defeat* would accelerate the revolutionary process. Hence war should not be condemned by Social Democrats, not even aggressive war. "Every futile war which costs heavy casualties must become the starting point of a revolution." *Die Neue Zeit,* XXIII/2, 371.

He pointed out that while strikes were very important, their real function was to contribute to the attainment of political freedom. He emphasized the role of the intelligentsia, favored an alliance with those elements of the bourgeoisie which were working for democracy, and did not oppose a liberal revolution. He argued that Social Democrats should organize the proletariat. The historical mission of the revolutionary intelligentsia, he believed, was to revolutionize the masses by instilling in them political consciousness, thus enabling them to wage the fight for freedom and democracy.

Lenin disagreed on some points: he was not really opposed to Axelrod's concept of allying the socialist movement with the liberal democrats, but he believed that "allies" change with circumstances and should be "utilized" for the time rather than considered as partners of long duration. He felt that particular care should be taken to insure the socialists' retention of their full independence, a point which had been made forcefully by Plekhanov in 1892.

A few years later, Plekhanov stressed the concept that the socialist party was to act as the "vanguard" of the proletariat, maintaining that organization was its primary undertaking. Other thoughts presaging *What Is To Be Done?* were set forth in the joint declaration of *Iskra's* editorial board, written in September, 1900, and in articles published by several contributors to *Iskra*.[17]

Lenin, grappling with the same problems in 1899, indicated the primacy of the political struggle; the need of adhering to the unadulterated Marxian doctrine;[18] the necessity of imbuing the proletariat with socialist ideas; the importance of the theoretical struggle; the need for the vanguard to possess an advanced theory;[19] the limitations of a spontaneous political movement (i.e., organizing from below rather than above, and contenting oneself with many local groups and unions instead of a unified political party); the need to carry consciousness into the proletariat from without; the role of the intellectuals; the importance of training and the need for the development of tactics; the difficulties of a struggle against a police state, hence the necessity of professional revolutionaries functioning in a disciplined centralized party; the importance of conspiracy; the need for proper selection of party members; and the necessity to prepare, systematically and on a protracted time schedule, for a national armed insurrection. All this had been said

[17]Geyer, pp. 113-117, 214-225.

[18]Potresov adopted the cover name of "Starover," the old believer, to emphasize *his* commitment to Marxist orthodoxy.

[19]Kautsky believed that the Russian proletariat might become the vanguard of the international proletariat. Lenin, at the end of the first chapter of *What Is To Be Done?*, took over this thought without, however, crediting it to Kautsky. Geyer, p. 244f.

before—by many people. But it was presented more logically and more convincingly by Lenin than by his socialist comrades. Where practically all the socialist writers (even Rosa Luxemburg and Parvus, and certainly Kautsky and Plekhanov) tended to be abstract if not vague, Lenin was clear, concrete, practical, imaginative, forceful—and infinitely more impatient.

As early as 1897, he was considering, with a great deal of tactical acumen, conspiratorial work, tactics, and organization. While others were hesitant, he was outspoken on the need for professional revolutionaries. It is entirely possible that his talk with Plekhanov during 1895, and the "old man's" recital of heroic deeds by conspirators and terrorists, impressed upon him the importance of training, discipline, and devotion to the cause.[20] But Lenin had had enough exposure to revolutionaries and their tales to recognize that a part-time revolutionary is unable to operate effectively. An energetic man like Lenin could not fail to worry about the predominance of talkers and babblers among his comrades. He was fully aware of the fact that many Russian youngsters considered it fashionable to pose as rebels for a few years, only to revert to their "class" after they had had their excitement and had grown a little older. Like Tkachev, Lenin preferred a party of action to a party of reasoning.[21]

Whereas all the other Marxists tended to let the social process— or capitalism, or history—assume the main burden, Lenin, constantly pondering the "unity of theory and practice," was an activist. Theoretical insight must serve as the handmaiden of revolutionary action. Analysis suggests opportunities; the activist requires the guidance of theory to devise effective tactics. One of Lenin's opponents considered tactics to be a process; the revolutionary was to be driven by social development like the sailboat by the wind. Lenin viewed tactics as plans that must first be executed and then modified

---

[20]Peter Scheibert, "Ueber Lenins Anfänge," *Historische Zeitschrift* (1956), V. 182, p. 561. Reflecting a remark by Boris Nicolayevski, Scheibert suggests this possibility but also points to Lenin's earlier contacts in Samara as the more probable origin of this Leninist merger between the new and the old revolutionary doctrine. Naturally, literary influences should not be overlooked. Tkachev, in 1874, stated that peaceful progress is made by the majority and revolution by a minority. The revolutionary's function is to call the people to an uprising. (Lenin, however, disagreed with Tkachev's notion that the timing of the insurrection is up to the revolutionary.) The rules of the *Narodnaya Volya,* which were well known, asked from the revolutionaries to give up friendships, loves and family ties, even individual will, and to give everything to the secret society. The professional revolutionary appears in Nechayev's *Revolutionary Catechism* but the concept can be traced back further. Among Marxists the concept, albeit under different terms, originated with Kautsky.

[21]Haimson, *op. cit.,* p. 17. Engels called Tkachev "a green high school kid of surprising immaturity." *(Werke,* Vol. 18, pp. 536-567.)

through experience. His chief concern was commitment to early and definite action, and his chief enemy was any form of inaction. *This* was Tkachev's legacy to Lenin.[22]

Lenin's originality has been exaggerated. There was, however, one innovation: the party leadership was to operate a "central organ" which was to organize the revolutionary striking forces, while developing technique and theory. Through the organ, the party was to guide the struggle in all its manifestations, advancing local conflicts into the class struggle of the entire Russian proletariat.

The concept of a central party organ had been tried before. In the period when Bismarck had outlawed the socialists, the German Social Democrats operated very effectively through such a central organ.[23] The idea actually had been suggested to Lenin by other Russian revolutionaries, members of the Jewish Bund. The plan carried some urgency, since the opposing faction's "organ," *Rabochoye Delo,* was exerting intellectual domination upon the movement. To increase his strength, Lenin needed an "organ" of his own.

But this practical requirement does not negate the novelty of Lenin's approach. Nor does the German precedent. The German socialists used their party organ merely as a defensive operation by which to keep the party together. Lenin conceived of the paper as an offensive weapon, a tool that could create a political force and prepare for the armed uprising. The broad scope which Lenin gave to this operational technique, his attempt to transform a newspaper into an instrument of thought, training, communication, and command, to use it as an organizational and conspiratorial device, and as an instrument of building and guiding a mass party toward insurrection, was entirely original. It constituted a highly creative solution to the problems posed by the tsarist autocracy. Lenin's critics, of course, sneered that a newspaper could not create a party, that it is the party that creates the newspaper. Actually, the significance of Lenin's approach lay not in the conception of *Iskra,*

[22]In his first article in *Nabat* (November, 1875), Tkachev argued against letting "today" pass. Procrastinating might mean the postponement of the revolution forever. In 1874, he opposed pauses and temporization. Andrei Zhelyabov, leader of the *Narodnaya Volya* and the guiding light behind the assassination of Alexander II, believed: "History moves too slowly, it needs a push." (Axelrod had known Zhelyabov.)

[23]This was *Der Sozialdemokrat,* edited by Bernstein. *Die Neue Zeit,* edited by Kautsky was the accompanying theoretical journal. The similarity of this setup to the *Iskra-Zarya* structure is apparent. The organizer of the German operation, Julius Motteler, in January, 1895, compiled its complete history, including an analysis of illegal border crossings and transports, and sent the manuscript as a handbook to Italian socialists for their benefit and initiation. It is unlikely that Lenin ever saw Motteler's explicit and instructive text but he had many contacts through whom he could have picked up this information. *See* Ernest Engelberg, *Revolutionäre Politik und Rote Feldpost, 1878-1890* (Berlin: Akademie-Verlag, 1959), pp. 112-283.

but in his devising of organizational and tactical arrangements suitable for the political-revolutionary struggle.

Lenin expostulated a number of ideas which went beyond the Marxian framework. He wanted to inculcate political knowledge in *all* classes of the population, and proposed that the theoreticians, propagandists, agitators and organizers of socialism should become "tribunes of the people." This was a strong modification of the doctrine that socialism was to be the work of the proletariat only. Lenin implied, though did not clearly state, that the political revolution could be "made." This idea was in accord with Russian precedents but constituted a fundamental modification of both the Marxist notion that the revolution would result from the social transformation of the capitalist system, and the frequent declarations of Kautsky that the course of the revolution was not predictable. Lenin argued that party membership should be restricted to professionals who were specialists in secret work; the party should consist of a core and its agents, trained to mobilize the "troops." This elitist concept of an "agents' party"[24] was a significant modification of the theory that the Social Democratic party should be a mass party, constituting a denial of intra-party democracy. Lenin specifically argued that since democracy would not work in the struggle against a police state, it should be replaced by rigid selection and training of professionals. If this "only serious organizational principle" were adhered to strictly, "something even more than 'democracy' would be guaranteed . . . complete, comradely, mutual confidence among revolutionaries."[25]

Perhaps the success of Lenin's book is explained, not by the novelty of his thoughts, but by the fact that the ideas he was expounding were familiar to his readers. Perhaps his work was successful because it filled the organizational void of Marxism—in Russia, at any rate. To my mind, his achievement was that he eclectically synthesized Marxism with the Russian revolutionary tradition and in so doing *preserved the essence of both.*[26] In brief, he contributed strategic-tactical realism to the vague image of the Marxian revolution. The success of this book was indeed no accident: Lenin was vastly superior to his comrades in his ability to think operationally and organizationally. The impact which this intellectual accomplishment exerted on his career as a political leader was enormous. It was of no matter to him whether he was original in a literary sense. Only political effectiveness counted.

[24]The term is by Dietrich Geyer.
[25]"What Is To Be Done?", *Selected Works.* (New York: International Publishers, 1943), II, 155.
[26]That is, of Marxism as based on the writings and actions of Marx and Engels before 1870-1872.

Organizational Build-up

The establishment of a party with a membership consisting al-most exclusively of disciplined agents was Lenin's foremost practical objective. Following the meeting at Pskov, Lenin went abroad to produce the newspaper; Martov remained behind to recruit agents for *Iskra* in Russian cities.

According to the scheme, the paper was to be sent to the agents through the transport organization. The resident agents were to distribute the paper locally, form party cells among the subscribers and readers, gradually enlarge membership, and establish new dis-tribution points. Working for *Iskra* was to be a paying full-time job, but the agents had also to obtain money from local resources, transmitting the surplus to the center. They were to supply the editorial board with information about political events and economic conditions, keep them posted on organizational matters, and carry out instructions.

By the time Martov left Russia, he had recruited about a dozen agents, mostly in the Ukraine. This "success" is partly explained by the fact that he came from a large family: one brother functioned in Poltava and another in Vilno. Lenin, Krupskaya, and Potresov had also "contributed" friends and relatives, as well as Siberian fellow-exiles. Upon Martov's departure, Krzhizhanovsky and his wife, after a short visit to Munich, proceeded to Samara, where they continued the recruiting effort Martov had initiated. Lenin, through a few trusted contacts, was molding the transport organization outside of Russia.

These undertakings were not outstandingly successful. Many agents left after a few weeks and others had to move before a local distribution point was properly organized. Recruitment of new members was lagging. The police arrested many of the active revolutionaries and infiltrated the transport and border crossing organizations. The distribution of *Iskra* frequently could not be accomplished, for the relative security of the various transport routes was in constant flux.

Consequently, it is impossible to determine the "deployment" of the *Iskra* organization, or to evaluate the effectiveness of the local agents in distributing the paper and performing their organizational tasks. But for most of the time, the net operated in St. Petersburg, Moscow, Samara, Arkhangel, Poltava, Kiev, Astrakhan, Pskov, Novgorod, Rostov, Vilno, Kishinev, and Baku, with a few traveling agents maintaining liaison.

The transport structure, which was quite unstable, included sea and land routes.¹ The paper was dispatched from the printing plant to an initial distribution agent who entrusted the packages to crew members of merchant ships or to locomotive engineers and border crossers; once the paper had been smuggled into Russia, it was transported to the primary centers of activity.

The shipping routes proceeded from London or Geneva via Alexandria, Egypt, to Kherson; from Munich via Marseilles to Batumi; from London via Vardø, Norway, to Arkhangel; from London to Libau; and from London via Stockholm to Abø, Finland, and then by land to St. Petersburg.² Land routes included smuggling from Tilsit, Germany, to Kovno and Riga; from Varna, Bulgaria, to Odessa; and from Tabriz, Persia, to Baku. The route from Lvov, Austria-Hungary, to Kamenets-Podolsk and Kiev was the most reliable.

Although the distribution scheme was extensive, very few copies of *Iskra* were actually distributed, far less than the original printing of 8,000. In some cases, the literature did not even reach Russia. Krupskaya recounts that some massive shipments dispatched via Sweden simply remained stored in the basement of the Stockholm People's House.³

The taunt by Liber and Jordania that Lenin ran a general staff without an army was a justifiable one. Yet the *Iskra* operation soon assumed a mythical aura about it. Interest was aroused; a cadre of relatively reliable followers was emerging. The steady growth of this group, coupled with the establishment of many subsidiary contacts among sympathizers, was of far greater importance than the distribution of reading matter to a few workers and intellectuals who would hardly have understood *Iskra's* contents. Moreover, through increasing resources and ingenuity, the *Iskra* organization gradually gained the upper hand over its Social Democratic competitors, in-

[1]Without the self-sacrificing assistance of the German Social Democratic party and individual German socialists, the smuggle of *Iskra* into Russia might have never succeeded. Communist literature, ungraciously, rarely acknowledges this crucial contribution. *See* Kurt Eisner, *Der Geheimbund des Zaren* (Berlin: Vorwaerts, 1905), which contains transcripts of a trial at Königsberg which the German government at the behest of Petersburg instituted against the German organization. The German socialists maintained a whole section for the publishing of Russian revolutionary literature and they also had a transport section to help the Russian revolutionaries. This fact should put the *Iskra* operation into its right perspective.

[2]Operations through Finland and Sweden were abetted by the wealthy Finnish nationalist Konni Zilliacus, largely with the intention of weakening Russia. Zilliacus (1855-1924) smuggled 16 tons of literature into Finland. On details of Lenin's *Iskra* transports through Skandinavia, and the historical origin of the Skandinavian route which dated back to the 1860's and to Bakunin and Ogarev, *see* Michael Futrell, *Northern Underground*, London: Faber and Faber, 1963, chapters I and II.

[3]For details on this episode, *see* Futrell, p. 44f.

cluding Lenin's friend Lalayants who was publishing a Social Democratic paper in southern Russia. The activities fell far short of Lenin's dreams, but there was established an initial core which provided him with the basis for effective political action.

Not surprisingly, the tsarist police were unhappy about this development—especially about *Iskra*. The Okhrana and the German police were then cooperating in their work against revolutionaries. Pressure was applied to the German Social Democratic party. Anna's room in Berlin was searched. It was finally decided to remove *Iskra* from Germany. To prevent a move to Geneva, where he would have fallen under Plekhanov's control, Lenin argued that London would provide less expensive quarters. On April 12, 1902, Lenin and Krupskaya, passing through Cologne (where they visited the cathedral) and Liège, went to England.[4] Emulating Marx, Lenin became a frequent visitor to the British Museum Library.

At that time, there was occurring a distinct upsurge of the revolutionary movement in Russia. The recently founded Social Revolutionary party—the descendants of the populists—were making significant headway. They successfully engaged in terrorism; *Iskra* immediately opposed this tactic. Though Lenin ought to have taken delight in the successes of the revolutionary movement, he spent much of his time making speeches opposing the Social Revolutionaries. This stance presumably pleased the Okhrana.

In July, 1902, with his mother and sister, Lenin vacationed at Loguivy, Côtes-du-Nord, in northern France. His dispute with Plekhanov having left him in a highly nervous state, he urgently needed relaxation.

On March 18, 1903, he lectured in London on the Paris Commune; until 1917 he was to give this commemorative lecture almost annually. He, incidentally, consistently misrepresented the Commune as a radical proletarian revolution. The Commune, however, aimed at neither the abolition of property, the establishment of socialism, nor at the dictatorship of the proletariat: it attempted only to preserve democracy from monarchistic restoration.

Differences within the editorial board became acute. The board decided to move *Iskra* to Geneva; Lenin was compelled to submit. He did not vigorously oppose the move, having come to realize

---

4At that time, there was unrest in Liège which culminated in shootings. Lenin also found there an opportunity to study the split in the Belgian Social Democratic party. The Okhrana at that time had an agent, V. G. Gudin, working among Lenin's contacts in Belgium. Krupskaya stated they visited in Liège Nikolai L. Meshcheryakov and his wife, "both old Sunday school friends." It must have been a strange Sunday school: Meshcheryakov initiated Krupskaya into illegal work, taught her secrecy techniques and helped her to become a Social Democrat by giving her illegal publications. Apparently this connection dated back to the beginnings of the Radchenko group. Krupskaya, 1959, p. 69.

that his position in London was an isolated one. Apparently, he also found it difficult to acclimate himself to British conditions. In May, 1903, Lenin and Krupskaya moved the *Iskra* management to Geneva. They took up residence near the lake, in a private house, with a large kitchen on the ground floor and three rooms upstairs. The elder Mrs. Krupskaya joined them, each member of the family occupying a separate bedroom. Lenin registered with the police as "Oulianoff, Voldemar, resp. Vladimir."

The move to Geneva pitted Lenin directly against Plekhanov, the *de facto* leader of the Russian Social Democratic party. Plekhanov's authority was grounded firmly upon his experience, prestige, and intellectual power, assets which Lenin could not match. But Plekhanov had fatal weaknesses as well: he was both lazy and lacking in organizational skill. Lenin was prepared to take advantage of these shortcomings.

Through 1902, Lenin had been suffering from agitated nerves. The imposed move to Switzerland angered him. His tension was mounting. In April, 1903, his skin broke out, particularly on the head. Krupskaya read portions of a medical handbook and diagnosed the ailment as ring-worm. They did not send for a doctor "as that would have cost a guinea,"[5] but rather received confirmation of the "diagnosis" from a Russian refugee medical student who advised putting iodine on the lesions. As a result, Lenin grew still balder; after that experience he forever distrusted socialist physicians. Apparently Lenin was suffering from shingles. A bad cold complicated the condition, and the trip was quite disagreeable; upon arriving in Geneva, he was compelled to stay in bed for two weeks. Insomnia aggravated the ailment. Fearing that he might suffer the customary end of a wounded shark, he succeeded in concealing his health troubles. Gradually he regained his strength, and consulted with "delegates" arriving from Russia. By late spring he was again in good health.

[5]Krupskaya, *Reminiscences*, p. 86. This estimate is ridiculous. In any event, Lenin could afford a doctor. Krupskaya's stories about Lenin's sickness vary. She herself suggests a psychosomatic disturbance, but shingles is a virus disease.

The Second Congress

Lenin's organizational career was gaining ground, but he still lacked authority. For that matter, there was no real party which he could have commanded. To overcome these shortcomings, he developed an astute plan: the *Iskra* agents were to contrive that in each local cell the faithful adherents of *Iskra* hold the majority. As a second step, the "safe" cells should join, in a majority agreement, with other groups in summoning a party congress. In the third phase, the congress was to be convened abroad; the cells and organizations were to send delegates—naturally, most of them were to be in *Iskra's* camps. Lastly, the congress, consisting of an *Iskra* majority and several split minorities, was to vote according to the wishes of the *Iskra* board, establishing the board's leadership over the entire party.

In its vague outlines this plan was known to Lenin's colleagues. What the theoreticians from Lac Léman failed to realize was that there was *a plan within the plan,* designed to transfer power to Lenin and to transform the board into a support element serving the foremost revolutionary. This super-plan envisaged that loyal followers of Lenin were to be appointed as *Iskra* agents and that a maximum number of delegates to the congress were to be personally accountable to Lenin. In other words, the *Iskra* organization only seemingly belonged to the board; in reality it was to be controlled solely by Lenin.

This project was complicated but, except for the interference of the police, turned out to be quite feasible. Lenin initially delayed the convening of the congress, concentrating first on strengthening his organization. As soon as he controlled sufficient power, he indicated, partly through his sister Maria and his brother, that committees inside Russia should begin to clamor for the congress. At that point he would join the rally.

The recruiting, stage-setting, and maneuvering were commanded by Lenin, under the noses of his "comrades." As much as possible, Lenin kept himself at a safe distance. Potresov was ailing from 1901 onward; Zasulich was unable to function; Leo Deutsch, who assisted Plekhanov, was ineffective. Plekhanov and Axelrod occasionally complained that Lenin did not keep them informed, but they had agreed to let Krupskaya function as organizational secretary, making no move to assume part of the workload themselves. Martov, the initial organizer, was really a *littérateur* and had moved to Paris where he lost contact. At one point he discovered that Krupskaya had engaged in "double bookkeeping," concealing Lenin's messages to Russia and hiding many replies.[1] But Martov did nothing to stop the abuse.

By December, 1902, an "organizing committee" inside Russia, whose steps Lenin had secretly guided and which appeared to be "representative" (it included rival groups and delegates of the

---

[1]This correspondence, mostly written in invisible ink, was directed through several towns, including Munich, Nürnberg, Darmstadt, and Liège. The purpose was to deceive the police, but many of these letters were read and intercepted. For details, *see Krasnyi Arkhiv* (Moscow, 1934), No. 1 (62), pp. 146-154.

Bund), resolved to convene the congress. Shortly thereafter, however, the Okhrana arrested scores of Social Democrats, almost destroying Lenin's meticulous plans. But Lenin's group was resilient and quickly appointed new delegates, though significant strength was lost.

Some of this rapid reorganizing was undertaken by Yelena D. Stassova, who lived in the house of her uncle Vladimir, a privy councillor, a foremost music critic and author of the libretto for Alexander Borodin's opera *Prince Igor*. Uncle Stassov was regularly receiving two copies of *Iskra*, one for his niece, the other for the secret archives of the Imperial Library. Stassova had been working with Krupskaya since 1896. She had participated in the *Iskra* distribution, and had illegally procured passports (through a janitor who secured the passports of persons just deceased).

Running short of suitable candidates, Stassova appointed A. V. Shotman to serve as delegate to the congress. As a Finnish sailor, Shotman would have no difficulty traveling. He had done some work on the *Iskra* committee, but having been abroad for a considerable length of time, he maintained no connection with the local comrades. Moreover, he was relatively uninformed about current problems, and was probably not very fluent in the Russian language. When Shotman insisted that he was not suited for the position, Stassova simply replied that he was required precisely because he was a worker. Stassova could find no other "Leninist" in St. Petersburg. So Shotman became "organizer" of the Vyborg district, the capital's center of industry.[2] According to his own version, he became one of *three* workers attending the congress of the proletarian party; according to the official version, however, there were *four* "proletarians."

Shotman was instructed to prepare himself by reading revolutionary literature, but he overlooked this part of the assignment. He soon departed for Geneva, where he was taken under the wing of Potresov and participated in a meeting in the apartment of Deutsch, whom he mistook for a liberal professor. A few days later, invited for tea at the Plekhanovs, he was perturbed by the great man's aloofness and the bourgeois opulence of his apartment. Plekhanov's daughters talked with their mother only in French.[3] Shotman was amazed to learn that Plekhanov sought no contacts with the "delegates" from Russia. Lenin found it easy to draw the delegate from St. Petersburg completely and securely over to his side. Shotman was impressed by the plainness of Lenin's quarters. Lenin was a master of the art of

---

[2]A. Schotman, *Wie der Funke zur Flamme wurde* (Moscow-Leningrad, 1935), p. 106.

[3]Mrs. Plekhanov, née Bogadev, was a physician who later practiced on the Riviera, where she enjoyed a fashionable clientèle.

politicking, and he employed it in dealing with the visitors from home. After a few weeks of "getting acquainted," the *Iskra* board and the official callers proceeded to Belgium. The day of glory was approaching.

The Second Congress of the Russian Social Democratic Labor party convened in Brussels on July 30, 1903. Meetings were held in a number of places (including one hall which had to be vacated due to an invasion of fleas). After the Belgium police expelled some delegates, the Congress moved to London on August 11, and met there until the final session of August 23. Although the move was expensive, there apparently was no difficulty in procuring the necessary money from as yet unidentified sources. Thirteen of the thirty-seven sessions had taken place in Brussels.

Of the forty-three delegates, some of whom held double votes, most were poor refugees living in revolutionary ghettoes throughout Europe. Some represented the Jewish socialist Bund; Lenin stated that about one-third of the delegates were Jewish.[4] Others were democratically-minded reform socialists who expected salvation from unionism and economic progress. Altogether twenty-six "organizations" were represented. Lenin represented the League of Revolutionary Social Democrats Abroad and Martov the *Iskra* faction. Of the fifty-one votes, between thirty-three and thirty-nine belonged to the *Iskra* organization, a number of which were directly controlled by Lenin.[5] In addition to some *Iskra* smugglers and a few delegates from local cells, Krupskaya had managed to provide votes for three women she knew from Ufa, the Volga, and Siberia; Lenin's brother Dimitri was also a delegate. Naturally, these "delegates" did not represent voters at home; appointed by Lenin, they represented *only* Lenin. (Nechayev invented the trick of pretending that he was running powerful organizations which, actually, were non-existent.) The strength of the *Iskra* group was inflated by the device of setting up a second cell in places where Lenin did not control the original cell, sending one delegate from each of the two groups, and then haggling about the seating of the delegates; usually Lenin's man was seated. Lenin had organized carefully. There was every prospect that the *Iskra* group would win every decision by a substantial majority so that it could run the party according to its will.

Plekhanov opened the Congress with a solemn address: this was a great day in the history of Russian socialism; the party of revolutionary Marxists had at long last been founded under the happy star of **unity.**

[4]Haimson, *op cit.*, p. 60.

[5]Schapiro, *The Communist Party*, p. 46f. contains the clearest discussion on the voting arithmetic of the Congress. For other information on the Congress, *see* Walter, pp. 115-123, and David Shub, *Lenin* (New York: Doubleday), 1948, pp. 58-63.

From the start, Lenin successfully maneuvered to get Plekhanov elected chairman. He himself managed to become vice-chairman, and contrived to elect another vice-chairman whom he could easily influence. Maneuvers of this type were quite possible among Russian revolutionaries, contemptuous as they were of formal parliamentary procedure.

Lenin was so convinced of his power over the Congress that he quickly overplayed his hand. The draft program was accepted with little difficulty, after a few debates, largely concerning trivialities. Anxious to obtain more control, Lenin called the *Iskra* supporters together in four private sessions. Acting as if he already were a dictator, he antagonized the more intelligent among his followers, including Martov. Lenin later admitted that he had behaved with "frightful irritation" and rage.[6] On August 5, the sessions adjourned for six days; the Congress was moved to London. During this time, Lenin was unable to influence the delegates.

When the Congress re-convened, the *Iskra* group was split, with Lenin enjoying the lukewarm support of Plekhanov, and Martov leading the opposition. The *Iskra* majority began to disintegrate by the sixteenth meeting. The cleavage was apparent at the twenty-second session, at which time the party rules were discussed.[7] The seemingly artificial argument of the session concerned the definition of party membership. By implication it bore on the problems of whether the party was to be composed exclusively of professional revolutionaries and whether it was to be under strict discipline, obeying the orders of the leadership committee. Martov's proposal would have afforded the party a larger membership than was possible under Lenin's restrictive wording. The difference could easily have been compromised; actually, Martov probably did agree to Lenin's formula when it was earlier shown to him. However, in the interim Lenin had acted in a highhanded manner. It became suddenly clear to Martov and many others that Lenin was striving to establish a personal dictatorship over the party.

Lenin prevailed upon Plekhanov to support the dictatorship of the proletariat. This proposal did not sit well with many of the delegates. However, V. E. Mandelberg, who under the pseudonym "Posadovsky" represented Siberia, sided with Lenin (the other "Siberian" delegate was Trotsky):

> Should our future policy be subordinated to some kind of basic democratic principles or should all democratic principles be subordinated exclusively to the advantages of our party? . . . There is nothing among the democratic principles that we should not

[6]Geyer, pp. 397 and 403.

[7]Schapiro, p. 48f.

subordinate to the advantages of our party [shouts: and the inviolability of the individual as well?]. Yes, also the inviolability of the individual. As a revolutionary party striving for its ultimate aim—social revolution, we should consider the democratic principles exclusively from the standpoint of the advantage of our party. If some postulate or other will be disadvantageous for us, we shall not introduce it.[8]

When the matter was brought to a vote, the friendship between Lenin and Martov was forever broken. Although Plekhanov sided with Lenin, the proposal lost by five votes. (The tally was twenty-eight to twenty-three.) Martov won through the support of the Bund delegates and two economists. Plekhanov subsequently returned to the democratic camp; though even in 1903 he was not as dedicated a supporter of dictatorship as Lenin, he concurred to placate his tempestuous comrade. The totalitarian philosophy was, of course, accepted in later years, providing the Russian party with its distinct position.

Shortly afterwards, the national question, which had been postponed, was considered. The vote concerned the retention by the Bund of autonomy in Jewish matters. The Congress voted negatively and the Bund walked out. Two additional delegates left because of another issue. As a result, the followers of Lenin suddenly acquired a slim majority of four votes. That Lenin regained the majority was due, in no small measure, to his endurance and persistence. Lenin was the only delegate to participate in each session from beginning to end. Many of the others, including Lenin's adherents, bored by the hair splitting, went sightseeing. Lenin certainly exerted the most energy among the Russian Social Democrats.

The word for "majority" in Russias is *bolshinstvo*. Lenin's group became known as the Bolsheviks, while the supporters of Martov were called the Mensheviks—from *Menshinstvo*—minority. Of the *Iskra* board only Martov, Plekhanov, and Lenin were delegates, both Martov and Lenin having two votes. The other board members and Krupskaya possessed merely voice, but no vote. Lenin and Plekhanov held twenty-four of the votes against nine votes firmly controlled by Martov. A six-man group of vacillators—contemptuously called "swamp" by Lenin—did not effectively oppose Lenin's manipulations. The remaining twelve votes were of little importance, since they rep-

[8]Rossiskaya Sots.-dem. Rabochaya Partiya, *Polny Tekst Protokolov, vtoroi ocherednoi syezd* (Geneva: Izdaniye Tsentralnago Kom., 1903), p. 168f. Plekhanov explicitly agreed with this speech. For a similar speech by Plekhanov delivered during the Congress, and on this entire debate, *see* Bertram Wolfe, *Three who made a Revolution*, New York, Dial Press, 1948, p. 236f. Plekhanov's later change of mind is discussed by Samuel Baron, "Between Marx and Lenin: George Plekhanov," in *Revisionism, Essays on the History of Marxist Ideas*, edited by Leopold Labedz (New York: Praeger, 1962), p. 50.

resented splinter groups. Hence Lenin felt free to pronounce that he spoke for the majority. So long as he represented the *whole Iskra* group this claim was true. But his tactics had resulted in the disruption of the *Iskra* group; his management utterly failed. On the specific issue which divided Martov from Lenin, Martov held the majority. But Lenin, a more skillful propagandist, followed Nechayev's advice, and artificially inflated his power by the use of propaganda.

Lenin succeeded in carrying out another complicated maneuver: he obtained approval of his proposal to limit the editorial board of *Iskra* to Plekhanov, Martov, and himself. He also placed three of his faithful supporters in the newly established Central Committee.

Lenin was intent upon establishing himself—in spite of inner conflicts—as the supreme leader of the party. Again, he planned: *Iskra* was to be the only party organ; the editorial board was to be controlled by Lenin, and persons not representing Russian organizations were to be eliminated from the board. A Central Committee operating in Russia was to be subordinated to the *Iskra* editorial board operating from abroad. The whole structure was to be maintained by rigid party discipline. The decision establishing this program was declared to be binding on the entire party—an extraordinary result, achieved through Lenin's voting strength in the rump congress. But the victory was hollow, for in the key ballot half of the authorized votes remained uncast. Lenin's strength was only superficial. Martov refused to serve on the *Iskra* board; Rosa Luxemburg commented that Lenin wanted only to control the party, and that he was not interested in its intellectual development. Plekhanov, who finally recognized Lenin's tactics, broke with him, remarking that Lenin had confused dictatorship *of* the proletariat with dictatorship *over* the proletariat. He even went further and stated that the "new edition of the Nechayev dictatorship" was a "criminal plot against the life of the Russian Social Democratic Labor Party."[9]

Dejected, Lenin returned to Switzerland. Long arguments with Plekhanov followed, Plekhanov endeavoring to reunite the quarreling factions, and Lenin insisting that it was impossible to cooperate with the Mensheviks. At this time, Lenin ran his bicycle against a streetcar and, almost losing an eye, he was for a while forced to keep it covered. His nerves were shattered. Plekhanov, as he was entitled to do, reinstated the former editors. Lenin was compelled to resign and *Iskra* passed to the control of the Mensheviks.[10] It was a shattering defeat. Lenin, his bid for power lost, had become isolated in an intellectual ghetto of his own making.

[9]Geyer, p. 413. *See also* a comment by Potresov, *ibid.,* p. 414.

[10]The French police at Annemasse reported Lenin's retirement from *Iskra* on February 4, 1904, and passed the information on to the Paris Okhrana. Document in Hoover Institution.

Early in 1904, Kautsky was asked by Axelrod what he thought about the split. He replied that the German proletariat disliked unnecessary squabbles. Unity was necessary, especially now when (as a result of the Russo-Japanese war) the German socialists were eager to aid their Russian comrades: it would be best if the German party did not learn of the Russian split. Kautsky explained that, in order to strengthen the party, Martov's formula on membership was preferable, despite the fact that the Russian party could function only as a *Geheimbund*. (Actually, in developing this point, Kautsky was confused: he used arguments which would have supported Lenin's position.) He stressed the role of mutual confidence, honesty, and communication among the party leadership, describing these factors as constituting a stronger organizational tie than formal centralization. Kautsky also criticized Lenin for having excluded Axelrod, Potresov, and Zasulich from *Iskra:* this kind of action was not conducive to the instilling of confidence. Solidarity among leaders was imperative; otherwise the organization would be disrupted. If two factions were to grow equally strong, the majority should not impose its will on the minority, especially since votes are often accidental. Differences should be composed loyally. At any rate, Kautsky declared, the organization question was not of primary importance. The Russian Social Democrats should cooperate with each other, exploiting opportunities to strike at absolutism. This dispute was paralyzing the party, and Lenin would have to be held responsible for having started the conflict.[11]

Kautsky offered to mediate, making every effort to moderate his criticism of Lenin. But he left no doubt that he considered Lenin's actions to be harmful to the cause of socialism. The unified Russian Social Democratic party proved to be a stillborn baby.

Yet most critics overlooked one point: Lenin had progressed in his personal political career. Although he had not emerged as *the* leader of *the* party, he had become the acknowledged leader of a small but clearly defined faction: he had assumed leadership over his own embryonic party. Since he also retained most of the offices he had held in the overall party, he had achieved double leverage. He had been defeated and he had won Pyrrhic victories. The essential result was the seizure of a major bridgehead on his road to power.

[11]*Ein Leben für den Sozialismus: Erinnerungen an Karl Kautsky* (Hannover: Dietz, 1954), pp. 83-89.

The War with Japan

In February, 1904, Japan and Russia went to war. An event of enormous political significance, it provided an unexpected chance that the revolutionary movement might be intensified. Yet, initially the war made little impression on Lenin. Practically ejected from the party, Lenin wrote a brochure, *One Step Forward, Two Steps Back,* expressing his version of the party dispute. Being virtually reduced to the position of a one-man party, he made efforts to enlarge his band of followers, recruiting such outstanding intellectuals as A. V. Lunacharsky and A. A. Bogdanov, a writer on philosophical questions whose real name was Alexander Alexandrovich Malinovsky. Krupskaya disclosed that Lenin was "not very familiar" with Bogdanov's writings, but that Bogdanov had extensive connections in Russia and "plainly was a man of caliber as far as the party was concerned."[1]

Lenin was again in poor physical and psychological condition; he needed absolute rest. According to the Russian police report of April 9, Lenin and his wife were leaving for a stay in the country of six weeks to two months. Lenin actually went on a lengthy hiking tour during which time he did not even bother to read the newspapers. In his absence, Martin M. Mandelstamm-Lyadov managed his affairs. Lenin returned in better health. His interests were now concentrated, almost exclusively, on the intra-party struggle. The Tsar's armies were being defeated and the revolutionary fever in Russia was rising. But Lenin's attention was riveted on fine points in Marxist theory, which he explored to strengthen his arguments against those socialists who were unwilling to subordinate themselves to his authoritarian rule. As late as December, 1904, he still was lecturing in Bern and Paris on such untimely subjects as "social democracy and liberalism." But, appearances were somewhat deceptive.

Sister Maria joined the Lenins in October. She and a young secretary of Lenin's, Lidya Alexandrovna Fotieva, became good friends, and the two often went bicycling with Lenin; sometimes the great man also bicycled with Krupskaya. There were musical evenings, with one Communist singing, another playing the violin, and Fotieva, a conservatory graduate, playing the piano. Fotieva reported that Beethoven's *Pathétique* sonata was Lenin's favorite.[2]

One curious discussion in which Lenin engaged some time during 1904 (or perhaps 1905) at Lausanne was with Georg Adolf Josef Lanz von Liebenfels, an erstwhile monk and priest, inventor of a race doctrine, and purportedly the "man who gave Hitler his ideas." Lanz had just published *Theo-Zoology,* in which he justified monarchy and aristocracy on the grounds of the inherited superior qualities of the rulers. The meeting of the two men was arranged by

[1]Krupskaya, 1959, p. 109.

[2]Fotieva, *Pages from Lenin's Life* (Moscow, 1960), p. 12.

a stunning baroness, Lanz related. The discussion was an animated one—Lenin had studied the book! He invited Lanz to join his movement and upon leaving, the "bolshi-chieftain," as Lanz called him, said: "I am sorry for you. Your ideas are right but before they win, our counter-ideas will prevail. For the Christians and Aryans on whom you rely no longer are Christians and Aryans but swine. . . ."[3] Soon, Lenin's life took a more serious turn.

Immediately after the outbreak of the war, suggestions had reached the Japanese government that it could greatly improve its position by stimulating the revolutionary movement in Russia. Some of these suggestions had been originated by the former Japanese military attaché in Russia, others by Joseph Pilsudski, who had testified at Alexander Ulyanov's trial and was now a prominent Polish revolutionary living in Austrian Poland. The Poles had effected contacts with Finnish nationalists, with whom they were eager to trade, for weapons and ammunition, their intelligence reports, as well as their influence on the numerous Polish soldiers in the Russian army. Pilsudski held that Japan was "the enemy of our enemy" and "the defeat of tsarism . . . our victory."[4]

Yet other Poles, as well as the British government, counselled against revolutionary warfare. The Japanese government was hesitating. After many months—and several successful Polish operations—the advice of some Americans, including the famed Henry Adams,[5] prevailed and the Japanese decided to place full support behind Russian revolutionary movements.

Actually, the Tokyo government merely ratified an activity that had been going on for some time. Colonel Motojiro Akashi, an outstanding intelligence officer, had been studying the Russian revolutionary movement attentively since 1902, when he was appointed attaché in St. Petersburg. After the outbreak of war, the Colonel met Konni Zilliacus in Stockholm and asked that he contact Russian revolutionaries living in Europe. Zilliacus had, during 1903, communicated with Russian revolutionaries to obtain their support for the Finnish independence struggle.[6] He went to Switzerland, France, and England and returned in June to Stockholm urging

---

[3]Wilfried Daim, *Der Mann, der Hitler die Ideen gab* (München: Isar, 1958), p. 99ff.

[4]Wladyslaw Pobog-Malinowski, *Najnowsza Historia Polityczna Polski, 1864-1945,* Paris, (no publisher), 1953, Vol. I, p. 130; and Witold Jodko-Narkiewicz, *Polska a Panstwa Neutralne,* Krakow, (no publisher), 1916, p. 18f.

[5]Report by special envoy Baron Kentaro Kaneko (Harvard classmate of President Theodore Roosevelt) to Japanese Prime and Foreign Ministers concerning conversation on January 13, 1905. *Archives,* Japanese Ministry of Foreign Affairs, Series MT5.2.18.33. Reel 804, p. 83.

[6]According to information obtained by the Okhrana, the Finnish separatists formally decided on July 16, 1903, to cooperate with Russian revolutionaries.

Akashi to get busy. The Colonel began to meet Russia's outstanding revolutionaries, negotiating with representatives of many parties. In July, Akashi saw Plekhanov in Geneva. This meeting was unprofitable; through Zasulich, however, Akashi met Lenin.

Shortly after his meeting with Akashi, Lenin called a conference of his followers to be held at the Lac de Bré in August. To confer was expensive, especially since some of the participants had to come from Russia. Also, several invitees presumably were not eager to work with Lenin. But the conference took place and revived Lenin's organization. Without tarrying, the Bolsheviks asked for the convocation of a new congress. After the meeting was concluded, Lenin vacationed by the Alpine lake till the end of the month.

By September 17, French police observers reported that Lenin no longer was exercising his party functions and that he probably would move from Geneva to Lausanne or Clarens; Lenin, in fact, expressed a desire to return to England. On September 26, 1904, Krupskaya wrote a plaintive letter to Odessa.[7] The Central Committee decided to relieve Lenin of his functions as its foreign representative, and appointed Victor L. Kopp to censor the writings of Lenin and his followers and to decide which Bolshevik manuscripts were to be published. Thereupon the Bolsheviks resolved to publish independently. Vladimir D. Bonch-Bruyevich, who had been acting as the Bolsheviks' financial secretary, was placed in charge of the technical work. Krupskaya stated that a number of brochures were ready. Publication would continue as long as means were available. The Central Committee wished to know upon whose request Lenin and Bonch-Bruyevich were embarking on this publication program. It was a pertinent question.

During October, Akashi and Zilliacus organized, and ran from behind the scenes, a conference of thirteen parties, which the Social Revolutionaries and national separatists attended. No Social Democrats were present. This conference contributed greatly to the unification of the revolutionary movement. The activity was under surveillance by the Okhrana; the Okhrana agents complained that they lacked sufficient funds for the job. (These agents procured the code used by the Japanese for a paltry 9000 francs: the professional standing of these agents was indeed high. Subsequently, Akashi and Zilliacus realized that their correspondence had been intercepted and that the Okhrana had been aided by the French police.)

Akashi met Lenin a second time, during 1904, perhaps at the Amsterdam congress of the Second International, where Plekhanov publicly fraternized with the Japanese socialist Sen Katayama. The Colonel reported:

[7]*Krasnyi Arkhiv* (1934), I/62, 165ff.

Lenin is considered by other socialists to be a rascal who uses all kinds of methods to reach his objectives. On the contrary, he is a sincere man and lacks egoism. He gives everything to his doctrine. Lenin is the person who can accomplish the revolution.[8]

This proved to be remarkable foresight. Zilliacus advised against supporting Lenin, but Akashi disregarded this recommendation and proposed to support him independently of the other groups. Lenin, he believed, functioned best by himself.

On November 27, the Okhrana reported from Berlin to St. Petersburg that Lenin was prepared to publish a newspaper. The first issue was to appear immediately—*Vperyed* came out on January 4, 1905[9]—and publication of fifteen issues was practically assured.[10] On December 3, 1904, the French police, noting that Lenin was still warring unsuccessfully against Plekhanov, reported that Lenin was now surrounded by a group of twenty to twenty-five students. Thus the unhappy time of organizational isolation and financial famine was suddenly over.

There is little doubt that the money had been supplied by the Japanese. How much money Lenin received is not known, nor are the methods of transference clear.[11] He was usually shrewd in these

---

[8]Komori, Tokuji, *Akashi Motojiro* (Taipeh, 1928), I. p. 142. *See also* Sugiyama, Shigemaru, *Akashi Taisho den* (Tokyo, 1921); Nishikawa, Torajiro, *Akashi, Taisho* (Tokyo, 1934); and Koyana, Katukiyo, *Sendo Dai Sendo* (Tokyo, 1930).

[9]*Vperyed* appeared until May 1905, when it was superseded by *Proletarii*. Lenin used *Vperyed* to attack Plekhanov furiously. The Central Committee proposed that the German socialist August Bebel arbitrate the dispute, but Lenin refused to accept this solution and reserved for himself freedom of action. (French police reports from Annemasa, February 16 and 27, 1905.)

[10]*Krasnyi Arkhiv, loc. cit.*, p. 170.

[11]The Japanese were not stingy. A Social Revolutionary who organized the Potemkine mutiny in 1905 received 40,000 rubles (Komori, *op. cit.*, p. 186). It appears from a note by Zilliacus (stolen in London by Russian intelligence from Akashi's suitcase) that on one account over 15,000 British pounds were available for a ship and rifles in the north. The Social Revolutionaries received 4,000 pounds and 1,000 rifles (valued at 800 pounds). 5,000 rifles (worth 4,000 pounds) were earmarked for Petersburg. (Okhrana note dated May 20, 1905; Document in Hoover Institution). A letter from Zilliacus to Akashi listed the expenditure of 20,000 pounds, mostly for rifles (Futrell, p. 81f.). Most of the other monies designated for political warfare presumably were destined for a projected assassination campaign and organizational expenses. Lenin, the man who was expected to lead the revolution, hardly could be neglected. But the sources merely indicate that he received a "pretty sum of money." Akashi's confidential report of January, 1906, on his operations against Russia does not provide financial information. For a well-documented study on the early relations of the Japanese with Polish revolutionaries, including Pilsudski, see Jerzy J. Lerski, "A Polish Chapter of the Russo-Japanese War," *The Transactions of the Asiatic Society of Japan* (Third Series. Tokyo, 1959), VII, 69-97.

matters. It is likely that the money was sent through "cut-outs."[12] It is known that Bonch-Bruyevich received paper and printing on "credit" from a French firm and that Lyadov secured cash for honoraria and distribution.

Vperyed's editorial board included V. V. Orlovsky, who in 1917 was to be one of Lenin's intermediaries with the Germans, and M. S. Olminsky, who, during World War I, published *Nasha Gazeta* in Saratov. Lenin in 1916 advised the Germans to support the Bolshevik group in that Volga town.

Reports state that by the end of December, 1904, Gorky had contributed 3,000 rubles for the newspaper. This sum might have been enough to start publication, but *Vperyed* was in print before Gorky's money could have reached Switzerland. Gorky asked Lenin to return to Russia to take personal charge of the party, but Lenin refused to go.[13]

The Gorky contribution probably included the 2,000 rubles that the eccentric millionaire Savva Timofeyevich Morozov had promised to give the Bolsheviks. In the presence of his friend Gorky, Morozov promised 2,000 rubles a month to Leonid Krassin, a wealthy electrical engineer who pursued revolutionary activities as a hobby. It is not certain precisely when this promise was made, but it was in the winter of 1904. Payments started forthwith, presumably. It is certain that Morozov gave money once; perhaps he contributed twice, but no more than three times. Other wealthy persons, including Gorbunov from Kaluga and Meshkov from Perm, also gave financial support. These contributions were not sufficient to finance entirely the sudden upsurge of Bolshevik activity, but they were useful in concealing the Japanese aid.

A foremost industrialist and the descendant of a slave, Morozov was a neurotic—possibly a manic-depressive—who dabbled in theater, reform, and revolution.[14] Concerned over the poor reputation among Russian liberals of the Morozov name, which dated back to the days of labor unrest in 1885, Savva was won over to the cause by Maria Fedorovna Andreyeva, a famed actress and *grande dame* and an enthusiastic supporter of the revolution. Morozov and Andreyeva had once had an affair, but she was now involved with Gorky. It

[12]This term is intelligence jargon and denotes a middleman, sometimes a whole string of intermediaries, to conceal the true origin of funds that are funnelled to agents or unsuspecting revolutionaries.

[13]Gorky did from time to time support the party financially. For example, in June, 1905, he transmitted, upon request, 2,000 rubles to Stassova. But Gorky's funds usually were used to keep the organization afloat inside Russia. *See* Shotman, *op. cit.*, p. 202. During World War I, Gorky again restricted his help to organizations in Russia.

[14]Morozov's brother Sergei was described by Savva as a hypochondriac, and his sisters as mentally ill.

seems, however, that Gorky attempted to dissuade Morozov from giving money to the Bolsheviks.[15] Rumors had it that Morozov gave "millions," but he was never in possession of that much money. In January, 1905, after Bloody Sunday (see below), Gorky was arrested and bailed out by Morozov for 10,000 rubles. Morozov's assistance to the revolutionaries did not help him personally: the Morozov factory became the object of a particularly venomous strike. As soon as Savva was replaced as director, the "workers" clamored for his return. When he appeared to talk to them, they threw stones and fired shots. Eleven men were killed and Morozov fell ill.

Morozov was finished and the Gorkys no longer had any use for him. He was deeply hurt: revolutionary proclamations were spreading lies about him. He objected to being thrown away like a "worn out shoe." Gorky countered that Morozov merely professed to being a revolutionary, that people were being killed at his factory. Morozov had accurately predicted that when he would no longer have money, no one, including Gorky, would need him.

Early in 1905, Savva's family, after considering his commitment, pensioned him and kept him temporarily confined at home. Serebrov visited him in a dark, neglected bedroom. Morozov, agitated, cried. He handed over a pile of money for the party, but a well-dressed woman, probably his wife, entered and complained that "ideologically-minded people" were robbing a sick man. Serebrov threw the money on the table and left. Through the closed door he heard Morozov yell: "I'll kill you." Something heavy crashed upon the floor.[16]

After the Russo-Japanese war, Morozov requested an audience from Prime Minister Sergius Witte, with whom he had been on friendly terms and whose portrait, together with one of Gorky, adorned his study. Witte admonished Morozov to abandon his revolutionary activities: "You don't understand a thing about politics. . . . Better get busy with industrialization."[17] Morozov was keenly interested in electrification but did not heed Witte's advice. He left Russia and went to Cannes, France, where he underwent psychiatric treatment.

Returning from a party congress in London, Krassin visited him. Morozov told him that he knew the party was not interested in his health, and that he had no money left. He handed Krassin a sealed

[15]Alexander Serebrov (A. N. Tikhonov), *Vremya i Lyudi, Memuary 1898-1905* (Moscow, 1955), p. 199f. On the Morozov story, see M. A. Aldanov, *Samoubiistvo* (New York: Literaturnyi Fond, 1958).

[16]Serebrov, *op. cit.*, p. 209f.

[17]Witte reported on this conversation in his *Erinnerungen*, (Berlin: Ullstein, 1923), p. 416f.

package for Gorky's wife. "This is all I have . . . I won't need anything any more."[18] The package probably contained a life insurance policy, naming Andreyeva as beneficiary, and permitting her to use the money as she saw fit.

The next day, some time in May, 1905, Morozov drew a heart on his chest with a chemical pencil and shot himself through the target.[19] He left no money to the revolutionaries. His widow married the police president of Moscow and squandered the remaining portion of her late husband's assets on herself.

Gorky and his wife were accused of having induced this suicide to obtain Morozov's money. There is no question that they treated the poor man brutally, making no effort to help him. The Okhrana, in a communication of April 30, 1907, seemed to accept the story that Morozov had settled a life insurance policy of 100,000 rubles on Andreyeva.[20] Rumors had it that 60,000 rubles were destined for the party and 40,000 for student organizations, etc.[21] According to the Okhrana, the Bolsheviks got 40,000 rubles; the police did not report on the disposition of the remainder, leaving open the question of whether the Gorkys profited personally from this policy. Since Morozov had been placed under tutelage, he could not have disposed of his money directly. The mystery remains as to why the insurance company paid upon suicide, especially since it appears the policy had been written shortly before Morozov's death. Apparently there was a considerable delay before the money was paid.

While Lenin remained preoccupied with party squabbles, on Sunday, January 22, 1905, demonstrators under the leadership of a priest, Father Grigori Gapon, attempted to present a petition to the Tsar. Gapon had been collaborating, off and on, with the police. There was some hope in court and police circles that the monarchy could be brought closer to the people—especially in view of the recent humiliating fall of Port Arthur to the Japanese—and that the Tsar would accept a petition by the workers to mark the beginnings of a new policy. Considerations of this type led to leniency by the police toward Gapon's strike and political agitation. The Austrian diplomat Consul General von Ugron reported a strange absence of police from the streets; he inferred that the demonstrators had been drawn into a trap to be taught a bloody lesson. In the European

[18]Serebrov, p. 211.

[19]Once he had discussed with Gorky the latter's suicide attempt: Morozov said Gorky had used a bad rifle; if his time came he would use a Browning.

[20]Okhrana note dated April 30, 1917 (Document in Hoover Institution).

[21]Schapiro (*The Communist Party*, p. 88) states that between 1906 and 1907, 60,000 rubles were given to Lenin, Bogdanov and Krassin by Gorky's wife, adding that the whole Central Committee budget (presumably the budget for the whole party) for the period between the Fourth and Fifth Congress was 80,000 rubles.

press it was openly predicted that the revolution would erupt on Sunday, January 22, at 2:00 P.M. It is certain that the police were aware of the preparations for the demonstration, but they made no serious attempt to stop Gapon and to prevent the incident.

Gapon, however, had joined forces with Social Democrats, including Gorky. Gapon, who, according to Akashi's subsequent report to his superiors, was prodded by the Social Democrats, deceived the police by aiming at objectives far more ambitious than the authorities were willing to permit.[22] Die-hard proponents of absolutism at the court may have encouraged Gapon's demonstration in order to find a pretext for slapping down the revolutionaries. When the demonstrators approached the Winter Palace exhibiting signs of a genuinely rebellious spirit, an order was given to fire. Whether this order was due to premeditation or panic is conjectural.[23] This massacre became known as Bloody Sunday and, together with alleged or real treachery which was ascribed to the Tsar and his uncle, sparked the revolution of 1905.

With Bloody Sunday prodding the masses out of their inertia, Lenin suddenly realized that, while history had been marching on, he had been wasting his time on trifles. He burst into activity; though he did not abandon the party struggle, he henceforth devoted most of his attention to the revolution. With characteristic boldness, he decided that what was necessary presently was the immediate preparation of an armed uprising. This notion was naturally quite in line with Akashi's wishes.

But Lenin soon discovered that his study of capitalism and party organization had not prepared him for active combat with steel and

[22]After his flight abroad, when he dealt with Lenin and was strongly coaxed by Akashi, Gapon returned and entered into very questionable relations with the police. Thereupon he was executed by Social Revolutionaries.

[23]Several years earlier, the government had experimented with "police socialism." To keep unrest under better control, the police itself established workers' parties and organized strikes, only to resort in several instances to repressive action. "Police socialism" came to be opposed by the Tsar's uncle, Grand Duke Sergei Alexandrovich, who promptly was assassinated by terrorists commanded by Yevno Azev, a police agent. It is not likely that Bloody Sunday was a deliberate provocation. My impression is rather that the police tolerated the operation to allow the masses to let off steam; and perhaps they hoped that the Tsar might receive the petitioner. (For some of the details see Father George Gapon, *The Story of my Life* [London: Chapman and Hall. 1905]). But Bloody Sunday showed how demonstrations and uprisings could be provoked, to provide a pretext and a tactical opportunity for violent repression. This lesson, I submit, was taken to heart by the Okhrana and heeded, just as they learned how to participate in and direct terroristic acts aimed at the regime, in the hope of deflecting terror from the important to the unimportant targets. One Okhrana document of January 12, 1909, dealing with the background of the Azev affair, clearly implies that the Okhrana was involved in the assassination of Duma deputy Jolles. This criminal operation was of considerable political help to the regime.

fire. A lesser man might have been satisfied with improvisation. Lenin went to the library and delved into the arts of war and uprising. He consulted the meager instructions which Marx and Engels had offered on the subject, and he probably read, for his own secret use, Auguste Blanqui's *Instructions pour une prise d'armes*.[24] He even translated— as the only suitable textbook he could find—a classical treatise which a *Communard* of 1871 had written on barricades and insurrection. Frantically, he wrote and lectured on the commune and its mistakes —which were not to be repeated. To the annoyance of his comrades, most of whom were revolutionaries of the pen, he belabored the "technical" aspects of revolution. He tirelessly called for the Third Congress, through which the armed uprising was to be prepared.

After having been hidden by Savva Morozov, Father Gapon escaped from Russia. In February, 1905, living in Axelrod's Swiss apartment, Gapon discussed with Lenin a united action of all revolutionary groups. In the meantime, stimulated by Bloody Sunday and the coincident advice of Henry Adams, the Japanese decided to embark on revolutionizing on a large scale. The revolutionaries sent emissaries abroad, notably to the German socialists, asking for help. The Okhrana reported on Russian revolutionaries bringing literature from the United States; Pilsudski and other Polish socialists were smuggling arms from Polish Austria into Russia.[25]

There took place another conference of Russian revolutionaries under Akashi's secret mentorship. This gathering decided upon preparing an uprising for summer, 1905, and began to increase the purchasing of weapons and their dispatch to Russia. Lenin and other Social Democrats initially participated but then left the conference.[26] A short while later, Lenin asked Maxim Litvinov, later Foreign Minister of the Soviet Union, to co-operate in the arms

[24]On April 23, 1885, Engels wrote to Vera Zassulich: "If ever Blanquism—that phantasy according to which a whole society is to be overturned by the action of a small conspiratorial group—had a justification of sorts, then surely at Petersburg. . . . Assume these people imagine they are able to seize power, what harm is done by this? If they only drill a hole which will cause the bursting of the dam . . . ."

[25]Circular from vice-director of Police to chiefs of Border Gendarmerie of January 28, 1905 (New Style).

[26]This information is contained in a memoir which Akashi wrote after his return to Japan. Akashi indicated that this conference took place in April, 1905. (Letter from National Diet Library, Tokyo, September 11, 1962). Other data show it might have occurred during February. The earlier date appears more probable, yet the April date is generally accepted (Futrell, p. 66f.). Incidentally, this may have been the conference which Pilsudski as well as the Okhrana's foremost *agent provocateur* Evno Azev attended. Zilliacus was intimate with Azev, who reported extensively on the Japanese machinations with the revolutionaries (Futrell, p. 69). Azev testified to the Germans during the war that he knew Lenin personally. The only meeting that I could discover was this Geneva conference. *See* Michael Sokolnicki, "Josef Pilsudski a zagadnienie Rosji," *Niepodleglosc* (London 1950), II, 55.

procurement operation; Litvinov was in charge of getting *Vperyed* into Russia.[27]

Lenin informed the Petersburg party committee that he had received money from an English workers' group to help the victims of Bloody Sunday. If such money did come from England, it would not have been channeled through Lenin. However, some of the money which was being collected throughout Europe may have eventually reached Lenin.

Krupskaya's version of these events is of interest. We know that the Japanese, who had great faith in Gapon, were grooming him to be the symbol of revolutionary unity. Krupskaya recorded, in a condescending vein, Lenin's dealings with Gapon, adding that "Gapon undertook to supply arms to the St. Petersburg workers. All kinds of donations had been put at his disposal, and he used the money to buy weapons in England." She disclosed further that Gapon received an illegal passport and secret addresses "from us" and left for St. Petersburg to organize the uprising. "To Vladimir Ilyich this whole enterprise was a passing from words to deeds. The workers had to receive arms at all costs."[28] Years later, Zilliacus commented to his son: "Half the people to whom Japanese money is distributed don't know where it comes from, and the other half don't care." Lenin knew and was unconcerned. In any event, the victims of January 22 did not receive any money from Lenin or the Bolsheviks, who were not interested in humanitarian ventures.

Lenin's enterprises boomed. His recent writings were translated into a number of Caucasian languages. The Japanese were particularly anxious to foment unrest in the Caucasus, and they distributed huge quantities of revolutionary writings and inflammatory appeals. It is only fair to reiterate that Lenin and his group were not the only revolutionaries inside Russia who collaborated with the enemy; on the contrary, treasonable collaboration was widespread among the revolutionary parties.[29]

Working without interruption and little sleep, Lenin was preparing for the Third Congress by writing a theoretical platform. His newest book, *Two Tactics of the Social Democracy in the Democratic Revolution,* was somewhat contradictory. It called for a "revolutionary and democratic dictatorship of the workers and

[27]According to Okhrana information of December 12, 1906, Litvinov possessed a German passport on the name of "Gustav Graf."

[28]Krupskaya, p. 116. She overemphasized Lenin's dealings with Gapon in order to conceal the Japanese connection.

[29]For example, N. V. Chaikovsky, a venerable veteran among the revolutionaries, performed Akashi's and Zilliacus' liaison missions at London.

peasants."[30] This dictatorship, though it would be unable to eliminate capitalism, could partition land property in favor of the peasants. Lenin argued that interrelated objective and subjective factors precluded "the direct liberation of the working class." He explained that "Marxists" were convinced of the bourgeois character of the Russian revolution: the social, political, and economic changes which had become inevitable would establish the rule of the bourgeoisie and further the development of the European, not the Asian type, of capitalism. Hence Lenin deemed it reactionary to seek the salvation of the proletariat in any manner other than the gradual development of capitalism.

However, apparently without noting the contradiction, Lenin also spoke of the "victory" of the socialist democracy. Merely to await this victory as inevitable would be "stupid," "half anarchistic," and even "reactionary." But if the European proletariat were to come to the aid of their Russian comrades, it would not be impossible. In 1883, Engels had offered the opposite judgment to the Russian revolutionary Gherman Lopatin: "Russia is what France was in a former century; to her belongs the revolutionary initiative."[31]

Lenin also inconsistently argued that the proletariat and the peasants should settle accounts with the monarchy and aristocracy in a "plebeian fashion": they should destroy their enemies pitilessly. Yet Lenin also proposed democracy. The interests of the proletariat and the aims of socialism, he argued, required complete political freedom. The provisional government was to ensure free elections on the basis of general, equal, direct, and secret suffrage, calling for a constituent assembly to express the true will of the people. Though many of these points were made only to facilitate cooperation with the liberals, Lenin was not yet fully convinced of the unsuitability of democracy.

Between April 25 and May 10, 1905, the Third Congress met in London. This time the Bolsheviks were entirely independent: Lenin controlled enough funds to select the participants. Less than two-thirds of the organizations entitled to be represented at a policy congress sent delegates, and some of these groups—including one

[30]The notion of "democratic dictatorship" can be traced back to Marx, in whose thinking the dictatorship was to be exercised by the majority. It differs fundamentally from the concept of a minority or elitist dictatorship which subsequently was elaborated by Lenin and Stalin.

[31]On Sept. 27, 1877, Marx wrote to Sorge: "This time the revolution begins in the East . . . . Compared with the crisis in the East the French crisis is quite a secondary event." On April 23, 1887, also in a letter to Sorge, Engels expected the beginning of the Russian revolution within months and considered that thereupon the German revolution could be started. For similar statements, see Helmut Krause, *Marx und Engels und das zeitgenössische Russland* (Giessen: Schmitz, 1958), p. 77f.

"committee" consisting of a single member—were of questionable standing. Lenin all but admitted that the Congress was illegal,[32] but this did not dampen his enthusiasm. The comrades reported, debated, and decided to endorse armed uprising, not necessarily because they entertained illusions of quickly seizing power, but because they were anxious to commit themselves to revolutionary deeds. It is difficult to determine whether this resolution resulted from Japanese instigation or whether Lenin and his followers, in view of the possibility that preparations for a rising might bring further assistance, were gripped by activist frenzy. The Bolsheviks discussed, quite prematurely, their possible participation in a provisional government,[33] but primarily concentrated on practical work: developing organizational plans, preparing cyphers and communication channels, exploring the problems of arms procurement, and ordering their finances.

Repeatedly Lenin declared to the Social Democratic committees in Russia that he represented the communications center of the party, and thus had to be kept informed of all activities; few people bothered to reply.

Subsequently, Lenin again negotiated with Gapon. The smuggling of arms was underway. Transports in the Baltic were supervised by Zilliacus (aided by an American lady of prominent social standing). Maxim Litvinov devoted most of his attention to transports in the Black Sea. Between July and September, 1905, Litvinov allegedly succeeded in shipping into Russia 15,000 rifles, 3,000 revolvers, and several tons of dynamite.

According to other reports, Litvinov's operations failed completely. Zilliacus, who had chartered a small steamer and two yachts, was able to discharge arms on islands near the Finnish coast early in September. However, after the first two unloadings, the steamer which was en route to a second hide-away ran aground. Two custom officials came on board and were held in friendly captivity for several hours. Then Zilliacus ordered the ship to be blown up. Although the tsarist government seized about 9,000 rifles, about 6500 were saved. Sizeable quantities of arms were secured by the Finns and hundreds or even thousands or rifles were used by St. Petersburg strikers and insurgents during October, 1905.[34]

Except for the Caucasus, where large numbers of weapons were landed, these efforts at weapons smuggling achieved only indifferent success. The operation could have been improved, but in the mean-

[32]Institut Marksizma-Leninizma, *Tretii Syezd RSDRP, Aprel- Mai 1905 goda, Protokoly* (Moscow, 1959), p. 46.

[33]*Ibid.*, p. 61.

[34]Futrell, p. 77ff.

time the war had been concluded, and the Japanese lost all interest in supporting and arming revolutionaries. Thus, the Japanese phase of the Russian revolution had drawn to its end.

Lenin's clamor for terror and armed uprising made it seem likely that he would rush home to assume command of his troops. But this was not in his plans. Many other revolutionaries, including Leon Trotsky and Alexander Helphand-Parvus, his friend and mentor, had returned to Russia immediately after Bloody Sunday.[35] But Lenin, except to travel in Europe, did not move.

Presently, Lenin went to Paris. Earlier, he had sent Fotieva to France in order to get the Paris Bolsheviks in line. He announced his arrival in a letter, saying that he was coming on unspecified business. Intending to lecture, he instructed Fotieva to rent "the largest hall."[36] Lenin stayed for three days, spending one free night at the opera; it bored him. On the other free night, Lenin, Fotieva and another male Bolshevik visited the Folies Bergères. "Vladimir Ilyich laughed . . . and really enjoyed himself that evening."[37]

[35]According to the Okhrana, Parvus may have returned later. His purpose was to publish a Social Democratic newspaper. The Paris agency informed St. Petersburg that he still was a Russian citizen. (Notes of November 13 and 14, 1905, from Garting to Rachkovsky.)

[36]Fotieva, *Iz Zhizni Lenina* (Moscow, 1959), p. 21.

[37]Fotieva, *Pages from Lenin's Life*, p. 30.

The Revolution of 1905

In the meantime, the war was drawing to a close. Russia had suffered defeat. Although she could have continued fighting, the simmering revolution prompted her to seek a compromise. As the Russian army was demobilized, the Japanese released their prisoners of war, many of whom they had indoctrinated in revolutionary thinking. Polish nationalists had deeply influenced Polish soldiers. With the financial help of a few American capitalists, George Kennan, an American newspaperman, had been distributing revolutionary brochures to imprisoned Russians and Ukrainians. Angered by treachery and defeat, irrascible after captivity, and aroused by new, stirring national, social, and political ideals, the soldiers were streaming back through Siberia into the heartland. Wherever they went unrest was precipitated.

The liberal parties, creating a united front, demanded the immediate institution of parliamentary government. The Tsar granted a few concessions but was still hesitating when a strike wave—amply financed by Russian industrialists who continued to pay the wages of the strikers—swept the country. The workers were supported by soldiers, by most of the moderate groups, and by the partisans of constitutional monarchy. Lenin and other Marxists had predicted accurately: this was essentially a "bourgeois-democratic revolution." A crippling railroad strike, as it rapidly developed into a general strike, forced the Tsar to concede. On October 30, he issued the so-called *October Manifesto,* which established a parliament, the Duma, and granted limited suffrage and freedom of speech. The *October Manifesto* transformed the autocracy into a semiconstitutional regime.

Four days earlier, the St. Petersburg Mensheviks had created a new, democratic body, the so-called soviet or Council of Workers' Deputies; it was to function as a sort of labor parliament in which industrial workers were to be represented. How did this come about?

Shortly after Bloody Sunday, the tsarist government had established a commission which was to investigate the causes of dissatisfaction among Petersburg industrial workers. The workers elected representatives to whom their grievances could be brought, and a few workers, selected by indirect voting, participated in the commission itself. At that time there were in Petersburg between 200 and 250 Bolsheviks who, after some hesitation and without Lenin's authorization, participated in this work. The commission did not function for long but the workers' organizations which it had spawned remained in existence.

Moreover, on January 16, 1905, a strike committee was created to negotiate with the management of the Putilov Works, Russia's largest armament plant. There also existed the workers' clubs which Gapon had formed with the permission of the Okhrana; Gapon cooperated with the Putilov committee.

In May, 1905, during a textile strike, a workers' council emerged in Ivanovo-Vosnessensk. This institution was the first recorded soviet (which used that name). It worked for free assembly, free speech, and the public debate of labor problems. Subsequently, similar organizations appeared, under different titles, in Kostroma and Moscow. In October, 1905, the railroad workers of Petersburg, along with liberal corporations and liberal entrepreneurs, authorized the establishment of such committees in many factories.

At this point, several Mensheviks, in concurrence with writings which had been contributed to *Iskra* by Martov, Axelrod, and Parvus, suggested the setting up of a strike committee for the entire Petersburg area. Who launched the idea is not known; possibly Parvus was the originator. On October 25, a young lawyer by the name of

George Nossar (who used the pseudonym of Khrustalov) [1] took the initiative and on October 26, the first meeting of the soviet was held, presided over by the Menshevik Zborovsky. Nossar became a Menshevik in November of 1905. (He was shot by the Bolsheviks in 1918.) Trotsky intended to propose a somewhat similar plan, but arrived at Petersburg after the soviet was already under way.

On October 30, 1905, the committee constituted itself formally as the Soviet of Workers' Deputies. This soviet was to play a leading role for only three months. For a while, the moderate parties, in the belief that this pressure was needed to consolidate the democratic gains, offered their support. The revolutionaries used the soviet to propagandize and lead the workers and demobilized soldiers, and above all to pressure government. Trotsky and Parvus were the dominating personalities.

At the time of the *October Manifesto,* Lenin was still in Switzerland writing about the armed uprising and discussing street fighting and "small battle groups." In a letter of October 16 to the Ukrainian Bolshevik N. A. Skrypnik, Lenin chided the comrades for over-organizing and not acting. Each group was supposed to procure its own arms, even if only rags dipped in petroleum. Informers and policemen were to be killed and banks raided to obtain funds for the uprising. In St. Petersburg alone, 200 to 300 action groups were to be established, each acting independently. The men were to be trained and were to undertake trial operations before striking. Yet Lenin, not anticipating the general strike which became the main act of the revolution, had not written or even thought about strike tactics. The most important revolutionary invention—the soviet—was a surprise for him. Since the Mensheviks were responsible for the innovation, he was opposed to the soviet, though the Bolshevik A. A. Bogdanov was sent to the assembly.

Thus, Lenin neither initiated nor influenced the revolution of 1905; it could hardly have been otherwise, since he was staying in Switzerland. Early in October, there was some talk that he should journey to Finland to participate in a meeting of the Central Committee. But only when, early in November, a very broad political amnesty was granted, did Lenin finally decide to move, after taking consider-

---

[1] Nossar began, shortly after Bloody Sunday, to give legal aid to strikers, and then formed a strike aid and liaison committee. He took the name of the factory worker Khrustalov to conceal his "class." *See* Voline (V. M. Eichenbaum), *La Revolution Inconnue,* (1917-1921) (Paris, Les Amis de Voline, 1947). For another but partially confirming version of Nossar, see Shotman, *op cit.,* p. 228f. During his subsequent emigration to Switzerland and France, Nossar got into considerable trouble and was suspected of unlawful transactions. After being discovered with the wife of a comrade, he was beaten and almost killed, as the Okhrana gleefully reported. The irascible husband tried to crack his skull with a sabre. Nossar, it was reported, escaped death because his head was shaped like a pear.

able time to make up his mind. The story that he was delayed two weeks waiting for his papers in Stockholm is a legend.[2] He left Geneva on November 15 or 16 and arrived in St. Petersburg five days later. At that time it was entirely safe for him to be in Russia. This hardly was the way to engineer a revolution.

[2]The implication of this version is that he was asking for a Russian passport. This is unlikely. According to another and more plausible story, he was traveling on a British passport which, of course, he may have picked up in Stockholm.

The Hero at Home

After his arrival in Petersburg, Lenin's ardor for the armed uprising temporarily cooled. Avoiding public appearances, he attended two or three sessions of the soviet as a spectator.[1] On his return home, he drafted an article (not published until 1940)[2] which stated that the soviet was supported by the masses and, pending the convocation of a constitutional assembly, should be transformed into a provisional revolutionary government. Upon his return, he scolded the comrades for permitting the Mensheviks to run the soviet, but since nothing could be done about this, he interested himself in a new party congress and in strengthening his own position within the Bolshevik Central Committee. Lenin met Maxim Gorky for the first time in the office of *Novaya Zhizn* (New Life),[3] which Gorky was financing and to which Lenin and other Bolsheviks were contributing articles.[4] (Lenin's first article was published on November 23.)

[1]According to K. Sharikov and G. Shidlovsky, *Lenin v Peterburgye,* Leningrad, 1940, p. 67, Lenin spoke on November 26, 1905, to the soviet on lock-outs. Since he was not a deputy, it is not clear whether he just talked in the building or had been invited to address the council or its executive committee. Prior to speaking, Lenin sought contacts with the workers of the Putilov works, the largest arms and heavy industrial corporation in Russia.

[2]Wolfe, p. 316ff.

[3]According to *Lenin v Peterburgye,* p. 70, Lenin met Gorky on December 10. However, he had been visiting the editorial offices of *Novaya Zhizn* almost daily since his arrival three weeks earlier: how then could he have failed to meet the famous editor? Gorky (*Days with Lenin,* New York, International Publishers, 1932, p. 5) asserted that his first meeting with Lenin took place in London during 1907. If Gorky's version were accepted, then the lack of contacts between the two men during the revolution of 1905 would cast considerable doubt on Gorky's alleged early financial support to Lenin's group.

[4]Krupskaya stated that Nikolai Schmidt, "a nephew of Morozov and owner of a furniture factory, provided money for *Novaya Zhizn.*" She disclosed that Schmidt became a Bolshevik in 1905. The editor of Krupskaya's book explained that the Morozovs were a family of millionaires who owned large textile mills but said nothing of Morozov's contribution to the party. Krupskaya, *op. cit.,* p. 185.

There is a curious story that Lenin spent much time with a coterie of female students and teachers and with *bourgeois* women who were rebelling against their class. Allegedly, he indoctrinated the girls for agitational work among women workers but it appears that his labors were not very successful.[5] Another presumably apocryphal story has it that he fell in love with an aristocratic lady to whom he was introduced by a comrade; the story also alleges that he used her as a courier and that she played for him Beethoven's *Appassionata*.

There were upheavals throughout Russia but, despite Lenin's earlier clamor, the Central Committee discussed armed uprising only on December 10.[6] On December 13, insurrections occurred in several cities. On December 15, the soviet, then dominated by Parvus, called for the financial boycott of the government.[7] This threat hastened the government into action: the entire Petersburg soviet was arrested on December 16.

On the following day, both factions of the Social Democrats decided on a general strike. The Moscow Bolsheviks, on December 18, proposed that the local Bolshevik-dominated soviet initiate a general strike culminating in a general uprising. The plan originated with Lenin and had been transmitted to Moscow by V. L. Shantser and M. N. Lyadov. The Moscow soviet accepted the proposal. The Petersburg Bolsheviks, under Lenin's prompting, decided to support the Moscow operation and to destroy the railroad connections between the two capitals.[8]

On December 20, the strike, originating in Moscow, was followed by strikes in Baku and a few other cities. The next day saw large-scale demonstrations and sporadic use of firearms. On December 22, barricades went up and for five days armed combat raged in Moscow; fighting also occurred in Rostov, Saratov, and Vilna. The Petrograd revolutionaries were unable to come to the help of their comrades; the government repressed the Moscow uprising on December 28. After considerable artillery fire, the last stronghold of the revolutionaries was subdued on December 30.

The Moscow uprising was the major battle of the revolution. Yet it may be seen as the dénouement of a revolution which had been successful, in effect, three months earlier. As the government inflicted a crushing defeat on those revolutionaries who preferred

[5]Nina Gourtinkel, *Lénine* (Paris: Editions du Seuil, 1959) p. 71.

[6]By the end of October, the police reported that weapons were smuggled into Russia across the Austrian and Rumanian borders. The border guards were inactive and sometimes helped the operation.

[7]According to *Lenin v Peterburgye*, p. 72, Lenin visited the executive committee at that time and discussed tactics; this would mean that, at a crucial moment, he was in contact with Parvus.

[8]*Ibid.*

insurrection over less violent techniques, it re-consolidated tsarism and broke the united front of the foes of autocracy.

The Moscow uprising was not a spontaneous outburst. It was brought about by deliberate decisions made by the Bolsheviks. Communist historiography has tried to conceal Lenin's role; only recently have they raised the curtain slightly.

Lenin ordered the uprising.[9] The Okhrana reported that the party allocated 11,316 rubles to prepare an armed uprising in Moscow and Petersburg.[10] However, at the time of battle, Lenin and forty comrades were assembled in complete safety at Tammerfors, Finland, where they discussed such pressing items as the agrarian question, their attitudes toward the Duma, and the need for a new congress, as well as "current affairs."

These current affairs included financial matters: since June 1, the party had received 78,000 rubles, spent 48,000, and paid debts to the amount of 20,000; thus about 10,000 rubles remained. The expenditures are not properly tallied, but income was reported as being received from two "semiparty" publishing houses, *Molot* in Odessa, and *Burevestnik* in Moscow, from the re-publication of Russian authors abroad, and from royalties received from theater performances. This publication activity supposedly netted about 100,000 rubles a year.[11]

The conference at Tammerfors convened five days after the general strike in Moscow had begun. It would have been sensible to postpone the meeting; yet the revolutionaries, instead of supporting their fighting comrades as they had promised, were concerned with their own problems. After five days the conference was adjourned as the last bit of resistance was crushed at Moscow. According to one version, Lenin proposed the "early" closing of the conference so that the Bolsheviks could participate in the uprising. According to a more recent Communist version, Lenin, on an unspecified day (approximately December 28), held a meeting in Gorky's apartment at Petersburg with the Central Committee, where he instructed Lyadov to cease

---

[9]The official call to rise was signed by the Moscow soviet and the Bolshevik committees as well as by the Menshevik group and the Social Revolutionary committee. Schapiro, *op. cit.*, p. 69.

[10]*Krasnyi Arkhiv* (1934), I/62, p. 186. Probably the entire amount went to Moscow.

[11]*Krasnyi Arkhiv, ibid.*, p. 186f. This disclosure is a little suspect. The trick of republishing Russian authors abroad and profiting from loopholes in international copyright legislation was invented by Parvus and *he* had run the operation. He might have supported the Bolsheviks but he was connected with the Mensheviks and had dropped the business which after his departure from Germany was never resumed. An income of 100,000 rubles was not obtainable in this fashion. Probably this was a camouflage item to cover the Japanese contribution. It is also possible that the Tammerfors conferees debated the budget of the *entire* party.

fighting; yet it is unlikely that Lenin was then in Petersburg. According to still another version the uprising came about because the inefficient Moscow Okhrana lacked advance information.

There is another side to the story: P. I. Rachkovsky, the leading strategist of the Okhrana, was rewarded with 75,000 rubles for his role in the suppression of the Moscow uprising. The police were no longer able to keep order by arresting agitators, for it was impossible to imprison and try thousands of people. No other choice remained but to crush the rebellion by force of arms. There is a strong possibility that the Okhrana provoked the uprising in order to put an end, once and for all, to the turmoil.[12] It is open to question whether the police indirectly provoked the Bolsheviks and the other revolutionary groups or whether they simply knew the insurrectional plan from agents operating among the Bolsheviks and allowed the operation to proceed while gaining enough time to prepare adequate countermeasures. It is evident that Lenin's tactics had played right into the hands of the tsarist government.

On December 16, the same day the leaders of the Petrograd soviet were arrested—after the Central Committee had resolved to instigate an armed uprising—Lenin established, temporarily, "legal residence" in St. Petersburg. This step was hardly taken out of naiveté or lack of information, nor is it likely that Lenin had reached some secret understanding with the police. But it is precisely this sort of riddle which the guardians of the Communist archives continue to obfuscate.

One bloody round was over and many party members criticized Lenin. Among them was Plekhanov, who asserted that it was wrong to take up arms. Lenin, however, remained convinced that the uprising had been justified entirely. Possibly so—but why was Lenin not on the spot to direct what, after failure, he called a "dress rehearsal"?

Krupskaya feared that Lenin, who was feeling ill, would become depressed. He himself expressed doubt that he would live to see victory, but the feared depression never occurred.

The failure of the insurrection necessitated a change in tactics. To win battles, arms were needed; to procure arms, money was need-

---

[12]Premier Witte "conceived the idea of ending the revolution with one blow. He would permit the Moscow revolution to take place. . . . The revolutionary leaders would all be dealt with, and the people would receive a convincing object lesson." He explained this idea to one of his assistants "who expressed his astonishment at the fact that the government should permit overt preparation for an armed revolt." V. I. Gurko, *Features & Figures of the Past* (Hoover Library Publication No. 14, California: Stanford University Press, 1939), p. 444. For further details see, V. K. Agafonov, *Zagranichnaya Okhranka* (Petrograd: Kniga, 1918), p. 289.

ed; hence, the first task was to obtain funds.[13] The Japanese were no longer interested; contributions were meager. To "expropriate the expropriators"—to rob the money from the state or the capitalists— would be merely an anticipation of the day when, the revolution victorious, the bourgeoisie would be expropriated as a whole. The Petersburg Bolsheviks, in January, 1905, had established under L. B. Krassin a combat bureau whose purpose was to prepare the uprising "technically." Krassin, a talented engineer, set up a laboratory in which he manufactured bombs.

During 1905, considerable activity occurred in the Caucasus, notably in Georgia, where the Japanese were agitating. A number of minuscule mountain republics sprang up, and in December, 1905, the Bolsheviks allegedly robbed 201,000 rubles from the treasury of the short-lived republic of Kviril. No attack took place, the rulers of the "state"—Caucasian nationalists, not Bolsheviks—simply absconding with the money before they were caught by the authorities.

In any event, the Central Committee got the money. In all likelihood the cash was brought to Lenin by a certain Dzhambul who wanted to enlist Lenin's help in purchasing arms for the Caucasian independence fighters. In the course of the conversation Lenin came to realize the advantage of expropriations: this was the way to get money for his publications and for the strengthening of the organization. Perhaps he remembered that Nechayev had been comtemplating expropriations in Switzerland and that Bakunin extolled the value of brigands for the revolution.

In January, 1906, Maxim Litvinov was sent to Europe to procure arms. Litvinov bought weapons and, through the help of the Macedonian revolutionary committee, chartered a ship. The venture came to nothing, probably because Lenin's most trusted agent in the West, a Dr. Jacob Abramovich Zhitomirsky, was a police agent, and because Litvinov's activities were under constant surveillance. There also was difficulty with the money; it was not released by the Central Committee, and the Bolsheviks claimed that the Mensheviks were unwilling to free the funds. This was probably untrue, if only because the Bolsheviks never lost control of the money. Some weapons were confiscated in Europe; intercepted, the ship was run aground. Typically, the ship's crew was composed largely of minority nationals, and the police reported that they were all members of the Social Revolutionary (not Social Democratic) party.

The weapons scheme was not of itself significant. What was important was that Lenin had resolved upon a new method of financing

[13]According to information in the files of the Prussian Ministry of the Interior (Abt. CB, Acta 5), considerable weapons smuggling took place during 1906 via Finland, Odessa, Cracow, one other Polish town, and various parts in Prussia. Much of this operation was conducted by foreign socialists and financed by liberal sympathizers.

operations. Krassin's combat organization, which had failed dismally in the Moscow uprising, was assigned to perform another task: robbery. Henceforth expropriations multiplied and considerable sums of money passed through Lenin's hands. Over 200 expropriations took place during January and February of 1906 alone, mostly in the forms of bank holdups, attacks on customs houses and ticket offices, and train robberies. Lenin liked to operate through members of other parties, notably the "maximalists," who often were (and even today are) confused with the Bolsheviks.[14] Some of them used the money on extravagant living. Highwaymen were transformed into "revolutionaries," and, of course, they retained most of the loot. The Bolsheviks gave the criminals a trademark of honesty—they were believed to be acting for political purposes—and received a percentage of the loot in return.

Krassin's operations sometimes extended beyond robbery. The maximalist Sokolov-Medvedj exploded a bomb in Prime Minister Stolypin's villa. He failed to kill Stolypin but crippled his daughter. Relying upon his facility of style with women, he wrote letters from jail coaxing the young lady to kill her father. . . . The bomb had been made available by Krassin.[15]

Lenin preoccupied himself with strategy in regard to the Duma. He decided that the Social Democrats should boycott the elections, a proposal on which there was much debate. Lenin later conceded—with considerable qualification—that his approach had been wrong. Actually, many Social Democrats, all Mensheviks, were voted into

[14]The Social Revolutionaries, according to police reports, decided in a conference at Terioki, Finland, to engage in partisan warfare in order to get money and sustain the fighting spirit. This decision was made on September 15, 1906. It is likely that these Social Revolutionaries were in reality "maximalists," i.e., a radical Social Revolutionary splinter group strongly influenced by Lenin.

[15]The police were well informed about Krassin's widespread activities yet never made a real attempt to put him out of action. Krassin's invulnerability bordered on the miraculous—or was there a more mundane explanation? Krassin, between 1891 and 1896, benefitted three times from police leniency, and in 1902 was allowed to live anywhere in Russia, including the capitals. The police registrar is silent on his activities between 1902-1907. Having been arrested in 1907, his case was subject to an intrapolice correspondence which disappeared. He was not exiled to Siberia but on March 6, 1907, was given by the St. Petersburg authorities passport No. 606 which allowed him to go abroad. In 1908, he was arrested again and turned over to the chief of the St. Petersburg Okhrana but was released for lack of evidence, and again allowed to depart. In March, 1908, he was imprisoned in Viipuri jail but was released after one month because the Russian authorities failed to supply to Finland the documentation needed to detain him longer (Futrell, p. 56). Although reporting about him and his exploits continued, there is no action file on him for the period after 1908. Yet Krassin held a prominent position in the German electric concern of Siemens-Schuckert and, therefore, should have been easy to watch. See M. A. Tsiavlovsky, *Bolsheviki, Dokumenty po istorii bolshevizma s 1903 po 1916 god byvsh. Moskovsk. Okhrannago otdeleniya* (Moscow, 1918).

the first Duma. This unexpected occurrence taught Lenin a lesson—a forceful one: the Mensheviks gained the majority in party membership. Lenin lost no time clamoring for "unity" within the party.

The Fourth Congress of the Social Democratic party met in Stockholm, in April, 1906.[16] The Mensheviks represented 20,000 and the Bolsheviks 14,000 members. The Bolsheviks captured only three of ten seats in the Central Committee. The party accepted Lenin's Paragraph Seven in the statute, the same one which had precipitated his breach with Martov in 1903. This acceptance of a basically dictatorial provision demonstrated Lenin's ascendancy over his more numerous, but vacillating, opponents. Emphasis was placed on party unity, while violent tactics and expropriation were de-emphasized. Lenin, in effect, was told to simmer down, and, on the basis of his own professed belief in party discipline, he was expected to obey.

But Lenin was willing to comply with discipline only when it fitted his purposes. He was determined not to allow "unity to tie a noose around our necks, nor to let the Mensheviks lead us by the rope."[17] He did not want to halt the expropriations. He prevailed upon the Central Committee to authorize "active tactics" of self-defense and to lend the technical combat bureau greater authority. This bureau was staffed exclusively by Bolsheviks. Expropriations were continued under the guidance of an ultra-secret finance committee created by Lenin and concealed even from the Bolsheviks. Lenin merely imposed the rule that prior to engaging in such actions, the "activists" were to leave the party.

The finance committee consisted of Krassin and Alexander A. Bogdanov, a philosopher-economist-physician and an intermittent psychiatric patient. Krassin and Bogdanov controlled the expropriations, obtaining the money which Lenin spent, possibly as much as one million rubles between April, 1906 and April, 1907.[18] The money was used to publish three papers and numerous pamphlets, to pay salaries and traveling expenses, to maintain a combat school in Kiev, to run smuggling operations—to keep the Bolshevik organization alive.

Strangely enough, Lenin also took heed of the Central Committee's

[16]This congress was permitted by the Swedish police, on the formal promise that it would be conducted in an orderly way. When the delegates were unable to buy their return tickets, the Swedish socialist Hinke Bergegren borrowed the funds from the chief of the Swedish police (Futrell, p. 47).

[17]Lunacharsky, *Vospominaniya o Lenine*, Moscow 1933, p. 21; *also* Shub, p. 86.

[18]An Austrian diplomatic report of December 14, 1906 stated that the Social Democratic Central Committee in Petersburg had been discovered; membership lists and 114,000 rubles were seized. According to *Proletarskaya Revolutsia*, No. 7, the Bolsheviks had 100,000 rubles in 1907, 40,000 in the districts and 60,000 in the hands of the Central Committee. These figures are suspect and may refer to some sort of an expense budget.

advice and, as a supplement to his clandestine activities, dabbled in conventional politics. Under the name of Karpov, he gingerly tried his hand at campaigning. On May 22, Lenin-Karpov, for the first time in his life, spoke at a non-party meeting, in the house of the liberal Countess Panin. (Communist historians conceal the lady's title, describing her house as a *narodny dom,* a people's house or socialist meeting hall.) In the following weeks, Karpov presented a number of public speeches; he and Krupskaya also paid a visit to his mother in the country.

This visit was abruptly culminated on July 21, when the first Duma was dissolved. Naval mutinies in the Baltic ports reawakened Lenin's interest in uprisings. Yet the Social Revolutionaries controlled the sailors. When he saw he could not progress, Lenin soon desisted. Early in September, the party, with Lenin's concurrence, decided to participate in the elections for the second Duma. Lenin prepared himself by vacationing for a few weeks in Finland.

It seems that Karpov became a candidate for election. This story has remained concealed: the Communists have claimed that Lenin was chosen to fill the office of elector in the workers' *curia* of the Vyborg district in St. Petersburg. According to another version, he was elected as a vote-auditor, and supervised for the party the counting of ballots in the Obvodnyi and Sapozhnyi sub-districts of the Moscow rayon at St. Petersburg.[19] Both stories are unlikely. According to one witness, Lenin actually was a candidate for election into the Duma, but he was not voted into office. This story is far more plausible, since a decision by the Bolsheviks to participate in the Duma implied, almost necessarily, that Lenin himself would be a candidate.[20] Lenin was hardly interested in ephemeral offices; and surely, no election campaign was needed to become an auditor on behalf of his party.

In any event, he conducted a lively campaign. His tactics were so underhanded, in fact, that he was forced to submit to a party tribunal on the accusation that he willfully slandered party comrades. He admitted his misdeeds cynically:[21]

I purposely and deliberately carried confusion into the ranks of the section of the St. Petersburg proletariat which followed the

[19]*Lenin v Peterburgye,* p. 94.

[20]There is some confirmation of Lenin's candidacy in the Austrian Archives, *Politisches Archiv I,* Karton 1070, letter by Trautmannsdorf to Foreign Minister, May 7, 1918.

[21]For details, see Wolfe, p. 355f. In 1907, Lenin in a brochure admitted that he wanted to evoke hatred, disgust and contempt against the Mensheviks and that he would wage a "struggle of annihilation" against his opponents. *Sochineniya,* 4th ed., Vol. XII, p. 383.

Mensheviks. . . . Are there any limits to permissible struggle? . . .
There are no limits to such a struggle set by any party standards.

His judges were so "democratically" minded that they did not expel
him from the party.

After the election, Lenin moved to Kuokkala, Finland. Since he
had not acquired parliamentary immunity, this was a safer place at
which to reside. He stayed in the large house of Lindov (Leiteisen),
and carried out much literary work, "practically" directing, Krupskaya said, "all the activities of the Bolsheviks."22 Actually, he mostly
wrote for *Proletary*, which was distributed from a house managed by
Komisarov, an Okhrana agent; the office work was carried out by
the agent's wife. The house also served as a "Bolshevik club." Not
quite as cozy was the arrangement in the Leiteisen house which had
before served as a "refuge for revolutionaries." Lenin's sister and
mother-in-law joined him.23 Lenin, Leiteisen, and Bogdanov often
played the Russian card game *durak*. Still, Lenin was in a "lonesome
mood."24

"Without revolutionary theory there is no revolutionary practice." Lenin inverted the venerable formula and in October wrote
an apologia of expropriations, which he dressed up as a theory on
"partisan warfare."25 This done, he called a conference at Tammerfors
to reorganize operations. By now, the expropriations served largely
to support the "expropriators" and were very damaging politically.
The disposal of the stolen money was also becoming an increasingly
difficult problem. The operation, though continued, was transferred to
the more distant Urals and Caucasus area.

During May, 1907, the Fifth Party Congress met in London.26
About 400 participants had been anticipated, but only a part of
that number appeared. Lenin, so his opponents charged, dominated
the Congress because of his great financial resources which allowed
him to dispatch a strong Bolshevik contingent; indeed, even Buchholz

22Actually, Krupskaya contradicted herself when she said that Bogdanov, who also
lived at Kuokkala, directed the work of the Duma deputies. (See Krupskaya, *op. cit.*,
p. 155ff.).

23There is no mention in this period of the whereabouts of Lenin's mother.

24Krupskaya, p. 153.

25For precedents on expropriations, see Alfons Thun, *Geschichte der Revolutionären
Bewegungen in Russland* (Leipzig: Duncker und Humblot, 1883), p. 269. Pilsudski's
group also used this technique.

26The Okhrana knew about this Congress since March. At first, they hoped that the
sessions would be in Copenhagen where extensive surveillance was prepared, but
Petersburg authorities vetoed Copenhagen for unknown reasons. Thereupon the
Danish police forbade the meetings at the last minute and the Congress moved to
London. The surveillance was largely in Zhitomirsky's hands. The Communists
never mention this incident.

appeared with his wife. There also was a certain Lett called Jansson, who was to be involved in future activities. Officially, the Bolsheviks gained control of only five of the thirteen Central Committee seats; but two Latvians tended to side with them, while two Poles were not fully committed. The Mensheviks and Bundists had only two seats each. Lenin was master with seven to nine votes against four opposing ballots. His manner was so overbearing that he was frequently interrupted by angry calls: "Don't play teacher. We no longer go to school."

But his victory was to prove hollow once again. He was forced to end the expropriations, though in the summer of 1907 a hold-up at Tiflis netted over 300,000 rubles. In this undertaking, Joseph V. Dzhugashvili-Stalin, whom Lenin had met at the first Tammerfors conference, played a prominent part.

The Okhrana reported that the Bolsheviks were in financial trouble, despite the fact that they had inherited 75,000 rubles from the writer Garin Mikhailovsky. The Mensheviks, by contrast, were receiving only token gifts: 6,000 francs from the Swedish party, 8,000 francs from the Danes, and 15,000 marks from the Germans. The Petersburg committee was budgeted at 1,000 rubles monthly, the Moscow committee at 500 rubles. The combined Central Committee was given just 100 rubles.[27] Wealthy benefactors were again sought. The total cost of the Congress had been around 100,000 rubles, but what was the practical value of such an expenditure? By the closing date of the Congress, 2,000 pounds were required for the delegates' transportation home. Lenin refused to pay; Plekhanov borrowed the money from an industrialist living in England. (After some prodding, the money was repaid after 1917.)

The Congress, under Lenin's presidency, debated the finances of the entire party. Total income of the preceding year was reported at 83,570.03 rubles. This included a contribution of 30,000 rubles by an unknown ('L. L') and 10,000 rubles by a foreign group. (This might have been an American subvention.) "Committees" produced 3,534 rubles. Forty thousand rubles remain unaccounted for. Expenses were as follows: salaries of prefessional revolutionaries, 4,200; agents of Central Committee, 4,554; Central Committee secretariat, 4,708; trips abroad, 5,829; organization, 4,494; passports, 1,868; bail, 2,055; liquidation of previous congress, 2,603; protocols of the congress, 2,180; help to exiles, 2,256; conferences, 4,079; Duma faction, 790; illegal literature, 13,400; and legal literature, 24,611; in sum about 78,000 rubles. This elaboration should dispose of the claim that the party made money by publishing its literature.

Lenin returned to Finland, seriously ill—his nerves were again

---

[27]Paul Olberg in Neue *Zürcher Zeitung* (February 7, 1957), Blatt 5.

giving way. The police reported in a top secret document that he was living on a German passport issued at Berlin for printer Erwin Weykoff supposedly born in Hameln, Germany, on July 16, 1862.

Shortly afterwards, the Social Democratic faction was expelled from the Duma. Most of the deputies were arrested on the grounds that the party was attempting an infiltration of the armed forces and was preparing new uprisings. (One of the infiltrators supplied the evidence.) A revolutionary ebb had set in, and Lenin realized that the time for violent action was over.

Lenin, however, did not intend to call a halt to the expropriation business. Together with Krassin, he resolved upon a final, major operation, the proceeds of which were to finance the Bolsheviks for five or six years: fifteen million rubles were to be seized, of which two to three million were to be held in reserve until 1908; the rest was to be burned.[28] Apparently the object of the raid was to be the Mendelssohn Bank at Berlin.

This plan was to be carried out by an experienced bandit, a young, cross-eyed Armenian, S. A. Ter-Petrosyan, known as "Kamo." About twenty-six years old, Kamo was the son of a tubercular mother and an impoverished father; the family had at one time been wealthy. Early in 1906 he highjacked 200,000 rubles on the Georgian Military Highway. In 1907 he executed, with considerable bravura, the Tiflis hold-up, which cost the lives of forty people and which was masterminded, at a safe distance, by Stalin. After this exploit, Kamo stayed close to Lenin in Finland, where the two, along with Krassin, planned the ultimate expropriation.

Kamo and Litvinov traveled to Paris, Liège, Geneva, Vienna, and Sofia, where they persuaded the Minister of War to sell them explosives and six infernal machines. From there Kamo proceeded to Berlin, traveling freely on an *Austrian* passport issued in the name of Dimitri Mirsky, from Gori, Georgia (sic!). There he was arrested, probably as a result of Zhitomirsky's reporting. An arsenal was seized in a Berlin house: the Bulgarian explosives were fished out of the Spree river a few days after Kamo's arrest. In Kamo's possession was found, in addition to fuses, 13,000 marks. Kamo feigned insanity; he was deported in 1909 to Russia where he was incarcerated in a fortress for sixteen months. Having been certified insane, he was then transferred to a mental hospital, from which he escaped, fleeing to France in 1911. Lenin, however, had no more use

[28]Note with neither address nor signature in Okhrana archive; approximate date: November, 1907. (Document in Hoover Institution.)

for this "childishly naïve man with the warm heart,"[29] and providing him with his own warm coat that had been given to him by his mother, he sent Kamo off on a wild goose chase. In 1907, however, Kamo's arrest abruptly invalidated the great five-year financial plan of the Bolsheviks: there was no one who could assume Kamo's place as robber chieftain, not even Stalin, whose talents no one now seemed to remember. From now on, Lenin was out of the expropriation business. For a while there was contrived a plan to forge money, and banknote paper was sent through the unsuspecting German Social Democratic organization to Lenin in Finland. But the operation was too difficult and dangerous; Lenin called it off.

Lenin strongly advocated participation in the elections to the third Duma, but did not himself run.[30] Against Bogdanov, he argued for the use of the Duma as a useful propaganda platform. He was active as a publicist and, in his role as a prominent theoretician, he issued a collection of his most important programmatic, tactical, and organizational writings since 1895. In the introduction to this volume, he explained the necessity of using Aesopian language, an unnecessary disclosure which illustrates the policy of tsarist censors to pass even the most radical writings if extreme terms were avoided.

After attending the International Socialist Congress in Stuttgart, Germany, (August 18-24, 1907), where he represented the left wing of the movement, Lenin settled down in Styrsudd, another Finnish hideout, where he largely devoted himself to literary work. Occasionally he returned clandestinely to St. Petersburg. His physical condition had so deteriorated that he avoided even political discussions; he frequently fell asleep. Soon he began to recover, benefitting from "the forest, the sea, nature at its wildest, with only another large summer house next door" inhabited by friends. Krupskaya and Lenin frequently went bicycling or spent a day near the sea. In the evening, they were often entertained by a singer, a relative of Lydia Knipovich whose family owned the houses. (Knipovich was one of Krupskaya's friends who attended the Second Congress.)[31]

[29]Krupskaya, *op. cit.*, p. 212. From France Kamo went to Bulgaria where he was arrested and then freed. In Constantinople he was arrested and released upon the intervention of the Georgian monks of Notre Dame de Lourdes. He returned to Russia, attempted an expropriation (probably with Lenin's agreement), was captured and given four death sentences. An amnesty on the tercentenary of the Romanov dynasty saved him. (Boris Souvarine, *Stalin* [New York: Alliance 1939], pp. 99-103). Kamo died during 1923 in the Caucasus, apparently deliberately running his bicycle downhill into a car. This was during the time when Stalin began a Russification campaign in the Caucasian area. (See below.)

[30]Among the five Bolshevik Duma representatives who were elected, there was the police agent V. E. Shurkanov, though he may have become an informer only at a later date.

[31]Krupskaya, *op. cit.*, p. 158.

In December, Lenin—who now went under the name of Paavo Kakko—detected signs indicating the police were on his trail.[32] He moved to Aggelby near Helsinki, but when it became clear that the police were continuing to look for him, he hurriedly departed for Sweden. He was anxious to leave Finland but did not dare board the steamer in the port. Accompanied by a Finnish policeman and another Finn, he crossed the frozen sea on foot to an off-shore island, from where he flagged down the ship. He recounted that he was afraid of drowning; actually, the ice had been thick enough. Apparently, Lenin panicked because he could not communicate with his Finnish companions.[33] After this adventure he stayed for a few days at the Hotel Malmsten at Stockholm, and soothed his nerves by listening to Swedish folk songs sung for him by Swedish comrades.[34] When Krupskaya arrived by the end of the month, the couple left for Berlin where they stayed for two days. Thereafter he made one of his mysterious visits to Leipzig. In the first half of January, 1908, after an absence of about twenty-six months, and a few days later than Communist historians want us to believe, Lenin was back in Geneva.

[32]Lenin was put on the "wanted" list under number 150034/II, St.2611 by the Okhrana on June 23, 1907. (Document in Hoover Institution)

[33]Futrell, p. 62.

[34]*Ibid.*, p. 49f.

The Hero Abroad

Lenin, at thirty-eight years of age, was the foremost radical of the Social Democratic party. Yet his policies had ended in bankruptcy: most of the party members distrusted and feared him, his own followers were lukewarm, he lacked contact with the masses, and his doctrines, whether Marxist or not, did not find general acceptance.

In addition, his physical condition was again poor. He had been suffering from his customary insomnia and lack of appetite; a slight tremor had appeared. His vacations in Finland had done him some good, but he brought back to Switzerland his constant "sputniks"— headaches and sleeplessness. The escape through snow and ice had not helped matters any. He had caught a severe cold, and in Germany he and Krupskaya both had fought a bout of food poisoning. When he finally arrived in Geneva, he was close to a state of collapse.

For a few weeks, he and Krupskaya went to the movies and the theater every evening (but rarely stayed to the end). At that time, too, Lenin and Krupskaya felt it necessary to study French, but neither of them was very successful. This effort was dropped as soon as Lenin had recovered sufficiently to bring his affairs into some semblance of order and to renew his contacts. He made his customary speech on the Paris Commune and went through Nice on his way to Capri where he stayed with Maxim Gorky, who, after an abortive money-raising trip to the United States, had settled on that island. Late in May, Lenin returned to Geneva and became the most assiduous visitor to the *Société de Lecture,* a well-stacked library with a large reading room. The reading room proved to be a very convenient place to work, since he was usually the only reader there. His card of admittance indicated that "W. Oulianoff" was a *"gentilhomme russe."*[1]

Lenin worked on the agrarian question, a subject to which he liked to return whenever he was not busy with current affairs, but, otherwise, he was little concerned with the problems of the revolution.

To some extent, as a writer, his name remained in the news. Plans had been made for a subscription issue of his collected works. When the first volume was published, 200 subscriptions had been received. The volume was soon confiscated. The first part of the second volume, dealing with agrarian matters, was not suppressed, but the demand was small; of 3000 copies printed, less than half were sold by 1917. The second part, when it appeared, was also confiscated. No attempt was made to publish the proposed third volume. These ventures were carried out, under different subterfuges, by the Zerno publishing house, a strictly party firm. By the end of 1907, they were offered "unlimited credits for paper" by a Danish firm in which the dowager Tsarina was one of the principal shareholders.[2]

Fortunately for his intellectual life, Lenin was enjoying participation in a continuing argument on religion and philosophy. He disagreed with Gorky, who had just written *The Confession,* in which he upheld the position of those revolutionaries who did not wish to abandon religion and who were grappling with the novel concepts of

---

[1]Istorik, *Novyi Zhurnal* (1961), No. 63, p. 287. It seems that when writing to his mother, Lenin addressed his letters to "Her Excellency M. A. Ulyanova" (Eye Prevoskhoditelstva). See *ibid.,* (1960), No. 61, p. 224. A passport exhibited in the Lenin Museum at Moscow indicates that Lenin possessed hereditary nobility. Inquiry by a friend of mine at the reference desk elicited consternation. After some hesitation the reply came that, as "everybody knows Lenin was a *Meshchanin* (i.e., member of the middle class)." The argument was advanced that the passport notation was wrong.

[2]M. J. Kedrov, *Book Publishing under Tsarism* (New York: Workers Library, 1932), pp. 17ff, 29.

"god-seeking"[3] and "god-building." Since Lenin did not want to quarrel with Gorky personally, he directed his fire at Alexander Bogdanov, who a short while before had been the executive officer of expropriations and was now prophet of the thesis that God did not yet exist but was to be built as a social being through the collective effort of humanity.[4]

When Lenin had been expropriating together with Bogdanov, he held that philosophical views were "completely irrelevant to the question of the social revolution." The first issue of *Proletarii* after the new period of exile appeared in Geneva on February 26, 1908.[5] In it Lenin stated that philosophy was a matter of personal opinion. As should be expected, the split with Bogdanov had, above all, an entirely practical basis, namely money. Bogdanov held funds—80,000 or 85,000 expropriated rubles—which Lenin wanted. The Bolsheviks, as we learn from Okhrana reports, possessed 100,000 rubles in 500-ruble notes. Of this amount, 35,000 rubles remained in Russia. Under Litvinov's leadership, an attempt was made to exchange the notes, but the police had been alerted, and many of the Bolsheviks, who were presenting the notes in different countries at the same time, were arrested.[6] Some 4,000 rubles were changed in Holland, but most of the money was seized and returned to Russia. A

---

[3]The term "god-seeking" was derived from the title of a novel by the Austrian writer Peter Rosegger.

[4]Bogdanov wrote a novel depicting life on Mars and designed a universal science of organization based on mathematics and computers. He is thus the direct forerunner of the space Communists. In the book *Red Star*, he built socialism on Mars. The Martians wanted to abscond an Earthian to study his impressions of Martian socialism. They needed a person of three characteristics: he had to be a Russian, a Social Democrat, and a Bolshevik. "Why didn't they take Ilyich?" The Martian replied that he did not take him because Lenin's absence would have caused too much trouble on earth. In Lenin's attitude towards Bogdanov and philosophy, *see* Walter, p. 183. On Bogdanov's life and philosophy, *see* Gustav A. Wetter, *Dialectical Materialism* (New York: Praeger, 1958), pp. 92-100.

[5]The French police at Annemasse reported that M. Nicolet, socialist deputy in the Grand Conseil of Geneva, who signed as responsible editor, was in relations with Mlle. Sarah Ravich. The police added that she was involved in the *"pillage de la Trésorerie de Douchet (Caucase)."* This raid was undertaken by a socialist splinter party and the 315,000 rubles which it netted were "confiscated" by the Bolsheviks. Ravich later was to travel with Lenin in the sealed train through Germany. There must have been a fair amount of money: between October, 1908, and November, 1909, *Proletarii* was sent by mail from Copenhagen to eighty-four addresses in fifty-six Russian towns, 4,000 copies altogether. Krupskaya wrote: "We pay the postal expenses" (Futrell, p. 63f.).

[6]Litvinov was arrested in Paris. The secretary of Georges Clemenceau, then Chief of Government, informed the Russian authorities; but before a request for extradition was presented, Aristide Briand, Minister of Justice, freed Litvinov and another Bolshevik and expelled him to Britain. (Paris Okhrana branch to St. Petersburg, January 22, 1908).

number of 500-ruble bills remained in Bolshevik hands, but this money could, of course, not be used.

Money therefore was short. Bogdanov proposed that party financing be handled through expropriations as had been done previously. Lenin felt that, while a single large expropriation was infeasible, numerous small hold-ups would be harmful. Lenin also was angry because Bogdanov was running on Capri a party school which Gorky was financing with money that Lenin felt could be better utilized for activities which he alone controlled. Unable to alter the situation, he infiltrated Bogdanov's school with his henchmen. As soon as the graduates returned to Russia, they were arrested: one of Lenin's protegés had been a police agent. Clearly, these were compelling reasons to wage a battle.

But an additional problem was involved. Bogdanov believed that economics was not merely an "adjunct to technological and ideological development," but was a more important factor. Hence, the seizure of the means of production was not in itself sufficient to build a classless society. It was also necessary to indoctrinate the workers in proletarian culture, an argument which Lenin was to grasp only fourteen years later. But Bogdanov also asserted that social and moral consciousness were inseparable; he saw in moral consciousness "the organizing principle of social practice." This argument Lenin never understood. He merely sensed that if Bogdanov's theory were right, his own approach was wrong. He chose to attack Bogdanov at his weakest point—his metaphysics.

Lenin went to London and worked studiously in the British Museum. In a remarkably short time he succeeded in ploughing through a large amount of philosophical writings. Late in June he returned from London, suffering from intestinal influenza. Yet he began writing without delay. Occasionally he took hikes and short recreational trips in western Switzerland. In September he moved into a more comfortable two-room apartment in Geneva, where he completed his current task.

His labors resulted in an extremely long volume entitled *Materialism and Empiriocriticism* in which he attacked positivism and religion, taking issue not only with the foremost "bourgeois" philosophers of the time, but also with Bogdanov and one or two other comrades. Caliph Omar, who burned the library of Alexandria and thus destroyed the ancient world's repository of knowledge, justified his act of barbarism by saying: "If those books contain what can be found in the Koran, they are unnecessary. If they contain what cannot be found in the Koran, they are harmful." Lenin wrote as though he believed that what was not to be found in Engels' *Anti-Duehring* could not have any value or validity.

Though Lenin, of course, did not think so, this was his poorest book. The whole, slightly paranoid, interlude is comprehensible only as a sort of intellectual vacation, an "abreaction," as psychologists term such periods.

In the fall, his sister Maria joined the Lenins at Geneva. She was in bad health and in need of an ear operation. Lenin informed his mother that Dr. Mermod, an ear specialist at Lausanne, four years earlier had operated on him (nothing is known about this incident); he recommended that the same doctor perform the operation on Maria. Presumably Lenin's advice was followed.

On December 12, 1908, Lenin and Krupskaya moved to Paris.[7] But no sooner had they rented a four-room apartment in a pleasant neighborhood than Lenin felt ill again. Apparently, suffering from a kidney infection, he was forced to diet. He took a "magnificent rest in Nice" early in 1909.[8]

Did Lenin at that time collaborate with the Okhrana? On September 30, 1908, an unsigned letter was received at the police section of the Russian Embassy at Paris. The writer stated that he wished to talk about a very serious matter, but, since he could not come to Paris, he requested a meeting in Switzerland, preferably near Lausanne. On the envelope there was marked: "Exp. Lenin, Lausanne P-[oste] R[estante] Bureau de St. Laurent." A cable of September 29, 1908, indicated that "Lenin" was salaried at 100 rubles monthly and for party reasons was unable to journey to Paris. Subsequent letters of February 22, 1909, (No. 124362) and May 31, 1910, (No. 125546) from the police department indicate that *Sotrudnik* "Lenin" received 200 rubles. "Lenin" was a secret agent of the Okhrana's foreign department.

This is a rather startling bit of information, but it turns out that there were two Lenins and that the second "Lenin" was an anarchist of the Burevestnik group. The operation which the second Lenin proposed had as its purpose the seizure of a secret printing plant abroad. Subsequently, Lenin II worked among the anarchists of Odessa and in June of 1910 was transferred to Paris.[9] Of interest is the fact that in both 1908 and 1910 he was in the same locality as

[7]The Paris Préfecture de Police reported on October 18, 1908, that Lenin and *"les membres dirigeants du parti S.D. russe"* were moving to Paris.

[8]*Letters of Lenin,* p. 277.

[9]Documents in Hoover Institution. The Burevestnik group was an anarcho-communist outfit and, as we have seen above, was secretly connected with the Bolsheviks. For example, Vera Velichkina, Bonch-Bruyevich's wife, published her translations of Engels at the Burevestnik publishing house. According to Agafonov (*op. cit.,* p. 335ff) Lenin II was Benzion Moiseyevich Dolin who worked for the Okhrana as early as 1904, first against the Bund in Zhitomir. After serving in Yekaterinoslav, he was lying low for a while, then betrayed an anarchist for 500 rubles and went abroad to get a listing of the Burevestnik membership. He traveled back and forth between Russia and Europe till 1910, and between 1910 and 1914 as "Charles" worked exclu-

Lenin I. Why the Okhrana selected this particular cover name is anybody's guess but probably it was a mere coincidence. For some reason Lenin I felt impelled to warn the comrades that the Okhrana was infiltrating provocateurs into Bolshevik ranks, as though this were not a standard operational procedure.

Lenin I, meanwhile, during most of 1909 was contributing to *Proletarii* articles which mostly rehashed subjects discussed previously. In January and February he gave a few lectures about which the Okhrana learned from intercepted letters and from the French police. One speech, delivered in the Hotel des Sociétés Savantes, rue Danton in Paris, concerned the current situation in Russia; but barely anything is known about these pronouncements. In March he joined other comrades—including Martov—in commemorating the Commune. A trouble-making comrade who ignored the French government's secret support to Russian revolutionaries, took the opportunity to attack the old *Communard*, Clemenceau, now Prime Minister, calling him a traitor who deserved to be shot. He was, as the French police reported, equally vehement against Briand.[10]

Suddenly a new problem arose. Krassin had borrowed, for the party, 3,000 rubles from a Petersburg widow who now requested the return of her money. The Bolsheviks refused; Krassin, furious, deserted Lenin. He was the treasurer, and it was immediately said that he took 140,000 rubles with him. This supposed amount was soon reduced to 38,000 rubles and it finally turned out that Krassin had taken only 25,000 rubles of the, as yet, unexchanged Tiflis money.[11] Presumably this constituted the remainder of the 35,000 rubles in 500-ruble notes. Lenin called for a meeting of the Bolshevik Center, an organization founded during the Fifth Congress at London, which had been kept secret from the Mensheviks and the national sub-parties, and which was camouflaged as the enlarged editorial board of *Proletarii*.

The Okhrana now considered the Bolsheviks the decisive element among the Social Democrats—they were well organized and had both the means and the program for executing definite plans. Hence the

sively for the Foreign Department in Paris. For alibi purposes he was arrested several times and allowed to escape, including once from Siberia. During the war, he served as a counter-intelligence agent, notably against Major Bismarck, the German military attache in Switzerland. His job was to interfere with German plans for sabotage operations. (*See* Serge Persky, *De Nicolas II à Lénine (1917-1918)* (Paris: Payot, 1919), p. 56-73.) Agafonov (p. 182) reported that after his suicide Dolin left much money. However, Dolin himself related to Burtsev (Persky, p. 73) that he turned over to the police the 50,000 francs received from the Germans and often he was compelled to help finance his operations himself.

10Report by the Préfecture de Police, March 19, 1909. (Document in Hoover Institution).

11Letters from Foreign Department to St. Petersburg, April 27 and July 16, 1909.

police prepared for surveillance of this meeting: Zhitomirsky, as could be expected, went into action. Also, among the approximately sixteen persons (including one Duma deputy) [12] who met on June 21 and 30, other "reporters" may have been hidden. In all, five members did not attend, Krassin being the most important absentee.

The conference dealt with philosophy and money. There occurred an argument about demands made by Bogdanov and his friends that the Duma deputies should be recalled or ordered to speak up more forcefully. A young assistant of Lenin, Grigory Zinovyev, analyzing Bogdanov's operations on Capri, maintained that Bogdanov intended to create his own "center." Bogdanov was expelled. The conference then dealt with the tasks of the Duma faction. They appointed a commission for the production of illegal literature, assigned the various comrades to party functions, appointed a small "executive committee" to run the Bolshevik Center, and decided to call for an All-Party Congress by winter.

The conference resolved to compose the conflict with Krassin and to repay the widow; the Bolsheviks were rarely so conciliatory toward a dissenter from the inner circle.[13] Krassin, however, remained aloof for many years afterwards.,

The new treasurer, Victor Taratuta, reported that the party was spending 6,000 to 7,000 francs a month (2,400 to 2,800 rubles) for *Proletarii* (this presumably was a subvention), transport of literature, the Foreign Bureau of the Central Committee, and subsidies to the Polish and Lettish sub-parties. The expenditure of an additional 2,000 rubles was approved for the establishment of a legal "Duma newspaper" and one or two small monthlies. With these matters out of the way, the conference devoted its attention to the big financial question, the so-called Schmidt inheritance.

It will be remembered that Nikolai Pavlovich Schmidt, a nephew of Morozov, had financed Gorky's *Novaya Zhizn*. Stirred by the revolution, the young man had joined the Social Democratic party. The Bolsheviks asserted that he had joined their ranks, a claim that the Mensheviks disputed; indeed, Schmidt hardly would have known the difference. During the Moscow uprising, Schmidt's furniture fac-

---

[12]This was I. P. Goldenberg, who had become an "unperson" because in April, 1917 he greeted Lenin upon his arrival in Petrograd from Switzerland via Germany: "Lenin has now made himself a candidate for one European throne that has been vacant for thirty years—the throne of Bakunin" and accused him of having raised "the banner of civil war within the democracy."

[13]Krassin, in the period of 1906-1907, "was the only man in the Bolshevik organization whom Lenin trusted fully and for whom he had real respect. Otherwise he respected no one and did not ask for respect toward himself. He was entirely satisfied with obedience which, incidentally, was given to him by the organization without fail." *See* V. S. Voytinsky, *Wehe den Besiegten!* (Berlin: Gutenberg, 1933), p. 68.

tory was utilized as an insurrectional stronghold. Schmidt was arrested and died in prison, allegedly as a result of police torture.[14]

Schmidt's money came into the hands of a younger brother who is said to have carried out his late brother's desire to finance the Bolsheviks. He is alleged to have turned over the money to his two sisters, Catherine and Elizabeth, who were to complete the transaction. Elizabeth wished to transfer the money immediately but since, according to Krupskaya, she was not yet of age, "it was decided to arrange a fictitious marriage." She "went through a form of marriage" with a certain Ignatyev, a member of the Bolshevik combat group—the specialists in expropriation. The official husband "consented" to the transference of the money to the party. The girl, according to Krupskaya, about seventeen at the time, "was actually the wife of another Bolshevik, Victor Taratuta." She could not, however, legally marry her true "husband," since he was sought by the police.

Lenin assigned a third Bolshevik, Nikolai Andrikanis, to court the elder sister, but this worthy suitor engaged in an affair with the girl and announced that he would turn over only a third of her share. Threatened by violence, Andrikanis agreed to a compromise at one-half of the total sum.[15]

This was the background. It was only fitting that the boyfriend of Elizabeth, the fictitious wife, act as treasurer of the Bolsheviks. Not surprisingly, however, Krassin and Bogdanov alleged that Taratuta had obtained the Morozov money and had kept it for himself. Taratuta now reported to the Bolshevik Center that the inheritance amounted to 490,000 rubles, of which the bigger part already had been given to the Center. It is believed that this larger part amounted to 280,000 rubles but Taratuta did not disclose the exact figure in his report.[16] As to the remainder, he stated that the money con-

---

[14]Krupskaya, p. 185.

[15]See the account by Schapiro, *The Communist Party, op. cit.,* p. 107f. *See* also Tsiavlovsky, *op. cit.,* p. 102. The trick of obtaining money by making love to rich and innocent girls originally was invented by Nechayev.

[16]A police report of March 28, 1909, stated that the Bolsheviks just had secured 200,000 rubles from an unknown source.

The data contained in police records and various disclosures by party writers and documents are so confused that it is impossible to ascertain the arithmetic of this transaction. The main difficulty consists in determining the principal. According to one report of June 13, 1908, the deceased Schmidt possessed 500,000 rubles, left to him by Vikulya Morozov; this money may have gone entirely to Elizabeth. (Police report of November 19, 1908 [Tsiavlovsky, *ibid.*]) But Catherine held another 170,-000 rubles, of which half was to go to the Bolsheviks. It is likely that the deceased left assets in addition to those he received from Morozov. In this case the amounts would be additive and it is naturally to be assumed that Schmidt provided for the sustenance of his brother and two sisters.

It will be noted that there were three children and that 170,000 is one-third of some 500,000 rubles. The surviving brother could have signed over his share only if

tinued to be invested in shares of the Morozov firm and would soon be available in cash. The Bolshevik Center, satisfied, voted its thanks to comrade Victor. Thereupon, the conference adjourned.

Difficulties concerning the Schmidt inheritance continued for quite a while; hence we must take a closer look at the real hero of this story. Aron-Shmuel Rafalovich Taratuta was born in 1881 at Yelizavetgrad. He had two sisters and a brother Hersh who became a stock broker at Kiev. At an early age Victor married Olga Rubin-

he were of age; otherwise a trustee would have been required. But there is no evidence of this sort of legal transaction. The whole deal was verbal and based on the testimony of M. A. Mikhailov, a lawyer.

If we assume that Schmidt left just these 500,000 odd rubles (and not his other assets) to the party, the three heirs presumably, in a first step, received the money in equal shares. Thereupon, in a second step, each would transmit his or her money to the Bolsheviks.

According to this interpretation, the brother might have signed over his share of from 160,000 to 170,000 rubles immediately. Catherine, by November, 1908, had transferred 45,000 rubles. One police report stated that she still owed the party 80,000 rubles but this may be a mistake: the reporter might have meant that she paid 45,000 of the 80,000 rubles owed by her. If so, an equal amount of 80,000 rubles might have been "owed" by Elizabeth. Supposing this to be true and that Elizabeth paid by 1909, the party might have received about 285,000 rubles from the three Schmidt's: 160,000 from the brother, 45,000 from Catherine, and 80,000 from Elizabeth.

According to another possible interpretation, the brother never paid any amount and the two sisters held more than a half-million. Catherine, by the time the Bolshevik Center met, had turned over her 80,000. If the party did receive around 280,000 rubles, Victor and Elizabeth must have paid 200,000 rubles, in which case, if they started with 490,000 rubles, they still were holding 290,000 rubles.

However, assume that the *total* was 490,000 and that Catherine's share was one-third or something over 160,000 rubles. If Elizabeth held both her own and her brother's share (altogether 320,000 rubles) and if Catherine contributed 80,000 rubles and the Bolsheviks received 280,000 rubles, then Victor and Elizabeth still were controlling some 120,000 rubles.

It is unlikely that Elizabeth got a worse deal than Catherine, i.e., *both* probably agreed to pay one half. In this case, assuming 280,000 rubles had been received by the party, 80,000 were paid by Catherine and 200,000 by Elizabeth, the latter still owned 45,000 rubles *if her exclusive total had been 490,000 rubles*. The remainder in Victor's and Elizabeth's hands would have been something like a quarter of a million.

If the total of around 500,000 rubles was divided only between the sisters, Catherine, according to the equal halves agreement, would indeed owe 125,000 rubles. This would support the police report (45,000 plus 80,000). Assuming 125,000 rubles were paid by Catherine and the party received 280,000 rubles, Elizabeth must have paid 155,000 rubles, or better than half. Such generosity would have endeared Victor to Lenin.

Presumably the party expected to obtain half a million rubles from the inheritance. This did not work out as planned because the heiresses were not that naïve and the comrades not that devoted. The money that remained unpaid by the Victor-Elizabeth couple can merely be estimated: some amount between 100,000 and 300,-000 rubles.

skaya, a very homely anarchist who was five years older than he. During his imprisonment, she passed into the hands of Ovsej-Meyer Gershovich Taratuta, described by the police as Victor's nephew. Ovsej and his sister Rakhil were associated, apparently at various times, with both the Social Revolutionaries and the Social Democrats, but were rather of anarchist and terrorist convictions. In 1905, Ovsej was arrested in Warsaw for possession of explosives; later in the year he participated in the Moscow uprising. Clearly a self-sacrificing revolutionary, he was arrested again in 1907.

A man of medium height and adorned with darkish-red hair and beard, Victor was arrested for the first time in 1898. Between 1900 and 1902 he was active in the Jewish Bund at Yekaterinoslav; at the end of 1902 he was, however, arrested at Odessa as a Social Democrat. In June, 1903, he was sent to Siberia for four years but fled in August of 1904. In May, 1905, captured at Baku, he was again convicted, but was freed as a result of the general amnesty proclaimed in November, 1905. Between 1906 and 1907 Taratuta was secretary of the Moscow Bolshevik organization, and during this time became the lover of Elizabeth Schmidt.

At that time, a morally inclined Bolshevik complained to Lenin about Victor, describing him as a scoundrel. Lenin replied that the party was no girls' college, that revolution could not be made with white gloves, and that a rogue could be useful precisely because he was a rogue. The best side of Victor was that "he isn't repelled by anything. Would you, for example—tell me frankly—live off the wife of a wealthy businessman? No! I wouldn't do it either, I couldn't overcome my disgust. But Victor accomplished this and helps party finances. He is irreplaceable."[17]

The details of Victor's departure from Russia are unknown, but there exists a gap in the financial report which he gave to the Bolshevik Center: since the portion of the money which had not yet been made available was in stock, it could have been sold without difficulty; moreover, stock prices being variable, it was not possible to assign specific monetary values to the assets.

On July 7, 1909, the Moscow Okhrana reported to St. Petersburg that they considered the "split" between Lenin and Bogdanov without substantial ideological basis, but rather one which Victor had intentionally provoked.

By 1910, rumor had it that Taratuta, then known as Victor Moskovsky, was a police agent. Martov even called him the "Azev" of the Social Democratic party. These insinuations probably were caused in part by Victor and Elizabeth's failure to relinquish the money.

A commission was appointed and it listened to fifty-four witnesses. Thereupon the commission presented its report from which the foreign bureau of the Central Committee published a short extract to the effect that Victor was cleared of all suspicions and reinstated as a party member with full right.[18]

A short while afterwards, Victor's legal wife died and he married Elizabeth. In December, 1911, Kamo passed through Brussels where he met Bogdanov. He then proceeded to Paris, talked with Vladimir Burtsev, the watchdog of the revolutionary movement, and again accused Taratuta of being a police agent. Burtsev felt that Kamo was mentally disturbed; however, Kamo had spent much time in prisons and may have discovered some valid indications. The police reported on Kamo's conversations on January 13, 1912, and during March and April sought to elicit more information. They found that Victor had become a respectable Monsieur Alexandre Kemmerer and was living under a passport issued in this name. He and his wife, along with their two children, were enjoying a rest at San Remo in Madame Plekhanov's sanatorium. No longer interested in politics, Monsieur Kemmerer was frequenting fashionable places and casinos where he liked to play cards!

It is therefore clear that Victor, having become well-to-do, had deserted to the ranks of the bourgeoisie. There may have been three sources of his affluence: first, the portion of the inheritance which was not given to the party; second, assets inherited by the sisters may have been concealed from Lenin; third, the unpaid amounts, reputedly in stock, might have been sold, perhaps through Victor's broker-brother, at a high price or the money might have remained invested and increased in value. All three interpretations probably apply; it is most likely that Victor paid less than Elizabeth's share on the pretext that the stock had been sold at a loss.

If the poor proletarian ended up with a quarter of a million rubles, as he probably did, and if he invested this at six per cent, his annual income would have been 37,500 francs—that is, 3,500 francs more than the party budget adopted at the Prague conferenec of 1912. Revolution can indeed be a lucrative undertaking. It should be added that according to some data, Taratuta returned to Russia after the revolution, rejoined the party, and faded out in a middle rank government position.

Lenin, after the conference, spent a leisurely summer vacation with Krupskaya and her mother at Bombon, a village in Saône-et-Loire. After returning to Paris, he accommodated himself to the working hours of the Bibliothèque Nationale by arising at eight o'clock;

18Copy of the Foreign Bureau's Bulletin dated July 21, 1910, in Okhrana Collection, Hoover Institution.

previously, he had seldom gotten out of bed before ten. But despite this heroic effort, Lenin's literary output was small. He spent some time in Brussels with the Bureau of the Second International, where he was accredited as a permanent Russian delegate.

Lenin was now forty years of age but looked far older; he was increasingly troubled by headaches and insomnia. Most of his time was taken up with squabbles about what should be published in the party press. He fought against "reformism" or evolutionary socialism. But in a speech he insisted that the revolutionaries trust the intellectuals who, by their continuing underground work, would defeat the tsarist regime.[19] The so-called "liquidators" who wished to abandon conspiratorial and violent methods including robberies and shady financial dealings were so powerful, while Lenin and his group were relatively weak, that he was forced into a *rapprochement* with the Mensheviks. His backing in Russia had shrunk to the support of a half-dozen "committees."

On March 29, 1910, he took the initiative in writing to Plekhanov. He also contacted the Polish Social Democrats, and later informed Gorky that "unity" had been restored. In July, together with Krupskaya and her mother, he vacationed in Pornic (*Loire Inférieure*). In the midst of his vacation, he traveled to Capri to spend a week with Gorky, after which he returned to Pornic, and on August 26 he met Plekhanov in Paris. The two were reconciled.

As was usual among Russian revolutionaries, the new friendship was cemented by a common hostility towards other persons—this time the target was Leo Trotsky. Relations with Plekhanov were temporarily running so smoothly that Lenin co-opted his old opponent to be a representative at the convening Eighth Congress of the Second International. After attending the Congress in Copenhagen, Lenin went for a week to Stockholm where he joined his sister Maria, and for the last time, his mother. He then returned to Paris.

On October 3, 1910, agreement was reached to publish with Plekhanov a new "party organ," *Rabochaya Gazeta* ("Workers' Newspaper"). Printing of *Proletarii* ceased and *Sotsial Demokrat* became the joint mouthpiece, with Lenin as the controlling influence. Lenin initiated, also with Plekhanov, the publication in Russia of the "legal" weekly *Zvezda*, or "Star," the previously proposed "Duma organ"; and of *Mysl* ("Thought"), which was to be produced in Moscow. The first issue of *Zvezda* appeared on December 29, 1910. Bonch-Bruyevich was responsible for its publication; to him Lenin wrote angry letters complaining that he was kept uninformed. Lenin was also worried that the editors might not wish to publish his articles. Despite his diatribes against the liquidators, Lenin, too, was placing

[19]French police report of November 27, 1909.

greater emphasis upon non-violent, legal forms of struggle. To reach the Russian audiences more effectively he turned to the "right."

But why was Lenin so eager to make overtures toward the Mensheviks? He had neither changed his mind (though he was lacking in fresh ideas) nor lost his combativeness. A practical, not a theoretical, matter was at the bottom of this appeasement: the foreign bureau of the Russian Social Democratic party was holding in escrow funds which the Bolsheviks claimed for themselves and needed to hold the "professional revolutionaries" together. These were portions of the Schmidt inheritance which Taratuta had turned over to the party. The police general, Alexander Spiridovich, disclosed that, according to his information, Lenin gave 100,000 rubles to the overall party and promised to pay the remaining amount of some 400,000 rubles, *provided* the Mensheviks restrict their struggle against the Bolsheviks to strictly within party confines.[20] This proviso, of course, was to free Lenin from his financial obligations. Soon Lenin was to argue that these funds belonged to the Bolsheviks anyway, and that the Mensheviks had no rights to them. The Mensheviks asserted that the money had been deeded to the entire party and that Lenin should therefore return the portion that did not belong to his faction. In these debates Lenin fared reasonably well, not only because he paid wages to his representatives whereas the Mensheviks by and large did not, but also because he was supported by the Poles and Letts, secretly subsidized groups within the party. He apparently concealed from the Mensheviks the fact that he ever received more than 100,000 rubles.

Much was becoming known about these matters. Bogdanov was talking, and perhaps Taratuta himself was not being discrete. Lenin's actions did not increase his popularity. To uphold the good name of socialism, the International arranged that a committee of three German socialists supervise the use of these dubious funds. Because the German trustees were aiming at conciliating the quarrelling factions, Lenin was to some degree aided. But it also proved to be a hindrance, for since he was running short of funds, money was obtainable only through exemplary behavior that would meet with the approval of the Germans.

After a few desultory moves toward unity, Lenin, on December 5, 1910, petitioned the party for release of the trust money, promising that there would be no further divisive tactics. But Lenin made the mistake of asking for the *entire* amount. The Mensheviks, naturally uneager to see Lenin re-financed, reiterated their claim that they

20A. I. Spiridovich, *Istoriya Bolshevizma v Rossii* (Paris: Franko-Russkaia Pechat, 1922), p. 206. This figure of 400,000 was too high, since it ignores the percentages to the heiresses and their boyfriends. *See also,* Schapiro, *The Communist Party, op. cit.,* p. 116f.

were entitled to their share. Agreement could not be reached on how the money could be divided "equitably." In addition, there were outside claimants; for example, one of the swindled sisters, and the representative of a Ural band of highwaymen whose leader, a certain Lbov, demanded repayment of 6,000—according to other sources 10,000—rubles once given to the Bolsheviks for arms which had never been delivered.[21] It also appeared that monies entrusted to a Bolshevik to defray party expenses had disappeared. The Mensheviks, who now knew that Lenin had received more than he admitted, told the Bolsheviks that they must return the money which had been extorted from the heiresses.

Early in 1911, Lenin paid a secret visit to Karl Kautsky, the most influential of the German trustees; little was achieved. In June, the trustees demanded that the Bolsheviks pay their debts. Lenin was forced to disgorge a sizeable amount. He agreed, readily enough, that the remaining 500-ruble notes which had become "hot money" be burned. But working through Clara Zetkin, the strongest pro-Bolshevik among the German trustees, Lenin arranged for the main portion of the requested "repayment" (30,000 francs or 12,000 rubles) to be re-transferred to the "technical commission" which Lenin ran. There was soon, however, a dispute in this commission also.

As chief editor of *Sotsial Demokrat,* Lenin had *de facto* control over a fund of approximately 100,000 rubles. The Bolshevik assistant editor, his young lieutenant Grigory Zinovyev, was entirely under his influence, while the two Menshevik editors Martov and Dan (as well as a Polish socialist) were easily manipulated. Nevertheless, disputes grew more acrimonious. Lenin concluded that collaboration with the Mensheviks would not provide the solution to his financial troubles. On May 27, 1911, Lenin's agent, Nikolai Alexandrovich Semashko, a physician, walked out of the foreign bureau of the Russian Social Democratic party, taking with him the records *and* the money.

The usually patient Martov, this time furious, disclosed details of Lenin's financial machinations. There was an uproar. In October, money for the November issue of the *Sotsial Demokrat* was refused; Lenin and Zinovyev, who had spent most of the allotted funds in

---

[21]Krupskaya (*op. cit.,* p. 155) indicates that these weapons were seized by the police and that the police agent Katya Kommisarov who ran the office of *Proletarii* had been in charge of delivering them. The wording suggests that she got the weapons to the Urals and that they were seized there. It is unlikely that a woman was entrusted with a substantial weapons assignment. Krupskaya apparently invented this cover story to hide the fact, then generally asserted, that the weapons were never dispatched. Olberg asserts that Lenin had received an advance of $100,000 (probably he meant 100,000 rubles) but this seems far too high.

futile attempts to build up their cadres, were compelled to borrow from the printer. Zinovyev staged a walk-out of his own, demonstratively leaving the organizational committee and taking along the cash and the printing press.

Even fiercely loyal Bolsheviks opposed these tactics, including A. I. Rykov, whom Lenin promptly denounced as a "conciliator." In August, 1911, Rykov returned to Russia to prepare for a party conference. M. I. Brendinsky, a Bolshevik police agent who later became secretary of the Moscow city committee, reported on his itinerary to the Okhrana. The police were intent upon keeping the party disunited, hence they were of one mind with Lenin concerning the "conciliators." Rykov (later Lenin's successor as "prime minister" of the Soviet Union) was arrested. Two other Bolshevik representatives in Russia were denounced and restrained.

The police and Lenin were doing each other's bidding. While arresting those of his comrades whom he could not handle, the police did not unduly interfere with the sale of his books in Russia. Lenin's exhortations on terror and uprising and his calls for the destruction of the ruling classes and the "bourgeoisie" were tolerated, yet Tolstoi's books extolling peacefulness and opposing violence were often seized. Possibly the police thought that radical ravings would discredit the revolutionaries, just as Nechayev's *Revolutionary Catechism* had served, in its time, to strengthen the existing order. At one point it would seem as though the Bolsheviks were little more than an operational arm of the Okhrana. For example, during 1908 and 1909, four of the five members of the St. Petersburg committee were police agents. This overly clever strategy was, however, bound to misfire.

Insofar as Lenin was concerned, the result of all these complicated moves and counter-moves, which probably even the intriguers themselves never fully understood, was quite simple: Lenin continued to retain at least 100,000 rubles under his full control. A similar sum was in escrow under German control, under the guardianship of Clara Zetkin, who attempted to preserve the money for Lenin. In the end, Lenin apparently obtained the entire amount: the last and major payments evidently occurred during the war, in 1915. At that time, the transfer had to be authorized by the government of Wilhelm II, Imperator Rex of the German Reich.

Amour

At this low point in his productivity and career, Lenin met Inessa

Fedorovna Armand.[1] Apparently for the first and only time, Lenin
fell in love. To this day, Communist puritanism contrives to conceal
this episode; Inessa is customarily referred to—even by ex-Com-
munists—as a "comrade who was close to Lenin" or "who worked with
him directly."

As seems fitting, Inessa was a revolutionary. French party historians, in an attempt to predate the beginnings of the French Communist party and to trace its origin directly to Lenin, allege that Inessa
met Lenin in the winter of 1903-1904 in Switzerland; If this is true,
it was purely a chance encounter. He may have met her during 1906
or 1907 in Russia, although this is unlikely since as late as 1909, the
Okhrana listed her as a Social Revolutionary.[2] Lenin most likely
met her either in 1909, at the International Bureau in Brussels,
or in 1910 at a meeting in Paris—Inessa was much sought after as an
interpreter since she could speak French and Russian without flaw,
and English and German quite fluently.

Inessa was born in Paris on June 16, 1875, and was thus five
years younger than Lenin.[3] Her real name was Elisabeth Pécheux
d'Herbenville. Her parents were well-known artists, the father a
comedian acting under the name of Théodore Stéphen, the mother
a pianist and vocalist, and also a music teacher. Her mother's name
is given as Natalie Wilde. Apparently the parents performed in
several European countries, including England, and took their

[1]For a Bolshevik biography see Jean Fréville, *Une grande figure de la révolution
russe: Inessa Armand* (Paris: Editions sociales, 1957); also Inna Armand, "Inès
Armand" in *Frauen der Revolution*, (No author) (Berlin: Dietz, 1960), pp. 73-90. For
a critical analysis, *see* Bertram D. Wolfe, "Lenin and Inessa Armand," *Slavic Review*,
Volume XXII, Number 1, March 1963, pp. 96-114. Wolfe also presents additional
references.

[2]According to Wolfe (*ibid.*, p. 101), she left her husband in 1904 and went to Sweden
where she interested herself in feminism. At that time she reportedly read Lenin's
What is to be Done?; apparently, as an admirer of Chernyshevsky, she was attracted
by the title. Wolfe claims that she was sent by the Bolsheviks to Russia but, on the
basis of information in the Okhrana file, this early tie with the Bolsheviks appears
doubtful.

[3]Wolfe, like other authors and even reference works, gives 1879 as her year of birth.
If this date were correct, she would have given birth to five children within six
years which is most unlikely for a woman of her circumstances. It would appear
that, in good bourgeois fashion, she rejuvenated herself by four years; and indeed
she was very young looking (Walter, p. 205). The editors of *Sochineniya* (4th ed.,
vol. 37, p. 601) give her birthdate as 1875. Moreover, her birth place generally is
given as Paris, but the Okhrana indicated that she was born in Moscow. This is not
quite as improbable as it sounds: it is, to say the least, surprising that not only her
aunt but also her reputedly English grandmother were living in Russia. Their professions were given as *"gouvernantes"*, music and language teachers. Also, Inessa's
Russian was too flawless to have been acquired after her fourteenth year. (Compare
Wolfe, *ibid.*, p. 99.)

children along on their travels. The father died young and left his widow and children penniless.[4]

Natalie Wilde allegedly was of English or Scottish origin, but in view of her Christian name and of the fact that her mother (Inessa's grandmother) was living in Russia, this appears doubtful. Natalie may have had an English father, but it is more likely that she was Russian[5] and had gone to England to study and perform as a musician. Presumably, she returned to Russia after her husband's death and died shortly thereafter. Thereupon Inessa went to live with her aunt (who allegedly was her father's sister but more probably was the sister of her mother). Inessa completed her education at Pushkino, near Moscow, where the aunt served as governess to the Armand family, wealthy textile manufacturers. The best evidence is that the girl moved to Russia when she was about fourteen years of age. She then adopted the orthodox religion[6] and presumably, at that time, changed her name to Inessa.

Vivacious, attractive, and gifted, the Okhrana described her as of medium height, with an oval and thin face, grey eyes, sharp nose, and red hair. (Lenin's remaining hair was also reddish.)[7] Inessa, at the age of eighteen, married one of the Armand sons, Alexander Yevgenevich, with whom she had five children.

Apparently bored with a life of wealth, she asked her brother-in-law, Boris,[8] to put her in touch with the revolutionary movement, for which she reportedly worked as an "agitator," first at Pushkino and then in Moscow. It is claimed that she joined a Bolshevik group in 1904, but this is unlikely. In any event, at that point, she hardly knew how to distinguish between bolshevism and other "isms." She was arrested in January, 1905, accused of possessing weapons and illegal Social Revolutionary literature in her apartment. Freed by the amnesty, she was held shortly in April, 1907, allegedly for Bol-

---

[4]According to her granddaughter Inna, Natalie Wilde was left with three children; the Okhrana reported in 1909 that Inessa had two brothers and three sisters, all living in Russia.

[5]If Natalie and the rest of her children had stayed in France, Inessa on her travels in that country would have met her relatives or stayed at their houses. Such meetings would have been recorded by the French police: apparently Inessa always stayed in hotels. If the supposedly English mother had returned to England (as would seem indicated), Inessa should have had contacts with English relatives; but apparently she never traveled to England.

[6]This also would indicate that her surviving family was Russian. It should be observed that the reason for these various discrepancies is not apparent; but there has been a deliberate attempt to conceal Inessa's antecedents.

[7]Krupskaya also was a redhead. The Bolsheviks may well be described as the red-head party, since many of the prominent members had this characteristic.

[8]A certain "B. Armand" was in trouble with the police in the late 1890's.

shevik activities in the armed forces,[9] and re-arrested in June, at which time she was condemned to exile. Shortly before the expiration of her two-year term, presumably several weeks before April 22, 1909, when she was put on the "wanted list,"[10] she escaped from the Arkhangel area to Brussels. She and her husband were now divorced, but he continued to support her financially until he was expropriated by Lenin's revolution. (In 1909, the Okhrana still listed her as married.)

Inessa had come to Paris to meet a close friend—probably Mikhail Vilonov, the organizer of the party school on Capri. As we have seen, Lenin objected to this school and through a number of maneuvers persuaded half of the students, including Vilonov, to join him in Paris. The students later returned to Russia where most of them were arrested. Vilonov, who suffered from tuberculosis which he had contracted in a penal regiment, went to Davos where he died on May 1, 1910. Inessa, heartbroken, decided to remain in Paris.

In her memoirs, Krupskaya related that Inessa Armand quickly became an "active member" of the Paris Bolshevik group.[11] She was living, said Krupskaya, with her two daughters and her son; actually Inessa had five children but two may have remained with the father. Soon Inessa was surrounded by a "certain number of our comrades." She must have caught Lenin's eye very quickly, for he entrusted to her the correspondence with Bolshevik cells throughout Europe.

On December 20, 1910, an Okhrana bulletin reported that a party school was being planned, with a faculty consisting of one Leninist and two Bogdanov Bolsheviks, two Poles, one Lett and one Bund member. The school, as we learn from another document, had been planned in January, 1910, but because of lack of energy and money, nothing further had been done. However, in November, 1910, Bogdanov established a school at Bologna, Italy; the money had come from a recent expropriation at Miass. Although he was invited to lecture, Lenin, as the leader of one of the three Bolshevik groups (one was to the right and the other, like Bogdanov, to the left of his), was perturbed. As the Russian Ministry of the Interior reported on March 10, 1911, Lenin produced 10,000 francs to finance a school for forty students. Police documents show that the school operated between June and August, 1911, when it was closed for lack of funds.[12] The

[9]Wolfe, *ibid.*, p. 101.

[10]In November, 1907, the police arrested Lidya Martinovna Armand, twenty-five or twenty-six years old, dark-brown hair, brown eyes, straight and free posture. Elegantly dressed, she would appear to be a sister-in-law of Inessa but her arrest card did not refer to suspect relatives.

[11]Krupskaya, p. 213.

[12]All the above quoted documents are in the Okhrana Collection of the Hoover Institution.

faculty was composed of many Social Democratic factions. There were merely ten students; five or six others were expected from Russia.[13] Some of these students presumably had been drawn from Bogdanov's school: Lenin was a great master at undermining opposing groups, even within his own party.

The party school was established at Longjumeau, approximately ten miles from Paris. Inessa, stepping into Vilonov's shoes as a school "organizer," rented a villa, where she lived and in which classes were taught.[14] Krupskaya took pains to point out in her memoirs that three comrades were "placed" into Inessa's house and that she and her husband were living in a proletarian abode "at the other end of the village."[15] Krupskaya also reported that there were two police agents among the students, including a young and "not very observant" person by the name of Andrei Malinovski. There is little doubt that Krupskaya's roster of police agents at Longjumeau was incomplete.

On the road to Longjumeau there was a little *bistro* that served good food and coffee; but since its prices were slightly above average, Russian *émigrés* seldom visited it. Lenin, however, frequented the place, for it offered him undisturbed solitude. Presently it was noticed that Lenin no longer drank his beer alone but was accompanied by Inessa who, it is said, drank only lemonade.

The relationship was quite unusual. The revolutionaries, after recovering from their initial surprise, heatedly debated whether this was platonic love or whether Lenin "was living with Inessa." Krupskaya often went to Paris in order to keep "comrades . . . from coming to Longjumeau," adding incongruously that the students intended to return to Russia and that "their stay in Paris had to be kept as secret as possible."[16] But rumors continued, and when Lenin appointed Inessa to lecture at the school, the consensus was that she exerted an enormous influence on *Starik*, the old man: unless he were in love, he would not have given such an important assignment to this novice.

Krupskaya, like most bourgeois wives, became wise to her husband's transgressions. The comrades noted how at lunch in school, Krupskaya's mother manifested open indignation whenever Lenin conversed with Inessa.

---

[13]Figures differ. M. I. Brendinsky, the Bolshevik shipping agent at Paris and a police agent, reported to the Moscow police chief on September 11, 1911 (New Style) that there were thirteen students from Russia and four local auditors. Each Russian student had been given a minimum of sixty rubles for the trip. They were recruited by a certain "Semyon"—presumably Semyon Schwarz. (Tsiavlovsky, *op. cit.*, p. 64f.).

[14]Brendinsky reported that initially the school was held at a different location (unnamed) and that the classes in Longjumeau were held in a former joinery.

[15]Krupskaya, p. 220.

[16]Krupskaya, p. 224.

But according to all indications, Lenin was undersexed; at least one close observer believed Lenin was impotent. He certainly opposed eroticism because it interfered with politics and revolution. But now his instincts were aroused. He had known Krupskaya for eighteen years. She was becoming a shrivelled and excessively thin woman incapable of continuing to work at the pace that Lenin set. She was about to fall victim to, or was already suffering from, Graves' disease, a glandular affliction which affects the libido. It is most unlikely, therefore, that Lenin could have found any sexual satisfaction with her; furthermore, there are no signs that Krupskaya was ever interested in sex.

In one of those strange and incongruous disclosures about Lenin's life, we learn that on May 21, 1911, he and Krupskaya made a one-day trip to Fontainebleau. Lenin had, in the past, hiked and bicycled with Krupskaya. This was certainly not the only spring morning which drew him into the beautiful forest of the Paris *banlieue*.[17] But apparently this excursion was memorable.

Krupskaya accepted her unpleasant situation with dignity, behaving politely toward Inessa. According to some reports, she proposed leaving her husband.[18] Lenin may have momentarily hesitated, but he stayed with Krupskaya and did not break with Inessa. The chances are that the walk in Fontainebleau led to one of those marital truce arrangements in which the wife accepts the mistress as a permanent fixture provided the husband makes a solemn promise that the marriage will remain intact.

Krupskaya did not lecture even once, and she never attended the Longjumeau school. Yet she was not kept very busy: the Lenins had a housekeeper, Katya Mazonova, the wife of an exile revolutionary. Krupskaya intimated that Katya was volunteering her services.

Inessa initially lectured on the history of the socialist movement in Belgium. But there was little interest in this topic and the course was dropped after only three lectures. Brendinsky informed the police that she was a poor lecturer. But apparently this was not Lenin's opinion. He probably considered Inessa's first lectures as a trial run and was satisfied. Inessa, who had earned degrees at the Sorbonne, was asked to conduct a politico-economic seminar. Preparing herself by diligent work lasting till late at night, she managed

---

[17]For example, Krupskaya stated that during their spare time at Longjumeau they went to a nearby airport where they often were the only spectators and Lenin was able to watch the planes "to his heart's content." She did not mention the May 21 excursion which was disclosed in the footnotes to Lenin's works, probably by Kamenev.

[18]Marcel Body, "Alexandra Kollontai," *Preuves,* April 1952, pp. 12-24; also Wolfe, p. 111.

fairly well. Lenin attended all of her performances, an honor he did not bestow upon any other lecturer.

Brendinsky produced interesting descriptions of the *dramatis personae*. Lenin was described as looking much the same as in years past except for being cleaner shaven and balder. Krupskaya was a little taller than Inessa; both were thin and had dark red hair and long, pale faces. Krupskaya, of course, was older; Brendinsky stated that her face appeared wrinkled and aged. The agent was impressed by Inessa's very full hair. Of her children, Brendinsky reported the presence only of her seven-year-old son. He described her as an *intelligentka* who had received her higher education abroad, adding that she spoke European languages fluently. He believed that she was Jewish.[19]

In his relations with Inessa, Lenin tried to emerge from his self-encapsulation. He listened to her play the piano—his love for Beethoven's *Appassionata* is again recorded. Gorky, years later, reported that Lenin, listening to a recording of this sonata, remarked that if he were to hear this music too often, he would become nice and stroke peoples' heads; but this should not be done for "the hand will be bitten off."[20] Although his sentiments when listening to Inessa's rendering of the *Appassionata* may have been truly aesthetic, he is said to have enjoyed most a passage of the third movement that reminded him of a revolutionary song.[21]

The musical interlude with Inessa lasted only a short while. In the first weeks of bliss, Lenin often promised Inessa not to talk about party business—a promise which was frequently broken. On her part, she tended—at least during the first period—to argue about ethics and morals. Lenin dismissed her ideas as petty bourgeois reasoning; as though his own fear of divorce did not bespeak of a petty bourgeois mentality!

Once, against Inessa's objections, Lenin fell into a long monologue. Speaking in a sharp tone and with anger, he asked her to identify the

---

[19]Tsiavlovsky, p. 67. This may be the explanation of the attempts at concealment. However, Inessa's father definitely was not Jewish and it is not likely (though not impossible) that her mother was.

[20]Gorky, *Days with Lenin*, p. 52.

[21]Wolfe, *Ibid.*, p. 112, quotes Angelica Balabanova as saying that "Inessa played beautifully." Lenin "deeply loved music, and this Krupskaya could not give him." She also mentioned Lenin's "beloved Beethoven." However, Balabanova probably exaggerated Lenin's understanding of music.

Krupskaya wrote from Cracow to Lenin's mother on December 26, 1913, that they once went to a concert and were planning to take out a whole subscription. The concert, on Inessa's testimony, was artistically first rate. A Beethoven quartet was being performed, but "somehow" the concert bored Lenin and Krupskaya "terribly". Clearly, of this series only one concert was attended. (Lenin, *Werke*, Vol. 37, Berlin, Dietz, 1961, p. 442).

"better elements of the bourgeoisie" she was discussing. He accused the bourgeoisie of having caused his brother's death; yet Inessa knew that Alexander and Lenin had not been close. Clearly, Inessa was unable to humanize Lenin, and gradually she became his obedient tool. But occasionally she was able to inspire in Lenin a spark of insight into values higher than those of revolution.

Return to Struggle

After school was over—Lenin had given forty-five lectures—the Lenins, late in August, 1911, returned to Paris. They moved to No. 4, Rue Marie-Rose, and Inessa with her children went to live in the adjoining house, No. 2. Shortly thereafter, Lenin traveled with Inessa to Switzerland, where he climbed Pilatus Mountain. Autumn was spent working with the International Socialist Bureau in Zurich and speaking in Swiss towns on Russian conditions. All of this undoubtedly Lenin enjoyed. But funds remained frozen. A new quarrel arose—over "liquidationism": the "liquidators" contended that the reconstruction of an underground party was impossible at the time and that the best tactical approach would be a democratic rather than a conspiratorial one. Lenin disputed this, but he himself used the methods the liquidators were preaching. Following his customary inclination to sow distrust, he alleged that the liquidators, and this term embraced most Mensheviks, were intent upon dissolving the party. Actually, they did not want to eliminate the underground party, perhaps only because it was not an effective force. Primarily, the liquidators distrusted the Central Committee which Lenin controlled through the votes of the Letts and Poles; the Mensheviks wished to reach the broad masses.

Lenin's attempt to reach an understanding with the Mensheviks—on his own terms and with himself as decision-maker—had not been effective. Many now agreed with Jean Jaurès, the French Socialist, who referred to Lenin with the German expression *Dreckgenosse*—"dirt comrade." Consequently, Lenin decided to attempt a new split, to be accomplished by a conference. On November 1, 1911, he wrote a letter to a Czech Social Democrat asking him to facilitate the holding of a conference in Prague. He warned the Czech that most of the delegates did not possess passports and were unable to disclose their real names.

This was a rather surprising step: heretofore Russian socialist congresses had been held in the democratic countries of Western and Northern Europe. The exiles traveled frequently through Germany and Austria-Hungary, but they usually avoided staying in the two imperial states. Krupskaya recounts that in 1908 Lenin wrote to Victor Adler, the leading Austrian socialist, and the Polish Bolshevik Felix Dzerzhinski, then living in Austria, concerning the possibility of publishing *Proletarii*. His letter said that since "Austria was closer to the Russian frontier, it would be more convenient in some ways to print the paper there, and easier to arrange transport facilities."[1]

But the plan proved infeasible for obvious reasons: despite recurrent disagreements, the two empires were collaborating with tsarism against the revolution. Germany had not been tolerant of Russian revolutionaries operating within her borders and the Austrian government was also unsympathetic to these agents. There were exceptions, of course. Trotsky, for example, had been living in Vienna unmolested since October, 1908, and was publishing *Pravda* ("Truth"), originally a Ukrainian paper. Initially, this sheet was financed by two wealthy comrades (one was the son of a Baku oilman); when it had been temporarily considered the main party organ, it had obtained money from the party. Trotsky probably was also supported by Austrian Social Democrats so that he was able to mail the paper to Russia.

Still, the Habsburg bureaucracy and police were notoriously difficult to deal with, especially in politically agitated towns like Prague. The Czech Social Democrats were nationalistic and reformist—there existed no possible basis of understanding between Lenin and them. Under these conditions, that Lenin decided to hold his conference in Prague is puzzling. Was the choice arbitrary or was there implied an offer to aid the Austrians in their struggle against the Russian-influenced Pan-Slavists? The very existence of the Russian revolutionary movement might have convinced the Pan-Slavic element in Bohemia that they could not have expected support from tsarist Russia. Krupskaya gave these reasons for the decision: there was no Russian colony in Prague, and "besides, Vladimir Ilyich knew Prague, for he had lived there . . . in the period of his first exile."[2] Actually, Lenin had just passed through while in transit.

A preparatory meeting was held in Paris between December 27 and 30, 1911.[3] The conference itself was held in the Bohemian capital between January 18 and 30, 1912, a remarkably short two-and-a-half months after Lenin had initiated the plan. The Prague conference was purely Bolshevik in composition. At least two, perhaps three, of the conferees were police agents, including a former student

[1]Krupskaya, *op. cit.,* p. 172.

[2]*Ibid.,* p. 227.

[3]This pre-conference gathering was duly reported to the Okhrana; it is interesting to speculate how they received the information: all six participants were Bolsheviks without any suspicion of police connections attached to them.

of the Capri school. Another agent, Brendinsky, was unmasked by Krupskaya in Paris and prevented from attending the conference. According to her version, Brendinsky never returned to Russia, but "the tsarist government bought him a villa in the suburbs of Paris for 40,000 francs." What services could have justified *this* munificence?[4]

Though billed as a "party conference," the meeting was not recognized by any but Lenin's followers. More specifically, those Bolshevik groups which did not obey Lenin slavishly had not been invited.[5] The Russian police, who allowed six of their agents to help organize the meeting, were interested in securing Lenin's independence, and arrested non-Bolsheviks who intended to attend the conference.[6] Lenin, on the other hand, had now become a virtuoso in creating a democratic façade by carefully controlling participants of the meetings. Subsequently he reminded one of his money-collectors that "we were victorious, since we had money at the January conference."[7] Yet this trickery did not pass unnoticed; on March 26, 1912, the German Social Democratic *Vorwärts* criticized the conference as unrepresentative. Criticism of this type was bound to hinder Lenin in his dealings with the German party.

It was the Prague conference which, at long last, established the Bolsheviks as an independent organization. Some formal ties with the Mensheviks were maintained even after the Prague conference, but their existence merely indicated for a long time the Mensheviks' hesitation to oppose the Bolsheviks strongly.

The Prague conference—which cost about 10,000 francs—called for the creation of illegal cells. *Rabochaya Gazeta,* a monthly published in Paris, was recognized as the official party organ.[8] The distribution of both legal and illegal literature was to be increased and the legal press inside Russia was to advance its output. As a result, the weekly *Zvezda* (Bonch-Bruyevich was still a member of the

[4]She confused the question further by indicating (p. 225) that Brendinsky was the shipping agent at Leipzig but that he was living in Dvinsk (p. 228). Actually he was stationed at Paris but presumably traveled a great deal.

[5]Gorky had been invited but declined on the grounds that his presence would tip off newspapermen. He added that he had no money to support any legal Social Democratic newspaper.

[6]Agafonov, *op. cit.,* p. 206f. Not all of the eighteen participants of this conference have yet been identified. Party historians are especially fond of manipulating this list of participants: police midwifery at the birth of the independent Bolshevik party is indeed too embarrassing. Nor have all the police ties of the participants yet been identified.

[7]*Istoricheskii Arkhiv* (1958), No. 6, p. 10. Money there must have been, but it is not clear how it was procured.

[8]Lenin, Zinovyev, and Kamenev were appointed editors with a monthly salary of 200 francs each. Tsiavlovsky, *op. cit.,* p. 100.

editorial board) was published twice a week during February, and in March began operating on a three-days-a-week schedule.

Lenin went to Leipzig after the conference, but made a detour via Marktredwitz so that he could talk briefly with Clara Zetkin on the train. Then, in the offices of the Leipzig socialist paper, he met with a newly elected member of the Central Committee who was a police agent, and two Social Democratic Duma deputies, one of whom was also working for the police. The meeting probably considered financial matters.[9] General Spiridovich reported that the Duma group (i.e., the Russian section of the party) had authorized the expenditure of 1,000 rubles for *Zvezda*,[10] but had rejected larger literary expenditures: apparently there was little money. It is asserted that the Leipzig socialists had been collecting money since 1907 for the "Russian class comrades."[11] But no money was offered now; moreover, it is asserted that the debates were ended early because the Bolsheviks feared a police raid. This story is unlikely.

Lenin proceeded to Berlin to negotiate with Kautsky and Bebel about the trust money. Bebel received him hostilely. "He looked like an animal," Lenin reported. Lenin said of Kautsky, that he was interfering with things he did not understand, that he did not even know the poet Nekrassov, and that he wanted to meddle in Russian affairs. Lenin wanted to sue but soon dropped this plan. While in Berlin, Lenin viewed a play directed by Max Reinhardt.

[9]These deputies had been too late for the Prague conference and Lenin improvised this meeting.

[10]One Duma deputy, Poletayev, insisted that this subsidy—the equivalent of 2,500 francs—continue to be paid, since *Zvezda* was the only legal paper of the Central Committee. The Prague conference had approved a budget of 12,000 francs for expenditures abroad and 18,000 francs for expenditures inside Russia.

[11]Xaver Streb, *Lenin in Deutschland* (Berlin: Dietz, 1957), p. 51.

Pravda

In April, 1912, there was established in St. Petersburg a legal Bolshevik paper, *Pravda* ("Truth"). It is alleged that the paper, whose name was the same as Trotsky's journal,[1] was published to implement the Prague decisions and that it was financed by Tikhomirnov, the son of a millionaire merchant from Kazan who supposedly gave 100,000 rubles.[2]

[1]In 1905, Lunacharsky and Bogdanov had published another *Pravda* in whose columns they attempted to merge Marx with the positivist philosophies of Mach and Avenarius.

[2]Wolfe, *Three who made a Revolution*, p. 559.

Yet the Prague resolution stressed the need for illegal publications far more strongly than the need for legal ones. There already was in operation a legal Bolshevik press in Russia; the acceleration of *Zvezda's* publication schedule would have amply fulfilled the directive. The injunction to enlarge the legal effort may be considered as an indication of a desire to establish a daily paper—as Communist historians assert—but the resolution did not state this. The reticence allegedly was due to "conspiratorial reasons"; it is true that the well-informed police reported nothing about such a decision. Others alleged that the resolutions were purposefully worded vaguely to guard against failure. But if the money were available (as it should have been if Tikhomirnov provided it), there would have been no need for such caution.

Tikhomirnov was abroad in 1911. It is reported that he met Lenin in Zakopane, Polish Austria; but that year Lenin was living in France. Tikhomirnov returned to Russia and in February, 1912, was arrested. He remained in deportation until 1914, at which time he went to see Lenin. He was there, as we learn from Krupskaya's memoirs, at the time of Lenin's arrest in August, 1914.[3] These dates preclude the possiblity that he was involved with the alleged Prague resolution about the founding of *Pravda*. Did he leave Lenin the money before he was arrested? Is there just confusion about his itinerary? By the end of 1911 the Bolsheviks, devoid of funds, financed the Prague conference only with difficulty. The allegation that Tikhomirnov gave 100,000 rubles to finance *Nash Putj*, the subsequently established counterpart of *Pravda*, bears greater validity. For that matter, Tikhomirnov has been put into the "memory hole" by Bolshevik historians. Thus, the tale of Tikhomirnov's money launching *Pravda* simply does not hang together.

No evidence has been produced proving that Lenin guided the establishment of *Pravda* from Paris. Perhaps the Prague conference did decide to publish *Pravda*, and it is possible that Lenin did try to finance the paper. If so, he was unsuccessful. The evidence suggests that after he had returned to Paris he *heard* about plans for a newspaper. On March 26, he wrote to the editors of *Zvezda* inquiring about the truth of the rumor. Two days later, he was furious that all contacts had been disrupted. The money situation was aggravated; he complained that no one was endeavoring to solve it. He requested a resolution which would enable him to bring suit against the German trustees; otherwise, he forecast, a collapse would occur within three to four months. The budget would have to be revised; bankruptcy was imminent.[4]

---

[3] Krupskaya, p. 279ff.
[4] *Krassnyi Arkhiv* (1934), I, 229f.

The answer Lenin received remains unknown, but it was surely a discouraging one, for he wrote his mother in April[5] that he was contemplating a move from Paris into the suburbs so that he might live in peace. Indeed his failure in Germany had brought him into a state of depression. In addition, he was having trouble with his memory and was suffering from his usual ailments. He needed the fresh air and he was happy to move away from *émigré* chatter. But would he have planned to go into temporary retirement if he had known that *Pravda* was about to be published? Shotman discloses that he was in Paris when the first issues of *Pravda* were delivered. Lenin went to Berlin and returned after two weeks. Nothing is known about this trip but is is likely that he again tried unsuccessfully to raise funds. Shortly thereafter, Shotman returned to Russia, bringing manuscripts with him. The implication of his confused account is that the local groups sabotaged publication of those contributions by Lenin.

Thus the evidence seems to indicate that the money for *Pravda* was raised in Russia, and that Lenin was not informed of the operation. According to the Communist version (which never states it definitely), Lenin had asked the Duma deputy, N. G. Poletayev in Leipzig, to organize the paper; but the police reported that they were haggling over 1,000 rubles for *Zvezda*. Poletayev did request a license to publish *Pravda;* but as a deputy he was likely to be asked for this service by whomever gathered sufficient funds. On April 10, 1912, with surprising speed, Poletayev was granted the permit. The first issue was composed in his apartment by Poletayev, Stalin, Pokrovsky, Olminsky, and Baturin. Poletayev played no further role in the history of the paper.

According to the Stalinist version, it was Stalin who arranged the publication, aided by Poletayev, Pokrovsky, two Bolshevik journalists, and other Duma representatives of a more Menshevik orientation.[6] Stalin himself wrote that he participated in creating the paper's "platform" and compiled the first issue in the house of a Duma deputy.[7] "The technical and financial prerequisites for the newspaper had already been provided thanks to the agitation conducted by

---

[5]*Letters of Lenin*, p. 299.

[6]Stalin had been co-opted to the Bolshevik Central Committee after the Prague conference. Lenin had met Stalin at Tammerfors in 1906, and at the Stockholm and London Congresses. The reasons why he was co-opted are not clear but the composition of the Committee indicates that Lenin apparently was anxious to emphasize work in the Caucasus. The "Russian" members of the Central Committee were in addition to Stalin, S. S. Spandarian and G. K. Ordzhonikidze—all Caucasians. There also was Goloshchekin as a fourth member but he was the "travel agent." All were on a salary of fifty rubles monthly (Tsiavlovsky, *op. cit.*, p. 101).

[7]See, for example, *Works*, Vol. II (Moscow, 1953), p. 412.

Zvezda, the sympathy of the broad masses of the workers, and the mass voluntary collection of funds for *Pravda* in the mills and factories." Collections were undertaken, but they did not bring sufficient money to begin publication.[8] *Zvezda* was ultimately merged with *Pravda*, but *Pravda* was set up more or less behind the backs of *Zvezda's* editorial board. In any event, Stalin did not claim that the funds were provided by him; he went out of his way *not* to take credit for the transaction. Why?

During the Prague conference into which Lenin had placed his most reliable Bolsheviks, the delegate from Moscow was a man named Roman V. Malinovsky. Lenin did not personally know him but had heard of his actions as a unionist, former Menshevik, and recent convert to bolshevism. His candidacy for the Central Committee was proposed by the energetic female party worker Lobova. Malinovsky, who allegedly had been "forced to volunteer" for military service during the Russo-Japanese war, had been a member of the Union of Petrograd Metal Workers since its founding on May 1, 1906, and had served as secretary to the union since 1907. In November, 1909, he was arrested while preparing an anti-alcoholism congress. After his arrest he went to Moscow, where he participated in a conference of factory physicians. Later he became active among the Moscow Bolsheviks. His wife, who was religious, almost committed suicide when she discovered he was an atheist; after that she suffered from nervous ailments.

Malinovsky, born in 1876, and probably of Polish noble extraction, was practically the only Roman Catholic among the party hierarchs. He was clearly in possession of leadership abilities, a keen intellect, oratorical talent, and conspiratorial experience. Lenin was so impressed by him that he appointed him member of the Central Committee and chief of the Russian bureau of the Committee. Thus, Malinovsky became Lenin's counterpart at home. Since Malinovsky was termed "comrade Bolshevik No. 2" and became the Bolshevik boss in Russia, he was responsible for organizing the publication of *Pravda*. Wherever the money came from, Malinovsky's position made him the person to handle it.[9] He, in fact, registered as the paper's publisher, listing a certain M. E. Chernomazov as the official editor.

It all seemed to be straight-forward except for one detail—both Malinovsky and Chernomazov were Okhrana agents.[10] At that time the intention of the Okhrana was to split permanently the Social

---

[8]Shotman stated (*op. cit.*, p. 289) that quite a few subscriptions were placed in Finland and among Finns in Russia, even "semi-illiterates" were subscribing.

[9]Krupskaya (*op. cit.*, p. 259) confirmed that Malinovsky helped start *Nash Putj*.

[10]Chernomazov committed suicide in 1917.

Democratic party. Malinovsky was operating under a mandate to this effect. The police, in fact, had influenced the Prague conference to achieve this very purpose.

Clearly, the best way to widen the Social Democratic split was to support the one man who consistently utilized "splitting tactics"—and that man was Lenin. If he were to gain strength, he would have to lead a strong and independent Bolshevik organization. This position was now achieved. But to sustain the organization, especially inside Russia where the police most needed the diversion, a party organ was indispensable. Little money, however, was available, the police learned from Malinovsky and Duma deputy V. Y. Shurkanov, the other agent who participated in the Leipzig discussions.

It is therefore highly probable that the police were providing the capital for *Pravda,* just as in previous times they had financed *Nachalo,* the first legal Marxist organ, as well as *Nash Putj.* However, the police did not contribute *all* the funds that *Pravda* required. Additional sums were obtained through subscriptions, collections, and benefactors of the revolution.

It seems strange that Lenin was not kept informed of *Pravda's* progress, and that no one attempted to enlist him as chief editor. In the early phases of this delicate operation, Malinovsky and his masters probably desired no interference from the quarrelsome Lenin. They probably also wanted to avoid a conspiratorial organization of the distribution apparatus. Apparently they planned to pursue a line somewhat different from that preached by Lenin. There is no question but that initially *Pravda,* dominated by "conciliatory" ideas, did not conform to Lenin's notions.

A slight mishap occurred. The police held contradictory aims—to expose and divide the revolutionaries as well as to calm them. But in the very first issue (May 5, 1912) there appeared an unsigned programmatic article which declared that *Pravda* stood "for unity in the proletarian class struggle, for unity at all costs. Just as we must be uncompromising towards our enemies, so we must yield to one another." This was precisely what the police did *not* want; Lenin did not want it either. The author of these lines was Stalin;[11] he was arrested immediately. Malinovsky also wanted Stalin's removal because as a recently co-opted Committee member he held too much authority.

Had Lenin been informed, he would have submitted an article for *Pravda's* initial number. But his first *Pravda* article, one of no special importance, was published three weeks after the first issue had appeared. He continued writing articles for other Bolshevik papers, entering into closer contacts with *Pravda* only by the middle of July.

[11]See Stalin, *loc. cit.,* p. 225.

His first communication to the editors was couched in a diffident tone: he asked them not to edit his material too freely. Only after *Pravda* had been appearing for almost two months did he become a regular contributor. In all, 636 issues of *Pravda* were published between 1912 and 1914. Lenin contributed 270 articles and "notes." But he did not reveal the truth about *Pravda*—if he knew it.

Deployment for War

Between the appearance of *Pravda* and Lenin's full-fledged editorial participation, Lenin moved to Cracow in Austrian Poland. His itinerary led him through Leipzig where he lectured on the revolutionary "upsurge." He also went to Stuttgart to visit Zetkin; Sepp Hahn, who was then staying with the Zetkins, recollects that Lenin arrived from Switzerland where Krupskaya, who had been ill for some time, had consulted a number of doctors.[1] The Lenins were met in Stuttgart by Adelheid Popp, the leading woman socialist in Austria, who apparently accompanied them to Vienna. Hahn also reported that Lenin and Zetkin argued, specifically about the *Vorwärts* criticism of the Prague conference.[2]

Lenin left a democratic country for a state where the police were strong and revolutionaries were unpopular. Why? It is said Lenin left France in order to be closer to *Pravda*. Unquestionably, this was an important motive; he had complained during the Prague conference of the difficulties of editing a Russian paper in Paris. Other motives included his eagerness to remove himself from a neighborhood where he had encountered trouble and humiliation. Also, Krupskaya's health was getting worse and it was considered advisable to move close to the mountains. (At that time, mountain air was considered the best cure for her affliction.)

Nevertheless, it was strange for an active Russian revolutionary to assume residence in Austria-Hungary. Communist historians assert that the Polish gendarmes hated Russia and her Tsar, and were thus more accommodating to revolutionaries than the French police who cooperated with the Okhrana. It is indeed true that the Polish area of the monarchy, which enjoyed a high measure of autonomy, constituted a center of agitation for Polish and Ukrainian nationalism and for the destruction of the "prison house of nations," as the tsarist empire was called. Does this indicate that Lenin, anticipating In 1906, Pilsudski and his group, after losing their Japanese support,

[1]Lenin arrived in Cracow on June 21, 1912.

[2]Sepp Hahn, "Lenin bei Clara Zetkin in Stuttgart," in *Unvergesslicher Lenin,* (No editor) (Berlin: Dietz, 1960), pp. 30-44.

that he would remain unmolested in his political and literary work, executed a costly and politically significant move, relying on the benevolence of the Austrian gendarme?[3]

In order to live near the border, Lenin had to obtain a permit, which required the approval of military authorities, specifically the Corps Headquarters in Cracow, and of the Vienna political police. The Austrian political police was under the control of Johannes Schober (later Chancellor of the Austrian republic). Schober was in charge of the Staatspolitische Abteilung in the Interior Ministry. He ran his office like a political warfare agency and for several years had been dabbling—not always with authorization from the Foreign Office—in revolutionary adventures, especially against Russia. Captain Josef Rybak (or, perhaps, his successor Captain Ludwig Morawski), the decisive man in Cracow, acted under the broad direction of army intelligence at Vienna, the so-called *Evidenzbüro*. Rybak also worked closely with Pilsudski and other Poles whose activities, which had commenced in Galicia during 1902-1903, were the subject of a continuing argument between Vienna and Petersburg.

By way of background: since 1908 relations between Austria-Hungary and Germany on the one hand, and Russia on the other, had been deteriorating. Russia was stimulating subversion in Galicia, Bukovina, Bohemia, Croatia, and Bosnia; Austria was similarly active in Russian Poland. As long as the pro-Russian party prevailed in Berlin, war by the Central Powers against Russia was unlikely. But by mid-1909, German foreign policy came under the control of the rather anti-Russian Chancellor, Theobald von Bethmann-Hollweg. During November, 1910, the German and Austrian intelligence services joined forces to uncover further information on the Russian situation.[4]

The Austro-Hungarian government was poor; it lacked the resources necessary to establish a strong espionage effort directed against Russia. During the 1905 revolution, the Austrian government had acquiesced in Polish revolutionary activities and had subsequently permitted the Poles under Joseph Pilsudski to train in Galicia guerrilla forces—to be used, perhaps, inside Russian Poland. In 1906, Pilsudski and his group, after losing their Japanese support,

[3]This is most unlikely: during 1911, 950 Russians were expelled from Cracow and 114 from Lvov, and several hundred more from the rural areas. This information was passed on July 1, 1912, by the Austrian Minister of the Interior to the Foreign Minister who had just been seized by a Russian complaint concerning Austrian support of anti-Russian subversion. The answer was slightly disingenuous because many of the Russians who were expelled were actually agents of the tsarist government carrying on subversion against Austria. But, though the Austrian authorities tolerated a few Ukrainian nationalists, they clearly were not infatuated with Socialist Revolutionaries.

[4]Max Ronge, *Kriegs-und Industriespionage, Zwölf Jahre Kundschaftsdienst* (Wien: Amalthea, 1930), p. 46.

offered to procure intelligence in exchange for logistical aid for their partisans; this offer was not accepted.[5] After the revolution abated, the relations between Pilsudski's group and the Austrian authorities, notably the Polish administration in Galicia and the general staff, though becoming weaker, were never ruptured. The Galician authorities, staffed largely by Polish nationalists, continued to aid Pilsudski, once even deliberately misinforming the Vienna Foreign Office when it queried in response to a strong Russian protest. The *Evidenzbüro* considered the Pilsudski group as a reserve force to be used when intelligence and insurgency operations would be increased.

Confusedly enough, this was an interlacing political war, for many Austrian intelligence officers surveying Russia were of Polish and Ukrainian nationality and thus favored the cause of the nationalistic revolutionaries. In this milieu, the Austrian intelligence service increasingly relied upon Polish revolutionaries as their primary source of information concerning Russia. Following the agreement with Germany, the service accepted, late in 1910, the offer of close cooperation which Pilsudski and Jodko had made earlier.

This arrangement had one drawback: though the Polish collectors of information were able to learn a great deal about Russian Poland, the largest portion of the tsarist empire was poorly covered. The Austrian intelligence service decided that other techniques would have to be employed. After securing, on November 24, 1911, permission (presumably from emperor Francis Joseph) to step up intelligence operations against Russia, the *Evidenzbüro* entered into relations with Russian revolutionaries in 1911, with the intention of securing the broadest possible coverage.

A continuing international crisis brought matters to a head. More was involved than just a war scare. Since 1908, when Austria had annexed Bosnia and Herzegovina, relations between Austria and Russia had been tenuous. This strain soon intensified to the point of partial mobilization in both countries. German diplomats reported, time and again, the danger of an Austro-Russian war; the intra-Austrian official correspondence often bore references to the "anticipated" war. The possibility was also mentioned in a letter from the Lvov authorities to the Interior Department at Vienna. By 1912, Vienna considered war to be almost inevitable.[6]

[5]Ronge, *op. cit.*, p. 23.

[6]Austrian Archive, *Politisches Archiv*, Krieg 8a, Karton 901, historical note dated September 14, 1916. On November 19, 1912, the German ambassador in Paris secured a letter by the chief of staff of the Petersburg military district, Count Nostitz, to his wife in France, reassuring her that war was not imminent. "We are not ready yet, we need still about two years, but this is just a postponement" *("ce n'est qu'une partie remise").*

In view of the war threat, the Austrian War Ministry felt that it would be neglecting its duties if it were not to take advantage of the political movements directed against Russia.[7] Actually, the circles around Archduke Franz Ferdinand, the heir apparent, were considering a "Gross-Habsburg" with Poland and the Ukraine. We know that in 1913 or 1914 Franz Ferdinand visited London, where he talked with Ukrainian separatists.[8] The Austrians, however, ill-equipped to deal at first hand with these political movements, depended upon the Poles to handle them. The task was essentially in the hands of Witold Jodko, who had played a part in the Japanese deal.

Jodko created a sort of Polish united front which culminated, in November, 1912, in the formation of a provisional independence committee. Polish deputies to the Austrian parliament announced in December, 1912, that they were undertaking the struggle against Russian tsarism. The Poles decided that Austria was their "natural ally" and that they had to cooperate with all suitable revolutionary movements, including the Russian Social Democrats; the Polish group included many Russo-Polish and Austro-Polish Social Democrats who were anxious to use their international connections to further the common cause.

Early in 1914, Jodko spoke with the Social Revolutionary Victor Chernov in Paris: since the liberation of Poland necessitated war, he maintained, it was best to side with the Austrians because Austria was weaker than Germany. He inquired whether Chernov would cooperate against the tsarist system if war came. Pilsudski, at the same time, predicted in a speech that the war would pass through two phases: first Germany and Austria would defeat Russia, after which the West would defeat the Central Powers.[9]

The Poles, admittedly, acted in accord with the motto of Adam Mieczkiewicz: "Oh Lord, we beseech you for the war of peoples." Chernov declined their request for collaboration. But how did Lenin get involved? We know that Zilliacus was Jodko's liaison man in Stockholm but he was hardly the main channel. It is also known that, sometime in 1912, Ukrainian Leninists approached the Austrian Embassy in London in an apparently unfruitful gesture.[10] Krupskaya disclosed that Lenin engaged in "several talks" with Jodko and other members of Pilsudski's P.P.S. and that the Social

[7]Austrian Archive, *Kriegsministerium.* Präs. No. 14.150, dated December 26, 1912.

[8]Interviews with, and unpublished memoirs by, V. J. Stepankowski, a Ukrainian nationalist who collaborated for many years with Austria and Germany.

[9]Ignacy Daszynski, *Pamietniki* (Cracow: Z.R.S.S. "Proletarjat", 1926), II, 116-120; V. M. Chernov, *Pered burei (vospominaniya),* (New York: Izd-vo im. Chekhova, 1953), p. 289.

[10]Stepankowski, unpublished memoirs.

Democratic member of parliament, Diamand, had vouched for him.[11] We learn from the memoirs of Pilsudski's widow that Lenin and Pilsudski had also met. But these contacts took place *after* Lenin had gone to Austria.

Upon their arrival in Cracow, the Lenins were met, as Krupskaya disclosed, by the neurologist "comrade Bagocki—a Polish political exile who . . . helped us with our everyday and secret work." Bagocki, secretary of a refugee organization, was on friendly terms with the authorities; he later became one of Lenin's liaison men with the Germans. Since Bagocki was a refugee himself, it is not likely that he was an intermediary either.

The credit for having arranged Lenin's move was claimed— probably justifiably—by Jacob Hanecki.[12] Yet the old revolutionary Felix Kohn may also have had a hand in the transaction.[13]

Why the move was considered initially is not clear. Jodko undoubtedly surveyed the Russian revolutionary groups; talks probably were held with Austrian Social Democrats at Vienna, presumably with Victor Adler, an acquaintance of Lenin. The unsolved question is whether Jodko approached Hanecki, or whether Hanecki, upon request of Lenin,[14] approached Jodko. The point is somewhat academic since Hanecki unquestionably was aware of Jodko's activities. It is significant that, according to Hanecki's memoirs, Vienna was well aware of Lenin; it can be surmised that they obtained the information from Hanecki himself or from Jodko, or both. Colonel Oscar von Hranilovic, a Croat, who later became chief of the Austrian intelligence service, was in charge of the overall operation.

Thus, it is likely that Hanecki informed Lenin of the Austrians' willingness to assist the revolutionaries. It is possible that Lenin held his conference in Prague, in part, to test the validity of this information. Since he was unable to settle his affairs with the German socialists, he must have been eagerly seeking new arrangements. When *Pravda* became a reality, Lenin, in order not to compromise

[11]Krupskaya, p. 281.

[12]Ganetsky, *Vospominaniya o Lenine,* Moscow, 1933, Ch. II. An Okhrana report of November 28, 1913, establishes that Hanecki participated in conferences with the "left P.P.S." and the Jewish Bund. *See* Wolfe, *Three who made a Revolution,* p. 567.

[13]The Lenins, especially Krupskaya, and Kohn had been friendly since Siberia; Kohn's party affiliations were somewhat fluctuating but, at the time under discussion, he was a "left P.P.S."; i.e., he stood to the left of Pilsudski's party. Late in 1916 Krupskaya worked briefly with Kohn in Switzerland. During the war with Poland in 1920, Kohn participated in the Bolshevik puppet government. Lenin knew Hanecki from the Second, Fourth and Fifth Congresses.

[14]Lenin might have been stimulated by the war talk to write to Hanecki. There were at that time no indications about a possible conflict between Russia and Germany, but he may have heard rumors that some Austrian consulates in Russia, notably in Kiev, were distributing revolutionary literature.

his position as leader, was compelled to move closer to Russia. The new prospect, Krupskaya related, transformed Lenin into "another person . . . he became less irritable" and better able to concentrate. The depression, which had caused him to doubt that he would see "the next rise of the tide," had vanished.[15]

It required just two months to arrange for the move—an indication that the Austrian bureaucracy, which was among the world's most inefficient, was anxious to cooperate. It also indicates that proper communications channels had been established. Lenin's (and presumably Zinovyev's) various permits were secured by Hanecki, who probably operated through Polish Social Democratic members of parliament, specifically Diamand and Daszynski. The Lenins were escorted into Austria by Adelheid Popp, probably at the suggestion of Victor Adler. In Cracow itself, Lenin established good relations with the local police, who in one instance asked him to vouch for a Russian revolutionary who had been engaged as a courier for the Bolshevik organization.[16]

Thus, at this point in Lenin's career, his place of residence was chosen in conformity with the intelligence and strategic interests of the Austrian general staff. More accurately, Austria was preparing for war and had "deployed" Lenin for political warfare purposes. His main propaganda outlet, *Pravda,* was being published with the assistance of the tsarist political police and through the instrumentality of police agents.[17] His communications with Russia were handled in part through Pilsudski's apparatus; the frequent border crossings of his couriers took place under the noses of friendly Austrian (i.e., Polish) border guards.[18] Lenin felt himself to be in an excellent position.

[15]Krupskaya, 1942, p. 174.

[16]Krupskaya, 1959, p. 237.

[17]It is interesting to note that in his first letter to *Pravda,* on July 19, 1912, Lenin submitted an article by a local writer who later turned out to be an Austrian agent: Lenin insisted that the author be paid before publication.

[18]On December 23, 1912, Lenin wrote to Gorky with whom he had made peace after disputes about "god-seeking" and the Capri school: "We shall stay here for the time being, taking 'advantage of' the Poles' desperate hatred of tsarism." See *The Letters of Lenin,* p. 314.

Malinovsky

It is quite certain that, at the time, Lenin received no money from the extremely parsimonious Austrian government, itself devoid of funds for such operations. The Bolshevik legal press in Russia was permitted to engage in extensive propaganda, but the party papers were not self-supporting. *Pravda* sold at one kopek per copy, which at 25,000 subscriptions yielded 250 rubles a day or, roughly, 7,000 rubles a month. Yet in January, 1913, as Lenin wrote to Gorky, *Pravda* was operating at a daily deficit of fifty to sixty rubles, or a monthly deficit of close to 2,000 rubles.[1] The editors seem to have been paid fifty rubles; Lenin's and Krupskaya's income was irregular, apparently paid according to the number of his articles published. In the period of October, 1912, to February, 1913, Lenin averaged approximately 200 rubles a month. Deficits of this magnitude were not overwhelmingly burdensome. Russian citizens had been aroused by a slaughter of miners in the Lena Basin (April, 1912) ; collections from the workers and the bourgeoisie were producing good results.

By the summer of 1912, Lenin, though a collaborator, had as yet little influence on *Pravda*. By September, Stalin reappeared and insisted on having a hand in the editing of *Pravda*. But he was not about to follow Lenin's instructions: in one case Lenin sharply ordered him to publish his article "in a prominent place and in large type," an instruction that Stalin did not follow; Lenin sent him to Vienna to write a brochure on nationalism.

From September, 1912, onward, the Mensheviks were publishing their own paper, *Luch*, which rapidly developed as a dangerous competitor of *Pravda*. Both groups used their newspapers for organizing purposes. Moreover, by 1912, the unions, gathering strength, provided the Bolsheviks with an open forum. In a reversal of roles, the Mensheviks attempted to structure an illegal party machine. By the end of 1912, the Bolshevik and Menshevik Duma deputies wanted to merge *Pravda* and *Luch*. Lenin and the police opposed the proposal. Lenin called to his aid Jacob M. Sverdlov, an energetic young Communist from the Urals, who in the fall of 1912 was placed on the editorial board. Lenin and Krupskaya bombarded N. I. Podvoisky with letters (most of which were intercepted) calling for a complete purge of the paper, a reorganization, and more intense radicalism.[2] On February 9, 1913, Lenin wrote to Sverdlov that it was necessary to get his hands on the money (income and subscriptions). He also asked Sverdlov to dissolve the board of editors and

[1]Intercepted letters of January 10, 1913, Lenin to Gorky and February 9, 1914, Krupskaya to N. I. Podvoisky and "Andrei" (probably Vlassov). A letter of April 5, 1913, by Krupskaya suggests that at that time there were only 5,000 subscribers. *Pravda*, of course, was not the only Bolshevik publication which was running a deficit. (Documents in Hoover Institution)

[2]Malinovsky had been instructed to bring about a split within the Bolshevik organization. P. P. Zavarzin, *Zhandarmy i Revoliutsionery* (Paris: Published by author, 1930), p. 195ff. This was traditional; Plekhanov's break from Narodnaya Volya which led to the establishment of the second revolutionary party, the Social Democrats, had been engineered by a police agent, Degayev. (Souvarine, *op. cit.*, p. 136.)

appoint his own assistants but to retain Malinovsky as the publisher. (At this point, another Duma deputy, Badayev, officially ran the paper.) However, on February 10, Sverdlov and other Bolsheviks were arrested, about a week after the purge, and the reorganization had been initiated. It is apparent that Malinovsky eliminated anyone who could challenge him. Yet the reorganization was carried out as Lenin had demanded it. And the letter, which informed him about the arrests, also made it known that 3,000 rubles might be raised.

Now Lenin, at long last *Pravda's* chief writer, was provided with an opportunity to display his journalistic talents. Actually, due to the arrests, *Pravda* was lacking writers; they simply needed Lenin. The articles which Lenin contributed to *Pravda* were factual, well informed, often timely, always pungent and politically effective. Lenin was definitely *au courant*. Evidence indicates that the number of subscribers quadrupled within a year. Lenin carefully planned his strategy. Sending one rude letter after another, he insisted that his troops in Petrograd and his family send him books, newspapers and magazines. Constantly complaining that he was not receiving enough material and that the mail was late, he supplemented his information by interviewing comrades who were passing through. Lenin also carefully studied *Pravda's* subscriber lists to determine prospects for party membership and to plan the establishment of new cells in suitable locations.

Early in 1913, plans were discussed with a publisher concerning the printing of a *large* daily newspaper. In one (intercepted) letter to the prospective publisher, Lenin explained that two papers were actually needed, one to be sold for five kopeks, and the other for one kopek; *Pravda* was to be used as the second paper. Books and brochures also were to be published. He implored the publisher to be more successful than in the spring of 1912—a cryptic remark which, however, seems to be relevant to the establishment of *Pravda*.[3] A small Social Democratic publishing house, Priboi, was established along "capitalistic lines" and given a party subvention of 350 rubles, but the larger newspaper was never published. Evidently, the police wanted to keep activities on a small scale. In fact, during the summer of 1913, *Pravda* was confiscated so often that Lenin considered establishing an illegal central organ. The police learned of this plan by June 12, 1913, and apparently took steps to squelch it.

During December, 1912, the Central Committee met at Cracow. The police department reported secretly on April 10, 1913, that personnel changes were made in *Pravda* and the danger of police

---

[3]These negotiations may have taken place with Bonch-Bruyevich, but this is a tentative identification.

infiltration was discussed. The Committee decided to send a Duma member to Kautsky with a request for 30,000 rubles; concurrently, Krupskaya instructed Podvoisky to have letters written to German socialists expressing approval of Lenin. It is not known whether the Germans were again opposed, but such a sum might have sustained *Pravda* to the end. However, *Pravda* went through several more financial crises. Another resolution appointed Malinovsky candidate to the International Socialist Bureau.

The arrangement, with Malinovsky functioning as number three man in the party,[4] led the police to decide upon a still bolder maneuver: they asked Malinovsky to run for a seat in the Duma. To legalize his candidacy, they expunged Malinovsky's criminal record —apparently three convictions for theft[5] were involved (1894, 1896, 1899) —and to ensure his victory they arrested his chief opponent. The election campaign cost them no less than 14,000 rubles. As soon as he was seated, Malinovsky was elected Deputy Chief of the Social Democratic Duma faction and Chief of the Bolshevik group.

Malinovsky became the most radical of all Russian parliamentarians, "almost a future Bebel," Lenin was to write later.[6] He was an excellent speaker with an impressive presence—he, too, was a redhead. Because Malinovsky was a poor writer, Lenin provided many of the ideas for his speeches, acting as ghost writer for some of his major pronouncements. Not to be outdone, the police, in the person of its director, Byeletsky, participated in this venture, primarily as a censor, but sometimes as a writer. Several of Malinovsky's masterpieces were written and edited jointly by Lenin and the Okhrana.

This was a remarkable set-up—but did Lenin know that he was "cooperating" with the police? Krupskaya made a feeble attempt to describe Malinovsky as a drunkard, but Lenin was personally very fond of him. That Malinovsky disclosed his police connections— which dated back to 1905—at his first meeting with Lenin is most unlikely. But subsequently, at the latest in 1914, Lenin learned the truth. During the war Lenin remained in contact with Malinovsky, three times affirming his confidence in print, in late 1914 and early 1917.[7] Malinovsky, while serving in the army, was taken prisoner by the Germans and participated in the revolutionary indoctrination of prisoners of war in German camps. This effort, similar to the pro-

[4]In their code, the Bolsheviks actually described Malinovsky as No. 3. (Letter of June 7, 1913, from Krupskaya to Podvoisky).

[5]According to another version, he had been convicted once for attempted rape (Futrell, p. 181). *See* also Walter, p. 214f.

[6]Walter, p. 224. Lenin also called him an "eagle" and a "remarkable worker-leader", *ibid.,* p. 216, 225; Wolfe, *Three who made a Revolution,* p. 542.

[7]Grigori Aronson, *Rossiya nakanunye revolyutsii* (New York: Novoye Russkogye Slovo, 1962), p. 53 ff.

gram which the Japanese inflicted on Russian prisoners of war during 1904 and 1905, was sponsored by both the German and Austrian governments. After the revolution Malinovsky insisted on returning from Germany to Lenin's Russia.[8] By this time, Malinovsky's connection with the police had become common knowledge. Yet Malinovsky firmly expected vindication by Lenin; unless we assume that he was insane, he must have had good reason for such belief. Interestingly enough, Krupskaya, after some sympathetic remarks, wrote: "The February revolution showed him up in his true colors. He returned to Russia of his own free will after the October revolution and gave himself up to the Soviet authorities."[9] Such actions would hardly be those of a police agent.

Malinovsky, in many ways a careerist, did much for money, but he also seems to have been a genuine revolutionary. In 1917, Lenin stated to an investigating committee that he did not quite see what the police derived from Malinovsky's services; assuredly, the Bolsheviks had been benefiting most from his activities.[10] Lenin's presumption was correct. During his trial in 1918, Krylenko, the prosecutor, stated that history had yet to decide whether Malinovsky had been useful or harmful to the revolution.[11] In 1923, Zinovyev, who probably knew the background of this affair, confirmed that Malinovsky did help the Bolsheviks. More than anyone else, Malinovsky contributed to the establishment of *Pravda* and *Rabochi Putj*, Zinovyev stressed. His behavior in German camps, vouched for in "dozens of letters" from co-prisoners, indicated that he really was a genuine Bolshevik. Yet, mantained Zinovyev, about a hundred of "our best people" were arrested because of him. Zinovyev hinted that his execution in 1919 was an act of vengeance by individuals he had betrayed. Was Sverdlov the avenger? Or perhaps Stalin? The fact is that during his trial (November 5, 1918), Malinovsky delivered a six-hour speech which was never published; the trial proceedings, too, were kept secret. The death sentence was pronounced and executed almost immediately—to prevent Lenin from saving him. Prosecutor Krylenko had induced Malinovsky's wife to testify against him and alleged that Malinovsky, in his closing remarks, stated that the death sentence had been deserved. According to Krylenko, Malinovsky asked to be executed—establishing the precedent for Stalin's purge trials during the 1930's.

It is said the Lenin attended the trial; this is unlikely. At the time Lenin was recuperating from two bullet wounds and, although

---

[8]Documents in file of German Foreign Office.

[9]Krupskaya, *op. cit.*, p. 276.

[10]For this text, *see* Wolfe, p. 553f.

[11]Aronson, *op. cit.*, p. 57.

he may have been present for a few moments, he did not possess the physical strength to sit through the lengthy proceedings. It is generally agreed that the trial upset him greatly. Contrary to expectation, however, he did not endeavor to save Malinovsky, perhaps because he lacked energy, or did not wish to oppose those of his aides whom he now needed, or possibly because he was simply too slow. But there occurred a curious incident: according to Krylenko, Malinovsky denied ever having called Lenin "a servant of the Austrian police," to which Krylenko countered that there was "contradictory evidence" in the Okhrana file.[12] Was this a broad hint to Lenin not to interfere?

Did the trial show that Malinovsky was a traitor to bolshevism? We do not know, but we may surmise that Lenin was told this. A one-day trial, in which the accused speaks for six hours, and which must evaluate a large and complex quantity of incomplete evidence, cannot be expected to arrive at a considered judgment. Malinovsky had returned voluntarily to obtain justice; and Lenin, for many years, steadfastly believed in his innocence.

Presumably Malinovsky, probably some time during 1913, succeeded in explaining to Lenin that he was under police orders but was a devoted Bolshevik whose loyalty would remain with the revolution. Lenin, excellent tactician that he was, took advantage of the opportunity. It was not the first time that the revolutionaries had infiltrated the police. One of the best known cases occurred in 1879, when *Land and Liberty* planted Salomon Ryss (Medved) into the center of the Third Section (as the political police were then called). This agent protected the terrorists of the *People's Will* who were plotting to kill the Tsar. Discovered in January, 1881, he was hanged, but by that time preparations were almost completed. Without the agent's work, Alexander II would probably not have been assassinated.[12a]

Lenin was no novice at this type of work. Ever eager to place agents into hostile organizations, he for years maintained an intelligence service among the Mensheviks. Why not then plant agents within the police? An idealistic Communist, Angelica Balabanov, years later remonstrated against this practice. Lenin looked at her ruefully and asked, "What can life do with you?", adding that he desired agents to infiltrate wherever possible.

Was this *Realpolitik* according to Marx? In 1850, Marx wrote:

> The conspirators maintain contact with the police, they clash with them continually; they hunt spies just as the spies hunt them . . . No wonder . . . the short jump from the professional conspirator to the paid police spy . . . is made so often.[13]

[12]N. V. Krylenko, *Za pyat lyet, 1918-1922 g.g.* (Moscow-Petrograd, 1923), p. 345.
[12a]For other cases, see Wolfe, p. 547.
[13]*Werke*, vol. 7, p. 274.

Marx stressed that conspiracy is self-defeating, especially if it is the primary revolutionary tactic utilized.

Vladimir Burtsev, who acted as a sort of chief of counter-intelligence for all Russian revolutionary groups, related that Malinovsky came to him in Paris in 1914, bringing a letter from Lenin suggesting a common plan against police infiltration.[14] Malinovsky told Burtsev that only he, Lenin, and Burtsev knew of this project.

Can we assume that Lenin would have placed such information in the hands of a double-agent? If so, perhaps Lenin discovered Malinovsky's role after January-February, 1914; this is also unlikely. The action might have been a cover maneuver intended to protect Malinovsky—and Lenin's own safety. Lenin was then in Paris and, in view of the importance of the matter, he would probably have accompanied Malinovsky. But perhaps Malinovsky undertook the trip on his own initiative, not especially to obtain information, but to ingratiate himself with Burtsev, who had excellent informants within the police; or again, perhaps Malinovsky had been ordered by the police to see that Burtsev and Lenin aided him by providing a cover story.

When Malinovsky was tried, he told the tribunal that he had repeatedly attempted to inform Lenin of the "abominations" in his past, but that Lenin refused to listen. In any event, Burtsev later disclosed that "according to Malinovsky, Lenin understood and could not help understanding, that his [Malinovsky's] past concealed not merely ordinary criminality but that he was a provocateur." But in 1914, Burtsev declared before a commission of inquiry that he had considered the evidence and believed the charge to be "improbable."[15]

In April, 1913, Lenin traveled to Leipzig, Germany, where he reportedly lectured on revolutionary conditions in Russia. In a letter sent to Russia, he cautiously described these conditions as a period of organizing.[16] In May, Lenin went to Poronin, a beautiful resort town in the Tatra mountains, where he found life more pleasant

[14]The Prague conference decided to enlist the services of Burtsev to improve Bolshevik defenses against "provocation." The conference had been impatient with the security commission that did exist and criticized it for its slow work. Lenin was charged to set up a new three-man board and accelerate the work. It took him two years for making the initial step to carry out this instruction. (Tsiavlovsky, *op. cit.*, p. 102).

[15]Krupskaya, p. 276.

[16]Intercepted letter of January 18, 1913. From letters to his sister Anna, it appears that his mother was then living in Saratov and that sister Maria had been exiled to Vologodsk during May, 1912.

than in Cracow. He rented what appears to have been a large and comfortable house.[17]

The change of location was largely prompted by Krupskaya's poor state of health. Unlike Lenin, who was feeling healthy and did a lot of walking in the summer and ice-skating in the winter, Krupskaya was weak, tired, dizzy, and suffered from headaches, fainting spells and trembling hands. Her heart was functioning poorly; she suffered from an irregular heartbeat. Despite electric treatment, her eyes and throat were bulging even more.[18] By June it became apparent that she had to be operated on for thyroid disorder, a condition Krupskaya described as "goiter." Lenin believed in always seeking the best doctors available. (When he ruled Russia, he advised Gorky not to seek help from Bolshevik doctors but instead to go to Germany or Switzerland.) On the advice of Bagocki, Lenin took Krupskaya to Vienna for consultations, and from there to Berne where I. V. Shklovsky, a delegate to the Third Congress, rented for them a house with an adjoining garden.

Lenin selected Dr. Emil Theodor Kocher[18a] to perform the surgery —the best and most costly choice he could have made. Dr. Kocher had become a Nobel Prize Laureate in 1909 for having succeeded in excising the thyroid gland and was an innovator in surgical technique as well. To Lenin's anger, the world-famous specialist was so busy that Krupskaya was compelled to wait for several days before he examined her. After she rested in the hospital for two weeks, the operation was performed on July 26, 1913, for a duration of three hours without anesthesia. Lenin was so impressed with the doctor he later recommended Kocher to another Bolshevik who was suffering from Graves' disease. Late in August, 1913, after two weeks in the Swiss mountains, Krupskaya was well enough to travel. After a few days in Munich, where according to his wife Lenin displayed an expert knowledge of beer, the Lenins returned to Poronin. In April, 1914, Lenin wrote that her trouble would disappear "soon."[19]

[17]A partial picture (Shotman, *op. cit.,* p. 303) indicates at least eight windows and two doors on the first floor, and at least one room on the second. Their Cracow apartment, as Lenin's mother wrote on August 19, 1912, to sister Maria (then in Saratov prison), consisted of two rooms with bath and shower, gas and electricity. A maid, Agasha, who had lived with the Lenins during the summer, was coming every day. *See* Walter, p. 220.

[18]Letter of May 12, 1913, by Mother Ulyanov from Feodosiya, Crimea, to Maria Ulyanov. Lenin had written these details to his brother-physician Dimitri, asking for his advice.

[18a]See Edgar Bonjour, *Theodar Kocher,* Berne, Haupt, 1950. Kocher's great accomplishment was that he reduced thyroid mortality from 18 to .5—1%. He also was considered one of the outstanding professors of surgery of his time.

[19]*Letters of Lenin,* p. 326.

Her health continued to fluctuate, but she was never really well again.

While Krupskaya was in the hospital, Lenin traveled through Swiss towns, where he spoke on the national question, a subject that must have surprised his socialist audiences. After he returned, party finances improved. The police reported on December 16, 1913, (New Style) that Lenin had printed in Austria 10,000 copies of a party resolution and 50,000 proclamations for the anniversary of Bloody Sunday; the materials were scheduled to be smuggled into Russia.

What had become of Inessa Armand? A short while after Lenin had settled in Cracow, she passed through the city, along with Georg Safarov; they were on their way to Russia allegedly to help in the Duma election campaign.[20] Actually, Lenin had asked her to organize border crossings and to examine the affairs of *Pravda*. She met N. V. Krylenko near the border in Lublin, made the required arrangements, and proceeded to St. Petersburg where she set up a regional bureau. She and Safarov were arrested on September 14, 1912, but it is not certain that she was correctly identified. She was released sometime in the summer of 1913. It is not clear why her imprisonment was so short; according to one source, there was not sufficient evidence; according to her daughter, her "husband," who visited her several times in jail, freed her on bail because she was ill.[21] As soon as she was released, she proceeded to Helsingfors and from there escaped with the passport of a deputy to the Finnish Sejm. She arrived in Poronin later in September, in time to participate in the so-called "summer conference" of the Bolsheviks.[22]

[20]On the occasion of the tricentenary of the Romanov dynasty, an amnesty was declared on February 21, 1913, and many revolutionaries returned home. Zinovyev also wanted to go and apparently asked his sister Lia about conditions. On March 13, 1913, Lia replied that she visited the vice director of police and was told there was nothing in the file which prevented his return; yet she would not really rely on this information. As to his becoming a Lutheran in Cracow, this would give him the right to reside in St. Petersburg and, also, theoretically to his wife and child, but in practice they would have to become Lutherans, too. Lia ended her letter with greetings from Papa who wanted to have the whole family together for (Jewish) Easter. The Bolshevik revolutionary preferred his safety to the family reunion and the Jewish festivity, and thus the Lutheran Church failed to acquire an unnecessary member.

[21]Inna Armand, *loc. cit.*, p. 80.

[22]This conference was attended, in addition to Malinovsky, by Alexei I. Lobov, who after the revolution was found to have been a police agent. He was shot on June 30, 1918. Lobov worked in Moscow and as one of his functions was checking on Malinovsky. He caused many arrests and was considered one of the major provocateurs. It is interesting that in 1912 Stalin traveled to Helsingfors and obtained from Shotman a passport to enable him to travel to Cracow. He appeared accompanied by Comrade Valentina N. Lobova who died in 1924 of tuberculosis (Shotman, *op. cit.*, p. 290). Lobova, of course, was Mrs. Lobov, and attended together with Stalin the Central Committee meeting at Cracow during December, 1912. Lobov began working for the Moscow police after March, 1913.

Inessa had lost none of her energy. But she had developed, according to Krupskaya, "symptoms of tuberculosis." She, however, "was just brimming with vitality and exuberant good spirits."[23] This description is patently contradictory, especially since Krupskaya was endeavoring to give the impression that they had barely known her in Paris but now were really enjoying her presence "in a small and friendly circle."

Inessa rented a room in Cracow, in the same house in which Kamenev lived.[24] The entire Cracow group, Krupskaya wrote, became attached to Inessa and even Mme. Krupskaya, the elder, who had displayed dislike for her in Paris, "grew very fond of her and often visited her to have a chat and a smoke. It seemed cosier and livelier when Inessa was present."[25] Inessa insisted that the Lenins attend Beethoven concerts, and she sometimes played the piano for them herself. "Ilyich was particularly fond of the *Sonate Pathétique* and he always asked her to play it."

In her memoirs, Krupskaya went to great pains to suggest that Inessa's affair with Lenin had terminated. She hinted that Inessa now was a "close comrade of G. I. Safarov with whom she had traveled to Russia and with whom she was arrested." It is unlikely that Krupskaya invented this liaison; yet, Safarov was in jail.

Krupskaya noted Inessa's quarters in Cracow, but she avoided mentioning that where Inessa was living in Poronin something like a *ménage à trois* had been established. Krupskaya related that she herself enjoyed walking with Inessa (and Ilyich) through the beautiful countryside. Of course, still only a few weeks after a serious operation and suffering from heart trouble, Krupskaya was in no condition to go for walks, especially the "long walks" of which she wrote. Those long walks were taken by Lenin and Inessa alone.

Inessa was now an experienced revolutionary. Adept with party jargon and familiar with Lenin's tastes, Inessa was probably the only person whom Lenin treated gently. She was highly intelligent and not afraid to oppose Lenin whenever she disagreed. Lenin took pains to educate her further and helped her write the articles which she wrote as "Lena (or, Illena) Blonina"—*blon* means "Meadow" in Polish. The first name is self explanatory;[26] the second is an allusion to those walks. Subsequently, she used the pseudonym "Petrova"; earlier Lenin had occasionally called himself "Petrov."

In October, they all returned to Cracow, and in December

---

[23]Krupskaya, p. 267f.

[24]Wolfe, "Lenin and Inessa Armand" (p. 103) dryly added to Krupskaya's statement: "The Kamenevs lived on an upper floor in the same building as the Ulyanovs."

[25]Krupskaya, 1942, p. 201.

[26]Years later, when after the revolution she edited *Pravda's* "woman page," she changed to "Yelena."

Inessa went to Paris. Originally, it was planned that she remain in Cracow and bring her children from Russia, but after long talks with Krupskaya "about women's work," she discovered that life in the Polish town was isolated and that she needed other outlets "for her abundant energies." Perhaps Lenin, in deference to Krupskaya, was making another attempt to break off. Yet shortly after her departure the two again met in Vienna and Paris.

Actually, Inessa's abundant energies, together with those of sister Anna Yelizarova, were used to produce *Rabotnitsa,* a magazine for female revolutionaries. This was not an unsuccessful venture: the police confiscated only three of the seven issues published. The idea originated with Lenin, who perhaps had an eye on American money: the emancipation of women was then a burning topic. The source of the money is not clear, though Inessa was definitely involved with the financing.

Krupskaya, Ludmilla N. Stal, and Inessa constituted the editorial board abroad. Correspondence reveals that Inessa addressed Krupskaya by the second person singular ("thou"), and Krupskaya wrote to Anna that Inessa had stronger principles than did Ludmilla. "Whatever she touches, she does well." In April, 1914, after reading *Rabotnitsa No. 3* (which was confiscated), Lenin wrote to Inessa: *"Mes félicitations à Ludm(illa) et toi!"* The "toi" and the lack of praise of Krupskaya, the other foreign editor, are revealing.[27]

Early in January, Lenin passed through Berlin and Paris on his way to Brussels where he delivered an address and discussed party matters with Lettish Bolsheviks. In Paris, he attended to party matters jointly with Malinovsky. This *séjour* in the French capital provided an amusing incident. Malinovsky (who, among other things, was interested in French picture postcards) purchased a reproduction by Boecklin, a third-rate romantic painter fashionable in sentimental petty bourgeois families. Proudly showing the picture to Lenin, he was surprised by the comment: "I knew that it would not go without Boecklin's *Isle of the Dead*. This is like hypnosis, people go after it. There are pictures which are a thousand times better." Perhaps this proves that Lenin possessed artistic taste after all. Lenin's attention to Boecklin and other painters had been drawn, a short while before, by Nikolai Bukharin, a young and gifted theoretician—and another redhead. Although Krupskaya once asserted that Lenin "was fond of paintings," there is little confirmation for this statement. She stressed that in the arts Lenin was "an out-and-out nationalist."[28]

[27]*Istoricheskii Arkhiv* (1955), No. 4, pp. 26ff.

[28]Krupskaya, 1959, p. 269; also 259. She stated that Lenin read *Anna Karenina* "about a hundred times." They left their fiction library in Paris but this was only "an insignificant part of what we had in St. Petersburg." A strange statement, for

Lenin returned via Leipzig where he stayed for twelve days, lecturing on the right of self-determination. By the middle of February, he was back in Cracow, initiating a campaign in *Pravda* on the national question. In one instance he declared that the national problem was being handled far better in Austria than in the tsarist empire. In April he wrote a Duma speech on the national question in Russia.

Lenin had put Stalin to work on the national question—a means of getting Stalin out of the way. When Stalin produced his manuscript, Lenin was unenthused. Finding faults with it, he began writing on the subject himself. This was only natural, for the national question was the foremost political problem of Austria-Hungary. The principle of self-determination had been introduced into the world socialist movement by the Poles and was exciting the Polish revolutionaries on whose support Lenin was dependent. Lenin remembered that, during the 1905 revolution, the struggle for national independence had garnered more recruits than the class struggle. There existed an organizational problem, since the Bolshevik party was comprised of several national groupings; party unity was imperative. The issue demanded immediate attention. But, the very concept of nationalism was the ideological weapon which the Austrian-Hungarian general staff intended to use against the tsarist empire. A Vienna university professor, who had taught many Russian students, including Bolsheviks, and had served as a clandestine collaborator of the Foreign Office, told a Ukrainian revolutionary that "Lenin was on Austria's side."[29]

On May 8, 1914, Malinovsky resigned from the Duma. During April he had been penalized by exclusion from fifteen Duma sessions. Shortly before his return, the Social Democrats drafted a radical declaration which, though supposedly kept secret, nevertheless became known to the President of the Duma. The information had been leaked from the Okhrana which also, apparently, let it be known that Malinovsky was a *sotrudnik*. This leak may have originated from a highly placed Okhrana officer who opposed "provocation" tactics.[30] Or did the police suspect that Malinovsky was not fully their tool? Malinovsky soon learned that his secret had been discovered. He probably felt relieved, for, as he later testified, his mental condition was beginning to disable him from

---

when Lenin lived in St. Petersburg, 1893-1897, he was not yet married. During 1905-1906, in the midst of a revolution, he scarcely had time to amass a substantial library of novels.

[29]Prof. Hans Uebersberger told this to Stepankowski.

[30]On some of the circumstances of Malinovsky's release from police service, *see* Wolfe, *Three who made a Revolution*, p. 549f.

continuing in his double role. He accepted a handsome gratuity from the police—and joined Lenin. This was remarkable: if Malinovsky had been a genuine informer, he would have disappeared. If he had been a true scoundrel, he could have made a good deal of money by writing about what he knew. But he went to the man whom he had betrayed and remained with his party.

With liberal-minded police officers fanning rumors that Malinovsky was a police agent, a few Bolsheviks became convinced of the truth of these stories. The Mensheviks accused Malinovsky openly in the press; many Bolsheviks resented his resignation and called him a deserter. Lenin ignored the hubbub at first, finally releasing sentimental "wishy-washy" statements. One of his followers sent him a telegram requesting a firm stand. Lenin wired back: "Who—from where?" Infuriated, the unknown Bolshevik wrote Lenin that the best answer to this question would have been: "Gladstone from Spanish parliament." He, furthermore, accused Lenin of negligence.[31] Lenin finally (in No. 4 of *Rabochy*) attested to Malinovsky's "political honesty"; this, of course, was still equivocal wording. He also requested that the Mensheviks agree to have the matter decided in a Swiss court, knowing full well that it would be impossible to obtain suitable witnesses.[32] A party trial [33] was held and Lenin supported Malinovsky. Naturally, the evidence against Malinovsky (which included his resignation) was inconclusive. But Malinovsky was staying at Poronin. Lenin was undoubtedly skillful enough to obtain the truth from him. The verdict, as the three judges wired to *Pravda,* was that they were "absolutely convinced of Malinovsky's political honesty." Malinovsky published a letter in *Pravda,* stating that he discontinued his political activity for personal reasons, but that he remained "a Bolshevik adherent."[34] The seeming gullibility of the eternally suspicious Lenin[35] can be explained only by his access to information of which the other Bolsheviks were unaware. General Spiridovich was later to assert that Lenin knew all about the case. The fact is that Malinovsky remained loyal to Lenin until his death—and Lenin remained loyal to Malinovsky *almost* to the latter's execution.

---

[31]Intercepted letter from St. Petersburg to Lenin, Poronin, May 24, 1914.

[32]Paul Olberg, *Vorwärts,* May 1, 1957.

[33]The tribunal consisted of Lenin, Zinovyev and Hanecki; the latter who knew all about secret operations, conducted the investigation (Futrell, p. 181). No documents about this trial have been published.

[34]Quoted from Shub, p. 126.

[35]In 1913 a revolutionary who was accused of being a police agent came to Lenin and asked for his assistance. Lenin made every effort to determine the truth of this case. *See* Shotman, *op. cit.,* p. 302f.

War is Coming

In April, 1914, political demonstrations took place throughout Russia. A protest strike was held in St. Petersburg in response to the alleged food "poisoning" of female factory workers. Sympathy strikes occurred in other cities, and Malinovsky, still in office, indulged in a good deal of oratory on "poisoning." The Petersburg Bolsheviks called for a general strike similar to that of 1905, but were unsuccessful. On May 14, 250,000 workers were striking in Petersburg, but only there and in Tiflis was the participation significantly large. A protracted strike in the Baku oil industry began on June 10, purportedly because of a plague epidemic among the workers.

On June 28, 1914, the assassination at Sarajevo of the Austrian heir to the throne plunged the world into crisis. Like almost all groups, the socialists were afraid of war. The Second International swung into action. To prevent the catastrophe, European socialists considered it necessary to reunify the Russian Social Democratic party. For this purpose a conference was called at Brussels, and Axelrod and Luxemburg were asked to write a paper considering methods by which Russian socialists could be reunified. Lenin, wishing to avoid a confrontation, did not himself go. Instead, he sent Inessa, arming her with a vitriolic speech rejecting unification on the grounds that the Bolsheviks were the only Social Democratic group of importance. However, the International was not satisfied and dispatched Emile Vandervelde, a Belgian socialist, to investigate.

A letter which Lenin wrote on July 15 to Inessa is *sui generis* among his writings. This letter, naturally, was written in the second person singular. After instructing her to argue that only the Bolsheviks constitute a party—the others being merely the "fiction of a bloc or little groups"—he added: "I am sure that you are one of those people who develop and grow, who become stronger and bolder, when they are standing alone on a responsible post. Therefore I refuse to believe the pessimists who say, you would scarcely be able, etc. This is sheer nonsense! I don't believe it! You will do this very well! With your skill at words, you'll smash them all."[1] From Lenin this was highest praise extended to a professional revolutionary; the personal attachment, however, is evident.

The purpose of establishing a legal press had been to develop mass support. The Okhrana no longer was in a position in which it could simply suppress revolutionary publications. Hence it had to play a sophisticated game. It "supported" the legal press, in its

[1]For further comments on this letter, *see* Wolfe, "Lenin and Inessa Armand," p. 106f.

fashion, for the purpose of splitting the revolutionary movement and depriving it of mass support. The record is clear: *Pravda,* at its peak, had a circulation of 50,000 to 60,000 copies. During March, 1913, circulation was 30,000 to 32,000 and on holidays 40,000 to 42,000. By the spring of 1914, readership had decreased to about 20,000; *Luch* had ceased publication in the fall of 1913.

This decline did not necessarily indicate that the Russian "proletariat" was turning away from the revolution. However, the Bolshevik "line" and the incessant feuding over trivial points lost many former adherents. Bolshevik cells operated in many factories, although there was no effective organization. The grand design of using the daily newspaper to create a revolutionary organization and, through a growing organization a unified cell in every town, to enlarge the newspaper's circulation, in turn, had been unsuccessful.[2]

But presently *Pravda* was again increasing its circulation. Vandervelde found that it was up from 35,000 to 40,000. Lenin argued that it had actually reached 48,000 (against 16,000 of a "liquidator" paper) ; therefore, he maintained, his group represented the large majority of the workers' movement, while the other parties consisted of general staffs without armies. Plekhanov commented that Lenin would not make peace because he was unwilling to release his money.

What money? Did the Bolsheviks uncover a major financial resource? Collections inside Russia, "to support strikes," yielded a few thousand rubles. Lenin was requesting money from Switzerland, and his old friend, Gorky, with whom he was on good terms during that period, may have been offering aid. Lenin received a salary and was paid for his articles. There existed no financial crisis; yet, neither was there an evident source of income.

Some recent Soviet disclosures indicate that Plekhanov may well have been correct. During the fall of 1913, the Bolsheviks decided to call a congress. Initially, the congress was to be held at Poronin or Cracow, but a Central Committee conference of April 15-17, 1914, decided to convene the congress at Vienna, shortly before the assembling of the Second International, scheduled to meet at Vienna on August 26, 1914.

But a congress required money. On December 14, 1913, Krupskaya inquired of Petersburg, from whom 2,000 rubles had been obtained: "It isn't from Pryanik, is it?" She requested half of the money, asserting that Lenin's operation in Galicia was without funds. "Pryanik," it transpired, was A. I. Konovalov, member of the

---

[2]Intercepted letter by Krupskaya to Krug of February 5, 1914. By "unified" was meant the inclusion of all nationalities into the party. (Furthermore, the aim was to absorb all other Social Democratic groups.) In this letter Krupskaya stressed the necessity of combining legal with illegal work.

progressist party, an industrialist, and one of Russia's wealthiest men.[3]

This was by no means a chance gift, but was rather a contribution in accord with a deliberate program. In February, 1914, Konovalov, together with two other millionaires, P. P. Ryabushinsky and one of the Morozovs, founded an "information committee," consisting largely of middle-of-the-road and middle-class politicians. The objective of this committee was to coordinate anti-governmental efforts of oppositional and revolutionary groups. The strategy was obvious (and in some ways modeled after the "bourgeois" strategy of 1905) : by strengthening the revolutionary groups it was hoped to pressure the Tsar into ever bolder reforms and thus to accelerate the trend toward constitutionalism or even democracy.

The Konovalov group, in all likelihood, was closely associated with the Free Masons. Russian Masonry, though it operated in a highly clandestine manner, had established significant international connections. The Germans occasionally used Masonic contacts for purposes of political warfare, but their influence on Russian Masonry was weak. Whether the more influential French had a hand in this venture is questionable: they did not suspect that war was imminent and may have been hoped for reform within allied Russia.

In any event, Lenin (signing as Frey), on March 4, 1914, wrote to Yelena F. Rozmirovich, secretary of the Bolshevik Duma faction, asking about possible sources of money, whether any rich people were being solicited, and urging that—since his own funds were depleted— finances be provided quickly.

Despite this lack of money, preparations for the congress were stepped up and efforts were made to select the Bolshevik representatives for the Congress of the International. The Bolsheviks could well proceed since, as the police reported on May 10, the information committee had eight days earlier promised 20,000 rubles for the party congress. The Bolsheviks negotiated with the committee through I. I. Skvortsov-Stepanov, party member since 1896 and one of the editors of *Nash Putj*; Skvortsov, a Mason, frequently functioned as Lenin's liaison officer with Masonic circles.[4] Skvortsov was entirely loyal to Lenin who apparently placed almost complete trust in him.[5]

During the April Central Committee meeting, as the police re-

[3]V. T. Loginov and A. M. Volodarskaya, "Podgotovka syezda bolshevistkoi partii v 1914g," *Istoricheskii Arkhiv* (1958), No. 6, pp. 3-35.

[4]Aronson, *op. cit.*, p. 131. In March, 1917, Skvortsov was present at the conference in the apartment of Kuskova, which established the provisional government.

[5]See exchange of letters between Lenin and Skvortsov of March 22 and 24, 1914, *Istoricheskii Arkhiv* (1959), No. 2, pp. 13-17.

ported forthwith, Lenin instructed Duma deputies Malinovsky and Petrovsky to negotiate on the payment of the promised money.[6]

In the meantime, a bombshell exploded: Malinovsky resigned from the Duma. He presented his resignation to Duma President M. V. Rodzianko, in the very presence of Konovalov. Perhaps this scene provides a clue to the police decision no longer to employ Malinovsky: they may have intended to prevent the emerging alliance between the revolutionaries and the middle-class reformers. If so, what better way was there than to prove to the naïve bourgeois politicians that the revolutionaries were corrupt and controlled by the police? Indeed when Petrovsky spoke to Konovalov, he was told that the matter of the large payment required further deliberation. But it also developed that 2,000 rubles had already been given to Malinovsky for the legal press (this probably was the payment referred to in Krupskaya's letter), and 3,000 rubles had been transmitted through Yelena Rozmirovich directly to Lenin—*this* payment had remained undisclosed to the party.[7]

By the end of May, Lenin, according to police reports, asked Skvortsov to resume negotiations and requested at least 10,000 rubles to begin work on the congress. In his letter of March 24, 1914, Lenin had told Skvortsov that it was not worthwhile to negotiate for less. Whether Konovalov paid, and how much, is not known. Soviet sources say that the money "apparently" was not obtained.[8] On July 17, Krupskaya wrote that the situation was desperate. "We cooked ourselves a dish of *kasha,* and now we have no money. Is there any hope?" But, on the same day, Lenin corresponded with Inessa about a meeting concerned with the preparation of the congress, exclaiming: "The situation is wonderful."[9] The Krupskaya letter, which was addressed to Moscow where the negotiations with Konovalov were being held, would indeed indicate that the bourgeoisie had finally realized what was happening, thanks to the police maneuver. But Lenin's letter suggests that another source of funds might have been found.

On July 14 to 15, a "political strike" at St. Petersburg brought 7,000 workers onto the streets. On July 16, 15,000 strikers, and on the next day 90,000, were mobilized. Some shootings occurred. On the 18th, 70,000 struck in Petersburg (but only 4,000 in Moscow) and on July 20, 130,000 Petersburg workers struck. The strikes were accompanied by large demonstrations. It seemed as if the revolu-

---

[6]*Istoricheskii Arkhiv, loc. cit.,* p. 10.

[7]*Ibid.,* p. 12f.

[8]*Ibid.,* p. 32.

[9]For Krupskaya's and Lenin's letters, *see Istoricheskii Arkhiv* (1958), No. 6, pp. 6 and 26.

tionary movement was rising from the ashes. What was happening?

On July 20, the president and premier of France arrived in Petersburg on a visit intended to warn Germany that the Franco-Russian alliance was very much alive. Since a large portion of the Petersburg police and garrison was used to guard the visitors and to march in parades, strikers and revolutionaries enjoyed considerable freedom of action.

How did the situation look from Berlin and Vienna? The Central Powers were not disinclined to fight, but they were most anxious to win a diplomatic victory without actually engaging in war. This did not seem impossible. For years, the Germans had been receiving two different types of intelligence reports. On the one hand, there existed considerable evidence indicating that a small group of Pan-Slavists, supported by Grand Duke Nikolai Nikolayevich and aided by the Montenegrin Grand Duchess Militsa working skillfully in the background, was plotting war. On the other, however, was weighty evidence that war, or even mobilization, would initiate revolution. No less an informant than Count Sergius Witte, a former prime minister, stated through an intermediary that Russia could not fight: thirty million non-Russians would act as spies and initiate civil war; in Finland and Poland revolutions would take place. Austria, he stated during February, 1913, was wise in defending herself against her enemies—the Russian political warfare infiltrators—"who stand already in the interior of her own home."

This sort of general information was supplemented by reports, beginning in 1913, on the re-emergence of the revolutionary movement. The mobilization of 1912-1913 had precipitated a certain amount of unrest among the reservists. The Germans and Austrians should have noted that *this* mobilization had *not* lead to revolution, and that there were indications that the railroad engineers and crews, who were predominantly Polish, would stir up trouble for the Russian army. On January 31, 1914, the embassy reported from St. Petersburg that the customary demonstrations on the anniversary of Bloody Sunday had been larger than ever before.[10] During March, strikes had occurred throughout the capital. About 40,000 strikers were involved but, the German ambassador, Count Friedrich Pourtalès, noted on March 28 that these strikes were clearly political in nature; they had no discernible cause and no demands were posed by the strikers. He stressed that the strikes were organized by "unknown agents."[11] Perhaps they constituted some sort of "dress rehearsal" for what was to follow.

[10]We know that Lenin had a large number of proclamations for this occasion.

[11]In view of the present disorganization of the German Foreign Office file, documents are identified by sender and date.

Strategy consists of action, not merely passive observation. To avoid war and obtain a free hand against Serbia, the Franco-Russian alliance would have had to be rendered inoperative. The Germans had already arranged disturbances in France, compelling the French government to enforce stringent internal security measures. By displaying to the French statesmen revolutionary unrest in Russia, the instability and military weakness of their eastern ally might be impressed upon them. In turn, the unrest might convince the Russian government that it should risk neither mobilization nor war, lest the long-predicted revolution overthrow them.

On July 21, the Petersburg Bolshevik committee distributed a leaflet requesting cessation of the strikes. It called for the strengthening of party organizations, emphasizing the need to mobilize the workers of the provinces, the peasants, and the soldiers, and to prepare for later demonstrations. On this day, 150,000 persons were on strike; *Pravda* was suppressed. On July 22, there were 120,000 strikers, on July 23, 135,000, and on July 24 (one day after the Austrian ultimatum to Serbia), 200,000 strikers. On the 25th, the strike movement declined. By July 27, 60,000 workers were still striking. Then, suddenly, the strikes subsided entirely. A few days later, Russia accepted the Austro-German challenge. The working premise of the war party had indeed been disclosed, long before this time, to a German diplomat by Peter N. Durnovo (who in 1914, however, opposed the war): war was required to crush the Duma (i.e., to undo the revolution of 1905) and to prevent future revolutions. "You mean a successful war?" Germany asked. "It does not matter," was the reply, "Russia remains Russia."[12]

Lenin knew that Engels had once told Gherman Lopatin that if unrest should occur in Russia, "Germany can exploit it to make gains at the expense of tsarism."[13] On July 18, Lenin wrote a letter to V. M. Kasparov,[14] his confidant in Berlin, inquiring about revolutionary developments in Russia. Lenin suspected something or he would have written directly to St. Petersburg.

Lenin played no role in this operation: the Germans had their own channels into the revolutionary movement (which, of course, does not mean that the series of strikes must be exclusively ascribed

[12]Stockholm to Berlin, March 9, 1915. For a highly prescient anti-war memorandum by Durnovo to the Tsar, of February, 1914, see F. A. Golder, *Documents of Russian History, 1914-1917* (New York: Century, 1927), pp. 3-24. Durnovo stated *int. al.*: "In the event of defeat, the possibility of which in a struggle with a foe like Germany cannot be overlooked, social revolution in its most extreme form is inevitable." (p. 21).

[13]See Wolfe, *Three who made a Revolution*, pp. 575 and 595, for other statements by Engels on a war between Russia and Germany.

[14]Kasparov was an expert on the national question. On his activities and correspondence with Lenin, *see* Krupskaya, p. 298.

to them or that they lacked "spontaneity"). Evidence indicates that the Germans were using impoverished aristocrats to serve as paymasters and masquerade as friends of the revolution.[15]

German reports from Russia, although belated, permit a glimpse at the real events. On July 23, three days after the French visitors had arrived, Pourtalès wired that the strikes could cause difficulties for the Russian government. Wilhelm II simply commented: "Yes." On the next day, Pourtalès was instructed to help the Austrian ambassador find intermediaries who could influence the local press financially, i.e., bribe politically important writers. This suggests, of course, that the Austrians took action before the Germans but, since Pourtalès never was very concerned about keeping Berlin informed, such an interpretation does not necessarily follow. On July 27, 1914, the German general consul at Moscow, reporting on labor unrest, added that the "workers" were bitterly opposed to mobilization—evidence, if this dispatch was to be believed, of the dangerous backfire effect possible in political warfare. On the same day, Pourtalès, in an ambiguously worded cable, announced: "Strike agitation under way." The very well informed and perspicacious daughter of the British ambassador bluntly asserted that the strikes were organized by German agents.[16]

No mass movements of this scope are entirely spontaneous. "Revolutionizing" tactics had been effectively utilized by Bismarck whenever that expert strategist wished to press the Tsar. In 1895, a secret fund had been authorized for use by the German embassy in St. Petersburg to obtain information and carry out various transactions by means of bribery. This operation was accomplished outside the embassy by a certain Freiherr von Stein, ostensibly a newspaper correspondent, who served till the end of 1913.[17] The operation first functioned on a small scale: less than 2,000 marks a year were expended between 1896 and 1898; but by 1913, Stein's salary alone amounted to 6,000 marks.

From March, 1914, onward, when another man was appointed—at the same salary—to this position, there are few records to be had.

---

[15]Information based on interviews with surviving German diplomats.

[16]Meriel Buchanan, *Diplomacy and Foreign Courts* (London: Hutchinson, 1928), p. 168. *See also* Alexander Spiridovitch, *Les dernières années de la cour de Tsarskoïe- Sélo (1910-1914)* (Paris: Payot, 1929), II, 478.

[17]Another Stein, a press man with the Christian name of Adolf, had a strong operation going during 1908. Through an official in the Russian Ministry of Interior, he placed articles into the Russian press. He proposed to enlarge his activities and requested money to set up a wire service. His proposal was sympathetically considered but it is not known whether the plan was accomplished. The Russian official, State Councillor von Grotthus, apparently continued working for the German and became involved, during the war, in a major espionage scandal, the so-called 'Myassoyedov Affair."

Yet there is located in the German Foreign Office files a document, dated a few months later, which indicates startling familiarity with the methods through which demonstrations and strikes could be organized in Russia. The document mentions the "wages" which the strikers must be paid daily; for strikes in the capital alone a fund of 1.5 million rubles was required. The author of this document is unknown.

Whether the strikes were spontaneous, called by the revolutionaries, organized by foreign agents, or resulted, as is most likely, from a combination of these factors, the tsarist government resolved to end them. They therefore used their own methods to suppress them. When, on July 21, the Bolsheviks endeavored to end the strikes, they undoubtedly feared a provocation, but it is most likely that the Okhrana agents operating within the revolutionary groups had already sprung into action. Yet the "masses" were paid by someone for waving the red flag; the "cadres" did not control their followers. The demonstrations were finally suppressed, but with difficulty. The police were aided by the national sentiment and war fever that were gripping the population. The revolutionary movement was crippled and the Bolsheviks seemed momentarily defeated. The liberal reform parties, by contrast, rejoiced at the prospects opened by the alliance between an autocratic Russia and a democratic Western Europe.

While war clouds were gathering and the socialists of all countries were preoccupied with the war danger, Lenin did not write a single line on this crisis. He busied himself with party matters. The Tories were not the only politicians who, in the face of catastrophe, tended to indulge in "business as usual." Even the assassination of Jean Jaurès seemed not to affect Lenin.[18]

It is said that when war finally came and the various socialist parties supported national defense, Lenin was stunned. Yet he had considered war inevitable.[19] At international congresses he had argued that since the socialists did not possess the strength to prevent war, war should be used to further the revolution.[20] For years he had been attacking those socialist leaders whose behavior now supposedly astounded him. In his opinion, many German socialists were lackeys

[18]Jaurès opposed the war. His removal greatly helped the French war party. In Russia, Rasputin was the main figure opposing the war. On the day before Serajevo, he barely escaped death by assassination; severely wounded, he was unable to influence events. The background of these two crimes has never been elucidated: obviously, the game of political warfare can be played by more than one side.

[19]At the end of January, 1913, Lenin wrote to Gorky that "a war between Austria and Russia would be a very useful thing for the revolution," though he doubted that such a war would occur. (*Sochineniya*, 4th ed., vol. 35, p. 48.)

[20]*See* Wolfe, p. 599f.

of the bourgeoisie, traitors, and counter-revolutionaries. Now he was surprised by the patriotism of the German Social Democrats.

Surely, there was no reason for astonishment. Lenin should have rejoiced at the position of the German socialist party, for had the German socialists decided to subvert the German war effort, tsarism would have emerged victorious. Only a few weeks earlier Lenin had described himself as the leader of four-fifths of the Russian proletariat. Yet he made not a single attempt to rally the Russian proletariat against the war. In reality, then, his own attitude was far more counter-revolutionary than that of the German comrades. He displaced his own guilt feelings by placing blame upon the German party which had nurtured him and which, by fighting tsarism, was following the injunctions of Marx, Engels, and Bebel.

War

Austria declared war on Serbia on July 28; Germany announced a state of war with Russia on August 1. For technical military reasons, Austria delayed, declaring war on Russia only on August 6, ten days after the first shots had been fired.

Lenin was a Russian citizen residing in Austria, close to the Russian border. It was to be expected that in time of war between Austria and Russia, Russian citizens would be placed under surveillance or interned. Hence, a cautious person, especially if he were a Russian revolutionary who intended to exploit the war actively for revolutionary ends, would not have voluntarily taken the chance of living in a country that was warring with Russia.

Lenin had the funds to allow him to depart for Switzerland without delay, but he did not budge from Galicia. On the contrary, on August 6, to prepare for war conditions, Lenin wrote to Copenhagen requesting that newspapers, letters and money be sent to Galicia.[1] He wanted "links" to be established through Scandinavia, to connect his headquarters with his followers in Russia. He must have had good reasons to assume that the Austrian authorities would not molest him or interfere with his political activities.

He had probably received some verbal guarantees of his freedom. Austria, however, was not a monolithic state: the excitement resulted in a spy scare and the gendarmes began to seek out Russian

[1]*Letters of Lenin*, p. 332f.

citizens. Lenin having just received some money from Russia,[2] the police may have thought that Lenin was a double agent. On August 7, Lenin's home was searched. The gendarmes suspiciously fingered lengthy statistical compilations; Lenin was told to report to the prison of Novy Targ.

The Russian police had received a report to the effect that Lenin did not possess sufficient money to get himself and his comrades out of prison and into Switzerland; hence he was waiting "impatiently" for Russian military forces to enter Cracow. On September 19, with Lenin already gone, the police department requested of the military that *Dvoryanin* (nobleman) V. I. Ulyanov and O. A. Radomyslki (Zinovyev) be brought to St. Petersburg. But Lenin had no intention of awaiting the approach of the Russian army which, for that matter, he did not expect to penetrate deeply into Austria.

The versatile Hanecki was asked for help; it was later alleged that he intervened with the Austrian Prime Minister, but it is more probable, as Krupskaya related, that he spoke to the district officer and helped Krupskaya compose a letter to Victor Adler, the cultured reformist chief of Austrian socialism. Adler, wanting to avoid summary proceedings, immediately went to the Austrian Minister of the Interior, Baron Heinold. In two conversations with him, he convinced Heinold that Lenin was a stronger opponent of tsarism than the Minister himself was. Thereupon, Heinold telegraphed the police at Cracow—confirming Adler's analysis of Lenin's political orientation. Cracow added that the arrest had been the error of a local gendarme. Two additional Social Democratic members of parliament, including Diamand, also interceded. Lenin was released on August 19—after a remarkably short period for Austria—and was permitted to settle in Vienna. Heinold explained the release by saying that Adler believed that "Ulyanov may render great services under present conditions."[3] He added that the same information was supplied by

[2]This was an inheritance of 4,000 rubles. The Lenins got the money out of Austria through a broker who "took exactly half of it for his fee." Krupskaya (*op. cit.,* p. 282) added that they lived "mainly on this money during the war, husbanding it so carefully that we still had some left on our return to Russia in 1917. And it was this money . . . that served as evidence" in 1917 for the contention that Lenin had received money from the German government. The Lenins stayed about 920 days in Switzerland. If, during this time, they used the 2,000 rubles, they could have spent a maximum of forty-six kopeks a day or, disregarding the expenditures for Krupskaya's mother, twenty-three kopeks per person (about twelve cents). And of this, they still retained money! Obviously the money was changed into Swiss francs. How could the possession even of a few hundred francs be used as evidence of anything, let alone of German payments? The fact is that the accusations against Lenin were *not* based on this sort of evidence.

[3]Various pertinent documents were published in the Vienna *Arbeiter Zeitung,* April 20, 1924, p. 4. *See also* Wolfe, *Three who made a Revolution,* p. 618.

Deputy Daszynski, who was then "in Cracow in connection with the organization of the Polish legion [Pilsudski's force] and . . . in constant contact with the military authorities."[4]

Lenin did not intend to reside in Vienna. He now recognized that he could not operate from an enemy country. He asked Adler, who epitomized everything he detested among the moderate socialists and who in earlier times had described Lenin as "crazy," again to intercede with the authorities. On August 26, Lenin was allowed to depart for Switzerland; on August 28, he left Cracow. The Austrians subsequently permitted Hanecki to forego military service and leave Austria to help in the revolutionizing of Russia.

On his way to Berne, Lenin was detained for several hours at the border crossing of Buchs. He was asked to deposit a bond of 100 francs and to produce identifying documents. He wired Karl Moor, a leading Swiss Social Democrat whom he had known from the international bureau. Moor maintained good relations with German authorities, and from time to time acted as an Austrian agent.[5] After vouching for the Lenins, they were permitted to proceed. Krupskaya stated that the veteran Swiss Social Democrat Hermann Greulich gave "surety" for them.

Greulich was later accused of pro-German activities. On August 25, 1914, Bukharin wrote Adler from Zurich that he had given Greulich 800 marks for Lenin in case trouble should develop, and that he was himself prepared to venture to the border to secure Lenin's admission to Switzerland.

Lenin arrived in Bern on September 5. No information exists as to why it took him eight or nine days to complete a trip that

---

[4]Documentation in Shub, pp. 131 and 406.

[5]The illegitimate son of a German aristocrat by the name of Birnette, who became an officer in the Austrian army, and of a Swiss (perhaps a Jewish-Swiss) woman, Moor did not inherit a noble character but received an excellent education. He had an excellent command of languages, was gifted in repartee, was active as a newspaper writer, and was a first-rate demagogue. He settled in Switzerland during the 1870's, joined the socialists, became the leading influence in the radical *Berner Tagwacht* and in 1894 was elected president of the *Arbeiterunion* which he led as a proponent of ruthless class struggle. His policy led to several splits but, in 1896, Moor was arrested on a morals charge—rape of a seventeen year old girl. The girl probably was bribed and did not press the charges. There had been similar incidents in earlier periods, but most of the complaints had been withdrawn. However, Moor was convicted once and he also was indicted on felony and embezzlement charges. In 1897, Moor was excluded from the party but was later reinstated. This "cross of Reinecke Fuchs, Richard III and Casanova" continued as the leader of the Berne socialists until 1917 or so when he began to act on the larger scene of the world revolution. Mr. Boris Nicolayevsky stated that, already at an early time, the German socialist Wilhelm Liebknecht suspected Moor of being an agent. Peter Bieler, *Albert Steck, 1843-1899, der Begründer der Sozialdemokratischen Partei der Schweiz* (Olten, Hauenstein, 1960), pp. 304f, 312ff, presents interesting biographic data on Moor.

usually endured only two or three days.[6] In good financial shape, he rented in a villa an apartment with an adjoining garden. Immediately after his arrival, Lenin wrote a four-page resolution on the "tasks of the revolutionary social democracy in the European war." This paper shows that his attitude toward the war was still in flux. The text contained a strong anti-German statement to the effect that the Prussian *Junkers* would use the war as a means of preserving tsarism, a remarkably inaccurate prediction. He called upon European social democracy to battle against their own governments, so that republics would be established everywhere. The task of the Russian socialists, he said, was to produce the defeat of tsarism as the "lesser evil" and to destroy the "dominion of the Great Russians over other nationalities." The ideas expressed in his paper were contradictory, for the destruction of the German monarchy before the overthrowing of the Tsar would have brought the victory of tsarism. A Duma deputy took Lenin's theses back to Russia. There they were rewritten, perfunctorily proclaimed, and filed. Socialists of all lines tended towards greater cooperation. Soon the police were busying themselves in carrying new dissension into the ranks of the revolutionaries.[7] As ever before, Lenin wanted no part of unity.

While still in Galicia, Lenin had been commissioned by a Russian encyclopedia to write an article on Karl Marx. After arriving in Switzerland he resumed work on this piece, completing it by the middle of November. The article, though idolatrous, was objective and descriptive; it was one of his more scholarly endeavors. Displaying considerable familiarity with Marx's life and work, Lenin also demonstrated acquaintance with anti-Marxist writings, but, except for two references to short articles, he mentioned only *one* of the important critics of Marxian economics, namely, Eugen von Boehm-Bawerk.

When writing his study of Marx, Lenin apparently felt the need for a better comprehension of dialectics: he did not once quote Hegel, of whom he had only superficial knowledge. After the article was completed, Lenin studied Hegel's two-volume *Logic* with great care. Until 1916, he repeatedly returned to philosophical research, as good a pastime as any to have during a "revolutionary ebb"; he also made a study of Clausewitz, the great theoretician of war who was an accomplished practitioner of Hegel's dialectics.

Lenin probably intended to write a book on dialectics. Judging from his extracts, marginal notes, and comments, it is a pity that he did not follow through with this project. The fragmentary drafts,

---

[6]Krupskaya (*op. cit.*, p. 282) asserted they stayed in Vienna "for a day" and took a whole week traveling from Cracow to the Swiss border. Undoubtedly these unlikely dates conceal conferences which Lenin presumably had in Vienna.

[7]Aronson, *op. cit.*, p. 28ff.

in which he classified dialectics into sixteen points, thus going far beyond customary interpretations, are among Lenin's most original and stimulating contributions. They demonstrate a grasp of philosophical problems of which he was not in possession when he wrote *Empiriocriticism*.[8] Most of his notes were remarkably free of dogmatism. For example:

> The thought that the ideal changes into the real is deep and very important for history. The personal life of man also shows that there is much truth in this thought. . . . Also the distinction between the ideal and the material is neither absolute nor enormous.[9]

Lenin, with the talent of a first rate scholar, was capable of objectivity. His most startling historical finding was put down as an aphorism:

> It is impossible to comprehend fully Marx's *Kapital* and in particular the first chapter, if one did not study carefully and understand Hegel's *entire Logic*. Consequently, after half a century, not a single Marxist had understood Marx!![10]

Lenin implied that this aphorism was also applicable to himself. But the discovery was not a new one. In 1895, Marx's son-in-law, Paul Lafargue, asked Lenin whether the Russian socialists were truly comprehending Marx. Lenin replied, "They do." Lafargue retorted :"You are wrong. We here, after twenty years of the Social Democratic movement—no one yet understands Marx."

This philosophical endeavor was undertaken as a matter of self-defense. Lenin was in the midst of one of his depressive periods.[11] He had not been functioning well since mid-July and, disregarding a short-lived flurry early in September, he resumed political activity only on October 11, at which time he debated with Plekhanov,[12] maintaining that socialists could fulfill their duty only when they fought against the "chauvinistic obsession of their own country." (Plekhanov supported the war effort.) Lenin brought fresh emphasis to the famous lines of the *Communist Manifesto* which stated that the Communists have no fatherland; he reiterated this theme in other speeches during the same month. But, inconsistently, on

[8]Lenin's summary of dialectics is given in an excellent English translation in Gustav A. Wetter, *Dialectical Materialism*, p. 119f.

[9]Lenin, *Aus dem philosophischen Nachlass, Exzerpte und Randglossen*, Berlin, Dietz, 1958, p. 31.

[10]*Ibid.*, p. 99.

[11]Krupskaya (p. 291f.) spoke of a "lovely autumn" in the "colorful picture of the Berne woods." "We lived in Distelweg . . . adjoining the Berne woods . . . Inessa lived across the road. . . . We used to roam for hours along the woodland paths. . . . Mostly the three of us went on these walks together . . ." On Lenin's experiences in Switzerland, consult Maurice Pianzola, *Lenin in der Schweiz* (Berlin: Dietz, 1956).

[12]Krupskaya, p. 286ff.

October 17, in a letter to Alexander G. Shlyapnikov, his contact man in Stockholm, he described tsarism as a hundred times worse than kaiserism;[13] therefore, the defeat of tsarism would have to be brought about without fail. Subsequently, he again reversed his position, arguing that the support which German and Austrian socialists were giving to the war could not be justified by the need to destroy tsarism. Instead of this "sophistry," he proposed the abstract and impractical formula that the imperialist war should everywhere be transformed into civil war.

But Lenin was himself not entirely certain of the validity of that slogan. To reconnoiter the political situation he arranged for Inessa to speak to Swiss audiences reporting on the various war policies of Russian Social Democrats, while he mixed with the public to study their reactions. Actually, many Bolsheviks had initially adopted a hesitant pro-war attitude. Gorky returned to Russia and sister Maria Ulyanova supported the war effort by becoming an army nurse (as did the Tsarina and her daughters). Sister Anna's husband, who was in the transport business, also contributed to national defense.

[13]*Ibid.,* p. 293.

Revolutionizing

The war did not come as a surprise to the Central Powers. They had, however, incorrectly estimated the number and strength of their opponents: they had expected a less burdensome war. Hence the Central Powers decided to engage in subversion and "revolutionizing." This by no means constituted a departure from precedent, especially in Russia: Karl von Clausewitz, pondering the lesson of Napoleon's war with Russia in 1812, had maintained that Russia could not be conquered, but "only subdued by its own weaknesses and by the effects of internal dissension."[1]

The decision to revolutionize is reflected by August 5, 1914, in several telegrams sent by the German military and in the traffic of the German Foreign Office, as well as the Austrian government. The first definitive German statement on revolutionizing appeared on July 29, when the Emperor rejected the request of a general who wished to leave Turkey: "He must stay and also fan the war and the revolution against England" *("Krieg und Aufstand schüren").* On August 8, 1914, Wilhelm wrote in the margin of an ambassadorial

[1]On some of the uses of this technique by Bismarck, see Gustav Adolph Rein, *Die Revolution in der Politik Bismarcks* (Göttingen: Musterschmidt, 1957), especially Chapters IV and V.

report from Vienna that the revolutionizing of Poland and the Ukraine should be financed on a larger scale. However, the revolutionizing operations predated the war by several months, notably in the Ukraine and in the Caucasus.[2]

The operations which had been conducted in countries like Russia for many years were *not* a prelude to revolutionizing: due to the war, the German operatives were compelled to leave, many of their agents were mobilized, and revolutionaries went underground or moved to other countries. The psychological climate had changed: a far more serious and radical operation had become necessary. For all practical purposes, the Germans had to make a fresh start.

They began by trying to locate revolutionaries, from whom they requested information from persons they considered knowledgeable. Contacts included bishops, rabbis, professors, Nobel Prize laureates, politicians, foreign diplomats, former agents, prisoners of war, deserters, and many classifiable as "swindlers, impostors, and fools." Schemes were hatched and discarded, gullible German agents were exploited by crooks, policies were continually altered and failures were more frequent than were successes.

The risings and revolutions that did occur were not "created" by the German Foreign Office, the "AA" or Wilhelmstrasse, as it was also called. Revolution is too complex a phenomenon to be caused entirely and specifically by human design—no matter how carefully organized. All the AA could do was to put at the revolutionaries' disposal money, legitimation papers, publication facilities, travel arrangements, communications and occasional information, weapons, and strategic decisions. But it *did* all this, becoming as a result the most important revolutionary agency of its time, substantially more significant than any of the "professional" revolutionary organizations. The stark fact is that the German Foreign Office was using many of these organizations for its own purposes.

The German and Austrian diplomats were not alone in their endeavors: the military occasionally participated, especially when requiring intelligence or contemplating sabotage. Individual politicians, using government funds, operated to some extent independently. Industrial concerns supported revolutionaries, assisted the AA, contributed funds (e.g., for the purchase of newspapers). Socialists, aristocrats, professors and artists were using their "international connections," sometimes in conjunction with the Foreign

[2]By June, or possibly as late as July, the Austrians spent 300,000 kronen to smuggle weapons into the Ukraine and were trying, amateurishly and unsuccessfully, to provoke a mutiny on the Black Sea fleet. In addition, there are indications, mentioned before, that the Austrians—and the Germans—had their hands in the strikes which occurred shortly before the outbreak of war.

Office and at other times for their own purposes. The Wilhelmstrasse attempted coordination of the maze of activity, but often the revolutionizers were working at cross-purposes.

The German diplomats, experts in revolution, did not select any one revolutionary to overthrow the government of his country. They assumed unpredictability and so supported many revolutionary persons and movements, betting, as it were, on *all* the horses in the race. They did *not* put these revolutionaries on their payroll, win them over to the cause of the German Emperor, dictate what they should or should not write, or issue orders guiding specific actions. The Germans used well instructed agents to influence decisions and events, but they left the revolutionaries to their own ideologies, tactics, and devices. Only rarely were direct contacts made; seldom were the revolutionaries cognizant of the source of the unexpected assistance. Many revolutionaries were willing to accept any help offered, on the grounds that they were upholding their own convictions and were actually using the Germans for their own ends. The Germans recognized this attitude, and to strengthen their political warfare capabilities, stimulated sentiments of this nature.

On the other hand, Germans were careful to select intermediaries or liaison agents who were realistic and cynical, willing to ally themselves with the Germans for the attainment of common objectives, and who had sufficient political ambition to carry out their assignments with the required zest.

Revolutionizing functions were not restricted to the fomenting of social revolution. In fact, the Germans, at first reluctant to foster socialism and anarchy, showed far greater interest in supporting national liberation movements. Eventually social and national revolutionizing were equally supported. Many cross-connections existed between the two efforts.

Revolutionizing entailed, however, more than lending support to the revolutionaries: it also required the infiltration and paralysis of the hostile government and military high command. A revolutionizing effort could succeed only if the "ruling class," while under attack, became psychologically defeatist.[3] (This was—during World War I— the condition of the tsarist regime but was not true of France and Italy.) The operations which the Germans undertook to weaken the tsarist regime were complex; the actual operations have been obscured by many legends. But massive German infiltration, espionage, and policy sabotage occurred, partly facilitated by the corrupting presence of many German Balts at the Russian court and in the bureaucracy, and partly by attempts to produce a separate peace with Germany. German connections with Russian financiers and banks, as

[3]The term "defeatism" was coined by Grigory Alexinsky, Bolshevik member of the second Duma and subsequently a firm opponent of Lenin.

well as the Tsarina's addiction to occultism and other mystical charlatanry, made possible many seemingly incredible operations.[4]

Between subversion above and revolutionizing from below, cross-connections arose from time to time. General Bonch-Bruyevich was close to leading generals who, in 1917, were instrumental in engineering the abdication of the Tsar. Certainly influenced by his Bolshevik brother, he contributed much to the poor military planning.[5] Some of the spies who operated around the Minister of War (who himself may have been maneuvered by the Germans) later participated in revolutionizing and, in a concealed fashion, in the German operation with Lenin. At one time, the person in the Russian legation at Bern supervising the activities of revolutionaries was in contact with the Germans. The Russian Minister of the Interior and one or two of his assistants heading the Okhrana were intent upon establishing a separate peace; they manipulated revolutionaries accordingly. And there were many similar cross-connections.

Other tactics were utilized: an immense peace propaganda at the front; bribery of Russian commanders to induce them to surrender fortifications (Kovno, for example); attempts, on the part of Russia's allies—especially Britain—to keep Russia in the war, so that urgent reforms which would perhaps remove the Tsar and Tsarina by a palace revolution could be instituted; popular dissatisfaction with poor government and poorer economic conditions; the impact of the war and of numerous defeats; and the massive dislocation of population, especially the removal of a large portion of the Jewish population from the border areas (to which they had been, more or less, restricted by law) to the interior of Russia. The efforts of the German Foreign Office must be seen in the perspective of this complex situation.

[4]Some of the salient events are described by W. K. Korostowetz, *Lenin im Hause der Väter* (Berlin: Kulturpolitik, 1928), esp. Chapters VII and VIII; and Mikhail D. Bonch-Bruyevich, *Petrograd, Erinnerungen eines Generals* (Berlin: Verlag des Ministeriums für nationale Verteidigung, 1959), Ch. 5-9. Korostowetz was an official of the Petrograd Foreign Office and specialized in communications intelligence. He was related to many high-ranking officials and aristocrats, and his information is, on the whole, dependable. General Bonch-Bruyevich, brother of Lenin's comrade, had many counter-intelligence assignments. A liberal during the war, he later joined the Bolsheviks and became something like the premier soldier of the Red army. The information by the two authors is largely corroborative.

[5]Nicholas N. Golovine, *The Russian Campaign of 1914* (Fort Leavenworth, Kansas: Command and General Staff School Press, 1938), p. 40.

Contacts with Austria

A few weeks before the outbreak of the war, there was created under Austrian auspices at Lvov, a Bund for the Liberation of the Ukraine. The purpose of this organization was to create a united front among the many revolutionary groups, and to stimulate an independence movement inside the Ukraine or, in case of an Austrian invasion or victory, to promote the installation of a suitable regime. It was not difficult, through salaries and other inducements, to organize enough Ukrainians, but the Austrian armies were halted. When Lvov fell temporarily to the Russians, the Bund decamped for Vienna. For a variety of reasons, including corruption among the revolutionaries and nationalistic conflicts in Vienna, the Bund was criticized within the Austrian Foreign Office, and it was removed to Constantinople. Turkey still was neutral, and it was hoped that it could be used as a base for revolutionary action against the Ukraine and the Russian fleet in the Black Sea.

These expectations were not fulfilled, but the move to Constantinople brought the Bund under the influence of Parvus, who had been residing there since 1910 and was now a wealthy businessman. During the Balkan wars he had specialized in grain purchases (and probably commodity and stock speculation), possibly had acted as a broker in arranging for oil concessions in Mesopotamia, and had given economic advice to the Turkish planners of railroad networks. It appears that he had worked together with the German embassy in various subterranean operations and shortly after the beginning of the war had assisted them in their efforts to purchase newspapers in the Balkans. Parvus wrote a short brochure for the Bund and suggested that the Bund publish a booklet by Martov. He also, rather foolishly, delivered public speeches and thus within a few weeks alerted the Okhrana to his activities. But he offered professional advice to the amateurish Bund, using these services as a means of establishing for himself effective relations with Germany (from where he had been expelled). The Bund soon fell into eclipse, though for years it remained the object of derision for the "defencists" among the Russian revolutionaries. Its significance was that it represented the true initiating activity of the revolution.

As we have seen, Lenin arrived in Switzerland carrying only enough money for living expenses. He soon complained about the lack of funds required for organized activities. Yet suddenly, on November 1, 1914, he published the magazine *Sotsial Demokrat* and transmitted money for party purposes to Scandinavia. After the first issue of 500 copies, there was a lapse of five weeks, following which three issues of 1500 copies each were published within a week of each other; another hiatus of five weeks then occurred. Thus, money came in irregularly, but sufficient sums were procured to resume political activity and establish a party organ.

On November 14, Lenin, according to Krupskaya, communicated

the information "that the paper had been delivered at a point near the frontier and would soon be forwarded on."[1] However, the accomplishment of such a feat would have certainly bordered on the miraculous: not only had enemy territory to be crossed in transporting the paper from Switzerland to the Russian frontier, but the long distance—not including detours—which was involved between the two points would make well nigh impossible the knowledge of their arrival within two weeks after dispatching the packages. (It required that much time for the Lenins themselves to proceed from Cracow to the Swiss border!) It is further difficult to believe that such a feat of transportation could have been accomplished under the aegis of an organization which had been badly splintered by the war.

Fortunately, the solution is found in an account which the Ukrainian Bund on December 14, 1914, submitted to the Austrian Foreign Office. The Bund report stated that of its total expenses of 220,000 kronen for the period from September to December of 1914, 30,000 kronen were used for "support to other revolutionary organizations." Under this heading, it was disclosed that the Social Democrats who joined the Bund did so on condition that their party would receive a subvention in order to enlist the cooperation of those who remained outside the organization. "The Bund has supported the majority fraction of Russian Social Democrats with money and assistance for communications with Russia. The leader of this fraction, Lenin, is not opposed to Ukrainian demands." This sentence was preceded by the disclosure that the Bund was cooperating with Parvus, supporting his work.[2]

The report indicated that support had been extended to Georgian Social Democrats and that it had been decided to aid in the publication of an organ of Ukrainian Social Democrats in Constantinople or Switzerland.

The contribution to the Georgians presumably was small; the group of "Ukrainian Social Democrats" was a bit mythological. Whether or not Lenin's paper was, in fact, the contemplated "organ of Ukrainian Social Democrats," the report, under this rubric, mentions money only *once* in connection with Lenin. The implication is that Lenin received the largest portion of this particular budget item: an amount not exceeding 5,700 dollars. In addition, the Bund paid for the transportation to Russia of two of his party members under another budget heading.

[1]Krupskaya, p. 295. By the end of 1915, the Petrograd Bolsheviks had received fifteen issues of *Sotsial Demokrat* in several hundred copies (Futrell, p. 102).

[2]Austrian Archive, Politisches Archiv, Krieg 8b, Karton 903, Ukrainische Aktion, *Provisorischer Bericht über die Tätigkeit des Bundes zur Befreiung der Ukraina.*

The problem sometimes arises about Lenin's knowledge of the source of payment—a question that assumes naive innocence on the part of one of the most professional of revolutionaries. The Bund report which asserted that Lenin was not hostile to "Ukrainian demands" added for proof of Lenin's attitude a speech which the Bund had reported in its paper.[3] In Zurich, Lenin indeed had given a speech in support of Ukrainian independence; it was reported by almost the entire Social Democratic press, including its two main organs, the Vienna *Arbeiter-Zeitung* and the Berlin *Vorwärts* (November 10, 1914). The *Hamburger Echo* (of the same day) juxtaposed the Lenin story with a report on a speech which Parvus made in Sofia, in which he stated that victory of tsarism would constitute a crushing blow to the revolution, whereas the defeat of tsarism would expedite the transformation to democracy. Krupskaya disregards the Zurich speech, mentioning merely that Trotsky objected when Lenin termed Kautsky a traitor.[4]

The Ukrainian Social Democrat Yurkevich, uncovering the secret ties between the Bund and the Austrian government, thought it his duty to warn the revolutionaries. Yurkevich was a capable Marxist scholar with whom Lenin had been friendly for quite some time. He was nonplussed when Lenin berated him about his disclosures. After Lenin committed the tactical error of angrily telling Yurkevich that this information should not have been published, the two men severed their ties.[5]

The Austrians now were having trouble with their own Ukrainians (called "Ruthenians") who were eager to attain independence. Vienna prepared to discontinue relations with the Bund. Two German revolutionizers investigated and by the middle of February, 1915, reported that henceforth the emphasis should be placed on the *overall* Russian revolution: the Bund had functioned to find the "bridge" which the revolutionizers had so long sought. In other words, the Bund put the Germans in touch with the *real* revolutionaries.

Between February 20 and March 3, 1915, Lenin assembled the leading Bolsheviks residing in Switzerland for a conference in Berne. The well-represented Okhrana reported extensively on the meeting.[6] Among the topics discussed were defeatist agitation among troops and the distribution of revolutionary literature to prisoners of war.[7]

[3]This attitude is still reflected, in a strongly attenuated form, in Krupskaya, p. 284.

[4]*Ibid.*, p. 290.

[5]Stepankowski, unpublished memoirs.

[6]Paris to Petrograd, March 15, 1915. (Document in Hoover Institution) The dates of the conference are as given by the Okhrana. *See also* Tsiavlovsky, *op. cit.*, p. 160ff.

[7]In an article in the Paris *Nashe Slovo* on February 9, 1915, Lenin supported, apparently for the first time, "fraternization" of soldiers at the front.

The latter task had been vigorously advocated by the Ukrainian Bund which had allocated during 1914 about 9,000 Austrian kronen for this purpose and had requested permission from the German government to begin this work in camps ùnder German jurisdiction. In Berne, the Bolsheviks expressed their eagerness to produce literature for these prisoners.

The conference opposed pacifism, advocated revolutionary war, denied the possibility of a "so-called democratic peace without revolutions," and proclaimed that the people of every country should engage in revolutionary propaganda as a preliminary to civil war and the overthrow of government. Russia's victory would produce worldwide reaction; hence, under all circumstances, Russia's defeat would represent the lesser evil. The Okhrana reported that, according to information revealed at the conference, 200 copies of *Sotsial Demokrat* were brought into Russia via Norway; and Paris might be the distribution point of 600 to 700 copies in the future. The implication is that the bulk of the *tirage* was shipped via Sweden, Finland, and Rumania.

The conference was dominated by the proposal to publish a "popular organ" abroad to be sent through Norway into Russia; simultaneously, an illegal paper was to be issued inside the country. This proposal presumably originated with Lenin and was an adaptation to wartime conditions of the *Iskra* and *Pravda* credos. Complaints ensued about the lack of good writers, but the material means were available, for both the newspaper plan and for the publication of brochures. The money source was Yekaterina F. Rozmirovich-Maish, a participant in the conference. She was the sister-in-law of Alexander A. Troyanovsky, a former artillery officer and future ambassador to the United States. Shotman says in his report that, while in Vienna, he lodged with the Troyanovskys.[8] Another visitor was Arshak G. Surabov, a Bolshevik from the Caucasus (from Tiflis, according to the Okhrana, from Batumi, according to Shotman). He had participated in the Second Congress and was a member of the second Duma. Surabov then lived in Constantinople and was a friend of Parvus; subsequently Surabov was a close assistant of Parvus in the latter's war operations, though finally they allegedly separated. Parvus was in 1915 a strong proponent of establishing a newspaper. The presumption is that Troyanovsky's sister-in-law, an insignificant party worker, was elected on the basis of personal contacts of long standing, to be the ostensible donor of money which was sent by way of Parvus.

This is just one interpretation. Other Ukrainian Bolsheviks who could have handled the financial liaison included a man named

[8]Shotman, *op. cit.*, p. 305. The time apparently was about August, 1913.

Bensya, and more likely, Marian Melenevsky, whose party name was Bassok. Lenin met Bassok in January, 1915, and Bassok presumably offered financial aid.[9] In an "Answer to Bassok," written on January 12, Lenin claimed that they were not traveling on the same road, but, strangely, this note was not published until 1924. Bassok remained with the party, became a Soviet official, and was eventually purged by Stalin: when an attempt is made to construe an alibi, there usually is something to conceal.

The newspaper plan was not pursued. After rumors had been rampant for some time, on February 20, 1915, Alexinsky gave a public speech at Zurich, in which he disclosed detailed and damaging (though somewhat exaggerated) information about the Bund, Parvus, and the German-Austrian influence on Russian revolutionaries. Lenin was told the Bund story by "Tria" (V. D. Mgeladze), the Georgian socialist who was in full possession of evidence on the case—but who was *not* a Bolshevik. Consequently, Lenin could not rely upon him. On the contrary, he assumed that if he were to continue working with the Bund despite Tria's warning, he would be very vulnerable. Security had been breeched: it was clearly advisable not to risk the exposure which the publication of a newspaper could entail.

Another feature of this Bolshevik conference merits attention. Maxim Litvinov, who had been a weapons smuggler during the 1905 revolution, was a participant who represented the Bolsheviks of London. Litvinov was living in London with another revolutionary, Nikolai Klyachko, who, ironically, worked as a technician at Vickers-Armstrong, Britain's foremost gun manufacturer. The Okhrana repeatedly reported at later dates that Litvinov possessed expert knowledge of weapons, obtained a great deal of information from Klyatchko, made many bicycle trips to British military camps, and reported the data to Lenin who, in turn, transmitted the intelligence to the Germans. The Okhrana may or may not have informed British authorities; in any event, no action was taken against Litvinov. There exists a document in the German file that indicates that Lenin made intelligence available, but it contains no suggestion of British data being involved.[10] Interestingly enough, Litvinov on March 8, 1906, received at Dresden a German passport in the name of "Gustav Graf." The implication of this Okhrana information is that the passport issued was genuine; a direct tie with German intelligence is clearly a possibility. But, for the period of 1915-1916, the Okhrana

---

[9] When traveling in Austria, Bassok conferred upon himself a patent of nobility and posed as "Ritter von Melenevsky."

[10] This document is printed in a watered-down English translation in Z.A.B. Zeman (ed.), *Germany and the Revolution in Russia 1915-1918, Documents from the Archives of the German Foreign Ministry*, London, Oxford, 1958, p. 16ff.

Ilya Nikolayevich Ulyanov, Lenin's father

House in Simbirsk where Lenin was born

Maria Aleksandrovna Ulyanova, Lenin's mother

Alexander Ilyich Ulyanov, Lenin's older brother

Lenin, at 17 (1887)

Maria P. Golubova

Nadyezhda Konstantinova Krupskaya, about 1895

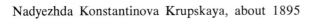

Lenin, at 27 (1897)

Dimitri I. Ulyanov, Maria I. Ulyanova and
Mark T. Yelizarov (1900-1904)

Inessa Armand, about 1904

Nadyezhda Konstantinova Krupskaya, about 1910

Anna I. and Maria I. Ulyanova in 1912

Lenin, about 1910

Lenin in 1914

Inessa Armand, about 1914

Lenin in 1917, in Switzerland before departing
for Russia

Lenin in 1917, in disguise

Nadyezhda Konstantinova Krupskaya,
about 1917

(Permission by Underwood & Underwood)

Smolny Institute, Bolshevik headquarters
during the uprising.

M. V. Fofanova

Lenin speaking at the unveiling of a memorial to Karl Marx and Friedrich Engels in Moscow, November 7, 1918

Lenin and Vladimir D. Bonch-Bruyevich (1918/1919)

Lenin, in March 1919

Lenin in 1919

Lenin (1919/1920)

Villa at Gorki where Lenin died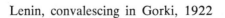

Lenin, convalescing in Gorki, 1922

Nadyezhda Konstantinova Krupskaya, toward
the end of her life

G. V. Plekhanov

N. Y. Fedosseyev

Y. O. Martov

A. M. Kalmykova   Maxim Gorky and M. F. Andreyeva

Motojiro Akashi, as Field Marshal

L. B. Krassin

Alexander Helphand (Parvus), L. D. Trotsky
and L. G. Deutsch

Alexander A. Bogdanov

Kamo

J. V. Stalin

G. E. Zinovyev

Bolsheviks in the 4th Duma: Badayev, Petrovsky,
Samoilov, Khaustov, Roman Malinovsky and Muranov

N. V. Krylenko
(Permission by Underwood & Underwood)

Count Ulrich
von Brockdorff-Rantzau

Karl Radek

G. Shlyapnikov

V. D. Bonch-Bruyevich

L. D. Trotsky, as military hero

Y. M. Sverdlov

G. M. Khzhizhanovsky

(Permission by Underwood and Underwood)

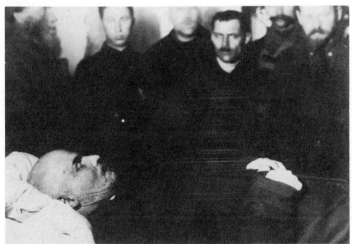

Lenin on his death bed
(Permission by F.P.G.)

J. V. Stalin, about 1923

(Permission by Brown Bros.)

Receipt by Parvus for one million rubles

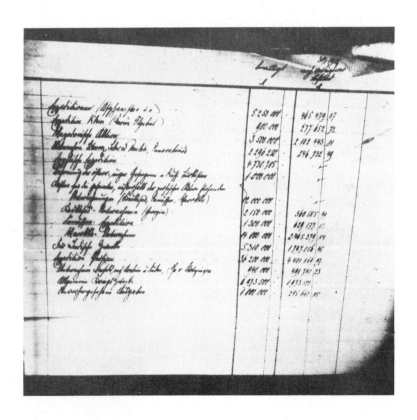

Top secret German list of political warfare
expenditures from beginning of World War I
to January 30, 1918

file contains no precise information beyond the observations of Litvinov's behavior.[11]

Years before the war, the Spanish anarchist Miguel Almereyda (subsequently accused of treasonable activities with the Germans) commented to a friend who was excited about the ethical ideas of Leo Tolstoi: "Forget about Russian novels . . . . The revolution needs money."[12] Lenin, of course, agreed entirely with this opinion.

[11]During the Kerensky regime, S. G. Svatikov investigated the Okhrana's foreign department. (*See Recueil de documents secrets tirés des Archives de l'ancien Ministère des affaires étrangères russe* (Geneva: Nouvelle Internationale, 1918).) Svatikov was a little naive, though he uncovered some interesting information. Litvinov complained to him about denunciations; Svatikov (p. 42) identified Nicholas Selivanov as the informer in this case, suggesting that Selivanov was a German spy. Svatikov had no proof whatever for this statement and also neglected to note that Selivanov was working at Vickers-Armstrong, as well as for the Okhrana. According to the German file, K. D. Nabokov of the tsarist embassy felt that Selivanov's information was dependable. The aggregation of Russian revolutionaries at Vickers is suspect and hardly accidental. It should be remembered that the Germans had difficulties in placing espionage agents in Britain. The use of Russians was a good technique. Nevertheless, the case against Litvinov remains unproven. On the possibility of Bolshevik espionage in Russia, *see* Futrell, p. 107f.

[12]Victor Serge, *Mémoires d'un Révolutionnaire* (Paris: Club des Editeurs, 1957), p. 28.

Contacts with Germany

As soon as the war started, German Social Democrats journeyed abroad to convince their brethren in the International that the overthrow of tsarism was the most important challenge facing civilization and progress. Among this group of travelers was Dr. Karl Lehmann, Parvus' companion on his trip to Russia during the famine. Lehmann, whose wife had preceded Krupskaya as the secretary of *Iskra*, ventured to Austria and Italy; presently following his convictions, he was killed as a soldier. It is not unlikely that he spoke of Lenin to the Wilhelmstrasse or the Prussian minister in Munich; certainly he mentioned Lenin to Parvus' friend, Adolf Müller, Bavaria's foremost socialist editor and another of the emperor's socialist missionaries. Müller traveled west. Wilhelm Jansson, a trade unionist from Russia's Baltic provinces and, according to his passport, a Swedish citizen, went to Scandinavia, arguing for the destruction of tsarism and asking for support for the revolutionaries. On October 9, 1910, the German minister to Stockholm reported that Jansson had told him that the Finnish revolution could be accomplished only through the Social Democrats. In line with initial thinking at Berlin on independence movements, Jansson had investigated such a possibility for Finland, although he doubted that much progress could be achieved. On October 13, 1914, another suggestion of Jansson's was recorded: the approach should be broadened beyond national revolutions (i.e., independence movements) and should aim at Russia as a whole (i.e., at a social upheaval throughout the tsarist empire). For this purpose, Jansson proposed that the help of Russian Social Democrats be enlisted—that is, of those who did *not* support the war effort.[1]

Previously, on July 12, Zilliacus had been contacted by a German officer in regard to the nearing war. This date is based on allegedly firm recollection; the discussion may therefore have been tied to the unrest fomented in St. Petersburg. Zilliacus is mentioned on August 8 as a person who could be useful in establishing an intelligence service directed at Russia. Zilliacus, however, was no longer in proper physical condition. But he probably suggested Lenin as an available veteran of the 1905 venture. Jodko visited Gisbert von Romberg, the German minister at Berne, to whom he proposed a scheme to help finance a French revolutionary newspaper editor. Romberg, an accomplished student of politics and undercover activities, hardly missed the opportunity to question Jodko about the revolutionizing of Russia.

But while more and more people were becoming involved, German diplomats were not quite sure whether the revolutionizing was to be taken seriously. The ambassador at Constantinople, upon inquiring, was told that revolutionizing was to be executed "ruthlessly and mercilessly" (*rücksichtslos und schonungslos*). On No-

---

[1]Okhrana documents indicate that Jansson was a member of the Latvian Bolshevik sub-party and in 1907 was accused by his comrades of treason. Another accusation was that upon being arrested in 1897, Jansson informed the police of the names of fellow socialist conspirators and provided details on printing plants and distribution points during the period 1893-1897. A report on his confession written by the police on December 17, 1897, was transmitted to Burtsev on May 29, 1913. Copied from Burtsev's document by a police agent, the new copy was sent to the police at St. Petersburg. In January, 1914, the Latvians, in Jansson's presence, discussed his case and it would seem that he purged himself of the accusation (Paris to Police Department, January 20, 1914). Lenin participated in this congress. How Jansson managed to disprove documentary evidence is not apparent. Why did the police put Burtsev on Jansson's track? This action suggests that in 1913, Jansson, working from Germany, was creating trouble inside Russia. However, there probably were two Janssons. The Jansson who was accused of treason went by the alias Braum and is now described in Soviet publications as a *founder* of the Latvian Social Democratic party during the period 1907-1914. The loyalty proceedings against this Jansson were not mentioned in *Istoricheskii Arkhiv* (1959), No. 4, p. 38, where it is alleged that Jansson became a Bolshevik at the beginning of the war. According to Tsiavlovsky, (p. 175), Jansson, who had lived for a while in Germany under the name of Vyacheslavov, attempted to journey from Britain to attend the Kienthal conference but was unable to obtain the necessary visas. According to *Istoricheskii Arkhiv*, he died in March 1917 on the way from England to Russia, when his ship was torpedoed. Braun-Jansson's first names were Jans-Jan Eristovich. The chances are that the two Janssons were close relatives and cooperated with each other.

vember 27, 1914, Undersecretary of State Alfred Zimmermann argued, in a lengthy presentation, that revolutionizing was an integral part of German strategy.

Romberg had anticipated Zimmermann's finding; experience had taught him that the Russian revolution was both inevitable and desirable from the German viewpoint. On October 5, 1912, he informed Berlin that he was starting a systematic search for revolutionaries.

Romberg found a remarkable scout. He was Alexander Eduard Keskuela, a thirty-two year old Estonian whose father seems to have been of German origin. Keskuela was rather tall and had blue eyes and bright blond hair. Born in Dorpat, he was raised as a Lutheran. Keskuela had been the object of about a dozen search warrants; in 1905 he had been an active revolutionary; captured, he benefitted from the Tsar's amnesty. Through 1906 and 1907, he served as a member of the executive committee of Northern Livland as well as in the municipal administration of Dorpat; he was also associated with the Bolshevik combat organization, the expropriation outfit.[2] He may have met Lenin at that time. After his arrest he succeeded in escaping. Apparently he continued his studies at the University of Zurich and (during 1912) at Leipzig; it is possible that he first met Lenin at the latter city. In 1913 he became interested in Estonian nationalism and shifted sharply to the right. Whether he abandoned socialism altogether is uncertain, but he undoubtedly desired a Greater Estonian state, a Baltic alliance between Estonia, Finland, and Sweden, the expulsion of Russia from the Baltic Sea, and the dissolution of the tsarist empire. A facile linguist, Keskuela was well educated. He possessed a true political mind and, despite his Estonian proclivities, impressed his German interlocutors with his authentic hatred of the Russian government and his usefulness as a political agent.

Keskuela first appeared in the German legation some time before September 12. It is likely that he and Romberg discussed the various revolutionary groups as much as they could with the available facts; at a later time the two men, as we know from handwritten notes,[3] surveyed the situation frequently. Thus it is possible to surmise that the compatibility of their thought patterns brought them together. It was readily apparent that further information was needed. By October 1, Romberg had asked Keskuela to undertake a reconnaissance trip; Keskuela was on his way to Sweden. A com-

---

[2]At this time, his party name was "Kivi" (stone). He used the name "Stein" in his correspondence with the Germans.

[3]Most of these notes were found in the file of the German legation at Berne; many of them are in the handwriting of Romberg.

munication of October 22 indicates that Keskuela still favored national revolutions, but it is also evident that the social revolution had been discussed and that Keskuela was evaluating its feasibility.

Lenin's name appears in the German file for the first time on November 30, 1914; earlier references have, at least, not been found. This was an incidental remark: the Duma deputies recently arrested in Russia are of Mr. Lenin's suasion. By itself, this arrest was not too important but Keskuela suggested contemptuously that the seizure might be useful to inflate the significance of the event. He said, in essence, that this is the type of thing with which Baron Romberg could toy. But, if insisted upon, it was possible to strengthen the Bolsheviks.

What Keskuela did not know was that on November 27, 1914, at Copenhagen, the German Minister Count Ulrich von Brockdorff-Rantzau, another specialist in Russian affairs, reported on a committee run by I. S. Sazonov that supported defeatist propaganda and urged preparations for an armed uprising. Sazonov, a Bolshevik, probably was the recipient of Lenin's productions in Switzerland. He apparently was in possession of funds, for his committee employed a secretary, Mrs. Rubinstein, who stood in favor with the Germans. Presumably this committee was the first Bolshevik group to receive German support.

On December 7, 1914—the time sequence is suggestive—an agent sent by a prominent unnamed Russian revolutionary asked Romberg a pertinent question: Should internal unrest compel the Russian government to enter into peace negotiations, would Germany betray the revolutionaries or protect them? Romberg gave a reassuring answer.

On his return trip, Keskuela talked with the German Secretary of State; no record has been found of the conversation. He proceeded via Switzerland to Austria to consult persons associated with the Bund. On February 24, Romberg reported that Keskuela had established contacts with revolutionaries; a cautious pessimism, however, was still dominant.

At this time, a well-placed Swedish observer whom the Germans had sent to Russia returned, expressing great optimism. His message about the social revolution was of special importance: he had discussed the problem with Count Witte (who was to die shortly afterwards, perhaps with the aid of the Okhrana). Apparently, at this point, there also was received a note (unsigned and undated) written by a revolutionary strategist who maintained that it would be necessary to foment both the national movements and the "internal revolution." The author advanced several proposals: contact with the Finns and Letts should be undertaken, large-scale strikes should be financed, and Lenin should be reached.[4] The contact with Lenin was soon to be established.

In the meantime, the Bolshevik conference was being held, through February and March. It was attended not only by the Okhrana but also by spies of Parvus and Keskuela, both of whom transmitted their intelligence to the Germans. But on one key problem the reports do not entirely agree: the Okhrana related that the Bolsheviks intended to unify the extreme left elements of *all* belligerent countries, and were anticipating a German mutiny to be organized by Liebknecht and his followers. If Lenin wished to aid Liebknecht, this news was surely welcomed by Petrograd. The German legation at Berne received no such information. The unrealistic belief that the revolution was to be instigated everywhere often appeared in Bolshevik arguments; it represented one of the very reasons why Keskuela had been so skeptical about Lenin and his policies: for if the revolution in Germany preceded Russia's, the autocracy would emerge victorious.

The Okhrana also reported that the Bolsheviks wanted to unify the various revolutionary elements operating in Russia. Parvus had received the same information; he noted that heretofore Lenin had been opposed to unification. But Keskuela found that Lenin had now adopted the *new* policy of working for the defeat of Russia as the lesser evil under current conditions. This policy may not have been "new"; it had been declared earlier. But Keskuela and Parvus, independently, concluded that Lenin had finally decided to pursue this policy actively.

Keskuela stated that he believed the new line would greatly impress Russia, where Lenin and his group still enjoyed a sturdy reputation, and he made an attempt to meet with Lenin. On March 25, Keskuela reported that he was going to see Lenin; an undated note of the same period indicated he would see him "tonight." However, on March 26, there followed a conference of female revolutionaries, largely organized by Inessa who, since Lenin had arrived at Berne, was undertaking most of the organizational work. (She had been elected Bolshevik representative to the International Bureau of Women Workers. Her children, who had joined her in Italy in 1914, had been sent back to Russia.) Lenin was steering this conference from a café across the street and talked with the delegates

[4]This document could be a memorandum of Keskuela's conversation with Secretary Jagow. But Keskuela would not have overlooked the Estonians in favor of the Letts and there is no sign that he was pushing Lenin's "candidacy." The emphasis on Finns and Letts, however, discloses great knowledge of the Bolshevik organization. Jansson may have been the author, but the style does not quite fit. I mentioned before that some Foreign Office operators were experienced in these matters. Count Pourtalès himeslf was continuously consulted about the revolutionizing activities. Prof. George Katkov believes the paper was written by Parvus while still in Turkey.

after the sessions. Hence he would have been unavailable before March 29. But he saw Keskuela shortly afterwards, either by the end of March or early in April, 1915.[5]

Keskuela, still alive in 1961, claimed that he saw Lenin only once, late in September or early in October, 1914; yet he admitted that he kept no notes or diary.[6] Since he left on or about October 1, he could have met Lenin only in September; but Lenin had just arrived on September 5. It is conceivable, however, that he saw Lenin briefly to obtain addresses in Stockholm, but his reports do not indicate that he engaged in a serious discussion with him. If indeed he talked with Lenin only once (which is doubtful[7]), then internal evidence of the German documents makes it clear that the conversation took place in the spring of 1915, after Keskuela had already infiltrated the Bolshevik organization of Stockholm.

As Keskuela told the story in the mid-1920's when his memory still was intact, Lenin greeted Keskuela, "Well, I hear you are now working as a German agent." Keskuela replied: "If it pleases you to interpret things in this fashion, go right ahead." Lenin: "The Germans may take Riga. The Germans may take Tiflis." Keskuela: "And Ingermanland?" Lenin: "Ingermanland? What do you mean? The area to the north or west of Petersburg?" Keskuela: "Ingermanland is Petersburg itself." Lenin fell into silence and changed the subject.

This story was related by Keskuela to a friend.[8] He also boasted that he was the person who drew the Germans' attention to Lenin. The story is consistent with both Lenin's and Keskuela's ways of thinking, as they can be determined from the record.[9]

Although the two men agreed on several points, there were a number of disagreements. Lenin clearly was reluctant to enter into firm commitments. To judge from Keskuela's reports, Lenin was still not eager to initiate aggressive action. Apparently, too, there existed widespread feelings of defeatism and—at the same time—opposition

[5]For some details on this conference, *see* Krupskaya, pp. 301ff.

[6]Michael Futrell, "Alexander Keskuela," *St. Anthony's Paper No. 12, Soviet Affairs No. 3* (London: Chatto & Windus, 1962), pp. 23-52. Keskuela died during July, 1963, in Spain.

[7]There is enough evidence to indicate that by 1961 Keskuela either misremembered things or did not want to disclose the whole truth.

[8]The source is a Swiss university professor who was interviewed by the writer and, earlier, by one of his assistants. The professor recounted the story even before the name of Keskuela became known.

[9]In a public speech during the fall of 1914 at Geneva, Lenin said that it would be good if the Germans were to take Warsaw and Tiflis. (M. Filia, "Iz davnikh vstrech," *O Lenine, Sbornik Vospominanii*, Moscow, 1927, p. 70.) Keskuela made his point on Ingermanland and Petersburg to A. V. Neklyudov, Russian Minister to Sweden. *See* his *En Suède pendant la guerre mondiale* (Paris: Perrin, 1926), p. 295.

to full concentration on the initial stages of the Russian revolution.

Years after the event, Keskuela asserted that following this meeting his communications with Lenin were transmitted through Arthur Siefeld, another Estonian Bolshevik, who was a friend of Lenin.[10] This assertion *is* compatible with the evidence in the German file. Keskuela also claimed that the Germans were not aware of Siefeld's activities. This is *not* so, for Siefeld's name appears in a note taken during discussions between Romberg and Keskuela, probably in the presence of Schuberth, the political officer.[11] Whatever the arrangement, Keskuela's reports and German correspondence about his activities suggest that contacts were very close and that Lenin was not quite as naively uninformed as Keskuela tried to hint in his later years.

Keskuela maintained that he gave Siefeld money to enter on Bolshevik collection lists, in installments of a few francs. Almost certainly, this is misleading information, for, though the Germans did contribute money in this manner, a few francs would not have been of any great importance, while larger donations would have made Siefeld suspect.[12] Keskuela received substantial sums to maintain the contact with Lenin;[13] there is no suggestion that he pocketed the money. If Siefeld actually "donated" only a few francs, the question arises of how Keskuela distributed the rest of the money.

Lenin did not at first receive German money. If he did not experience a sorrier financial state, it was probably because, in that period, the money which was held in escrow by the German socialists was transmitted to him. It would not be unlike Lenin to demand payment of this money which he felt belonged to the Bolsheviks as a token of earnest of the groups which wished to do business with him.

In May, Lenin met Parvus-Helphand, who was mobilizing Russian revolutionaries for the Germans. Parvus had been received by the German Secretary of State and had long discussions with Dr. Kurt Riezler, the political warfare adviser to the German Chancellor. To these men, Parvus, the ambitious graduate of 1905, had submitted a grandiose plan for revolutionizing Russia. The scheme contained impractical features, but the impressed Germans gave Parvus one

---

[10]Futrell, *Northern Underground*, p. 146f. On Siefeld himself, see *ibid.*, p. 149.

[11]The writer has a microfilm copy of this document.

[12]Actually, any substantial donation by a penniless party member would have aroused doubts.

[13]Keskuela, it says in a German document of May 8, 1916, has "maintained his extremely useful contact with Lenin" and must "therefore continue to be provided with the necessary means in the future" (Zeman, p. 17). Keskuela was then living with his pretty Swiss wife (and servants) in an elegant villa in North Stockholm where he was giving "lavish parties" (Futrell, p. 122).

million marks and later another 500,000 marks to be pumped into Russia.[14]

The conversation between Lenin and Parvus (which was later confirmed by Parvus in one of his brochures) occurred when Parvus accosted Lenin in a restaurant at Berne. Lenin was there eating with Siefeld. Parvus asked Lenin to talk and the two men departed for Lenin's home. Lenin later told Siefeld that upon hearing Parvus' proposals he sent him away. Yet the fact remains that after this conversation Lenin announced plans to move to Scandinavia.[14a] This project did not materialize and a German confidential report of August 1915 disclosed that Parvus would support Lenin only after the tension had been smoothed out. Thus, Lenin's explanation to Siefeld is suspect. It seems rather that Parvus refused to support Lenin's personal efforts. Indeed, there is enough evidence to show that before March, 1917, Parvus financed and used Bolshevik operators without consulting Lenin. The German aid to Lenin came mostly via Keskuela.

Lenin did not wish to associate himself with Parvus, partly because Lenin considered him a competitor, and partly because he feared leaks of information. On his part, Parvus was interested primarily in obtaining access to the Bolsheviks and arranged employment for some of Lenin's men.

Hanecki, authorized by Lenin to go to Copenhagen, traveled through Paris (where he talked too much) and presumably through London. It is remarkable that, in the middle of a war, this Polish revolutionary was able to move freely in enemy countries. Though years earlier he may have had a Russian passport,[15] he must have been traveling on false papers, probably provided by Schober. Was Hanecki sent with the mission of reporting intelligence to Vienna?

In Copenhagen, Hanecki became Parvus' assistant.[16] On July 6, five million marks were budgeted by the German Foreign Office for revolutionary propaganda. Three days later, Parvus for the first time met Rantzau, and discussed the feasibility of revolutionizing Russia. The talk resumed on August 9 and resulted in the establishment by Parvus of a rather complicated enterprise. It consisted of a front

[14]Zeman, pp. 1-5.

[14a]Futrell, p. 172f. Parvus probably knew next to nothing about Keskuela, but Keskuela was informed of Parvus's activities and sought to undercut that "uncommonly fat and paunchy gentleman" who despite "very expressive intelligent eyes" looked "like a tightly stuffed sack with a quivering belly," as Siefeld described Parvus. Lenin's report to Siefeld hardly was designed to disclose the content of the conversation but rather to conceal it.

[15]He originated from the Russian part of Poland.

[16]On Hanecki's biography, and his attempt to postdate the time of his arrival in Skandinavia to 1916, see Futrell, p. 168f.

research organization, ostensibly to study the social effects of war, but whose real purpose was to create a *cadre* for the penetration of Russia. Parvus did indeed recruit some outstanding intellects who were destined to leave their mark on the Russian revolution—A. G. Zurabov, V. D. Perazich, V. G. Groman (later a specialist in economic planning and victim of the purge of the Mensheviks in 1931), G. I. Chudnovsky, and M. S. Uritsky. (He almost got N. I. Bukharin, next to Lenin the outstanding Bolshevik theoretician, but Lenin, who did not want to compromise on ideological matters and may have feared Bukharin's naiveté with respect to subversive operations, persuaded him to stay away from the Parvus institute.) This "intellectual" outfit was tied to a business firm which traded coal with Denmark and was designed to engage in smuggling to and from Russia.[17] When the Germans found it difficult to secure enough rubles, Parvus determined a method of retaining earned rubles within Russia for intelligence, subversion, and insurgency. In 1915 Russia imported from Germany products worth about twenty-four million rubles; in 1916, goods valued at 9 million rubles were imported. Included were such commodities as copper and salvarsan. There was also some trade from Scandinavia to Russia. A significant part of these transactions went through Parvus' hands, directly or indirectly; naturally, not all of the money was left within Russia.[18] Hanecki devoted most of his time to a smuggling operation which he did not advertise on the "affiches": he smuggled, on a fairly large scale, rubber articles, mostly contraceptives, into Russia. In addition, his firm handled drugs, syringes, thermometers, stockings, pencils and haircutters.[19] As the Austrians reported on the arrangement, Parvus dealt with the

[17]The Okhrana, already on July 22 and 30, reported that Parvus had rented an office for 1,100 crowns and had leased a private apartment in a wealthy suburb. *"Il est homme de moyens."* He has with him a *"dame de compagnie allemande,"* Marie Schillinger, twenty-two, from Munich, and a Danish *"gouvernante"* (probably they meant she was a *"bonne").* They stated he started a big library and the institute on war, a *"compagnie de commerce et d'exportation,"* and a publicity outfit, *"colonnes d'affiches de Copenhague,"* with Jacob Fürstenberg (Hanecki) as director. (Fürstenberg, they said, was born on March 15, 1879, in Warsaw). In addition to all this, Parvus was doing literary work. The reports indicated Parvus' political objectives— overthrow of the Tsar and a more liberal constitution—and added it could not be proven he received money from the Germans. Otherwise, this was fairly sound reporting.

[18]Parvus prided himself upon earning money by making scarce commodities available; by the end of the war he had amassed a fortune of thirty million Swiss francs (about six million dollars).

[19]Futrell, p. 183ff. Contraceptives which apparently were fabricated in Denmark from rubber which the British had allowed to pass through the blockade also were sold to Germany. The salvarsan was procured in Chicago (p. 187). Much of the trade with Russia went via the Russian Red Cross (p. 171f.). The contraceptive trade may have been initiated by a Russian importer, the Bolshevik S.M. Sachs-Gladnev, or been suggested by Eduard Fuchs, well-known socialist historian of sex mores.

Germans, Hanecki with the Russians; the liaison between Hanecki and Lenin was accomplished through an unidentified "German-Jewish Swiss national."[20]

The significance of Parvus' dealings with the Germans really was not that he placed them in communication with Lenin. Parvus became the adviser of the Germans on overall strategy directed towards Russia. Much of his advice was funnelled through Brockdorff-Rantzau, an advocate of revolutionizing and later Foreign Minister and Ambassador to the Soviet Union, who transmitted ideas to Parvus and periodically arranged for him to talk to the policymakers in Berlin. Parvus' schemes often evoked ridicule. He once, however, proposed the forgery of ruble bank notes. (This idea was used, *sans recherche de la paternité* by the Nazis in World War II.) The relevance of the information Parvus procured through his organization, his profound knowledge of Russian and revolutionary affairs, and the clarity of his objectives, had a great impact upon the course of the war. Of equal importance was the fact that through his "commercial" operations he built up assets in the amounts and, above all, in the currencies that were required for Germany's political warfare.

Keskuela and Parvus probably did not provide the only German contacts with Lenin. There existed a third, as yet unidentified, channel between Lenin and the German Foreign Office, probably Karl Moor. Another "friend" of Lenin, Dr. Kornblum was reported by the Austrians to have great influence and to display good judgment; Kornblum did report on Lenin to Busso von Bismarck, the military attaché. There were Bagocki and Shklovsky, and Buchholz who ran a chemical laboratory which paid Zinovyev a salary for his skill in "political chemistry." All of these individuals dealt with the Germans for some periods of time.

Karl Radek, a friend and compatriot of Hanecki, had for years been an editor in Germany, and now worked on the *Berner Tagwacht,* a very much socialist paper. Radek had numerous connections in Germany[21] and, though he did not agree with Lenin on many points, he maintained close contact with him, and, later joined him in the venture of the sealed train. The German legation often used his paper to "leak" information and to provide documentation harmful to Germany's enemies. There were also a dozen or so people who knew Lenin or Zinovyev and who were affiliated with newspapers and universities or who simply met in cafés frequented by revolutionaries and writers. The military authorities also were involved.

20This person is unidentified, but if Moor's mother was Jewish, which seems likely, the description would apply to him. The Austrian document of November, 1917, was published by Helga Grebing in *Politische Studien,* Munich, 1957, p. 232ff.

21Schub, pp. 136f. and 406.

German military intelligence had placed well-selected agents every-where.[22] Some of them were on military furlough, including Bismarck's preferred intermediary, Dr. Walter Nasse.

As suggested by General Moltke, the military had established prisoner-of-war indoctrination programs (which in 1916 led to a protest by Petrograd). There is evidence from the Okhrana that this operation was gradually following more radical and Bolshevik lines, with Malinovsky playing a significant role.[23] This operation influenced events far more than is generally recognized. A recent Soviet publication has shown the extent to which Lenin and Krup-skaya were involved.[24] Lenin's efforts extended to fourteen camps in Germany and seven camps in Austria. He knew the number of prisoners in each camp and was well informed on camp conditions. Packages were sent, literature was distributed (mostly during 1916), and contacts were maintained, especially through Krupskaya, with forty-six prisoners and three libraries and study circles. In one in-stance, Lenin sent money for book purchases. A total of 119 letters were dispatched, including five to Malinovsky at the camp of Alt-Grabow.

The military, always searching for saboteurs and spies, also went bodily after the revolutionaries. Unfortunately, the military files were destroyed and details are missing. It is reported that the military wanted Lenin to go to Russia to organize a sabotage pro-gram.[25] They reiterated this request, which Lenin continued to reject as nonsense, several times through a "V-Mann" (*Vertrauensmann* or "man of confidence"). Major Bismarck, nephew of the "Iron Chancellor," concluded that Lenin was a coward. Lenin, however, did procure a sabotage expert who came from Russia to Stockholm: the old highwayman Lbov, whom Lenin had cheated. Lbov was supposed to blow up bridges over the Volga; this time it was Lbov—not Lenin—who was dishonest.[26]

---

[22]On Nasse and Moor, *see* Gustav Mayer, *Erinnerungen* (Zurich: Europa Verlag, 1949). Mayer was a historian of German socialism and the biographer of Engels. He had entrée to socialists of all lines and transmitted somewhat naive information to the German Foreign Office.

[23]*See also* Ruth Fischer, *Stalin und der deutsche Kommunismus* (Frankfurt: Frankfurter Hefte, no year), p. 35f.

[24]*Istoricheskii Arkhiv* (1961), No. 5, pp. 101-107.

[25]Interview with a former member of the German legation at Berne.

[26]There was cheating but the identity of the cheater is not certain. The Germans thought they dealt with Lbov, and presumably Lenin had promised him. According to other information, he was hung. The man who wanted the Bolsheviks to pay their debt may have been Sasha Lbovets. Lenin probably did not know the differ-ence, and Lbovets may have been the dishonest saboteur. There is a possibility that this affair was connected with the counter-intelligence activities of Lenin II (Dolin).

The Germans occasionally checked to ascertain whether political funds were reaching their destination. Reportedly, there occurred some embezzlements of Bismarck's funds destined for the Bolsheviks; but details are no longer traceable. German purchasing agencies held "black funds" to sustain revolutionaries. Some of these men were employed commercially; others made money through speculation and black-marketeering.

The Austrians were busy, too, especially in Berne and Geneva.

The historiographical difficulty is not in identifying "liaison agents" between the Germans and the Bolsheviks, but rather in distinguishing the busybodies and story-tellers from those who, in possession of relevant contacts, accomplished their aim. There is no doubt, however, that the "defeatist" Russian revolutionaries—especially those in Switzerland—were heavily infiltrated by German and Austrian influences; this penetration is true of the Social Revolutionaries, the internationalist Mensheviks, as well as the Bolsheviks. Few were political prostitutes; many were marionettes—and practically all of these alleged idealists were manipulable. However, history has been kind to them: but for a different sequence of events, they all would have earned the reputation which, in World War II, Vidkun Quisling gained for himself and the tribe of "Quislings."

Lenin Realizes His Power

In March, 1915, Krupskaya's mother (who had been living with the Lenins) died; her body was cremated. Late in May, Krupskaya was again afflicted by her glandular disease. The Lenins departed for a hotel in Soerenberg, one of the most beautiful spots in the Berne uplands. During the summer, Inessa, who in Berne was residing across the street from the Lenin's, came to visit them, often playing the piano. Krupskaya reported another series of *promenades à trois.*[1] But it was not all idyllic: the Bolshevik Central Committee was not invited to attend a meeting preparatory to an international conference scheduled for the fall. Lenin angrily sent Inessa to pursue the Swiss hosts of the conference.

The conference was held at Zimmerwald between September 5 and 8. The Zimmerwald movement, which emerged from this conference, was an internationalist-socialist protest against war. The Germans took a deep interest in it: the stronger the movement became, the weaker would be France and Italy—and Russia. Whether they had quietly engineered the meeting is conjectural. The Germans were worried about the defeatist attitude in Germany. Although

[1]Krupskaya, p. 307.

Lenin officially preached the thesis of revolution everywhere, he played no active role, signing the moderate resolution passed by the conference. It was only subsequently that his opposition to the "soft" line was noted.[2] Inessa's talents as interpreter were very much in demand. Edmundo Peluso, a Portuguese socialist and one of the participants who directly or indirectly reported to the Germans, was employed by the local correspondent of the United Press. But the wire services did not feature the meeting.

After the Zimmerwald conference, Lenin exhausted, returned to Soerenberg where Krupskaya was still under treatment. Inessa completed her French translation of Lenin's and Zinovyev's brochure, *Socialism and War,* and then proceeded to Paris to plan its distribution throughout France and to investigate the possibility of propagandizing within the French army. She also helped to establish in Paris a committee for the resumption of international relations—a classical front organization which in due course was to grow into the Communist party of France—together with similar outfits, including an anti-war committee of French and Russian women. It is asserted that Lenin's brochure, as Inessa had demanded out of a sense of revolutionary justice, was widely distributed in Germany; this claim is untrue.[3] The Germans did not bother to smuggle this bulky theoretical treatise into Russia; they were content at that moment to concentrate on defeatist propaganda in France.

This visit by Inessa to France brought forth documentary references on her relationship with Lenin: the Paris *préfecture de police,* in its notes to the Okhrana on April 14 and April 19, 1916, stated that "*demoiselle* Sophie Popoff," called "Inessa," is "*la maitresse de Lénine.*"[4] According to this information Inessa remained in Paris from January 9 to April 11, when she returned to Switzerland. The purpose of her activities was to induce the soldiers to instigate revolution.[5] The police reported that Inessa seemed to be on good terms with Trotsky and that she made quite an impression in a talk to the Jeunes Syndicalistes because of her knowledge of the French and Russian revolutionary movements, as well as her "*manières*

[2]The French police, on April 11, 1916, reported that Lenin proposed a resolution on civil war. After this resolution was rejected, he went along with the majority.

[3] It is, however, true that a German translation was made, and distributed at the Zimmerwald conference (Krupskaya, p. 310).

[4]A third but undated police note, probably of October, 1916, repeats the phrase "*maitresse de Lénine*" and speaks of "*son amant Lénine.*" According to this information, the purpose of Inessa's trip was to propagandize the point of view of the left Zimmerwaldians. This was probably correct: the international defeatists were then preparing for a second conference.

[5]Her daughter (*loc. cit.,* p. 84) reported that Inessa was engaged in propaganda activities among Frenchmen interned in Switzerland. They were, of course, chiefly deserters.

insidieuses" and her facileness at speaking. However, plans for an illegal paper could not be realized and the revolutionizing of French soldiers was unsuccessful. It is interesting to note that Bolshevik attention was focussed upon France rather than Russia. Perhaps this represented a *Liebesdienst* for the Germans.[6]

In the fall of 1915, Lenin negotiated with Keskuela, either directly or through an intermediary, seriously committing himself to a joint-action program. He was careful enough to conceal his true intentions: the socialist "minimal program"—establishment of a republic, expropriation of large estates, and initiation of an eight-hour workday—was to be the basis of the collaboration between Germany and Russia. Such goals interested the Germans only mildly. Nor did they attach much significance to the "condition" that there were to be no Russian indemnities or territorial concessions to Germany. But the Germans were highly elated when Lenin promised autonomy to non-Russian nationalities, and offered no objection to the establishment of buffer states between Russia and Germany. He also stipulated the evacuation of Turkey by the Russian army. Thus, Lenin agreed to the disestablishment of the Russian empire and to German economic penetration of the Middle East. But most remarkable was his promise of a Russian attack on India. This constituted, in effect, a proposal to engage in an alliance between Russia and Germany against Britain.

This document is most significant.[7] The only man among the Russian revolutionaries who committed himself to a secret aggression pact with imperial Germany later became the ruler of Russia. The war against India did not take place,[8] but, in due course, Lenin

---

[6]Safarov, Inessa's friend, was expelled from France, probably in January, 1916, for defeatist propaganda among the sailors at St. Nazaire.

[7]Zeman, p. 6f.

[8]When asked about Lenin's promise concerning India, Keskuela in 1961 explained that this must have been a garbled version of what he told the German Minister in Berne, namely that a future revolutionary regime would assist in an anti-imperialist war of liberation. This "rectification," which merely broadens the commitment, still constitutes assistance to Imperial Germany. The German Minister, incidentally, was an accurate and intelligent reporter. He hardly produced "garbles" like this, but based reports of this import on thorough discussions with the man who brought the information. Keskuela's memory, forty-one years later, is less trustworthy than a contemporary document. (Romberg would not have reported about Lenin's offer without knowing who Keskuela's intermediary was and satisfying himself, so far as possible, on his reliability.) In 1961 Keskuela also denied having offered money in 1914 to Lenin's collaborators, Alexander Shlyapnikov and Alexandra Kollontai; yet these two rather honest revolutionaries asserted this fact when Keskuela's real role was not known to them. Keskuela struck the pose that he had been employing indirect methods of financing. But he also boasted: "Lenin was my protegé . . . It was I who launched Lenin." Futrell (pp. 147 and 151), who generally gives Keskuela the benefit of the doubt, admits that the version of indirect financing is not compatible with the documentary evidence.

was to redeem his other promises. In 1940 Stalin and Hitler negotiated over a similar alliance against Britain.

Keskuela, in a report dated September 30, 1915, warned that "social patriots" like Plekhanov and Axelrod were working for the defeat of Germany, and that they possessed ample means from the "government," presumably the tsarist government. By October, German funds were flowing to Lenin. On December 21, 1915, Rantzau transmitted to Berlin Parvus' estimate that the Russian revolution would cost twenty million rubles (40 million marks or about 10 million dollars).[9]

Yet it should be added that the monetary aspects of the unholy alliance were less important than the organizational support which the Germans were providing. Up to that time, Lenin had been unable to maintain adequate contact with his organization. The key Petrograd committee, for example, received from him only one letter during 1915.[10] The contact with the Germans permitted him to remedy this situation to a considerable extent. Equally important, the Germans reprinted, in large numbers and on "cigarette paper," Bolshevik materials, much of it on the Admiralty's press,[11] and transported these from Germany via Denmark, Sweden, and Finland into Russia. Reproductions of Bolshevik writings were also distributed at the front. In concealed fashion, German "cut-outs" took command of the Bolshevik organization in Sweden and from there exerted influence on the Bolsheviks in Russia. During 1913 and 1914 Lenin had analyzed systematically the list of *Pravda* subscribers and, though the war had brought about dislocations, a substantial portion of the old structure had remained intact. One of the contact points was Lenin's sister, Anna Yelizarova, but she probably knew nothing about the German support. However, she as well as Shlyapnikov and Skvortsov were visited by one of Keskuela's contact men, a Danish socialist by name of Alfred Kruse.[12] Contacts also extended to the Volga area, specifically to Saratov and Samara, once Lenin's residence. In addition, Parvus' two-way smuggling operation served to transmit funds to the Bolsheviks and other radicals. From time to time, messengers traveled back and forth into Russia. Thus, by the end of 1915, a number of professionals operating under the direction, and with the logic support of, the German Foreign Office had assumed leadership of Bolshevik groups. The German revolutionizers were also infiltrating other parties.

[9]Zeman, p. 9.

[10]Statement by N. I. Podvoisky, *Istoricheskii Arkhiv* (1956), No. 6, p. 112.

[11]Keskuela stated that plans to have this literature printed in Stockholm did not work out (Futrell, *Northern Underground*, p. 148).

[12]*Ibid.*, p. 137f.

Lenin exerted little influence. The Germans transmitted his various communications to Sweden, occasionally neglecting those with which they were not in agreement; they also relayed news from Russia to him, carefully reading the information before delivery. Lenin told them—through "cut-outs," no doubt—what else he knew. Hans Steinwachs, the "case officer" who supervised Keskuela for the German General Staff[13] considered Lenin an important source of intelligence.

In October, 1915, Lenin returned to Berne. With his financial stability assured, he did not yet burst into any great activity. In fact, he barely worked during the remainder of the year. Krupskaya reported that they saw *The Living Corpse,* a play by Tolstoi.[14] In December or early January of 1916, Lenin was invited to contribute a volume to the "Europe Before and After the War" series, to be published in Petrograd. He decided to write a book on imperialism—a subject which German propaganda was exploiting eagerly and which under the circumstances was directed against Britain and France, rather than Germany and Russia. Lenin began work by January 11, and completed his book on July 2, 1916. A short while later, the Lenins left for an extended vacation.

By February 11, 1916, Lenin had moved from Berne to Zurich, the latter city's library being larger.[15] There had again been a clash with the Mensheviks who, the Okhrana reported, wanted the 140,000 francs held in Germany.[16] Lenin refused; he had already obtained 100,000 francs. The Mensheviks were indignant: the International Socialist Commission required money. They proposed a compromise with Lenin receiving the largest portion. Lenin claimed he was not authorized to make any decisions but would query the Central Committee in Russia.[17] There the matter rested. Perhaps the Mensheviks

[13]Zeman, p. 13.

[14]Krupskaya, p. 311.

[15]There are discrepancies in these dates. According to information which the Okhrana obtained from the Swiss police, Lenin stayed at Zurich from May 22 till July 20, **1916.**

[16]The confusion in the figures persists. As reported above, Lenin allegedly gave the trustees 100,000 rubles or 250,000 francs. The German trustees might have paid the 110,000 francs and, if they did, both Bolsheviks and Mensheviks would have received money. Though it is possible that Lenin never paid 100,000 rubles, this residual figure of 56,000 rubles (140,000 francs) is so unusual that it suggests payments by the trustees. From vague indicators at the time of the Prague conference, there is a possibility that the Bolsheviks received 30,000 francs a year. This would account for 90,000 francs during 1912-1914. If then the Bolsheviks received 100,000 francs in 1915, there is a discrepancy of 20,000 francs which the Mensheviks (or someone like Martov) might have obtained. This would explain why there was no acrimonious quarrel about these funds before 1916. For a slightly different interpretation, see Schapiro, p. 129.

[17]Paris to Police Department, Petrograd, May 29, 1916.

were pacified with the remaining 40,000 francs; Lenin, however, may also have appropriated this money.

In Zurich, Lenin studied for two hours each morning and two hours each afternoon. During February and March, he studied the problems of national self-determination—another political line which the Germans were strongly advocating and the importance of which, Keskuela stated in 1961, Siefeld was told to impress upon Lenin. Strangely enough, at this time almost every one must have been happy with Vladimir. The Okhrana, on February 9, 1916, belatedly reported that the German left-socialists expected support from Russian revolutionaries. Lenin is said to have replied that the situation in Russia depended in large measure upon the revolutionary development in Germany: the Russian proletariat, he believed, would follow a revolution in Germany. In what Parvus described as a sentimental policy, Liebknecht advocated immediate peace with Russia—on the grounds that Russia had already been defeated.[18] It was fortunate for Lenin that the Germans did not read the mail of the Russian Okhrana.

In April, Lenin participated in the conference at Kienthal, the second meeting of the Zimmerwald group. Though the debates of this conference are now viewed by Communist historians as signifying a move to the left by international socialism, Kienthal actually had little practical significance. It is interesting that Inessa Armand, who had just returned from France and was then living in the town of Clarens, was a delegate in these congresses; Krupskaya was ailing again and did not participate.[19]

The choice of Clarens as a home base illustrates the conditions under which the Bolsheviks were then functioning. In Clarens there existed an excellent library which was well stocked with Russian materials. The library was owned by Nikolai Rubakhin, a non-denominational socialist and pacifist, who popularized scientific books. He was the brother of Julian Reichesberg, professor in Berne who contributed to *Die Neue Zeit* and headed the committee for assistance to Russian prisoners-of-war in Germany. Both Reichesberg and Rubakhin had contacts with the Germans—as could be expected.

During this period, the Swiss police thought they detected a transitory love affair between Lenin and a German countess who,

---

[18]Copenhagen to Berlin, December 7, 1915. If Liebknecht had prevailed, Lenin's suggestion that the people oppressed by Germany also should be liberated could not have become effective either. (He published this thought in May in a *legal* Petrograd magazine.)

[19] Early in 1916, Lenin wrote to his mother that Krupskaya again was suffering from Graves disease (Basedow) and though they now had a new apartment, with bath and shower, near the woods (Waldheimstrasse 66), they would have to go to the mountains.

they believed, functioned as his liaison with the printer, supposedly a Count von Ostheim; the nobleman seems to be a mythical figure. Probably the "printer" was Baron Friedrich von der Ropp, a Balt who worked for the military and later briefed General Ludendorff on Lenin. It is quite possible that Ropp was paying some of Lenin's printing bills, but perhaps only at a later time when Ropp was receiving large sums to propagandize the cause of the minority nations in Russia. Ropp's brother was still in Russia where the police suspected him of espionage. The report on the love affair, in all likelihood, was mistaken. The German countess presumably was Inessa Armand. But there is the implication that Inessa was aware of Lenin's financial dealings.

In May, Lenin spent some time in Geneva, lecturing and using the library. Krupskaya fell ill again and Lenin, too, was suffering from tension. The Lenins went for a rest in the mountains. Renting for twenty-five francs a month a little house in a French-speaking canton, they lived there from sometime in July until August 14, and then moved to a sanatorium in the German-speaking area, paying 150 francs per month for room and board. On this sum they enjoyed simple comforts. Actually, a few months earlier, sister Anna had written Lenin to inquire whether he needed money; he rejected her offer. The vacation was marred by news of the death of Lenin's mother on August 7, near Petrograd. She was buried under a Christian cross. Lenin's last letter to the ailing woman was dated March 12, in answer to a short note of February 1 in which, in a postscript to Anna's letter, she told about Maria's teaching in Moscow and acquiring many friends.

In August, while still in the mountains, Lenin wrote a letter to G. L. Shklovsky, one of Lenin's contacts with money sources, complaining of a lack of money. There were two parties within the German Foreign Office, one advocating the revolutionizing of Russia and the other seeking a separate peace with the Tsar. By summer of 1916, the latter party, benefitting from the failure of revolutionizing attempts, had gained the upper hand. There had been received information that the Tsar had been persuaded the war would be followed by revolution, hence he wanted to continue the war to delay the catastrophe. Wilhelm, on March 11, 1916, commented in a marginal note: "Heavens, is this stupid! And for this thousands must bleed to death."

Perhaps discreet overtures were made. Rumor had it that the Germans were willing to guarantee the Russian throne against the revolution. There seems to have been some response, especially after the visit to Russia of the French Minister of Munitions, Albert Thomas. Thomas was a socialist who genuinely wished to defeat Germany and who attempted to encourage enthusiasm for the war among Russian "defencist" socialists. It is certain, however, that he promised them aid in reform or even revolution after the war. The Tsar, it appears, was furious about Thomas' contacts, the importance of which undoubtedly was exaggerated by the Okhrana. Sazonov, the pro-Entente Foreign Minister, was dismissed and a new Minister, Boris V. Sturmer, who was generally deemed to be pro-German, was installed. His confidential secretary, Ivan L. Manasevich-Manuilov, was soon arrested. He was an old hand at the most devious phases of intelligence and political warfare and had often been used by the Germans for the press activities inside Russia.[20] Sturmer placed him in charge of controlling Rasputin's activities.

On August 7, 1916, Wilhelm II suggested that a separate peace was the best solution, a judgment that reflected the success of a Russian military offensive under General Brusilov and that was related to the appointment of a new German military High Command.

On November 27, 1916, the widow of Grand Duke Konstantino-vich,[21] a German-born princess, conveyed through the Queen of Sweden a broad hint (*"politische Andeutung"*) to Prince Max of Baden. The Germans were prepared to act upon this suggestion. Keskuela had noted the reversal in German policy on July 26, and had attempted to continue his operation by briefing Romberg on the deployment of the revolutionary movement in Russia, especially the Bolsheviks. He marshalled arguments against the separate peace policy. Although the handwritten notes which Romberg kept of the conversation are not very readable, it can be determined that Keskuela suggested the novel coordination of uprising with the offensive utilization of Zeppelins. In any event, Romberg did not relay this choice suggestion, probably knowing that to argue for revolutionizing would be futile at that precise moment.

Keskuela said in 1961 that Lenin quarreled with Siefeld over the national question. Romberg's notes, so far as they can be deciphered, do suggest some friction between Lenin and Keskuela. On October 14, Keskuela complained that the revolutionizing effort lacked momentum. Accommodating himself to the new German policy aiming at a separate peace strategy, Keskuela reverted to advocating the Estonian

---

[20]Golder, *op. cit.,* p. 157.

[21]The Grand Duke, the poet of the Romanov family under the pseudonym "K.R." was the protector of the Russian capital's foremost "fixer," Prince Mikhail Andronikov, who also was Rasputin's main financial agent and his contact with pro-German Jewish bankers. The Germans were supposed to be in contact with these circles all along, but the Foreign Office file refers to a conversation with a friend of Rasputin only on March 9, 1916—other data have not yet been found. On September 11, 1916, there appears a list of persons who could be used as intermediaries in separate peace negotiations. The Germans had then very exact knowledge of the situation at Petrograd. Compare also Buchanan, *op. cit.,* p. 245. According to Persky, Andronikov stayed with the Bolsheviks in 1918.

cause; but this provoked hostility towards him on the part of the many German Balts influential in the Wilhelmstrasse.

The flow of German money to the Bolsheviks ceased. Lenin learned of this turn in his fortunes when he returned to Zurich in mid-September.[22] Compounding his troubles, the publication of *Imperialism* proved infeasible. There was no money at all. Lenin wrote to Shlyapnikov[23] that unless money were forthcoming, "we are going to croak."[24] Lenin even considered putting the ailing Krupskaya to work; but this was unnecessary, although for a few days she did help Felix Kohn. It is not clear how money was procured. In an emergency, Inessa may have been able to help. Possibly Lenin received assistance from Karl Moor. Yelizarov, the wealthy brother-in-law, was called upon and occasionally sent 100 or 200 rubles. To a great extent, this was "window dressing": it is unlikely that all of the organizational money had been spent; therefore Lenin was capable of drawing on his party salary. We know from Krupskaya that not all of the inheritance from the aunt had been spent. But the primary source of money was gone. It was politically advisable to publicize the fact that the Bolsheviks had no funds: perhaps some of the comrades could be goaded into raising money.[25] And the undesired penury could be put to good use to disprove the ugly rumors about unsavory money sources—a classical deception maneuver.

Late in 1916, Lenin resumed loose contact with the Germans, through uncertain channels.[26] The hopes for separate peace had been disappointed again, and the Berlin revolutionizers, though they did not regain control, were able to function, preserving the option for revolution as a sort of reassurance against failure with the

[22]The Lenins lived at Zurich in Spiegelgasse, adjoining a sausage factory (which caused a "terrible stink," according to Krupskaya. The flat was opposite a "dadaist" cabaret (Futrell, p. 153).

[23]Shlyapnikov was an engineer who had lived several years in France and was traveling on a French passport. He also spent some time in Britain and worked temporarily at Vickers-Armstrong. From the Spring of 1916, he spent most of his time in Petrograd but, apparently, returned several times to Scandinavia. He served via Stockholm as Lenin's main liaison with the Bolsheviks in Russia. The son of Old Believers (who did not record his birth, which occurred probably in 1885), he was dependable and clear-headed, and "had the ability, rare among Russians, to organize" (Futrell, p. 106).

[24]Lenin, *Sochineniya,* 4th edition, Vol. 35, p. 187.

[25]For what it is worth, a survivor from the Berne German legation personnel told me that Lenin was unsure about the outcome of the war and insured himself against a possible necessity of leaving Europe. If he had been forced to flee, he intended to go to Brazil. For this purpose he allegedly kept a money reserve.

[26]By December 16, 1916, Romberg again showed interest in renewing the contact via Keskuela. There may have been small German contributions *à fonds perdu* to keep the Bolshevik organization going, but it is unlikely that significant payments were made before January or even February, 1917.

Tsar. This group, very skeptical of the advisability of a separate peace with the tsarist system, argued that it was not sufficient merely to frighten the Romanovs with revolution, or even to overthrow the dynasty. They insisted upon the destruction of the Russian state. Lenin collected Marxist quotations on the need for the proletarian revolution to demolish the bourgeois state. These notes were later included in one of his best known books, *State and Revolution,* which was published in an incomplete form in December of 1917. At that time, the Russian legation at Berne received a report that Lenin had visited the German legation. Probably the claim was false; no corroboration of the denunciation exists in the Okhrana file. Nevertheless, the Russian legation complained about Lenin, apparently describing him as a deserter—perhaps an attempt to have him arrested or extradited. The Swiss police investigated and, in January, Lenin presented a written declaration denying the charge: "Since the 1905 revolution, I have been a political refugee." Lenin moved to Zurich on January 2, 1917, and reported to the police on January 5.[27] A few days later, a Swiss police agent estimated that the Lenins had a monthly income of 200 to 250 francs.

Lenin was almost inactive. He gave his customary speech commemorating Bloody Sunday. Despite the current "tomb-like stillness," he claimed, Europe was pregnant with change. Yet, "we of the older generation may not live to see the decisive battles of this coming revolution." As he offered his melancholic remarks, the Russian Revolution was beginning.

[27]While at the police, Krupskaya was asked where they had been between July 20 and January 2. She replied that they had been on vacation but was unwilling to state precisely *where* they had spent their time.

The Throne Collapses

The assassination of Rasputin had ended the inertia. To the disgust of the Tsar, the British insisted upon internal reforms. By the end of February, 1917, the Tsar decided to discuss terms of peace with Austria. The Germans, under a Red Cross cloak, were about to send Prince Max of Baden to Stockholm.[1] Partly to forestall peace moves and partly to eliminate the virtually insane Tsarina and

[1]The Tsarina's brother, Grand Duke Ludwig of Hesse, reportedly went to Russia *incognito* late in 1916. The Hesse family has continued to deny this story and it would seem foolish for the Grand Duke to travel, in the midst of war, to enemy Russia. A trip to Finland would have been more easily arranged but would have been pointless if personal contact was desired. Communications between brother and sister could be easily maintained through Sweden.

replace Nicholas II by an energetic Romanov, the military was backing a palace revolution scheduled for March or April.[2]

Early in March, socialist groups in Russia, still debating whether strikes and insurrections were premature, were warning against police provocations. Shlyapnikov, who led the Petrograd Bolsheviks, was trying to restrain action. Yet a strike flared up in the Putilov works and the old revolutionary "Cherevanin" (F. A. Lipkin), a creature of Parvus, initiated conversations about the reestablishment of a soviet. There were arrests, but labor leaders were simultaneously being released from prison. On March 12, a steering committee was formed. Within a few hours, this committee constituted the Petrograd soviet.

There were various moves by the Okhrana which suggest that an operation similar to that used in the 1905 Moscow uprising was being organized. The plan was to eradicate the revolutionary organizations, to use a pseudo-revolution to forestall the palace *coup d'état,* and ultimately to bring about a separate peace with the Central Powers. Unrest was an indispensable element of the separate peace: it was needed to release Russia from her obligations to the allies and to ensure their financial benevolence.

On September 29, 1916, Alexander D. Protopopov, a Duma vice-president, was appointed Minister of the Interior, supposedly to improve relations between the throne and the legislature. Actually, Protopopov had attempted to negotiate with the Germans at Stockholm. The figurehead of *Volya Rossii,* a newspaper whose German attachments were notorious[3], he was close to the Rasputin clique and the mystics at the court. The latter connections and his Stockholm discussions rather than his Duma membership are the clues that disclose the more important intentions of his appointment.

The allies knew that there existed no military reason that would justify Russia's quitting the war: both army morale and war production had been improving. There were economic difficulties, but they could be managed. The issue was political: the country lacked an efficient government able to inspire public confidence. To achieve this the Tsarina would have to be eliminated as an active political figure, a vigorous step toward constitutionalism would have to be risked, and perhaps the Tsar would have to be supplanted by a

[2]Communist writers (e.g., Trotsky) denied that a palace revolution was in the making. There is, however, ample confirmation, including the recent autobiography by General Bonch-Bruyevich (*op. cit.,* pp. 124ff) who also asserts that the British and French Ambassadors knew about the plot. According to many uncorroborated reports in the German file, the British desired the *coup d'état* to ensure an effective Russian contribution to the war and block the separate peace maneuver. Rightly or wrongly, the British seem to have been convinced that the separate peace between Russian and Germany had become unavoidable unless Nicholas II were eliminated.

[3]Golder, *op. cit.,* p. 173.

Romanov regent. The Tsar was, of course, unwilling to adopt this course: he had little choice but to try to defend existing conditions.

There were good reasons for the Tsar to fear a separate peace which might lead to uprisings and also might deliver him to the mercies of his cousin, Wilhelm II. Nevertheless, he was in a quandary, for he realized that, for compelling political reasons, the war could not be continued indefinitely. The time for negotiation had not yet arrived, but Nicholas had to determine the basis on which the Germans would be willing to negotiate. The conditions of 1916, as reported by Protopopov, were unacceptable.

There is evidence which indicates that the Tsar opposed a separate peace. Much of this evidence, however, should be considered with caution since it is derived mainly from statements made prior to these critical days. There is no documentation to indicate whether the Tsar, during the last weeks of his regime, wanted or did not want a separate peace. But ample evidence exists that peace discussions (not negotiations, in the technical meaning of the term) had been going on since mid-1916; that leading personalities of the Russian government were involved in these discussions; and that by February-March 1917, Germany and Austria, hardly without Russian encouragement, were preparing to step up these contacts.[4] The Tsar, in fact, did nothing to halt these activities. On the contrary, he furthered the career of some of those who had been seeking contacts with the enemy.

To understand the separate peace problem, a number of key factors must be distinguished: first, German agents in Russia agitating for separate peace; secondly, Russian politicians and businessmen who wanted an end to the war;[5] thirdly, more or less authorized

[4]Much of the evidence from the Russian side was collected by S. P. Melgunov, *Legenda o separatnom mirye* (Paris: no publisher, 1957). This work was published after his death before the author could finalize his conclusions. Melgunov showed that there was no formal negotiation and he argued that the Tsar did not really know or approve of these transactions. He failed to understand the technical difficulty of such an undertaking, and also underrated the momentum of the effort. He did not have pertinent information from the German and Austrian files. By arguing that only Russian personalities of secondary importance were involved, he misinterpreted the role of the Prime Minister, the Minister of the Interior and other high-ranking personalities, and also misconstrued the function of intermediaries who by necessity must be able to operate anonymously.

[5]One such group centered around the financier Manus, many of whose interests were devoted to the transport industry. Manus had connections with several banking firms influenced by German capital. He supposedly distributed German secret funds in Russia. The validity of this theory appears doubtful, since Manus was primarily attracted by the cause of money-making. However, once a week he had Rasputin for dinner, and these regular dinners always were attended by two or three important court officers from the Tsarina's immediate entourage. The classified information revealed during these evenings presumably was passed on, and many of the "counsels" given to the Tsarina through Rasputin (notably with respect

"hints" or "feelers" from both sides—largely within the aristocratic and dynastic internationals; fourthly, occasional exploratory talks, such as Protopopov's conversation at Stockholm; fifthly, projects for contacts (even *Austria* made a request on February 26, 1917, to enter into negotiations, perhaps designed to accelerate action within the government at Berlin) .

Finally, it must be noted that the Germans waged psychological warfare: they leaked misleading stories about separate peace negotiations to the *Berner Tagwacht*. These rumors were spread by the world press and, despite immediate denials from Petersburg, created a great deal of suspicion, especially in London. The Russian nationalist and liberal opposition utilized these tales against the government during November, 1916; they were, to a degree, responsible for a more acute fear of the Tsar's policies in London and Paris, for the assassination of Rasputin, and for the preparations for the palace coup.

The Germans took an *open* initiative during December, 1916, calling for peace negotiations between all belligerents. The Russian Foreign and War Ministries drafter a declaration intended to squelch all premature peace talk. They stated that Russia's war aims were Constantinople and an independent Poland incorporating the Polish territories of Germany, Austria, and Russia—and that these aims had to be realized before peace could be discussed. The Tsar signed this paper. Although the declaration of December 25 was written in a tone of determination, it actually constituted a counter-

---

to incessant changes of Cabinet Ministers) presumably originated during these Wednesday soirées. Banker D. L. Rubinstein, who stood to Rasputin in a relationship similar as did Manus, specialized in acquiring shares of requisitioned German firms and helped the Tsarina to transfer money to Germany; he was more obviously interested than Manus in politics, for he acquired shares of newspaper corporations. However, Manus associated with a former secretary of Witte, a State Councillor named Josif Y. Kolyshko who, after leaving government service, had become a political commentator. Several times, during the 1915-1917 period Kolyshko negotiated with the Germans gaining their implicit trust. It is likely that Manus passed much of his intelligence through Kolyshko. The German industrialist Hugo Stinnes, in agreement with the Wilhelmstrasse, gave Kolyshko two million rubles to establish or buy a newspaper (in August, 1916). Kolyshko broke with Stinnes and after the fall of the Tsar was pressed by the Wilhelmstrasse into the service of the second revolution. Parvus advised the Germans that Kolyshko should be taken seriously—apparently the two men met. Gorky's *Novaya Zhizn*, which started publication in May, 1917, was financed in part by the Stinnes money (transferred through Kolyshko) who also had acquired the *Petrogradskii Kuryer*. Kolyshko apparently was the main disbursing agent for the Bolshevik unrest in April and May, later boasting that he had "worked hard" to evict from the provisional government P. N. Milyukov as Foreign Minister and A. I. Guchkov as War Minister. Kolyshko was arrested by the end of May, released on bail in September, and then escaped abroad. This story demonstrates the continuity and interrelationships of the German effort but it does not indicate whether people like Manus were themselves agents or used by agents. It does indicate the enormous impact a well-placed agent can have and retain even while circumstances are changing.

proposal to Germany's demand that Russia free non-Russian nationalities in Eastern Europe. The paper signified that a compromise was possible in relation to Poland, provided Germany would sacrifice Turkey for a Russo-German understanding.

But how could Russia negotiate seriously with the demanding Germans? It was not feasible to improve Russia's bargaining position through military means. Yet, destruction of the internal opposition would strengthen the Tsar's position.

Even more pressing than these considerations was the need to forestall the impending palace coup which had been stimulated (though not caused exclusively) by a German rumor campaign of a non-existing negotiation that had led to closer relations between the "defencist" opposition and the British and French in Russia.[6] The Allies now were cajoling the Tsar to reform his regime. This single fact lessened perceptibly his enthusiasm for the alliance. It was not a question of whether the Tsar was about to "betray" the allies; after all, the Allies had fallen for a German propaganda trick and were now opposing the Tsar, though the Tsar's misgovernment was an equally potent cause in their change of attitude. In so far as Nicholas was concerned, however, the important factor was that he no longer could depend upon the loyalty of the governments in London and Paris. And he hardly was oblivious to the fact that if he had followed the advice which he was receiving from London (and to a lesser extent from Paris), the Russian government would have been seized by strongly pro-British elements. The Tsar, undoubtedly, was convinced that he needed more freedom of action against his own allies, quite irrespective of the separate peace question.

It is unlikely that the Tsar feared a socialist insurrection—the socialist leaders were trying their best to quiet their restless followers. It is more likely that because the revolutionary inclination of the populace were underrated, the fanning of a "little" unrest was considered to be without risk. Hence under the cloak of trouble, the government might move against the aristocratic, military, and bourgeois opposition preparing the palace coup. Several dates had been set for the coup, but it seems that the government had obtained intelligence which led it to expect the action by about March 24 (New Style). Preventive action, then, would have to be underway two to three weeks earlier: "P-Day" ("P" for provocation) would be some time near March 10.

Early in 1917, the Tsar's relations with Britain worsened and the military district of Petrograd, which had been under the commander of the northern front, was established as an independent command headed by the Minister of War. The purpose of this maneuver was to

[6]For a summary of the various *coup d'état* projects, see Michael Smilg-Benario, *Der Zusammenbruch der Zarenmonarchie* (Wien: Amalthea, 1928), pp. 89-108.

deprive the generals, who were believed to be implicated in the palace coup plot (including the commander of the northern front), of operational command authority in the capital. German communications intelligence noted this change and, on the basis of several additional indicators including cessation of messages transmitted abroad, deduced the probability of a strong governmental action. On February 20, 1917, Ziese, a German agent, submitted in Stockholm a rather foresighted prediction of the events that were soon to transpire. On February 26, an Englishman passing through Sweden from Petrograd decided that the situation in Russia would soon turn against British interests.[7]

In the meantime, rumors spread that bread was becoming scarce in Petrograd and that bread lines were forming before bakeries. Since there was no shortage of flour, the trouble could have been remedied easily; proper actions, however, were not undertaken in time. The police, trained in the use of machine guns, placed an unknown number of these weapons on roof tops to control the main thoroughfares of the capital.

Months later, when Protopopov was indicted, it was alleged that he had asked the Tsar for 400,000 rubles to crush the revolution. The money was to be used to train the police and to buy machine guns. The Tsar approved of the measure but allocated only 50,000 rubles, to be paid on February 25. No money was required, of course, to train the police or even to purchase machine guns, since they could have been requisitioned from the army; obviously the special funds were to be allotted to operations not yet financed by the government. In any event, a payment on February 25 would have come too late for the training of the police, as well as for the acquisition and deployment of the machine guns. For that matter, it is not known whether the 50,000 rubles were paid, although it *is* known that 200,000 rubles from the Tsar's secret fund were requested *by Nicholas* early in March and given to him on March 9—a most unusual transaction. The agitators, who were to become active within one or two days, were paid from unknown sources.[8] According to one witness, they each received seven rubles a day, but this figure seems high.[9]

If the amount allocated for the provocation was 200,000 rubles

---

[7]The unnamed Englishman's remarks were reported to German authorities.

[8]Gurko, *op. cit.*, p. 272.

[9]According to W. K. Korostowetz, the patriotic demonstrators who, late in July, 1914, were called into the streets to counter the impression created by the "revolutionary" demonstrators, were paid three rubles. (*Lenin im Hause der Väter* (Berlin Kulturpolitik, 1928), p. 146.) Since apparently the Germans paid only one and one-half rubles, this must have been the start of the inflation in the business of revolution.

and, if indeed seven rubles were paid per demonstrator, then the plan may have been to have ten thousand men demonstrate for three days—a minor demonstration—but it is likely that not every demonstrator was to be compensated for his enthusiasm. Unquestionably, the police could use funds appropriated in the usual manner in addition to the special ones. In brief, the financial evidence seems to suggest that demonstrations by twenty or thirty thousand revolutionaries were planned. This order of magnitude would fit the challenge of such a provocatory operation in the midst of war. In order to serve its purpose, the unrest would have had to have been "significant"; but to retain control and to avoid encouraging the enemy, the unrest would have had to have been kept within bounds.

Provocation is a precarious operation. In 1905, Tsar Nicholas was served by a team of experts headed by Durnovo, Minister of the Interior, General Trepov, Palace Commander, and Rachkovsky, the tactical Field Commander. All of them were guided by the crafty Prime Minister, Witte. In 1917, the Prime Minister, with only two months experience in his job, knew nothing of the "black arts." The military District Commander not only lacked energy, but was also quite incapable. He may not have even been informed of the operations being planned. He obviously had no plan of his own, exercised no effective command, and delayed redeployments and orders to use arms until it was too late. Protopopov was the strategic commander in charge but he lacked the skill and intelligence necessary to carry this task to a successful conclusion. There exists ample evidence to prove that Protopopov was mentally unbalanced;[10] possibly he was syphilitic.[11] Underestimating the strength of the organized revolutionaries at Petrograd, he believed that the core did not exceed 300 men; there were probably about five to ten times that number. Protopopov's private secretary, a certain Orlov, who was arrested after the overthrow of the Tsar, was later liberated by Lenin, and reportedly joined the Bolsheviks.[12]

Another person who may later have made his peace with the Bolsheviks was police General Mikhail Stepanovich Komisarov.[13] (His wife was previously mentioned as Lenin's aide.[14]) While still a captain, Komisarov had received instructions from Rachkovsky himself and had run the anti-semitic operation through which, in 1905,

[10]P. E. Shchepolev (ed), *Padeniye tsarskogo rezhima,* vol. I, Leningrad, 1924, pp. XXIX, 111-181; Melgunov, pp. 229, 264.

[11]The Tsar wrote about this affliction of his minister to the Tsarina on November 10, 1916.

[12]Persky, *op. cit.,* p. 273.

[13]Ibid., p. 272.

[14]See page 100.

the Okhrana hoped to deflect the revolution.[15] Whether or not Komisarov possessed the ability to handle this super-provocation of 1917 as its tactical field commander can never be ascertained, because on or about March 12, this master of ceremonies was unexpectedly abducted and thus neatly prevented from demonstrating his talents.[16] Komisarov was later released unharmed; the identity of his abductors is not known. But the action was a masterful strike in intelligence operations. It is most unlikely that any Russian organization would have shown so much dexterity. The Germans certainly were not involved either, but they themselves were sure that they detected the hand of the British in this incident.[17]

The abduction of Komisarov, however, was not the only or even the primary cause of the provocation failure. The tactics planned by the police were inept; the intended employment of machine guns from predetermined fixed positions was especially faulty. The Petrograd garrison of 160,000 men was sufficiently strong numerically, but the soldiers were mostly those beyond the age of active duty or those convalescing from former wounds. Both groups of soldiers were naturally strongly against war and therefore oppositional. The better caliber of soldiers consisted mostly of "minority nationalities," especially Ukrainians and White Russians; there also were Letts, Lithuanians, Finns, and Estonians. These troops had become strongly anti-Tsar.[18] The morale situation among the military was aggravated by poor logistics which resulted in a scarcity of warm food and drinks and the overuse of troops to beyond the fatigue point. The men who were used most extensively and broke first were in undisciplined reserve units. The Cossack units consisted largely of untrained recruits who were obviously not suited for action against civilians. The officers assigned to the Petrograd garrison were sick in large numbers, wounded, or desk types unaccustomed to leading troops and imposing discipline. In addition, many of the reserve officers sympathized with the revolution.

The tsarist government had for years failed to provide indoctrination courses for its troops. It did not even practice civilian "public relations." During 1916 five million rubles had been allocated for this purpose but by March, 1917, none of this sum had been spent.

The situation got out of hand when the management of the Putilov armament works, the largest concern in Russia and in Petro-

[15]A. A. Lopukhin, Otryvki iz vospominanii (Moscow, 1923), p. 88.

[16]Louis de Trywdar-Burzynski, Le Crépuscule d'une autorité et quelques crises en Allemagne, (Extraits de Souvenirs) (Florence: Rossi, 1926), p. 151f.

[17]The Germans adduced many data to show the similarity of the February revolution with British activities directed in 1908 and 1909 against the Sultan of Turkey.

[18]Keskuela reported that the Estonian infantry men were foremost among those who refused to obey orders and put down mass unrest.

grad, took advantage of a desultory strike (on March 7) to institute a complete lock-out of its 30,000 workers. This created a strong emotional reaction. A. A. Putilov was in favor of Nicholas' elimination, and he may have initiated the lock-out to aggravate the situation.

Moreover, March 8 was the "Day of the Female Worker." For this date, demonstrations (mostly of women) had been planned. Except for the Okhrana agents among them, such as V. Y. Shurkanov, the revolutionary organizers still insisted on a relatively peaceful demonstration. But the Putilov workers, being idle, joined the women; the police, whose orders were to be accommodating, became entirely passive in the face of female wrath. Such police behavior stimulated many would-be demonstrators. As the news spread that the government seemed to have lost control of the situation, the columns grew longer and more and more demonstrators appeared in the streets.

Only at this point did the revolutionary organizations take action. The Bolsheviks were particularly slow; they are, to this day, in their historical writings attempting to predate their revolutionary actions. Yet a small Social Democratic splinter unit, composed chiefly of intellectuals (the so-called *Mezhrayontsi* or inter-burrough organization), was the first revolutionary group which, through posters and appeals, sprang into action and advanced the revolution. This group was under the leadership of I. K. Yurenyev and was associated with Trotsky, who was then in New York.[19] In addition, local Bolshevik cell and factory leaders, notably V. N. Kayurov[20] and Chugurin, in defiance of such party hierarchs as Shlyapnikov, called out their troops. Due to the initiative of such men, the demonstrators, who had been stopped at the Neva bridges, were led across the ice into the central sectors of town; the crossing, which could have been blocked easily, was unopposed. Mensheviks and Social Revolutionaries joined the soldiers, inciting them to mutiny; this effort was seconded by Bolshevik and other agitators who were serving under the colors. The garrison which was ordered to support the now powerless police

[19]I. Yurenyev " 'Mezhrayonka, (1911-1917),' " *Proletarskaya Revolyutsiya* (1924), Nos. 1 and 2. The *mezhrayonka* may have been in touch through Larina with the Parvus organization. There is no good evidence where the money went, which Parvus and Hanecki earned to finance the revolution. At a minimum, several tens of thousands of rubles, and perhaps more than 100,000 rubles must have been available, granting that profits were far smaller than turn-over and that profits had to be split. (For the basis of this estimate, *see* Futrell, p. 188.) The Petrograd Bolshevik organization remained without substantial funds. There is hardly any doubt that Parvus and Hanecki pumped substantial amounts of money into the *Mezhrayonka*. Prof. George Katkov, with whom the writer discussed this problem, also is inclined to accept this interpretation.

[20]*Proletarskaya Revolyutsiya* (1923), No. 13, *Istoricheskii Arkhiv* (1956), No. 5, p. 148.

refused to shoot. One regiment after another mutinied, placing itself under the orders of the Duma which had suddenly become a revolutionary command center.

On March 10 the Tsar wired Petrograd, "I order to liquidate . . . by tomorrow the unrest in the capital."[21] (This command sounds almost like Xerxes ordering the Hellespont to be whipped.) But if the telegram is read simply as a counterorder to the stage directors of the provocation, it loses its tone of imbecility; Nicholas II should not be considered a comic opera prince.

The order was sent too late. The leading generals told the Tsar that the moment of abdication had arrived. Tsarism was at its end.[22] The aims of the palace revolution had been achieved. But in the process, the political earthquake and the social upheaval which the plotters had wanted to avoid by a neat surgical operation had taken place after all. The revolutionary Mephistopheles held the promise of everything to everybody—happiness, pleasure, whatever one could dream of or desire. The Russian people, similar to Faust, answered eagerly, *"Eh bien, pauvre démon, fais-moi voir tes merveilles."*[23]

Keskuela, the devil's disciple, immediately wrote for *Die Neue Zeit* an article calling for the completion of the revolution. Nicholas Murray Butler, a leading American intellectual, commented that Jean-Jacques Rousseau again had been proven the greatest political force in the world. Butler described the Russian revolution as the "product of philosophy and letters"[24] and wished it godspeed. Such are the delusions of some intellectuals.

---

[21]Smilg-Benario, p. 140.

[22]Contrary to the superficial interpretation of many historians to the effect that the February revolution was "spontaneous," Lenin, far more correctly, ascribed it to the collusion of three forces: English-French finance capital, "the entire bourgeoisie and the landowning-capitalist class in Russia (and the higher officers in the army)," and the revolutionary proletariat, including the revolutionary soldiers. (*Werke,* vol. 36, p. 410f.)

[23]Goethe, as translated by Gérard de Nerval.

[24]*New York Times,* April 24, 1917.

The Sealed Car

In Zurich, Lenin knew nothing about these momentous changes. The morning of March 15, as he was leaving for the library and Krupskaya had finished washing the breakfast dishes, a friend ran into their apartment and reported that the revolution had begun. Lenin and Krupskaya proceeded to read the newspapers which were hung up in display boxes. On March 16 the Tsar's abdication was confirmed.

But Lenin belittled the event: the bourgeoisie had legalized the political power that it already possessed *de facto*. He did not expect that a labor party would be legalized. If it were, the unification of the Bolsheviks and the Mensheviks would be unavoidable!

The news had been electrifying to the revolutionaries. Some Bolsheviks living in Sweden had started for home already. Lenin's initial response was a strengthening of his belief that the Bolsheviks would have to continue existence as an independent party. He did not consider returning to Russia. Lenin wrote to one of the Bolshevik Duma deputies who had been arrested in 1914 that, upon his release, he was to go to Scandinavia in order to organize Lenin's liaison with Russia. On March 17 Lenin proposed the establishment of a communication point in Norway and called for the organization of revolutionary cells within the army. This demand could not but curry favor with the Germans, who were reading Lenin's mail. On March 18 Lenin calmly traveled to western Switzerland, met Inessa, and gave his customary talk on the Paris Commune.

Lenin assumed that "it will not be possible to get away early from this damned Switzerland."[1] Yet German diplomats already were planning the return of Lenin to Russia. A few weeks later, the German Chancellor, Bethmann-Hollweg, reported to the Emperor that "immediately" upon learning of the Russian revolution—he received this news during the afternoon of March 14—he instructed the German Minister to Switzerland to offer the Russian exiles passage through Germany. It is not clear which channels were to be used; the Germans had a large number of contacts. These included Dr. Kornblum who participated in the Bolshevik conference of 1915, and who at that time apparently was in contact with von Bismarck; Buchholz, whom Lenin had known from Samara and Berlin; Bagocki, who had been involved at Cracow and who soon became the executive secretary of a committee working for the return of the revolutionaries from Switzerland to Russia; Shklovsky, who during 1916 was one of the persons who transmitted money to Lenin. Also of importance in such work were the correspondent of the *Frankfurter Zeitung*, Dr. Deinhard; the German left-socialist Paul Levi; the promotor of the Youth International and Lenin's young German adherent, Willi Muenzenberg; the Polish socialist and former German journalist, Karl Radek; a Swiss socialist, Hermann von Boetticher; finally, the several contacts which the military attaché had among the international Mensheviks; and, of course, Keskuela and Moor.

It was indeed simple to plant the idea. Already in 1915 Parvus

[1]Krupskaya, p. 337.

had dispatched Russian revolutionaries through Germany. The German military wanted Lenin to organize sabotage campaigns. On December 29, 1916, Okhrana agent "Gretchen" reported that Lenin was still in Switzerland and would not leave via Germany: even if he were able to obtain the visa he would not use it—to avoid giving for a second time the impression of collusion with the Central Powers. It would be interesting to know the background of this perplexing "premature" document.

Financial support to Lenin was probably resumed before the overthrow of the Tsar: the Germans knew through their intelligence service that major changes were impending. On February 17, Lenin wrote that numbers three and four of *Sbornik Sotsialdemokrata* (a collection of theoretical articles) were ready, but "how sad—we have no money."[2] During that period, surviving witnesses have reported, Zinovyev often paid Lenin's restaurant bill. On March 10, however, the German Minister dispatched to Berlin the two previous *Sbornik* issues (which Keskuela secured and which the experts in the Foreign Office never read) and added, "I hear that publication of numbers three and four is assured." On March 17 money was available and was offered to the comrades in Scandinavia.

The Petrograd bureau of the Central Committee sent a telegram through Norway on March 18 which Lenin presumably received on March 19. It stated: "Ulyanov must come immediately." The revolution had been underway for more than a week and the Tsar had abdicated three days earlier, but only *now* did the Bolsheviks remember their leader who had not yet bestirred himself. He had merely tried to establish contact through Alexandra Kollontai, a woman comrade in Stockholm, but she had returned to Russia without waiting for the leader's advice.

Despite this invitation, and another to go at least to Finland, Lenin took no serious action. Unlike other revolutionaries he did not go to the British and French consulates. He asked Safarov to lend him his passport so that he could travel through France under a false name. Yet Safarov had been disseminating defeatist propaganda to the French army. With his passport Lenin would have met with more trouble with the French authorities than if he had been traveling under his own name; preparations for the trip were discontinued.

But presently, Lenin's old enemy, Martov, suggested at a meeting at Geneva with Bolsheviks on March 19, that the revolutionaries be permitted to pass through Germany in exchange for Austrian and German prisoners of war.[3] This proposal was contingent upon

[2]*Letters of Lenin*, p. 411; *also* Werner Hahlweg, *Lenin's Rückkehr nach Russland 1917, die Deutschen Akten* (Leiden: Brill, 1957), p. 10.

[3]Krupskaya, p. 338.

approval by the Petrograd government.

Martov made the unfounded assumption that France and Britain would deny passage. It was not unreasonable to expect difficulties, but the proper course of action would have been to request instructions and diplomatic and consular assistance from Petrograd. Yet Lenin and his temporary allies of Menshevik loyalty did not even consider applying for passage through allied territory, despite the fact that many Russian émigrés were returning home via the West, usually in allied ships.

The Bolsheviks and international Mensheviks, as well as the left Social Revolutionaries, the Jewish Bund, Polish socialists, and other defeatist groups had had dealings with the Central Powers.4 The key men in these groups, uncertain as to what extent their secret contacts had been detected, did not wish to risk indictment for espionage. The German legation believed, however, that the revolutionaries feared the sea voyage with its peril of submarine attack.

The revolutionaries resolved to contact Berlin through the Swiss government and requested that the Swiss socialist deputy, Robert Grimm, act as negotiator in their behalf. Grimm was leading the Zimmerwald movement. The revolutionaries probably suspected that he maintained close contacts with the German legation. In Lenin's judgment (expressed in January, 1917), Grimm had gone over to the "social patriots" and was destroying the movement;5 Grimm was guilty of "complete treason." Yet he was now chosen to conceal the true nature of the transaction—or selected with the expectation that he would do nothing.

On March 20, Lenin resumed a rather desultory literary effort. On March 21 Parvus saw in Copenhagen Brockdorff-Rantzau to whom he proposed mobilization of the more radical socialists against the new Russian government which was democratic, pro-Entente, and "defencist." The next day Parvus transmitted to Adolf Müller, the Bavarian socialist who had excellent connections with the Berlin government, a program which was to be accomplished by their Russian "party friends." It called for the arming of workers, indictment of the Tsar, proclamation of a republic, confiscation of crown lands, convocation of a constituent assembly, partition of large land

4The leader of the left Social Revolutionaries was the veteran revolutionary Mark A. Natanson. He was the subject of an Okhrana report of February 20, 1905, which stated that he was in close contact with police agents with whom he sometimes spoke quite candidly. Victor Chernov, leader of the Social Revolutionaries and their foremost Zimmerwaldian defeatist, was in contact with the Austrians and later with the Germans through Alexander Evgenevich Zivin, whose role was partly confirmed by an Okhrana report of September 28, 1916. Zivin also was known as "Pyatnitsky," and was associated with Natanson. There were several channels into the "international Mensheviks," including Axelrod, probably via Moor.

5See, for example, *Letters of Lenin,* p. 406. On Grimm, see Hahlweg, p. 51.

holdings, eight-hour workdays, and peace. Parvus' prodding forced Rantzau to formulate a new strategy of revolution which was to replace conventional warfare. Parvus was sent to explain the concept to the German Chancellor shortly after March 21. (Subsequently, Rantzau demanded that Parvus be received by the unsympathetic Secretary of State.) Crucial was the return of Lenin to Russia. Berlin approved and Parvus' agents (notably Hanecki, who was then at Christiana) undertook the task of persuading Lenin. A German apparatus in Scandinavia also accelerated its operations.

On either March 22 or 23, the Swiss Foreign Minister informed the German legation that "outstanding Russian revolutionaries desire to return to Russia via Germany since they are afraid to go through France on account of the submarine risk."[6] This was the first *official* communication.

Lenin knew that the revolutionaries in Denmark—Parvus and Hanecki—had established a close rapport with the Germans and were in possession of substantial financial resources. On March 24 he wrote to Hanecki.[7] There were earlier communications, perhaps through intermediaries, and it seems that this message to Hanecki was preceded by a receipt of money, but this is the earliest letter published. With his customary caution, Lenin spoke mainly of better communications with *Pravda*, a problem of secondary importance. But in Aesopian language he informed Hanecki that he was willing to cooperate: he pointedly ended his letter by employing a slogan which Parvus had just expounded to the Germans: "Long live the proletarian militia which is preparing peace and socialism."[8]

Opposition still existed in Berlin. But on March 24 Lenin acquired a new "ally" when the German Emperor let it be known that he intended to support the socialists against the new Russian government, and the High Command informed the Foreign Office[9] that they had no objections to the passage of Russian revolutionaries through Germany.

To this point, Lenin's interest in returning to Russia had been weak. Because many revolutionaries were on their way home and virtually all exiles were talking about their return, Lenin, who was supposed to be an active revolutionary leader, was forced to go through some motions, but he was play-acting. On March 25, however, he informed his comrades in Copenhagen that he was unhappy

---

[6]Text of this telegram in Hahlweg, p. 65.

[7]Hanecki, after a short term of imprisonment, had been expelled from Denmark for smuggling and was now operating from Christiana (now Oslo), Malmö, and Stockholm. On Hanecki's trial in Denmark, see the fascinating account by Futrell, pp. 179-190.

[8]*Letters of Lenin*, p. 417.

[9]Zeman, p. 26.

about the delay. Still, he found time for doing what he liked best—to attack other socialists: as though it were a matter of the greatest urgency, he polemically argued against Gorky.

On March 27 Parvus' emissary, who also was an agent of the German General Staff,[10] visited Lenin and suggested a solution. Passage through Germany would pose no difficulties; the real task was to smuggle Lenin and Zinovyev through Denmark and Sweden into Russia. The German Bolshevik organization in Scandinavia had been smuggling literature and merchandise into Russia for years. Hence it undoubtedly was able to transport Lenin into the country without danger. This project, it seems, had been suggested earlier and apparently Lenin had sent passport photos of himself and Zinovyev. Now the false Swedish passports were being delivered by Parvus' agent but Lenin was not willing to take the "risk." The risk was merely that the Swedish border officials might have noticed that these alleged citizens did not speak Swedish and they might not have believed the cover story that the bearers of these authentic-looking passports were deaf-mutes. The risk actually involved was only detention for a few hours or days.[11]

Lenin telegraphed Hanecki that he could not agree to the plan. Instead, Lenin wanted an entire Swiss railway carriage to transport him to Copenhagen, or an agreement about the exchange of Russian refugees for interned Germans. The exchange agreement would have required lengthy negotiations between Berlin and Petrograd through a neutral power and would have entailed inordinate delays. Hanecki, who was then in Stockholm, could do little to obtain a Swiss railroad carriage. Lenin probably knew that the Swiss would not agree to such a transaction in order to preserve their neutrality. In sum, Lenin was procrastinating.

Meanwhile, in Copenhagen on March 28, 1917, Sazonov talked to Siegfried Goldberg, who was an agent of Matthias Erzberger and, as a German Reichstag member of the Catholic Center party who was amply supplied with funds, guided many psychological and political warfare campaigns outside the Foreign Office structure. Sazonov and Goldberg discussed methods of achieving peace. Sazonov, who was about to leave for Russia, told Goldberg that Lenin was the *real* revolutionary leader and promised to contact him. It is believed that Erzberger then applied pressure on the Wilhelmstrasse to get Lenin underway.

[10]This probably was Georg Sklarz, one of the financiers of Hanecki's trade in contraceptives and after the war exposed as a racketeer (Futrell, p. 190 and Hahlweg, p. 15).

[11]Hanecki found a way to utilize Lenin's picture: He inserted it in the Stockholm daily *Politiken,* with the caption: "The leader of the Russian revolution" (Walter, p. 260).

On March 29 Lenin again changed his mind. He wrote to Hanecki asking him to spare no costs and go to Petrograd, adding that the first bourgeois government to be eliminated was that of Russia. An agent of the German military attaché assisted at a Bolshevik meeting and reported that Lenin now was willing to pass through Germany *without* the permission of the Russian government; Lenin's comrades remained entirely unconvinced.

The Germans discussed the technicalities of the proposed trip. The military, foolishly fearing that the Russians might agitate while passing through Germany, suggested that the revolutionaries travel under escort in a collective transport. This notion was transmitted to the revolutionaries; whether it was a feedback from Lenin's suggestion to Hanecki is difficult to determine. On March 30 an agent of the General Staff, in a report to his superiors, suggested that the trip be authorized without delay.

Alleging that England would not allow him to pass through, Lenin wanted the soviet to arrange an exchange with interned Germans, a time-consuming project. However, on March 30, Lenin again desired approval from Petrograd.[12] On the same day, the German legation at Berne received an agent's report which stated that Lenin had deliverd a speech lasting two-and-a-half hours in which he called for the liberation of colonies and oppressed nations, opposition against bourgeois governments, notably in Russia, and revolutionary war. This type of language conformed well with the supposed needs of German strategists.

On March 31 Lenin and Zinovyev wrote to Martov and Natanson (who then used the name of "Bobrov"). They objected to the hesitancy shown by the other revolutionary groups; they affirmed that they wished to proceed. It was the first forceful insistence on departure. It also represented one time when Lenin did not want a split, for he needed support for purposes of self-justification. Significantly, the letter added that Grimm's proposal—to pass through Germany—was acceptable, but Grimm had insisted that Petrograd be contacted and permission secured. Lenin, Zinovyev, and Krupskaya immediately wired Grimm from Zurich notifying him that they would assume no responsibility for further postponement: "We absolutely cannot agree to further delay . . . Send us decision tomorrow."[13] They added that they numbered "over ten passengers" and would be traveling "alone," that is, without waiting for the revolutionaries from other parties.

But the genuineness of the hurry seems doubtful. On the previous day Grimm had informed the revolutionaries that he could not

[12]*Letters of Lenin*, p. 421.

[13]*Ibid.*, p. 421.

continue to negotiate. Yet, after receiving the telegram, he spoke again with the Swiss Foreign Minister. This time he advised against contacts with Petrograd. The Minister told Grimm to stay out of the affair and informed the German legation that the revolutionaries would make contact the following day.[14] Grimm telephoned (it is not known to whom) to say that his mission was terminated; he proposed finding another intermediary. In the meantime, the legation waited. It was as though Lenin became active at the moment he lacked an intermediary. Yet two weeks after the Tsar's abdication it was obvious that no serious risk was involved in a return to Russia.

On April 1 the Wilhelmstrasse requested five million marks for political use within Russia—a major decision had been made.

On April 2 the Mensheviks and Social Revolutionaries stated that without the approval of the Petrograd government, passage through Germany would be a mistake; they would not move before it was clear that proper authorization was unattainable.

If Lenin had been anticipating such a declaration in the hope that it would provide an excuse for his own inaction, he had miscalculated. On the morning of April 2, the German Minister in Berne received a peremptory communication from Berlin ordering him to expedite the transport of Russian revolutionaries through Germany:[15] clearly Berlin thought that the deepening of the Russian Revolution should no longer be delayed. The means were available but the actors were still wanting.

Romberg, seeking an excuse to explain the loss of tempo, answered that some émigrés were awaiting instructions from Russia and "others still seem uncertain as to whether or not they wish to avail themselves of our offer"[16] (which had not yet been made officially). He recommended waiting, but sprung into action and contacted Lenin through Paul Levi. Within a few hours, Lenin liquidated his household furnishings and proceeded to Bern.

In the evening of the same day, Anna (Lenin's sister in Petrograd) received a telegram from her brother informing her that he would arrive on the evening of April 11.[17] The telegram must have been dispatched on the morning of April 2, almost immediately after the German Minister had been told by Berlin that Lenin should depart without delay. At that time the Bolsheviks had not even initiated formal negotiations with the Germans. The telegram has been available for years: if interpreted through the background of the

[14]Zeman, p. 29.

[15]*Ibid.*, p. 33.

[16]*Ibid.*, p. 34.

[17]*Letters of Lenin*, p. 421.

German files, it proves that, far from acting like a tiger in a cage, Lenin started to move only after the Germans forced him.

Fritz Platten, a Swiss socialist who had participated in the Russian revolution of 1905 and who was married to a Russian, was the new intermediary recommended by Grimm. Lenin had described Platten as a "good for nothing" in February, 1917.[18] Now he found him acceptable, partly because his views were similar to Lenin's and partly because he was a political weakling. Platten may not have been a German agent, but he was a corrupt individual seeking personal gain and notoriety.[19]

On April 3, Lenin conferred with Platten who then went to the German legation for a preliminary contact. Platten proposed to the Germans the establishment of an intelligence service in Stockholm. His suggestion was not accepted, although the Germans later used him as an occasional communications channel.[20]

In the evening of April 3 Lenin wrote to the Bolshevik section in Zurich that he was in possession of "a fund of over 1,000 francs to cover the cost of the journey"; he enclosed 100 francs to be loaned to an unnamed comrade.[21] On April 4 Platten held a long conference with the German Minister. On April 5 an "agreement" was worked out; it was approved by Berlin on April 7. Also on April 5, the German Foreign Office had reported agreement among the General Staff and their promise that an "understanding officer" would accompany the train. But there were further delays. The Germans attempted to persuade a number of the unwilling revolutionaries to accompany Lenin; they also negotiated the transit through Sweden.

Lenin, on April 7, asked a few international socialists to compose a statement "approving" of the trip; this act, according to Russian law, constituted high treason. He also requested the approval of the well-known writer Romain Rolland but failed to gain it.[22] Finally on Monday, April 9, the revolutionaries and their friends consumed a farewell luncheon at the Zähringer Hof. Lenin read the draft of a

[18]On Platten, see Hahlweg, pp. 18 and 77.

[19]There is no record that Platten was paid before this transaction, but on May 29, 1918, "Friedrich" informed the German legation at Berne that Platten was in financial trouble. It appears that he was helped within five days, with Nasse acting as intermediary.

[20]Platten's expressed wish to die in Russia was fulfilled when he succumbed in one of Stalin's slave labor camps. He moved to Russia permanently in 1924, lectured at an agricultural school, was arrested in 1939, died in 1942 in a camp near Arkhangel, and was rehabilitated under Khrushchev. He once made a speech to the effect that hundreds of thousands of corpses meant nothing if the happiness of the proletariat was at stake. *Neue Zürcher Zeitung*, October 9, 1956.

[21]*Letters of Lenin*, p. 422.

[22]Walter, p. 276f.

letter to the Swiss workers[23] saying that while "the Russian proletariat has the great honor to commence a series of revolutions engendered by the imperialist war . . . socialism cannot win immediately" in Russia, "one of the most backward countries of Europe." The task was to give impetus to the bourgeois-democratic revolution and to make a "small step" toward the socialist revolution. Lenin concluded: "The German proletariat is the best and most reliable ally of the proletarian revolution in Russia and of the world revolution."

The travelers left the restaurant at 2:30 P.M. In the station, there were shouts and unrest. Lenin, with Platten and Zinovyev, walked solemnly to the train through a *cortège*.[24] Shortly after boarding, he bodily evicted Oscar Blum, a socialist from Riga, whom he suspected of being an Okhrana agent. Thereupon the train with thirty-two revolutionaries and fifteen minutes delay, left Zurich at 15:10 o'clock.[25]

The Germans had expected sixty travelers. According to Communist count there were nineteen Bolsheviks. Actually, there were not more than about a dozen true Bolsheviks, almost all of them members of Lenin's "enlarged" family: Krupskaya, Inessa Armand (whom an Okhrana report of November 16, 1916, described as Lenin's "right hand"), her former and perhaps current boyfriend, Georg Safarov, and his brother, Zinovyev, with his wife and child, and Olga Ravich, a friend of Krupskaya.[26] There were two other reasonably prominent Bolsheviks present: G. Y. Sokolnikov and the Caucasian, Mikha C. Tskhakaya,[27] Chairman of the Third Congress

[23]*Ibid.*, p. 277f.

[24]Communist writers stress the dignity of this departure, yet German eye-witnesses described an unruly scene, with the Leninists and their opponents calling each other dirty names (see Walter, p. 278; Hahlweg, p. 96f. and *contra* p. 101).

[25]Krupskaya (*op. cit.*, p. 345), playing tricks with the two calendars, after she had given dates according to the Western calendar, suddenly switched to the Russian practice and put the departure date on March 27. Even then she cut one day: Lenin departed on March 28 (Old Style). The effect of this manipulation is to advance Lenin's return by fourteen days.

[26]Krupskaya describes the little boy as the son of a Bundist woman, but from the list of signatures it is clear that it was the son of Zinovyev's wife. Yet the relations between the Lenins and the Zinovyevs supposedly were very close!

[27]A Caucasian agent of the Germans, Keresselidze, informed Romberg that he wanted to ensure further contacts with the Georgian who was traveling with Lenin. There also was a Soulichvili on the train but he apparently did not belong to the Bolshevik group. Keresselidze participated in the German financial support to the Bolsheviks during the summer of 1917. He and his brother, with the relative of another German agent, Dumbadze, had implicated the Russian Minister of War in an espionage charge. The checkered career of Keresselidze cannot be detailed here, but *one* fact is noteworthy: according to an Okhrana letter of May 21, 1907, it appears that the brothers Keresselidze were given money by the police to be paid to a revolutionary committee but that a portion of the amount was embezzled by them and banked in Switzerland. "So are they all, all honorable men."

and later President of the Central Executive Committee of Trans-caucasus and finally of Georgia. There were also two Russian workers who had joined the Bolsheviks in Zurich, a Bolshevik of the criminal type and one other revolutionary, "A. Linde," who either was a German agent or the brother of one (or both). The total is thus thirteen; Radek may be added to the list of Bolsheviks,[28] but Radek's relations with Lenin had not been close. The rest of the group consisted of persons who then and now remain totally unknown. Some, to judge from the signatures, were quite old. It is apparent that the supposed number of the "revolutionaries" was padded to impress the Germans.

The trip was uneventful. Krupskaya said that the "cook served up good square meals to which our emigrant fraternity was hardly accustomed."[29] Lenin, who disliked the odor of smoke, severely rationed cigarette smoking. The train, incidentally, was not "sealed"; nor was it a box car, but rather a wagon. The revolutionaries, however, were separated from the other passengers.

The train was given such high traffic priority that it delayed the train of the German Crown Prince for two hours.[30] Yet a connection was missed at Frankfurt and a few hours delay resulted. It was reported that a British spy was evicted from the train, but this probably occurred without loss of time, either after crossing the border or, according to interview information, at Celle. The train was scheduled to arrive at the Baltic port of Sassnitz on April 11 at 1:00 P.M.[31] Due to the delay the train was not expected to connect with the ferry to Sweden and plans were made to quarter the revolutionaries overnight in Sassnitz. However, the train remained overnight *in Berlin,* departing on April 12 at 7:15 A.M. It arrived at Sassnitz at 3:15 P.M.—a delay of twenty-six hours. Apparently the train stood for at least twelve hours and possibly as many as twenty hours in Berlin. Strangely enough, this fact is seldom noted. Reports of other passengers state that the train stood for a "few hours" on a Berlin siding. The official report of the escort officer, Cavalry Captain von der Planitz, was delivered to army intelligence.[32] If there existed a copy, it has vanished from the files of the Foreign Office.

---

[28]During the purge trials, Sokolnikov, Radek, and Rakovsky, all of whom took part in the German-Bolshevik operation, were practically the only prominent Bolsheviks who received relatively light prison terms.

[29]Krupskaya, p. 345.

[30]Hahlweg, p. 23.

[31]The scheduled travel time of thirty-two hours was quite long, an average speed of only twenty-two miles per hour for an express train. However, wartime conditions may explain this schedule.

[32]German military files, it seems, have not been preserved.

Time and again, the German documents refer to the need *not* to compromise the passengers. Still, there are vague hints about chance conversations in Frankfurt. It is said that in Berlin, Platten was not allowed to leave the platform "without permission"—implying that he did leave, even if only after obtaining approval. Krupskaya reported that just before they came to Berlin, "several German Social Democrats" entered a special compartment but "none of us spoke to them."[33] Zinovyev told Fedor Raskolnikov that Scheidemann, the leading German Social Democrat, tried to see Lenin on the trip. Platten disclosed that three representatives of the German government accompanied the train and that Jansson brought greetings from the trade unions but added that Lenin did not meet Chancellor Bethmann-Hollweg or Scheidemann.[34]

The train would not have been delayed in Berlin without compelling reason. The rumors that Lenin met Bethmann-Hollweg or even Scheidemann seem far-fetched indeed. It is conceivable that Lenin, alleging upon disembarking from the platform that he was Platten, did confer with German officials. If so, it is possible that he saw Kurt Riezler, Bethmann's assistant for political warfare. Riezler later told a friend that he had sent an emissary to the train but that the talk took place only on the ferry between Germany and Sweden.

The Germans, pretending to act upon a suggestion by *Swiss* trade unions, had insisted on Jansson joining the transport. When Berlin accepted Platten's "conditions" concerning the modalities of the trip, they added that Jansson would have to be among the passengers. Whether Lenin and the others were told about this modification is not clear. Jansson, a few days earlier, had returned from Sweden where he had spoke with Russian revolutionaries and, together with Parvus, had "briefed" the socialist leaders on the Russian problem.[35] He entered the train, presumably at Stuttgart, but it is said that Lenin refused to talk to him. Incidentally, the delay at Berlin violated Article Six of the agreement which Platten had negotiated with the Germans. What happened on the siding at Berlin is one secret that may never be pierced. As will appear presently, however, Lenin changed his mind about the Russian revolution after he left the Zähringer Hof, at Zurich, and before he arrived at the Finland Station at Petrograd.

Late on April 12 the revolutionaries passed into Sweden and were in Stockholm on April 14. Parvus had planned to meet the

[33]Krupskaya, p. 345.

[34]*Magdeburger Volkstimme*, May 16, 1917. Scheidemann had returned to Berlin from Scandinavia on April 10.

[35]Philipp Scheidemann, *Memoiren eines Sozialdemokraten* (Dresden: Reissner, 1928), I, 421.

party at Malmoe; he had expected Axelrod and Martov to be accompanying Lenin. The meeting did not occur. Lenin refused to be seen with Parvus, and Parvus probably did not care to meet only Lenin. Instead, the arrivals were met by Hanecki, who commented on the unexplained delays in his memoirs. But Parvus did negotiate with "the Russian émigrés from Switzerland" and reported upon his conversations to the German Social Democratic party and to the Foreign Office.[36]

Upon his arrival in Stockholm, Lenin spoke with Swedish socialists, asking them to "approve" the passage through Germany; he also requested money to continue the trip. The travelers had signed a statement confirming that Platten had "guaranteed" the trip only to Stockholm. Money was granted by the Swedes but Lenin asked for an additional 1,000 kroners for himself.[37] Thereupon he took time to buy himself shoes and pants which he needed badly, protesting all the while that he was not going to Russia to open a haberdashery. He then made a public statement to the effect that he had negotiated with Social Democrats "of various countries" and that the German Social Democrats would send representatives to a peace conference in Stockholm. Although the statement may have been based upon his conversations with Hanecki, it is likely that this declaration was preceded by contacts with German socialists. Since he had not negotiated with German socialists in Switzerland, contacts must have taken place elsewhere.

Before leaving Sweden, Lenin appointed Hanecki to be the foreign representative of the Bolshevik Central Committee; thus, in essence, Hanecki inherited Lenin's position. Lenin knew full well, of course, that Hanecki was working closely with and through the Germans and that he belonged to Parvus' organization. Karl Radek, who as an Austrian citizen was not permitted to enter Russia, became Hanecki's assistant. V. V. Vorovsky also was in Sweden to help.[38]

Upon entering Finland at Torneo, Lenin completed a form in which he stated that he was a Russian Orthodox, a political refugee, and a journalist. Furthermore, he stated that he was traveling on a certificate issued by the Russian Consulate General in Sweden. Platten was turned back by the British officers who were then in control of the Russian border crossings. The Germans made a feeble attempt to put the Danish socialist Borgbjerg on the train: a contact

---

[36]Hahlweg, p. 22; Zeman, pp. 42, 45f., 50.

[37]Paul Olberg, *Vorwärts*, May 1, 1957.

[38]Vorovsky was employed by the German industrial concern of Siemens-Schuckert; of that firm's Petrograd branch, Krassin was then the managing director (Futrell, p. 156).

of Parvus, he had been traveling to Russia but had just been turned back by the well-informed British. Russian counter-intelligence later believed that a German military agent named "Müller" did get through with the transport.

Finally Lenin and his group arrive at Petrograd's Finland Station, several hours late, at 10:30 P.M. on Monday, April 16, 1917. They were greeted by a huge crowd of workers, soldiers and revolutionaries, an honor guard of Kronstadt sailors, and an official reception committee of the Petrograd soviet. Accompanied by the sounds of the "Marseillaise," Lenin was guided to an armored car which had been brought by the Bolshevik military organization.[39] He mounted it and made a short speech of congratulations and of warnings about the possibility of becoming slaves of capitalism. The crowd howled and carried him into the Tsar's reception room where he was presented with a large bouquet of flowers. He held the flowers clumsily in his hands as he listened to a speech by Menshevik N. S. Chkeidze, who spoke in the name of the soviet and expressed the "hope" that Lenin would not split the ranks of the revolutionary democracy. Lenin turned away. Pointedly ignoring Chkeidze, he made a sharply radical speech before exiting. He stopped again to speak before the station and then stepped into an automobile.

The crowd, however, was so large that the car could not begin to move. Lenin climbed upon the hood, spoke, and then tried again to get into the car, but Podvoisky asked him to mount upon a second armored car that the Bolsheviks had brought. Clad in a dark suit, white shirt, blue tie, black hat and shining shoes, Lenin, standing on top of the tank and overcome by emotion, presented a fiery speech calling for action. Then, illuminated by searchlights from the Peter and Paul Fortress, Lenin rode in the armored car to Kshezhinskaya Palace, formerly the home of the Tsar's mistress,[40] and now headquarters of the Bolsheviks. (They had secured the palace by tolerated expropriation.) The rest of his party, including Krupskaya, presumably followed by car after the crowd had dispersed. Lenin again addressed the "masses" from the balcony and talked to his friends inside. To get a merry party underway, he proposed the singing of revolutionary songs.[41] After 3:00 A.M. he and Krupskaya went to the

[39]G. V. Yelin, the Bolshevik headquarters commander, had to be persuaded to release the armored cars for this social occasion. He thought tanks were needed for other purposes. The government did not bestir itself to disarm the private armies of the various parties. *See* N. I. Podvoisky "V. I. Lenin v 1917 gody," *Istoricheskii Arkhiv*, 1956, V. 6.

[40]This relation had occurred many years earlier.

[41]Yelena Stassova reported that he asked for the singing of the "Internationale" but the comrades did not know this song and just mumbled something.

rich bourgeois apartment of Yelizarov, where the Lenins were given a spacious room.[42] A servant girl stood ready for their use.

To everybody's surprise, Lenin, before he even reached the streets of Petrograd, had advocated a *second* revolution. His listeners thought the job was to turn the first revolution into success. It was this "second revolution" theme which induced one of the German political warfare managers to telegraph, on April 17, from Stockholm to Berlin: "Lenin's entry into Russia successful. He is working exactly as we would wish."[43]

---

[42]Yelizarov apparently had participated on the Russian end in the Parvus-Hanecki smuggle operation, largely in partnership with the left Social Revolutionary Spiro, who at one time had been connected with the Okhrana and who later served for a few weeks as Commissar of Post and Telegraph. (General A. Niessel, *Le triomphe des bolshéviks et la paix de Brest-Litovsk, souvenirs 1917-1918* (Paris: Plon, 1940), p. 122).

[43]Zeman, p. 51.

Sudden Prominence

Lenin had expected to be arrested for treason. Instead he received a hero's welcome—except that his well-wishers did not know for which heroic deeds and social accomplishments he was to be praised. He was acclaimed as the "leader of the Petrograd masses, workers, soldiers and sailors," yet he had never led them. Lenin's mystique was born during those hours of darkness in the parade which started at the Finland station and which the Mensheviks of the soviet had helped to organize in the naive hope that a triumphal reception would soften the radicalism of the nostalgic homecomer.

But Lenin could not be bribed by flattery so transparent in purpose. The entire Russian Bolshevik organization, at the time of the overthrow of the Tsar, had not numbered more than 5,000 members and 100 to 200 trained "cadres" and propagandists. There were at first only thirty Bolsheviks in the Petrograd soviet and most of these had not been elected but were co-opted by the members of the soviet. Such prominent leaders as Kamenev and Stalin arrived by the end of March from Siberia. Though membership had climbed to about 25,000, and soon was to reach 40,000, the question of seizure of power was considered untimely, and was conceived, in the image of the American spoils system, as seizure of the state apparatus by the socialists. There was some confusion, but most of the Bolsheviks, while debating within the soviet, gave qualified support to the government. For a few days, though they asked for immediate peace negotiations, the Bolsheviks even advocated measures of defense. One revolutionary asserted that the Bolsheviks had become "de-bolshevized."[1] Lenin's first words at the Finland Station, so much at variance with his last public words in Switzerland, should have destroyed the illusion that he would support a moderate policy. But it was thought he would soon learn more about the "situation."[2] In the meantime, his new views shocked even Krupskaya who reportedly exclaimed: "I am afraid it looks as if Lenin has gone crazy."[3] *Pravda* described Lenin's view as "unacceptable in that it starts from the assumption that the bourgeois democratic revolution is ended."[4]

Still, sudden glory endowed Lenin with immunity. On the day after his arrival, the Petrograd soviet, albeit by implication, sanctioned Lenin's trip. His case was ably defended by Zurabov, who for years had been connected with the Germans in Denmark. He was on the allied "control list" but returned to Russia as soon as the new government cleared him. Masquerading as a left Menshevik, Zurabov now functioned as a deputy in the soviet.

The soviet's acquiescence to Lenin's trip was not surprising. All the delegates were socialists, and they were not about to oppose one of their prominent comrades, irrespective of his lack of loyalty. The fear of helping the "counter-revolution" was an overriding consideration. But there was another point: the Germans had pumped money into several socialist groups and they had maintained contacts with others. These transactions were secret, but the politicians on the Executive Committee—the soviet's only functioning body—knew enough not to take chances.

Still, the government could and should have taken forceful action. But it was composed of impractical "idealists" who had destroyed the counter-intelligence organization. Hence they were not equipped to prepare a strong case. The Minister of Justice harbored sentiments of socialist solidarity. He was Alexander F. Kerensky, son of the Simbirsk school principal who had helped young Lenin to graduate after his brother's execution. There also existed some reluctance to initiate an open fight with the soviet. The moderates in the government expected Lenin to discredit radicalism. Since he could be relied upon to resort to his favorite splitting tactics, he might weaken the soviet which prevented the cabinet from governing by functioning as a second government.

Lenin struck as soon as the soviet had accepted his explanations of the trip through enemy territory. He vehemently opposed "defencism," though he carefully avoided offending the "defencist"

[1]Walter, p. 286ff.

[2]Shub, p. 190; also Schapiro, p. 161f.

[3]Raphael R. Abramovitch, *The Soviet Revolution 1917-1939*, (New York: International Universities Press, 1962), p. 30.

[4]Quoted from Schapiro, p. 164.

socialists. The revolution had to be propelled immediately into its second phase: the state was not to be simply "taken over" but demolished. Lenin hinted, without making the point explicit, that the socialist revolution would mean seizure of power by the Bolsheviks.

Lenin proclaimed that Russia was under a regime of "dual power"—that of the government and of the soviet.[5] The Bolsheviks must run the soviet, directly or indirectly. The soviet would have to be developed primarily as an "organ of uprising." It would assume full political power and create a new form of state (a parliamentary republic would be "a step back"). To begin with, agitation should be based upon the slogan "all power to the soviets" (i.e., destroy the government). The Bolsheviks were to strengthen their positions within the soviet while agitating for power to the soviet as a whole.

The idea expressed tactical genius but it shocked the party. The members thought that the notion of "smashing the state apparatus" constituted anarchism—which it was—and that Lenin's tactics of "permanent revolution" were unrealistic—which they were not. The Petrograd party committee voted down his proposals. Against his opposition, a strong part of the Bolshevik Central Committee came out for reunification with the Mensheviks.[6] Lenin was more or less isolated, but he remained unperturbed. He called Sverdlov from the Urals to Petrograd and they combined with Zinovyev in using their excellent knowledge of pre-war party membership to rebuild an organization loyal to Lenin. He did not neglect to establish "shock units" in Kronstadt, Petrograd, and Helsingfors, recruiting or hiring radical Social Revolutionaries, anarchists, and criminals.

After some delay Lenin succeeded in drawing Stalin to his side, gaining a majority of one with a five to four edge in the Central Committee. This control enabled Lenin to select the delegates for the so-called April party conference and to gain a clear mandate for his policy. Initially he achieved this victory through his tactical skill and his abuse of intra-party democracy, but by the end of April or early May money became available.[7] This helped enormously, especially in the hurried recruiting of goon squads.

[5]This was not original with him. The formula was first expressed by Y. M. Steklov on March 17, 1917. *See The Russian Provisional Government 1917, documents,* ed. Robert P. Browder and Alexander F. Kerensky (3 Vols., Hoover Institution, Stanford University Press, 1961), III, 1224.

[6]Many local party organizations until the Bolshevik seizure of power remained, despite Lenin's efforts, jointly Bolshevik-Menshevik in their composition (Schapiro, p. 164).

[7]On April 25 Lenin wrote to Hanecki and Radek complaining that so far "exactly nothing" had been received; "no letters, no packages, no money from you." *Letters of Lenin,* p. 424. On May 4, he confirmed receipt of "2000" from Kozlovsky *(Proletarskaya Revolyutsiya,* No. 9 (21), 1923, p. 231).

Lenin entered what might be considered the most satisfying three months of his life. Shortly after his arrival he became editor of *Pravda*, which had started publication again on March 18. Lenin could indulge in venting his hatreds against other socialists, and, he venomously attacked those who were accusing him of subversive dealings with the Germans. Though a pedantic writer when discussing theoretical problems, Lenin was a gifted journalist. Some of the fiery short articles he wrote were examples of prime polemic writing.

Lenin's private life was quiet, however. Inessa had gone to Moscow, which suggests that love had abated and that, perhaps, she took the initiative in terminating the affair.[8] In any event, too obvious a relation was not advisable. Since at long last Lenin was able to operate as he wished, politics was now of overriding and absolute importance.

By early May Lenin had acquired enormous authority and personal prestige. He was treated as the formal and undisputed head of the Bolshevik party. He opened and closed party conferences. However interminably and rudely he spoke to the soviet of peasants and at the All-Russian soviet, he was listened to with respect. Opposing the government, he incessantly called for "all power to the soviets." Indefatigably he agitated for national self-determination of the non-Russian peoples, the dissolution of the army, fraternization at the front,[9] the immediate termination of the war, and a *de facto* truce on the front; to keep face, he protested against separate peace with Germany. At this point the Germans had adopted a strategy of virtual inaction but had increased propaganda at the battlefront. Parvus was one of the instigators of this strategy. Thus advanced the world revolution.

These exhortations and hopes had become meaningful to millions of Russians. It so happened that Lenin's slogans coincided with

[8]"During the war Lenin wrote more letters to Inessa Armand than to any other person, whether relative or disciple . . . Lenin wrote more frequently and at greater length to her than to anyone else. . . . From November 20, 1916, to . . . the February revolution in 1917, he wrote . . . more to her than to all the rest put together. In his letters to Inessa, as always, preoccupation with politics is uppermost. But tone and depth reveal facets of his nature exhibited in no other letters." (Wolfe, "Lenin and Inessa Armand", p. 104f.) During January 1915, Inessa sent Lenin the outline for a pamphlet on the women's question which elicited a critical reaction by Lenin on the subject of "free love" and "freedom of adultery." Inessa was deeply hurt (Wolfe, p. 109) but Lenin succeeded in explaining himself. In his last letter to her written in Switzerland between March 25 and 31, 1917, he still assumed they would be unable to go to Russia (*Sochineniya*, 4th ed., Vol. 35, p. 248). Although he chided her for being nervous, the relationship appears to have remained intact. (In his wartime letters, Lenin no longer addressed her by *ty* but by *vy;* Wolfe interprets this, correctly, as a conspiratorial move to deceive wartime censorship.) There are no data to indicate the reasons why, upon arriving in Russia, the two separated.

[9]Lenin's first article on this subject appeared in *Pravda* on April 28.

German interests except, of course, for his muted calls for a revolution in Germany. Since the summer of 1915 the Germans had been particularly interested in defeatist "disorganizing" and "disintegrating" propaganda within the Russian army. Now the tempo of this effort increased. On April 28, a few days after Lenin's arrival, *Soldiers' Pravda* (shortly afterwards renamed *Trench Pravda*) began publication. Lenin's confidant during the publication period of the first *Pravda*, Podvoisky, took charge of the operation which gave fraternization at the front a clear political meaning. The paper, which was officially issued by the Social Democratic military organizations in the Latvian region, rapidly achieved wide circulation at the front but, on June 17, the editor, a certain Khaustov, was arrested as a German spy. (Even before Lenin's return, a member of the *Pravda* staff had been arrested as an enemy agent.) Little incidents like this passed unnoticed in the general enthusiasm for the new political life. Lenin's socialist comrades had decided that the opposition to Leninism should be based purely on ideological differences.[10]

Though Lenin was the formal leader of his party, there exists ample evidence that outside forces were agitating. Lenin's interests did not entirely coincide with those of the Germans. The latter, vitally concerned about the military effort of Russia, were anxious to create unrest to as great a degree and as rapidly as possible. Lenin, by contrast, was anxious to seize power, but for this very reason had to be careful not to undertake premature moves. His timing had to be in harmony with the attitudes of the masses rather than with the interests of the Germans. He later commented that the existing government, though it would eventually have to topple, could not be overthrown immediately. "We are no Blanquists. We do not want to rule with a minority . . . against the majority."[11]

In April, 1917, Lenin favored peaceful demonstrations as a means to strengthen the party and spread his slogans. Yet, early in May, the government announced its loyalty to the Allies and supported national defense. This created a sore point with the Germans. There was little spontaneous unrest, but German agents rapidly got busy. On May 7 Riezler received a report from "Uno" (probably Jansson) advising means of aiding the "activists" in Petrograd. On May 14 the Wilhelmstrasse was told that Jansson and Steinwachs had established contacts with *all* groups of the Social Democratic party. Bolsheviks had built up cells in two or three regiments by incessantly delivering speeches to soldiers in their barracks. A Bolshevik specialist

[10]For an example, see Browder-Kerensky, *op. cit.*, II, 1094.

[11]Lenin mainly criticized Blanqui's disregard for the importance of the masses. His main statements on Blanqui appear in *Sochineniya*, 4th ed., Vols. 10, p. 360; 12, p. 88f.; 15, p. 337ff.; 17, p.129f.; 24, pp. 21, 29, 119, 186f., 206, 233, 288f.; 25, pp. 282, 406; 26, pp. 4f., 181; 28, p. 281; 29, p. 132; 30, p. 458; and 31, pp. 48, 69.

in military work, F. F. Linde of the Finland Guard Reserve Regiment,[12] led the rebellious soldiers into the streets.[13] Investigation showed that the demonstrations were prepared in advance: there were banners and placards, many with expertly executed drawings. The demonstrators were led by agitators and accompanied by armed men. "Provocative shots" were fired and casualties resulted.[14] The government's palace was surrounded and the mutinous soldiers were preparing to arrest the government. Such a step would have boomeranged. After a few shots were fired, the soviet, which had full authority, called a halt to the operation. The military wanted to suppress the demonstration, but the leaders of the democratic government, G. E. Lvov and A. F. Kerensky, decided to rely on "moral influence."

An insurrection attempt would also have been a grave mistake from the Bolshevik point of view. Later Lenin, who had been surprised, counseled moderation and admitted that this operation "was not organized by the party." He asserted that those who stood to the left of the Central Committee were "crazy." He reminisced later that this upsurge—"somewhat more than an armed demonstration and somewhat less than an armed uprising"—opened his eyes to the potentialities of a popular insurrection.[14a]

Lenin's behavior was unusual and did not quite fit the legend. It

[12]Abramovitch, (p. 37) described "Fedor Linde" as a teacher of mathematics and philosophy, then serving as a private.

[13]Linde poses an interesting puzzle. On March 24, 1916, the Paris Okhrana agency reported to Petrograd on a German secret agent, von der Linde, who was working against Russia and was then in Switzerland. A "Linde" returned with Lenin on the sealed train. This may have been the same Linde whose archive Shotman in 1913 brought to Lenin in Poronin (Shotman, *op. cit.*, p. 300f). Another "Linde" sometimes also described as "F. F. Linde" was in Petrograd on March 14. He was one of the first soldier delegates to the soviet, and apparently had a hand in drafting the soviet's Order No. 1 which, by instituting soviets throughout the army, greatly weakened Russia's military strength. The above Linde was identified as a Social Democrat and left intellectual who was a member of the soviet's executive committee by April, 1917, and later became a political commissar and was killed on the front in 1918. A Fritz Linde, also known as Karl Y. Pechak, was arrested in November, 1914, together with several Bolshevik Duma members, and, was sent to Siberia because of "cooperation with German and Austrian military interests" (Tsiavlovsky, *op. cit.*, p. 156). One element of confusion is that "Fritz" also seems to have used "Alexander" as his first name. The odds are, however, that there were two Lindes. There were quite a few teams of brothers and cousins acting in unison.

[14]Browder-Kerensky, *op. cit.*, II, 1242. The examining magistrate requested the soviet to make available the results of their finding on this unrest. This request was complied with only after long delays. Hence the organizers were not identified. In September the prosecutor dropped the case. This example of inefficiency, procrastination, and unwillingness to stop subversion was typical of the way "Russian democracy" handled the "internal threat."

[14a]"Noviye dokumenty V. I. Lenina," *Voprosy Istorii KPSS*, No. 5, Moscow, 1958, p. 16.

could not but disappoint the Germans who expected more than agitation for an international socialist conference. Lenin turned to the land question and sometimes obliquely, other times vehemently, suggested to the peasants that they should set up committees and seize land: there was no risk of prematurity in localized rural uprisings. This tactic (which can be traced back to Bakunin) was well coordinated with the Germans who in their front propaganda were telling the Russian soldiers the same thing as Lenin and, to induce mass desertions, were spreading the rumor that the land was being grabbed by those who had stayed at home. This propaganda technique had been suggested to the Germans, not by a revolutionary but, on April 17, 1917, by an otherwise unknown Count Corvin Milewsky, who during World War I was a resident of Holland. This effort was most effective in revolutionizing Russia.

The Bolsheviks were flourishing. Under Vyacheslav M. Molotov, a press bureau (*byuro pechati*) was established and with "special funds"[15] furnished by the Central Committee it financed and enlarged ten provincial party papers plus *Trench Pravda* and the chief organ, *Pravda,* in Petrograd. The considerable source of the "special funds" which supported a dozen papers is unrecorded, but the historian of this effort was I. S. Sazonov, who participated in the labors of the bureau. This fact suggests that Berlin was the main source of the funds.[16] However, given Sazonov's contacts with an agent of Erzberger rather than the Foreign Office, presumably these funds were funneled through Erzberger's organization which did specialize in "press work." These funds would have been used *in addition* to those budgeted by the Foreign Office. Incidentally, the first issue of the bureau's *Bulletin* contained an article by Stalin. It is open to speculation if he and Molotov knew or surmised the financing of the bureau's farflung operations.[17]

When Shotman visited Lenin by the end of May or early June, Lenin proudly showed him a new and modern press which was capable of increasing the output of *Pravda.* Lenin related that the printing press had been made available by the Finnish party, a most unlikely source of such supplies.[18] In any event, on June 3,

[15]*Istoricheskii Arkhiv* (1955), No. 5, p. 200f.

[16]*See also* Schapiro, p. 177.

[17]It is not a foregone conclusion that all this financing was done with genuine money. There are indications that forged rubles were used also, though apparently largely in connection with "demonstrations." It will be recalled that Parvus proposed an ambitious "strategic" scheme for money forging. Perhaps the Germans followed up this suggestion, but only on a "tactical" level. The Russian government had been informed to the effect that the Germans possessed plates for the printing of 10-ruble notes. B. V. Nikitine, *The Fatal Years* (London: Hodge, 1938), p. 114.

[18]Shotman, p. 386. The Finnish socialists did make available paper to Bolshevik and other socialist newspapers. On two or three occasions they reportedly also gave the Bolsheviks several thousands of rubles (Futrell, p. 159f.). This money, which came

1917, Berlin informed Romberg that Lenin's peace propaganda was getting stronger and that the disorganization of the Russian army was progressing.

To disprove this kind of talk, the Russian government again felt the need to display its army's power and the firmness of Russia's alliance with France, Britain, and the United States. They decided upon a military offensive. This decision soon was known and openly debated in the press. A victorious Russian offensive might have changed the entire military situation. German propaganda outlets immediately became active. Lenin, maintaining that an offensive would entail the slaughtering of Russian workers and peasants, demanded an immediate peace offer to the suppressed classes of all countries, a peace anchored to the destruction of capitalism.

At the beginning of June the Petrograd municipal elections were held on the basis of universal suffrage and the Bolsheviks polled one-sixth of the vote. This percentage was still quite small, but on June 4, Lenin declared in the All-Russian soviet that the Bolsheviks were prepared to assume power, a declaration that was received with some applause and much laughter. *Pravda,* the Germans reported, was selling 300,000 copies daily[19]—a large circulation, especially when one considers the other subsidiary organs.[20] But trouble was brewing: one of the Bolsheviks who had returned with Lenin through Germany was implicated in a criminal affair (theft of jewelry) and the Malinovsky story broke. The debate about the offensive was an excellent diversion but the Germans, who had determined the approximate battle date through radio intelligence, desired action.

On June 19 the Bolshevik military organization of Petrograd, over which Lenin exercised little control, began preparations for an ostensibly peaceful—but actually armed—demonstration. Austrian diplomats in Stockholm were told by one of their academic agents that Olof Aschberg, director of Nya Banken, had discovered that Lenin was preparing to strike within a few days.[21] If successful he

through Karl Wiik who in turn was tied in with Hanecki, may have been of German origin. Naturally, small Finnish collections may have been used to cover up for the larger sums.

[19]Austrian documents put this figure at 400,000.

[20]On December 3, 1917, the German Secretary of State, Richard von Kuehlmann, stated in a report for the German military High Command, "It was not until the Bolsheviki had received from us a steady flow of funds through various channels and under varying labels that they were in a position to be able to build up their main organ, *Pravda,* . . . and appreciably to extend the originally narrow basis of their operation." (Zeman, p. 94) Unfortunately, there are no exact figures. From related data in the German file it would appear that a paper with a printing of 400,000 would run a deficit of at least 500,000 dollars annually. This would be equivalent to close to 100,000 rubles per month (pre-war parity).

[21]Austrian Archives, *Politisches Archiv,* Rot 834, Krieg 3, Russland, June-September, 1917.

would take power, but it was likely that the attempt would fail. On June 21 Lenin was prevailed upon to approve of the planned demonstration. The plan envisaged that in case of popular support, the main government buildings were to be occupied, the government arrested, and power seized by the Central Committee. A lengthy proclamation was issued, the substance of which was that the soldiers should join the workers in the streets and that not a single regiment or division should remain in the barracks. It called for the control and organization of industry, for the concentration of all power in the soviet, and for "bread, peace, liberty." The text emphasized that there were to be no secret treaties with the allies and no separate peace with Germany. This phrase was telegraphed by a *Pravda* editor, Bronislav Veselovski, to Hanecki and thereupon was published in the German press.[22]

The demonstration took place on June 23, but there was little support. The All-Russian soviet, thirteen per cent of whose delegates were Bolsheviks, asked the Bolsheviks to end the operation. The Bolsheviks rejected the request. Thereupon the Petrograd soviet forbade demonstrations for three days. The Bolshevik military leaders wanted a "test of strength" but Lenin interfered and cancelled the operation. Chernov, a Social Revolutionary leader of strong Zimmerwald convictions who enjoyed direct or indirect Austrian and German support,[23] commented that Lenin was shrewd enough to avoid political suicide.

It was suggested in the soviet that the Bolsheviks be disarmed and the mutinous regiments disbanded. Martov, who had recently arrived via Germany, protested that there was no enemy on the left and that the most important task was to prevent a counter-revolution. The Menshevik Weinstein alleged that, lest the counter-revolution win, Bolshevik force should be subdued by *non-violence*. Of course, Weinstein was in communication with German socialists in Stockholm.

On June 25 the soviet, surprisingly, announced open support of the offensive. This meant that the Germans were forced to create unrest again. A revolutionary center was formed inside the Bolshevik party to put pressure on Lenin. However, countermoves were made and, on June 29, the Bolshevik military organization decided to restrain from demonstrating as yet.

On July 1 the Russian military offensive began. The event rapidly swelled the Bolshevik ranks. The Bolsheviks proposed a demonstration. Partly to neutralize this effort and partly to bring about

---

[22]Browder-Kerensky, *op. cit.*, III, 1369. The Russian government established that there was only one outgoing telegram discussing Bolshevik slogans.

[23]Through Zivin, his intermediary with the Germans.

reconciliation, the Mensheviks decided to join with the Bolsheviks in this demonstration. The Bolsheviks stole the show with greater numbers, large quantities of streamers and leaflets, and forceful slogans, but the demonstration had no national impact. The Germans were so worried about Lenin's failure to stop the offensive that they established relations with the anarchists, who attacked the main prison, liberating criminals and deserters. Bolshevik and anarchist agitators, propagandizing military units, advocated rebellion and mutiny. The Germans and Austrians increased their front propaganda and stepped up distribution of their own Russian language publications. Fraternization was reoriented to conduct "peace negotiations" from regiment to regiment.

The Russian offensive soon weakened. According to Lenin's interpretation, a turning point in the revolution had been reached; but he feared a blood bath in which the groups which wanted to advance the revolution would be exterminated. Kamenev and Stalin supported him against Raskolnikov, a lieutenant and Bolshevik leader of the Kronstadt naval base, and Ensign A. Y. Semashko,[24] both of whom were insisting on an uprising. On July 5, Bolsheviks from the Central Committee, the Petrograd committee, and the military organizations resolved to begin the uprising. Lenin undoubtedly disagreed with the decision. Though the uprising was expected to spark a German counterblow at the front, it was politically premature.

By July 11 the Russian offensive had turned into defeat and a German counteroffensive was about to be initiated. The next day Lenin went to Finland, accompanied by Demyan Bedny, the poet, to take a summer rest with his sister Maria in Bonch-Bruyevich's *dacha* in the village of Naivola—a vacation "in a sea of trouble." He was completely exhausted and suffered from such insomnia that sleeping pills were prescribed.

The uprising started late on July 15.[25] It was launched by a machine gun regiment following Semashko's orders. Other military units, notably a sailor detachment from Kronstadt, and a few civilian groups joined.[26] There was a fair amount of popular unrest. Yet to

[24]This was not Dr. Semashko, Lenin's medical friend and party treasurer after Victor Taratuta, but presumably his cousin. Semashko was ordered to go to the front in April but refused and concentrated on organizing Bolshevik cells in the Petrograd garrison.

[25]The timing was in accord with German tactical requirements. The Bolsheviks were well informed on events at the front because of their infiltration into the communication and telegraphic services. Through these same infiltrators rumors were spread to the front that the Bolsheviks had assumed power in Petrograd and were calling off the war.

[26]According to the *London Times* of July 19, 1917, there were also demonstrations by national groups clamoring for self-determination.

get large masses of demonstrators and soldiers into the streets, money was necessary. And indeed, German agents were distributing money freely in 5, 10 and 25-ruble notes.[27]

The rising really got under way in the afternoon of July 16. In the evening the soldiers and workers of Petrograd were called into the streets. The soviet was surrounded and vainly was requested by the demonstrators to assume governmental power. The Central Committee had very little control. The insurgent troops (altogether five reserve regiments) were firmly in the hands of the Bolshevik military leaders. Lenin returned early on July 17 and made an insipid speech but did not call a halt to the uprising.

By the evening of July 17, despite government counteractions, the Bolsheviks, for all practical purposes, still controlled Petrograd. Yet there was no real mass support; the operation was in the nature of a *putsch* rather than an uprising. The continuing lack of visible success, as well as food, water, and other bodily needs caused restlessness among the masses.

At this time, some enterprising souls disseminated information demonstrating "definite proof of Bolshevik treason." Yet before the insurgents were handed newspapers and leaflets accusing Lenin of being a German agent, an assistant of the Minister of Justice, N. S. Karinsky, secretly informed Bonch-Bruyevich that there was a plan underway to indict Lenin. He warned that there was adequate evidence. Between seven and eight o'clock that night, the Central Committee, with Lenin's approval, called off the "manifestation." Lenin went into hiding. The government deployed loyal military forces; many Bolshevik units, shocked by the disclosures, were easily disarmed. Other Bolshevik troops inadvertently began to fire upon each other. Panic ensued, and immediately thereafter a thunderstorm followed by a heavy downpour emptied the streets. Within a few weeks the party was to lose half of its membership. Bolshevism seemed to be crushed forever.

[27]Nikitine, p. 111f.

Accusation of Treason

Subversive warfare stood the Germans in good stead. The great Russian offensive, which had been undertaken with a considerable numerical superiority and with an ample supply of weapons, had not been successful. The failure was largely due to the unwillingness of the troops to fight. Desertion and self-mutilation rates reached unprecedented heights. The German counteroffensive routed the

Russian army so quickly that the Germans were unable to apply their encirclement tactics.

The entire calamity, however, was not due to the Bolsheviks. The main cause of the military disaster lay in disorganization. Each unit and every group of specialists had formed its own soviet.[1] The soldiers spent much time debating and voting. Many soviets, particularly those under Bolshevik influence, thought it their duty to countermand military orders. All socialist parties bore responsibility for this state of affairs. The defencists called for the offensive but at the same time refused to rectify the disorder within the army. The soldiers were weary, but still were susceptible to firm leadership. The Bolsheviks, of course, concentrated on deepening and giving ideological meaning to the "pacifist" mood of the soldiers. But without the help—mostly through inaction—of the other socialists, Bolshevik subversion would not have succeeded.

The Germans had taken great pains to protect the security of their clandestine operations. Their payments to the revolutionaries were concealed according to the wishes of the recipients. These were the rules as stated in one German document: "1) The personality of the donor would guarantee that the money came from an unobjectionable source. 2) The donor or the bearer of the money should be enabled . . . to cross the Russian frontier. 3) . . . ready cash, . . . Swiss currency could be turned most easily, most efficiently, and least obtrusively into liquid and useful form."[2]

Despite precautions the secret was not well guarded. In April the socialist French Minister Albert Thomas had warned the Russian government after studying intelligence reports. In May the military High Command had given to the Department of Justice a voluminous dossier on the case. French officers in Petrograd who specialized in communications intelligence had volunteered their services. The government itself had taken the case under advisement and a cabinet committee was investigating. Yet no action was undertaken to stop Bolshevik activities, though one armed demonstration had

[1]This, together with the undermining of discipline, was the main result of Order No. 1. The issuance of this order against the will of the moderate parties often has been ascribed to German agents, but if there was a diabolic plan behind this event, the planning and tactical ability of a few anonymous German political warriors would have bordered on the miraculous. Still two points seem worth mentioning: the order was due essentially to two persons, Linde and N. D. Sokolov, a shadowy figure who was a cross between Bolshevik and Menshevik. He was a close friend of the Bolshevik Kozlovsky of whom we shall hear more presently. It should be remembered, too, that the order was written for the most part by Sokolov to inhibit the Tsar from throwing troops into the capital and chasing away the revolutionaries. The order fulfilled its purpose of depriving the Tsar of his army. *See* Tarasoff-Rodionov, *La Révolution de Février 1917* (Paris: Gallimard, 1930), Chapters VII and VIII; and Smilg-Benario, p. 216ff.

[2]Zeman, p. 55f.

taken place, another had been attempted, and now an operation which bordered upon a mass uprising was in progress.

As the crisis became more acute, permission was obtained from the Minister of Justice to publicize the presumed treason. Alexinsky, who knew a great deal about these matters, and who for many years had been very close to Lenin, and V. S. Pankratov, an old reputable revolutionary who had spent a long period in Schlüsselburg prison at hard labor, were elected to act as "channels." Invoking their "revolutionary duty," these two men warned Russian citizens of the dangers to their liberty and security. This warning was put into a letter to the committee of journalists attached to the provisional government. Several cabinet members and delegates to the soviet speedily intervened to prevent publication of the letter; it was printed in only one obscure newspaper.

The Alexinsky-Pankratov letter consisted of two parts, the first explanation based upon counter-intelligence and the second largely on censorship intelligence. In the first part of their letter, Alexinsky and Pankratov stated that on May 8, 1917, Ensign Yermolenko a Russian prisoner in Germany, was dispatched behind Russian lines to agitate for a speedy separate peace. German officers Schiditzki and Lübbers told him that peace propaganda was being disseminated by A. Skoropis-Yoltukhovsky, of the Bund for the Liberation of the Ukraine, and by Lenin, who was commissioned to undermine the confidence of the Russian people in the government. Money for this purpose was transmitted through a certain Svendson at the German legation in Stockholm.[3]

The report stated that Yermolenko's file had been forwarded to the Ministry for examination on April 28, i.e., before Yermolenko crossed back into Russian territory—an indication that Yermolenko may have been a counter-intelligence agent who had originally been dispatched by the Russians to the Germans.[4]

It was impossible to confirm the existence of Captain Schiditzki, who may have been Yermolenko's interrogator. However, the existence of Captain von Lübbers is substantiated by documentary evidence. He was assigned to the Unterkunfts-Departement of the German War Ministry, where he was placed in charge of prisoner-of-war propaganda. If Yermolenko did talk to Lübbers, he was, indeed, in communication with one of the top men. Although it is improbable that the Germans would have given secret information to a Russian prisoner, they might have acted incautiously if they had

[3]Browder-Kerensky, *op. cit.*, III, 1365.

[4]This was confirmed by Stepankowski, who also stated that the man's correct name was Yaremenko. The Russian agent posed as a leader of the Ukrainian independence movement and thereby won German confidence quickly. According to other indications, he was a counter-intelligence expert of long standing.

believed they were dealing with a prominent leader. Possibly Yermolenko was able to present adequate credentials or offer references from Ukrainian socialist and nationalist politicians.

Alexander Skoropis-Yoltukhovsky did run the Ukrainian Bund. This was rather widely known, but Lenin's connection with the Bund had been successfully concealed. Though the report did not suggest such a connection, Lenin must have been shocked and frightened by the juxtaposition of himself with Skoropis, even though he probably did not know much about the rest of the information.

The second portion of the letter stated that the Germans were transmitting money and instructions through Hanecki and Parvus in Stockholm, who then were communicating with Mecheslav Yulevich Kozlovsky, a Bolshevik attorney, and Eugenia Mavrikievna Sumenson, a woman relative of Hanecki. Kozlovsky was described as the chief recipient of the German money that was transferred from Berlin through the Diskonto-Gesellschaft to the Stockholm Nya Banken and thence to the Siberian Bank in Petrograd where Kozlovsky presently held a balance of over two million rubles.

The Minister of Justice was upset over the leaking of this detailed information which undoubtedly allowed some culprits to seek cover. Kerensky stated that Hanecki was preparing to cross the border with incriminating documents which would have clinched the case, but the leak kept him in Sweden. Hanecki hardly was so inexperienced as to carry compromising evidence on his person: Kerensky's complaint about the leak was not entirely genuine.

In the main, the information about Hanecki was correct, but Parvus did not, so far as is known, communicate directly with Petrograd. Sumenson's and Kozlovsky's names do not appear in German documents. Whether Sumenson was related to Hanecki is not known, but she worked for the firm of Fabian Klingsland which was the Petrograd correspondent of Hanecki's export firm.[5] Kozlovsky was described as a Polish socialist, but he served on the initial executive committee of the Petrograd soviet for the Latvian Social Democratic party. A certain Kozlovsky from Russia was a member of the Ukrainian Bund in Vienna during 1914, but the first names do not coincide. However, there is evidence that Kozlovsky, already in 1915, was connected with Parvus. He offered money to publish a socialist paper, and before the revolution traveled several times to Scandinavia dealing in revolutionary finances.[6] He also

[5]Futrell, p. 166.

[6]*Ibid.*, p. 171f. Kozlovsky and Hanecki attempted to recruit N. D. Sokolov, who wielded great power among the Mensheviks. Whether they succeeded or not, Kozlovsky had a room in Sokolov's flat which he used "as an accommodation address for most of his correspondence" (Nikitine, p. 167). Sokolov did much to shield Lenin and the Bolsheviks.

acted as legal adviser to Parvus. After the Bolshevik seizure of power, ironically, Kozlovsky was appointed to prosecute Alexinsky's case. (Kozlovsky died in 1927.)

The Diskonto Gesellschaft, a foremost German bank, certainly was uninvolved in these matters. A German diplomat, reading the text of the letter, wrote between the lines that "probably Parvus' firm" was meant, but the Germans later intercepted a telegram sent by the London *Times* correspondent in which he stated that the money was transferred through the Loan and Discount Bank at Copenhagen. No further explanation is found in the German file.

The Nya Banken, under Aschberg, affiliated with Swedish socialists, had handled many ruble transactions for the Germans during the war. Aschberg, who had dealt with tsarist Russia and American bankers, had arranged a Russian commercial loan in the U.S. and later related in his memoirs how he had succeeded in traveling back and forth across the Russian border by using bribes. Aschberg had assisted at Protopopov's conference with a German diplomat during 1916, and also was acquainted with Krassin. After 1917 the Bolsheviks apparently employed him for bank transactions abroad. For many years he was, in Sweden, considered to be something of a "Red banker." The intercepted—and unpublished—telegram by the *Times* correspondent stated that Aschberg had confirmed the business transactions but "thought" that they served honest business purposes. Years later he reasserted the same version adding, however, that possibly Hanecki sent money to Russia (i.e. to Sumenson) in small amounts.[7] Unfortunately, Aschberg died before he could bring himself to discuss these matters frankly.

As soon as the story broke, the Germans hurriedly organized a denial campaign. *Dagens Nyheter,* on July 22, published a denial by Hanecki, Radek, and Vorovsky.[8] Sumenson suddenly was described personally as a man who acted as managing clerk of a Petrograd firm which represented the Swiss chocolate firm Nestlé and an export company run by Hanecki. Hence Hanecki had sent money to Stockholm but not the other way around.[9] There are indeed some vague indications that Nestlé[10] was abused for some transactions but, in

---

[7]*Ibid.,* p. 166.

[8]According to Scheidemann, Vorovsky was in close contact with Parvus, *op. cit.,* I, 127).

[9]According to Futrell, Aschberg's belated admission destroyed this denial by Hanecki (p. 166f.).

[10]Three intercepted telegrams between Hanecki and Sumenson contained these phrases: "Nestlé not sent flour. Agitate." "Cable what funds in your hands Nestlé." "Cable bank balances then pay Nestlé account if possible." (Nikitine, pp. 120f.) Nikitine, a counter intelligence chief, stated that Sumenson was a demi-mondaine and was not employed by a commercial firm (p. 123f.), but this probably was an error.

any event, no evidence was submitted to prove the alleged remittances from Petrograd to Stockholm.

The denial also stated that Hanecki had no connections with Helphand (Parvus), incongruously adding that he had business dealings with him. Moreover, many Social Democrats maintained business relations with Parvus; the name of a prominent Menshevik was brought up to exculpate the Bolshevik suspect. Hanecki denied knowing "Svenson." ("Svenson" probably was a pseudonym of Hans Steinwachs, who before 1917 had acted as Keskuela's case officer and who now was handling finances for revolutionizing at Stockholm.)[11]

On July 24 Vorovsky telegraphed to Sklarz in Berlin requesting him to deny under oath, before a suitable forum in Copenhagen, that he gave money to the Bolsheviks or to Lenin through Hanecki or other persons. This telegram is odd in that Sklarz's name had not yet been mentioned publicly. The Germans deemed it inadvisable to fulfill the request. Hanecki also sent a telegram asking "Alexander" (i.e., Parvus) to travel to Copenhagen immediately.

On July 26 *Soldati i Rabochii,* then the name of *Pravda,* acknowledged that Hanecki and Kozlovsky had been working for Parvus. On July 31, 1917, Hanecki, in *Russische Korrespondenz Prawda,* admitted that he had worked in a trading firm connected with Parvus. He did so, he said, to support his family and the Social Democratic party in Warsaw (then occupied by the Germans). But he added that he considered Parvus to be an honorable man: "Only history can show who was right in judging the man Parvus: Lenin or Hanecki."[12]

In the meantime, Karinsky, who had warned Bonch-Bruyevich of the case against Lenin, had—in a typical switch—been put in charge of prosecuting the affair. (He resigned this office by mid-September.[13]) Despite his inauspicious attitude he had gathered extensive documentation. He reported part of his findings on August 4. The indictment was drawn up for treason and organized armed rebellion. Those who were indicted for rebellion were not necessarily accused of treason and vice versa. The accusations against Semashko, Raskolnikov, Kollontai, Trotsky, and Lunacharsky dealt with rebellion; those against the group headed by Lenin, Zinovyev, Parvus, and Hanecki, with treason. There was no mention of Hanecki's probably not being a Russian citizen; Parvus was not either, but perhaps this was not known.

Concerning the rebellion, it was stated that a search of Bolshevik

---

[11]It is also possible that he was a Swedish socialist by that name. The Swedish socialists, as Futrell shows, were very helpful in these transactions.

[12]Futrell, p. 167f.

[13]Browder-Kerensky, *op .cit.,* III, 1370ff. 1702.

headquarters had revealed that the revolt had been ordered by the Central Committee. From those headquarters instructions had been issued to military units ordering them to place armored cars and a cruiser at the disposal of the Bolshevik military organization. The search disclosed deployment lists of suitable military units, "armed workers," cell leaders, contacts, and Bolshevik intelligence operators. An interesting discovery was literature of the arch-reactionary *Union of the Russian People* and large numbers of post cards illustrating ritual murder. Presumably this material was to be used to stimulate the fear of counter-revolution—a chief factor preventing socialists and liberals from taking action against the Bolsheviks.[14]

The indictment stated, with respect to Lenin's treason, that "while residing in the German part of Switzerland" Lenin was in contact with Parvus, frequented camps of Ukrainian prisoners of war, and carried on propaganda for the separation of the Ukraine from Russia.[15] The evidence, it was stupidly alleged, pointed to Lenin as a German agent[16] who had an agreement with Germany and went to Petrograd "to aid Germany in her war with Russia." It was this unfounded allegation which vitiated much of the later discussion of Lenin's relations with the Germans.

Further, it was stated that in April an attempt was made from Stockholm to publish a newspaper to oppose England and France, that Lenin and Zinovyev were arrested in October, 1914, in Austria, that they were released upon order by the Austrian Prime Minister, and that Hanecki played an important role in their release.

In addition, it maintained that Hanecki had worked closely with Parvus in Copenhagen, that Kozlovsky had traveled to Copenhagen and acted as legal adviser to Parvus, who was proposing the financing of a steamship company in Russia, and that Parvus, Hanecki, and Kozlovsky visited Berlin. It was held that the telegraphic correspondence which Sumenson, Lenin, Kollontai, and Kozlovsky in Petrograd had with Hanecki and Parvus in Sweden was "a cover-up for relations of an espionage character."[17] During the past six

[14]Paralyzing fears are an excellent tactical device. Since 1956 the Communists have been using the fear of nuclear war as a psycho-strategic cover for their operations.

[15]Browder-Kerensky, III, p. 1374.

[16]*Ibid.*, p. 1375.

[17]Twenty-nine of these telegrams were published, without dates, by Nikitine, but the French intelligence officer who intercepted them had a considerably larger number. One telegram points to the pressure exerted by and on the Bolsheviks. It reads, "Funds very low cannot assist if really urgent give 500 as last payment pencils huge loss original hopeless instruct Nya Banken cable further 100 thousand." This telegram was sent by Sumenson to Hanecki. The text suggests that the July uprising may have been hampered by low funds. For a general analysis, *see* S. P. Melgunov, *Zolotoy nemetskii klyuch bolshevikov*, Paris, La Maison du Livre Etranger, 1940, pp. 104-116. Melgunov stressed that Hanecki was paying for Sumenson's "imports" and

months, Sumenson had withdrawn 750,000 rubles from her account; the balance was 180,000 rubles.[18]

Other data could not "as yet be made public." But the information pointed to the fact that the accused were assisting in the disorganization of the Russian army and that they were conducting propaganda to inhibit military actions against the enemy. The armed insurrection, moreover, "was accompanied by murders and violence."

Lenin replied on August 8 and 9 in *Rabochy i Soldat*. He first commented on his role in the rebellion. He had left Petrograd on July 12 "on account of illness" and returned only on July 17, when he delivered a single speech—and that lacked significance. This was true enough, except that he overly stressed his illness. He assumed full responsibility, he wrote, for all steps and measures taken by the Central Committee and the party, but failed to say how he was able to discharge this responsibility. As to the accusation about relations with Germany, Lenin felt that this was another "Beilis case."[19] Lenin claimed that the accusations "parrotted" the slanders of calumniator Alexinsky; but Alexinsky had simply distributed information which had been leaked to him from the Justice Department. Lenin corrected the claim that Zinovyev had been arrested in Austria; he could have added that he himself had been arrested in August and not in October. He also related that he was arrested not as a Russian subject but as a spy. He denied that Hanecki played a part in his release but this denial was false. He said it was "a contemptible lie" to assert that he had relations with Parvus; but he had such relations, and Parvus soon mischievously confirmed in print one of his meetings with Lenin during this period.[20] Lenin stated that it was untrue that he had visited military camps; he was correct in adding that "nothing of the kind happened, or could even

added that according to Beletsky, former Okhrana chief, Sumenson had been known for years to be a German agent. Incidentally, for most of his communications with Petrograd, Hanecki used the diplomatic pouch—the government unwittingly, helped in the conspiracy (Futrell, p. 155).

[18]Browder-Kerensky, III, p. 1376. It was also stated that in the early days of the revolution "sums of money (800,000 rubles, 250,000 rubles and other sums) were remitted to Russia from Stockholm through one bank that received orders from Germany" (p. 1375).

[19]This is an allusion to the celebrated trial in 1912 of Jacob Beilis, a hapless Jew, on contrived charges of ritual murder. Beilis sought his day in court and was acquitted. It would have been more correct for Lenin to refer to the *Bonnet Rouge* affair that just had broken in France. The Germans financed a radical revolutionary and pacifist paper to undermine French resistance. He could also have cited the case of his old Zimmerwald crony, Robert Grimm, who had been expelled from Russia because he was plotting with Germany to facilitate a separate peace. Grimm was exposed because a telegram of his to Berne was deciphered.

[20]Russian counter-intelligence had seized three letters by Lenin to Parvus, presumably of May-June, 1917. (*See* Nikitine, *op. cit.*, p. 118).

happen." He denied, untruthfully, any connection with the Ukrainian Bund and ignored the allegation about Ukrainian separatists' propaganda.

A telegram seized in Bolshevik headquarters about a money deal in Stockholm had been misunderstood by the prosecutor. Lenin seized upon it and disproved more than the error warranted. He denied "financial dealings" with Hanecki. However, letters already mentioned disprove this denial. It is also noteworthy that Lenin's address book showed three different entries for Kozlovsky's home, office and his extension in the soviet:[21] this fact indicates that Lenin was quite well informed about the secret machinations of his aides.[22]

In his reply in *Rabochy i Soldat* Lenin frankly admitted Hanecki's relation with Parvus. Offering no explanation why he maintained contact with Hanecki, who was a friend of the "social chauvinist" Parvus, Lenin poked fun at the point that "commercial correspondence" might serve as a screen "for espionage" and asked how many of his political opponents could be accused "according to this wonderful prescription." He ignored the fact that the evidence did not point to espionage at all, and took the prosecutor to task for not having presented a better analysis of the Sumenson account, detailing the source of the money and the recipients.

The point was valid. There obviously were a number of mistakes in the prosecutor's story, but much had become known. The Justice Department and counter-intelligence knew considerably more than they revealed, and Lenin had no way of knowing if Mme. Sumenson, who was not politically motivated, did not reveal everything under interrogation. Insofar as the prosecution was concerned, an orderly development of the case could have been quite effective. But the investigation was allowed to linger. The order for Lenin's arrest which was issued, after some delay, on July 19, was not revoked; it remained in force until he seized power. Actually, however, the case had been dropped by the middle of August. Some of the more illusionary members of the government—especially N. V. Nekrassov,

[21]Futrell, p. 177f.

[22]After the seizure of power the Central Committee refused to appoint Hanecki to be diplomatic representative in Stockholm. Lenin, in a vigorously worded letter, came to his defense without, however, enlightening the comrades about Hanecki's true role *(Leninski Sbornik,* vol. 36, Moscow, 1959, p. 18ff.). Lenin argued that it was not forbidden by any party resolution to work in commercial firms. Hanecki's and Kozlovsky's case was discussed in eight meetings of the Central Committee between April 1917 and February 1918 but the published minutes of these meetings omit these debates (Futrell, p. 174f.). Some debates, presumably, were influenced by M. S. Uritsky who had lived between 1915 and 1917 at Copenhagen and also was connected with Parvus. The whole affair was a replica of the Malinovsky story; only this time, Hanecki was the accused and not the judge. In any event, Hanecki made a moderately distinguished career under Lenin but in the late 1930's he seems to have fallen victim to Stalin's purges. Subsequently he was rehabilitated.

who later joined the Bolsheviks—objected to accusing an authentic revolutionary of high treason. P. N. Pereverzev, the Minister of Justice, who authorized the disclosures, was forced to resign. In his place, Kerensky appointed A. S. Zarudny, who had served as Trotsky's defense lawyer in 1906. Thus, Kerensky took no serious initiative to make justice prevail. He affected criticism of the premature disclosure which had allowed Hanecki to escape arrest. But it was known that Larin had served as a courier between the Petrograd and Stockholm Bolsheviks and nothing was done to get the truth from him.[23] The fact that he was neither a Bolshevik nor a Menshevik apparently provided him with ample political protection.

[23]Nikitine, *op. cit.*, p. 117. *See also London Times*, July 20, 1917.

In Hiding

The Bolsheviks were given ample opportunity to cover their tracks. Lenin hid in Stassova's plush apartment (this would have been an obvious place to search) and was given a choice diet—Maria had left instructions to take care of Lenin's sick stomach. On July 18, Lenin stayed with Sverdlov at the apartment of M. L. Salimova, then went to that of V. N. Kayurov and to the flat of N. G. Poletayev, a Duma deputy. The choice of the last two apartments is quite surprising. Finally, he proceeded to the residence of S. Y. Alliluyev[1] and in a secret meeting of party leaders refused to present himself for trial, on the invalid and transparent pretext that he could expect no justice from a "counter-revolutionary government." An innocent man would have seized the opportunity to cleanse his record. This is precisely what Trotsky did. But obviously Lenin could not take the risk, even though he probably knew that he had little to fear from prosecutor Karinsky.

Not all of the party leaders present knew about Lenin's deals with the Germans. Stalin hardly was privy to these secrets, but he possessed a first-rate conspiratorial nose and argued most strongly against risking a confrontation with the law. Krupskaya asserts that Lenin and Zinovyev, even against Maria's objections, decided to present themselves for trial at the appointed time. Lenin asked Krupskaya to inform Kamenev. As she arose hastily, Lenin checked her with, "Let's say goodbye . . . we may not see each other again."[2] They

[1]Alliluyev was Stalin's father-in-law.

[2]Krupskaya, p. 366. Walter, p. 335, relates that Stassova reported a rumor according to which evidence had been found in the police archives that Lenin was an *agent provocateur*. Was this perhaps the documentation on "Lenin II"?

embraced. The tale goes that a few hours later Stalin persuaded Lenin not to appear in court and thus "saved his life." This is a touching but thoroughly untrustworthy story.

In the evening of July 20, the room which the Lenins still occupied in Yelizarov's house was searched;[3] two days later the entire flat was examined and subsequently a third search was made. The searches, however, were incompetent and too late. Lenin slipped out of town on July 22, at 11 P.M., walked for nine kilometers to an outlying railroad station, and quietly traveled to Razliv, near Sestroretsk, where he stayed in the house of the worker N. A. Yemelyanov.

On August 3 Lenin was formally indicted but the government made no real effort to locate him (which should have been easy). The Mensheviks, dreading that an investigation might backfire on them, loudly cried "slander," saving the Bolsheviks.

Since May Trotsky had been Lenin's closest collaborator: he was a more forceful orator and clearer thinker than other Bolsheviks, and he possessed more energy and tactical sense. But he had no money and therefore, though he had the most able collaborators, was unable to sustain an effective newspaper.[4] Formally he and his group had remained independent and, since the government had not implicated him in its accusations, Trotsky remained at liberty. He wrote a cocky letter to the government saying that he shared Lenin's convictions and was as responsible as Lenin for the July events. Why was he not indicted? For about two weeks, Trotsky constantly made speeches in which he defended the Bolsheviks and goaded the government. After a long period of this performance, he was arrested. Trotsky—formerly described by Lenin as a "swine"— was not afraid to take personal risks.

Once in this period Lenin reacted to a prediction that he soon might be premier by saying, "This wouldn't be so strange."[5] But he was thoroughly dejected.

It seemed to some that Lenin's career was nearing its end. Fearing that someone might "do him in," he asked Kamenev, in strict confidence, to edit the manuscript which later was published as _The State and Revolution_. He wanted Kamenev to ensure post-humous publication. "I think it is important" he said, "because Plekhanov and Kautsky are not the only ones who blundered."

His concealment did not lack its romantic aspects, but it hardly improved his health. He had left the Yemelyanov house and moved

---

[3]Shub, p. 216.

[4]Trotsky had been associated with the _Mezhrayonka_ which presumably was supported before March, 1917, by Parvus; at that time, Trotsky was living in France, Spain, and the United States.

[5]Shotman, _op. cit.,_ p. 396.

into the woods. Lenin, now known as Konstantin Petrovich Ivanov, could be reached by one of Yemelyanov's children acting as guide. The road led through the village to the seashore, from which point a boat had to be taken. After rowing for half an hour, mostly through sedge, there was another ten-minute walk through swamps before reaching a barn. There "Ivanov" was living, *sans* beard and mustache. Inside the barn a sort of bedroom had been created, but because it was filled with hay there could be no fire, so that it was quite cold at night, even in July and August. The vapors from the swamp were unpleasant and dangerous. Another inconvenience was the difficulty in getting supplies to Lenin. In order to attract little attention, the faithful Shotman alternated with a female comrade, A. N. Tokareva, in bringing things.

In almost complete isolation, it was surprising that Lenin snapped out of his depression by mid-August. He was able to write several articles and work on *State and Revolution.* Yet he feared that the "Bonapartist" phase of the revolution was about to begin. This expectation kept him politically inactive.

On August 8, a party conference convened which allegedly represented about 150,000 party members.[6] Siefeld attended as a delegate from Odessa. Lenin was honorary president, but the conference was dominated by Stalin. It ratified the formal adherence of the jailed Trotsky and his group to the Bolsheviks. More than any other socialist group, Trotsky's *Mezhrayonka* contributed to the Tsar's overthrow. Trotsky also held strong support from the sailors. His "apparatus" was better organized than Lenin's although Lenin had broader mass support and a stronger propaganda machine. The merging of the two groups was in line with German wishes, for together they created a truly effective insurrectional force.

The conference preached a united front of the internationalists against the defencists, and formulated a hold-the-line resolution which held the seizure of power to be the goal of the revolutionary classes. But what else could it say? There was a suggestion that socialism could be built up even if there were no proletarian revolution in the West; this constituted an abandonment of a basic tenet of the creed, and one which fitted German interests. The most visible change was that the slogan advocating "all power to the soviets" was revoked: the soviet had turned strongly against the

---

[6]This figure probably should be much smaller since party membership was down significantly. The best evidence is that the 100,000 mark was reached only late in 1917. It is also asserted that the Bolsheviks were now publishing forty papers, printing 1,500,000 issues *per week.* (*Istoricheskii Arkhiv* (1955), No. 5, p. 201). This means that the *tirage* of the average paper was very small and that organized party membership must be counted merely in the tens of thousands. *See also* Schapiro, *Origin,* p. 167.

Bolsheviks. For Lenin, any institution was an instrument of power. If it served his political interests, it was good; it if did not, it was bad—no organization could have a genuine value for and in itself.

The Bolshevik conference aroused much ire and evoked criticism of the government for not finding Lenin. On August 15 an *ukas* was issued authorizing administrative arrest and deportation of persons dangerous to the defense and internal security of the state and "to the freedom achieved by the revolution." Two days later, another decree threatened with prison terms, of indefinite periods at hard labor, persons guilty of violence with the intent to change the state structure, to sever from Russia any of its parts, to remove the organs of supreme state power, or to prevent the exercise of state authority. Revolution was thus outlawed, but Lenin could not know that these laws would be invoked only against generals trying to defend their country against the external enemy.

On the face of it, Lenin's legal jeopardy had worsened. There was fear that hunters might inadvertently discover Lenin's hide-out which, for that matter, would become uninhabitable in cold weather. The decision was made to remove Lenin to Finland, but the border was well guarded. Shotman and another Finn, Ejno A. Rakhya, systematically tested all nearby border check points; they decided that a simple crossing with false papers was too dangerous. It was decided that Lenin should travel as a stoker on a locomotive operated by a friend of Shotman.

One day, allegedly early in September but more likely by the middle of August, Lenin and his party left the barn and walked about six miles through the bush to a railroad station. This walk at night was slightly hazardous; Yemelyanov, who acted as guide, lost his way. A river had to be crossed and a brush fire caused trouble. At the station, Yemelyanov was arrested as a suspect, but Lenin and Rakhya, who had been hiding in the dark, jumped on the train in the best American hobo tradition. Finally they reached a place near the border at which point they waited till the next evening in the apartment of comrade Kalske. By nightfall, G. Jalawa, the friendly engineer, was ready. Wearing a wig, make-up, and appropriate clothing, Lenin mounted the locomotive and began to toss wood into the fire. The train reached the border check point. When it appeared that the control was strict, the engineer drove the locomotive forward, as though to take water, and put Lenin across.[7]

While Lenin changed roles from stoker to revolutionary, he asked Shotman to return the manuscript of *State and Revolution* which he had entrusted to him. A car was waiting to carry Lenin to a safe apartment. The next day he traveled to Lakhti, where he remained

[7]For more details, see Shotman, pp. 400-411.

for two days. Then he moved to the village of Zhalkala, to the home of the parents of the very young and pretty Lidia P. Parviainen, Rakhya's wife. There he is said to have stayed for about ten days and to have enjoyed the home-made sweets. Finally, "Constantin Petrovich Ivanov" disguised himself as a pastor and moved to Helsinki, the Finnish capital, where he stayed with a comrade, Kustaa Rowio who, since the February revolution, had been in charge of the city police! Rowio had a fine Marxist library; Lenin began to work. During one night (we do not know exactly when), he stayed in the house of Karl Wiik, who had been deeply involved in the "northern underground." There Lenin read Jules Michelet's account of the terror in the French Revolution.[8]

The Germans, meanwhile, were not satisfied with Lenin's performance and were hesitating. They wanted the Bolsheviks to concentrate more on organizing and less on agitating. For a while the Germans attempted to pull additional socialist groups into their net and through an international conference at Stockholm (September 5-12, 1917) sought to enhance socialist "unity." But this tactic failed, partly because of Bolshevik sabotage and partly because the moderate socialists wavered.

By the middle of August the military joined conservative and middle-of-the-road politicians to map out a program of restoring order in Russia. Rumors of an impending military coup were thickening.

Early in September, a conflict pitted the government against the high command. The military, under General Lavr Kornilov, attempted to seize control.[9] The frightened socialists rallied around the soviet. The Bolsheviks, who had recently treated the soviet, the Mensheviks, and the Social Revolutionaries as traitors, reversed themselves and joined the socialist "counter-revolutionaries" in

---

[8]Futrell, p. 18.

[9]The attempts by the right to restore an orderly regime in Russia prove that, to make revolutions or counter-revolutions, money is not enough. One group collected four million rubles but they did not know how to spend the money and spent only about 500,000 rubles for ineffectual propaganda. A maximum of 800,000 rubles was given to Kornilov for operations to support his military action. (Actually, the amount turned over may have been far less.) Hence there was, in orders of magnitude, just as much money available to this group as to the Germans. But the ingredients of leadership, organization, and purpose were lacking. Money is indeed just *one* of the prerequisites of revolution. Incidentally, the planners of the counter-coup had intelligence that the Bolsheviks were planning another demonstration or uprising by September 10. This was countermanded. (The change may have been connected with Lenin's departure for Finland.) Thereupon, the military decided to stage a "Bolshevik" coup themselves, and 100,000 rubles were allotted. By the time 26,000 rubles were spent, a high ranking general vetoed the scheme. (Browder-Kerensky, *op. cit.*, III, 1527-1542.)

opposition to the military counter-revolutionaries. Suddenly there occurred a resurgence of the cry, "All power to the soviet!"

No one bothered to ask Lenin's advice. However, three days after the united front had been improvised, Lenin provided tactical advice: the Bolsheviks should join with the other socialists in fighting Kornilov but should not support the government. This was a typical Lenin prescription on the subject of how to swim without getting wet.

The Bolsheviks exploited the opportunity to enlarge their militant organization and pressed forward to obtain the weapons which the government was distributing. After Kornilov was defeated (largely through railroad strikes and sabotage), the Bolsheviks ignored the government's request to return the weapons. The Kornilov affair provided the Bolsheviks with an unexpected gain, for it discredited most of the parties that were represented in both the government and in the soviet.

For the first time in the incessant voting exercised to keep the soviet "representative" of public opinion, Petrograd factory workers during September returned a slim Bolshevik majority. In the Petrograd soviet the military deputies sided with the Bolsheviks. The Bolsheviks also gained a majority in the Moscow soviet, and early in October won an election in the Moscow district. This major reversal occurred at a moment when practically all of the ranking Bolshevik leaders were in prison or in hiding. A few days later, partly as a result of this switch, Trotsky was released from jail and elected president of the Petrograd soviet. The government instituted a purge of military officers, but by now it lacked any real power. A front organization (the Committee for the People's Struggle Against Counter-revolution) insisted upon the release of all those who had been "unjustly" accused. Virtually all the perpetrators of the July uprising, including Trotsky, were released outright or set free on bail. The amount set for bail was no less than 8,000 rubles for the main defendants, but the Central Committee was able to pay.[10] Chaos was spreading.

On September 13 the Petrograd soviet adopted a resolution calling for a cabinet which would be responsible to the soviet. The next day Lenin wrote an article, entitled "Compromises,"[11] advocating all power to the soviets and a government of Social Revolutionaries and Mensheviks responsible to the soviets. He went on to say that, if the new government were to guarantee full freedom of propaganda under conditions of real and complete democracy, there would be a possibility of "peaceful progress of the revolution"

[10]Yelena D. Stassova, *Stranitsy zhizni i borby* (Moscow: Gospolitizdat, 1957), p. 99.

[11]*Selected Works*, Vol. VI, pp. 208-214.

and of a "peaceful solution of the party strife within the soviets." Such a possibility occurs only extremely rarely in history, Lenin added, and the present opportunity may last for only "a few days, or for a week or two," but it still would be "extremely valuable" to utilize the unexpected chance. Zinovyev had stated more clearly a few days earlier, in an article *What Not To Do,* that an insurrectional attempt would herald the fate of the Paris Commune for the revolution.

But on September 16 Lenin added in a postscript that the proposal for a compromise was "already too late" and asserted that Kerensky was about to "consolidate his position with the help of the bourgeoisie." There seemed to be no basis for this statement—no significant political change had occurred to invalidate Lenin's compromise proposal. But Lenin's thinking had for some reason suddenly taken a dramatic turn. Why?

The Armed Uprising

Through Wiik Lenin resumed contact with Hanecki in Stockholm. He wrote him an unofficial letter saying he could not consult with the Central Committee, "nor even get in touch with them." Yet, in the same paragraph he added that he would forward a report from Stockholm to the Central Committee.

The point of this Aesopian letter was that the comrades in Stockholm should take action themselves. The Central Committee "cannot help," hence, how are money affairs? Did they manage to collect money "through the Swedish left?" Lenin hinted that Karl Moor might provide a source of funds, or since the old channels were clogged, could serve as a cover man for further money "collections." Lenin may also have feared that the German link was broken, and wanted Moor to reestablish relations. Since his letter might have been intercepted, Lenin observed the rules of conspiracy. He asked: "But what is Moor like? Has it been completely and absolutely proven that he is honest? Has he never had any direct, or indirect hobnobbing with German social imperialists?" Of course, Lenin had known Moor for years. (Note that Lenin did not ask whether Moor had connections with the German government but merely professed interest in his associations with the German Social Democratic party.[1])

[1]The editors of Lenin's *Sochineniya* (3rd edition, XXIV, 365) asserted that on October 7 the Central Committee declined a money offer by Moor because it was not feasible to check the real source of these funds. There may have been such a vote, especially since most members of the Central Committee were left in the dark about these affairs . . . but the funds were hardly declined.

Lenin's liaison men must have acted quickly. On September 29, 1917, the German Foreign Office informed the high command that their military operations were being substantially bolstered by "intensive undermining activities inside Russia on the part of the Foreign Ministry. . . . The Bolshevik movement could never have attained the scale of the influence which it has today without our continual support. There is every indication that the movement will continue to grow."[2] In other words, the Bolsheviks were receiving help again.

The telegram further said that Russia "is only barely held together by English agents," and added that the English influence depended upon rail communications through Finland. The message reported: "The preparations for the Finnish rising are . . . busily underway and are being supported to a considerable extent." Lenin was in Finland at that time.

For a number of reasons, the Foreign Office proposed the occupation of the Aaland Isles. The operation would have to be accomplished in the first half of November in order to improve in an "eminently important manner" the German "position in the West and the North." This action would affect "the whole outcome of the war." Since the occupation of the Aalands was not feasible, the high command proposed instead—over the signature of General Erich Ludendorff—to continue the revolutionizing of Russia. The plan gave thanks to the Foreign Office for the generous financial support it had extended to this activity. (Note the timing on which the Foreign Office insisted: "first half of November.")

Lenin had changed his mind on September 16. But he procrastinated for another nine days. On September 24, Ludendorff, after considering the lessons of the Kornilov uprising, expressed the fear that another military coup might succeed. In order to forestall this danger, he asked the Foreign Office to apply more radical measures. On September 25, Lenin notified the Central Committee that the current strategy would have to be modified: the Bolsheviks should assume state power. It is possible that he had learned that the Germans were again backing him.

Lenin took two days to write his message. The thoughts and suggestions reflected his entire experience of twenty-four years. He stated that the Bolsheviks were gaining the majority in Petrograd and Moscow, and that it was time to replace speech-making with action. "History will not forgive us if we do not assume power now. . . . We will win absolutely and unquestionably."[3] He felt that an uprising was essential but that it should be carefully prepared. Lenin

[2]Zeman, p. 70.

[3]*Selected Works*, Vol. VI, p. 217.

outlined his concept of insurrection as an art, offered suggestions concerning organization and tactics, and emphasized that further delays were inadmissible.

The letter horrified the Central Committee. Kamenev suggested that Lenin's proposal be rejected. It was decided to burn the letter, but a vote of six to four with six abstentions resolved to preserve a copy for the party archieves.

As had often occurred before, Lenin was out of step with his contemporaries; but in this instance he was in step with history. Chaos was gaining the upper hand. During September agrarian disorders erupted throughout the countryside and an increasingly intense peasant civil war was underway. Inflation was rampant and the value of the ruble declined precipitously. (There were now three types in circulation.) Labor productivity had declined by one third or more. Production of many key commodities was at a virtual standstill, and with about 1500 locomotives out of order, transport bottlenecks were disrupting the distribution system. Food was scarce, especially in the army. The government, in the midst of a rapidly increasing deficit, was unable to distribute the social benefits it had promised. There were outbursts in the Urals and Siberia and rebellions by independence movements in Turkestan and the Caucasus. The situation in Finland gradually became unmanageable. On October 1, 1917, Ludendorff issued a new directive on front propaganda; "fraternization" was immediately stepped up. The Russian government displayed utter impotence, while running what was alleged, even by Lenin, to be the freest democracy in the world.

Perturbed by the Central Committee's failure to acknowledge his letter, Lenin concerned himself with the technical aspects of the insurrection. He pondered the possible means of employing the Baltic fleet, the Kronstadt garrison, and the troops stationed in Finland.

The Central Committee continued on its conciliatory course. The Bolsheviks attended a democratic conference which resolved to establish a "pre-parliament." The Bolsheviks voted to join with the other parties in participating in that body. Lenin was furious and demanded that the conference and the pre-parliament be boycotted. Trotsky and Stalin supported him, but the conciliators held the majority.

Lenin was impatient; he departed from Helsingfors for Vyborg. On the pretext that the border crossing was very dangerous, the Central Committee forbade Lenin to return to Petrograd. Shotman was dispatched to intercept Lenin and inform him that his return to Russia had been "forbidden" by the party.[4] Strangely enough,

4Shotman, *op. cit.,* p. 415. For a biography of Shotman, see *Istariocheskii Arkhiv* (1960), No. 2, p. 34.

although he was infuriated, Lenin not only obeyed this order but apparently did not protest it. However, one source who should be knowledgeable asserts that Lenin traveled to Petrograd on Friday, October 5.[5]

Lenin's anger increased when he noted that the "central organ," then edited by Stalin, was not including his criticism of party tactics. On October 12, he wrote to the Central Committee that he recognized the "subtle hint of gagging me and of proposing that I retire." He continued, "I am compelled to tender my resignation from the Central Committee . . . leaving myself freedom of propaganda in the lower ranks of the party and at the party congress . . . . It is my deepest conviction that if we . . . let the present moment pass, we shall ruin the revolution."[6] The party leaders "conciliated" and decided to quit the pre-parliament.

The current dispute concerned the feasibility of awaiting the opening of the Congress of Soviets—in which the Bolsheviks might gain influence and perhaps a majority—before solving the question of a rising. Lenin considered the discussion "a childish play of formality" and insisted upon immediate action.

On October 16 the Central Committee "approved" Lenin's move to Petrograd; he had not asked for such consent. This act implies that the Bolsheviks were telling him not to stand at a distance and preach, but to prepare the uprising himself—and to do so at the locale of danger.

Lenin wrote another letter on October 20 demanding immediate insurrection; he submitted a detailed tactical program. In the press he published an article asserting that the "third" period of the world revolution was beginning. He interpreted the signs as indicating an incipient uprising in Germany. He wrote, "The crisis is here. The future of the Russian revolution is at stake. The future of the international workers' revolution for socialism is at stake."

The state of affairs in Russia can be gauged by Lenin's brazenness in announcing his intentions openly. But the Central Committee still was not replying to his communications; he again offered his resignation. By October 20 Lenin recognized that he could not accomplish his objectives by remaining in Finland. This time, a convenient vacation at the critical moment would mean the end of his political career. Again posing as stoker on the locomotive, he slipped into Petrograd, hiding in the apartment of Marguerite Fofanova, a female party member. Party writers have attempted to suggest that this was a poor worker's apartment in a proletarian quarter,[7] but Fofanova

[5]M. V. Fofanova, "Posledneye podpolye V. I. Lenina," *Istoricheskii Arkhiv* (1956), No. 4, pp. 166-172.

[6]*Sochineniya*, 4th ed., Vol. 26, p. 61f.

[7]Krupskaya, *op. cit.*, p. 373.

was an agronomist, and the apartment, which was situated on a broad thoroughfare, was large and spacious. The apartment building stood next to a house with garden which formed an approximate border between a district of workers' dwellings and a suburban villa development. In October, "the family, including the servant" still were "in the country, where they had gone for the summer," Krupskaya related.[8] Yet Marguerite Fofanova indicated that she had been told in August to have her apartment ready and that her sister took the Fofanova children to their grandparents in Ufa province in order to leave the apartment free.

Marguerite Fofanova's version of the date of Lenin's arrival in Petrograd is doubtful: it does not correspond with other reports. More significantly, Fofanova reported that Lenin was chiefly concerned with the agrarian question; she claimed that while he lived at her apartment the literary argument with the party was over. This story would put his arrival in the middle rather than the early part of October. Fofanova probably is correct in remembering that Lenin arrived on a Friday afternoon; she has a vivid recollection of his staying a long time. If the arrival date of October 5 is excluded as too early, and if Lenin appeared on a Friday, he may have appeared on October 12 or October 19 (rather than October 20). The October 12 date is the most plausible. Thus, Lenin stayed at least eighteen, and perhaps twenty-five, days at Marguerite Fofanova's apartment.

There is an eerie quality about this interlude. Lenin had fought a bitter struggle with his own party and he was preparing a violent uprising which might have entailed his own death. There was chaos and trouble all around. Yet here he was, by force of circumstances, on a little island of peace, a Robinson Crusoe with a girl Friday who provided him with shelter and food, and who acted as his courier.

Marguerite Vasilyevna Fofanova (born in 1883) was completing the last year of her studies in agronomy. Apparently an alert and intelligent girl, there is no doubt that there existed a close mental rapport between her and Lenin. Though they had not met previous to his arrival at her apartment, Lenin soon talked to her confidentially about his tactics in dealing with the peasants and, even more significantly, discussed with her the top secret correspondence he received from Zinovyev. She reported that Lenin suffered from insomnia and displayed irritability and hastiness. She also recounted that Krupskaya visited her husband on the first day of Lenin's arrival and again on October 31, when she "stayed with us overnight." The next morning Krupskaya came to Marguerite's room and inquired about possible treatment for Volodya's insomnia. Fofanova's chronicle hints that she and Lenin kept in contact during the following

[8]*Ibid.*

years and that their letters were often about books, and sometimes discussing Goethe's *Faust,* and opera. It is noteworthy that Communist historians describe this interlude as lasting only a mere two or three days.

Lenin, at forty-seven, was confined for three weeks with a young woman to whom he was attracted. Normally, the inference would be plain, but Lenin might not have been tempted. Still, the tone of Fofanova's reminiscences and also the flavor of Krupskaya's recollection do suggest a somewhat intimate bond. Psychologically, the matter is of more than passing interest: this was the peak of Lenin's life, the only time when he threw himself into the midst of the fray. Perhaps he did feel the inner need to prove himself as the great conqueror during the Indian summer of his emotional life. All that is definitely known is that during these climactic days, Lenin was in close contact *only* with Fofanova, a woman thirteen years younger than he. It would be unreasonable to assume that her influence was trivial.

After Lenin had focussed upon the uprising as a military operation, he became anxious to broaden his political base. He sent Marguerite to obtain for him back numbers of *Krestyanskiye Izvestiya,* the organ of the peasant soviet, in which the left Social Revolutionaries were playing the radical role. Many of their leaders had returned to Russia through Germany. Lenin's political strategy was designed to neutralize the Mensheviks in order to confuse public opinion and to seek a temporary alliance with the leftist Social Revolutionaries in order to obtain peasant support. Winning the good will of this revolutionary group presented a problem. The Bolsheviks had no convincing agrarian program. Lenin studied the copies of *Krestyanskiye Izvestiya* for two full days, working late into the night. After he had read thoroughly the articles and speeches of left Social Revolutionaries, he found a "mandate" which local peasant electors had produced. Lenin showed the paper to Marguerite, saying, "Here's a ready-made agreement with the left Social Revolutionaries. . . . We shall use [this mandate] as the basis for our law concerning the land and see if the left Social Revolutionaries dare to reject it."9

Lenin carried out the plan and the left Social Revolutionaries behaved as he anticipated. Lenin abandoned, temporarily, the notion of the large farm run like a factory and advocated partition of the land. In order to achieve power, he promised the peasants exactly what *they* wanted, and thus was empowered to accomplish, later, what *he* wanted. This procedure is offensive to the ideologist, but displays great tactical skill.

On October 21 Lenin turned to a purely military argumentation.

9Krupskaya, *op. cit.,* p. 390f.

He said, "Only the immediate movement of the Baltic fleet, of the Finnish troops, of Reval and Kronstadt . . . is capable of saving the Russian and the world revolution. . . . Delay means death."[10] Two days later he wrote to Ivan T. Smilga, who controlled the Bolshevik units within the forces stationed in Finland, telling him to be ready within approximately two weeks. Lenin later asked Podvoisky to brief him on the military units at Petrograd which might be sympathetic to the Bolsheviks.

On October 22, Trotsky, skillfully exploiting the unexpected announcement by the government that the Petrograd garrison no longer would be exempted from front duty, suggested to the soviet the establishment of a military-revolutionary committee to supervise military moves. The moderates were unconcerned and the soldiers, who were anxious to avoid the discomforts of the trenches, applauded. Trotsky appointed a committee consisting of Bolsheviks and one member of the left Social Revolutionaries. This representative was a boy of eighteen.

Trotsky, upon announcing that all orders to the garrison would have to be approved by his committee, dispatched committee representatives to the units. This was the decisive military move:[11] his commissars had the "legal" and moral power to prevent the government from using the garrison against the Bolsheviks and, in some instances, the commissars succeeded in switching the units to Trotsky's command.

At this point Lenin could not tolerate his isolation any longer. On October 23, (still wearing his wig) he participated in a ten-hour meeting of the Central Committee held in Petrograd. The meeting was attended by only twelve members and took place in the apartment of N. N. Sukhanov, a Menshevik whose absence had been contrived by his Bolshevik wife. Lenin argued, entirely fictitiously, that the Entente was going to make a separate peace with Germany and that the result would be the crushing of the revolution. He insisted that if the Bolsheviks took control, the West would follow suit. Kamenev and Zinovyev argued with him, but Lenin had a more forceful personality and was in a violent state. He persuaded the Central Committee to accept the uprising on the grounds (as they stated mendaciously in their resolution) that the government was about to deliver Petrograd to the Germans.[12] Thus, the uprising was accepted in principle, but the persons to whom the technical preparations were entrusted were unsure about what steps to take. One leading Bolshevik thought that, although lengthy preparation was

[10]*Selected Works,* Vol. VI, p. 302.

[11]For further details, see my *A Century of Conflict* (Chicago: Regnery, 1953), pp. 62-66.

[12]Lenin, *Sochineniya,* 4th ed., Vol. 26, p. 157f.

required, the uprising eventually would take place, perhaps within a year.

Zinovyev and Kamenev, who had voted against the resolution deciding upon the insurrection, wrote a secret letter to party committees warning against uprising and revolutionary war.[13] The Bolsheviks, though they were increasing in mass strength, still did not have the majority. Hence they were unwilling "to stake on one card not only the fate of our party, but also the fate of the Russian and international revolution." Not realizing that Lenin and Trotsky were planning to use military detachments, in addition to party forces, the two oppositionists proposed to make every effort to win electorally in an attempt to establish a radical coalition government which the Bolsheviks could dominate.

German agents were busy buying, almost openly, machine guns and rifles from delinquent soldiers. The weapons were distributed to the Bolshevik Red guards. Such activities had been occurring for several weeks.

At that time, foreign currency was the preferred tender in Russia. The German Minister in Berne had been requested to procure Swiss francs without revealing the involvement of the legation. This operation was accomplished. On October 25, 1917, Diego von Bergen, who controlled political warfare in the Wilhelmstrasse, and who had been masterminding the revolutionizing of Russia,[14] before Dr. Jordan, one of his aides in the Russian business, handed a sealed envelope to Herr Sennefelder, a courier. Sennefelder signed a receipt and it was noted that he did not have knowledge of the contents of the sealed envelope (100,000 francs) but would transmit the packet instantly to the *Vertrauensmann* (confidential agent). It was perhaps not a very large sum but the Swiss franc was valuable in inflation-ridden Russia.

In Petrograd, however, matters did not advance. On October 29, a Central Committee meeting was attended by representatives from the Petrograd Bolshevik organizations. Lenin, who briefly emerged from hiding, called for an immediate insurrection and managed to have the dissenting voices overruled.

Suddenly, the struggle within the Central Committee broke into open print. There had been a leak and Kamenev and Zinovyev immediately denied that a day had been fixed for an uprising. Furious about the leak Lenin attacked his opponents in three articles. Without mentioning names, Zinovyev replied. Stalin published a mollifying note. Kamenev, writing in Gorky's paper, strongly opposed

---

[13]Text of the letter in Bunyan and Fisher, pp. 59-62. *See also* Lenin, *Selected Works*, Vol. VI, pp. 325, 329ff.

[14]Zeman, p. IX.

the uprising. Lenin demanded the expulsion of Zinovyev and Kamenev from the party. Stalin was determined to preserve unity, but Kamenev resigned. An anti-Bolshevik newspaper published the Bolshevik operational plan, whereupon Trotsky and his friends launched deceptive rumors to discredit the new leak. But the disorganization of the government had gone too far. Even the disclosure that the Bolsheviks were about to initiate an insurrection did not stimulate effective counter-actions.

On November 3, a party council was convened. Theoretically such a council consisted of the Central Committee and the leading party functionaries. If a genuine council with the appropriate membership had been convened, the uprising probably would have been cancelled. Hence, Lenin resorted to one of his old tricks: the participants were not invited *ex officio* but were selected by Sverdlov, Shotman, and Rakhya's brother; Stalin later added two or three names. Those who were invited were notified by trusted persons like Shotman—or not notified if the wrong name had slipped on the list. In the end, twenty-five persons assembled in the municipal building of the Vyborg district, which was close to Lenin's hiding place. Lenin talked for two hours, then a long debate followed. Many of the participants withdrew to adjoining rooms to nap. By seven the next morning Lenin's resolution to seize state power was accepted by a vote of nineteen to two, with four voters abstaining. The council had been well selected.

November 4 was a holiday (the Day of the Soviet), complete with street demonstrations, manifestations, and mass meetings. The Bolsheviks used the opportunity to hold trial maneuvers, concealing this bold operation by mingling their troops with the demonstrators and strollers.[15] On November 5 Trotsky persuaded the soldiers of Peter-Paul Fortress to change sides; this daring coup gave the Bolsheviks about 20,000 rifles and a topographical position commanding the capital. On the evening of Tuesday, November 6, the Bolshevik leaders assembled in their Petrograd headquarters. Lenin wrote: "The matter must absolutely be decided this evening or tonight. History will not forgive delay by revolutionists who could be victorious today (and will surely be victorious today); while they risk losing much tomorrow, they risk losing all . . . . The government is tottering, we must deal it the death blow at any cost."

The government, which expected the rising to occur on the next day, was positioning guards on the Neva Bridges. Lenin was warned that if the bridges were raised, the city would be divided and the uprising could be suppressed piecemeal. Lenin sent Marguerite with

---

[15]Curzio Malaparte, *Tecnica del Colpo di Stato* (Milan, Bompiani: 1948), p. 117f.; James Mavor, *The Russian Revolution* (London: Allen and Unwin, 1928), p. 147f.

a note to the Vyborg headquarters, his liaison point, and called for immediate action. She was told that Lenin should stay in hiding. Lenin sent her back. She returned with the same answer and apparently tried to convince Lenin to exercise caution. But he sent her off for a third time saying, "Ask them . . . what they are afraid of? . . . Do they have a hundred reliable soldiers . . . with rifles? I don't need more for my protection." The Vyborg committee denied Lenin for the third time during the night.

When Marguerite returned to the apartment, Lenin had gone. On the table there was an unfinished dinner. A note was fastened to his napkin. It read, "I went where you did not want me to go. *Au revoir,* Ilyich."

Marguerite fell into her bed. Suddenly, the doorbell rang and Marguerite saw Krupskaya standing there. Fofanova told her through the closed door that Lenin had gone to the Smolny.[16] Krupskaya returned to the Vyborg committee.

Lenin had good reason to leave. He was worried that his comrades might hesitate or draw back and feared that the bridges might be raised after all. But he did not go alone: he met Ejno Rakhya who had appeared suddenly, perhaps with an order to keep Lenin away, and ended by going with Lenin, who could no longer be restrained. Armed with false papers, Lenin put a bandage over his face as though he had a toothache and donned an old cap. At eight in the evening, accompanied by Rakhya acting as his bodyguard, Lenin began his trek. A streetcar took them a good part of the way; during the rest of the distance they walked and were stopped twice. When Lenin reached headquarters in the Smolny Institute, the guard did not recognize him and he was forced to sneak into the house. Everything went according to his fondest hopes. The order to rise had been issued hours before, the telegraph agency already had been seized, and the insurrection was in full swing.

Now, when for the first time in his life Lenin had moved to the battlefield himself, he occupied himself with drafting proclamations and statements. Fully convinced that his words were as necessary as bullets and shells, he worked until he was utterly exhausted. He interfered with military operations to a point where Podvoisky, who was acting as chief of staff, became furious and resigned. Lenin ordered him to continue if he did not wish to be shot. Podvoisky wrote later that at that moment, "I felt for the first time that we had a dictatorship."[17]

The Smolny was brilliantly lighted. Couriers came in rapid succession to receive instructions, the telephone worked perfectly,

16Fofanova, "Ilitch à la veille d'Octobre 1917", *Lénine tel qu'il fut*, Vol. I, p. 732.
17Podvoisky, "Les journées d'Octobre," *ibid.*, p. 752.

girls were sorting incoming telegrams and typing order.[18] The house was protected by a field gun, machine guns, and armored cars. The Bolsheviks did not even erect barricades. There was no government interference.

Rarely, if ever, had the headquarters of an uprising functioned so openly. This was possible because of the strong influence Trotsky's military revolutionary committee exerted upon most units of the Petrograd garrison. The insurgents claimed that they were simply defending the garrison and the democratic regime against the counter-revolution.[19] The government was relying upon the Cossack regiments, but the Cossacks distrusted Kerensky and were unwilling to fight without infantry support. They decided to spend the night discussing politics and saddling their horses.[20] The City Commander took an ambiguous attitude, displaying no energy whatever, and soon disappeared. The Minister of War, to whom the city commander reported directly, had been relieved of his duties.[21]

But was there really an uprising? The workers had remained on their jobs and there were no mass strikes—not even workers in the streets. The Red guards, few in number, played an insignificant role; some detachments were mainly composed of Chinese laborers, released prisoners of war, and unemployed Letts. The ultimately decisive factor was the landing of 2,000 or 3,000 Kronstadt sailors and the demonstration by seven warships. These forces participated on their own initiative, not because they had been called from Smolny headquarters.

The fall of the government was announced prematurely. At ten in the morning of November 7 Lenin issued a proclamation about the change of government and, again prematurely, claimed that power was in the hands of the soviets. He stated, "Here is the cause for which the people fought: immediate peace offer on democratic

[18]The government had disconnected the telephone but the Bolsheviks had seized the central switchboard and reestablished service.

[19]For an example—the line taken by Gorky's *Novaya Zhizn*—see *Novy Zhurnal*, No. 69, New York, 1961, pp. 199.

[20]Serge Oldenbourg, *Le coup d'état bolchéviste, 20 octobre-3 décembre 1917*, Paris, Payot, 1929, p. 154ff.

[21]The Minister of War, A. I. Verkhovsky, was a socialist general who, on November 2, had openly called for separate peace. There were over ten million men in the army, of whom five million were fighters, but two million could not be fed; in addition, there were two million deserters. Verkhovsky had changed his line without consulting the government and was furloughed. The impression is that he changed when he recognized that the government was hopeless. Verkhovsky had been assistant military attaché at Belgrad during 1914 and probably played a minor role in the Serb-Russian intelligence arrangements which led to the assassination of the Austrian crown prince. He later served in the Red Army.

principles; abolition of land ownership by landowners; workers' control of production and creation of a soviet government."22

Lenin did not remind Russia that the uprising contradicted Engels' declaration of 1895 which read, "The time has passed for revolutions to be accomplished through the sudden seizure of power by small minorities at the head of unconscious masses."23

Later in the day, four insurgent battleships were in operation in the Neva estuary and 1,500 sailors arrived by train from Helsingfors. Sufficient troops were available to lay siege to the winter palace, the seat of the government. As the Bolsheviks were massing, the government forces disappeared. At six that evening, Gregory I. Chudnovsky, a former assistant to Parvus, asked the government to surrender.24 Lenin became impatient about eight! He decided to speak to the All-Russian soviet as soon as the government had been deposed. Between nine and ten o'clock there occurred desultory shooting and sailors penetrated the palace through a back door that conveniently was left open. About eleven, the guns of Peter-Paul Fortress fired a few shots, achieving two hits. The light cruiser Aurora fired a blank shell. At two in the morning of November 8, Chudnovsky negotiated the withdrawal of the troops who were "defending" the palace. After the defenders had departed, the palace was taken by "assault."

The Petrograd insurrection could have been easily suppressed by one or two front divisions. Kerensky issued the requisite orders but before action was taken the orders were countermanded by General V. A. Cheremisov, commander of the northern front, who was acting in close liaison with the military revolutionary committee of his headquarters in Pskov.25 Cheremisov, a political careerist, behaved more radically than the radicals: his personal ambitions made him thoroughly unreliable. He justified his action by claiming that the task of the army was to hold the positions currently occupied and not to concern itself with the political struggle at Petrograd. (The most interesting aspect of this story is that late in 1915 or early 1916

22Sochineniya, 4th ed., Vol. 26, p. 207.

23Marx and Engels, Werke, Vol. 7, p. 523.

24According to an Okhrana report of February 2, 1916, Chudnovsky had then resigned from Parvus' organization and wanted to go to London. He later came to the United States and returned to Russia with Trotsky. It is possible that he was an intermediary between Trotsky and Parvus.

25The food situation in the army had become critical. Deliveries during October were down by one-third, partly due to troubles with the railroads. Stocks were down to a two to three day supply. The situation in Cheremisov's command was so "catastrophic" that even the baking of bread had stopped. (Browder-Kerensky, op. cit., II, 651, 657.) For further details, see my A Century of Conflict, p. 72f.

Cheremisov was involved in an affair of German espionage.[26] He maneuvered to become commander-in-chief under Lenin but found he betrayed in vain: Lenin did not want him.)

On November 8, 1917, Riezler asked Berlin for two million in war bonds.[27] He also asked for Jansson, whom he needed urgently. On the following day, the Wilhelmstrasse requested fifteen million marks for political propaganda in Russia. On November 15, Vorovskyl the Bolshevik contact man in Stockholm, sent a telegram to an agent in Switzerland (probably Moor) who was organizing the transfer of German money to the party in Russia: "Please fulfill your promise immediately. We have committed ourselves on this basis." He added, "Great demands are being made on us."[28]

On November 10, one million rubles were on their way. Riezler was informed, by means of an ultra-secret code, that the balance would follow shortly and that more was available.[29] Insurrections can be less costly than the retention of power.[30] The German military elatedly told the foreign office on November 9 that the victory of the soviets was in the German interest.

[26]Browder-Kerensky, *op. cit.*, III, 1526, 1804; *See also* W. S. Woytinski, *Stormy Passage* (New York: Vanguard, 1961), pp. 355, 374 and Mikhail Bonch-Bruyevich, *op. cit.*, p. 92ff. Bonch-Bruyevich added that he should have been relieved of his post and, at best, retired, but someone helped the "dear fellow." He was promoted and given command of an infantry division. He owed his later promotions to Kerensky, whom he betrayed.

[27]War bonds had held their value better than ruble banknotes, whose value had dropped to about one-third of parity. The telegram (Zeman, p. 72) did not specify the currency, but obviously rubles were requested.

[28]Zeman, p. 85.

[29]*Ibid.*, p. 79.

[30]On November 28, Berlin wired Romberg that the Petrograd government was in financial difficulties; hence it was desirable to send money. Zeman, pp. 75 and 93.

Chief of Government

The term "seizure of power" aptly describes what had happened: there was no insurrection, for the democratic government had become utterly impotent, so that the Bolsheviks simply took possession of the power that no one claimed. Lenin's critics contended that forceful seizure was unnecessary and that the Bolsheviks possibly could have assumed power by democratic means. But the elections which were soon held proved that the Bolsheviks had no chance of winning a majority. The Bolsheviks did not merely aim at ministerial chairs; their goal was to establish a dictatorship. This could be attained only through force; that the operation entailed few risks was their sheer good fortune. The application of force created the myth of the October revolution: it was *this* important tale that provided bolshevism with its world-wide significance and established Lenin as a first-rank leader. Lenin's mystical faith in force and violence was better attuned to the irrationality of the historical process than the "reasonableness" of those who hoped that the revolution would evolve naturally and needed not to be artificially executed.

On November 7 at 10:45 P.M. the Second All-Russian Soviet Congress was called to order while the winter palace still was under siege. The opening of the session was delayed to provide Lenin time to speak. Since Lenin's opponents had left the soviet, the Bolsheviks functioned as the majority party.

The Presidium consisted of fourteen Bolsheviks and seven left Social Revolutionaries who occupied the seats vacated by right Social Revolutionaries. The Kronstadt sailors who participated in the coup were mostly left Social Revolutionaries and anarchists. The left-wing Mensheviks also sat in this rump congress along with a single Ukrainian socialist. Lenin could have made his victory appearance by three in the morning after the fall of the palace, but he did not appear. Lenin was too exhausted. He went to the home of Bonch-Bruyevich, could not fall asleep, and worked on the land decree.[1] The soviet waited until six o'clock and then adjourned.

Later in the morning Lenin delivered his victory speech. He claimed that the old state apparatus would be demolished. A new soviet government would be created without the bourgeoisie. Lenin's government would report to the soviet. The third Russian revolution would bring the victory of socialism, but the liquidation of the war was the immediate task. The international proletariat would help the Russian proletariat. The second task was to expropriate agrarian property. (In 1921, Lenin was to explain to the Third Congress of the Communist International that the "masses" wanted peace and the soldiers did not want to fight. But one cause was insufficient. The congress stole the left Social Revolutionary agrarian program and soon the majority of the peasants were persuaded. This was the strategy which, according to Lenin, rendered victory simple.)

During the evening of November 9, Lenin participated in another meeting; thereafter he did not appear for three days in the Smolny, the Bolshevik headquarters which had now become the seat of government. During the following week he was busy at the headquarters, then eclipsed himself again on November 19, 20, and 21.

The Bolsheviks introduced the eight-hour working day and expropriated land and certain other types of property. They bestowed upon all nationalities in Russia the right to self-determination

[1]Vladimir D. Bonch-Bruyevich, *Na Boyevikh Postakh Fevralskoi i Oktyabrskoi Revolyutsii* (Moscow, 1931), p. 119f.

(including the right to secede) and abolished religious privileges. All existing secret treaties were cancelled. A three-month armistice was offered to all belligerents, and hostilities were suspended early in December. Hostile newspapers and counter-revolutionary activities were suppressed.

Many Bolsheviks argued that, since a purely Bolshevik government could maintain itself only through terror, a coalition government should be established. Lenin demurred. The first government crisis occurred within the first week of Lenin's administration.

The Poles, Ukrainians, and Finns declared their independence. By contrast the Bolsheviks maintained their power in Russia by relying on Lettish and Chinese mercenaries: those were the only troops they could depend on. The Germans paid for the military services rendered in behalf of the Bolsheviks. A few weeks earlier, Lenin had told Shotman that for the Bolsheviks to stay in power all money would have to be "annulled." Shotman asked what would replace the currency. Lenin replied, "We shall put all printing presses in motion and within a few days print as much as we need."[2] Things were not that simple, but the printing presses were run for more than eight hours every day.

The Germans had used fraternization tactics throughout the preceding months in an attempt to weaken the Russian army and stimulate the Bolshevik revolution. Now this same weapon was available to the Bolsheviks to initiate the next round of the world revolution and to revolutionize Germany and Austria-Hungary. Quite a few prisoners of war had joined the Bolsheviks so the maneuver was entirely feasible and fraternization was increased. Yet the Germans forced Lenin to stop all fraternization with German soldiers immediately.[3] The Germans obviously could hold the threat of black-mail over Lenin, who was now beginning to pay the penalty for his Machiavellian politics. His great dream of using the Germans to make revolution in Russia and then carry the revolution into Germany could not be fulfilled. This much became evident within the first month of his rule. And to leave no doubt about this, the German Minister at Stockholm, Hellmuth Freiherr Lucius von Stoedten, warned Vorovsky "in a discussion lasting several hours . . . emphatically against trying any experiments with internal German affairs."[4]

On December 15 a formal armistice was concluded with Ger-

---

[2]Shotman, p. 417.

[3]Fraternization was stopped on November 13, 1917, at 11 P.M., and on November 14, *Prikaz No. 3*, signed by Krylenko, ordered the immediate cessation of firing and fraternization on all fronts *(Istoricheskii Arkhiv* [1957], No. 5, p. 156-160).

[4]Zeman, p. 105.

many, and on December 17, Lenin signed a decree ordering the demobilization of the Russian army.[5] Simultaneously, the Bolsheviks established a terror machine, the dreaded "Cheka" or Extraordinary Commission. On December 23, 1917, the Menshevik organ, *Novy Luch*, summarized the situation by saying that the Bolsheviks were ruining the country by controlling production and creating unemployment. The Bolsheviks had originally favored the dismemberment of the Russian empire, but now they were fighting the autonomous states which refused to submit to their rule. They resuscitated the tsarist police system; and, instead of introducing a dictatorship of the proletariat, they established a personal dictatorship by Lenin.

On January 11, 1918, in the midst of a war which had merely been interrupted by a truce arrangement, two additional military decrees were issued. One abolished all ranks; the other stipulated that commanders were to be elected by soldiers' committees and commanders of units larger than regiments be chosen by soldiers' congresses. The military commanders were to have no disciplinary prerogatives. These decrees effectively destroyed the army. The massive desertion rate, which had characterized events so far, degenerated into a spontaneous demobilization.[6] The Bolsheviks claimed that the army had to be destroyed to preclude army counter-revolutionary attempts; naturally, other measures could have been taken to attain the same objective. No attempt was made to build up new and dependable units or to halt progressive demoralization. For two months, the Bolshevik strategists eagerly busied themselves destroying the remnants of Russia's military power. The Germans could not have asked for more.

Indeed, on January 3, 1918, an unnamed German socialist— probably Kurt Eisner—complained in Gorky's newspaper, *Novaya Zhizn* (which had been partially financed by German money[7]), that the Bolsheviks were enabling the Germans to start an offensive in the West. The German socialist warned that by resuming economic relations with Germany, the Bolsheviks would replenish the Kaiser's food and raw material reserves; thus, the Bolsheviks were saving Imperial Germany and were aiding in the preparation of "the most cruel triumph of German militarism." Gorky's paper commented that the Bolsheviks were misleading the masses by claiming they could obtain a "democratic peace" from Germany. Gorky described the delaying tactics as a sham. In response, the Bolsheviks spread the rumor that they were delaying negotiations until a revolution would break out in Central Europe.

[5]*Istoricheskii Arkhiv*, loc. cit., p. 154.
[6]Mikhail Bonch-Bruyevich, *op. cit.*, p. 260ff.
[7]Zeman, p. 92.

The Bolsheviks were not sufficiently accommodating to the Germans. On January 7, 1918, the German Foreign Secretary cabled his agents that the time had come to provide a few broad hints through the available safe channels but not in public. "If the truth were to become known in Russia . . . then the Bolsheviks will be finished. Their own dishonesty will ruin them."8 Subsequently, Lenin improved delivery and the Germans never found it necessary to disclose the truth.

Lenin, Krupskaya, and Maria Ulyanova spent Christmas at an unnamed place in Finland. They apparently left Russia on Christmas Eve (January 6, 1918, New Style) and enjoyed "that spotless Finnish cleanliness with its white curtains everywhere."9

Lenin was experiencing his customary health troubles. He began the composition of three articles but could not finish them. The Germans reported from Petrograd that he was spending a few days in a Finnish sanatorium but had been recalled to the capital. There was not much opportunity for relaxation after his return. Krupskaya reported that between the middle of January and the end of February she and Lenin went for walks along the Neva. This sounds a bit too hazardous for a dictator's health treatment.

On January 15 someone fired at Lenin while he was riding in his car. The vehicle was struck by four bullets. Lenin's life was saved by Platten, who was sitting beside him and pushed his head down.10 Platten was slightly wounded in the hand.

In an extremely difficult situation, Lenin had insisted upon coming to power. It seems that he should have had a formulated program through which the great promise of socialism (or communism) could be fulfilled. The old vexatious system of ranks and classes (*chin*) had been abolished by the democratic regime. The Bolsheviks instituted a few reforms, such as the adoption of the Western calendar and the eight-hour day (which for many years was ignored), whose introduction required no revolution. They abolished the institutions through which the economy had been directed, but were unable to invent better instruments. They advocated self-determination but did not permit it. They adopted the agricultural program of the Social Revolutionaries, but did not fulfill this program either;

8Zeman, p. 112f., prints an instruction from Berlin to the legation at Stockholm that it was "necessary to have serious words with Vorovsky." "Appeals to our nation, which include revolutionary matter and calls to our soldiers to disobey orders and lay down their arms . . . we must regard as improper and intolerable interferences in our internal affairs."

9Krupskaya, *op. cit.*, p. 425.

10Platten had succeeded finally in being admitted to Russia; Radek also had arrived. On December 20, 1917, the Associated Press offered Radek the post of chief Russian correspondent, which he declined.

yet they destroyed genuine agrarian reforms which had been accomplished by the tsarist regime.

Thus, the Bolsheviks cheated both the minority nationalities and the peasants, and alienated and destroyed the middle and upper classes. They claimed to speak for the proletariat but betrayed the workers. The Bolsheviks in power were not a labor government but a group of intellectuals with a slanted education. They claimed they knew how to build socialism and they promised the proletariat better treatment. While they were able to disrupt the existing system, they did not know how to fashion a workable socialist system. They even betrayed the soldiers: though they released many from duty, they failed to tell them that this act was at Germany's bidding. They cared nothing about democratic peace, but soon were to establish a new army to fight a protracted civil war. They had lied and cheated their way to power. Now that they had seized the government, they knew how to preserve and enlarge their power but proved unable to use their strength constructively for their professed purposes.

Several socialist parties and socialists from practically all groups were willing to participate in constructive work. If there had been a positive program, a broadly based government could have commanded the loyalty of the people in the true sense of the word. In the absence of constructive ideas, it would have been advisable to permit —in fact, stimulate—discussion on socialist policy. But the Bolsheviks were terrified of free debate and abolished free speech without delay. Nor did the Bolsheviks wish to share their power. They intended to rule by unrestricted dictatorship, not in the sense Lenin originally had promised (i.e., active participation by the masses in public affairs and total suppression of bureaucracy), but in the sense of unrestricted power exercised by a small minority. The Bolsheviks had so little confidence in their own ability to create that they preferred fear to mass support. They lacked the wisdom and humility to use their undoubted victory to make peace with their fellow socialists and thus spare their country an era of endless anguish.

Some of the Bolsheviks with more intelligence and integrity recognized that this policy would have catastrophic results. But this program was Lenin's brainchild and reflected his psychology. He had become the inviolate and infallible ruler. To paraphrase Santayana: after he had forgotten his aims, he was strongly motivated to redouble his efforts.

The Destruction of Democracy

Shortly after Lenin's seizure of power, general elections were held for the constituent assembly. Throughout their history the Bosheviks had given lukewarm support to the concept of a constituent assembly gathered to write a basic constitution for the new Russia. After the end of tsarism, the assembly should have been convened speedily, but the government procrastinated on the pretext that such technical difficulties as improper voting lists which needed correcting prevented early elections.

When Lenin came to power, the Bolsheviks expected a comfortable majority and posed as champions of democracy; thus, they allowed the scheduled elections to be held. To their great chagrin, however, only twenty-four per cent of the votes cast were definitely in their favor, and another five per cent endorsed the left Social Revolutionaries who sympathized with the Bolsheviks. The Mensheviks won only about four per cent, and the bourgeois parties polled about fourteen per cent. The Social Revolutionaries, with fifty-four per cent, were the theoretical victors.[1]

Within the army and navy, the Bolsheviks gained forty-five per cent and the Social Revolutionaries, forty-three per cent, but threefifths of the soldiers failed to vote.[2] However, the Bolsheviks showed strength in the military units around Petrograd and on the decisive front which faced the bulk of the German army.

Thus, Russia had voted for "socialism"—no less than eighty-six per cent of the votes had been cast for the socialist parties—but Russia had not endorsed the Bolsheviks. On the other hand, the Bolsheviks were the second strongest party and could rely on support from other parties for nearly all reasonable policies.

The enormous socialist majority in the constituent assembly offered Lenin the opportunity of constructing socialism by democratic methods and with the full support of the population.[3] This would have entailed a coalition government, which would have constituted a genuine "dictatorship" by the proletariat. As Marx really understood this concept, the dictatorship was to represent the overwhelming majority and was to be based upon universal suffrage of the nation's "healthy elements" (with the exclusion of the "wealthy capitalists").

A coalition government could have been formed under Bolshevik leadership and the rules of democracy could have been observed. It would have been easy for Lenin to obtain acceptance of most of

---

[1] O. H. Radkey, *The Election to the Russian Constituent Assembly* (Cambridge: Harvard, 1950), pp. 16f., 21. For Lenin's analysis of the election results and his ostensible reasons why democracy could not be risked, see *Werke*, Vol. 30, pp. 242-265.

[2] Radkey, p. 37; Bunyan and Fisher, p. 46.

[3] This was also the opinion of Krassin. *See* Lyubov Krassin, *Leonid Krassin, his Life and Work* (London: Skaffington, 1929), p. 64; *see also* Shub, p. 266f.

his program. The socialists were in agreement on the crucial step of nationalizing the land. They hardly would have balked at the nationalization of banks or objected to Lenin's vague proposals concerning production control (which were at that time meaningless anyway) ; they would have accepted the federalization of Russia. There would have been no slowdown in the "construction of communism" because Lenin lacked a plan for such construction; in fact, he might have found new ideas emerging from the democratic debate. As leader of a coalition government, Lenin would have had a stronger hand in dealing with the Germans. Terror and civil war could have been avoided and the overall development of Russia would have been less catastrophic.

Lenin had made his peace with Trotsky and for a while permitted a few left Social Revolutionaries to participate in the government, though they were not given their share of power. But this concession was the greatest he would make. A genuine coalition would have meant that Lenin would be compelled to share power with those he hated most and that his ideas might not, in every particular detail, have prevailed. Lenin's intellect was sufficiently forceful that he could expect to wield enormous influence; with a little patience and applied statesmanship, he could have become a constructive leader. But presently Lenin discarded this historic and unique opportunity and asserted that the constituent assembly, virtually all of whose members were socialists, constituted the "dictatorship of the bourgeoisie."

Did he lack greatness of soul and character and was he too cowardly to risk the hazards of democratic leadership? He probably sensed that his judgment was not always the best and that in the past his opponents had frequently been right. Abrupt changes in policy and adoption of the opposition's viewpoint were two characteristics of Lenin's leadership which would not have permitted political longevity in a democracy. Krassin thought Lenin was irresponsible and had lost his mind.

Perhaps a more fundamental explanation can be offered. Lenin, probably aware of the basic flaws of socialism, judged democracy and socialism to be incompatible. Martov was dreaming of a situation where the proletariat had united "about itself 'all the healthy elements' . . . that cannot but benefit by the revolutionary transformation" and will "recognize the advantage to them of this transformation."[4] Such a hope was utopian: for most "elements" the transformation was and could not but be harmful. Lenin scarcely harbored any illusions to the contrary. However, as Krassin remarked, the

---

[4]Yu. Martov, *The State and the Socialist Revolution* (New York: International Review, 1938), p. 64.

notion that socialism could be introduced immediately was "a utopian ideal pushed to the very limit of folly."[5]

Lenin's concern about the saleability of socialism must not be confused with doubts about socialism itself. Lenin still consciously believed in his socialist image. But he feared that, if he ruled by majority, the dream could not materialize: the majority accepts only what *is* to its benefit. It follows that only a non-democratic minority rule would be able to build socialism. Therefore the primary objective would be to retain and strengthen power.

When the constituent assembly met on January 18, 1918, in the Taurid Palace,[6] it was besieged by sailors under the command of Anatoly Zheleznyakov, a semi-anarchist who, on November 7, had led the Kronstadt detachment into Petrograd. Lenin arrived carrying a revolver in the pocket of his overcoat. (The revolver was soon stolen from his coat as it hung in the palace's special apartment set aside for Lenin to use for holding meetings and for resting.[7] When Lenin discovered the theft, he rebuked P. Y. Dybenko, who commanded the guard, and called for heightened discipline. The thief, a soldier of the guard, was apprehended a few hours later and shot.)

Lenin was as pale and tense as a commander in battle directing the Bolshevik faction. When he could not gain domination of the proceedings, he ordered his followers to sing the "International." Whenever the opposition brought out a speaker he particularly disliked, he stretched out on the steps leading to the podium and feigned sleep. He moved that it be deemed illegal to oppose the "soviet regime" (meaning his own government) and suggested that the assembly abdicate its function to the All-Russian soviet. He blocked a vote which would have had beneficial constitutional impact and slyly had this decision announced by a left Social Revolutionary (who later had ample time to repent his duplicity during his American exile). Lenin did not even make a speech to the constituent assembly. Perhaps he hoped that military demonstrations both outside and inside the assembly hall might help him to obtain something like a vote of confidence. But his dictatorship was rejected—the assembly's fate was sealed. Probably according to plan, the Bolsheviks demonstrated, leaving the hall noisily. Lenin did prevent the sailors from massacring some of the non-Bolshevik deputies.[8] But in the early

[5]Quoted from Shub, p. 267.

[6]For data on the constituent assembly, *see* Bunyan and Fisher, pp. 338-389; N. Shaveko, *Oktyabrskaya revolyutsiya i uchreditelnoye sobraniye* (Moscow, 1928); and Mark Vyshniak, *Vserossiskoye uchreditelnoye sobraniye* (Paris: Sovremenniye Zapiski, 1932).

[7]On his way to the assembly, Uritsky was held up by bandits who took his coat: "You have warmed yourself enough. We are cold!" (Shub, p. 289).

[8]Walter, p. 408.

morning hours of January 19, the sailors turned off the lights and dispersed the assembly.

The assembly neglected several opportunities: they could have continued their session in a factory, as the workers at one plant proposed, or they could have reassembled out of town. The assembly proclaimed Russia to be a democratic republic but failed to nominate a government. Lenin was correct on one point: the delegates lacked strength and will. Previously these politicians had been responsible for the poor performance of Russian democracy. Now, they did not have the ability to guide a government which had barely come to life.

Subsequently, Lenin asked the Third Congress of the All-Russian soviet to proclaim the soviet as the source of revolutionary power. This was his contribution to fictional "constitutionalism."

When Lenin told the left Social Revolutionaries that he wanted to dissolve the constituent assembly, they objected on the grounds that the action was not moral. Old Vera Zasulich was indignant and took her former protégé to task. Lenin lifted his eyebrows and replied, "There are no morals in politics; there is only expediency."[9]

[9]S. Mstislavsky, "Zapiski o Lenine," *O Lenine*, Vol. IV, (Moscow, 1925), p. 107.

The Shameful Peace

Lenin's past overshadowed the crucial problem of conducting peace negotiations with Germany. The severity of the peace agreement made at Brest-Litovsk has been exaggerated by those who fail to see that this arrangement, in most respects, conformed to the nationality principle: many of the states which Russia had lost were re-established as independent nations. It is true that Germany wanted to control some or all of the new states indirectly and arranged for alliances and military mergers, integration of railroads, economic preferences, trading blocs, and the like. It is also true that the transformation of the tsarist empire into a set of national states, including the national state of Russia, satisfied German power interests. Nevertheless, if the national principle was valid, the structure of the Brest-Litovsk treaty had a certain plausibility. Moreover, the alignment of frontiers and economic relationships was definitive only on paper. Regardless of the peace treaty, finalization obviously could not be accomplished before the World War was concluded on *all* fronts.

The practical problem was that by eliminating Russia from the war and arranging for trade, Germany could improve her acute raw material and food scarcity and mass her military power against the

Western front. A "democratic" peace would also have affected the political situation in the Entente countries, presumably to the benefit of Germany. Thus, the treaty of 1918 provided Germany with a chance to win or, at any rate, achieve a compromise peace even after the United States had assumed a belligerent position. The potential of this opportunity was proportionate to Russia's cooperativeness and to Germany's foresight.

There were a number of key factors involved in the strategic situation confronting the Bolsheviks. First, the continuation of the war between Germany and the West would have placed the Bolshevik regime in an increasingly favorable position, for the Germans required the aid of Bolsheviks, along with Russian supplies. This aspect was fully grasped by Lenin. Secondly, to maintain some pressure in the East, Britain and the United States were interested in strengthening Russia and helping her economically and financially. The Bolshevik government knew this. Thirdly, from the point of view of world revolution, there was an excellent possibility of carrying the infection into Germany, notably through continuation of hostilities and fraternization at the front. Fourthly—and an even more promising approach—if moderate and socialist parties would enter the German government, Germany might cooperate honestly with Russia and, in due course, the socialist elements could take full power at Berlin. This development would pave the way toward general peace and a world-wide upsurge of socialism.

The way to put the revolutionary process into motion was to continue fraternizing and to negotiate a German-Russian peace on a popular basis. Instead of negotiations between governments (i.e., diplomats and soldiers), a conference on neutral soil could be attended by representatives of various German and Russian parties, speaking for the Reichstag and the soviet, and empowered by legislative resolutions to establish the groundwork of a democratic peace. Various combinations were possible: the conference could be preparatory to a subsequent regular peace negotiation; it could be advisory; or it could devote itself to an exploration of a peaceful international system. The conference could be expanded, in time, to form a meeting of representatives from all belligerent countries. Under any combination, an international conference in a neutral country would have furthered the cause of socialism and peace, while neutralizing the militaristic and aggressive forces within Germany. Here was an extraordinary opportunity to make real progress toward peace.

The concept of a conference of parliamentarians was put forward by the moderate parties in Germany (the so-called majority group) which authorized the Catholic deputy Mathias Erzberger to negotiate on this basis with the Bolsheviks. The Austrians, who had moved toward peace while Kerensky still was in power, also were anxious to end the war and were willing to negotiate in a conciliatory fashion and even to institute substantial constitutional reforms for this purpose.

The Social Democrats favored a more revolutionary but similar concept postulated by Parvus.[1] He argued that, since the German socialists had helped Lenin to power, Lenin should now be in a position to assist the German socialists.[2] Cooperation among Russian, German, and Austrian socialists would probably enable the Social Democrats to enter the governments at Berlin and Vienna, and thus would ease the Bolshevik position. Several Bolsheviks, notably the representatives in Stockholm, agreed that this approach was very promising. Lenin would not have risked much if he had attempted to apply this concept. To gain full support might have necessitated a socialist coalition. Hence the constituent assembly should not have been dispersed: perhaps the moderate socialist would have offered Lenin tacit support.

Naturally, the Imperial Foreign Office refused to participate in such a scheme. It was not interested in undermining the German monarchy and did not desire the strengthening of the German socialists. It aimed at creating chaos[3] in Russia, and wanted to use the Bolsheviks as an instrument for this purpose. The Foreign Office took two steps: it contrived for the negotiations of Erzberger and Parvus with the Bolsheviks to be cut short, dropped Parvus as an advisor, and maneuvered him out of Stockholm; and it informed the Bolsheviks that a conference on neutral soil was an impossibility. Instead, the Imperial Foreign Office asserted, the negotiations would have to be conducted on a government-to-government basis at the front (i.e., at Brest-Litovsk). The Bolsheviks (who by November 13 already had sent parliamentarians across the front lines to request a truce) were told, in no uncertain terms, that they would have to comply with this demand.

The Austrians wanted to force the Wilhelmstrasse into an early compromise peace, but they were asked to permit the Germans to handle this situation since Berlin had maintained communication

[1]Some of the documents on Erzberger's and Parvus' efforts were published by Zeman (documents 86, 89, 90, 100, 102, 106, 108, 109, 110, 111, and 112).

[2]On November 17, 1917, Hanecki and Radek wired Lenin that they were coming to Petrograd, after seeing Parvus, who entrusted them with an important mission (Niessel, *op. cit.,* p. 100).

[3]Kurt Riezler who later taught political ethics at an American university, wrote to the Reichskanzler on November 12, 1917, that the Bolsheviks would try to eliminate "the existing administrative machinery. If they are successful in this, even for only a few weeks . . . the country will cease to figure in military and economic calculations concerning the World War." It would take "years to restore order among the chaos" (Zeman, p. 83).

with the Bolsheviks and also possessed "organs" to supervise Bolshevik activities.[4] The Austrians were also informed that the scheme for negotiating peace through the international socialist movement was unfeasible since the Entente socialists, to the best knowledge of the Bolsheviks, would not cooperate; this claim was true, but a change in the policy of Germany—and of Lenin—might have resulted in a different attitude.

What could Lenin have done? Continued fraternization and systematic propaganda would have helped his cause. If Lenin had cooperated with the German socialists and the Reichstag majority, the German government might have been compelled to go to Stockholm. But, for obvious reasons, Lenin could not risk a rejection of the wishes of the German Foreign Office.[5] He had no choice but to comply. The Germans told him to call a halt to the fraternization which had been launched on a massive scale less than a week before. Lenin did so.

In December, 1917, the German Foreign Secretary wrote to Wilhelm II that it was in the German interest to utilize the Bolsheviks' "time in power, which may be only very short, first of all to bring about an armistice and then, if possible, to achieve peace."[6] Trotsky, until he allowed himself to be persuaded otherwise by Lenin, believed a separate peace to be "inconceivable." In a letter to Stockholm intercepted by the Germans, he stated that his objective was to prolong the peace talks as a screen for the "mobilization of international Social Democratic forces promoting a general peace."

Yet German radical Marxist Kurt Eisner (in an article which was published by Gorky and is often falsely ascribed to the reformist Eduard Bernstein) wrote that Lenin's policy was blocking the revolution in Germany and might facilitate German victory. The Bolsheviks, Eisner wrote, were playing a comic role and the German military seemed satisfied with these "good revolutionaries." The triumph of German militarism was being prepared and the faithful Bolsheviks were protecting it against its enemies. Eisner was no casual observer. He subsequently established in Bavaria a semi-Communist regime and died a martyr's death. His credentials as an honest revolutionary are beyond reproach. He was not the only German socialist who let it be known that Lenin should hold fast. And these suggestions were not merely pious wishes: the German socialists possessed considerable power and were capable of applying pressure to Berlin. But to

[4]Kuehlmann to Czernin, November 16 and 17, 1917. The substance of these communications was transmitted to the Austrian Emperor on November 18, notably the reference to the "Organe, die die Taetigkeit der Bolschewiki ueberwachten."

[5]On December 8, 1917, Vorovsky reassured Lucius that "calls to peoples to start the revolution" were meant "platonically" (Zeman, p. 100).

[6]*Ibid.*, p. 96.

be able to act, the schemes of the German militaristic diehards had first to collapse. Bolshevik resistance was the prerequisite for the acceleration of reform or revolution in Germany.

If the Germans had not had their secret hold over Lenin, could the Bolsheviks have resisted German demands? A key consideration was whether Russia would have been capable of continuing the war, or of conducting a revolutionary war which many Bolshevik leaders proposed. The argument that Russia could not continue to fight has superficial plausibility. Russian military power was indeed disrupted. There is no argument that the Russians could have done anything but fight defensively, execute a retreat, and harass the enemy by guerrilla activity. The main question is the *extent* by which military power had declined: was acceptance of the German *diktat* necessary or was resistance still possible? This question has been debated for years; yet, after the publication of General Bonch-Bruyevich's memoirs, much of the doubts can now be resolved. During the critical period Bonch-Bruyevich served as chief of staff to the "supreme commander" Krylenko (i.e., he was the leading military professional of the Communist regime).

Bonch-Bruyevich indicated that the army included a great many aged soldiers who should not have been mobilized. By demobilizing them immediately, the supply and morale situation of the army could have improved markedly. Experience showed that the Bolsheviks, through their commissar system, had little difficulty in enlisting the cooperation of the army; for example, the order to salvage military matériel and transport it away from the enemy's reach was executed with considerable success. Bonch-Bruyevich foresaw the troubles ahead and proposed the establishment of a defense screen by creating formations of reliable troops, a strengthening of the existing functioning units, and redeployment of the forces for protection of the main roads of advance (i.e., the railroads), since a cross-country advance would have been very difficult for the Germans and would have been halted by the spring thaws. However, Krylenko ordered specifically that those units which still could be used in combat and which could have formed the proposed screen be disbanded without delay.[7]

Naturally, the various decrees which transformed the army into a debating society should never have been issued. There already were more than enough soviets throughout the army, but early in December a decree strengthened the grip of this organizational cancer. To ensure the survival of the military soviets, their members were paid five to ten rubles a day. (Though the value of the currency was about one-fourth of parity, this was still a handsome

7Bonch-Bruyevich, *op. cit.*, p. 262.

income.) It was further decreed that each military chief be elected for a term of only three months and that his office could be revoked at any time.[8] Ranks were abolished in a frenzy of "left radicalism."

A demobilization committee was formed during December and Lenin queried it at length. The situation was poor; Lenin learned of the conditions. That the units where the Bolsheviks predominated should have been so demoralized was particularly disheartening. But precisely because the Bolsheviks did have a disciplined party, the situation was remediable. Still nothing was undertaken until January 12, when it was decided to institute a military reorganization. This decision, too, was followed by inaction.[9] Such an amazing display of apathy is certain to have been deliberate.

The plan to establish a Red army and eliminate the old structure was conceived at the latest by early January, but the decree was signed only on January 28 and then its publication was delayed. The plan required further details for an orderly transition from the old to the new army but these were not offered; not even a planning organ was created. The *Stavka* (G.H.Q.) was abolished at a very inopportune moment, despite the fact that it was completely in the hands of Bolsheviks and pro-Bolsheviks. The process of disbanding was completed on the very day the Germans attacked. It was estimated that about one-fourth of the infantry and three-fifths of the soldiers serving in the other divisions were prepared to remain in military service. However, the initial Red army concept was *not* to build a better army for defense, let alone for revolutionary war, but to establish an instrument to fight a *civil war;*[10] it is unlikely that the Germans objected to this idea.

The German army was exhausted. They were preparing for the supreme effort in the West in the realization that they had to win quickly, before the American forces appeared on European battlefields.[11] Between November 1 and February 1, 1918, the German army in Russia was reduced from eighty-one to fifty-seven divisions, mostly second-rate units.[12] In addition, a majority of the soldiers under thirty-five were shipped to the West and the remaining units were below normal strength. The Germans had withdrawn 5,000

---

[8]Niessel, *op. cit.*, p. 141.

[9]Leonard Schapiro, *Origin of the Communist Autocracy* (London: Bell, 1955), pp. 98, 105.

[10]Bonch-Bruyevich, *op. cit.*, p. 267.

[11]The Bolsheviks were fully aware of this German plan (see Zeman, p. 111).

[12]General E. A. L. Buat, *L'Armée allemande pendant la guerre de 1914-1918* (Paris: Chapelot, 1920), pp. 53-59.

guns.[13] The bulk of the Austrian army was now deployed against Italy; the Austrians did not intend to resume operations against Russia, a fact which the Bolsheviks realized. It also was clear that a sustained eastern offensive could not have been mounted simultaneously with the offensive in the West. Even a limited offensive would have been politically impractical for the Germans, partly because of unrest at home (there had been massive strikes in Berlin and Vienna). Above all, contact with the revolutionary Russian army had to be carefully avoided, because of the danger of mutinies at the front.

It is difficult to determine the state of the Russian army with some degree of accuracy. At the time of Bolshevik seizure, nine to ten million men were armed. The War Ministry was planning to demobilize the soldiers over forty, to reduce the number of divisions to 165, and to keep two and one-half million combatants and about five million service personnel. Furthermore, it was planned to reorganize the army according to the nationality principle (an operation begun in 1916 with the establishment of Lettish regiments[14]). An overall reorganization would have been difficult but feasible, provided it had been entrusted to expert technicians. General Verkhovsky, who was a socialist, might have been able to complete the job, and at first the Bolsheviks spread rumors that he was to stay on. General Cheremisov, who sympathized with the Bolsheviks, V. A. Antonov-Ovseyenko, a party member, and General Bonch-Bruyevich, who was entitled to the Bolsheviks' full confidence, were all capable. But the Bolsheviks overlooked these competent commanders and appointed Krylenko as head of an army which already had been disorganized by Kerensky, its first civilian commander.

Nikolai V. Krylenko had been a Bolshevik since 1904; during Lenin's sojourn in Austria he served as organizer of transport and border crossings at Lublin. During that period he apparently associated himself with a right-wing Russian party (which suggests some tie with the Okhrana). In the summer of 1917 he induced a regiment to withdraw from the front, thus causing defections and defeats of neighboring units. This act of "revolutionary anti-militarism" was responsible for the Germans' victory in the battle of Tarnopol.[15] Krylenko lacked military talent and was by no means an obvious choice in a party which counted within its ranks men with

---

[13]Winston S. Churchill, *The Unknown War, the Eastern Front* (New York: Scribners, 1931), p. 381.

[14]The Lettish regiments became the most thoroughly bolshevized units in the Russian army (Niessel, p. 137).

[15]Niessel, *op. cit.*, p. 122f. The French officer observed that this "generalissimo" hardly was possessed of "la vocation de la bataille."

proven military abilities. Lenin would not have appointed Krylenko if he had intended to preserve military strength.

What could a "defencist" Bolshevik commander have done? The most demoralized units were those in which the Bolshevik commissars had the greatest influence. Hence, the primary task was to pass the correct line to these commissars. The second task was to eliminate most of the military soviets, reducing their activity to reasonable proportions; this could have been readily accomplished by not paying bonuses to the delegates of the soviet. The third job was to stop the deserting soldiers from taking goods from warehouses and selling them, a problem that could have been solved by paying the bonuses earmarked for the soviet delegates to the units guarding the warehouses and establishing detachments of reliable troops to catch and punish deserters. Fourth, the many newspapers which were printed for the soldiers could have been reoriented—even Krylenko in a proclamation of November 14 had said, "The strong alone will attain his objective."[16] Perhaps the situation was beyond repair, but not a single constructive step was ever attempted: Krylenko's efforts were directed toward destroying what remained of the army. The induction years of 1895 to 1899 had been released previously and now Krylenko dismissed the classes of 1900 to 1907, without interference from Lenin.

Lenin was unable to obtain a majority. In a party conference held on January 21, 1918, he received only fifteen votes as opposed to thirty-two in favor of revolutionary war and sixteen for a compromise formula. (This party conference is usually "forgotten" by Communist historians.) Trotsky's "no war—no peace" concept subsequently was adopted in the Central Committee (nine to seven votes) and by a large majority in the soviet. These votes implied that revolutionary resistance against a German advance must be prepared and, indeed, the Central Committee voted unanimously to create a Red army. But Lenin took no action on this mandate.

French intelligence discovered on January 30 by reading the telegrams exchanged between Lenin and the Bolshevik delegation to the peace conference at Brest-Litovsk that Lenin was determined to accept German conditions.[17] The dissident Communists knew this, too. As early as January 24, Uritsky stated that Lenin's error was the same as that of 1915, "to consider matters from the point of view of Russia, and not from the international point of view."[18] The French thought that Trotsky was in agreement with Lenin but did not want to sign immediately. It is difficult to determine whether this delay was

[16]*Istoricheskii Arkhiv*, (1957), No. 5, p. 160.

[17]Niessel, *op. cit.*, p. 228.

[18]In this evaluation, which was correct, Uritsky reflected the thinking of Parvus.

designed to take advantage of strikes in Germany and Austria (as was asserted) or was mere window-dressing. The Germans disliked the delay and assumed a harder stance. Krylenko released the draft groups of 1908 and 1909. On February 10 Trotsky ceased negotiations, announcing to the Germans that Russia was withdrawing from the war but would not sign the peace treaty. He added, somewhat ambiguously, that the order was being relayed to the Russian troops to demobilize on all front lines.

This was an unprecedented military situation. It had come about because Lenin had run into strong opposition towards his surrender policy. Trotsky conceived the "no war—no peace" formula as a stratagem to placate both the opposition and the Germans. Kuehlmann, the German Foreign Secretary, was willing to accept this formula but was overruled by the military, who wanted a peace treaty. They perceived no risk in waging a sham war. The question was whether or not the Bolsheviks would call upon the country to defend itself.

On February 11 Krylenko decreed the complete demobilization of the army at the exact moment the Germans were about to resume hostilities. Lenin suddenly awoke and attempted to invalidate the decree. Krylenko proceeded anyway, releasing the classes of 1910 to 1912 and, a few days later, of 1913 to 1915. Still functioning were 175,000 men on the northern front and 150,000 men on the western, with only 15,000 and 20,000 men, respectively, in the trenches; and these apparently were given the order *not* to resist.

In the Central Committee, on February 17 and 18, Lenin was twice defeated by a narrow margin. A rapid German advance— the fall of Dvinsk without a single shot being fired—aided Lenin in exacting from thirteen select people's commissars an agreement to offer to the Germans to sign the peace treaty forthwith. This vote was seven to five with one abstention. Lenin was supported by Zinovyev and Sokolnikov, companions on the sealed train, Smilga, who may have received German aid during the days of the uprising, Stalin, who had been vacillating and did not care much about the world revolution, and Sverdlov, who fastidiously followed Lenin's orders.[19] Lenin would again have been defeated except for Trotsky's sudden reversal, and for the unexpected cooption of Stassova, secretary of the Central Committee, as a voting member: she abstained. Trotsky explained his turnabout by saying that, although Lenin's arguments were unconvincing, and a revolutionary war was feasible, the disunity in the party left no choice but to ask for peace.[20]

[19]Uritsky, Joffe, Lomov, Krestinsky, and Bukharin voted for resistance.

[20]For a useful summary of these moves and votes, see Giorgio Migliardi, "I protocolli del comitato centrale: 1917-1918," *Annali* (Milano; Instituto Giangiacomo Feltrinelli, 1960), III, 781-800.

But the Germans did not accept this capitulation. They took their time, and then imposed new conditions. On February 21, exactly ten days after the demobilization decree had been issued, Lenin ordered general mobilization.

What was the German military situation? In numbers of usable divisions, the Germans now undoubtedly enjoyed a massive numerical advantage, except that they were unsure of the number of Russian units still capable of offering resistance. But their main concern was that most of the German force had to be used for garrison duty in a vast hinterland, so that barely more than one-third of the total strength (some twenty or so divisions) were available for offensive operations. As the Germans advanced, they would have been compelled to divert additional forces to garrison duties; gradually the offensive contingent would have decreased in size even if there had been no Russian resistance. The number of divisions was so small in relation to the enormous expanse of Russian land in which the Germans would have to operate that the entire force ran the risk of piecemeal destruction. The small size and poor quality of the force and the inadequacy of German logistics, as well as the lack of roads, the Russian distances, the rigors of winter, and the coming of the thaw within six to eight weeks precluded a cross-country advance. The Germans did not even contemplate such an operation and did not halt the withdrawal of their combat divisions to the west. The only practical way to advance was to move along the railroads. This would have enabled the Germans to reach Petrograd within "a few months," but, as Kuehlmann wrote on February 10, the Bolshevik government could withdraw further inland and the situation would remain unchanged. Kuehlmann did not mention that a small German detachment might have found it quite impractical to conquer a large metropolitan city. Actually, the German High Command was fearful of an explosion of Russian patriotism and therefore, apparently, did not contemplate a deep penetration.[21]

When the truce was abrogated, the Germans embarked on what their Chief of Staff, General Max Hoffmann, called the "funniest war" he ever fought. A few foot soldiers were put into a train, or placed in automobiles wherever there was a road, and sent to the next locality where they arrested the local authorities—Soviets, Bolsheviks, and all—and moved on to repeat the operation at the next stop. Obviously, resistance would have been possible against *this sort of attack.*

Whether or not there remained intact over ten Russian divisions to oppose more than twenty German divisions is not clearly discernible from the available data. Assuming that there were really

---

[21]N. Rutych, *La parti communiste au pouvoir en U.R.S.S. 1917-1960* (Paris: La Table Ronde, 1961), p. 143.

no military units left, it still would have been possible to sabotage the railroads by the railroad personnel—who were more or less "defencist"—or by other workers. This tactic had been twice used successfully, during the February revolution against the Tsar and against the Kornilov rising: the Bolsheviks knew this tactic well. Perhaps railroad sabotage might not have halted the Germans, but it would have aggravated their manpower problems and delayed them considerably. No orders for the defense and sabotage of railroads were given.

When the Germans resumed their advance, however, General Bonch-Bruyevich and a few other generals were ordered to Petrograd to report to Lenin and to organize defenses. Lenin told Bonch-Bruyevich that Petrograd would have to be defended by the workers since there were no soldiers. According to the most recent news, the Germans were advancing on Narva, but Bonch-Bruyevich replied that it was unlikely that large German forces could break through. Possibly a few small units had been dispatched in the expectation that they would encounter no resistance. The general also estimated that the German army could not really penetrate very deeply with strong forces. Lenin agreed, adding that, since the attack on Narva involved only weak elements, the Bolsheviks were preparing to repel it "only with workers' forces."[22] Defenses were improvised, the Germans were pushed back, and the "screen" which Bonch-Bruyevich had requested was organized effectively, though two to three months too late. Thus, it was not difficult to recreate a fighting force; all that was required was a firm decision and energetic execution. Even the war-weariness of the troops was highly exaggerated; after all, the supposedly exhausted troops were easily swayed by indoctrination and firm leadership and continued to fight for another four years.

Prominent party members under the intellectual leadership of Bukharin proposed that the Germans be opposed by guerrilla warfare. This concept was not entirely new but it was unusual and therefore lacked persuasiveness. Yet such strategy did not lack logic and was vindicated in many wars in due time. It is unlikely that Lenin failed to grasp the value of the proposal.

Bukharin and his friends argued that it would not matter even if the Germans advanced to Moscow; the deeper they penetrated, the more vulnerable they would become to sudden raids. The numerical advantage soon would be on the side of the guerrillas, the German supply lines would be cut, and the massive employment of propaganda plus thousands of prisoners of war who had been converted to communism and organized in international brigades, would lead to

22Bonch-Bruyevich, p. 285.

the dissolution of the German forces. Bukharin did *not* propose this course of action simply to satisfy Russian national interests and preserve old frontiers, but in order to carry the revolution into the German army and create from German soldiers, deserters, and prisoners, communist forces capable of revolutionizing Germany and all of central Europe.[23] He conceived of revolutionary war as the logical sequel to the October revolution; he probably was correct.

Lenin opposed these ideas as mere talk. Nevertheless, the Bolshevik government decided to establish an army of one million men to be developed systematically from existing units. A little later, obligatory military service was proclaimed. But since Lenin did not call for defenses of the railroads, he enabled the Germans to play an enormous bluff: in rapid order they occupied a number of towns situated close to old front lines without encountering resistance. Since these "conquests" included cities like Minsk, Pskov, Reval, and Kiev, the impression was created that the German advance could not be repelled—precisely the impression Lenin needed to prove his point.

Naturally, the conduct of a "revolutionary war" might have jeopardized the survival of the Bolshevik regime; but it also could have brought about its stabilization, although at the price of broadening its political base. No doubt, by February, 1918, the military situation was almost hopeless; but there had been no over-riding reason to demobilize before an agreement with the Germans was reached. It is most unlikely that Lenin did not realize that he was violating his own political rules in relinquishing power un-necessarily in the midst of a war or a world revolution. There was no absolute necessity to accept the *diktat* of Brest-Litovsk and certainly no military reason which forced the Bolsheviks to forego a genuine *political* offensive against the German government. The majority of the Bolshevik leaders was in favor of fighting; Lenin was compelled to resort to one subterfuge after another to make his policy prevail.

The proponents of revolutionary war may have been incorrect and Lenin's ostensible arguments for caution may have been most realistic. But Lenin's acquiescence to German demands had far-reaching consequences. Inside Russia, civil war became inevitable, while resistance might have forged a united front. Lenin's move enabled the Germans to maintain their armies intact despite the heavy fighting in France. Most important, the "separation" of the German troops from the Russian armies through armistice and peace *broke the chain of the world revolution.*

[23]Ruth Fischer, *op. cit.*, 47ff. Niessel (p. 227) was skeptical about the practicality of the "holy war'" but, being an orthodox soldier, he was bound to underrate the potentialities of new forms of warfare.

It is important to note, however, that Lenin was unable to consider the case for revolutionary war on its own merits. Being controlled by the Germans, Lenin simply was forced to deliver the peace. As mentioned before, his emissary on December 8, 1917, told the Germans that "calls to the people to start the revolution" were meant "platonically." German intelligence reported that the Bolsheviks had entered into no agreements with German socialists to foment a German revolution but that they were active against Hungary (March 20, 1918). Subsequently, Riezler reported to Berlin that the making of the peace required the "use of special arguments."24 This was not just a matter of bribery. On March 13, 1918, Count Wilhelm von Mirbach, German ambassador-elect to Moscow, argued that it was in Germany's best interest that the Bolsheviks remain in power. So the arrangement was for Lenin to deliver the peace and for the Germans to help him remain head of government. If Lenin could not have arranged the peace, they would have used every means at their disposal to overthrow him.

Lenin found difficulty in inducing the party to close ranks behind him.25 Without the help of Trotsky, he would not have succeeded.26

24May 27, 1918, Riezler to Nadolny, "Einsatz besonderer Argumente."

25Rutych, chapter 11; Schapiro, *Origin,* Chapt. 6.

26The vacillating role of Trotsky is not easy to interpret. It is clear that he wanted to continue the war (after all, he was the world revolutionary *par excellence*) but he carefully avoided putting Lenin into an untenable position and in extreme situations supported him. Trotsky was too intelligent to misunderstand Lenin's predicament. His own implication is questionable. Accusations that he cooperated with Austrian authorities before World War I never have been substantiated and are dubious, except that his activities were tolerated. More significant is the fact that late in 1914, he showed up in Paris with considerable funds. Apparently he traveled as war correspondent of *Kievskaya Mysl* and was accredited by the Russian war ministry. (The then Assistant Minister of War, General A. A. Polivanov, played a double game and was not above helping the revolutionaries.) In Paris, Trotsky first helped in the financing of Martov's paper *Golos.* Later he founded *Nashe Slovo* which undertook an effective defeatist campaign among the many Russians living in France and contributed to a mutiny of Russian soldiers on French soil. The paper was forbidden in the course of the anti-defeatist operation of the French government and Trotsky was expelled from France and via Spain went to New York. A note in the Okhrana file states that Trotsky's financial resources had come from Christian Rakovsky, the leading Social Democrat in the Balkans. This note (dated May 16, 1916) was written by a well-informed French observer and it would seem as though there was corroborating evidence. The German archives revealed that Rakovsky worked closely with the Germans and was considered by them almost as an agent. (Previously the Austrians had dealings with him which *did* involve money.) Rakovsky probably was given funds through the German Social Democratic deputy Suedekum but there were several other German channels (including Parvus in 1914 or early 1915). Also Trainin, a Bulgarian socialist military physician, was active. Trotsky may not have known of Rakovsky's connections but the Germans did and they may have warned the foreign commissar at an opportune moment. (On Rakovsky and his German connections, see for example Zeman, p. 85f.). The possibility of

Lenin propagandized for the treaty as much as he could. Under the name of "Karpov" he wrote articles in *Pravda*. German advances were publicized but the Bolshevik success at Narva was concealed. The Central Commitee, though Lenin controlled attendance, remained rebellious. The vote to accept the new German terms was seven for, four against, and four abstentions. The vote he needed to conclude the peace legally was finally obtained and then not in the party, but in the Central Executive Committee of the *soviet*—after the Germans had bribed a large number of the deputies.

The Seventh Party Congress voted subsequently. Lenin had prudently used his old trick of carefully selecting the delegates. The Congress should have been attended by about 250 representatives, but only fifty-eight delegates assembled, of whom forty-six were entitled to vote; less than a quarter of the party was represented. The vote was twenty-nine in favor of peace with nine opposed and a number of abstentions. The data on these figures are of course variable, but there is no doubt that Lenin's policy was approved by only twelve to fifteen per cent of the party. However, the advocates of revolutionary war were even weaker.

On the same day (March 6, 1918), the Germans dissolved the Stockholm agency to which the imposition of a peace treaty on Russia by political warfare had been entrusted.[27]

Between March 14 and 18, the Fourth Congress of the All-

German support to the *Mezhrayonka*, with which Trotsky was affiliated, was mentioned before.

Another interesting aspect was that early in 1918 Edgar Sisson, an American agent, procured a number of documents bearing on German relations with the Bolsheviks. Some of these documents were authentic, others were forged, but some of the forgeries contained much accurate information. It seems that these documents were played into Sisson's hands by Alexander Gumberg, a Russo-American socialist who was very close to Trotsky. Trotsky took great interest in these documents and events related to them. This might have been a deliberate plant to neutralize in advance possible German disclosure. Or perhaps it constituted an attempt by Trotsky to undercut Lenin. The "leak" coincided approximately with moves to enlist Allied support (moves which largely were in Trotsky's hands). Whatever the true story of the Sisson documents may be, Trotsky's behavior sprang from very complicated motivations. The allies told Trotsky about their concern toward Lenin's attachment (Niessel, *op. cit.*, pp. 119, 337). Trotsky told one of the intermediaries that he would be glad to take money from the French and would use it to foster revolution in France. His later writings show that the "German deal" was a matter of great concern to him and he tried every trick to deny the allegations. The Sisson documents must have been fabricated by a professional intelligence outfit engaged in "black propaganda" and political warfare. (On this point, see my *Jahrhundert des Aufruhrs*, Munich, Isar, 1956, p. 82.)

27In May, the German General Staff recalled from Stockholm Steinwachs who through Keskuela had maintained the connection with Lenin. One of his assistants was a certain Buchholz who may have been Lenin's old friend (Zeman, pp. 13 and 97).

Russian soviet ratified the treaty. In his speech asking for ratification, Lenin stated that the "hope that a German revolution will start immediately is nothing but self-deception."[28] The text of the treaty was not disclosed; but German money circulated in considerable amounts. Martov congratulated Lenin, saying that now he would be "under the protection not only of the Red guards but also of Kaiser Wilhelm." Martov apparently did not suspect that the Germans were paying the Red guards.[28a]

On March 12 Lenin and the government moved to Moscow. The move had been decided upon to deprive the Germans of an unnecessary temptation.[29]

Lenin and Krupskaya moved into two rooms with bath at the Hotel National. Maria, who was functioning as Lenin's executive secretary, remained with them. Inessa, who during the preceding eleven months had been living in Moscow, opposed Lenin's peace policy and kept to herself. A few days later, the Lenins were provided with two rooms in the Kremlin and then, after a thorough cleaning job, moved to their permanent apartment. It consisted of three rooms with a kitchen which adjoined Lenin's office and the office of the Council of People's Commissars.[30] It would have been fitting for Lenin, moving into the old castle of the Tsars, to read Shakespeare's *Richard III:*

> Within the hollow crown
> That rounds the mortal temples of a king,
> Keeps death his court, and there the antick sits,
> Scoffing his state and grinning at his pomp;
> Allowing him a breath, a little scene,
> To monarchize, be fear'd, and kill with looks,
> Infusing him with self and vain conceit,
> As if this flesh which walls about our life
> Were brass impregnable; and humor'd thus
> Comes at the last, and with a little grin
> Bores through his castle wall.

[28]*Sochineniya,* 4th ed., vol. 27, p. 157. For negative German socialist reactions to the peace, *see* Shub, p. 415.

[28a]A strong international brigade was the key element both of the Red guards and the incipient Red army. This brigade was composed of several national units and had an estimated strength of 50,000, including 20,000 Letts, 10,000 Poles, 10,000 Chinese and Koreans. The rest was composed of German and Austrian (largely Czech and Croat) prisoners of war. These men were well supplied and well paid, often in hard foreign currency. (Rutych, pp. 169-172).

[29]The German army may not have been able to reach Petrograd by land, even if they wanted to, but an amphibious operation was feasible—and feared.

[30]Krupskaya, p. 451f.

The Grind of Government

Despite the fact that he had established a strong personal dictatorship, Lenin found himself in a very difficult position. The left Social Revolutionaries withdrew from the Bolshevik government and a purely Bolshevik regime again came into existence on March 16. Lenin frequently invoked party discipline but was able to prevail only through manipulations: for example, on February 23, 1918, he threatened to resign from the Central Committee and the government.

As the peace negotiations ran into trouble, Lenin could not but give some attention to the planning of a German revolution. Unable to disclose his handicaps, he was forced to prove through deceptive maneuvers the seriousness of his intention to advance the revolution. A newspaper, *Die Fackel*, was printed in large numbers (about one million) but gradually was diverted for use by German-speaking prisoners in Russia. Another paper distributed on the front, *Völkerfriede* ("Peace Among Nations"), served its purpose during the negotiations. Radek, who had been in charge of stimulating a German revolution, was dispatched to Brest and removed from operational planning. The newly formed Liebknecht brigade did not make much progress, and soon was lost from sight.

A well-informed German negotiator, Ernst Jaeckh, reported from Stockholm on the basis of his contacts with Bolsheviks that the revolution would erupt in France and Italy, but would bypass Germany. Edgar Sisson, President Wilson's special representative in Russia, relayed essentially the same information from Petrograd.[1] On February 6, 1918, "left Zimmerwald revolutionaries" conferred in Petrograd about advancing the world revolution, but no Germans or Austro-Hungarians participated. An effort was undertaken to propagandize the Rumanian army (Rumania had entered the war against Germany). Extensive plans were formulated to send expert revolutionizers to Europe: Kamenev, who for two weeks had been chairman of the Central Executive Committee (i.e., "president" of the state), was to go to France, Central Committee member Alexandra Kollontai would go to Scandinavia, an assistant of Trotsky would be sent to Switzerland, and a ferocious and unknown revolutionary was assigned to Britain. But since the Germans were blocking the Finnish exits, the plotters remained in Russia. Lenin enunciated *Theses on Peace*, asserting that all questions had to be solved for the purpose of developing and strengthening the "socialist revolution which has already begun." But no deeds followed.

[1]Edgar Sisson, *One Hundred Red Days* (New Haven: Yale, 1931), p. 354.

In all this political chaos Lenin had to make good his economic program. In December, 1917, he signed a decree for the nationalization of banks and trusts; in January, 1918, a decree on forced labor (mainly to accelerate snow removal in Petrograd) ; in April, 1918, three decrees on nationalization of corporations, registration of securities, and abolition of inheritance. On February 23, 1918, in an attempt to ram Brest-Litovsk down the throats of his comrades, he alleged that the economic reorganization of Russia would be feasible within a few months of peaceful work on the basis of the dictatorship of the proletariat, the nationalization of banks and industry, and barter exchange between towns and small farmers. It is possible that he believed his statement. Subsequently, Lenin regretted many radical features of the early decrees, which were written for the most part by Mikhail A. Larin, a former internationalist Menshevik. Larin, né Lurye, was employed during the war as a correspondent of a bourgeois newspaper in Stockholm. His connection with Parvus was probably the reason he understood so much of the German war economy which he praised as a model to be used in socialist planning. Larin emphasized Parvus' point that socialism was constituted of more than simple expropriation. A Menshevik since 1906, Larin joined the Bolsheviks in 1917. Without him, there would have been provided no concept of "socialist construction." It is interesting to note that Larin's wife, before March, 1917, served as a communications relay for liaison with revolutionaries inside Russia and during the summer of 1917 acted as one of the couriers through whom the Germans maintained contact with the Bolsheviks at Petrograd.

During this period Lenin worried about the secession of various nationalities, as well as counter-revolutions in many of the non-Russian areas. He maintained the outer appearances of a workers' democracy by appearing to consult with the soviet; he even issued a decree on the freedom of "conscience" (not of "speech," by any means) .

Lenin usually began his daily conferences at four in the afternoon, often refusing to receive diplomats and high officials. He liked to speak to "delegations" from factories and villages, telling them that the Bolsheviks were the only friends of the workers. After such meetings, he worked through the evening until early in the morning, when he was almost completely exhausted. Still unrecognized in the streets, he risked evening walks, sometimes visited balls and, like Harun el Rashid, mingled among the people. He went to the market to talk to traders and to listen to talk critical of him. There were some stories that he was enriching himself; he heard these with an indulgent smile. But the proletarian style *was* changing: he now had an automobile at his disposal. "Whenever he had a moment to spare he would go motoring outside Moscow with his sister Maria" and Krupskaya, "always visiting new places, riding and thinking and filling his lungs with the fresh air."[2] Krupskaya related that when they returned home Lenin could not fall asleep, restlessly moved about, telephoned orders and, when he finally dozed, slept badly and dreamed violently. From time to time, Lenin withdrew, and read history, from which he intended to marshal better arguments to support his surrender to Germany. (Similarly, the German Foreign Secretary refreshed his historical knowledge while in Brest.)

During May and early June Lenin was busy guiding the affairs of Russia. Once (June 20) he went to the theater and then took a short vacation. Heretofore, Lenin had been concerned with concepts, negotiations, and speeches; but now the details of daily affairs were pressing down on him. The ideological obligations he had assumed in the past proved to be a millstone around his neck. As the doctrinaire program was put into practice step by step, the economy collapsed. Lenin was compelled to work out a theory opposing "left childishness."

Food shortages, especially in the capitals, were acute. In characteristic fashion, Lenin tried to remedy the situation by organizing the poor peasants against the "kulaks" (the "middle peasants") who were producing most of the food. He also incited the rural workers to confiscate grain. They did this with alacrity, taking even the seed grains and consuming them. The better-run farms were ruined but very little was delivered to the towns and to the "industrial workers." Lenin had to concern himself with the rationing of coal, the production and transport of oil, the control of sugar industry, and manipulation of state finances. He worried about the sharply declining labor discipline and productivity. He dealt with wages and prices and, most unsuccessfully, with the ever growing black market. The country was in the throes of an uncontrollable inflation; nominal wages had to be boosted frequently while real wages declined catastrophically.

The People's Commissars, who orginally were paid the same wages as skilled industrial workers, were granted a substantial pay raise on July 16, 1918. This was one of the earliest modifications which the new regime introduced into its original program. Some industries were being "nationalized," but proposals for the nationalization of others were shelved temporarily. Lenin began to understand that the bureaucracy that had emerged as the key instrument of his rule was also becoming the chief obstacle to the realization of his dreams. It rapidly became apparent that socialism could not be introduced in one dramatic clean sweep.

[2]Krupskaya, *op. cit.*, p. 469.

During that period the Germans were in complete control of the situation. They had entered into close relations with a moderately socialist regime in the Ukraine. Lenin, not wishing for trouble, in May countermanded a Bolshevik invasion and discouraged Bolshevik takeovers in most parts of the Ukraine. Yet the Bolsheviks maintained bridgeheads throughout the Ukraine; many of Lenin's orders were disregarded by the local revolutionaries. Rumor had it that during May Trotsky agreed to help organize an uprising in Germany. Lenin was dissatisfied over the various revolutions his Bolshevik comrades were organizing against nations which had been naive enough to take seriously Bolshevik statements about self-determination.

On May 13, 1918, the German Ambassador in Moscow requested funds to supply the Bolsheviks with the minimum of necessary goods to maintain them in power. Five days later Kuehlmann authorized him to spend what was needed, since it was in the German interest to keep Lenin in power. On June 5 the German Foreign Minister informed the Minister of Finance that Germany would have to keep the Bolsheviks from another orientation. "This costs money, probably much money."[3] Five days later, the Germans issued an ultimatum that the Russian naval vessels in the Black Sea that had fled to Novorossisk be interned at Sevastopol under German control.[4] The order was followed, but some of the ships were scuttled. Somewhat earlier there had been a dispute concerning the Russian ships in the Baltic. Trotsky insisted that they be scuttled and that the sailors be paid for blowing up the ships—a strange way of getting sailors to execute official commands. Admiral Shchastny, the fleet commander, demurred. The scuttling was unnecessary, since the German fleet had been withdrawn. There was no immediate danger and the fleet could be easily protected. Admiral Shchastny, who tried to reason with Trotsky, was arrested, tried, and on June 21 shot after being found guilty in a rigged trial dominated by Trotsky.[5] But the ships had not been scuttled.

Trotsky's fury at Shchastny is difficult to explain, since the Admiral had saved the ships from an extremely foolish order. Shchastny had rescued the Russian fleet once before, when the

[3]Zeman, p. 133.

[4]The Germans wanted to preserve the Russian ships in the Black Sea where they lacked naval power. In the Baltic the Germans had enough ships, and it would have been difficult to find a suitable port to intern 168 Russian warships. Scuttling was a better solution from the German point of view. On August 27, 1918, a Russo-German exchange of notes authorized, "in case of need" the German use of the Russian ships in the Black Sea for military purposes. (*See* Rutych, p. 155).

[5]Report by U.S. Consul De Witt C. Poole, June 24, 1918, reprinted in Sisson, *op. cit.*, p. 437ff.

Germans attempted to blockade the ships at Helsingfors. The man should have been decorated, yet his was the *first case* in which the death penalty was applied through a phony legal procedure. Trotsky pretended to be particularly enraged because the Admiral had in his possession four documents, purportedly forgeries, showing that the Bolsheviks followed German orders. These documents had been sent to the Admiral by mail just as he was leaving to report to higher headquarters, where he was arrested.[6] The outward signs of a provocation are all too apparent.

Outside their direct support to the Bolsheviks, the Germans tried their hand at various political warfare schemes. One program which proved effective was the training of Bolshevik soldiers by German prisoners of war; in some instances, the prisoners joined Bolshevik units. But the Entente powers were not idle either; they too were experimenting with the game of revolutionizing. During February and March they had tried to enlist Ukrainian forces against Germany, but had failed despite considerable outlays; now they had mastered some of the strategy and were becoming active within Russia. By the middle of June a German diplomat who was a political warfare expert reported from Moscow that the Bolsheviks were becoming nervous and believed that their regime was approaching its end.[7] Presumably in response to this and similar reports, the Germans expanded their Russian budget.[8]

[6]The documents were of a similar nature to those given to Sisson by Gumberg. *See also* Schapiro, *Origin,* p. 115 and 119. According to other data, however, a German commanding officer communicated to the Russian Admiral documents purporting to prove that the Germans were authorized to occupy a certain naval fort (Rutych, p. 153). Shchastny was not allowed to call witnesses in his defense.

[7]Zeman, pp. 133, 137f.

[8]*Ibid,* p. 137.

Murder

At the end of June, M. M. Volodarsky, a Bolshevik commissar, was killed in Petrograd. This individual had played a key role in the inner councils of the party and had been functioning as the party's propaganda chief. On June 26 Lenin returned from his vacation to protest very strongly Petrograd Bolsheviks' lack of reaction to this assassination: mass terror should have been unleashed, said Lenin. Zinovyev, the Petrograd boss, was opposed to the tactics of terror. Lenin insisted that the "energy and the mass character of terror against the counter-revolutionaries" would have to be encouraged.[1]

[1]*Sochineniya,* 4th ed., Vol. 35, p. 275.

At this time, as British troops were landing at Murmansk, Lenin became apprehensive about the possibility of counter-revolution. Bolshevik bankruptcy was apparent to all. Pitirim Sorokin, a sociologist who had been a moderate socialist and was following events with an open mind, stated, "I am no longer a revolutionist because revolution is catastrophe. I am no longer a socialist because socialism is wrong." He added that if the people desire a government "of the people, for the people, and by the people," they must be willing to do something to achieve it. But the temper of the masses was still revolutionary and radically socialist, and the strong opposition to the Bolsheviks did not come from the moderates but from the left Social Revolutionaries.

These radicals believed that the dictatorship of the proletariat had developed into a dictatorship of Mirbach, the German minister at Moscow; that the Brest treaty was harmful both to the Russian and the world revolution; and that the existing arrangement should be overthrown by revolutionary means. German intelligence reported that the left Social Revolutionaries were supported by the Entente, notably the French. On June 24 the left Social Revolutionaries decided to resume terrorism directed at "prominent members of German imperialism," but they did not resolve upon the overthrow of the Bolsheviks. By contrast, on June 28, Lenin gave three speeches, advocating civil war and boasting that local uprisings could easily be suppressed by local Bolsheviks.

Lenin's pro-German policy was highly unpopular in Russia, even within Bolshevik ranks. The Bolsheviks needed economic collaboration, as did the Germans, but German decision-makers were split into pro-Bolsheviks (centered mostly in the Foreign Office) and anti-Bolsheviks (centered mostly in the High Command[2]). Due to this division, German diplomacy moved slowly. Meanwhile, the military was applying pressure inside Russia. On May 16 Lenin spoke to Count Wilhelm Mirbach, warning him that the Germans were overplaying their hand; if his government were overthrown, he continued, German interests would be hurt. Neither Mirbach nor the German eastern command was convinced that the Lenin regime was indispensable.

Lenin endeavored to abolish the remaining opposition parties one by one. In April Lenin succeeded in crippling the anarchists. The social revolutionaries were now receiving support from the Entente, and the military and Cossacks were organizing resistance in the south.

The Bolsheviks decreed another mobilization but Mirbach considered this to be merely a paper measure. Still, he advised the German press to portray this Bolshevik decision as one indicating

[2]*See*, for example, General Ludendorff's memorandum of June 9, 1918 (Zeman, p. 134ff.).

power and vigor. A few days later, on June 3, he informed Berlin that, in view of strong "competition" from the Entente, Bolshevik vigor required for its sustenance three million marks each month. The German government quickly budgeted forty million marks.

Early in June, the German Foreign Office was told by its Moscow legation that within a few weeks it might become necessary to restore "a bourgeois order" with which Germany could reach an agreement. On June 25 Mirbach warned that bolshevism "has reached the end of its powers." He feared that the revolutionaries financed by the Entente might lead Russia back into the war and advised that Germany should seek to fill the expected vacuum "with a regime which would be favorable to our designs and interests."[3] The German political warfare experts were negotiating with several suitable candidates, including a Romanov grand duke.

The Bolsheviks, suspecting a change in German policy, increased their intelligence coverage of the German legation. Jakob G. Blyumkin, a twenty year old left Social Revolutionary who was a member of the secret police, was in charge and apparently did an expert job of penetration.

On July 4 during the Fifth Soviet Congress, the left Social Revolutionaries, comprising about one-third of the delegates, very effectively attacked Bolshevik policy, putting Lenin in a bad position. Their criticism was highly popular. Many Bolshevik leaders feared that they were losing control. In the evening, Blyumkin contacted a leading left Social Revolutionary (probably Maria Spiridonova) and offered to kill Mirbach. On July 6, he and another terrorist, equipped with documents bearing the signature and seal of Felix E. Dzerzhinski, chief of the secret police, requested an audience with Mirbach. In the course of the interview the minister was murdered, probably by Blyumkin's companion.

This killing kindled shootings throughout Moscow: the Bolsheviks were subduing an alleged left Social Revolutionary uprising. It proved to be an exceedingly easy task. It is true that one or two Bolshevik leaders were briefly held as prisoners: these were the police chiefs who were negotiating with the Social Revolutionaries. It is also said that the telegraph office was seized for an hour or so and that a revolutionary proclamation was broadcast. Presently, however, the rebels were disarmed.

The alleged insurrectionists were subsequently brought to trial. Despite the prevailing harshness of the terror regime, only light sentences were meted out. Blyumkin was not found. He surrendered in 1919 and was rehabilitated on the grounds that the assassination of Mirbach did not justify his imprisonment. He was admitted to the Bolshevik party in 1921, rejoined the secret police (which he seemed

[3]Zeman, p. 138f.

to have betrayed), and became a special assistant to Trotsky in the Commissariat of War.

All this is highly irregular and hence suspect, especially since the "uprising" occurred at a moment when almost all left Social Revolutionary leaders and the party's main cadres were busy debating in a soviet session. The alleged plotters were all arrested together in the Bolshoi Theater—after the Bolshevik delegates had been duly informed about events and had left the hall and before the Social Revolutionaries heard the news. It is true that the Social Revolutionaries ventured some military actions but it is likely that they were just defending themselves against the Bolsheviks; it is also possible that their attacks were staged by Bolshevik infiltrators. (The Bolsheviks had many left Social Revolutionaries under their discipline.)

In brief, the assassination of Mirbach was probably a Bolshevik provocation; if so, the plot must have been directed by Lenin. Indeed, the elimination of Mirbach was highly desirable since he was the one German who was most capable and most willing to remove the Bolsheviks. This death eliminated the threat and served as a warning to the Germans against overreaching themselves at the expense of Russia. German power within Russia was substantially reduced by Mirbach's murder.

Naturally, Lenin ran the risk of reprisals, but the Germans were not interested in ousting the Bolsheviks. They eagerly accepted the accusation of the Social Revolutionaries. Wilhelm II ordered that the Entente should be held responsible in all propaganda outlets, stating that "even in the absence of direct proofs . . . it will be difficult for them to prove the contrary." And, most important, the incident enabled Lenin to subdue the Social Revolutionaries who had become difficult to deal with. Lenin had told Krassin that he intended to obtain all the benefits from the incident, yet preserve Bolshevik innocence by making "an internal loan among the left Social Revolutionary comrades."[4] Krassin replied that he never suspected "such profound and cruel cynicism" in Lenin. The cynicism is beyond argument, but the tactical genius required to undertake such an operation should not be overlooked.[5]

Nevertheless, trouble was not restricted to Moscow. The French had been busy. A left Social Revolutionary Red army commander, M. A. Muraviev, to whom the Germans had paid "considerable financial subsidies," was bribed to defect.[6] He did so, after the liaison

[4]Shub, p. 317. Lenin meant that he was sacrificing left Social Revolutionary comrades in the interest of the Bolsheviks.

[5]George Katkov, "The Assassination of Count Mirbach," *Soviet Affairs* No. 3, p. 53f. (St. Antony's Papers No. 12, London, 1962.)

[6]On an earlier British attempt to bribe Muraviev, *see* Sisson, *op. cit.*, p. 269ff.

man between him and the Germans was arrested and his funds were running down. In a few provincial towns, the left Social Revolutionaries deemed the assassination and the related shootings a signal to rise. Insurrections occurred around Yaroslavl, Rybinsk, and Murom, and unrest spread temporarily into Petrograd. The insurgents probably received some support from the Entente and the peasants, about one-third or even one-half of whom Lenin and his comrades had described as "bloodsuckers and vampires," and against whom they were conducting a vigorous expropriation campaign. Yet the peasants and the left Social revolutionaries were poorly organized and, within a week, the rising was suppressed.

The time was propitious for squaring old accounts. On July 19, 1918, the Moscow press disclosed that "the wife and son of Nicholas Romanov were sent to a safe place."[7] The report represented a classical case of Communist mendacity. The truth was that during the night of July 16 the Tsar, Tsarina, the heir apparent, four daughters of the Tsar, his brother (who had been his successor for less than two days), and other members of the Imperial family were assassinated at three different localities.[8] To exculpate themselves, Moscow suggested that local Communist authorities had acted on their own volition. The truth is that the Tsar and his family were shot in a well-coordinated operation in which, many hundreds of miles apart, the various branches of the Romanov family were being exterminated. No Communist of any locality ever was indicted for the deed.

This grisly operation was supervised for Moscow by Sverdlov, a former pharmacist apprentice, who was chairman of the Central Executive Committee—and thus had rank equivalent to president of Russia. Since November 21, 1917, he had been Lenin's closest confidant and his *alter ego*. There is no question that Sverdlov acted under the precise instructions—and in any event with the authorization—of Lenin, who was his *de facto* (though not legal) superior. Lenin had been for months calling for terror measures against all opponents and was building organizations specializing in fear. Immediately after the Bolsheviks had come to power, the actual terror campaign began with the brutal muder, in a hospital, of two ill members of Kerensky's cabinet. It is not known whether Lenin ordered this initial assassination himself. In any event, no attempt was made to apprehend the murderers; accomplices who had been arrested were released after a few days.

On July 17, at a meeting of the People's Commissars (as the ministers were then called), Sverdlov told Lenin of the murder of the

[7]Shub, p. 319.

[8]For a short and vivid description of the assassination of the Tsar, *see* William Henry Chamberlin, *The Russian Revolution 1917-1921* Vol. II, (New York: MacMillan, 1957), p. 89ff.

tsarist family. Lenin rose, interrupted the speaker and declared he had just been informed "that the former Tsar has been shot in Yekaterinburg by order of the Ural regional soviet." Sverdlov added, "The Presidium of the Central Executive Committee has decided to approve this act." Lenin supposedly continued, "Now, let us proceed to read the draft point by point."9 This scene obviously is an anti-climax that may be legendary. Lenin's conscience was not much troubled. He approved this story about his reactions. Hence he must have been eager to convey an image of himself as an assassin.

The murder of the Tsar was more than a crime: it was an act of the highest psychological significance. It symbolized the end of the old regime and buried the hopes of a restoration. It satisfied the cravings for revenge of many revolutionaries, and demonstrated the power of the new men. Yet these individuals lacked courage both to assume unequivocal responsibility for their act and to try the Tsar in open court, as proposed by Trotsky, who volunteered for the self-aggrandizing role of prosecutor. Since Lenin and Sverdlov could not afford to advance Trotsky's political fortunes, justice gave way to crime.10

The Tsar's life and rule were lacking in higher values, but the death that made him a sacrificial lamb ennobled the Tsar and his memory. Their murder recovered for the Romanovs the glory of innocence and the bitter but most moral reward of duty and rectitude. However, the destruction of the old did not signify the birth of a better society. It merely heralded regression into barbarism.

It may be granted that the Bolsheviks worried about the role the Tsar might play in civil war. There were reports that his liberation was being planned and there was danger that anti-Bolshevik forces might conquer the area where the Romanovs were held prisoners. There exist data suggesting that the Germans insisted on the release of the tsarist family and had requested the Tsar's extradition; yet the Germans probably did nothing of the kind, and after the event Wilhelm II instructed his diplomats to shift the blame for his cousin Nicholas' murder to his other cousin, George V of England.

Immorality was not a Bolshevik monopoly. The assassination of the Tsar and of one or two potential pretenders to the throne

9Quoted from Shub, p. 319.

10*Trotsky's Diary in Exile 1935,* Cambridge, Harvard, 1958, p. 81f, quotes Sverdlov to the effect that Lenin believed "we shouldn't leave the Whites a live banner to rally around." Trotsky explained that "summary justice" was expedient and necessary. "Under judicial procedures, of course, execution of the family would have been impossible."

might possibly be "justified" on the grounds of political expediency, but the murder of the Tsarina, who was physically and mentally ill, the Tsarevich, who suffered from hemophilia and was not expected to live for long, the grand duchesses, and household personnel without significance, indicated a crime of simple revenge.

The murder was plotted by three of Lenin's most trusted agents, but the actual executioners were apparently Hungarians. Lenin's personal representative was Philip Isayevich (or Shaya Itskovich) Goloshchekin who, at the Prague conference of 1912, had been taken into the Central Committee by Lenin. Goloshchekin was a professional revolutionary who had gained a great deal of experience in expropriations and partisan operations during 1906. He had been arrested five times, in each instance for cause. Yet every time, his sentence had been commuted or he was allowed to escape—a pattern that arouses the suspicion that he might have been a police agent. If this man was vengeful towards the Tsar, his hatred was most unjustified. Goloshchekin, who was close to Lenin and enjoyed the full confidence of his friend Sverdlov, was killed during the Stalin purges.

Georg Ivanovich Safarov, the second of the trio, had been arrested in his youth but his sentence permitted him to go abroad. In 1912 Lenin sent him back to Russia to work on *Pravda.* He traveled with Inessa Armand, whose favors he probably enjoyed when Lenin was not with them. He was arrested again, presumably because of Malinovsky's machinations. According to explanatory notes in Lenin's *Works,* Safarov was a member of the Central Committee; this association is not confirmed by other sources. During the war, Safarov was in Switzerland, and then engaged in defeatist propaganda in St. Nazaire, France. Inessa worked with him during her French mission. Expelled for pro-German activities, he returned to Switzerland, and later traveled with Lenin to Russia in the sealed train. Subsequently, he edited the Leningrad *Pravda,* and together with Inessa opposed Lenin's Brest policy. Interested in nationality problems, he opposed Great Russian chauvinism. He was ejected from the party in 1927, re-admitted, convicted for counter-revolution in 1935, and purged in 1938.

The third member of the murder team, Peter Lazarovich Voykov, had returned to Russia in May, 1917 (probably in the second transport passing through Germany), joined the Bolsheviks in August, 1917, and participated in the strengthening of Bolshevik power in the Urals. In 1924, he became the Soviet Ambassador to Poland and was murdered on June 7, 1927, in Warsaw.

The man who actually shot the Tsar, Jakob M. Yurovsky, allegedly was a Trotskyite (according to subsequent nomenclature) and was killed in a Communist purge. Whether any political orientation can be ascribed to him is questionable. He was practically illiterate and, at least in later years, was almost demented. Before killing him, the Soviet state paid him a pension and allowed him to live in reasonable comfort without requiring him to work.

Grand Duke Mikhail Alexandrovich, the brother in whose favor the Tsar had abdicated, was murdered by G. I. Myasnikov, who later opposed the party's policy by extolling freedom of speech. According to him, Soviet power should emulate that of the Roman emperors and maintain, at its own expense, a body of detractors. Myasnikov's calls for freedom of criticism were condemned, but as long as Lenin was in power, his most serious punishment was a one-year suspension from the party. Banished in 1928, he went to Paris. He returned to Russia after World War II and disappeared.[11]

Alexander G. Beloborodov, the murderer of four grand dukes, one prince, and the Tsarina's sister, was imprisoned during the 1930's, tortured, and executed. It is reported that he, of course, violently objected to his own torture, but the manner in which he had killed his own victims was exceptionally brutal.[12] Thus the chief murderers "perished by the sword."

The fiction that local Communists were responsible for the murder of the Romanovs was not for long maintained. Yekaterinburg, where the Tsar and his immediate family had been killed, soon was renamed Sverdlovsk. At this writing, the city still bears this name in honor of the murderer.

[11]*See* Schapiro, *Origin,* p. 327f.

[12]For more details see Nicolas Sokoloff, *Enquête judiciaire sur l'assassinat de la famille impériale russe* (Paris: Payot, 1924), and Paul Bulygin, *The Murder of the Romanovs* (London: Hutchinson, 1935).

Lenin is Shot

Terror was now rampant. The British naval attaché was murdered on the steps of his embassy. A German field marshal was assassinated in Kiev. To obtain bread, which was becoming ever more scarce, Lenin increased "reprisals" directed at the peasants.

After an abortive peasant uprising in Pensa during August, Lenin instituted (as we read in his telegraphed instruction to Evgenia B. Bosh) "a merciless terror against the kulaks, priests, and White guards. Suspects to be imprisoned in concentration camps outside of town." Upon receipt of this order, 152 persons were executed by Bosh to avenge the death of one Communist. (Remember that Bosh was a woman.)

On August 30, one of the chief terrorists, M. S. Uritsky, was killed by Leonid Kannegiesser, a gifted poet.[1] Anatol V. Lunacharsky, an aesthete who was determined to advance culture through the Bolshevik revolution, described Lenin as an *"al fresco* colossal figure who in the moral dimension literally has no equal." Lenin's "rage is also extraordinarily attractive. Although his thunder lately did kill several thousand people, he always dominates his wrath which assumes a jesting form. This thunder . . . comes from a blue sky."[2]

Not everybody took such a view of things and on August 30, the day of Uritsky's murder, Lenin was shot by a Social Revolutionary, a twenty-eight year old girl named Fanya (or Dora) Kaplan, who under the Tsar had been punished by eleven years of hard labor.[3] She had resolved to kill Lenin because she considered him to be a "traitor to the revolution," and because Lenin's continued existence was "destroying the faith in socialism." Though she may have been a friend of Spiridonova, there is no real evidence that she was anything but a "free-lancer." There was, however, every indication that the girl was sick: in tsarist hard-labor prisons since she was sixteen, she was, at intervals, suffering from blindness, probably hysterical in nature.[4] Still, the author has interview data which suggest that the attentat might have been instigated by a foreign power. These data include a complaint that the planner of the attempt should have determined beforehand whether Kaplan was a good shot.[4a]

At that time, Lenin had discontinued his walks in the streets, exercising within the confines of the Kremlin which was guarded by well-paid Lettish soldiers. The hours he spent in the courtyard were irregular, sometimes during the day and occasionally at night. But he was obliged to make speeches in public. On August 30, at about 10 P.M., Lenin was addressing the workers of the Michelson factory in Moscow on the "dictatorship of the bourgeoisie and the dictatorship of the proletariat." As he was returning to his car, Kaplan, who

[1]Uritsky had only recently turned from Menshevism to Bolshevism and, for a while, had functioned as Plekhanov's secretary. Uritsky knew Kannegiesser and talked to him on the phone shortly before the murder. Kannegiesser apparently acted on his own, to avenge the killing of a friend. A few hours before his deed, he played chess with his father. *See* M. A. Aldanov, *Zeitgenossen* (Berlin, Schlieffen, 1929), pp. 319-361.

[2]Aldanov, *ibid.,* p. 302.

[3]Schapiro, *Origin,* p. 153. Schapiro says that Social Revolutionary writers invariably called her Dora; the police called her Fanya. Her original name was Feiga Yefimovna Roidman. She was born in Vilna *guberniya,* the daughter of a Jewish teacher. Four brothers and three sisters, together with her parents, moved to the United States in 1911.

[4]Abstracts of her five interrogations in *Proletarskaya Revolyutsiya,* No. 6-7 (18-19), 1923, pp. 282-285.

[4a]The Bolsheviks suspected the British, yet Kaplan did not talk or there was nothing to say. The two main suspected organizers were speedily released upon instructions from G. V. Chicherin, Foreign Commissar. See R. H. Bruce Lockhart, *British Agent,* New York, Putnam, 1933, p. 314-317.

was standing in the crowd, wounded him with two bullets. One bullet struck Lenin's left shoulder, while the other pierced the neck from left to right, grazed the left lung, and lodged near the right collarbone. No vital organs were wounded.

Communist myth-makers claimed that one bullet passed into the thorax cage and that the other went through the carotid artery. This sounds as though they wanted to prove the immortality of their leader. According to Bolshevik writers, Lenin was lying on the ground and losing blood but he did not lose consciousness. In a typical gesture, he forbade being carried to the hospital and ordered that he be taken home. After more than an hour, they reached his apartment. It is said that he walked two floors up to his lodging. (Naturally, he was carried upstairs.)

Bonch-Bruyevich was summoned. His wife was a physician, and Lenin's chauffeur, Stepan K. Gil, brought her medical bag. Maria Ulyanova and Anna P. Kizas, the Lettish maid of the Lenins, arrived. Bonch-Bruyevich gave instructions to apply iodine to the shoulder wound. Then his wife and another party wife who also was a physician, Vera Krestinskaya, came and gave somewhat more professional treatment. Lenin complained of pains in the heart; Bonch-Bruyevich told him he had been wounded in the arm only. Lenin fell back to sleep, then awakened to ask, "Why are they tormenting me? Why didn't they kill me right away?" Lenin was convinced that he was dying. He kept repeating, "When will the end come?" Vera M. Bonch-Bruyevich (Velichkina) injected morphine.

At long last, more competent doctors arrived. Professor Mints, a surgeon, did not believe there was just one wound and examined Lenin carefully. He found the second wound on the side of the neck. The concern was whether a vital organ had been harmed. In the meantime, Lenin's lungs had filled with blood and he began to cough and spit. There was such a large quantity of blood in his chest that his heart had been pushed to the right and caused great pain.

Krupskaya, who had been attending a meeting, was herself quite ill. She entered the room and remained in a chair for the rest of the night. Party leaders kept vigil in Lenin's office. A nurse remained in attendance. Lenin suffered from thirst during the night. The next day, Lenin was spitting blood again, his temperature was higher and his blood pressure was irregular.[5] A doctor's council convened with N. A. Semashko, Commissar of Health, presiding. Examinations indicated that Lenin's wounds were not serious. On September 10 he was reported out of danger. However, his left arm was immobilized

[5]Vladimir D. Bonch-Bruyevich, *Pokusheniye na V. I. Lenine v Moskve 30 Avgusta 1918* (Moscow, 1924); Krupskaya, p. 480ff; V. Rozanov in *O Lenine, Vospominaniya* (Moscow, 1925), *op. cit.*, III, 121-136.

for two weeks. Within three weeks the wounds were healed, but the bullets remained in his body.

As an after-effect, Lenin complained of pains in his left thumb and forefinger, due to a nerve that was affected. But it was determined by physical examinations (repeated daily for over a month) that he was generally in sound shape. There was, notably, no sign of sclerosis.

The better side in Lenin's nature was featured in Communist propaganda in this instance. Lenin was alleged to have ordered that Fanya Kaplan not be executed. Throughout the years occasional stories were printed about her serving as a prison librarian in Moscow or somewhere in Siberia. As late as January, 1958, a report concerning her recent natural death in a concentration camp was cabled from Moscow to the United States.

This line of writing was soon proven false by those interested in preserving the image of the true Lenin. The rectification came through the publication of the memoirs of Pavel D. Malkov, the erstwhile commandant of the Kremlin and sailor of the Baltic fleet.[6]

Gil reported that upon hearing the shots he ran after Kaplan but then returned to Lenin who had been left alone. Lenin's first question was, "Did they catch him?" Krupskaya does not breathe a word about leniency toward Kaplan but quotes a statement issued in the evening of August 30 by Sverdlov that the "working class will respond . . . by a ruthless mass terror against all the enemies of the revolution."[7]

Malkov reported that V. A. Avanyessov, Sverdlov's secretary, ordered him to transfer Kaplan from the prison to a cell in the Kremlin.[8] Within four days after the attempt, as it became apparent that Lenin would survive, the *Vcheka* (as freely translated, "state security commission") sentenced Kaplan to death; Malkov was ordered to execute the sentence by shooting her immediately in the courtyard near the garage. Sverdlov answered Avanyessov's question about the place of burial with, "We shall not bury Kaplan. Destroy her remains so that no trace be left." Malkov removed several trucks from the garage and started the motors. Then he fetched the victim.

In the interim Demyan Bedny, the poet whose apartment was located above the court, had come down to investigate the noise. There was no concern about his witnessing the killing. Malkov ordered Kaplan to walk toward a car. She stepped forward and

---

[6]*Zapiski Komendanta Moskovskogo Kremlya* (Moscow, 1959 and 1960).

[7]Krupskaya, p. 482.

[8]At one time Avanyessov acted as the supervisor of the imprisoned family of the Tsar. Apparently he was considered too lenient towards his prisoners.

Malkov shot her from behind. On September 4, 1918, *Izvestiya* announced the execution of right Social Revolutionary Fanny Roid (alias Kaplan) in accordance with the decree of the *Vcheka*.

The Bolsheviks now resorted to "wholesale terror." On September 5 the Commissariat of Justice issued a decree entitled *On the Red Terror,* which empowered the police to place "class enemies" in concentration camps and to execute opponents of the regime.[9] It is said that in Petrograd alone more than 500 hostages were slain. According to other figures, 800 hostages were shot throughout Russia. A literary "chekist," Martin Y. Latsis, had written earlier that laws which were once held sacred no longer applied. "To slaughter all those who were wounded by taking part in the battles against us—such is the law of civil war." Incriminating evidence was no longer required. The decree said that the prisoner was to be asked to "what class he belongs, what is his origin, his education and profession. It is those questions that should decide the fate of the defendant—therein lies the meaning of Red terror."[10]

"Death to the bourgeoisie! — this should be the slogan of the day," *Krasnaya Gazeta* wrote.[11] These were not mere phrases. The avowed program was to "exterminate the bourgeoisie as a class"; no one was keeping accurate statistics on the program's progress.

In the days preceding the attempt on his life, Lenin had not been feeling well. In a photograph of that period he looks as though he had just undergone a cruel sickness. Krupskaya reported that he could not write or sleep. He managed to keep going by imposing upon himself strict discipline and a careful diet. Krupskaya, who was Vice-Commissar of Education, was also in ill health. In one instance, it is reported that Lenin officially ordered her, in his position as head of the government, to take a two-week rest; actually, she was forced repeatedly to discontinue her work.

Yet Lenin possessed a robust physique; the enforced rest helped his recovery. On September 6 and 11 he dispatched telegrams and by September 15, though still weak, he took interest in affairs again. Then, on three consecutive days, he surprised everyone by participating in Central Committee and cabinet meetings. But he had over-extended himself. Sverdlov secretly ordered Malkov to locate a suitable house in the country in which Lenin could recover. Malkov found a superb villa near Gorki, in the woods surrounding Moscow.

9Simon Wolin and Robert M. Slusser (eds.), *The Soviet Secret Police* (New York: Praeger, 1957), p. 5f.

10M. Y. Latsis (Sudrabs), *Chrezvychainyye Komissii po borbye s kontr-revolyutsiyei,* Moscow, 1921, p. 8. On the testimony of Martov, the Cheka also took wives and children as hostages and frequently shot them (quoted from Shub, p. 326).

11Quoted from G. P. Maximoff, *The Guillotine at Work* (Chicago: Alexander Berkman Fund, 1940), p. 75ff.

It was almost a castle which formerly belonged to A. A. Reinbot, ex-governor of Moscow, whose wife was the widow of one of the Morozovs.[12] Krupskaya described it as "a fine house with verandas, a bathroom, and electric lighting, richly furnished and standing in an excellent park."[13] There even was a little lake.

Lenin moved to Gorki on September 24, and was put under the protection of ten Lettish "chekists." There was no telephone. Malkov served as courier between Sverdlov and Lenin, and Sverdlov visited Lenin frequently. Bonch-Bruyevich and Dzerzhinski also saw Lenin several times and Stalin visited upon his return from the civil war front. Lenin soon felt stronger and was eager to return to his home. His apartment in the Kremlin had been enlarged by one room and was being redecorated. Sverdlov gave orders to delay the work. Early in October Lenin wrote an article opposing Kautsky, and justifying terror. He asserted that terror had been forced upon the Bolsheviks, but this was untrue. Unlike Trotsky, he did not state that the guillotine "will be ready for our enemies" but on January 24, 1918, at the time when he was destroying the constituent assembly, he proclaimed: "When violence is exercised by the toilers . . . against the exploiters—then we are for it."[14] And on August 9, 1918, he ordered the soviet of Nizhni-Novgorod to institute mass terror.[15] He had been shot—but he had not yet reaped what he had sown.

[12]Probably the hapless Savva Morozov.

[13]Krupskaya, p. 484.

[14]*Selected Works,* Vol. VII, p. 269.

[15]*Sochineniya,* 4th ed., Vol. 35, p. 286. Compare also the seven subsequent telegrams, all of which advocate terror (pp. 287-293).

The World Revolution Aborts

Gradually Lenin became aware that he was deliberately being held in Gorki. He realized that the renovation of his apartment had been completed. Thereupon he simply ordered Malkov to transport him to the Kremlin. He returned to Moscow on October 22, but remained politically inactive for another two weeks.

During this period revolution gripped Austria-Hungary and Germany, but Lenin was not guiding operations; Sverdlov was handling most of the practical business. Lenin apparently trusted Sverdlov to a greater extent than anyone else, and Sverdlov undoubtedly kept Lenin informed. He had organized the Bolshevik government and, while the others were maneuvering in grand strategy, he was administering the state. Without Sverdlov the

Bolshevik government could not have survived. He accomplished most of the things for which Stalin later assumed credit. Though a competent administrator, he was a poor strategist.

The military situation with Germany had been developing auspiciously. In summer the German military wanted to overthrow the Bolsheviks but was overruled. In August a supplementary treaty was concluded between Russia and Germany which was designed primarily to pave the way toward economic cooperation. The Foreign Office, as Karl Helfferich, Mirbach's successor in Moscow, asserted, was deliberately disseminating pro-Bolshevik news, not only in Russia but in Germany as well. Helfferich resigned his post when he was unable to gain acceptance of an anti-Bolshevik policy. The military again pressed for the elimination of the Bolsheviks but a decisive defeat of the German army on the western front early in August deprived the Germans of this option. On August 11, 1918, before Lenin was shot, the Bolshevik Ambassador at Berlin, A. A. Joffe[1] (Trotsky's old friend), offered the Germans an alliance against the Cossacks and against the British at the Murmansk front. On August 30 the new German Foreign Secretary, Admiral Hintze, decided again to use the Bolsheviks for as long as they stayed in power in order to keep Russia relatively weak and to give Germany a free hand in the buffer zones of Eastern Europe. On September 9 Ludendorff was informed that Joffe wanted 200,000 Russian rifles, 500 million cartridges, and 20,000 machine guns for the civil war. But these negotiations were overtaken by events: the Germans presently started to withdraw on all fronts and their forces began to disintegrate.

Under the circumstances, the key strategic requirement for the world revolution would have been to establish close contact with the German and Austrian armies and to revolutionize them, an achievement which would have involved pressuring of the Austro-German forces, resuming fraternization propaganda on a large scale, and organizing large-scale desertion and mutiny. The German army in Russia was reduced to thirty-two divisions (including twelve divisions in the Ukraine) plus occupation detachments. Two-thirds of this force were second-rate reserve units composed of old soldiers. But the Bolsheviks were busy fighting a civil war in the east and their forces in the west were marauding. Trotsky was in charge of the army and supposedly was the chief strategic planner. But apparently no plan had been prepared for the contingency which now was arising and which had been predicted by Lenin when he had argued for acceptance of the Brest treaty. At a minimum, a command and

[1]At this time Hanecki and Krassin also were in Berlin negotiating about supplies to Russia. Hanecki was dealing with Parvus to get coal for Petrograd industries (Futrell, p. 193).

logistics structure could have been established and elite shock troops could have been deployed at key points. There was a possibility of creating international brigades from the prisoners of war, in accordance with earlier proposals. But no action had been undertaken.

On October 1, 1918, the convalescing Lenin wrote to Sverdlov that the revolution in Germany was progressing rapidly. The world revolution had to be reckoned with "as an event of the nearest days."[2] Yet the Communists were lagging behind. Hence, a considerably intensified effort was needed in order to prepare food and other reserves for Russia and the German workers. An army of three million troops should be established by spring to assist the international workers' revolution. Lenin asked Sverdlov to send a car: he wished to discuss the problem with the Central Committee.

The Central Committee meeting took place on October 3, 1918, but Lenin did not attend. The speech which he had prepared was read, telegraphed to all corners of the world, and published in *Pravda*. Lenin repeated his points. The task of the Russian proletariat was to aid the German proletariat. Yet, incongruously, he added that he was not contemplating canceling the Brest treaty at a moment when "the anti-imperialist elements inside Germany are fermenting." There is no record that the Communist government came to a decision even faintly resembling the program outlined by Lenin. In a speech delivered on October 22 to the Central Executive Committee, the Moscow soviet, and the miners—in his first public address after the *attentat*—Lenin reversed himself and, by implication, *stopped* all attempts to help the German revolution.

Lenin's change of policy seems extreme. On November 5, he is said to have attended Malinovsky's trial, which is doubtful. (It is certain, however, that many leading Bolsheviks were taking precious time from the world revolution effort to exact their price of vengeance from the alleged sinner who had come to repent.) Lenin talked about the Austrian revolution and delivered eight speeches commemorating the first anniversary of his own revolution. But above all, he was quite concerned with completing a long book he was writing to criticize Kautsky. Circumstances provided the long awaited opportunity to carry the world revolution forward into Europe; yet Lenin was back at his old hobby of engaging in polemics. He urgently needed to preserve his strength. Lenin probably felt a compulsion to defend terrorism, but he could have helped the revolution in a more constructive manner.

For example, it would have been a wiser course, at that crucial moment, to be reconciled with Kautsky rather than to attack him. The German Social Democrats had taken over the government, and Kautsky had been appointed as Undersecretary for Foreign Affairs.

[2]*Werke*, Vol. 35, p. 340.

At the price of democratic concessions in internal policies, Lenin easily could have achieved a mutual defense arrangement with Germany. The Bolsheviks anticipated a Franco-British attack. For a while, some Moscow Bolsheviks did entertain the idea that Germany and Russia should join in mutual defense and continue the war against the West. There exists no evidence indicating that Lenin himself pushed this concept or that he even seriously considered the matter. Yet, this was precisely the type of problem the self-appointed leader of the world revolution should have been analyzing at that time.

According to Krupskaya, the first anniversary of the Bolshevik revolution, which coincided with the German revolution, provided the happiest days in Lenin's life.[3] If he was euphoric, his elation did not lead to action.

On November 13 he is supposed to have "organized" the liberation of the Ukraine. The truth is that the German and Austrian armies were withdrawing and that Bolshevik local bands were taking over—spontaneously in most instances—areas that had been evacuated. Lenin merely established a Ukrainian command and, for the remainder of the year, intermittently considered military problems. He was too weak to exert leadership. He returned to writing but was unable to conclude the literary project he had undertaken. He clearly was in the midst of a period of depression.

Besides seeking a *rapprochement* with the German socialist government, Lenin could have revitalized the concept of an international socialist conference or cooperated with the revolutionaries in Poland, the Baltic states, Austria-Hungary, and Germany. The Bolshevik envoy in Berlin paid small sums of money to the rather unlikely German "revolutionary" Oskar Cohn and to Emil Barth, who ran the revolutionary shop stewards. There was undoubtedly some help offered to a few leftist publications. These contributions to the German revolution represented mere window-dressing; not surprisingly, the effort was highly publicized and the amounts of money exaggerated. Envoy Joffe, a genuine revolutionary, was intent upon proving subsequently that he had done everything he could but that the Bolsheviks really had been too weak to accomplish anything. Joffe bought information from German officials and passed some of it on to socialists for speech-making and publication. The Germans accused him of having spent 105,000 marks for arms and ammunition; Joffe corrected this by saying he had given Barth several hundred thousand marks for this purpose.[4] But the mark of that time had

[3]Krupskaya, p. 489.

[4]Louis Fischer, *The Soviets in World Affairs* (Princeton: Princeton University Press, 1951), p. 75ff; James Bunyan, *Intervention, Civil War and Communism in Russia, April-December 1918, Documents and Materials* (Baltimore: Johns Hopkins Press, 1936), p. 156.

been devalued by at least half; at best this amount was insufficient to bring about an uprising even in Berlin alone. Joffe claimed that he put ten million marks at Cohn's disposal, the implication being that the money was transferred after Joffe was expelled on November 5;[5] Cohn, who was the lawyer of the Soviet embassy in Berlin, claimed that he received money to assist Russian prisoners of war in Germany.[6] The fact is that the German government confiscated twenty-two million marks of embassy money that had been desposited in the Mendelssohn bank to serve revolutionary purposes. This was an unlikely institution, for Mendelssohn had handled many financial transactions of the tsarist government and was closely affiliated with the Wilhelmstrasse.[7]

The German-Bolshevik cooperation, with respect to the revolutionizing of France and Italy, continued in a desultory fashion.[7] Shortly after coming to power, the Lenin government had allocated two million rubles for the purpose of fostering the world revolution. On December 28, 1917, Riezler reported that the money would be funneled through Stockholm but that Bolshevik propaganda would not be extensive. Efforts were made by the Germans to divert this sum for use in Western Europe, but there is doubt that the money ever left Russia. During the summer of 1918, the Germans discussed with the Bolsheviks in Switzerland the possibility of establishing an agency to stimulate a revolution in France; Berlin was reassured that the Bolsheviks considered the German revolution to be more remote. The talks took place through Peluso, who had international connections. In August, 1918, Shklovsky, who had returned from Russia, obviously through Germany, discussed the same problem. The Germans were

[5]The expulsion was officially motivated on the grounds that Joffe was getting vast amounts of revolutionary propaganda through the diplomatic pouch and was distributing these materials. One of the boxes of the diplomatic mail was "inadvertently" dropped (the porters had been trained in this operation) and conveniently revolutionary pamphlets came out. The fact, though, was that these materials had not been written in or dispatched from Russia but originated in Germany and were put into the broken box by the Germans themselves. (*See* Scheidemann, *op. cit.*, II, 252f; and Eric Waldman, *The Spartacist Uprising of 1919* [Milwaukee: Marquette University Press, 1958], p. 66.)

[6]The Germans wanted to send Cohn to Moscow to negotiate the repatriation of Russian prisoners. Thereupon Moscow announced, by radio, that Cohn was being given money to arm German left radicals. This announcement, of course, ended Cohn's mission. The purpose of this stratagem has never been determined but it illustrates the specious character of Soviet revolutionizing. Incidentally, the Russian prisoners of war, more than a million, constituted a potential revolutionary force, which Lenin neglected. (*See* Herbert Helbig, *Die Träger der Rapallo-Politik* [Göttingen; Vandenhoeck and Ruprecht, 1958], Ch. 2).

[7]According to some sort of evidence in German hands, Cohn was holding money which was to be transmitted to Radek for Bolshevik propaganda in France and England. See Otto-Ernst Schüddekopf, "Karl Radek in Berlin," *Archiv für Sozialgeschichte* (1962), II, 104.

willing to finance additional efforts against France. Buchholz (whose travels may or may not have taken him back to Russia) offered to act for the Germans as a liaison agent with key revolutionaries. But it is not certain that the conversations produced concrete results; time was running out anyway.

Shortly after November 12, 1918, Radek sent a radiogram from Moscow to Berlin suggesting a common struggle on the Rhine against the capitalist Entente.[8] In January, Buchholz and Inessa Armand traveled to France (ostensibly on a Red Cross mission) to investigate the chances of revolution. All this does not signify that Lenin was more serious about the French than about the German revolution, it simply suggests that potent reasons existed why the Bolsheviks were *not* found in the forefront of the German revolution.

Acknowledging that the German upheaval was the most important "link" of the world revolution, Lenin had based his strategy on the concept "that our intervention should not damage their revolution." In the only speech he made on the subject (October 22, 1918), he preached "caution"—and inaction.[9]

On December 5, after the German revolution had been underway for one month, Lenin sent Joffe, Bukharin, Rakovsky, and Radek to Berlin. The German government refused them admission and the revolutionizers went home. Only Radek smuggled himself through the lines, disguised as an Austrian prisoner of war but traveling under his real name. (Since Radek was most easily recognizable, this version is not very convincing. It is possible that the Germans permitted his entry.) Joffe had demonstrated recently his ineptness as an organizer of revolution, Bukharin was a theoretician and little else, and Rakovsky was vulnerable to German pressure—a fact of which Lenin hardly was ignorant.[10] This group, therefore, seemed most unsuited for making the German revolution a success.

By the end of December, Radek appeared in Germany to aid the revolutionaries. Despite his abilities and experience as a propagandist, he was unfit as an adviser. Radek was quite intellectual and his eccentricities kept him from achieving contact with a mass party; he lacked personal experience in the art of insurgency and he had been expelled from the German Social Democratic party, justly or not, for thievery.[11] Rosa Luxemburg, now the most prominent

[8] Emil Barth, *Aus der Werkstatt der deutschen Revolution* (Berlin: Hoffmann, 1920), p. 68.

[9] *Sochineniya*, 4th ed., Vol. 28, p. 108.

[10] In a telegram of November 16, 1917, sent by the Foreign Office and signed by von dem Bussche to its representative with the Emperor, it was stated about Rakovsky, "Previously he was in relations with us in Rumania and worked for us."

[11] Radek's name was Karl Sobelsohn. His pseudonym was formed from the Polish *Kradziez* for thief.

revolutionary in Germany, had opposed Radek in this unsavory affair and refused to accept Radek as a trustworthy co-revolutionizer. Radek was implicated in the German-Bolshevik deal and, while in Switzerland, was in contact with agents (*Verbindungsleute*) of German military intelligence.[12] He also helped the German Foreign Office to publish in the *Berner Tagwacht* its controlled leaks and trial balloons.

Lenin hardly overlooked these factors which made Radek unacceptable to the German revolutionaries. Radek may have been sent as a signal to the German military that Lenin had no serious intention of revolutionizing Germany. In his own memoirs, Radek recounted that before leaving for Germany he and Lenin talked.[13] He found that Lenin—now that "Germany is broken" and "the road of the Entente into Russia is free"—feared an Allied invasion of Russia. He wanted Radek to work in Germany, which he considered to be the enemy's rear, the enemy being France and Britain. The amazed Radek objected that the German revolution could hardly be developed as a diversionary attack. "Right," said Lenin, "I don't propose that you should force events."[14] Actually, Radek opposed the Spartacus uprising of January, 1919, and favored an alliance with Germany.

On February 12, 1919, Radek was arrested, a few weeks after the seizure of Luxemburg and Liebknecht. The military had ordered Luxemburg and Liebknecht to be shot "while trying to escape," and, subsequently, had Leo Jogiches shot; Radek's life was spared by another order.[15] On February 15, Moscow denied that papers had been taken from Radek which indicated that Russian troops would help Communist insurgents in Germany. Moscow stated that Russia was not planning an invasion.

Upon being arrested, Radek declared that the Paris government could now be relieved, for he had been attempting to transplant

[12]Schüddekopf, *loc. cit.*, p. 94.

[13]Karl Radek, "November—Eine kleine Seite aus meinen Erinnerungen," *Archiv für Sozialgeschichte* (1962), II, 125.

[14]*Ibid.*

[15]Wilhelm Pieck, later the Communist "president" of East Germany, was placed against a wall and was about to be shot. He requested to talk to the officer alone. This done, he was released with a letter of protection by the intelligence officer of the unit. The incident was investigated by German Communists in 1930 and the investigator, upon Pieck's request, was liquidated in 1936. (*See* Waldman, *op. cit.,* p. 195.) According to Captain Waldemar Pabst, whose unit arrested Liebknecht, Luxemburg and Pieck, the latter betrayed his comrades. He disclosed the secret quarters of the Communist leaders, the location of weapons depots, assembly areas, the warning organization, etc., and explained the content of his notebooks to Pabst. This information made it possible to suppress the Spartacist uprising. (*See* the interview with Pabst in *Der Spiegel* [April 18, 1962], p. 38f.).

bolshevism to France. Later Radek wrote a letter to the German Foreign Minister, socialist Hermann Müller, avowing that he had been critical of the German Communists because they failed during January, 1919, to demonstrate to the masses that seizure of power was unfeasible. Gradually, the German authorities were coming to understand the situation. Radek was given a large cell in Moabit prison and was assigned a secretary and permitted to conduct extensive political negotiations from jail. He was visited by former Foreign Secretary Hintze, future Foreign Minister Walter Rathenau, then a director of the German General Electric Company (A.E.G.) , a leading German publicist, a former Turkish premier, a former Turkish War Minister, many German Communists, and other politically active persons. After a while Radek was transferred to the apartment of a German baron who was a "national Bolshevik" and a friend of General Ludendorff. There he also conferred with Colonel Max Bauer, who had been Ludendorff's operational planner and who during the 1920's tried to undo Germany's defeat through political warfare. In all the unusual undertakings (strange if it had been Radek's task to revolutionize Germany, but not if the intention was to ally bolshevism with Germany) , he was given the services of a liaison officer who managed Radek's business through the general staff to which he had ready access. That officer was Karl Moor![16]

Early in 1919 Lenin sporadically looked after military matters related to the civil war. He gave some attention to the food problem and he again began an article which he left unfinished. The assassination of Rosa Luxemburg and Karl Liebknecht in Germany prompted him to write a speech of less than ten lines. Lenin asserted that democracy was a system of violence and implied that the German Social Democrats were responsible for the murders—a deliberate and multiple lie. Ignoring his own role of terrorist, he ended with "death to the executioners!"

Shortly before Lenin spoke on the assassination of Luxemburg and Liebknecht, he himself was almost murdered. Krupskaya had suffered a serious health relapse and was in a sanatorium at Sokolniki. Christmas (according to the Old Style calendar) was

---

[16]Ruth Fischer, *Stalin und der deutsche Kommunismus*, p. 251f. The general staff issued fake passes to Radek's visitors. *See also* Radek's biographical remarks about Moor in "November," (*loc. cit.*, p. 152). Radek stated that Moor kept him informed about activities in Russia and had good contacts with German Social Democrats (who were in power) and the German military, among whom he had many relatives. Radek stated that Moor was a member of the First International. He also asserted that Moor's parents had died before the war and left him a considerable inheritance which, Radek implied, allowed him to help the Bolsheviks. Radek said that before this inheritance, Moor was poor. Since Moor was born in 1850, it is a little unlikely that his parents lived that long. In any event, Moor took Austrian pittances in 1917. The inheritance story presumably was a cover for German funds.

approaching. Bonch-Bruyevich took presents to the children at the sanatorium. Accompanied by a bodyguard and Gil, his chauffeur, Lenin and his sister Maria were driving there to celebrate Christmas.[17] Their car was held up by bandits. Lenin, who carried no money, surrendered his coat but kept the milk bottle he was taking to his wife. He also lost his revolver. It is not clear what happened to the presents. The bandits took the automobile and drove away. Suddenly they realized who their victim was and turned around to kill Lenin. But he had prudently disappeared from the road.

Rosa Luxemburg rated a solemn and serious funeral oration. She was one of the foremost socialist brains, an accomplished leader, and a genuine martyr. But she also was a severe critic. She wrote:

> Freedom only for the supporters of the government, only for the members of one party—however numerous they may be (even the proverbial 'fifty-one per cent')—is no freedom at all. Freedom is always and exclusively freedom for the one who thinks differently.

> Socialism . . . cannot be introduced by ukase.

> With the repression of political life . . . the Soviets also must become more and more crippled. Without general elections, without unrestricted freedom of press and assembly, without a free struggle of opinions, life dies out in every public institution. . . . Only the bureaucracy remains as the active element . . . a dictatorship . . . not of the proletariat but only of a handful of politicians.[18]

Lenin was not familiar with these words but he was aware of her attitude: had he acknowledged her criticism, he could have taken advantage of the situation that emerged after the end of hostilities to move toward normalization, democracy, and freedom. Many catastrophes would have been avoided by routing the "experiment" into constructive paths. Unlike Luxemburg, Lenin suspected that socialism was an artificial system incapable of functioning under freedom and democracy. But Luxemburg saw more clearly than Lenin that dictatorship and bureaucratic tyranny would not produce socialism, much less the emancipation of the "wage slaves."

> The tacit assumption underlying . . . the dictatorship is this: that the socialist transformation is something for which a ready-made formula lies completed in the pockets of the revolutionary party, which needs only to be applied energetically. This is . . . not the case. Far from being a sum of ready-made prescriptions . . . the practical realization of socialism . . . is something which lies completely hidden in the mists of the future. . . . Our program is

[17]Krupskaya alleged that Lenin visited her "almost every evening, in most cases with Maria." It is more likely that he only came for the holiday.

[18]For a slightly different translation by Bertram D. Wolfe, *see* Rosa Luxemburg, *The Russian Revolution* (New York: Workers Age Publishers, 1940), p. 45ff.

nothing but a few signposts and . . . indications . . . mainly negative in character.[19]

Luxemburg concluded that only the "creative force" of free
political life would allow the socialists "step by step . . . to feel out
the ground, try out, experiment, test now one way, now another"
and in this way to build socialism. "The negative, the tearing down"
(e.g., expropriation) "can be decreed; the build-up, the positive,
cannot."

Lenin did not grasp this point. The psychology of a combative
dogmatist prevented him from having the insight to acknowledge
that power must have a purpose beyond its realization. The worst
aspect was that by establishing his personal dictatorship, Lenin had
eliminated (with a few exceptions) those socialists who could have
provided effective and creative leadership. Now, at a time when he
could have derived maximum advantage from his personal power
and enormous prestige and could have established new goals, he
lacked ideas. Partially incapacitated, he was barely able to handle
routine tasks. He found nothing better to do but work on the party
program, and went into the exactly opposite direction from the one
which Luxemburg had proposed.

Early in 1919 revolution was stalking Eastern and Central Europe.
Unrest was prevalent everywhere, Communist parties were multi-
plying, socialists were gaining mass support, governments were
being overthrown, and new governments installed. Zinovyev predicted that within a year Europe would be communistic, and the
"struggle for communism would spread to America and perhaps Asia
and the other continents."[20]

Energetic Communist leadership unquestionably could have
advanced the revolution. Belatedly, Lenin called for the establishment
of the Communist International. This organization should have been
functioning six months earlier and should have been designed to
effect an international united front of all activist socialists. According
to the testimony of an honest and knowledgeable revolutionary, this
operation was a farce, designed to bluff through the motions of
revolution but to do nothing to progress it.

On March 2, 1919, the First Congress of the Communist International was held in Moscow. Lenin made a speech on each of the
four days and wrote an article. It was a dismal affair: most of the
representatives were either Russians speaking for foreign countries or
foreign nationals living in Russia.[21] The German representative,

---

19*Ibid.*

20"Perspektivy proletarskoi revolyutsii", *Kommunisticheski Internatsional,* No. 1,
1919, p. 42.

21For a vivid description of the founding of the Comintern, *see* Angelica Balabanova,
Lenin (Hannover: Verlag fuer Literatur und Zeitgeschehen, 1959), pp. 70-75, 87.

Hugo Eberlein, followed Luxemburg's concept that the establishment of the International was premature or even unnecessary; he did not sign the founding charter. The most impressive work of the enterprise was an enormous world-wide propaganda effort. Lenin appointed Zinovyev president of the Comintern. Though an agitator of great abilities, Zinovyev possessed a cyclic temperament, vacillating between enthusiasm and depression, energy and inactivity. He was devoid of willpower. Lenin, who knew him well, said, "If he is not afraid, it only means that there is nothing to be afraid of." Lenin deliberately put the Comintern into the hands of a coward who could be expected to do little more than "bark."[22]

Early in March, Mark T. Yelizarov, Lenin's brother-in-law and the most stable element of the family, died in Petrograd. Upon returning from the burial, Lenin received a second cruel blow: Sverdlov had caught pneumonia while speaking at Orel but refused to be nursed. He died suddenly on March 17. Sverdlov had been the "indispensable man." In his funeral speech, Lenin hailed him as the true organizer of the soviet power. With the only Bolshevik he really trusted dead, the physically weakened Lenin was alone.

Strange forces were already at work. Stassova recorded that the documents of Sverdlov's office (including the files of the Central Committee from March, 1917, to March, 1918) were transferred to the Moscow party center. Most of these papers were lost without trace.[23]

Between March 18 and 23, a party congress met. Lenin spoke on military matters and agriculture. For the first time he voiced a doubt, when he asked if food production really could be boosted through violence.

The congress revamped the higher party organization. The position which Sverdlov had occupied was assumed by a newly established political bureau. This decision-making body was supplemented by an organizational bureau which was to execute orders, allocate forces, and control activities on all party levels. Stalin was assigned to both organizations and thus, in reality, became Sverdlov's successor. Lenin did not return to the practical activity in which he had been engaged before the *attentat* but concentrated on formulating policy and defining strategy. The conduct of civil war, notably in the Ukraine, demanded most of his attention.

As the Austrian-Hungarian army retreated, they took with them former prisoners of war who had in Russia become Communists. Some of the prisoners had been given specialized training, and on March 21 a detachment of repatriated soldiers seized power in

[22]Compare *ibid.*, pp. 76-85.

[23]Yelena D. Stassova, *Stranitsi Zhizni i Borby* (Moscow, 1957), p. 102.

Hungary. In Rumania, the Bolsheviks were less successful, but they too stirred up trouble. Bavaria had been governed by a radical regime since November, 1918, and gradually was moving toward the left: on April 4, a Bavarian Soviet Republic was established in which, however, the local Bolshevik party did not participate. This radical seizure of power in Bavaria had occurred more or less spontaneously, with the anarchist Erich Muehsam proclaiming a socialist republic. Zinovyev boasted that the Third International had three "Soviet Republics" which would constitute its "main basis." With respect to Bavaria, which was run by three highly impractical *littérateurs* —two of whom were anarchists—this statement was highly optimistic. Their socialist republic was a farce, but when effective counter-moves did occur, the Communists took control through three party intellectuals who seized power.[24] The men were Russian Jews who had studied in Germany and had become naturalized citizens. At least one of these men knew Lenin, but they were not orthodox Leninists. Communist power in Bavaria and Hungary was in jeopardy. The situation urgently required remedies, but Lenin was not ready to move. Perhaps there was nothing that could be done for either claimant; but it is quite possible that a decent method of disengagement might have been found.

Lenin asked the Hungarians to guarantee that their government was Communist and not a "socialist-treacherous" government; that it was committed to the dictatorship of the proletariat. He queried the Bavarians about their agrarian program and about their "nationality" policy.[25] (There were no national minorities in the country: Lenin had lived in Munich, yet seems to have had absorbed little knowledge about the country.)

On April 29 Lenin greeted the Bavarian Soviet Republic, asking if it had yet established workers' and servants' councils, armed the workers and disarmed the bourgeoisie, confiscated stores, expropriated agrarian ownership, doubled and tripled the wages of rural and unskilled workers, taken control of paper and printing shops in order to propagandize the masses, introduced the six-hour day together with an obligation to work for two to three hours on public works, restricted the bourgeoisie to less living space and moved workers into rich apartments, confiscated all banks, taken

---

[24]The style of the government was indicated by a telegram which its "foreign minister" sent to Moscow. Among other things the minister "asserted that his predecessor had taken away the key to the toilet", he talked about "hairy hands of gorilla dripping with blood," and added: "We want peace forever. Immanuel Kant, *On Lasting Peace, 1795,* Theses 2 to 5." It is unlikely that the Kremlin bothered to look up the reference. This "minister" was a Dr. Lipp, probably one of the agents through whom Radek was in touch with German military intelligence during World War I.

[25]Helmut Neubauer, *Muenchen und Moskau 1918-1919* (Munich: Isar, 1958), p. 56.

members of the bourgeois as hostages, increased the workers' food
rations to the detriment of the bourgeoisie, mobilized the workers
"to the last man" for defense, and carried propaganda to the
villages.26 This formidable list provided a most explicit action program, but Lenin's government would itself have been unable to
follow it through. The program was totally inapplicable in Bavaria.
Lenin might have wanted the Bavarians to set a radical Communist
example before being destroyed, or he was perhaps seeking a pretext
so he would not have to intervene. Lenin apparently misread the
situation, for on May 1 he praised the Bavarian "working class" for
having liberated itself, after the first soviet republic in Germany had
already been destroyed.

It is painfully obvious that Lenin did not know what he was
doing. References in soviet military dispatches indicate that some
time before May 7, 1919, and perhaps as early as April 1, an order was
communicated to the Red army to attack in the direction of Buda-
pest. Another fact, one usually forgotten, is that on May 18, Russia
declared that a state of war existed with Rumania.

But the revolution directed at Hungary from without was as
ineffective as the revolution in Bavaria from within: the latter was
left in the lurch. The attack army, which was partly composed of
Hungarians recruited in Russia, began to pillage, encountering
popular resistance even before it crossed the borders. The anti-
Bolshevik army operating in the Don basin created a diversion and
the Communist forces which were preparing to invade Rumania and
Hungary had to turn back.

By the end of May failure was apparent. Except for composing a
few articles and telegrams and writing a report warning against
espionage, Lenin faded from the picture. Stalin did not even bother
to advise him of military developments. Lenin sent strongly worded
telegrams requesting that he be kept informed at least twice a
week,27 but he was unable to exercise command effectively. On
August 1, the government of Hungary resigned. The leading Communists fled to Vienna where they were interned in the local insane
asylum for about a year. In 1920 they were permitted to go to Russia,
where they were given governmental and party jobs. Bela Kun, the
individual most involved, was later purged by Stalin. Matyas Rakosi
became a Stalinist and one of the chief perpetrators of the Hungarian
tragedy of 1956.

Sobered by the Hungarian failure, Lenin told Italian socialists

26*Ibid.*, p. 74f.

27*Werke*, Vol. 35, p. 368, also compare p. 356.

that they should avoid premature revolutionary risings.[28] A revolution in Italy would be a tragedy: it would endanger the security of the Bolshevik regime. Yet he accused the Italian Communist leader who acted on this warning of being a traitor; at one point, the Communist press even asserted that this man was a spy in the pay of the Italian government. The image of the relentless revolutionary movement had to be preserved at all costs.

The policy of deemphasizing the invasion of Europe was a realistic one. But in the opinion of Trotsky, who still was posing as chief strategic planner, the revolution could be pressed in Asia. India, for example, could be invaded by an expeditionary cavalry corps. On August 5, 1919, Trotsky suggested that strategy be reoriented on the concept that the route to Paris and London might pass through Kabul, Calcutta, and Bombay. History did not conform to the Marxist predictions, but seemed "to be unwinding her skein from the other end." This "Eastern orientation," which in a more primitive formulation had been preached by Stalin, became very significant later. At that time it largely provided a theoretical excuse to shelve the "Western orientation."

[28]Ruth Fischer (*op. cit.*, p. 141) makes the not unreasonable point that the well organized and powerful socialist parties of Austria and Italy might have helped Hungary; and thus a Central European revolution might have begun. But no leadership was forthcoming from Moscow. The undercutting of the Italian socialist party contributed much to the emergence of Mussolini.

The Polish War

Lenin delivered a long speech on July 4, 1919. A week later he spoke at the University of Sverdlovsk, at which place he appeared again on August 29. On both occasions he discussed, of all timely subjects, the theory of the state. Otherwise, he made several routine speeches, wrote a few articles, leaving one uncompleted, and apparently went on vacation late in July. He stayed away during most of August and September and did not return until October. In the fall, he began work on a book which he never finished. Krupskaya confirmed that he was in poor health.[1] Late in 1919 Lenin engaged in polemics with foreign newspapermen, criticized the activities of foreign revolutionary parties, carried out ceremonial functions, and was involved in numerous minor affairs. Petitions were brought to him and he often redressed injustices by sending sharp or solicitous telegrams. Like the Tsar had done before him, he was particularly

[1]Krupskaya, p. 534.

punctilious about addressing military recruits. The year drew to a close with the customary speech celebrating the anniversary of the revolution, a talk to a congress of Eastern people, and an appearance before a party conference.

Lenin was increasingly becoming an icon. Nominally head of government, Lenin acted as if he were propaganda minister and chief inspirator. His contact with actual affairs was sporadic. Nevertheless, the major decisions of the Bolshevik government were made by him or in accordance with his instructions. He formulated policies that others were instructed to implement; yet, he had no way of checking on the results. By necessity the dictator lived in a vacuum which only freedom of the press could fill.[2] The political practitioners, headed by Stalin, carefully insulated Lenin from reality.[3] Lenin was too clever not to sense what was being done. Yet he could do little more than try to prevent his underlings from acting contrary to his wishes.

Early in 1920 the military position had improved. The threat to Petrograd (which at one point had been very serious) had been beaten back, the forces of the White (i.e., anti-Red) group in Siberia were crippled and, progress was considerable on the southern front. Lenin, believing that a more constructive policy was in order, lectured his comrades on administration, the evils of bureaucracy, and the advisability of decreasing terroristic methods. Following the suggestions of his old friend, G. M. Krzhizhanovsky, Lenin proposed the electrification of the country as a major step toward socialism. In a first break with classical Communist economics, industrial workers were offered premium payments for better and faster work. Lenin also dealt with transport and oil questions, and in March he ordered his troops to hasten the conquest of Baku. Upon the intercession of Gorky, Lenin provided starving scientists with better food and equipment.

Lenin was now effectively running affairs. His fiftieth birthday marked the zenith of his career. His work capacity was so great that, despite his enormous schedule, he completed an entire book. In *Left Radicalism, an Infantile Disease,* he argued that a revolutionary must know how to use any and all means, but that Bolsheviks must learn to make better use of indirect means and of the parliamentary institutions of their enemies. The book's ink still was wet when Lenin resorted to open and direct means.

During 1919 there had occurred desultory fighting between

[2]Myasnikov wrote two articles arguing that in a dictatorship, abuse and error can be avoided only by free criticism and debate, which required freedom of the press. Lenin countered that freedom of the press meant suicide for the Bolshevik regime; therefore Myasnikov's proposals would not be accepted. (*Werke*, Vol. 32, pp. 528-533).

[3]See, for example, the dialogue in *Werke*, Vol. 33, p. 309.

Bolshevik and Polish forces. The Poles were, to some extent, supported by the French. In November the two belligerents secretly concluded a cease-fire agreement. The Poles notified the Soviets that they would not cross a certain demarcation line. Led by Pilsudski, the Poles informed the Kremlin that they did not want a "White" victory over the Bolsheviks. Pilsudski miscalculated that a "White" government would be highly nationalistic and, hence, would threaten Polish independence more than would the Bolsheviks. The Poles did not attack when General Yudenich and his Bolshevik forces were four miles from Petrograd and General Denikin was approaching Orel. If the Poles had struck, they probably would have defeated the Bolsheviks. Continuous Polish inactivity enabled the Bolsheviks to regroup their forces and expel their opponents from the Ukraine.

However, it proved difficult to advance from this tacit and secret truce to a formal peace treaty. On January 22, 1920, Trotsky informed the Politbureau that Pilsudski was preparing to resume hostilities. Whether this was a personal judgment or an intelligence evaluation is not known. In any event, on March 11, 1920, Lenin ordered his military forces to group near the Polish front.

On April 25, the Poles launched a full-scale offensive and were able to take Kiev on May 7. The attack was described as an aggression but it probably represented a genuinely preventive operation since Polish intelligence had reported that a Bolshevik attack on Poland was impending. It is entirely possible that both sides misinterpreted each other's intentions.

There is evidence, however, which suggests that Lenin had formulated ambitious plans. First, the Bolsheviks were discussing openly the doctrine of the revolution from the outside.[4] Secondly, by February, they were making strenuous efforts to improve the railroads in the west and had mobilized numerous party members for transport work. Thirdly, a Cossack congress in Moscow (which Lenin addressed) passed a resolution calling for action against Poland and opposition to Wrangel, who was the commander of the residual "White" army on the Crimean. Fourthly, the Bolsheviks did not respond to a Polish peace offer, but instead made evasive counter-offers. Fifthly, Lenin had made speeches on March 1, 6, and 29 in which he warned of a presumed danger of war with Poland. He argued that Poland was in the throes of internal crisis and that Germany was experiencing a revolutionary upsurge. He prophesied that if Poland did engage in a conflict, the country would be defeated and "rotten capitalism and imperialism would fall down." He urged, "Try it, you will be taught a lesson you'll never forget." Talking vaguely about a Soviet Republic in Poland, he asserted that

[4]Compare my *A Century of Conflict*, pp. 110-114.

the Soviet Republic of Russia "never had such a chance of victory as now."[5]

It was necessary to build morale. The traditional holiday of May 1 fell on a Saturday and this year was declared a "Communist Saturday"—a day of collective work to complete an overdue job of cleaning litter left from the war and uprisings. Lenin decided to aid in the clearing of an area littered with wooden and metal debris. Krupskaya and Maria tried to dissuade him, but he spent four hours carrying wooden posts. Alexandra M. Syssoyeva,[6] Lenin's servant, proceeded to the area to observe her master at work. Presumably this exhibition (his presence was duly noted by his co-workers and the numerous bystanders) took place near the Kremlin. When Lenin returned home, his shirt was thoroughly moist with sweat and the sole of one shoe was torn.

After the Poles had attacked, the main Soviet army was launched in the direction of East Prussia and the Vistula estuary. Its principal goal was the invasion of Germany. The conquest of Poland was entrusted to two weaker columns. The Bolsheviks announced that it was their objective to cause a proletarian victory in Poland, Hungary, and Germany. They claimed that the first phase of the war was to be national in character. The second phase was to be a German and Hungarian war of liberation in which, Karl Radek explained, "the national and socialist aims would be fused." On May 5, Trotsky exclaimed, "We move vigorously toward the West, to meet the European proletariat which knows that we can join it only on the body of White Poland, in a free and independent Poland of workers and peasants."[7] Lenin later commented, "If Poland had become Soviet . . . the international system (established by the Versailles treaty) would have collapsed."[8]

Lenin was busy organizing the hinterland, speaking to soldiers, and writing instructions on psychological warfare and on the purchase of war materials abroad. Following a sabotage wave—including the destruction of an artillery depot in Moscow—terror was reinstituted. Lenin's responsibilities ranged far and wide. The food

[5]*Sochineniya*, 4th ed., Vol. 31, p. 251.

[6]Syssoyeva was employed in 1908 by the Ulyanovs till Maria went abroad. She later worked for the Krzhizhanovskys from whom she was borrowed when Lenin journeyed to Gorki to recover. She went back to the Krzhizhanovskys but joined the Lenins on January 24, 1919, and stayed with them till June 10, 1923. Sania, (as she was called) claimed that she ran the household. Krupskaya's reference to Zhuravlyova (see below) would seem to indicate that there may have been two servants. It is known that two servant girls were on duty between March and June, 1923; Syssoyeva and Evdokia M. Smirnova remained with the family till 1927.

[7]Trotsky, *Kak vooruzhalas revolyutsiya*, Vol. II, book 2, (Moscow, 1924), p. 116.

[8]*Sochineniya*, 4th ed., Vol. 31, p. 251.

supply situation embraced the whole gamut of raw material needs; his concern for railroads fused with worries about oil and motorization; the housing shortages demanded his attention; and difficulties in arms production compelled him to undertake a thorough study of industrial management. As Lenin's awareness of the role of science and technology rapidly deepened, he issued instructions for the establishment of research institutes. Lenin's interest in international questions became more practical: his former belief, expressed a few years earlier in a conversation between him and Trotsky, had been that foreign policy consisted in issuing a few revolutionary proclamations and appeals, "and then close down the shop." Now, Lenin had to establish a political warfare machinery to prevent war supplies from being delivered to Poland. Considerable resources were used to organize transport workers' strikes in Europe.

By early July the Polish forces were being pushed back. British Foreign Secretary Lord Curzon proposed mediation. Most Bolshevik leaders, notably Trotsky, were willing to accept this proposal. Lenin, insisting upon revolutionary war, ordered a "furious speed-up of the offensive on Poland," an attack on Warsaw, and an invasion of the Polish corridor through Germany. Polish and German Communists warned him against optimistic assumptions, but Lenin's resolve was firm. He intended to revolutionize Poland and Germany, and to "probe Europe with the bayonet of the Red army."

As the offensive took shape, the Second Congress of the Communist International convened. The delegates were regaled with victory communiqués, most of which Zinovyev fabricated in order to create a suitable atmosphere. Lenin consented to this comedy and enthusiasm ran through the international Communist movement.

Actually, things were going badly. The southern army, led by Stalin as political commissar, was determined to fight its own war. Lenin asked Stalin to submit reports at least twice weekly,[9] but Stalin was so eager to win the laurels of victory for himself that he seldom replied. A little earlier, on March 31, 1920, Lenin had stated that "the Soviet socialist democracy is in no way inconsistent with the rule and dictatorship of one person. A dictator . . . sometimes will accomplish more by himself."[10] He added that this interpretation of the proletarian as a one-man dictatorship was approved by the Central Executive Committee on April 29, 1918. Hence it would have been the job of the dictator to coordinate strategy, to compose differences between army commanders and commissars, and to direct the overall war. But there existed no high command or central

[9]*Werke,* Vol. 31, p. 192. Incidentally, in an earlier telegram Lenin told Stalin he should answer by phone: "I am able to understand you well, if you speak distinctly" (*Werke,* Vol. 30, p. 365).

[10]*Sochineniya,* 4th ed., Vol. 30, p. 444.

staff to assist the dictator in controlling the field commanders. Trotsky, Commissar of War, contented himself with routine administration; Bonch-Bruyevich reported that even in war councils Trotsky often displayed his boredom by reading French novels, totally ignoring the debates until they related to him personally. Lenin obviously could not function effectively on the basis of merely two weekly reports, yet he did not understand the command problem and thus failed to establish a suitable system.

Suddenly, the two main Russian armies diverged. Lenin noted the gap, but, with his loose arrangements, could or would do nothing to correct it. He sent a note to E. M. Sklyanski who, though merely Trotsky's deputy, was in effect functioning as civilian commander-in-chief. The message read, "Warsaw must be taken within three to five days at any cost." Lenin had still another idea: he proposed to Sklyanski that an imaginary peasant guerrilla force be established, to operate as though they were anti-Bolshevik "green guerrillas." This force would advance "ten to twenty versts and summarily hang the kulaks, priests, landlords. The premium: 100,000 rubles for each one hanged."[11] Later, the blame for these murders was to be shifted to the opponents of Bolshevism. This plan was typical of the man. Yet treachery is not always useful.

The Poles, ably assisted by the French General Maxime Weygand, inflicted a resounding defeat on the Bolsheviks near Warsaw. By August 17 the Red army was in full retreat. The Polish and German "proletarians" had not allied themselves with the Bolsheviks, preferring national independence and democracy to communism. Politically, this was an even more devastating blow than the military defeat. The White armies under General Wrangel had been grimly holding a last beachhead and now broke from the Crimea and advanced toward the Russian industrial heartland. The Bolshevik forces were numerically vastly superior. The Red army, which numbered five million men, was regrouped hastily to defeat Wrangel. But the Polish "revolution from outside" had ended in disaster.

[11]August, 1920. Note in Lenin's handwriting, No. 565, in Trotsky Archive, Houghton Library, Cambridge, Mass.

The End of Love

For Lenin the shock was severe. He lapsed into almost complete passivity until early October except for a few minor appearances. At this point another tragedy hit him: Inessa Armand died.

The nature of his relations with Inessa after spring, 1917, is not known. No letters from Lenin to Inessa have been published for the period after March 31, 1917, and, of course, not a single letter from Inessa to Lenin has yet been released. The significance which must be attached to Inessa's relations with Safarov is uncertain.

Inessa had returned to Russia with the Lenins, but had settled in Moscow. After Lenin's move to Moscow, she became a member of the Moscow Executive Committee (i.e., the local government) and of the local economic council. She conducted the women's department of the Central Committee. According to some reports, she also was a member of the Central Executive Committee, the key organ of the government. There is no question but that she opposed Lenin's Brest policy. It was reported that she argued with him, signifying that the two were seeing each other. But late in 1918 she was leading an unhappy existence, clearly estranged from Lenin and neglecting herself.[1] There is no reference to any visit she might have paid Lenin after he was shot.

Early in 1919 Inessa was sent to Paris as a delegate of the Russian Red Cross. Some Red Cross business may have been transacted but she was sent mainly to report on the political situation. There was taking place a struggle between various French left groups, and Inessa reported about these dissensions. After her return, she wrote a brochure, began to edit the women's page in *Pravda,* participated in the founding and operations of the Comintern, and functioned as "chairman" of an international women's conference. Krupskaya reported that Inessa visited the Lenins frequently in the latter half of 1919. One of her daughters, on September 25, 1919, participated in a meeting at the Moscow party committee, at which a bomb was detonated by a left Social Revolutionary and anarchist group.[2] Lenin learned of this incident first from Inessa.[3] This same daughter also was active at the front. Krupskaya remembered that Inessa, with whom Lenin "liked to discuss the prospects of the movement,"[4] once brought her youngest daughter, Varya. A young girl at that time, Varya later became a staunch party member. Somewhat inconsistent with the assertion that Varya had come only "once," Krupskaya related that Lenin "used to indulge in day-dreaming in their presence; I remember how Varya's eyes used to sparkle."[5]

[1]Wolfe, "Lenin and Inessa Armand," p. 110.

[2]This terroristic act was due to the influence of the left Social Revolutionary Cherepanov but was condemned by the main body of the anarchists. Some of the terrorists later were pressed into Cheka service. Many anarchists were arrested as hostages. The Central Committee, with the deciding vote cast by Kamenev, resolved against wholesale shooting of these hostages. (Maximoff, *op. cit.,* p. 359.)

[3]Krupskaya, *op. cit.,* p. 507.

[4]Krupskaya, p. 539.

[5]Krupskaya, *op. cit.,* p. 539. Not too much should be read into this suggestive prose. Timewise, it is unlikely that Varya was Lenin's daughter. Krupskaya added in the

In the spring and summer of 1920, Inessa exhausted herself while preparing for the Second Comintern Congress.[6] As soon as the Congress was over, she and her son Andrei, who was also ill, went to Kizlovodsk, a favorite vacation spot in the North Caucasus. Though thoroughly exhausted and unable to sustain a conversation, she recovered soon in a sanatorium. As a result of Wrangel's advance, the Bolsheviks evacuated the area. Caught in the military turmoil, Inessa contracted cholera while passing through Vladikavkaz. She became ill on the train and died within a few days. She was buried on October 12, 1920, on Red Square in Moscow.

Though a chief of state may find it difficult to carry on a love affair secretly, Lenin had ample opportunity to see Inessa. He might have assigned her a bureau or apartment in the Kremlin, but he did not. Lenin spent many weeks away from Moscow in the countryside and used his car for weekend trips when he traveled incognito. There is an account by Lenin's chauffeur, Gil, who took great pains to describe Lenin as a "good husband," a "good family man," and a "good brother."[7] Lenin was accompanied by Krupskaya whenever she was well, but this was not often. Gil stressed Lenin's concern for Krupskaya's health and his visits to her when she was in the sanatorium, but he did not mention Inessa. Inessa's name usually was deleted from reports and later Communist histories also fail to mention her. Even her important role in the Comintern remains concealed.

Alexandra Kollontai, reminiscing about Inessa's "theses" to women's congresses, said that they were always fascinating and interesting. She added, "But we knew that they were inspired and edited by Lenin himself."[8] Kollontai was not referring to the 1915 conference, which she did not attend, but to the one held in 1920. This, of course, does not mean that the affair was continuing: Lenin could have remained "close" to her in a platonic sense. Yet during the last year-and-a-half of her life, she was again in the midst of work that was of prime importance to Lenin. The Central Committee hardly would have ordered Inessa to the Caucasus if she had been merely a minor staff worker of the Comintern. Lenin wrote a personal letter to Ordzhonikidse, his lieutenant in the Caucasus, and reminded

same breath that Lenin also talked in the kitchen where "by force of old habit he liked to have his meals," with the servant woman Olimpiada Zhuravlyova, mother of a woman writer and formerly office cleaner at *Pravda*. "Ilyich liked to talk with her about the future victories."

[6]This Congress was very carefully prepared by Lenin. See Branko Lazitch, *Lénine et la IIIe Internationale,* Neuchâtel, Baconnière, 1951, third part.

[7]S. K. Gil, *Shest let s V. I. Leninym* (Moscow, 1947), p. 70f. Compare Fofanova, *Pages from Lenin's Life,* p. 71.

[8]Balabanova made the same point (see Wolfe, p. 101).

him of his promise to ensure her first-rate treatment.[9] In this letter, Lenin provided Ordzhonikidse with a code sentence which he was to use in his reply—an indication that Lenin wished to conceal from the office his concern about Inessa. But it remains doubtful that the two had become "close" again. It seems that both were worrying about health and politics; the atmosphere was hardly conducive to love. Lenin was probably no longer interested in sexual relationships. But there is no doubt that Lenin still was deeply attached to Inessa; and if we accept the image which Krupskaya was trying to convey, the two rivals had become friends.[10]

There exists a description of Lenin's behavior during Inessa's burial. Lenin was suffering intensely, yet he tried to control himself

[9]Letter of August 18, 1920 in *Leninskii Sbornik*, Vol. XXXIV, (Moscow, 1945), p. 345f. On the previous day Lenin wrote a letter to the Administration of Sanatoria at the Caucasus: Inessa and her sick son "who are known to me personally" should be given all cooperation. (*Ibid.*, Vol. XXXV, p. 143).

[10]Balabanova believed that Inessa had a daughter by Lenin and that she married the German communist Hugo Eberlein (who participated in the first Comintern conference, later became a Comintern official and ultimately was purged by Stalin). Wolfe disputed, quite correctly, that Inessa had a daughter by Lenin (p. 112) and stated: "When Inessa died, the Ulyanovs adopted her daughter, Inna, and took her to live with them. It was at Lenin's home that Eberlein met Inna Armand." This version does not appear to be entirely accurate. 1. At the time of Inessa's death, Inna must have been around twenty and may have been even older; hence she scarcely would have been adopted. 2. Inessa's youngest child was a son Andrei, born approximately in 1903 (Inna Armand, "Inès Armand", p. 76). 3. Her youngest daughter was Varya (Krupskaya, p. 539), who therefore must have been born in 1902 or 1901, and who also was too old for adoption. Inna wrote, however, that after her mother's death the Lenins watched over the welfare of the three youngsters (I. A. Armand, "Poyezdka vo vkhatemas", in *V. I. Lenin o literaturye i iskusstvye* [Moscow, 1957], p. 620). Since Inna herself by that time already was married to Eberlein, or was to marry him presently, and since there seems to be no other reference to Lenin's interest in Andrei, Varya apparently was the object of Lenin's affections; this, indeed, is made clear by Krupskaya.

Thus, the question arises again whether Varya was Lenin's daughter. If so, Inna must have produced misleading information. For Varya to be fathered by Lenin either Lenin must have known Inessa by 1904-1905 or Varya must have been much younger and been born by 1911. The early meeting between Lenin and Inessa is not impossible but unlikely; if Inessa had given birth in 1906, she hardly would have involved herself in seditious activities leading to arrest and banishment in 1907. By contrast, if Varya had been born in 1911, Lenin would hardly have sent Inessa to do underground work in Russia in 1912. Moreover, it does appear that in 1920, Varya was considerably older than nine. Hence there is no likelihood that she was his daughter. In summary: none of the Armand children was adopted by the Lenins, and the daughter who was most closely integrated into the family, did not marry Eberlein.

During Lenin's lifetime, Inna's husband Eberlein enjoyed the confidence of the Kremlin and was one of the channels through which the Communist uprising in Germany during November, 1923, was financed with more than one million dollars: in the midst of the German inflation, this was an enormous sum. (See Ypsilon, *Pattern for World Revolution*, [Chicago: Ziff-Davis, 1947, pp. 68-75.] "Ypsilon" was the pseudonym of Johann Rindl and Julian Gumperz. However, these particular pages appear to be written by neither but are parts of an unpublished diary by Eberlein.)

and conceal his feelings. He hid his face beneath his hat so that his tears would not be seen. Hardly able to stand upright, he walked with closed eyes, unwilling to leave the coffin.[11] A man of Lenin's nature hardly would have acted as though he had lost his own will if his love for Inessa had been entirely a matter of the past. This is the only well-documented case of a deep emotion gripping Lenin.

Yet Lenin was a self-disciplined leader. As soon as the burial service was concluded, he returned to his work and approved a preliminary peace arrangement with Poland. Two days later he gave orders to crush the White forces on the Crimea. Perhaps in memory of the departed, he ordered an enormous artillery bombardment against General Wrangel's forces, which constituted the last of the White armies. The guerrillas of the anarchist Nestor Makhno, who had made a pact with the Bolsheviks, now opened the Isthmus of Perekop to the Red army. At this point, the Bolsheviks turned against them and executed most of the guerrilla leaders.[12] The officers of Wrangel's army were offered amnesty for which they were instructed to register; most of these officers were then executed by order of Bela Kun, the unsuccessful emulator of Lenin in Hungary. This orgy of blood and treachery marked the end of an epoch in Russian history. Soviet power, at long last, was firmly established.

[11]The description of the funeral, without identification of the deceased, is in Angelica Balabanova, *Lenin* (Hannover: Verlag für Literatur und Zeitgeschehen, 1959), p. 48ff. Kollontoi's account confirms Balabanova's description: "Lenin was unrecognizable. He walked with closed eyes; at every moment we thought he would collapse." (Wolfe, p. 113.)

[12]Maximoff, *op. cit.*, p. 124-129. Makhno was a significant factor in saving the Bolshevik regime from General Denikin's attack during 1919. *(Ibid.*, p. 110f.)

The Dogma Weakens

The unceasing wars, the tendency to solve problems by sheer force, and endless experimentation with "communism" had crippled the economy. Stringent food shortages resulted in the imposition of a "tax-in-kind" upon the peasants: agricultural produce, even seed, was confiscated. The famine, which affected about five million people, was aggravated both in the cities and the rural areas. Transport was in deplorable shape. Lenin, together with Trotsky, decided to "militarize" labor and establish "labor armies," as the *Communist Manifesto* had proposed. Lenin had envisaged in September, 1917, before coming to power, the imposition of state service and use of the labor book, first for the rich and eventually for the entire population.[1] Now, the transport industry was to be militarized; Trotsky was put in charge. Thus Trotsky, who still acted as Defense Commissar, became the most powerful man in the government. The slave-labor boss position did not, of course, increase Trotsky's popularity. The opposition toward him surfaced rapidly and furiously.

This opposition was secretly guided by Zinovyev. Trotsky hoped to reduce the power of the unions and eliminate them as "representatives" of the workers. The union leaders, together with Zinovyev, argued for greater democratization, including the free election of union officials. The deeper question being debated was whether the Communist government was to be responsive to the workers' needs or whether the workers were to be mere instruments of the government. Lenin struck a pose that was new for him: he acted as the great compromiser. Basically supporting Trotsky, he assigned an "educational" role to the unions and called upon them to serve as "transmission belt" between party and "masses." This meant that the unions, while *appearing* to act for the workers, were transformed into a tool of the dictatorship.

Yet Lenin was vaguely uneasy about his position. He now doubted the efficacy of force in economics and worried about the problems of bureaucracy. More than his comrades, he realized that Russia badly required foreign capital and technical assistance. He pressed for the wider availability of electricity, proposing the "electrification of all houses." To facilitate peace on *all* fronts, he adopted a general "line" that was relatively moderate.

The theories about the sudden upsurge of production under socialism, especially the expectation—as Lenin had set forth in *State and Revolution*—that the state would wither away, had been proved to be entirely unfounded. The notion that once socialism was constructed, any female cook—like Syssoyeva or Zhuravlyova— could administer the state, was a fairy tale. Lenin still was impressed by the class struggle, but he understood that, since the so-called bourgeoisie had been eliminated, the struggle really had become one of the "hard" revolutionists against the "faltering" and "wavering . . . elements of the toiling masses themselves." He dimly sensed that this conflict was harming the workers and the peasants. The "will of the majority," perhaps, did have some meaning.[2]

Lenin decided to write about these unexpected complications, but his effort was not completed. In his public speeches, Lenin still

[1]The idea was that terror could only break active resistance but could not eliminate passive resistance. Other means of compulsion considered by Lenin were the grain monopoly and the bread card. For a discussion of this program, *see* Maximoff, *op. cit.*, p. 45f.

[2]Compare *Werke*, Vol. 32, p. 218.

upheld the old arguments, with a few new tones which included a realization that a dictatorship does not constitute progress in statecraft if mistakes are defended and concealed and if incompetent and dishonest officials are retained in office.

On December 30 Lenin admitted for the first time, in a public speech, that he was extremely ill;[3] and on January 1, 1921, he went to Gorki to rest. But conditions were critical. Stalin was recuperating from an especially acute appendectomy and Trotsky, who had his own solution to practically all major policies, was quite inactive and concerned himself solely with military matters and literary work. Lenin wrote on January 19, "The party is sick."[4] He realized he could not risk being sick and returned several times to attend meetings.

At this juncture, Lenin made his peace with Maxim Gorky and investigated other approaches. Gorky convinced Lenin that he should finance Ivan Pavlov's physiological work[5] and persuaded him to put more emphasis on scientific endeavors.[6] Gorky gave Lenin a sober appraisal on how the dictatorship was building socialism. These conversations were in the nature of Lenin's great confession. His thinking changed after these meetings with Gorky. Lenin's personal librarian, Chuchanika M. Manuchariants, said that Lenin considered writing a treatise on the scientific organization of work.[7] The plan never matured.

Despite his physical handicaps, Lenin met with an educational commission for several days. He sensed the effectiveness of propaganda and agitation for destructive purposes but recognized that the construction of a well functioning society was dependent upon genuine education. He became highly solicitous about Gorky's personal well-being; Gorky used his position as a favorite to intercede on the behalf of persons who had been wronged.

---

[3]*Werke*, Vol. 32, p. 1.

[4]*Sochineniya*, 4th ed., Vol. 32, p. 23.

[5]*Werke*, Vol. 32, p. 56f. "Pavlov wrote to Lenin in 1922 and said that an account of the distressing conditions in Russia, he would like permission to leave Russia . . . Lenin wrote him a very considerate letter, saying that on account of Russia's need for scientists like him, it was impossible to give him that permission, but that he would assign to him the rations that were given to Communists at that time." In a letter of 1927 written to Stalin, Pavlov said "On account of the way that you are torturing, depraving, and demoralizing the intelligentsia, I am ashamed to be called a Russian." (Mary A. B. Brazier, ed., *The Central Nervous System and Behavior* [Washington: Josiah Macy Foundation, 1959], p. 183f.)

[6]*Werke*, Vol. 33, p. 346f, where Lenin emphasizes the great technical significance of radio and the potential of the new technology for propaganda and agitation. He recommended that an English invention for the secret transmittal of messages by radio should be bought because of its military significance.

[7]"Mon travail à la bibliothèque de Vladimir Ilitch," *Lénine tel qu'il fut*, Vol. II, p. 765.

In February union leaders established a "workers' opposition" which was led by Lenin's old comrades-in-arms Shlyapnikov and Kollontai. Encouraged by Zinovyev, they argued that, instead of bureaucratic management, organized workers should administer the economy through the unions; moreover, the workers should elect their representatives freely and the unions should approve major nominations in the economic bureaucracy. They contended that this arrangement would provide the party with mass support. Some of the oppositionists argued that the unions—not the party—should be considered as the "vanguard of the proletariat." In the Tenth Party Congress of March, 1921, Lenin opposed these uncomfortable arguments with a great deal of hairsplitting, but conceded that the Communists had not succeeded in convincing the broad masses.

At the beginning of February, 1921, in another "revolution from the outside," the Red army invaded Georgia, where the Bolsheviks had polled only three per cent of the vote. This time the attack was directed, not against a bourgeois, but against a Menshevik socialist government; on May 7, 1920, the Kremlin had reorganized by treaty the independence of the country.[8] It is said that this operation was undertaken on Stalin's demand. Yet Lenin, who was grooming Stalin for more important posts, approved the plan when it suddenly was presented to him as a *fait accompli*.

Zinovyev, in March, also entered the limelight: he and Bela Kun were attempting to foment a revolution in Germany. Zinovyev was completely ignorant of the German situation and, together with Lenin, had overriden the councils of prudence offered by German Communists. The error was extraordinary, and it revealed to the world the incompetence of the Comintern and of Lenin.

But there were further difficulties. Zinovyev had endeavored to get the Baltic fleet to side with him against Trotsky and, thus, had greatly weakened the party's influence among the sailors.[9] Zinovyev's Petrograd soviet, unwilling to act for the benefit of the people, was imposing such harsh economic regulations that martial law had to be established. Strikes erupted and strikers and demonstrators were dispersed by the Cheka. Mass arrests followed and Zinovyev decreed a lock-out at some factories: this meant starvation for many of the workers.

Though the Petrograd proletariat had been considered firmly in the Bolshevik camp, this unwarranted repression aroused resistance. The government feared that the unrest might cause national repercussions. (There had been a peasant rising in the Tambov area

[8]*Facts on Communism, The Soviet Union from Lenin to Khrushchev,* (Washington: Government Printing Office, 1960), Eighty-sixth Congress, 2nd Session, Committee on Un-American Activities, II, 114ff.

[9]Schapiro, *Origin, op. cit.,* p. 259.

during 1920 and there was now widespread unrest in the Ukraine.) Asian troops were dispatched to the city. Thereupon, the Kronstadt sailors, who were the actual instigators of the revolution, declared that they would support the Petrograd strikers. A provisional revolutionary committee, authentically composed of enlisted men of proletarian and peasant origin, was established on March 2. At least one-third of the Communists in the fleet supported the committee.

In view of the enormous prestige of the Kronstadt sailors, this was a devastating blow. In a resounding proclamation, the sailors affirmed that labor had not been transformed into joy as had been promised, but rather into a new form of slavery. They called for several changes: elections on a democratic basis with secret ballot, freedom of press and assembly, the liberation of all arrested revolutionaries, an end to one-party dictatorship, freedom of political action by all socialist and anarchist parties, the establishment of democratic socialism, the abolition of Communist control units in the army and factories, freedom of action by the peasants with regard to the land (this was to include the right to keep cattle but not the right to employ hired labor), freedom of production by artisans (again without the right to hire labor), and an end to terror. "The third revolution has begun in Kronstadt," the proclamation of March 1, 1921, stated. It was a pointed reminder that without the Kronstadt sailors the Bolsheviks never would have come to power and that the sailors were now supported by soldiers and workers.

The rebels asked that democratic freedoms be bestowed upon socialists only. They did not oppose the Communist party but objected to bureaucratic tyranny and careerism. They called for a revolution of a non-violent nature and accused the party of having thrown mud "on the beautiful idea of communism."

Led by Lenin, the government reacted ruthlessly. The country was told the lie that a French-supported tsarist officer, General Kozlovsky, had organized an uprising from Kronstadt.[10] Although there had been merely political action and not an uprising, large military forces were concentrated. Trotsky ordered that the island be assaulted across the ice, demanding that the Kronstadters surrender unconditionally. The peasant soldiers were induced to attack by promises that the forcible collection of grain would be discontinued and the farmers allowed to trade.

The Kronstadters proclaimed that they were fighting "for the genuine power of the laboring people, . . . the sanguinary Trotsky

---

[10]Lenin himself initiated the lie that the Kronstadt rebellion was incited by foreign intelligence services. (*See* Maximoff, *op. cit.*, p. 161ff.) The sailors who did not believe Zinovyev and Trotsky anyway had not expected that Lenin would associate himself with the hypocrisy in the party. (*See* Schapiro, *Origins, op. cit.*, p. 303 and Lenin, *Werke*, Vol. 32, p. 274ff.)

and the fat Zinovyev for the power of the party which betrayed communism." After a ferocious two-day bombardment, Kronstadt was occupied *on Lenin's order* (March 17). Bloody and cruel repression and a wholesale slaughter of honest socialists followed, in which perhaps as many as 18,000 persons were "liquidated."[11]

As a diversion (though contrary to all the rules of the art of uprising as formulated by Lenin), the German Communists were ordered to rise immediately.

While the Kronstadt rebellion still was critical, the Tenth Party Congress continued in session. Lenin admitted that "our state is a state with a bureaucratic perversion," but he rejected the argument that there should be greater "freedom of criticism."[12] Lenin participated in drafting a decree on the improvement of living standards, but still upheld the "tax-in-kind." He insisted on party unity in opposing both the "workers opposition" and the radical Bolsheviks. Lenin protected Trotsky from attacks by party hacks, which Zinovyev and Stalin stimulated. Lenin deliberately set a course based upon compromise: the party was to move along a middle road in order to remain together. To enforce this line, Lenin imposed a fateful decision: factions, and therefore genuine intra-party discussions, were outlawed.[13] By imposing party unity, Lenin was threatening deviant individuals or groups with punishment. Members of the Central Committee were faced with demotion and as an extreme measure, with expulsion from the party.[14] Lenin hoped that the measure would never be used,[15] but it was not in effect long before Lenin attempted to expel Shlyapnikov[16] and to silence Myasnikov for complaining that the jaws of the workers (and not of the bourgeoisie) were being cracked.

The resolution on party unity was adopted at a moment when about half of the delegates to the Congress had left to deal with the Kronstadt crisis. The vote which selected the new Central Com-

---

[11]Consult Robert Vincent Daniels, *The Conscience of the Revolution, Communist Opposition in the Soviet Union* (Cambridge: Harvard, 1960), p. 144.

[12]*Sochineniya*, 4th ed., Vol. 32, p. 171ff.

[13]*Werke*, Vol. 32, pp. 245-248.

[14]This provision was contained in article seven of Lenin's resolution which, however, stipulated that major penalties could be pronounced only by a plenary meeting of the Central Committee and of the Control Commission. The article was kept secret till January 17, 1924, and later served as the "legal" basis for Stalin's purges (*Werke*, Vol. 32, pp. 248 and 560).

[15]*Ibid.*, p. 263.

[16]Shlyapnikov later was to die (utterly exhausted and disappointed) a miserable death from exposure in a political isolator. During the purge trials he and other prisoners were put into an unheated cellar for mass punishment. Krylenko was in the neighboring bunk and survived a little longer. Shlyapnikov was one of the purest figures within the Bolshevik party.

mittee was rigged by the sending of a large percentage of the opposi-tionists to the front.[17] Trotsky lost ground against Zinovyev, whose role in provoking the Kronstadt incident was ignored. Stalin placed a number of his personal followers on the Central Committee and in the key positions of the enlarged and upgraded secretariat of the Central Committee. (The secretariat handled increasingly the daily business of party and government.)

The resolution did not create the dictatorship, for it already existed. But it did eliminate the remnants of creative political life within the party and established a structure which could be managed only through the unfettered dictatorship of a single man. Since Lenin suffered from his physical handicaps and was unsure about his succession he should have been more cautious.

Lenin was aware of the hollowness of these measures. The per-sonal crisis which he was undergoing can be discerned from his contradictory behavior. While he still was talking about the tax-in-kind, he took steps to alleviate the misery of the peasants. He wired instructions to Georgia requesting reconciliation instead of oppres-sion,[18] yet he still supported those who were ravaging the little country. For several weeks, there was fanfare about the re-emphasis of established policies and the search for new approaches, but harsh conditions could no longer be removed by arguments. The national income of Russia had been reduced to one-third of what it had been in 1913. Industrial production had declined by eighty per cent, coal production was down ninety per cent, and steel production was off ninety-five per cent. The famine was becoming still more acute, affecting some thirty-five million people (*Pravda,* on June 26, admitted twenty-five million). Food production was adequate chiefly in the Western Ukraine; in wide areas crops did not even cover seed requirements.[19] Lenin was struggling within himself, finally recog-nizing that policies had to be modified and that the alterations had to be profound.

[17]For details, *see* Schapiro, *Origins,* p. 319.

[18]*Werke,* Vol. 32, p. 328.

[19] H. H. Fisher, *The Famine in Soviet Russia 1919-1923* (New York: Macmillan, 1927), p. 501; *see also Facts on Communism,* II, 130ff.

On the Extreme Right Wing

In one speech after another, and often in harsh and hectic language, Lenin drew the lessons from past errors. The system of "war communism" had not been a "policy to implement the economic tasks of the proletariat,"[1] it was an improvisation to muddle through a difficult time. When the communists came to power, they had no "economic system," nor an "economic plan of policy" to offer.[2] Enormous stupidities have been committed.[3] The peasants and the workers are dissatisfied with the proletarian dictatorship, and they are right, because their needs are not being satisfied.[4] Communists have proved unable to solve the problems of economics.[5] "Oblomovs" are to be found all over the society, and also among workers and party members.[6] The state apparatus is "miserable."[7] The proletarian dictatorship possesses enough power but it did not and does not use it properly—what it is lacking, is culture.[8] There is a great danger that the Oblomovs might defeat the Communists through cultural conquest.[9] No foundation existed as yet for the building of socialism.[10] There was no chance of an immediate transition to communism.[11] Without a big industry, socialism could not be established, certainly not in a peasant country like Russia.[12] There was no economic basis for the withering away of the state, and no withering away of economic inequality was taking place.[13] To move the economy in the proper direction, compulsion must be avoided.[14] "To want to build the communist society only with the hands of Communists is a childish, a very childish idea. The Communists are a drop in the sea, a drop in the sea of the people."[15]

All this, to be sure, was accompanied by protestations about the continuing validity of the creed and by professions of faith in ultimate

---

[1]*Werke,* Vol. 32, p. 355. This and all subsequent quotes from Lenin's *Werke* are from the 1961-1962 edition.

[2]*Werke,* Vol. 32, p. 298.

[3]*Werke,* Vol. 33, pp. 92f., 209, 414f.

[4]*Werke,* Vol. 32, pp. 177, 209.

[5]*Werke,* Vol. 33, p. 259.

[6]*Werke,* Vol. 33, p. 209. An "Oblomov," of course, is just the Russian version of "good old Adam." The Communists live with the illusion that in a communist society "discipline from the outside" will be replaced by "simple joy of work by normal socialized man." Hence, "compulsion in whatever form will disappear forever." (N. I. Bukharin, *Oekonomie der Transformationsperiode* [Hamburg: Hoym, 1922], p. 183.)

[7]*Werke,* Vol. 33, p. 288.

[8]*Werke,* Vol. 33, pp. 215, 274f.

[9]*Werke,* Vol. 33, p. 275.

[10]*Werke,* Vol. 33, pp. 260 and 289.

[11]*Werke,* Vol. 33, p. 49; this was precisely the point Krassin had made earlier.

[12]*Werke,* Vol. 32, p. 428.

[13]*Werke,* Vol. 32, p. 337.

[14]*Werke,* Vol. 33, p. 410.

[15]*Werke,* Vol. 33, p. 277.

victory. Lenin left no doubt that he intended to keep power,[16] and that he wanted the party to stay at the helm. He claimed that he merely was seeking practical solutions to practical difficulties. But how the solutions he proposed could be effective if the theoretical tenets of socialism were correct, Lenin did not explain.

Lenin proposed, at first in broad outline, a "new economic policy." What did he have in mind? First, he reformed the currency and returned to orthodox principles. He ordered that inflation be halted, budgeting and finances placed on a conservative basis, and interest-bearing bonds issued. Since it was of prime importance to rekindle commerce and trade, a hard ruble was established on the basis of gold; and gold was to be sold dearly and used to buy commodities cheaply.[17] "Why does it follow that the 'great, victorious, global' revolution can and should apply only revolutionary methods?" Revolutionary methods failed but their replacement by reform methods does not prove that the revolution as such was a mistake, Lenin added hastily.[18] N. N. Kutler, a foremost financial adviser to the Tsar, was assigned to establish monetary order.

Secondly, Lenin re-interpreted the tax to permit free trade.[19] Once the peasant delivered his quota, he was to be given the right "freely to exchange the remainder of his grain." Internal trade was to be stimulated to the point of "freedom of trade." Cost accounting, competition and individual initiative suddenly were re-emphasized as economic values, and the small peasants were allowed to return to capitalism.[20] Lenin added pointedly, "This freedom of exchange means freedom for capitalism."

The third change in policy was the most surprising. Lenin, to the stunned amazement of faithful Communists, proposed that foreign capitalist firms participate in, and profit from the development of Russian industry.[21] He argued forcefully[22] that Communists should learn from capitalists.[23] He proposed the adoption of a system of

[16]*Werke,* Vol. 33, p. 205.

[17]*Werke,* Vol. 33, p. 95.

[18]*Werke,* Vol. 33, p. 91f.

[19]Larin, not quite as "doctrinaire" as Lenin had accused him of being, had advocated a modified form of free trading with the villages late in 1918. Schapiro, *Origin,* p. 216.

[20]*Werke,* Vol. 32, p. 220f., vol. 33, p. 260.

[21]*Werke,* Vol. 32, pp. 130, 310-326.

[22]*Werke,* Vol. 32, p. 367, vol. 33, p. 261f.

[23]One lesson had been learned: Communist salaries no longer were spartan. Lenin's monthly income during that period was 13,500 rubles. To be sure, there was a great deal of inflation but, with free quarters and many free services, this was a substantial salary.

"state capitalism."[24] The new economic policy, he stated bluntly, signified "the transition to the restoration of capitalism to a considerable extent."[25] He capped all this by asserting that the new economic policy would have to be implemented "seriously and for a long time."[26] This implied that the destruction of capitalism had been a mistake. A generation earlier the detested Struve had called upon the socialists to go "to the school of capitalism." Now, at long last, he was vindicated.

Lenin's greatest disappointment was that it was practically impossible to find experts. "The Communists have become bureaucrats." He estimated that of 100 persons only one would qualify, but among Communists—"God willing"—only one out of 1000 has real know-how, he wrote to Sokolnikov in February 1922. This insight, however, did not prevent him from suggesting (on January 28, 1922) that French workers and peasants should be told that within three to five years they could become three times richer and work only six hours daily if there were a soviet government in France that would work for the electrification of the country. . . .

Lenin was now too incapacitated for sustained work.[27] He relied on his enormous willpower but was no longer able to run the government. Instead, he restricted himself to theoretical work. In a speech of July 5, he admitted that he had been too ill to prepare himself properly for the report he was to present.

On July 11, 1921, Lenin addressed, haltingly and with difficulty, the Third Comintern Congress. He opposed "left stupidities" and called for more flexible and "opportunistic" tactics, more thorough preparations, a closer coordination of the Communist world movement, the avoidance of risks, and patience and caution. Propaganda was to remain uncompromising and the retreat was to be tactical and temporary. Russia could hold out for five years or more; there was no reason to worry or fear that the Communists might be too late. Lenin promised that, as the masses were won over by these conciliatory tactics, victory on a world scale was certain and would occur perhaps in two to three months, perhaps in two to three years, or later. "We cannot come too late but we might begin too early." The masses must be conquered by a reasonable opportunistic and rightist policy. It was impossible to advance the "calendar of the revolution."[28] A few months later he confessed ruefully that on the third Comintern

[24]*Werke*, Vol. 32, pp. 237, 347, vol. 33, pp. 265, 296, 413.

[25]*Werke*, Vol. 33, p. 44f.

[26]*Werke*, Vol. 32, p. 450.

[27]*Werke*, Vol. 32, pp. 525, 537, vol. 33, pp. 237, 242, 260, 356.

[28]"Noviye dokumenty V. I. Lenina," *Voprosy Istorii KPSS, loc. cit.*, p. 17.

Congress he stood "on the extreme right wing" and was convinced that this was the only correct position.[29]

Ostensibly Lenin was teaching the tactics of retreat to foreign Communists. The discussion raged around the failure of Comintern strategy in Germany. Lenin defeated attempts to unseat Zinovyev and to penalize Kun but was adamant against the chief German critic, Paul Levi, who held such views as opposing violence in almost all forms, insisted that bolshevism was an Asiatic phenomenon, and objected to Russian political advisors whom he described as "Turkestanians." Klara Zetkin, Lenin's old comrade, supported Levi and permitted the German police to obtain documents that were incriminating to Comintern leadership. (These papers were taken from her at the border as she was going to the Congress.) Lenin again played his newly cast role of compromiser and pacifier, but the left wings of the various parties grew critical of him.[30]

Lenin's own realization of what was failing went deeper than an acknowledgement that the Communists had made mistakes. It went beyond an injunction to foreign comrades to admit mistakes so that they might attract the masses by overcoming their fear of communism. His own, still muted insight was displayed in a single sentence which was offered as a historical digression. "We are not Blanquists," he said, "we do not want to rule with a minority of the workers's class against the majority." But it was too late for Lenin to dismantle the dictatorship. A comrade suggested that the cabinet system be adopted. Lenin replied, "This man is finished forever."[31]

Still another grim reality was the failure of the Bolshevik regime to overcome the famine. No alternative remained and Lenin allowed Gorky and Patriarch Tikhon to ask for help. Gorky addressed himself on July 13 to "all honest European and American people for prompt aid to the Russian people. Give bread and medicine." Bolshevism suddenly rediscovered the values of honesty and humanitarianism—at least as a tactical expedient.

On August 2, 1921, Lenin himself signed an appeal asking for food. The famine, he admitted, "seems to be only a little less severe than the disaster of 1891."[32] Lenin's old hometown of Samara was also ravished by cholera. In other districts typhus was rampant. A famine, for which tsarism was responsible, had made Lenin a revolutionary. The present famine was caused by his own regime. Lenin realized that he had not discovered the panacea which he once believed had been revealed to him.

[29]*Werke*, Vol. 33, p. 192.

[30]Ruth Fischer, *op. cit.*, p. 216f.

[31]*Werke*, Vol. 33, p. 303.

[32]*Sochineniya*, 4th ed., Vol. 32, p. 477.

After making these enormous admissions to the Communist movement and the entire world, the exhausted Lenin departed for a vacation which lasted for over two months, except for attendance at one cabinet meeting and the writing of several short articles.

Lenin had formulated a new rationale by autumn. The proletariat had conquered "quite enough political power" and was holding it in order ultimately to achieve socialism. But capitalism had to be reintroduced to preserve the political system of communism. As the capitalists began to amass wealth, they could be taxed and the revenues could be invested in the socialist causes. Then, well managed firms owned by the state would prove their greater productivity. While capitalism was supporting the entire system, socialism would supplant capitalism step by step. Because state management, Lenin held, was intrinsically superior to private management, socialism was inevitable.

The interim capitalist system was not to consist of an entirely free market system. It was to be state capitalism wherein the entrepreneurs were to be restricted to small-scale production, trade, and agriculture. The production of goods which the Communist government deemed unnecessary was to be prohibited.

This was a reversal to the original Marxist postulate that socialism would be the successor to mature capitalism. Lenin had defended this line in his youth but had rejected it during and after the revolution when he adopted the populist thesis that direct transition to socialism, without the detour through capitalism, was feasible and desirable. Now he emphasized that industrialization and the transformation of psychology and habits were prerequisites to socialism. This would take time, not centuries perhaps, but decades and generations.[33]

This change was more than a mere reversal. Lenin grasped some of the advantages which a free enterprise system would possess over a state-controlled economy. He did not understand that the "classical" economics which he was rediscovering had general applicability; or, if he discerned this point, he did not admit it. But he realized that socialism was as yet unfeasible in Russia. He predicated the feasibility of socialism on a substantial raising of cultural levels of the entire country, at best a very protracted process.

Increased productivity, he maintained, must be obtained at all costs, but could be achieved only through "a partial reversion to the system of state capitalism." Lenin insisted on the necessity of personal incentive. So far the capitalists were able to supply commodities but the Communists were not. The capitalists were able to conduct business efficiently but the Communists were not. Capitalism's production costs were high, but Communist production was ten times more costly. He requested that the Communists learn the art of management from the capitalists and insisted that they must become capable of applying "commercial . . . [and] capitalist methods." "Only when you do that will you be able to build up the Communist republic." Communist administrators were lacking in administrative abilities.

The task no longer was "to break up the old social economic system, trade, small production, small proprietorship, capitalism, but to revive trade, small proprietorship, capitalism, while cautiously and gradually getting the upper hand over it or creating the possibility of subjecting it to state regulation only in proportion as it revives . . . . Compared with the previous revolutionary approach this is a reformist approach." The new task was to carry the bourgeois revolution to its culmination.[34]

Lenin decided that the Communists must help the peasants in overcoming ruin, impoverishment, and starvation; if not, the peasants would overthrow them. The achievement of a prosperous economy seemed more important than worrying about "remote socialist ideals." The new economic policy was to be "the application by . . . Communists of commercial methods, of capitalist methods."

Lenin realized that Communists were devoid of culture and, therefore, were being led by the bureaucracy. Lenin enjoined the party to fight against bureaucracy, bribery, "Communist vanity," and illiteracy. He claimed that political and military victories are not difficult to achieve, but that cultural progress is. Precisely this sort of victory was required as a prerequisite for the victory of socialism.

Lenin's opposition to bureaucracy can be traced to his youth when he and his family read the first *Iskra*. The newspaper was run by a friend of Chernishevsky and opposed bureaucracy and red tape as its prime target.[35] In *State and Revolution* and other pre-October writings, Lenin attacked "appointed officialdom," argued for the election and control of officials, and actually favored direct self-administration by the people. On April 12, 1919, in a decree signed by Kalinin, Stalin, and Lenin, it was stated: "The old bureaucracy has been destroyed but the bureaucrats remain . . . . The Soviet government . . . will not tolerate bureaucratism in any form . . . ." These were brave words. Lenin did not recognize the inconsistency inherent in enlarging on the one hand state power to the utmost and entrusting the state apparatus with the management of the economy, education, and practically all other affairs; and on the other hand in deploring the tyrannical impact of the state. He did not understand

---

[34]Speech of March 27, 1922, *Selected Works* (New York: International Publishers, 1943), IX, 324-369.

[35]Krupskaya, *op. cit.*, p. 521.

the near identity of state and bureaucracy; and aside from a few utopian notions, he proposed no measures through which bureaucracy could be improved.

Lenin wanted a purge of the party.[36] By now its members were almost exclusively bureaucrats and careerists: only two per cent of its membership had joined before the Tsar had fallen and less than one-third had held membership in November, 1917. Lenin now doubted that the proletariat was the chosen class. Not all factory workers are proletarians—some of them were just shirking military duty.[37] The proletariat had no longer a real economic base and therefore was weak, demoralized and in mental disarray; likewise, the "alliance" between workers and peasants, and even the proletarian dictatorship, lacked a proper economic base.[38] The proletariat which as a class might grow only slowly, may have ventured too far forward.[39] In fact, Lenin considered the Russian proletariat *déclassé.*[40] Lenin's disillusionment was so extreme that he doubted whether his government represented the proletariat. He wrote, "What do you describe as proletariat? That class of laborer which is employed in large-scale industry. But where is the large-scale industry? What sort of a proletariat is this? Where is the industry? Why is it idle?"[41] His old friend Shlyapnikov replied "Vladimir Ilyich said yesterday that the proletariat as a class in the Marxian sense did not exist. Permit me to congratulate you on being the vanguard of a non-existing class."[42] Some Communists became even more radical proponents of capitalism than Lenin himself. Stalin slyly suggested the restoration of land property to the richer peasants.

The doctrinaire revolutionaries were completely discomfitted because, unlike the socialist system which never had fulfilled its promises, the new economic policy dramatically produced progress rapidly and massively. Food reappeared as by magic (granted that much of it came from America), stores were cleaned and proper service was given; after years of deprivation people were able to purchase clothing and other necessities. There was even some entertainment available. The "old filth of former times" was returning—gambling, drunkenness,

---

[36]*Werke,* Vol. 32, p. 27, vol. 33, p. 19.

[37]*Werke,* Vol. 33, pp. 243, 286. What Marx wrote on the characteristics of the proletariat is correct for "capitalism as a whole" and for a "period of six hundred years . . . but does not apply to the Russia of today. Many of those who go into the factories are not proletarians but haphazard elements." (p. 286).

[38]*Werke,* Vol. 32, pp .430f., 443, 479, vol. 33, p. 3.

[39]*Werke,* Vol. 33, pp. 6 and 144.

[40]*Werke,* Vol. 32, p. 483, vol. 33, p. 50.

[41]*Werke,* Vol. 33, p. 158.

[42]N. N. Popova (ed.), *Protokoly syezdov i konferentsii vsyesoyusnoi kommunisticheskoi partii (b), XI syezd RKP (b),* (Moscow, 1936), p. 109.

prostitution, and a growing chasm between re-established classes. The "old believers" were shocked that "wealth" appeared again. They had a distorted perspective and failed to grasp that the new "capitalism," though weakened, was creating more than "filth." Supporters expressed fear that the proletarians would lose their faith in socialism. Certainly, replied Lenin, "If you can propose another road . . . ." But there was no other road.

Sickness and Terrorism

The strain on Lenin was enormous. Early in August, he had written Gorky about his sense of futility, adding, "I am so tired that I cannot do a thing."[1] In fact, he was reigning but not governing. He talked to people and sent notes to his ministers but the state was administered by others.

In November, Lenin interrupted his work several times and early in December wrote Gorky that he was "devilishly tired"[2] and suffering from insomnia. He vacationed and on December 16 requested, in accordance with his doctor's advice, that his leave be extended for two weeks. Yet he did not adhere to his own schedule and returned to Moscow to participate in a Soviet Congress. At this time, his severe headaches were almost incessant. Their extreme pain caused him to sit down, clasp his head with both hands, and remain immobile for many minutes. He also suffered from vertigo and was often forced to catch hold of objects to avoid falling. He believed that these were the first signs of his end and predicted that he would become paralyzed. Late in December he resumed his vacation but apparently did not go to his house located at Gorki but instead chose the village of Kostino because of its proximity to the Kremlin.

During these absences, Lenin showed himself to be the solicitous dictator. He cabled the Soviet envoy in Persia concerning the care of Varya Armand, Inessa's daughter, to send her back with an escort, and to supply her with warm clothes. He intervened with the Central Commission, which had expelled Nadjezhda S. Alleluyeva, Stalin's bride, claiming that he had personally observed her work as a secretary; moreover, her family hid him during July, 1917, and rendered the party excellent "conspiratorial services." Alleluyeva was reinstated and later committed suicide (or was murdered by Stalin himself). On January 9, 1922, Lenin asked that the village of Alakayevka be given bread and seeds. "Since I was personally acquainted with this village, I think it would be politically advisable

[1]Gorky, *Days with Lenin*, p. 52.
[2]Walter, p. 466.

if the peasants do not go back without having received some help."[2a]

During January, 1922, Lenin was only sporadically participating in affairs. He began to concern himself over the selection of his replacement. He believed the fiction that the Central Committee and the Politbureau were acting as collective decision-making bodies but without strong leadership were incapable of cohesive action. In the absence of Lenin the Politbureau proved itself to be especially weak. There seemed to be, he said, "absence of executive control." The directing bodies of the Communist state had been reduced by the bureaucratic machinery "into the scribbling of documents, the talking about decrees and the drafting of decrees, while vital work is being submerged in this morass of paper."[3] He wanted to get rid of all the paperwork and have the "good-for-nothing Soviet apparatus" supervised by good Communists. He thought about ways of dividing his own functions among several deputies. But Lenin failed to solve the succession problem.

By early February, the Central Committee ordered him to take a rest. Late in March he asked for another extension of his leave. However, he changed his mind. When the Eleventh Party Congress convened on March 27, Lenin appeared to deliver a long speech in which, with a great deal of verve, he expounded the philosophy of the new economic policy and the necessity of trading with the capitalist world. He confessed, in his speech, that during the past few months he had been unable to deal directly with affairs. He said that he visited Moscow rarely, stayed for only a short time, and did not attend the meetings of the government or the Central Committee. He added, "It is hardly likely that I shall return to work in the near future."[4]

This appearance was to be his last major one and the effort weakened him immensely. Actually, medical specialists brought from Germany were unable to diagnose any specific organic trouble. Lenin's condition worsened and he was forced to abandon the trip he had planned to Geneva where he was to have met the British Prime Minister. Instead, on April 16, the Bolsheviks concluded the Rapallo treaty with Germany. This treaty, through which they ended their diplomatic isolation, was in accord with the new tactics Lenin was advocating.

On April 2, 1922, Lenin appointed Stalin as the party's secretary-general. The secretary's function was to enforce decisions made by the Politbureau and the Central Committee and to strengthen discipline within the ranks.

[2a]*Leninskii Sbornik,* Vol. XXXV, p. 312.

[3]*Sochineniya,* 4th ed., Vol. 33, p. 171.

[4]*Werke,* Vol. 33, pp. 242, 260; Walter, p. 467.

Stalin was the only person to hold membership in the four decision-making bodies—the Central Committee, the Politbureau, the Orgbureau and the Secretariat.[5] Stalin also controlled the Commissariat of Nationalities and acted as the government's Inspector-General. Lenin created this new executive position to energize and rejuvenate the party's leadership. Stalin impressed Lenin as the most forceful among the younger leaders and, above all, one endowed with exceptional organizational and managerial talent.[6] Still, the choice was somewhat surprising, for Stalin never had been entirely loyal. Lenin apparently believed that Stalin took a neutral position between the contending forces and that therefore he could rely upon him. Probably, the thought never passed through his mind that a person like Stalin would himself eventually reach for supreme power. He assumed that Stalin would be like Sverdlov and serve as chief coordinating and executive officer and implement orders without questioning Lenin's authority. This appointment was *not* intended to coach Stalin into becoming the "dictator."

A week after Stalin's promotion, Lenin proposed that Trotsky be appointed deputy chairman of the Council of Peoples' Commissars. The two existing deputies were dealing with economic and administrative affairs. Trotsky would have become deputy in charge of political decisions. He disagreed with Lenin and the majority about several political and economic questions and declined the offer, alleging that this post did not provide him with real authority. According to the program that Lenin had prepared, power was to be vested in the party as a collective entity. But Trotsky's refusal placed the party in Stalin's hand.

On April 7, 1922, Lenin wrote to Ordzhonikidze complaining of continuing headaches. "My nerves are still hurting."[6a] At this time, Lenin was advised to have the bullet extracted which had been lodged in his shoulder since the attempted assassination in 1918. A German specialist, Professor Klemperer, believed that Lenin's troubles were the result of the two bullets poisoning his system. (There had been assertions that the bullets were coated with curare.) Other doctors demurred, but a compromise was reached: the bullet near the collarbone would be excised. Lenin entered the hospital and Dr. V. I. Sokolov transcribed the patient's medical history. He noted general nervousness, insomnia, headaches. "Specialists diagnosed neurasthenia due to overwork."[7] Surgery was performed

[5]Radek later was to joke about Marxist theory and practice: "From the Matriarchat through the Patriarchat to the Secretariat."
[6]Lenin thought Stalin highly qualified for the highest administrative posts and in particular believed him to be a good listener (*Werke*, Vol. 33, p. 301).
[6a]*Leninskii Sbornik*, Vol. XXXV, p. 344.
[7]V. A. Rozanov, "Iz vospominanii o Vladimire Ilyiche," *O Lenine, Vospominaniya* (*Moscow*, 1925), p. 131.

on April 23 at the Soldatski Hospital, by Professor Borchardt from Berlin, and Lenin returned to his home the next day. By the end of May the wound was healed. But this operation did not aid Lenin's condition. Lenin's headaches, insomnia, and bad moods continued. He wrote to the Caucasus to arrange for a rest, but rejected the proposed location as being "too high, requiring too much climbing for Krupskaya, and being unsuitable for sick nerves."[7a] On April 26, Lenin informed a foreign Communist by letter that he no longer was functioning as chairman of the Council of Peoples' Commissars.[7b]

It might have been expected that his illness and his new insights into the deficiencies of socialism would have moderated him. Instead he resumed his unnecessary struggle against the politically defunct Mensheviks. Increasingly more police and surveillance methods were instituted within the party, notably directed at Stalin's opponents in the higher party bodies. In February, 1922, a Finnish comrade was executed after a sham trial because his political line had induced a few other comrades to commit a terroristic act. The condemned man was not personally involved in this crime.[8] Lenin unquestionably was cognizant of the facts of this case. On March 27 he asked that the persons who publicly professed to be Mensheviks be shot. This hardly was a suitable method to establish a majority or democratic rule. Lenin, of course, always favored the death penalty. Immediately after the Bolsheviks came to power, Kamenev contrived the abrogation of the death penalty for deserters which a few weeks earlier had been reinstituted by Kerensky. This policy greatly upset Lenin. He questioned, "How can a revolution be made without executions?" and insisted that the "most drastic revolutionary terror" was needed. He acquiesced only when it was decided to retain the new decree to placate public opinion but to execute people anyway.[9]

On May 15 Lenin instructed the Commissar of Justice that, though Mensheviks and Social Revolutionaries were to be shot, occasionally a foreign exile might be substituted for the execution. The opponents should be indicted under "a formula that would place these activities in connection with the international bourgeoisie and her struggle against us (by bribery of the press and agents, war preparations, etc.)."[10] Two days later Lenin requested

---

[7a]*Leninskii Sbornik*, Vol. XXXV, p. 345.
[7b]*Leninskii Sbornik*, Vol. XXXVI, p. 476.
[8]Maximoff, *op. cit.*, p. 277f.
[9]Trotsky in *Pravda*, January 23, 1924, quoted from Maximoff, *op. cit.*, p. 30.
[10]*Facts on Communism*, II, 136ff. In 1908, Lenin conversed with a tsarist official. Lenin stated that if it were to cost thirty to forty million lives out of a population of 180 million, this sacrifice would be justified if it would get mankind closer to the goal of socialism. (W. K. von Korostowetz, *Neue Väter—Neue Söhne* (Berlin: Kultur-politik, 1926), p. 279).

that a paragraph be inserted into the criminal code explaining "the essence and justification of terror, its necessity, its limits. The court must not eliminate terror."[11]

Lenin's renewed interest in terrorism had been heightened when a show trial was staged against Social Revolutionaries during his absence early in 1922. The trial represented nothing more then an act of revenge against some of the foremost figures of revolution. Accusations were manufactured and false witnesses produced. Foreign socialists protested these illegal procedures and offered to serve as defense lawyers. To Lenin's great fury, Bukharin and Radek, perhaps with a view toward healing the socialist schism and reconciling the German socialists, promised that no death penalties would be imposed; yet twelve death verdicts and ten prison sentences were issued. Trotsky authored a compromise whereby the death sentences were pronounced but not carried out. The hapless victims of Bolshevik justice were held in prison or labor camps for about fifteen years and were killed during Stalin's purges. (Incidentally, most of the Bolsheviks who participated in this operation also perished at Stalin's hand.)

Although the show trial was organized without Lenin's participation, he opposed the leniency and bore the moral guilt for this scandal. In considering famines to be progressive and in favoring terrorism, Lenin remained within the revolutionary tradition. The Jacobin Jean-Baptiste Carrier cried, "We shall make a cemetery out of France rather than fail to regenerate her in our way." (Carrier was executed before this project was realized.) Marx also subscribed to the maxim, writing on November 7, 1848, "The cannibalism of the counter-revolution will convince the peoples that there is only one means in order to shorten, simplify, concentrate the murderous death pangs . . . of the old society, the bloody birth pangs of the new society, only one means—revolutionary terrorism."[12] But after the experiences of *his* revolution, Lenin should have known better.

The tonic of terror did not improve Lenin's health. He continued to deteriorate rapidly. On May 20 he left for Gorki and on May 26, 1922, he suffered a light stroke. He was attended by his family physician, Dr. Guetier, but Maria called five additional doctors, including their brother Dimitry. Lenin had stomach pains, vomitted, and suffered from excrutiating headaches. For about three weeks, his speech was impaired and his right arm and leg were partially paralyzed. During May, June, and July he suffered from periodic attacks lasting between thirty minutes and two hours. These left no permanent paralysis. When he recovered speech after his

[11]*Werke*, Vol. 33, p. 344; see also p. 205.

[12]Marx and Engels, *Werke*, Vol. 5, p. 457.

initial stroke, one of the first questions he asked his doctor was, "Tell me the truth, is this paralysis and will it progress?" The physicians could not tell him.

Lenin did not trust Communist doctors; he was also suspicious of Russian physicians. Professor Otfried Foerster, a foremost German neurologist, was called and attended Lenin throughout his illness. Foerster recalled that when he first visited his patient, Lenin was resting in a small, stuffy room and it took much effort to persuade him to move into a larger room with more air. Lenin often returned to this little room, even when he found it difficult to climb the stairs which led to it. Foerster noted that Lenin was drawn to this room whenever his affliction took a turn for the worse.

The accommodations at Gorki consisted of three houses. The largest house was inhabited by the Lenins, one of the small houses was fitted as a communal dining hall, and the third house was inhabited by A. A. Preobrazhensky, the manager of the estate. V. Zorin recounted that until 1921 Lenin lived in Preobrazhensky's house. He may have resided there when he came for short weekend visits, but the large house always was kept ready. It had been reserved for Lenin and since he had gone to Gorki for a long sojourn, it is most likely that he and his family had moved into the more spacious quarters. But he did occasionally return to the little room in the manager's house.[13] It seems peculiar that Lenin used the other house, inhabited by someone else. Perhaps he wanted to be separated from Krupskaya. But there probably were ample opportunities to humor this need in the big house. Probably he was drawn into the little dark room because he was suffering from agoraphobia.

In July, Lenin, in a fashion, was back on his feet. On July 11 he received his first visitor, Stalin. The next day he informed the Kremlin of this "recovery" and requested books. Stalin visited Lenin twice again in August. Early in September Lenin wrote a one-page article. On September 11, he telephoned Stalin and requested that the Politbureau again discuss the appointment of Trotsky as Deputy Chairman; but Trotsky had left Moscow. On September 14, Stalin, presumably with Lenin's approval, asked the Politbureau to censor Trotsky for dereliction of duty. On September 17, Lenin sent a letter saying "this is the first time since my illness that I am able to address a Congress even though in writing."[14]

The national question came up at this juncture (together with a painful toothache which was bothering Lenin in addition to his

---

[13]In addition to Foerster, the fact also it attested by Rozanov (*O Lenine, op. cit.,* pp.133, 205).

[14]Lenin, *Werke*, Vol. 33, p. 356.

other ills). Stalin strongly criticized the Georgian Bolsheviks. (Georgia had been invaded early in 1921.) On September 27, 1922, Lenin wrote to Kamenev that Stalin "is somewhat inclined to hurry" and voiced doubts that the Georgians were as guilty as Stalin had asserted. In commenting on this letter to the Politbureau, Stalin reversed roles and criticized Lenin for his "haste." Offensively he referred to the "national liberalism of comrade Lenin." To what was Stalin referring? Lenin, on March 2, 1921, had instructed Ordshonikidze to arrange for a compromise with Georgian Mensheviks and to grant substantial concessions to the petty bourgeoisie. He wanted a Georgian Red army[15] and proposed that retail trade not be nationalized but, to improve Georgia's economic situation, small trade be permitted. Special conditions made it mandatory *not* to apply the Russian model to Georgia. Stalin's policy was diametrically opposed to this concept and he now felt himself to be sufficiently strong to risk a confrontation. But Lenin was too weak to rebuke his rebellious subordinate.

On October 2, Lenin returned to Moscow and resumed his duties. He was ordered to adhere to a schedule of working only five hours during five days, but he nonetheless worked seven hours. After a few weeks he admitted that he had been forced to slow down considerably. When he learned that the Georgian Central Committee had resigned, he became increasingly apprehensive about Stalin. He still maintained good relations with him outwardly but wrote a letter to the Central Committee in which he said, "I am declaring war on Great Russian chauvinism, a war not for life but *for* death; as soon as I get rid of this accursed tooth of mine I shall use all my healthy ones to eat it up."[16] Lenin appointed a commission to investigate party problems in the Caucasus.[17] Actually, while he correctly sensed national oppression, he failed to notice that Stalin was quietly placing his own henchmen into party positions.

Lenin's long absences had alienated him from the Politbureau and the Central Committee. He opposed a decision on foreign trade which, in his judgment, would have reinstituted capitalism to a higher degree than he considered necessary. He was delighted that Trotsky agreed with him.

Lenin was relatively active through October and November. In one instance, he argued that socialism no longer was "an abstract

[15]*Ibid.*, p. 185.

[16]*Ibid.*, p. 358. He also proposed that the central executive committee be presided over *seriatim* by "a Russian, a Ukrainian, a Georgian, etc."

[17]On Lenin's struggle with Russian chauvinism and his last writings on the national question, see Richard Pipes, *The Formation of the Soviet Union, Communism and Nationalism 1917-1923* (Cambridge, Massachusetts: Harvard University Press, 1959).

picture or an icon."[18] On October 31, he delivered a most uninspired speech celebrating the conquest of Vladivostok. On November 13, he addressed the Fourth Comintern Congress. Speaking haltingly in German, and often losing command of the language, he ended prematurely after three-quarters of an hour when he became too weak to continue. In his speech Lenin attempted to compose the disputes in the German Communist party and criticized a Comintern resolution on the structure and methods of Communist parties as being too closely modeled after the Russian experience. The resolution was "too Russian" and therefore could sever the Communists from the "path to further progress." This comment startled both his Russian and non-Russian listeners.

On November 20, 1922, Lenin made his last public appearance. In his speech to the Moscow soviet he disclosed that he had delegated his duties to Tsurupa and Rykov, both Deputy Chairmen of the Council of Peoples' Commissars. But when both of them went to Germany for medical treatment, Kamenev assumed control. Lenin reiterated that socialism was not to be abandoned, but that the Communists had much to learn. In particular, they needed to learn how to calculate and to do business so that they could produce profitably.

> The masses, the whole population must test our road and be able to say, 'yes, this is better than the old system.' . . . The masses of the peasants and workers should be able to say 'you are not praising yourselves, we are praising you. We say that you have achieved the best results and not a single sensible person will ever dream of returning to the old system.' But this is not the case yet. That is why the new economic policy continues to be the principal, urgent, and all-embracing slogan of the present day. . . . Socialism is no longer a question of a distant future or of an abstract scheme or of a solemnly painted icon.[19]

A melancholy farewell of a revolutionary whose life had been dedicated to the icon of socialism.

[18]*Sochineniya*, 4th ed., Vol. 33, p. 405.
[19]*Werke*, Vol. 33, p. 428f.

The Testament

On November 25, 1922, Lenin's physician prescribed absolute rest for one week. It seems as though Lenin, too, expected his incapacitation to be only temporary. But he soon realized that he needed a long rest; he decided to undertake less work after a Politbureau meeting on December 7. He participated in a three-hour session of the conference and continued working afterwards. In the evening he left for Gorki. During the first half of December, he suffered repeated attacks which temporarily paralyzed his right extremities. Nevertheless, between December 7 and 12, he transacted business from Gorki by phone and drafted a speech to be made to the soviet.

In the few notes he managed to put down, he pointed out that the civil war had united the proletariat with the peasants and had educated and hardened all toilers. The enemies of communism were excellent teachers; the best workers had been those who had served in the army. Now that the war was over, economic build-up was the chief task.[1] This notion had cropped up in 1919 when, in a letter to Hungarian Communists, he stressed that the dictatorship of the proletariat consisted not just of violence, and not even primarily of violence, but of discipline and organization; its purpose was to achieve socialism and to put an end to the exploitation of man by man. But Lenin never acted vigorously on this concept.

The way in which to construct socialism, Lenin continued in his draft, was through the new economic policy. He felt that both external and internal trade would have to increase. Small industry was progressing, but heavy industry would be finding itself in the midst of difficulties. He continued to believe that the state apparatus was poor. The bureaucracy was so large that often the staff did not belong to the Communists—the Communists belonged to the apparatus. This thought preoccupied Lenin. For example, on December 9, he wrote to the Kremlin that it was of greater importance to improve the state than to lose time chatting with people.[2] Thus he proposed a rule to be adhered to strictly, "whereby each vice-chairman should spend no less than two hours weekly inspecting the most diverse parts of the apparatus, both in higher and lower levels, and the least expected ones at that."

The draft for the speech cautioned that Communists had remained on a cultural level lower than that attained by the bourgeoisie. It would require many years to develop the necessary cultural background. As Lenin now viewed the situation, the problem of building socialism was primarily one of cultural development.

At eleven in the morning of December 12, 1922, Lenin returned from Gorki to Moscow. He proceeded to his office at 11:15 A.M. but stayed only a short time. He returned to the office at noon and spent two hours talking with Rykov and Tsurupa. He went back to the office at 5:30 P.M. to make a few short phone calls and to give

[1] *Werke,* Vol. 36, p. 571f.

[2] On February 21, 1922, Lenin had a different pitch: "The state apparatus is dung. Decrees are dung. To look for people, to check the work—that is the point." (*Sochineniya,* 4th ed., Vol. 36, p. 549).

instructions regarding letters to Italian Communists. He was suspicious that the messages might not be sent.

Dzerzhinski came to see Lenin at 6:45 and apparently stayed for one hour. Then Lenin received the soviet trade representative from Berlin and discussed foreign trade with him for thirty minutes. At 8:15 Lenin went home. This was his last working day in his Kremlin office.

Lenin suffered two minor attacks on December 13. The doctors now insisted that he take a long rest. Lenin promised them that he would immediately put his affairs in order. After the doctors had left, Lenin dictated three letters. At 12:30 P.M. Stalin came and remained until 2:35 P.M. Lenin was dictating again by six that evening.

His activities on the following day are somewhat obscure. (The available information is contradictory.) It is certain that Lenin had some bad business with Stalin and did not know quite what to do. However, he was anxious "to plan the battle." He finally sent a letter to Stalin, with the apparent intention of later adding a postscript. At 10 P.M., Fotieva, Lenin's confidential secretary, was told that he would dictate that night.

On December 15 he dictated another letter to Stalin. He began dictating on the telephone at 8:30 P.M. but completed the dictation after he had called Fotieva to his flat. Lenin wrote that he had liquidated his affairs and could leave without worry. He wanted still to deliver the address which he had outlined. He asked that someone replace him as the main speaker and that time remain reserved for him; Lenin felt that he perhaps would be able to talk for about forty-five minutes.[3]

Lenin's condition worsened during the night of December 15: he suffered his second stroke. The attack lasted for more than thirty minutes. Yet the next morning he dictated another letter. The doctors did not arrive until 11 A.M. on the 16th—long after the seizure. The delay is extraordinary: doctors were on twenty-four hour duty in the Kremlin.[4] Did the family fail to call the physician, was the telephone out-of-order, or could the doctors not be found?

The doctors ordered rest. This stroke had permanently disabled Lenin's right arm and right leg. He was bedridden.

In the evening Krupskaya called the Secretariat and asked that Stalin be informed that Lenin would be unable to speak at the Soviet Congress. But Lenin could not travel to Gorki: the roads were impassable for automobiles and the sleigh was considered too tiring for him.

[3] *Werke*, Vol. 33, p. 446.

[4] On the delay of the doctor's arrival, see L. A. Fotieva, *Pages from Lenin's Life*, p. 165.

On December 23, the doctors allowed Lenin to dictate for five minutes. In the evening he dictated a four-minute letter to the soviet; he did not know what day of the month it was. On the following day he dictated for ten minutes. He repeatedly instructed Maria A. Volodicheva, one of his secretaries, to keep these materials confidential.

It seems that on December 23, Lenin dictated to Krupskaya a short letter addressed to Stalin which, one would presume, dealt with the national question and with Stalin's future role. Stalin directed "an unusually rude outburst" towards Krupskaya and threatened her with the control commission: apparently he was taking exception to Lenin's correspondence with him. Krupskaya wrote to Kamenev, "What one can and what one cannot discuss with Ilyich I know better than any doctor because I know what makes him nervous and what does not. In any case, I know better than Stalin." She asked Kamenev and Zinovyev to protect her from "rude interference . . . and vile invectives and low threats."[5] Yet it is likely that Krupskaya, to guard Lenin's health, did not immediately inform her husband of this quarrel.

On the same day (December 24), Stalin held a conference with the doctors. (The members of the Politbureau allegedly also participated, but this is doubtful.) It was decided that Lenin would be permitted to dictate for five to ten minutes daily but that he should not receive any replies. Visitors were forbidden and no political news was to be conveyed to him. But he was allowed to call in Fotieva and Volodicheva. Lenin may not have been informed of these arrangements, which, in effect, isolated him. That he was unhappy is clear, for on December 25 he dictated what has become known as his testament.[6]

It was a letter of advice on his succession, describing Stalin and Trotsky as the "two most able leaders." Trotsky was "the most able man in the present Central Committee" but he was too self-confident and overly impressed by administrative elements. Stalin "has concentrated enormous power in his hands and I am not sure that he always knows how to use that power with sufficient caution." Lenin emphasized that the party would have to avoid a split between Trotsky and Stalin. Lenin tried not to offend anyone, but he clearly ruled out Zinovyev and Kamenev as possible successors. He had encouraging words for two younger members of the Central Committee, G. L. Pyatakov and N. I. Bukharin, and designated the areas in which they needed improvement. By implication, Lenin antic-

---

[5]N. S. Khrushchev's *Secret Report* of February 24-25, 1956, in Bertram D. Wolfe, *Khrushchev and Stalin's Ghost* (New York: Praeger, 1957), p. 98.

[6]*Werke*, Vol. 36, pp. 577-582.

ipated that leadership would be shared between Stalin and Trotsky, but his misgivings were transparent.

Meanwhile, the Congress of the Soviet concerned itself with a crucial task: the creation of the Soviet Union as a so-called "federation of soviet republics." The chief promoter of this sham federation had been Stalin, whose project was adopted after a speech on December 26, in which he did not mention Lenin even once. The tenth All-Russian Congress of Soviets was transformed into the first Congress of the Soviets of the U.S.S.R., and on December 30, Stalin delivered a victory speech. He proclaimed that this was "the day of triumph of the new Russia over the old Russia, . . . the new Russia which has smashed the chains of national oppression." Pointedly adding that "we Communists are often abused and accused of being unable to build,"[7] the speaker hinted that he shared none of Lenin's worries. Stalin's assertions represented classical examples of what Lenin had called Communist lies and Communist vanity. Stalin was boasting about a subject, the national question, which was close to Lenin's heart and which had caused him special concern. Stalin's disrespect was blatant and deliberate.

On December 28, 1922, Lenin dictated for about twenty minutes and the next day was permitted to read. Krupskaya said that he read a book on the Revolution (which he did); but he probably also covered the Congress proceedings and examined Stalin's speech. He certainly realized its significance. On December 30 and 31, he dictated three notes on the national question.

The commission which Lenin had appointed to investigate the Caucasian situation exonerated the national policy which Stalin had imposed and which Ordzhonikidze was executing. However, Lenin spoke to one of the members of this commission, Felix Dzerzhinski. He learned that Ordzhonikidze, in a party discussion, had resorted to physical violence. This information distressed Lenin and increased his fears. "One can imagine the rut we have gotten into," he lamented.

On the night following the conversation with Dzerzhinski, Lenin had the two minor attacks. It is not known if he discussed the problem with Stalin on December 14; presumably he did and Stalin probably promised to reform his ways. Lenin subsequently conveyed his concern to Zinovyev. He now gathered his waning strength to write about the nationality problem, which worried him almost as much as did bureaucratic degeneration.

Lenin began by stating that he was guilty in the eyes of the Russian workers for not having intervened with sufficient energy and

[7]Stalin, *Works*, Vol. 5, p. 161.

incisiveness.[8] The "single apparatus" which was to emerge from the founding of the Soviet Union would be nothing more than a bourgeois-tsarist mechanism, "only barely anointed with the soviet chrism."[9] The right of secession would be merely a scrap of paper and the minorities would be subjected to the "scoundrel and violator which the typical Russian bureaucrat is." In all this, a fatal role was played by Stalin's anger, hastiness, and administrative practices.

On the next day (December 31), Lenin continued to dictate laboriously. He implied that Stalin was a "social chauvinist" and a crude and complacent imperialist who lacked caution and courtesy. Though the new union would have to be retained and strengthened, Lenin proposed that the constitution be reconsidered at the next Soviet Congress. Perhaps it would be necessary to turn back and "retain the Union of Socialist Soviet Republics only in the military and diplomatic spheres and in all other respects restore the full independence of the separate commissariats." This suggestion, of course, was not followed.

Lenin suggested that exemplary punishment be meted out to Ordzhonikidze. "Stalin and Dzerzhinski must be held politically responsible for this truly Great Russian nationalist campaign."

On January 4, 1923, Lenin deduced an eminently practical conclusion from these premises. In a postscript to his "testament," he proposed to replace Stalin as General Secretary with an individual "more patient, more loyal, more polite, and more attentive to comrades, less capricious, and less rude."[10] Lenin added that Stalin's removal was required to prevent a split "from the point of view of the relation between Stalin and Trotsky," a remark implying that he wanted Stalin to continue in a prominent party position and that he still considered him to be as important to the party as Trotsky, his rival. Lenin was torn between a vain hope for a *duumvirate* and the fear of a split. His cornered position made him unable to propose effective action beyond Stalin's demotion. The time it took for Lenin to oppose Stalin seems long: perhaps Krupskaya finally informed Lenin of Stalin's rudeness in December. Lenin's reaction was probably due both to Stalin's speech and Krupskaya's disclosures. He summed up his attitude by telling his wife that Stalin was lacking in "elementary honesty."

[8]Lenin's important notes on the nationality question were originally published by Pipes, *op. cit.*, They have now been released by Moscow. See *Werke*, Vol. 36, pp. 590-596. There are, however, differences in the various versions.

[9]*Werke*, Vol. 36, p. 591.

[10]*Werke*, Vol. 36, p. 580.

The Last Struggle

Lenin was not really on good terms with Trotsky. He had known him for twenty years and during most of this period had been quarreling with him. Lenin thought Trotsky flighty, arrogant, and ambitious. In turn, Trotsky had described Lenin, in 1912, as an intriguer, a disorganizer, and an exploiter of Russian backwardness.[1] Yet Lenin and Trotsky joined forces in 1917; without their alliance the October revolution never would have taken place.

After their union Trotsky regarded Lenin as a hero, professing a high opinion of his leadership abilities. Lenin relied on Trotsky as his chief strategist and organizer and, on the whole, provided him with unstinting support through the civil war. Lenin and Trotsky lived within the Kremlin in adjacent apartments and had joint dining and bathrooms. Lenin is said to have enjoyed playing with Trotsky's children. However, disagreements between them occurred during 1921 and 1922 and the friendship cooled perceptibly. Stalin fanned Lenin's basic animosity toward Trotsky. The contacts between the two men gradually decreased to a minimum.

A fundamental dispute arose over economic concepts. Trotsky conceived something like the NEP, the new economic policy, about a year before Lenin did, but he also favored the "militarization of labor." Lenin found it difficult to accept Trotsky's reasoning on this matter.

Trotsky promoted the "single" economic plan. This was the notion that the entire economy should be developed and managed from one bureaucratic center. But Lenin, on February 19, 1921, wrote to Krzhizhanovsky that such a plan would entail the possibility of over-bureaucratization. The "single plan" represented "bureaucratic utopia." Subsequently, Lenin criticized most of the 1918 nationalization decrees. Actually, he had disclosed on March 27, 1922, that the purpose of these decrees had been only to present to the workers and peasants the Bolshevik *ideas* of politics and to gain the confidence of the masses—the decrees which allegedly were designed to build socialism were no more than propaganda.[2] Lenin now insisted that electrification of the country, rather than a comprehensive plan, constituted the proper approach to the construction of socialism.[3]

[1]Isaac Deutscher, *The Prophet Armed, Trotsky: 1879-1921* (New York: Oxford, 1954), p. 232f.

[2]For a discussion of this point, see Maximoff, *op. cit.,* p. 27.

[3]Lenin was infatuated with electric power and between 1920 and early 1922 tried to press for the development of an electric plow. This venture was unsuccessful.

"Life pokes fun at plans." Warning against "bureaucratic illusions." Lenin advised running a minimum number of the most important plants, and merely to keep informed about the plants of secondary importance.[4] A plan is nothing but a "yardstick, a criterion, a lighthouse, a signpost."[5]

Lenin reexamined the planning concept during October and November, 1922, when he and Trotsky were in agreement on the foreign trade monopoly. He continued to hold reservations about Trotsky's notions.

Early in December, he summoned Trotsky to a private conference. Lenin invited his guest to join him in opposing the growth of bureaucracy and offered him the post of Vice-Premier. Trotsky hesitated. Reading Trotsky's mind, Lenin proposed to fight also against the organization bureau of the party; this, of course, implied Stalin. When Lenin went further and suggested the formation of a "bloc," Trotsky accepted. (Lenin apparently forgot that he had outlawed party "factions.") The details of the joint fight against bureaucracy were to be resolved later.

On December 15, Lenin, realizing that he was strongly opposed in the Politbureau, decided to carry the fight about the trade monopoly into the Soviet Congress. But the battle was unnecessary. The agreement between Lenin and Trotsky had become known and the opposition never got underway. On December 21, 1922 (with the German doctor's permission), Lenin dictated a letter to Trotsky: although they had captured the position without firing a shot, he proposed that they should not stop but continue the attack.

On December 27, Lenin notified the Politbureau that he had found common ground with Trotsky on state planning: they had agreed that the state planning commission was to become "a meeting center of the leading experts and representatives of science and technology." Lenin was willing to compromise with Trotsky and enlarge the functions of the planning commission, but it is apparent that in his mind the commission was to concern itself largely with modernization, rationalization, and the location of industry. This concept was compatible with the market concept characterizing the new economic policy and was very much unlike the "bureaucratic

[4] *Werke*, Vol. 32, p. 520f.

[5] *Ibid.*, p. 334. Bukharin who at first did not believe that planning posed any scientific problems, was in charge of elaborating a theory of planning. Bukharin sensed that a centrally planned economy needed a potent state; he argued that the state would nevertheless whither away, as classes disappeared, and that the planning administration would be purely functional in character. It can safely be said that Bukharin, though he went about this problem more systematically than Lenin, Trotsky and Krzhizhanovsky, proved unable to develop a coherent planning doctrine. (Compare Peter Knirsch, *Die ökonomischen Anschauungen Nikolaj I. Bucharins* [Berlin: Duncker und Humblot, 1959], pp. 220-225.)

utopia"[6] which Stalin established, years later, by vesting all major management decisions in a centralized administration.

After Lenin had secured his "bloc" with Trotsky, he penned his postscript to the "testament." After this, he was more firm in his resistance to Stalin. Lenin followed his habit of collecting a full dossier concerning his opponent. Yet work proceeded very slowly and there existed little documentation. With Lenin isolated from political life, it does not appear that Trotsky provided him with effective support.

It is likely that Stalin was informed, at least to some extent, of Lenin's plans. Since he did not know whether or when Lenin would return to office, Stalin acted cautiously, concentrating his attack on Trotsky: in the event of Lenin's recovery Stalin might have succeeded in splitting the two but if Lenin were not to recover, Stalin's attacks would have at least served to weaken Trotsky. Trotsky still refused to become vice-premier. He aroused the hostility of other Bolshevik leaders by foolishly proposing a reorganization which might have diminished their influence. His general behavior lent credence to Stalin's insinuations that he wished to succeed Lenin. Some of the other men (notably Zinovyev), had the same desire.

In his lonely struggle from his sickbed, Lenin was supported by three secretaries.[7] Lidya A. Fotieva, whom he had met in 1904, had been his most important aide since he had been installed in the Kremlin. There is a remote possibility that she was "close to him" in a personal sense. Lenin also was helped by two other assistants, Krupskaya and his sister Maria (who was a close friend of Fotieva). Maria seems to have been in charge of practical matters and gave all the orders in the household.

On January 24, 1923, Lenin instructed Fotieva, Maria I. Glyasser (Lenin's third secretary), and N. P. Gorbunov to collect and carefully study the data on the "Georgian question." Lenin said that he needed the analysis for the party congress; he did not know that the "Georgian question" had been placed on the Politbureau agenda. Why had he not acted earlier? The Caucasian question had been troublesome for many months. But there were good reasons for Lenin's hesitation: his own record in this area was not without blemish. He had advocated violation of self-determination in Georgia as early as 1917 and had countenanced the military invasion of that little socialist-ruled country in 1921. Apparently the invasion had been secretly prepared by Stalin, and Lenin had permitted him

[6]Compare Krzhizhanovsky "Lénine et le travail de planification", *Lénine tel qu'il fut,* Vol. II, pp. 737-744.

[7]Trotsky mentioned three. Krupskaya alleged that Lenin also dictated to Manucharaints, but this person was listed as Lenin's librarian.

this breach of discipline. Now the issue was really not so important: Stalin eliminated many of the Georgian Bolsheviks[8] and placed his own followers in power. (Stalin was, in fact, beginning to apply similar tactics in Russia.) Lenin's fury can be explained only by assuming that he sensed Stalin's intent to wreck the old party.[9] The Georgian Communists who opposed Stalin were saved by Lenin. (This rescue was only temporary, for Stalin killed all of them during 1936 and 1937 as members of a "Trotskyite center for spying, wrecking and terrorist activities."[10])

Three days later (January 27) Dzerzhinski told Fotieva that Stalin possessed the facts on the "Georgian question" but that he happened to be away from Moscow. On January 29, Stalin told Fotieva on the telephone that he could not give her the data without the permission of the Politbureau. "He asked me," Fotieva wrote, "if I was not telling Vladimir Ilyich more than I should, since he seemed to be well-informed about current matters. . . . I replied that I told Vladimir Ilyich nothing and had no reason to believe that he was fully informed on current matters."[11] Fotieva informed Lenin about this conversation. He said that he would insist on obtaining the materials. On February 1, the Politbureau agreed to give to Lenin the documents of the Georgian commission.

By that time Lenin's condition seemed to have improved. His color had returned, he was cheerful, and he dictated without pausing and searching for words. On February 2, he was able to dictate for forty-five minutes.

Lenin spoke to Fotieva for a few minutes on February 3. He requested further information concerning the Georgian affair. When told that the papers were less numerous than had been expected, Lenin wanted to know if the question was being discussed by the Politbureau. Fotieva replied that she was not permitted to say. "Have you been forbidden to speak to me about this particular matter?" Lenin asked. She answered that she was forbidden to speak to him about current events. When Lenin pressed Fotieva further, she disclosed that the Georgian commission had reported to the Politbureau and that, on the whole, the bureau had approved of the conclusions. As the doctors entered the room, Lenin concluded,

[8]Boris Souvarine, *Stalin* (New York: Alliance, 1939), pp. 203, 301 .

[9]Stalin apparently also was planning a resettlement of various Caucasian peoples but it is not known whether Lenin heard about this or would be concerned. *See* Artur Müller, *Die Sonne, die nicht aufging, Schuld und Schicksal Leo Trotzkis* (Stuttgart: Cotta, 1959), p. 256.

[10]Abdurakhman Avtorkhanov, *Stalin and the Soviet Communist Party* (New York: Praeger, 1959), p. 198.

[11]Fotieva, *Pages from Lenin's Life,* p. 181.

"Well, I believe you will give me your account in about three weeks from now, and then I shall write a letter."[12]

Lenin's condition continued to improve. On February 10, he ordered about a dozen books; most of them dealt with economics, but he also asked for Arthur Drews' *The Myth of Christ*. Dictation time was extended. He was allowed to exercise and was able to move his hand a bit. Elated by the prospect of better health, he laughed often and heartily. But occasionally he stumbled in the midst of his dictation, and his health varied daily. He insisted that the examination of the Georgian affair be completed soon.

In the meantime, he was filling his dossier on Stalin with incriminating materials. The nature of the accusations is unclear. The terror regime in Georgia hardly differed from the terror which Lenin had instituted in Russia. It is possible that the evidence indicated that the Georgians were replaced by too many Great Russians in the administration; this, however, was nothing new and had been condoned by Lenin for years on the grounds that the Russian-speaking element predominated within the party and the centralization of the state required working through Russians. But Lenin, for some time, had insisted upon moderation; this advice was not heeded.[13] Perhaps the data also showed that Stalin and Ordzhonikidze were settling personal accounts: both had made enemies during their early revolutionary career. Whatever the evidence, Lenin took particular pains writing a comparatively lengthy article on inspection. On this subject he had been collecting data for quite some time. Lenin judged that the Commissariat of Inspection was the worst in the entire Soviet government. Since Stalin had led this commissariat until recently, Lenin's sharp criticism would be recognized by every knowledgeable reader to be aimed directly at Stalin.

Toward the end of February, Lenin asked that the article be published in *Pravda*. Lenin knew his comrades well: he asked to be shown the issue carrying the piece. The Politbureau did not intend to oblige Lenin. Bukharin, who controlled the press and propaganda, was opposed and Stalin, Molotov, Rykov, and Kalinin supported him against Trotsky. Kuibyshev, one of Stalin's henchmen, proposed that a single issue of *Pravda* containing the article be printed to show to Lenin.[14] Kamenev, who had appeared late, agreed with Trotsky that an article by Lenin could not be kept from the party. Grudgingly, the Stalin faction accepted this view. Lenin recorrected the article on March 2 and it was sent to the printer.

---

[12]*Ibid.*, p. 183f.

[13]Schapiro, *Communist Party*, p. 223f.

[14]According to some data, Stalin later contrived the assassination of his friend Kuibyshev.

On March 3 Lenin's staff gave to him their memorandum on the Georgian question. Their findings are unknown; probably they rendered a soft verdict. But by now Lenin understood the meaning of Stalin's nefarious actions in Georgia.

On March 4, Lenin's article appeared in Pravda. It was an open signal that the campaign against Stalin was starting in earnest. Accordingly, on March 5, Lenin asked Trotsky "to undertake the defense of the Georgian affair. . . . It is now being 'persecuted' by Stalin and Dzerzhinski. . . . I cannot rely on their impartiality. Indeed, quite the contrary! If you would agree to undertake its defense I could rest easy."[15] Trotsky suggested bringing Kamenev into the fight but Lenin vetoed this because "Kamenev would show the letter to Stalin, and Stalin would make a rotten compromise in order then to deceive."[16]

Lenin's return to political activity heralded Stalin's end. Stalin understood this clearly, whether or not he had specific intelligence, and on March 5, he initiated a counteroffensive.[17] The nature of his thrust is seen in a note Lenin wrote to Stalin castigating him for rudely summoning Krupskaya to the telephone and harshly reprimanding her.

> I have no intention to forget so easily that which is being done against me and I need not stress here that I consider as directed against me that which is being done against my wife. I ask you, therefore, to weigh carefully whether you are agreeable to retracting your words and apologizing or whether you prefer to sever relations between us.[18]

On March 6, Lenin appended a sentence stating that he was breaking "all personal and comradely relations with Stalin."[19] He instructed Fotieva to hand the letter to Stalin personally and to bring back an answer. It seems that Stalin did not hurry. When his answer arrived, Lenin's health had drastically deteriorated. Lenin never read Stalin's reply[20] and it is not known if Stalin surrendered, or declared war on the crippled man. The document still remains unpublished. Krupskaya reportedly told Kamenev that Lenin "would never have ventured to break off personal relations, if he had not thought it necessary to crush Stalin politically."[21] Lenin's decision came too late.

[15]Leon Trotsky, *Stalin* (New York: Grosset and Dunlap, no date), p. 361.
[16]*Ibid.*, p. 362.
[17]During a session Stalin noted an exchange of communications between Glyasser and Trotsky. Glyasser had, for Lenin, summarized Trotsky's attitude on the national and Caucasian questions.
[18]Khrushchev in Wolfe, *Stalin's Ghost*, p. 100.
[19]Trotsky, *Stalin*, p. 375.
[20]Fotieva, p. 193.
[21]Trotsky, *Stalin*, p. 374.

Medical Crime?

On the same day, March 6, Lenin resolved upon strong action. He cabled the Georgian Bolsheviks, saying that he was outraged and that he supported them with all his heart. He added, "I am preparing for you notes and a speech."

On the same day Kamenev visited Trotsky. Kamenev surely knew of Lenin's rupture with Stalin for, according to Trotsky, he offered to mediate. Trotsky reassured him that Ordzhonikidze would not be punished. Trotsky added that he opposed the removal of Stalin, provided he would apologize to Krupskaya, stop persecuting the Georgians, and behave loyally. Trotsky took the opportunity to suggest to Kamenev that the opposition against himself (notably by Zinovyev and Stalin) was pointless, and suggested that Stalin select his words carefully if he wished to continue as General Secretary. Stalin, finding a way to save his career, was of course agreeable and for many months thereafter went out of his way to be polite to his opponent. In turn, Trotsky promised not to press the issue and, probably underrating Stalin, agreed that the entire dispute be dropped. He later "explained" this treachery against Lenin by asserting that he was then feeling unwell.[1]

In the meantime, Lenin had changed his mind about Kamenev and had asked that a copy of his Georgian telegram be sent to him. Fotieva on March 7 called on Trotsky, who lay in bed suffering from lumbago. The observer is impressed by the difficulties of communication between Lenin and Trotsky. They were now living in separate houses within the vast Kremlin compound, but it seems there would be a telephone. Lenin was forbidden by his doctors to use the telephone; presumably there was no instrument in his bedroom. But Trotsky could use one easily and could have talked with Krupskaya, Fotieva, and Glyasser. Apparently, the telephone was shunned deliberately: the two ostensibly most powerful rulers in Russia must have presumed that the line was being tapped by an organization which obeyed Stalin's orders.

Trotsky asked Fotieva why Lenin had changed his mind and why

[1]Trotsky frequently had debilitating fever bouts, sometimes aggravated by colds. For many years the diagnosis was uncertain and a tonsillectomy, in 1926, did not help. It also was determined that he suffered from colitis and podagra. (Artur Müller, *op. cit.*, p. 339). These afflictions did not, however, prevent him from going hunting. It is apparent that he was psychosomatically affected and that his passivity during the period of Lenin's last illness was due to a profound mental disturbance. Trotsky himself ascribed his illnesses to "nerves," adding, however, that "the physicians diagnosed an infection . . . in 1923. It is possible that . . . my 'nerves' . . . give such a wide range to the external manifestations of the illness" (*Diary*, p. 145).

he insisted on hurrying. He was told that Lenin was feeling worse and wanted to do everything he could. Fotieva added: "Ilyich does not trust Stalin. He wants to come out openly against him before the whole party. He is preparing a bombshell."[2]

The incidents of March 8 are unknown.[3] However, on March 9, 1923, Lenin suffered his third stroke, so far the severest one. He ran a high fever and suffered a great deal of pain. The already weakened right extremities were paralyzed again. At first he was able to utter a few words like "Lloyd George" and "conference" but then he lost his powers of speech. But not until March 10 did the Kremlin doctors arrange for the service of night nurses.[4]

The "bloc" between Lenin and Trotsky had come to its natural end. Trotsky did not attempt to fulfill the mission which Lenin had entrusted to him; instead he followed the agreement with Kamenev. Stalin was saved.

To understand the significance of these events, Lenin's family doctor must be considered. He was Dr. Fedor A. Guetier, by then 60 years old and an old friend of the Trotsky family. He kept Trotsky informed of Lenin's health. By the end of February, Trotsky inquired about Lenin's prospects. Guetier told him that Lenin could get on his feet again. The decline in cerebral arteriosclerosis is not constant, and partial and short-lived remissions occur. Lenin at that time had shown some improvement. Yet, Guetier's diagnosis was incompetent: Lenin's condition could at best improve for a very short time. Judging from the descriptions of their German colleagues, the Russian physicians tending Lenin were quite second-rate. The German doctors, however, apparently did not care to make a firm diagnosis either, although it would appear in retrospect that the symptoms of Lenin's disease should have been abundantly clear.[5] But the medical problem is not at stake: the point is that some medical authorities professed belief in the possibility of Lenin's recovery.

There is little doubt that Stalin, an experienced collector of

[2]Trotsky, *Stalin,* p. 362.

[3]It is important to realize that the Khrushchev regime, by and large, has allowed the publication only of those pertinent documents which already were known in the Free World.

[4]Fotieva, p. 193.

[5]The Swedish neurologist S. E. Henschen and the German expert Nonne served as consultants from Europe in addition to Bumke and Foerster. "There was no disagreement in the diagnosis of arterial disease, but Henschen alone was correct in the prognosis, namely that the disorder would be rapidly progressive." Henschen based this prognosis on the family history. (Webb Haymaker, ed., *The Founders of Neurology* [Springfield: Thomas, 1953], p. 182f.) The data of this family history at his disposal seemed garbled, but it is interesting that they contained a reference to a relative from the side of Lenin's father, who had his leg amputated because of arterial disease.

intelligence, also kept close watch over Lenin's health. The later writings of the German physician, Professor Foerster, showed the author to be pliable; undoubtedly he was then reporting to the "authorities." There are indications that he underrated the seriousness of Lenin's condition. Perhaps old Fotieva, who had a good career under Stalin and whose existence was pointedly ignored in the writings of her friend, Maria Ulyanova, was one of Stalin's main sources of information; but apparently she was on Lenin's side politically.[6] Glyasser (another of Lenin's secretaries), who quoted Stalin in her memoirs profusely and demonstratively, seems to have worked for Lenin for only a few weeks. Thus, she might have been planted by Stalin but apparently she did not obtain relevant information. By contrast, Volodicheva did; she apparently was connected with Stalin during the August conference of 1917. Initially, she and Krupskaya were the only persons who knew of Lenin's testament: Volodicheva had recorded it.[7] It should be noted that none of the three secretaries fell victim to Stalin's purges.[8]

The problem was twofold for Stalin. One question was whether Lenin would recover sufficiently to resume office; regardless of the diagnosis, this contingency seemed remote. The other question was

[6]As Secretary of the Council of People's Commissars, Fotieva signed on July 10, 1923, a resolution of thanks to the American Relief Administration and Herbert Hoover, "in the name of the millions of people saved." "The people inhabiting the Union of Soviet Socialist Republics will never forget the help given them by the American people . . . seeing in it a pledge of the future friendship of the two nations." Kamenev, Acting President of the Council of People's Commissars, also signed (H. H. Fisher, *op. cit.*, p. 398).

[7]Trotsky, *The Suppressed Testament of Lenin* (New York: Pioneer, 1946), p. 14. It is now known (*Werke*, Vol. 36, p. 580) that Volodicheva typed the testament. However, the postscript on Stalin of January 4, 1923, was typed by Fotieva. Thus Stalin probably knew about the testament which was slightly critical of him and, in essence, favored Trotsky to be Lenin's successor ("certainly, the most capable man in the present central committee"), but he may not have yet known about Lenin's recommendation to consider Stalin's replacement. Thus, there was no urgency for him to take any precautions early in January.

[8]At an earlier time, approximately by 1920, Stalin became interested in Nadezhda Alliluyeva, daughter of the veteran Sergei Y. Alliluyev, in whose apartment Lenin hid briefly in 1917. Alliluyeva worked in Lenin's secretariat and Stalin courted her to obtain information—Nadya was Lenin's code clerk. She became pregnant and since she belonged to a family that was prominent in party circles, Stalin was forced to accept her as his common law wife. She was rather pretty and bore him two children. As soon as her political usefulness ended, Stalin's roving eye sought other interests. In 1927, she took part, together with Krupskaya and Maria Ulyanova, in a protest directed against Stalin. In 1932, she made a violent scene at home with Stalin. He was probably intoxicated and lost his temper, hit her temple savagely with the butt of his revolver, and then choked her to death. The only eye witness to this murder, Natalia Trushina, was put into a "political isolator" where she told the story to Elisabeth Lermolo. (*Face of a Victim* (New York: Harper, 1955), pp. 217-232.)

whether Lenin might improve to the extent that he could interfere from his sickbed, or even return briefly to the Central Committee, the Politbureau, or a Party Congress, to use his prestige to destroy Stalin. This danger appeared to be very real. Meanwhile, Stalin "was trying with all his might to prevent Lenin from communicating his views in writing."[9]

Trotsky reported that by the end of February, 1923, Stalin informed him, Zinovyev, and Kamenev that Lenin had expressed concern about his health. Lenin told Stalin (according to hearsay evidence repeated by Trotsky) that he was losing the faculty of speech, anticipated a new stroke, did not trust his physicians, and considered his situation hopeless. Lenin asked Stalin for poison.[10]

When disclosing this story many years later, Trotsky brought up an obvious point: since Lenin at that time was preparing his "bombshell" against Stalin, why did he ask his strongest enemy to "help" him? Perhaps, Trotsky hypothesized, Lenin reasoned that only Stalin would do him this "favor," or perhaps he wanted to test Stalin. The four parted, Trotsky reported, with the "implicit understanding" that they would not even consider sending poison to Lenin. The incident took place before the final rupture. It is, however, quite unlikely that Lenin made such a request of Stalin or that he even invited Stalin to his sickroom.[11]

If Trotsky did not fabricate the incident, which is unlikely, it must be assumed that Stalin was not telling the truth. But the concoction of such a story raises a question of timing: if Stalin did contemplate killing Lenin, why did he suddenly want to take action by the end of February? It was only on March 4 that the threat became serious. Did he then learn about the postscript to the testament? The stark fact is: Lenin suffered a stroke which was *not* caused by poison.

It is certain, however, that on March 5 (after Lenin had fired his opening gun), Stalin behaved very rudely to Krupskaya. His manner, in fact, was so brutal that despite her otherwise strong inclination to shield Lenin from worry, she immediately asked her husband for help. According to one version Stalin termed her an

[9]Trotsky, *Diary*, p. 33.

[10]Trotsky, *Stalin* (New York: Grosset and Dunlap, 1941), p. 376ff. This story is corroborated in Trotsky's *Diary* (pp. 32-35), where he referred to a statement by Maria Ulyanova in defense of Stalin. The statement was made to the July-August 1927 Plenum of the Central Committee and the Central Executive Committee and was to the effect that Lenin broke with Stalin "for a purely personal reason" (an assertion which Trotsky disputed), and that Lenin valued Stalin as a revolutionary, otherwise "he would not have turned to him with a request for the kind of favor that could be expected only from a real revolutionary." This request was for poison so that Lenin could "join the majority" (p. 34).

[11]No such visit seems to be recorded anywhere.

"intriguing woman" and called her insulting names. But she hardly was shocked by vulgar expressions. It was rumored that at one time Stalin put pressure on Krupskaya by telling her that if she did not do his bidding, he would disclose that for many years she had been Lenin's wife only in name. He may have made this remark years later when, for a short while, Krupskaya went into open opposition. Yet it is equally possible that he referred to Inessa Armand on this critical March 5, 1923. This type of remark was bound to stir up a hornets' nest.

It is known that through 1921 and 1922 an elaborate investigation was made of Lenin's and Krupskaya's family background.[12] The investigation was ordered to facilitate the diagnosis. Presumably Inessa Armand's medical history also was investigated. Lenin himself feared that he was suffering from syphilis.[13] Apparently a number of doctors and some Bolsheviks shared this suspicion. Naturally, Lenin knew his life better than anyone else. But Lenin's sex life was not such that there was a high probability of his having been infected.

However, Lenin may have suspected hereditary syphilis. Modern medicine no longer accepts the belief in hereditary syphilis and even a diagnosis of congenital syphilis (which was unlikely in Lenin's case) would be most rare at present. But in 1922 the diagnostic situation was different: hereditary syphilis was thought to occur frequently. The investigation apparently did not uncover any firm information that there had been syphilis among Lenin's ancestors, but reportedly it unearthed a great deal of "dirt" which the Politbureau thought would be best forgotten. The "dirt" may have been information regarding Lenin's father or his maternal grandfather, or it may have been culled from Lenin's own life (e.g., police dossiers). It is possible that Stalin used this material to blackmail Krupskaya.

After Stalin had visited Lenin in the summer of 1922, he wrote a short comment which demonstrates that he was fully aware of the possible danger of excitement and worry upon Lenin's health. The doctors insisted upon sheltering Lenin from disputes and conflicts. Lenin's second stroke had been preceded by excitement. This, unquestioningly, was known to Stalin. It is obvious that he had surrounded Lenin with his agents or, in any event, with persons who reported to him. It is also apparent that by one means or another he exercised some degree of control over Krupskaya and Maria.

Stalin was a most calculating individual. If he had wished to placate Lenin, he could have been most solicitous. Undoubtedly, his rude behavior was *designed* to upset Lenin and subject him to

[12]*Sotsialisticheskii Vestnik* (May, 1961), No. 5, p. 967.

[13]Walter, p. 471 .

enormous strain from which he would collapse or die. Years later Stalin was to prove his mastery of "imperceptible murder." Perhaps, Lenin was the first victim of this black art.[14]

Whatever Stalin used, his attack was not political but personal in nature. Lenin, who politically was almost invulnerable at that time, obviously was hit at a sensitive spot. Krupskaya was thoroughly cowed: Lenin's "testament" had been written for the forthcoming Twelfth Party Congress but was held back by Krupskaya for more than a year and transmitted to the Thirteenth Congress not until May, 1924.[15] The release was preceded by a consultation with Trotsky. He may have told her that he did not plan to take any action. By that time Stalin was firmly entrenched. Zinovyev averred that Lenin's fears had proved groundless. Kamenev argued that Stalin should remain in office but if he did the contents of the testament would have to be kept secret. Krupskaya objected and Trotsky said nothing. The Central Committee finally voted forty to ten to ask Stalin to continue in office. (Trotsky voted with the majority.) The testament was published abroad as a "leak" but the authenticity of the text was denied.[16] Within the party, it was given a brief reading at the Congress, but within the Soviet Union the testament remained unknown—supreme treason! "The evil that men do lives after them."

[14]A. A. Joffe, who committed suicide in 1927, was driven to this act by political despair. But he also was quite ill and depended on medicines from the Kremlin pharmacy. When he did not give in to Stalin, the supply of these medicines was stopped. The art of camouflaged murder was not new in the history of socialism nor was it necessarily a Russian phenomenon. The death of Karl Marx's daughter, Eleanor, apparently was compelled by Edward Aveling, her boyfriend who did not want to marry her. *See* Lewis S. Feuer, "Marxian Tragedians, a Death in the Family," *Encounter* (November 1962), p. 23ff.

[15]Schapiro, *The Communist Party*, pp. 272, 283. Lenin's notes on the Georgian question, which Lenin wanted to keep from Stalin until the Twelvth Congress, were distributed by Fotieva to the politbureau (*Ibid.*, p. 269). Fotieva, allegedly acting on Maria Ulyanova's advice, stated that the notes had not been edited to be suitable for the printer. This constituted considerable service to Stalin who with Trotsky's acquiescence easily resolved the Georgian question on his terms. (*See* Wolfe, *Stalin's Ghost*, p. 278.) Maria at that time was in Stalin's camp. (Trotsky, *Diary*, p. 33.)

[16]Such denials perplexed many writers à la Walter (p. 472).

Death

There were complications in the area of internal medicine, but we have no information on their nature.[1] Bumke, Foerster and six Russian physicians consulted daily up to five hours in Lenin's recep-

[1]Oswald Bumke, *Erinnerungen und Betrachtungen* (Munich: Pflaum, 1953), p. 96.

tion room, and Bumke complained about the inactivity of his Russian colleagues. Many Russians, he added, were then hoping that Lenin would live on, because Lenin had finally realized that communism was not workable; but only Lenin would be capable of abandoning communist ideas and guiding the evolution toward a different system.[2] Previously, Lenin had firmly disputed that he was trying to create "socialism on the island of Utopia." "We will destroy everything and on the ruins we will build our temple . . . for the happiness of all. But we will destroy the entire bourgeoisie, grind it to a powder."[3] It was now clear that Lenin had been little interested in building his "temple" but that he had acted "from insurpassable hatred against the tsarist regime and its supporters."[4] The execution of the Tsar and his family had been the fulfilment of "the only personal ambition" of his life.[5] Thus, he did not regret anything that had been done to destroy the old system, but he realized that the system he had built was not functioning as he had wanted it to work.[6] He knew that his comrades were turning from him. "Princely counsel in his face yet shone, majestic though in ruin."[7]

After a few weeks Lenin improved slightly. On May 5, he was examined by a group of German and Russian specialists. On May 12, Lenin was carried by stretcher to a car and transported to Gorki. To relieve his pain, he frequently was put into hot baths. He took speech lessons and tried physical therapy. He also watched movies. In June he had a setback but in July there was some improvement. His spirit, appetite, and ability to sleep were relatively unimpaired. In good weather he spent about three hours a day in the fresh air and picked mushrooms. He walked with help, and twice a day Krupskaya coached him as he exercised his speech.

Quinine was prescribed but he disliked it and ultimately refused to take it. He also ceased to take iodine preparations. As he had done in his childhood, Lenin seems to have flown into tantrums when he was not given his way. But when he felt better, he sometimes picked a flower and offered it to his sisters; it is not reported

[2]*Ibid.*, pp. 110 and 117.

[3]Quoted from Shub, p. 268f.

[4]Balabanova, *Lenin*, p. 9. She added: "As time went on, this more or less instinctive attitude was supplemented by objective, theoretical motives."

[5]Ralph H. Major, *Disease and Destiny* (Lawrence: University of Kansas Press, 1958), p. 20.

[6]Schapiro's analysis of Lenin's last writings (in ignorance of other recollections) states, "As Lenin nears his death, we catch glimpses of his thought which suggest that he was attempting to console himself for his disappointment over the failures of Communist party rule to live up to his expectations." (*The Communist Party*, p. 228.)

[7]John Milton, *Paradise Lost*, book II.

that he gave flowers to Krupskaya (who at this time was lending her name to a concerted party drive to eliminate undesirable books from the libraries).

By September, Lenin was able to descend stairs unassisted, his speech allegedly was improving through the exercises he was taking with Krupskaya, and he was practicing writing with his left hand. Dr. Rozanov, who was medically in command at Gorki, felt free to go on vacation and the nursing attendance was curtailed. Lenin became irritated by Dr. Foerster; the fact that he remained as a consultant was kept from Lenin. Lenin was able to walk with a cane in October and had newspapers read to him. Once, after he had felt especially uncomfortable, he insisted on returning to the little room (although it was very hot). Supported by a cane, he walked to the house himself and even negotiated the stairs. His will power was still strong. Intruders into the small cubicle infuriated him; his sister wanted him to return to the larger house, but he remained in the little room until the next day.

Sometimes Lenin dropped in to see the visitors Krupskaya received from the Department of Education. Once, it is reported, a workers' delegation came to greet him. In October, Ossip Pyatnitsky and Ivan Skvortsov were permitted to visit Lenin one Sunday. Lenin entered the room, followed by Krupskaya, holding his cane in his left hand. He extended his hand and smiled. Pyatnitsky was surprised that he had changed so little. The visitors told him about elections in Moscow and summarized affairs of the Italian, German, and English parties. Lenin was not very attentive, but on two occasions Pyatnitsky believed he was interested, when his eyes became more expressive. Lenin spoke the only word which he still was able to utter clearly: "Tak!" ("That's it!") Krupskaya wrote to Trotsky that at an even later date she read aloud a passage Trotsky had written on Marx and Lenin: Lenin wanted it reread and then read the piece himself.

But it is likely that these stories are highly exaggerated and that Lenin actually did not understand what was being said. One eyewitness reported that he had regressed to the puerile stage. Photographs tend to confirm this impression. The autopsy later suggested that he must have been entirely demented through this period.[8] Some doctors allege that he overcame portions of his cerebral defects through his enormous will power. To some extent, he might have, but his physiological decline did not allow him much leeway.

Reports say that on October 18 he walked through the garden to the garage and ordered the chauffeur to drive him to Moscow. In

[8] Stefano Stefani, "Psichiatria nel Mondo, Il Cervello di Lenin," *Minerva Medica*, (No. 61-62), August 1957, p. 15.

the Kremlin he walked around his office, looked into the conference hall, and spent the night in his apartment. The next day he was driven through the capital, and after stopping shortly at an agricultural exhibition, returned to Gorki.

There are several versions of this trip. It is not even certain that Lenin spent the night in the Kremlin. (This is quite improbable, in fact, although several witnesses assert that he did.) According to one version, he removed a document from his desk. According to another, he noted with consternation that his files had been rifled; he searched for a document and, when he did not find it, shouted loudly and incoherently. According to a third version, he looked with great emotion at the place at which he had done his work and walked around his office as though taking leave of his life. According to a fourth version, he looked into the Politbureau conference room, took some books from his library, asked to be driven to the exit of the Kremlin and, after passing through the exhibition, was driven back to Gorki.

All accounts agree that he was unable to speak. How then could he have given these various orders? Perhaps one of the "factions" was exhibiting him to suggest that he would return to power; or another group may have been displaying him to make it known that he had become a blabbering idiot. The latter version is more plausible —Stalin's masterful hand is faintly visible.

All stories agree, in the best mystical tradition, that it was as though a dead man had arisen. But politically, Lenin, though he was still officially President of the Council of Commissars (if only because in his zombie-like state he was physically and mentally unable to perform the act of resignation), was already dead. Stalin was just about to complete the building of his machine. In November, Trotsky became ill with malaria. It was of little importance, for he had neither the power nor inclination to forestall Stalin's rise to autocratic rule.

Little is reported of Lenin's life after his ghostly visit to the Kremlin. He often sat deep in thought with tears in his eyes. He displayed growing hatred towards his doctors, perhaps a not abnormal attitude. In good weather he was taken on car and sleigh rides. On Christmas eve, Krupskaya is said to have decorated a Christmas tree for him—a curious way of bringing joy to a hardened atheist.[9]

His tremor had gotten worse by the end of the year and he often lapsed into unconsciousness. On Saturday, January 19, 1924, he indicated that he was unable to see. On Sunday he did not get up for breakfast. His vision continued to fail. The doctors were summoned

9V. D. Bonch-Bruyevich reported that in 1918, presumably after the hold-up incident, Lenin played with children around a Christmas tree in the sanatorium where Krupskaya was recuperating.

hurriedly. During the night, Lenin suffered an attack and lost consciousness. He recovered, but was very much weakened. During the afternoon of January 21, he felt ill again and did not want to eat.

After dinner, he lay back. Suddenly, a severe attack hit him. Around five o'clock he was unconscious and his temperature was rising. Hot water bottles were ordered. Maria burst into tears and told Smirnova, the servant girl, that there was no hope; she disappeared into her room. Smirnova carried the hot water bottles into Lenin's bedroom. Three doctors were around his bed and a few male nurses sobbed in the corner. Krupskaya, sitting by the bed, was holding Lenin's hand. Lenin died of a massive cerebral hemorrhage at 6:50 P.M.

Lenin's death was announced on January 22. A German and two Russian doctors officially certified that Lenin's death had been caused by paralysis of the lungs and excessive body temperature. The government issued a statement saying that, though Lenin had been sick for some time, he had recently appeared to be improving but had suddenly fallen sick on January 21 and had died within a few hours.

In the morning and early afternoon of January 22, in the veranda of the villa at Gorki, an autopsy of Lenin's corpse was performed by Professor Aprikossov in the presence of nine Russian doctors, a German doctor, Semashko, the Commissar of Public Health, and the medically untrained Stalin. The autopsy disclosed a high degree of sclerosis of the blood vessels, with marked changes in the brain arteries, considerable softening in the left and partial softening in the right lobes of the brain, and a recent hemorrhage. The severe and extensive sclerosis of cerebral blood vessels was of long standing; it was stated to be partly ascribable to an inherited disposition.[10]

Dr. V. P. Ossipov, who was present at the death scene, later wrote that Lenin had inherited the arteriosclerotic disposition from both father and mother. According to contemporary Soviet press accounts, however, the sclerosis was due to overwork.

Semashko, who was a better revolutionary than a physician, subsequently disclosed that he had never seen so much calcification: the surgical instruments sounded as though they were cutting stone. Some of the vessels had become so narrow that not even a hair could have passed. He asserted that the doctors were unanimous in saying that the case was unique. Semashko was amazed that the sclerosis was restricted to the brain and had not affected other vessels. He wrote as though he had never heard of cerebral arteriosclerosis.

According to Dr. Foerster's interpretation of the autopsy, the

---

[10]No evidence of sclerotic deterioration was found in 1918 after the attempt on Lenin's life nor during his operation during 1922; of course, his brain was not examined at these times.

heavy damage which the brain had suffered made the restoration of Lenin's speech, reading, and writing capabilities scientifically inexplicable. How was this non-Communist German professor prevailed upon to detect a miracle that never occurred? Perhaps the answer is that Foerster, who had stayed on against Lenin's desire, was compelled to stay for one year in an adjoining room and reduced "to watch Lenin through a keyhole." Foerster ascribed the alleged partial recovery to Lenin's will power. But perhaps Foerster was induced to find a miracle because his diagnosis had been grievously wrong.[11]

Semashko asserted the sclerosis was due to hypertension; in all likelihood, this was partially true. But the communiqué on the autopsy alleged (presumably at Semashko's or Stalin's insistence) that Lenin's sclerosis had resulted from "excessive brain activity." In other words: he "thought himself" to death.

To prevent any blame's falling upon the doctors, the report added, "Lenin suffered from an incurable disease of blood vessels which, in spite of all medical measures, inevitably would have led to the fatal end."

Lenin had been attended by no less than twenty-five doctors, including six Germans and one Italian, many of them enjoying the highest reputation. The autopsy report which all present signed was especially strong, since one Russian *lumen* of medical science had insisted, almost to the bitter end, that Lenin was just suffering from overwork. But most of these doctors had merely been consulted and had taken no part in the treatment. Otfried Foerster had the international reputation of making the lame walk and the blind see. He was deemed to be the foremost neurologist in "depth and breadth of knowledge, in the wide range of investigative work, in the happy blending of physiology with neurology and neurosurgery. . . ." "He was on hand at the autopsy,"[12] but for months he had not been treating Lenin unless observation through a keyhole is called "treatment." The impression which was cultivated that Lenin had been given the most elaborate medical care was misleading.

These indications of untruthfulness raise a doubt as to the validity of the entire autopsy report. In her odyssey through "political isolators," Elizabeth Lermolo ran into an old Bolshevik, Gavril Volkov, who had become in 1923 the kitchen chef at Gorki. Later, in a prison hospital, she also met Liza Semyonova, Volkov's sister-in-law, whom Stalin used to "monitor" telephone conversations of party leaders. Volkov reported that Stalin came to Gorki "a few times" and that Lenin was improving. By the end of 1923, Krupskaya was called to Moscow for two days and Lenin took a turn for the worse.

11Haymaker, p. 423, and Foerster in *O Lenine,* Vol. IV, p. 206.
12Haymaker, *ibid.*

Yet he improved. Krupskaya, some ten days later, was recalled to the Kremlin and Lenin again felt very ill. When Volkov brought Lenin his morning tea, Lenin succeeded by gestures to signal Volkov that Krupskaya should be called home. At eleven on the morning of January 21, as Volkov brought Lenin his second breakfast, Lenin slipped a note into his hand, uttering an unintelligible sound. Dr Yelistratov, the attending physician, ran into the room, carried Lenin back to his bed and gave him an injection to quiet him. Lenin closed his eyes and never opened them again. The note allegedly read, "Gavrilushka, I've been poisoned . . . go fetch Nadya [Krupskaya] at once . . . tell Trotsky . . . tell everybody you can."[13]

Elizabeth Lermolo has been found to be a dependable witness. Consequently, there is no reason to doubt that Volkov told this story substantially as she recorded it. Nevertheless, the account raises grave questions. According to Volkov, Dr. Yelistratov appeared to suffer the "torment of a deeply hidden secret," but this is not elsewhere recorded. This does not invalidate the story but rather, if the tale is accepted for argument's sake, would point to him as the administrator of the poison. Indeed, if the poison were not given medically, it would have had to have been given with the food, and this would mean that Volkov himself was the poisoner. However, if Yelistratov were poisoning Lenin by injections or medications, why was the poison so ineffective that Lenin recovered after Krupskaya's return and again, after her second departure, found sufficient strength to write a note? For that matter, if the poison were administered medically, the absence of Krupskaya was unnecessary. On the contrary, her presence would have been desirable.

Stalin may have reasoned that an autopsy would be unavoidable; hence poison had to be given in very small doses lest the crime be discovered. But doctors cannot be deceived that easily. It is unlikely that Stalin, if he ordered Lenin poisoned, would have taken the risk of an elaborate autopsy, even in his presence. Rather he organized the autopsy on a grandiose scale to foreclose any talk of foul play. He could risk this bravado because Lenin had died of natural causes.

There really was no need to poison the disabled man. It appears unlikely that Lenin still was able to write notes. It would seem that the announced finding of the autopsy (death due to cerebral arteriosclerosis) is fully verified by Lenin's medical history[14] and there

---

[13]Lermolo, p. 135ff. The existence and function of Yelistratov is authentic: he cosigned the death certificate. However, the physician in attendance may have been a Doctor Rukavichnikov.

[14]The diagnosis of cerebral arterio-sclerosis seems beyond doubt, according to Bumke (p. 109), Major (p. 21), and Haymaker (p. 182). Stefani (p. 15), however, allows also for the possibility of severe circulatory disease and hematic dyscrasia.

can be no doubt about his strokes. It is therefore virtually impossible that Lenin still was in a position to compose a coherent note of a dozen words on the day of his death with most of his brain already destroyed. Granting such an act *could* occur, it is puzzling how Lenin would *know* he was being poisoned. He merely could *suspect* it, and he probably did. Whether one accepts the story of Lenin's note, or other specifics of Volkov's recollection, the kitchen chef undoubtedly conveyed a correct impression of the emotions and the atmosphere which then permeated the stricken dictator's abode. He probably gave an accurate glimpse into the frame of mind of Lenin at the terminal point of his consciousness.[15]

Trotsky's disclosure that Lenin requested poison from Stalin must also be considered. Perhaps Stalin himself was terrorizing the Kremlin by planting rumors of poisoning. And perhaps the unlikely note was planted by one of Stalin's henchmen precisely in order to induce Trotsky into making an accusation which could not be sustained. This interpretation would seem to fit the known facts. Such a tactic offered an added attraction to Stalin, since rumors about poisoners would have given the ailing Trotsky cause for concern about his own illness which the doctors found so difficult to diagnose.[16]

After embalmment (also supervised by Stalin), Lenin's coffin was

[15]Volkov's and Lermolo's recollection as to the precise time of this story may easily be erroneous: the incident could have occurred weeks and months before Lenin's death.

[16]It should be noted that Krupskaya may have fallen victim to a cup of poisoned coffee. After Lenin's death, Krupskaya was afflicted (for a while) by a nervous disease which manifested itself in extreme weakness of her limbs. After recovering her health, she adopted an attitude of weak and ineffectual opposition. Soon she was demoted from her position of Assistant Commissar of Education and became a lowly librarian. She helped the Lenin Institute with their collection of memoirs, and occasionally rebelled against too blatant distortions; these included tales claiming that Lenin had thick, reddish hair (he was bald); that he drove in 1919 without a bodyguard; objected to getting his shoes shined; received persons clad in rags; arrived in his office at 9:00 A.M. (he was a late riser). She even protested many stories about his playful relations with children as sentimental twaddle. Her activities were innocent enough, especially since her complaints were not taken into consideration. But her very existence was bothersome: too many of the old Leninists who were being purged by Stalin wrote her to ask for help. On her 70th birthday (February 27, 1939), Krupskaya was scheduled to speak to a teachers' conference. She prepared a draft (supposedly slightly anti-Stalinist) which the wife of Solomon A. Lozovsky took for clearance. Mrs. Lozovsky acted as watchdog over Krupskaya. Upon her return from the unknown censor, Lozovskaya served Krupskaya a cup of coffee. A few minutes later, the old woman was dead (*Novoye Russkoye Slovo*, June 14, 1961) Lozovsky (Dridzo) was an old "internationalist" and for most of his pre-1917 career was associated with the Mensheviks. Expelled from the party in 1918, he was re-admitted in 1919. During the above episode, he served as Director of Book Publications. From 1939 he was attached to the Foreign Ministry and between 1940 and 1949 taught international relations at the higher party school. He was arrested in 1949, died in jail or camp during 1952, and was "rehabilitated" under Khrushchev. Whether this rehabilitation signified approval of Krupskaya's presumable murder by Lozovsky's wife remains an open question.

transported to Moscow on January 23. The temperature was —30 degrees. A funeral procession, organized by Kalinin and, fittingly, by police chief Dzerzhinski, accompanied the body to the House of Soviets where Lenin lay in state. In four days about 700,000 people were marched past the catafalque. On January 25, the soviet mourned Lenin's departure by speech-making in the Bolshoi Theater; Krupskaya also addressed the deputies. On Sunday morning, January 27, the body was brought to Red Square. Guns thundered and the Kremlin bells rang, with the sirens of factories providing a cacophonic background. In the evening, with the beat of drums and orchestral accompaniment, Lenin's body was placed in a ramshackle mausoleum.

Trotsky was en route to the Caucasus for a cure. He had known from Guetier that Lenin was about to pass away and he never should have left: his disease was not so severe that he was unable to stay. But apparently he wanted to escape. Now, Stalin tricked him into not attending the ceremonies: he wired him the wrong date for the funeral. But Trotsky made no effort to return, obviously not inclined to honor the departed. Thus, it fell to Stalin to deliver the funeral oration. It was as though Brutus had exchanged places with Mark Anthony.

Instead of Lenin's enemy, his former friends, such as Bogdanov or Shlyapnikov, could have spoken. Would they have repeated what they were saying so often, that the socialist character of the revolution had been destroyed? A representative of the Russian people might have noted that under Lenin's rule 200,000 to 1,500,000 persons had been killed through terror, about five million had died from famine, and that more millions had become casualties in the civil war—that Lenin had cost the Russian people ten million or more lives. If his Holiness Tikhon, Patriarch of Moscow and All-Russia, had been permitted to officiate, he could have quoted from his letter of November 7, 1918, to the Council of Peoples Commissars:

> The blood of our brothers, who have been killed mercilessly by your orders, has formed rivers and cries out to heaven. . . . Regardless of the names by which you cover your evildoings, murder, violence and robbery are always grave sins and they are crimes which cry to heaven for revenge. . . . You promised freedom. Freedom is a great value if it is properly understood as freedom from evil and freedom from oppression. . . . But you did not give us such a freedom. . . . You use your power for the persecution of your neighbors and the destruction of the innocent. . . . The truth is this: you have given the people a stone instead of bread and a serpent instead of fish (Matt. 7:9-10). . . . The words of the Prophet are fulfilled: "Their feet run to evil, and make haste to shed innocent blood; their thoughts are unprofitable thoughts; wasting and

destruction are in their way" (Is. 59:7). . . . "All they that take the sword shall perish by the sword" (Matt. 26:52).[17]

[17]Original in Hoover Institution. I am indebted to Father P. N. Kurgaz, O.P., for calling my attention to this document and allowing me to use his translation.

. . . and Transfiguration

But the end of Lenin was not yet. Some Communists deduced that since Lenin was the greatest genius of history, his brain obviously had to be a unique product of nature.

At the suggestion of a Russian neurologist, Professor Lazar Salomonovich Minor, the Soviet government invited Professor Oskar Vogt, Director of the Kaiser-Wilhelm Brain Institute in Berlin, to set up a vast research program for the exploration of Lenin's brain.

Together with his French wife Cécile, Vogt was a leading proponent of cyto-architectonics,[1] a particular school of brain research which concentrates on the analysis of the cellular structure of the brain, notably the layers of the cerebral cortex. This school is also interested in identifying the specific functions of the various cortical areas. This was one approach among many and it was by no means undisputed. It has been pointed out, for example, that while the cyto-architectonics of the brain should be known as accurately as possible, and while reflex functions may be dependent on specific areas, non-reflex functions and complicated processes of mentation use a large number of brain areas, in addition to specific areas that may be specially involved. Processes of integration necessarily involve the entire brain. Furthermore, it has been known since 1914 that "the functional topography of the excitable cortex" could undergo changes in a person's lifetime; therefore, localizations must "be expressed not only in terms of space, but also in terms of time."[2] The functioning of the brain, moreover, was dependent upon numerous metabolic processes and on external factors. "While politely admired, the teaching of the Vogts had little influence."[3] However, Vogt's approach had many deep roots in the history of materialism and held considerable appeal to the ideologues in the Kremlin.

In 1925, after the German Foreign Office had prevailed upon Vogt to accept this assignment in the interests of German-Russian

[1]For a contemporary textbook, see Constantin von Economo, *The Cytoarchitectonics of the Human Cerebral Cortex* (London: Oxford, 1929).

[2]Walther Riese, *Principles of Neurology* (New York: Coolidge Foundation Publishers, 1950), page 91.

[3]Percival Bailey and Gerhardt von Bonin, *The Isocortex of Man* (Urbana: University of Illinois Press, 1951), page 8.

scientific collaboration, Vogt organized the systematic dissection of Lenin's brain; that is, since the left hemisphere was almost totally destroyed, of the right hemisphere of Lenin's *cerebrum*. This work was finished in the first half of 1927. During the second half of the same year, Vogt examined the slices. It seems that most of his analytical work was done in Berlin from micro-photographs.

On November 15, 1927, *Pravda* reported on a lecture which Vogt had read on November 12 to Soviet high officials at Moscow. Vogt disclosed that he had compared 34,000 slices with preparations from average people; this must have been quite a chore during the few months which Vogt had set aside for the assignment.[4] Lenin's granular cells were considerably larger and more clearly defined than those of most people. His pyramidal cells—which, Vogt explained, serve as the foundation of higher psychic life—were particularly large and well formed, and also possessed numerous well-developed and long dendrites. These factors, *Pravda* quoted Vogt, provided an explanation of Lenin's psychological characteristics.[5]

For comparative purposes, Vogt displayed specimens from the brain of Nobel Prize laureate Wilhelm Ostwald (who, strangely enough, had dabbled during 1914 in Russian revolutionizing) , and of a murderer, whose pyramidal cells were small and few in number.[6]

On November 19, People's Commissar of Health N. A. Semashko published an article in *Pravda*. He disclosed that in 1925 an institute for the study of Lenin's brain had been set up in Moscow under the supervision of Prof. Vogt. Of Lenin's brain, 31,000 slices were taken; apparently there was no agreement on the number of specimens. Semashko repeated the information about the pyramidal cells and added that not only were these cells larger and more clearly

---

[4]The number of slices appears incredibly high: the very thorough analysis of Pilsudski's two hemispheres was based upon 13,000 slices which in a two year period were analyzed far more extensively than the Lenin specimens. (M. Minkowski "Maksymilian Rose: Le cerveau de Joseph Pilsudski," *Schweizer Archiv für Neurologie und Psychiatrie*, Vol. XLIV, No. 2, p. 408.) There may be many purposes for making brain slices. To be of use in cyto-architectonics, sections must be "absolutely perpendicular to the cerebral cortex and perpendicular to the course of the convolutions." Each convolution must be cut perpendicular "in all its parts." This requires "a vast number of slices." After making these points, Economo demonstrated a hemisphere which had "been cut into more than 200 such slices." (Karoline von Economo and Julius von Wagner-Jauregg, *Baron Constantin von Economo, His Life and Work* [Burlington, Vt.: Free Press Interstate, 1937], p. 73f.) It is possible therefore that Lenin's brain was cut up too much and that many slices were really unsuited for proper examination. (On the whole subject, see Economo "Wie sollen wir Elitegehirne verarbeiten?", *Zeitschrift für die gesamte Neurologie und Psychiatrie*, Vol. 121, 1929, pp. 323-402.)

[5]This whole argument was initiated by Albert Wilson, *Unfinished Man* (London: Greening, 1910), who asserted that psychopaths, including mental defectives and criminals, have only few pyramidal cells.

[6]I am indebted to Dr. Marguerite Vogt for this information.

defined than those of average people, but also the third cortical layer was wider. This, he argued, proved that Lenin's brain represented a higher type of development of the central nervous system.

According to Moscow releases, "200 fields of localization" had been found in Lenin's brain, many of the same type as had been found in the brains of apes.[7] Vogt was quoted as having said that the

> marked development of the pyramidal cells produced, of necessity, an intensification of the general activity of the various divisions of the brain. This in itself explains the outstanding nature of Lenin's intellectual life. The large number of paths proceeding from the pyramidal cells . . . uniting portions of the brain otherwise widely separated explains, furthermore, the wide range and multiplicity of ideas that had developed in the brain of Lenin, and, particularly, his capacity for quickly getting his bearings when confronted with the most complex situations and problems. The abundance of centers in which Lenin's ideas arose, and the manifold paths through which these ideas passed explain likewise Lenin's ability to comprehend new situations and face conditions as they actually are. The multiplicity of ideas, together with the wide range and rapidity of his powers of conception, produced in Lenin unusual powers of intuition.[8]

All this constituted "the basis of what was universally recognized as a peculiar type of genius. Thus, the key to a materialistic view of Lenin's genius has been found."

Although Vogt may have been carried away by the occasion, it is most unlikely that he made those statements, but far more probable that the materialistic interpretation was invented by Semashko or his propaganda office.[9]

It is noteworthy that no data were published about the weight and volume of Lenin's brain, the peculiarities of its fissature,[10] the

[7]*American Journal of Physical Anthopology*, Vol. XI, No. 2, Jan.-March 1928, p. 389. The Vogts' identification of brain areas "was imposing but also quite bewildering . . . Not everyone saw the subtle distinctions which the Vogts described" (Bailey and Bonin, *loc. cit.*). This general comment on Vogt's work does not refer to his examination of Lenin, for the pertinent information, if any, was not disclosed. The Vogts had identified these two hundred fields of location in their previous work and published this information during 1919. ("Allgemeine Ergebnisse unserer Hirnforschung," *Journal für Psychologie und Neurologie*, Vol. 25, pp. 279-461.) Thus, it is more than doubtful that the reference to Lenin's brain areas represented new research rather than a program which Vogt was advocating.

[8]*The Journal of the American Medical Association* (Chicago: March 3, 1928), p. 708.

[9]Political neurology was initiated by Paul Emil Flechsig, a pioneer in his science and a staunch conservative. Upon looking at the brain of a well-known socialist, he remarked: "My, what disharmonic convolutions!" (Haymaker, p. 34).

[10]"It appears that the brains of prominent people exhibit a strong asymmetry in their fissural patterns." (See Walther Riese and Kurt Goldstein "The Brain of Ludwig Edinger," *Journal of Comparative Neurology*, Philadelphia, Vol. 92, No. 2, April 1950, p. 153.).

differences between the hemispheres, nor even about the lobes and specific areas where the pyramidal cells and the third lamina allegedly showed progressive development.[11] Not a single measurement was given on the size and density of Lenin's cells or the width of the cortical layers. Hence it was impossible to evaluate the magnitude and significance of the supposed deviation.

Soon, some of Vogt's colleagues reminded him gently that perhaps far-reaching interpretations were not entirely supportable. Professor Mingazzini[12] recalled that in 1883, Ernst Haeckel, one of Vogt's most respected teachers, had produced the chain argument that the pyramidal cells control motion, hence will, and since will presupposes thought, he risked to call these cells the "thinking cells." This deduction had been speedily refuted by Rudolf Virchow. At any rate, where *were* the data to support Vogt's theses?

It seems that Vogt also was in trouble with Communist purists who were angered by his remarks on the hereditary character of Lenin's affliction. For two whole years Vogt stayed away from Moscow. In the fall of 1929, he dedicated an issue of his journal to "Professor" Semashko, whereupon he was invited to return.

On November 10, 1929, Vogt spoke in the Brain Institute at Moscow.[13] He repeated that he found "in the third layer, and particularly in its lower parts, in many areas pyramidal cells of a size otherwise not observed by me, or large pyramidal cells in a quantity not yet observed by me." He disputed that this finding could be due to functional hypertrophy of the intact hemisphere and also denied that the size of the cells was caused by *post mortem* changes.

The greater width of the third layer, at the expense of the fourth lamina, appeared to Vogt to be of genetic origin. He called the pyramidal cells "association cells," reiterated that feeble-minded criminals have few such cells, and that progressive mental debility usually is connected with disease in the third layer. But Vogt failed to specify whether this cell-layer peculiarity applied to Lenin's entire cortex or only to parts. A devotee of localization should have been expected to provide precisely *this* type of information.

Lenin's large cells indeed constituted "a progressive phenomenon," Vogt asserted. Hence the pyramidal cells may explain Lenin's feats

[11]On the methodology of brain analyses, see Riese and Goldstein (*ibid.*, pp. 133-161) and the literature quoted therein; furthermore Walther Riese, "The Brain of Dr. Trigant Burrow," *ibid.*, Vol. 100, No. 3, 1954, pp. 525-567.

[12]G. Mingazzini, "Die Zytoarchitektonik der Hirnhemisphären Lenins," *Psychiatrisch-Neurologische Wochenschrift*, Halle, No. 39, 1928, p. 451-453. See also Stefani, *Il cervello di Lenin*, p. 9f, where the point is made that the term "genius" is an abstraction, and hence could not be correlated in a simple way to histological factors.

[13]"Erster Bericht über die Arbeiten des Moskauer Staatsinstitutes für Hirnforschung," *Journal für Psychologie und Neurologie*, Vol. 40, No. 3-4, 1929, pp. 108-118.

in comprehension and thought, and his sense of reality. Lenin was an *Assoziationsathlet.*

However, Vogt did *not* use the flowery language that was reported about his 1927 lecture. "My findings show that cyto-architectonics is able to make anatomical and physiological contributions to the understanding of Lenin's personality." This, undoubtedly, was true. "From now on the task is to undertake the detail work." In other words: nothing serious had yet been done. Vogt hoped that the minute examination of Lenin's brain could begin by spring of 1930. In brief, the professor needed funds to finance his research program.

What was to be done? First, it was necessary to investigate the architectonics of 200 areas in Lenin's brain and relate those areas to his performance and behavior. For this purpose an elaborate questionnaire on Lenin's personality must be produced. This request could not but sour the Kremlin on the project.

Second, other brains must be studied for comparison purposes, and fortunately, Vogt told his listeners, thirteen elite brains were already at hand. Those included the brains of Bogdanov, Skvortsov-Stepanov and Tsurupa, and of the neurologist Rossolimo who had been one of the physicians attending Lenin. In Berlin, Vogt had the brains of Dr. Henschen, another of Lenin's physicians. Subsequently, the Moscow Institute was to acquire the brains of Gorky and Karpinsky as well as of Mayakovsky, poet of the Revolution (who was unappreciated by Lenin and at the time of his suicide at thirty-six, was suffering from advanced cerebral arteriosclerosis), of Tsiolkovsky, the space pioneer, and of Pavlov.[14] In this scientific *danse macabre,* Lenin's brain obviously had a rendezvous with many of the brains with which it had communicated *in vivo.* It was an excellent sample of bolshevik types *in vitro*—a philosophical expert in the application of violence, a master in the art if clandestine financing, a liaison man with a foreign intelligence service, a statistical economist who died a bureaucrat, two propagandists, the non-political inventor of brainwashing, the proponent of advanced revolutionary technology, and a few foreign experts who had been practicing peaceful coexistence; and, of course, Lenin, the master planner. It is not known whether in 1949, the brain slices of Semashko, the physician without patients who promoted himself to top medical administrator, and those of the executioner of communists, Stalin, who was suffering from a mania to persecute and murder people, joined the reunion. What discoveries

---

[14]Haeckel's brain had been analyzed thoroughly in Germany. But neither it, nor the brain of Gambetta, the first political brain that was put in formalin, was to be used for control. The purges of the 1930's could have made available thousands of elite brains but the scientific interests of the Soviet government did not at that time bear on brain research.

on comparative brain characteristics the Russian neurologists still owe the world!

Brain research, Vogt argued, was of great social significance. It could shed considerable light on the question of whether the backwardness of certain races was due to milieu or to genetic factors, and it might detect which functions are best developed among the various races. Vogt thanked Semashko who presided over a Russo-German commission on race biology, for permitting the establishment of a race research section in the Brain Institute. But his most ambitious expectation was that the "analysis of the elite brain and its genesis would prove to be the most important prerequisite for the genetic improvement of the brain."[15]

This insistence on race biology, genetics and eugenics hardly endeared Vogt to the Communists who, at that time, were busily downgrading those very sciences. But Vogt was vulnerable on purely professional grounds: it does not seem that during 1927 and 1929 he had undertaken any new research on Lenin's brain. In those two years he—or the Moscow Institute—could have come up, perhaps not with new discoveries, but certainly with additional descriptive data. At the very least, a description of Lenin's fissurization, information about the destroyed hemisphere, gross comparisons with other brains, and a catalogue of the major distinctions of the Lenin hemisphere were in order.[16]

But nothing had been happening. Vogt just repeated in 1929 what he had said in 1927. Perhaps the reason was that the Russian brain scientists, all of whom Vogt had trained, essentially on Lenin's brain, began to have second thoughts on the validity of Vogt's theories, methods and findings.

The problem was fourfold. On the highest level was the question of whether the "materialistic" base of genius had been found. Obviously, the materialist must stipulate that *all* the relevant material factors need be known and evaluated before a phenomenon can be fully explained. Perhaps Lenin's cells and third cortical layer were significant but were they *solely* responsible for his accomplishments? The discussion on this self-evident point never got started.

On the second level was the question of whether Vogt correctly

[15]Compare Cécile and Oskar Vogt, "Hirnforschung und Genetik," *Journal für Psychologie und Neurologie,* Vol. 39, No. 4-6, 1929, pp. 438-445. This was the issue dedicated to Semashko.

[16]For a drawing showing with great clarity the peculiarities of the fissures in Pilsudski's brain, see Karl Schaffer, "Einiges über das Gehirn der Hochtalente," *Schweizer Archiv für Neurologie und Psychiatrie,* Vol. XLIV, No. 2, 1939, p. 349. The Polish government, within less than four years after Pilsudski's death, published the first part of an analysis of his brain, with seventy large photographs and more than two hundred pages of explanatory text.

assessed the role of the pyramidal cells and of the third layer. On this point, many neurologists agreed with Vogt to a large extent, although the evidence was (and still is) inconclusive.[17] Yet it is also true that a high level of cerebration could be a function of an enlarged cortical surface due to heavy fissurization and that many or large cells could simply be compensating for inadequate fissurization.[18] Thus, data on cells, even assuming them to be more than mere impressions, are not by themselves informative but must be supplemented by other facts. Moreover, a potent neurological endowment of the associative functions does not need to result in high combinatory intelligence but can also be the basis of mental disturbance, including excitability, lack of concentration, etc. Much depends, *inter alia,* on synaptic thresholds and on the density of connections between the *specific* areas of the brain. Even if Vogt's

[17]Haymaker (*Neurology* [Minneapolis: Minn., Vol. 1, No. 3, 1951], p. 201) writes that the third lamina is "said to be concerned with associative function." According to James Papez, "Neuranatomy," *American Handbook of Psychiatry,* Vol. II (New York: Basic Books, 1959), p. 1611, "layer III may be regarded as the dominant layer fired by incoming sensory, thalamic and association systems for perceptional and memory images." The third layer also is connected with awareness, sensation, discrimination, perception, knowing and comprehending. The same author (p. 1612) contends that all large nerve cells are "probably true tape recorders." According to Riese, the pyramidal cells are "effectors" (*Principles of Neurology,* p. 41). However, according to Lorente de Nó, no layer may be called "effector," "receptor" or "associative," since nearly all layers contain afferent, efferent and associative elements. (J. F. Fulton, *Physiology of the Nervous System,* third edition [New York: Oxford, 1949], pp. 288-312.) Also, larger numbers of neurons are necessary for fuller conceptualization and finer analysis (R. W. Gerard, "Neurophysiology, Brain and Behavior," *Handbook,* Vol. II, p. 1635). But in addition, thresholds, metabolism, hormones, vitamins, sugar, enzymes etc., are involved. During 1936, Wilder Penfield was beginning to wonder, on the basis of the examination of conscious brains, whether the "indispensable substratum of consciousness lies outside the cortex, not in the new brain but in the old . . . probably in the diencephalon." He agreed (1959) that the cortex is more than a relay system and hypothesized that it may reorganize streams of impulses. Professor Lashley did not believe in the centrencephalic integrating system because the brain stem does not have enough cells or circuits for this purpose; yet the location at which the cortex should store the required engrams has not yet been found. Jasper suggested that the "relative simplicity of neuronal circuits in the reticular system" of the stem and the diencephalon may allow the selectivity required for "unity of performance . . . of the conscious mind and behavior," and also stressed that lesions in the reticular system have the most profound effect upon conscious behavior. Sir Russell Brain (1958) synthesized the old and the new view by saying, "Function of the cortex is the integration of those neural processes upon which consciousness depends, but this cortical function of integration in turn depends upon the integrity of the diencephalic and brain-stem activities." (Herbert H. Jasper, "Evolution of Conceptions of Cerebral Localization since Hughlings Jackson," *World Neurology,* Minneapolis, Minn., Vol. 1, No. 2, 1960, notably pp. 103-108.) Hence while Vogt's main thesis may have been strongly modified by more recent findings, cortex, third layer and pyramidal cells still are recognized as crucial elements of intelligent performance.

[18]Schaffer, p. 348.

postulates were entirely valid, on these questions Lenin's brain apparently yielded only fragmentary information.

The third question was whether Vogt properly correlated the histological facts with Lenin's behavior and intellectual activity. This question, we may be sure, was in 1929-1930 hardly discussed openly within the Brain Institute. But the Russian specialists were aware of this problem, which we might pursue for a moment. Vogt was told about Lenin's memory[19] and indeed large pyramidal cells might have been its basis; except that Lenin's memory, though good, was not outstanding. Vogt's notion that Lenin had exceptional associative powers and was able to do many disparate things simultaneously was most certainly wrong.[20] Far from being an *Assoziationsathlet,* Lenin's thinking moved in narrow and repetitive patterns. Lenin had no outstanding "multiplicity of ideas," nor a "wide range of thinking," let alone "unusual powers of intuition." He had an excellent sense of realism and often (though not always) his perceptions were rapid. But Vogt did not explain how these supposed talents were cyto-architectonically conditioned. If it be true that the "impulsive murderer" whose brain Vogt exhibited in 1927 did have a wide fourth and a narrow third layer, while Lenin's case was the obverse, this could at best mean that Lenin was no "impulsive murderer." As a matter of fact, he was not; but he deliberately caused the death of many people. Could a wide third lamina be associated with calculated political crime?

But the decisive question was this: How good were the observations on which all this theorizing was based? It soon transpired that Vogt's observations were anything but tenable.

I. N. Filimonov, who by the end of 1927 became the assistant director of the Brain Institute and in effect was running it, confirmed that the pyramidal cells in the third layer are growing after birth; this was interpreted to mean that Lenin's cells *could* be larger than those of other people. But Filimonov also called attention to the fact that the time which elapses between the moment of death and the fixing of the brain is of crucial importance for accurate measure-

---

[19]Information from Dr. Marguerite Vogt. However, there is no reference in Vogt's speeches to Lenin's memory capability.

[20]Vogt had been impressed by tales about Lenin but did not refer to facts like simultaneous dictation of several letters in his publications. Some of the tales originated with Foerster who probably got most of his information second-hand from Lenin's family. Foerster was one of those who held Lenin to be a "genius," basing this evaluation on long daily talks during the last two years of Lenin's life (*O Lenine,* Vol. IV, p. 206f). Actually, Foerster's contacts were by no means that close and Lenin scarcely debated with him matters which would allow such an evaluation. Foerster, however, stressed Lenin's willpower, which Vogt seems to have ignored.

ment.[21] If the time difference is more than five hours, findings might be very misleading.

The data do not disclose the methods used to fix Lenin's brain, but probably it was placed in formalin.[22] Nor was the time of fixation reported. However, we know that a minimum of 16 hours and 20 minutes, and a maximum of 21 hours, elapsed before fixation was accomplished.[23] The researchers in the Brain Institute were well aware of this key fact.

Presently, one of the Russian researchers, S. A. Sarkissov,[24] ostensibly taking issue with the argument that wild animals show better cell definitions than domesticated animals, explained that when the brains of dogs, rabbits, rats and foxes were put into solution 24 hours after death, they invariably showed beautiful large pyramidal cells. This suggested that Lenin's cells had been pathologically altered after death. The point which demolished half of Vogt's thesis should have been clear long before, because the granular cells *also* appeared enlarged, as Vogt himself had pointed out and promptly forgotten.

Subsequently, Filimonov (and others) politely criticized Vogt's cyto-architectonic theories. He complained pointedly about the difficulties with elite brains which, because of the time span between death and fixation, just do not allow "satisfying results." Delays, "as it was proved and as it was shown several times in the literature . . . cause great differences in the size of cells and the width of layers." Filimonov made two guarded references to the *cerebrum* of Lenin but in his clinical analyses apparently made no use of the Lenin specimens. Yet he counted large and numerous pyramidal cells in the third layers of control brains belonging to persons of only moderate talents.[25] Another blow was struck when an Austrian scientist proved that the staining method which Vogt had been using to argue that the pyramidal cells are association cells, did not show the cytological material accurately and was highly unreliable.

The work which Vogt wanted to start in earnest during 1930 never got under way. Vogt did not return to Moscow and never saw the new building in which the Brain Institute was eventually housed.

[21]*Journal für Psychologie und Neurologie,* Vol. 39, No. 4-6, 1929, pp. 328, 377ff.

[22]"The unsuitability of the brains removed many hours after death, and fixed in the usual way by immersion in formalin, should be evident to every one, and the histological preparations made from them show clear evidence of pathological alterations." (Bailey and Bonin, p. VIII.)

[23]*Proletarskaya Revolyutsiya,* No. 3, 1924, p. 17.

[24]S. A. Sarkissov, "Zur Frage nach dem Einfluss der Fixierung auf das Zellbild der Grosshirnrinde," *Journal für Psychologie und Neurologie,* Vol. 41, No. 5, 1930, pp. 265-272.

[25]*Journal für Psychologie und Neurologie,* Vol. 42, Nos. 3-4, pp. 213 and 262; and Vol. 44, Nos. 1-2, 1932, pp. 1-96, especially p. 23. It should be observed that Vogt was the editor of the *Journal* and loyally printed all the articles which, if only by inference were highly critical of him.

In a short release published in 1938,[26] it was alleged that the Institute, which in the meantime had been branching out into the study of Pavlovian techniques and electro-physiology, was founded in 1927—an obvious attempt to conceal the early connection with Vogt. The Institute's first efforts, so it was stated, had been devoted to the study of cortical cyto-architectonics. Yet *no* reference was made to the study of Lenin's brain, or even to the fact that this brain was preserved in the Institute. In 1940, at a Moscow congress devoted to cerebral localization, the whole theory of localization was given the brush-off as a phase in the history of neurology. "The complex brain function is to some extent as independent of separate brain areas as planned movement is of any single muscle." This was considered a victory of dialectical over mechanistic materialism.[27]

In 1950, the Vogts reiterated that, according to their experience, elite brains always display anatomical peculiarities; either throughout the entire cortex, or in several or single areas, or in the type of cells. Lenin's brain, Vogt recalled, showed a wide third layer, however, the size of Lenin's pyramidal cells was now forgotten.[28]

In 1951 the Vogts wrote in an American journal:[29]

We have been able in all cases thus far examined to demonstrate anatomic peculiarities or alterations in the brains of individuals whose mental achievements were far above or below the average, in congenital or acquired idiocy, in schizophrenia and other psychoses. . . . As far as our present knowledge goes, it is permissible to correlate these alterations with the degree of mental ability or with the disease process, in spite of the fact that some of these conditions had previously been considered to be functional psychoses or neuroses.

However, still another point was involved. The study of a brain must always be "gross and cyto-architectural." "Always when one part of the brain was exceptionally well developed, other parts were in the realm of normal or were underdeveloped; hence universal genius was considered impossible."[30] But there were no gross data

[26]*Acta Medica* USSR, Vol. 1, No. 3-4, Moscow, 1938, p. 6ff.

[27]Walther Riese and Ebbe C. Hoff, "A History of the Doctrine of Cerebral Localization," *Journal of the History of Medicine and Allied Sciences*, New York, Vol. V, No. 1, p. 68f.

[28]"Wie weit lassen sich schon heute bei Funktionsanomalien des Gehirnes anatomische Besonderheiten nachweisen?" *Der Nervenarzt*, Wuerzburg, Vol. 22, No. 8, August 20, 1950, p. 337ff.

[29]"Importance of Neuroanatomy in the Field of Neuropathology," *Neurology*, Vol. 1, No. 3, 1951, p. 209.

[30]Webb Haymaker, "Cécile and Oskar Vogt on the Occasion of her 75th and his 80th Birthday," *Neurology, ibid.*, p. 201. Incidentally, Vogt was fired by the Nazis from the directorship of his Institute at Berlin. In 1950, he received, though living in West Germany, a prize from East Germany, and he also was conferred an Honorary D. Sc. by Oxford (*ibid.*, p. 195).

on Lenin's brain, let alone information about those parts of his cerebral equipment which, *ex hypothesi*, must have been under-developed.

While Lenin's brain was being abused to enhance the cause of materialism, his decorticated body was on a more mundane Odyssey to serve in the cause of twentieth century idolatry.

By 1926, rumors were rife all over Moscow that the embalmed body of Lenin, which was exhibited in the mausoleum and worshipped every day by thousands of faithful Communists, was actually only a doll. To dispel these rumors, the Russian government invited a German physician to participate as an "objective observer" in the labors of a commission investigating the authenticity of Lenin's corpse. This doctor happened to be a tourist visiting Moscow and was not known to be an expert. Apparently he was simply a general practitioner with somewhat leftist leanings. The doctor duly reported that he had seen Lenin's body under a 2000-candlepower light. Different shades of skin, spots, and little hairs were visible. Blemishes such as minor frost bites were noted on the cheeks and ears. The forehead looked as though there was perspiration on it. The figure impressed the doctor as that of a sleeping sick man. But honest fellow that he was, he added that there was a strange discoloration on the right thumb which the Russian experts assured him would vanish.

The same witness elucidated the history of the embalmment as it had been told to him in 1927.[31] Initial preparations were made during the autopsy. This was an important alibi point; but it is unlikely that a decision had then been made to embalm the body for permanent exhibition. However, the doctor negated the alibi through his disclosure that the body already was damaged at the time the autopsy was undertaken. This indeed is confirmed from other sources which reported that putrefaction was very rapid.

After the initial embalming, the witness continued, the body deteriorated within six weeks. Two Russian professors were ordered to reprocess the corpse. They began their task two months and nineteen days after Lenin's death. In cold, wet weather they labored for four-and-a-half months, under poor working conditions in a leaky wooden structure which lacked air conditioning. In the course of the autopsy and the initial embalming, most of the vessels necessary for embalmment had been destroyed. This would normally have precluded the preservation of the body, but the Russian experts invented a new process which overcame this "difficulty." This new technique was so successful, the witness asserted, that he could

[31]Dr. Victor Schilling. "Vor der einbalsamierten Leiche Lenins," *Die Umschau, Illustrierte Wochenschrift über die Fortschritte in Wissenschaft und Technik* (Frankfurt, 1927), pp. 266-268.

bend the corpse's ear; the cheeks felt soft and cool; and when he lifted an arm, it fell back without stiffness.

This accomplishment was hailed as a sensational breakthrough in the science of embalming. However, the two Russian experts, so the German was told, were not sure of their achievement and wanted to wait for another three years before divulging the process. Actually, the process had been divulged during 1925 and was that of Professor Melnikov-Razvedenkov, as modified by Professor Vorobiev. It was disclosed that Aprikossov, the autopsist, had been asked originally to preserve the body only for six days but that after the body had been lying in state, the actual embalmment was begun by Professors Vorobiev and Zvarsk after one month. (It is not known where the body was kept during that time.)

When the embalmment was begun, putrefaction had progressed and mummification, especially of the face and the head, had become apparent. Since as a result of the autopsy, embalmment by intravascular injection no longer was feasible, another procedure was employed. The body was immersed in water, then in a mixture of water and weakly concentrated acetic acid, and finally in peroxide of oxygen. The objective was to conserve the body without desiccation. For this purpose potassium acetate was used but in order to allow that this hygroscopic salt became truly effective, deep incisions were made all over the body. Ultimately, the body was immersed in a solution of alcohol, glycerine, formalin, and potassium acetate. The whole process lasted about four months, after which the "spots" disappeared, and the tissues again resembled normal tissues.[32]

By 1927, rumors about the body forced the authorities to take such counter-measures as inviting "inspections" by foreign observers. However, by 1928, the body had clearly deteriorated, and the mausoleum was closed for one month. For the "repair work" Vorobiev and Zvarsk were joined by an Austrian specialist, Professor Ferdinand Hochstetter, who had perfected a method to preserve bodies for indefinite periods.[33] This method, in contrast to the one used before,

[32]Information by Doctor Lauer in *Revue Franco-Russe de Médicine et de Biologie,* May 1925, as quoted in *Chronique Médicale,* Paris, Vol. 33, 1926, p. 82; also Ricardo Royo-Villanova y Morales, "El Cadaver de Lenin," *Cronica Medica,* Valencia, vol. 39, 1935, p. 587f. Note the discrepancies between this information and that given to Schilling on the timing of these operations. According to Royo-Villanova, the embalmment process used by Vorobiev was a modification of procedures used already by the ancient Chinese, from whom the old Egyptians took over most of their techniques.

[33]Hochstetter, a well-known anatomist, also was a brain specialist and was particularly knowledgeable about the processing of brains and brain slices. The Brain Institute apparently used his methods for the preparation of fetal materials. (Filimonov in *Journal für Psychologie und Neurologie,* vol. 39, No. 4-6, 1929, p, 326). Since Hochstetter was in Moscow during 1928, and the Brain Institute began to use his procedures at about this time, he obviously was in contact with Filimonov *et al.* This suggests that he might have been consulted on the problem of Lenin's brain.

aimed at bringing about the complete desiccation of the body, and then to impregnate it with paraffin. Whether or not Hochstetter used his customary method in reprocessing Lenin's body was not disclosed. It is, of course, possible that the three professors invented a new process to fit this unusual problem of achieving a third embalmment. However, extensive reprocessing of a perforated body which originally was to be kept life-like, and its transformation into one which was to be completely desiccated, would appear to be impossible, especially if life-likeness continued to be desired. Was this ever attempted? One is reminded of Dr. Johnson's remark on a dog walking on its hindlegs: "It is not done well; but you are surprised to find it done at all."

In the early 1930's observers visiting the mausoleum noticed that there existed no protrusion where the feet should be located: in later visits, such a protrusion was visible.[34] It also was noted that Lenin's head displayed more hair than he possessed at the age of thirty. At the occasion of the tenth anniversary of Lenin's death, Vorobiev and Zvarsk examined the body. Finding it in a state "better than expected," they were rewarded and decorated by the Soviet government. Indeed the likeness, with its colors and even its expressions, has been attested to by many of those who knew Lenin during his lifetime.

But the trouble was that, as of that time, "science did not know of any method to conserve a human body for a long time and without any changes."[35] Mummies can be preserved for indefinite periods, but they are completely desiccated and parched. Lenin, by contrast, looked as though he were alive!

The Soviets may have discovered the ideal embalmment process, but so far they have not seen fit to disclose their secret. (Nor has the secret been leaked in Professor Hochstetter's homeland.) Imagine: if there were such a method—how many immortal politicians would be remaining among us?

The visitor to the marble mausoleum on Moscow's Red Square can gaze, through indirect lighting, at Lenin's head and hands. Whether there is a body beneath the velvet and the flag of the Paris Commune which covers the middle portion of the catafalque, he is unable to discern. Perhaps the hands and the head were preserved, after all. . . . But the odds are overwhelming that when in 1928 the paraffin treatment was rejected or did not work, an unnamed practitioner of Mme. Tussaud's art modelled Lenin's hands and head from wax. (There are a number of processes through which a wax face can be fitted with authentic hair and a lifelike skin.)

During World War II, Lenin's "body" was removed to Kuybyshev

[34]Royo-Villanova, p. 587, is just one of many who remarked on this point.

[35]Royo-Villanova, p. 592.

—a town named after the man who had once wanted to deceive Lenin by printing his article on inspection in a single issue of *Pravda*. After the war, the "body" was returned to the mausoleum. It seems that during the move, several "improvements" were made. In 1953, the corpse of Stalin, Lenin's most deadly enemy, was placed by Lenin's catafalque. Stalin's body remained there until the end of 1961[36] when it was evicted and unceremoniously reburied inside the Kremlin. Yet Stalin's grave is known, marked, and prominent.

Such is not the case with the corpse of Lenin: If he ever was in the mausoleum, his remains probably had to be disposed of during 1928. But the location of his grave or his urn is unknown. One story has it that his ashes were scattered over the banks of the Volga. Since his mother, at least two of his sisters, and his brother-in-law were given burial, this story seems groundless.

A strange ending for a life whose heritage, accomplishments, and memory have been held in careful esteem by his successors and admirers.

The Communists, who do not believe in immortality, fabricated a wax dummy to establish *their* claim on eternity. To worship the idol, they deprived the human of an honorable burial and denied him a last resting place. The desecration of the dead is an ever recurring and repulsive hallmark of totalitarianism. But there was no Communist Antigone to sacrifice her own life in protest against this ultimate denial of humanity and personal freedom. The Communists with their dead souls hardly understand, even now, the enormity of the sacrilege. *Animus meminisse horret.*

[36]The assumption is that Stalin's corpse was effectively treated and properly kept from the start.

APPENDIX

every kumrad is a bit
of quite unmitigated hate
(travelling in a futile groove
god knows why)
and so do i
(because they are afraid to love).
                    e. e. cummings

The Psychology of Destruction

Although an explanation of the complex Bolshevik revolution cannot be attempted in this work, a study of the psychology of Lenin, the man, may be relevant.

Lenin was short in stature, presenting a squat appearance. The police gave his exact height as 2 *arshin* 5½ *vershok* (5 feet, 6½ inches). With a certain statistical regularity, such a "pyknik habitus" is correlated with a cyclothymic or cycloid personality type. The "rotund, robust type" is most "apt to suffer a cerebral hemorrhage."[1]

As has been shown, Lenin's ego structure was exceptionally strong; despite frequent setbacks, he exhibited few signs of deep frustration, never relenting in his ultimate purpose. Although he often suffered from psychosomatic gastric and vascular disorders, Lenin experienced no serious "illness" until he was forty-eight—as a result of two bullet wounds acquired in the assassination attempt. When he was fifty or fifty-one, he was struck by the cerebral arteriosclerosis that killed him at the age of fifty-four.

Lenin was capable of considerable concentration on his intellectual work and lengthy expenditure of high energy, yet he was not interested in athletics, preferring mainly occasional hikes. In his youth he did some swimming and hunting, in his exile years, he relaxed walking in the mountains, and later made several hunting trips during his tenure at the Kremlin. A reasonably good shot, he liked to hunt mainly because it divorced him from the telephone, from letters, and from decision-making. Otherwise, Lenin, who had a pale complexion, was an indoor type. Yet he was not addicted to the typical "indoor vices," was extremely frugal, and disliked drinking, smoking, and overeating. Krupskaya emphasized that he liked to sleep with his windows open. Servants commented on his cleanliness and sense of order, and Krylenko asserted that, even while hunting, Lenin did not use swear words. The latter is somewhat suspect, since in his literary work Lenin expressed himself in the strongest words printable.

[1]Franz Alexander, *Psychosomatic Medicine* (New York: Norton, 1950), p. 71.

Lenin had an excellent sense of finance. Completely uninterested in earning money for his personal comfort, he was extraordinarily adept at raising funds, if often by illegal and criminal means. Money was an instrument of the political struggle, wholly unconnected with morality—and the single-minded Lenin knew how to spend effectively the money he had, whether to finance propaganda, procure arms, or buy votes and souls. His ability to obtain funds and his skill in using them are among the key conditions of his success.

Lenin's brother and two of his sisters died young. While Lenin left no offspring, it is asserted that he and Krupskaya loved children. This may be a legend; an occasional romp with children does not necessarily denote such love. Considering the vagaries of a revolutionary career, the Lenins may have decided against parenthood; but even in this case the probability of accidental pregnancy would have been high in a sexually normal couple living in situations where contraceptives were practically unavailable, as in the Siberian exile.[2] Krupskaya contracted Graves' disease ten years after her marriage, and in view of the nature of this malady, a considerable decline, if not disappearance, of her libido must be assumed. But this occurred after many years of marriage; undoubtedly the marriage was consummated. In view of the assertion of one well-informed witness that Lenin and Krupskaya very much wanted a child,[3] the presumption of infertility is strong.

The question of sterility is of great importance, since sterility, especially if it occurs in whole families, may be safely considered as a symptom of genetic trouble. Lenin himself was not unaware of this possibility and suspected some syphilitic impact somewhere. Biological weakness also may have been due to the fact that Lenin's father was conceived when the grandfather was 66 and the grandmother 41 years of age.

Medical science during Lenin's lifetime often associated sterility with degeneracy. According to the thinking of the period, the various classes of "degenerates" included people suffering from neurasthenia and individuals with "unimpaired intellectual processes . . . who have a disturbance of their feelings and impulses."[4] While the nomenclature of "degeneracy" no longer remains in use, and while modern scientists prefer to coin less opprobious terms, the phenomena and their interconnections, which have been described under this heading of "degeneracy", are real enough and are again attracting well

2The use of such devices was as yet very infrequent: the first birth-control center was opened in 1890 in Amsterdam.

3G. A. Solomon, *Lenin i ego semya (Ulyanovy)* (Paris: no publisher, 1931), p. 51.

4Richard D. Walter, "What became of the Degenerate? A Brief History of a Concept," *Journal of the History of Medicine*, Vol. XI, No. 4 ,1956, p. 423.

deserved attention. The Ulyanov family had a very high incidence of "neurasthenics" and moral eccentrics. It is unlikely that there were no genetic factors involved.

While it is true that Krupskaya's father was sickly and died quite young, the indications of infertility in the Ulyanov family are more relevant to the question. There exists a picture of Lenin in 1922, with "a nephew" who appears to be about six years of age. His identity is uncertain, yet we know that Anna and Mark Yelizarov, who were unable to produce offspring, adopted in 1913 a young boy named Georgi Y. Losgachev. He had come to their attention through newspaper articles featuring the gifted child: son of a janitor and a washerwoman, he was able to read at three and by the time he was five was studying the classics. The well-to-do Yelizarovs persuaded the parents to give them the child and provided him with a good middle-class education. During the February revolution, when street battles were taking place, the Ulyanov sisters used the little boy as courier and instructed him to paint slogans on the walls of houses. Losgachev ultimately became a military judge and reportedly retired at the age of forty. Born in 1906, he was sixteen in 1922, and so could not have been the nephew shown in the picture. A single Soviet source claims that this nephew Victor[5] was the son of Dimitri Ulyanov. If so, Dimitri would have been about forty-two or forty-three when he became a father. He was married to Antonina I. Neshcheratov but, at the time the boy was conceived, Dimitri was serving in the army and probably was away from home. The few data that are available about his life suggest that he was

[5]There is a short two-page recollection by Victor about Lenin. This report purports to be written by a child and bears all the earmarks of ghostwriting. According to this paper, Victor during the winter of 1921 was living in the environs of Moscow, then moved to Anna Yelizarova's. He spent the summer of 1922 at Gorki, apparently was there during 1923, staying through Christmas of that year. Dimitri spent part of this time in the Crimea and it is not reported that he visited Lenin at Gorki, except once as a doctor in May of 1922. If Victor were Dimitri's son, he would have stayed with him in the Crimea or at Moscow, and he probably would not have stayed outside of Moscow and then moved to Anna's flat. Naturally, Dimitri might have been visiting Gorki more often than appears from the available evidence, but Victor hardly would have spent Christmas there without his alleged parents also being present. But apparently Dimitri and his wife were not there. Victor's own report hinted that he was staying at Gorki all the time, and certainly Dimitri was nothing more than an occasional visitor. However, Maria was living at Gorki continuously during Lenin's illness. It would be hard to believe that a household with the chores imposed by serious illness would adopt a child who belongs to a successful relative living somewhere else.

[6]Anna Kunze, "Da waren alle Einwände widerlegt," in *Der unvergessliche Lenin, Erinnerungen deutscher Genossen,* edited by Institut für Marxismus-Leninismus (Berlin: Dietz, 1960), p. 151. Trotsky, who had no use for Maria, described her as "an old maid" who concentrated all the strength of her unspent love on her brother Vladimir." Trotsky also mentioned her rivalry with Krupskaya (*Diary,* p. 33).

childless. However, there is a reference to such a son by one of Lenin's sisters. This sister (who must have been Maria) brought a German woman Communist, in the Tsar's automobile, to visit a children's home, where her own child was being raised.[6] There is no particular reason to question this suitably detailed story. The chances are, therefore, that Victor Ulyanov was Maria's son. If so, she became a mother when she was about thirty-nine. The confusion seems to result from the fact that if Victor was Maria's son, the child was illegitimate. Hence the puritanical Communists preferred for many years to treat Lenin's nephew as an "unperson," and it is only recently that they have identified him by any name.

It is probable that Victor was fathered by Stanislav Stanislavovich Krzhizhanovsky. Virtually nothing is known of him except that he was presumably a relative—perhaps a cousin—of Lenin's friend, Gleb Krzhizhanovsky. Maria and Stanislav had known each other from an early period, were implicated together in a political affair at Saratov, and between 1911 and 1912 were both exiled at Vologda. Since they were arrested together, it is to be presumed that they petitioned the police for a common place of exile residence, claiming that they were engaged to be married.

Stanislav was wounded in the war and again met Maria in a military hospital at Lvov where she was a nurse. Apparently the two were living together, or near each other, in Moscow during 1916. Maria, who was a devoted daughter, delayed visiting her sick mother in Petrograd almost until it was too late. This behavior was unusual and could be explained by a reluctance to disclose her pregnancy. From known dates it can be deduced that the child was born during May or June, 1916; however, the Soviet source asserts he was born in 1917.[7] Krzhizhanovsky is described as a "near friend of Maria I. Ulyanova, a Social Democrat, Bolshevik."[8] It is by no means clear why the two did not marry, but perhaps he died of his wounds.

Shortly after Lenin's death, Maria was stricken by a light form of tuberculosis. She had not been well previously. Family correspondence, especially her mother's letters, indicate that she was a constant source of worry. Apparently she was nervous, excitable and unstable.[9] Maria died of a cerebral hemorrhage. She and Lenin inherited their disposition towards arteriosclerosis from their father. Lenin's older sister, Anna, apparently succumbed after a series of strokes. Lenin's mother suffered several times from unspecified illnesses which, in one or two instances, may have been psychosomatic.

[7]The same source indicates that Victor, an engineer, was running a laboratory; he became a member of the Communist party only in 1944 when he was twenty-seven. He was decorated with the Red Star and several medals.

[8]*Istoricheskii Arkhiv*, No. 2 ,1958, p. 22f.

[9]For examples, see *ibid.*, pp. 7 and 14.

She lived, though, to the age of eighty-one. However, according to one of Lenin's doctors, she too was afflicted by arteriosclerosis; presumably hers was a light case.

One sister and one brother survived a normal life span, another sister and Lenin died in their fifties, a third sister died at a very young age, another as an infant, and, of course, one brother was executed. It is reported that all Ulyanov children were sickly in their youth. There are frequent references to Anna's and Maria's sicknesses and to surgical operations.

Not surprisingly, the life of the Ulyanov parent family has been described as ideal.[10] Allegedly it was entirely harmonious and marked by mutual love. The facts, however, disclose something else. The relationship between the parents may have been outwardly peaceful, but there was manifested little love, warmth, or tenderness. Tensions, though generally suppressed, were strong. The father was frequently absent on trips; as a result, the children were brought up as half-orphans. (Krupskaya, in 1938, admitted that Lenin "did not idealize his father."[11]) It is to be presumed that their father's returns were experienced as disturbances. Ilya Ulyanov maintained only minimal sex relations with his wife and there are indications that he wanted no children.

Lenin was close to his three sisters and they apparently reciprocated in their affections. Anna and Maria aided him in his political work. Maria, who was considered by the family to be dull-minded, often lived with the Lenins. Throughout his last illness, when Krupskaya functioned only intermittently, Maria cared for the patient. Anna, who was described as mean, ugly, difficult, and domineering, enjoyed Lenin's full confidence, even with respect to conspiratorial matters. Lenin and Anna were similar in many respects; apparently they got along with each other quite well. Lenin's relations with his older brother Alexander were constructive in early childhood but later became competitive and hostile. (Krupskaya averred that he did not admire his brother blindly.) Apparently, Alexander's execution did not throw Lenin into a psychological crisis, let alone produce a trauma. There is no question that it impressed him as one of the most important experiences of his early life. Lenin's attitude to Dimitri was condescending and contemptuous; he considered his younger brother a fool.

In later years the family, under Anna's leadership, indulged in an elaborate mother cult. Anna insisted that visitors be particularly nice to her and tried to insure some gaiety to counteract the oppressive

10A similar legend has been spun about the allegedly happy and entirely harmonious relationship between Marx and his wife. The true story of that marriage still remains to be written.

11*Istoricheskii Arkhiv*, No. 4, 1958, p. 76f.

and depressive atmosphere exuded by their mother. It is said that Maria Ulyanovna fell sick after Alexander's execution and Anna cared for her. Thereafter, she remained nervous and preoccupied, and her children avoided discussing revolutionary affairs in her presence. There is no doubt that she was held in great affection. Lenin himself, otherwise ice-cold, changed his countenance when he talked about his mother, often describing her as "a saint."[12] As a youth and until he was about forty, he remained very close to her.

Lenin's relations with his father were ambivalent. It is said that as a child he was obedient. Lenin learned from his father self-discipline and a respect for learning. Yet his father was harsh, distant, and forbidding, and allowed no warmth to enter into the relationship.

After his father's death, Lenin demonstratively turned to atheism. Of course, the father probably was not genuinely religious: at that time most Russian natural scientists tended toward agnosticism. Hence, Lenin's manifestation of irreligiosity may have had a political tinge. Against the wishes of his father, Lenin may have decided to oppose religion as a pillar of the tsarist state. After the assassination of Alexander II, the elder Lenin was so jarred that he put on his uniform and went to mass.[13] Since his father was a staunch upholder of the existing system, a negative attitude toward his father provided at least one root of Lenin's hatred of tsarism. This hatred preceded his infatuation with socialism and stayed with him until the end of his life, even when his socialist convictions were growing weaker. Lenin was an exceptionally vehement hater, and his distaste for dissenting socialists was not much weaker than his hatred of tsarism. He apparently did not hate Krupskaya and Inessa, but was contemptuous of many of his close collaborators. In general, hatred was his predominant sentiment; and it seems to have come to the fore again toward the end of his life, after a decline at the beginning of his illness.

Naturally, Lenin's hatred of tsarism had multiple sources. In addition to his attitude toward his father, his complex national background, the execution of his brother (and the temporary ostracism of his family), his loneliness after being dismissed from the university, and his professional difficulties both as a farmer and lawyer, there existed a highly objectionable political condition. Painful childhood and adolescent impressions such as a devastating famine, police oppression, and the intellectual milieu of thought control and

[12]Solomon, p. 26.

[13]Krupskaya, trying to prove the political precocity of Lenin, asserted that he was much taken aback by his father's action. (He was then eleven years old.) (*Istoricheskii Arkhiv*, No. 4, 1958, p. 78.) The important part is that this incident was symptomatic of the father's general attitude.

political criticism formed part of Lenin's conditioning.

In a well-known psychological reaction, lack of parental and environmental tenderness engenders anxiety in the child. Anxiety, in turn, leads to aggressive behavior and destructiveness. Further development is influenced by the stereotypes to which the juvenile is exposed.

Revolutionary ideas undoubtedly were discussed at the Ulyanov home and probably were expressed by Lenin's mother over the objections of her husband. These ideas acquired emotional associations, for they were interwoven with the parental struggle. Had these ideas not possessed emotional coloring, it would be difficult to explain why *all* the Ulyanov children, in varying degrees, committed themselves to the revolutionary cause. The true role of their father can be deduced from the fact that all the children sided against him. Characteristically, the resentment of the younger children was weaker and that of the youngest son was weakest: the father was almost constantly present when the older children were growing up but frequently was absent while the younger children were being raised.

Alexander, the eldest son, was the most strongly and personally committed. His case displays definite oedipal characteristics. Alexander was nursed by his mother and manifested strong competitive emotions against his father. As formulated by Freud, terroristic acts against a father-image (e.g., the Tsar) are psychologically rooted in parricidal wishes. Alexander's psychology demonstrates manic-depressive traits and his voluntary assumption of responsibility, along with his suicidal refusal to ask for clemency, suggest intense guilt feelings. His warm relationship with women—he was engaged to be married when he was only twenty—fits this picture perfectly.

Alexander, a close replica of Dostoyevsky's Raskolnikov, differed psychologically from Vladimir. One notable difference was the apparent lack of guilt feelings in Lenin. It would seem that, as an infant, Lenin considered the whole environment—rather than a single person—to be hostile; only when he was a bit older did he direct his opposition against the two competing males, his father and older brother. Endowed with an exceptionally strong "will," he early exhibited a drive for dominance which manifested itself in a variety of ways, including an unwillingness to walk before he was three, a tendency to fall and hurt his head, and frequent destructive rages.

Unless this behavior is explained entirely on the basis of inherited factors, Lenin must have undergone severe psychological stress during the first period of his life. "Oral deprivation" is implied and may have been caused by his mother's lactation difficulties which required the services of a wet nurse; it may account for the lack of "fellow feeling," which characterized Lenin's interpersonal relations. It should be added that the analysis of psychopathic personalities with characteristics similar to those of Lenin sometimes discloses that the patient as an infant had observed his parents in the act of love-making. Since the Ulyanov parents slept separately and infant Vladimir probably slept with his mother, this "explanation" may be applicable in this case.

At school, Lenin was a good—almost a perfect—student. There is no evidence of truancy, misbehavior, or rebelliousness towards teachers. In fact, both the older Ulyanov boys and girls were model students. Maria experienced difficulties only at the university level. The third son, who became a physician, apparently was an indifferent student. Though Lenin depreciated him as a politician, he often asked his medical advice. The intellectual talent of the family is beyond argument.

It is likely that the death of the father created uncertainty and anxiety. The circumstances surrounding Alexander's arrest and execution must have been cause for immediate fear. But there is no evidence that in the long run the family was harrassed or inconvenienced. Still, Lenin was not permitted to attend university classes. This banishment from the university imposed upon him long periods of solitude, isolating him from human relations outside of his family. For several years he experienced uncertainty concerning a professional career.

After the death of the two senior males, Lenin moved easily into the role of family boss, a position his psyche had craved. His drive had not been to be the father's successor vis-à-vis the mother: he wanted to be the leader of the clan. He longed to be the person who is always right, who controls people and things, who is admired, who does not render but who receives service—and who may use a "family" to enhance his ego and satisfy his power urge. Lenin felt little sense of responsibility toward his relatives; he was willing to render advice but expected them, especially his mother, to provide assistance, often in the form of money.

Like a pasha in his harem, Lenin was always surrounded by women. Yet his attitude toward women was basically one of paternal authority, devoid of erotic love and intimacy; however close women were to him, they were expected to function as servants and professional assistants. Women were "useful" as couriers, code clerks, secretaries, translators, and *perhaps* as companions. In his underdeveloped emotional life women had no inherent value as women. Stunting of emotional and sensuous capabilities or lack of full emotional satisfaction often is related to an irrational and irrepressible drive of destructiveness.

Lenin's relations with his classmates, colleagues, and contemporaries seem to have been cool and impersonal. During his life, he was prone to enter into close but, almost invariably, only temporary intellectual and functional relations with men. Practically all the "friends" who helped him were eventually discarded, often in a humiliating manner. Those who worked for him had to do his bidding. Slight disagreements, often over trifles and usually about power, led to hasty and spiteful "splits." These ruptures were healed only occasionally. It was as though Lenin, unable to bear an association for any length of time with one person, felt a psychological compulsion to destroy the closeness, lest anyone become too intimate with him. In the period of 1908 to 1912, he broke with nearly all his associates and ended in almost complete isolation.

Lenin did not have a single life-long friend. He was friendly but distant with Yelizarov, his hen-pecked brother-in-law,[14] and maintained a not very deep friendship with Krzhizhanovsky. Only for a man like Martov, who was his equal, did he maintain some semblance of personal loyalty despite political enmity. But it was only when he thought he was dying that he touched briefly upon his attraction to the human characteristics of Martov. Gorky and Plekhanov functioned somewhat as father-images and personal ruptures were followed by partial reconciliations. Lenin ended in good relations with Gorky and had ultimate regrets about the break with Plekhanov, but this personal "warmth" did not appear before he was very ill. He respected Krassin.[15] With genuine competitors like Trotsky relations were very unstable and basically hostile. He betrayed Malinovsky, to whom he had been personally attached and to whom he was bound by conspiratorial obligations. Only with a few of the "younger comrades," such as Bukharin, did he assume a genuine paternal attitude and show an inclination to forgive. Sverdlov and, to a lesser extent, Dzerzhinski were the only high ranking party functionaries whom he trusted. The builders of the Bolshevik party broke with him at one time or another; usually because they objected to immoral actions on his part. The uprising of 1917 would not have been realized had Lenin not been joined by former enemies, Mensheviks, and other Social Democrats, who had opposed his divisive tactics and had pleaded for unity. On the other hand, the October revolution never would have happened but for Lenin and his ability to lead, rather than conform to his "peer group."[16]

[14]Yelizarov, who for a short while served as Commissar of Transportation, did not think Lenin was quite "normal." (Solomon, p. 28.)

[15]The affection was by no means mutual. In 1916, Solomon approached Krassin to obtain money for Lenin. Krassin did not want to talk about Lenin and said that he did not merit being supported. (Solomon, p. 77f.)

[16]Trotsky (Diary, p. 46) pointed out that both he and Lenin made the revolution. It could not have happened if only Trotsky had been available. Trotsky thought that Lenin could have seized power without Trotsky's help but this is highly questionable.

Despite Lenin's vitality and intellectual precocity, his sexual libido was very weak. It is quite possible, of course, that his sex life was of a greater intensity than is evident from the record. But his psychological characteristics, as well as his ascetic convictions and living habits, support the hypothesis of a low libido. Only one woman appeared in his younger years and she was nine years his senior. The initiative for his marriage was taken by Krupskaya, who was slightly older.[17] A mother fixation is thus transparent.

It is quite certain that after 1909 Lenin and Krupskaya no longer lived as man and wife. Several times, it seems, Krupskaya, indicating her willingness to leave her husband, asked for a divorce, but Lenin requested that she stay. This would be in consonance with his lack of sexual initiative and his fear of compromising revolution with love. Perhaps Lenin was hesitant to live with the vivacious and sexually alert Inessa. But Lenin was a great philistine, almost in the puritan tradition. His character had the authoritarian traits which practically forbade gratification, let alone the abandonment of the head of the family role. In opposition to the rumors begun by some of his disenchanted associates that he was impotent from his youth, it would seem that there occurred in him no loss of self-esteem, as should have been expected if there had been genuine impotence. Perhaps his low activity was in the nature of ego defense, but it is more likely that, being overly occupied with his other drives, he had little interest in and time for sex.

Irrespective of whether his sex drive was merely weak or was in fact repressed, such abstinence may produce irritability, insomnia, and vindictiveness (or it could reinforce these traits if they are symptomatic of other problems). Abstinence also contributes to a stunting of the personality, especially in its emotional aspects.

After Lenin met Inessa Armand, he overcame a long period of depression. For a while, a moderate interest in the emotional and sexual aspects of life became visible. Yet Inessa, a fertile woman still in the child-bearing age, did not bear him any children. In its middle phase, their relationship was frequently interrupted by long and seemingly unnecessary separations. The nature of their relationship after 1912, and even more so after 1917, is in doubt. The fragmentary data that are available are not incompatible with the interpretation that Lenin had no sexual life after returning to Russia in April, 1917. On the other hand, there is the remote possibility that his sexual interests may have reawakened briefly during 1917 with Fofanova,

---

[17]This reversal of the usual relationship often appears in Russian literature (e.g., Tatyana's letter to Eugen Onegin) and seems to happen often to Russian men. See Boris Shub and Helene Zwerdling, "Sex in the Soviet Union," *The Encyclopedia of Sexual Behavior,* edited by Albert Ellis and Albert Abarbanel, vol. II, New York, Hawthorn, 1961, p. 989f.

but this hardly was a lasting liaison. There is the doubtful possibility of an affair with Fotieva, and after a lengthy break he may have resumed closer relations with Inessa shortly before her death. In any event, Lenin's sexual life, at the latest, ceased with Inessa's death in the fall of 1920. While he was the ruler of Russia, information indicates that most of the time Lenin was sexually inactive. The evidence suggests that after the age of fifty he was impotent: a case could be made for advancing the onset of his impotency by several years.

When he was twenty-three or twenty-four years old, Lenin began to manifest psychosomatic diseases. Initially, he suffered nervous stomach cramps and digestive troubles; for considerable time he was on a strict diet. At 25, he had a bout with pneumonia.[18] Subsequently he was afflicted by occasional skin eruptions. However, most somatic difficulties seem to have disappeared after he was thirty-eight. This is the normal course of psychosomatic illness, but it is also noteworthy that this health improvement coincided with Inessa's appearance. Restlessness, headaches, insomnia, violent dreams, and talking in his sleep never disappeared: these afflications plagued him during his youth in minor ways and became worse after 1903. Symptoms of tension became very pronounced after he was forty-five and often paralyzed him in situations of crisis.

Continuous tension may result in somatic sickness; it almost invariably entails psychological consequences. Lack of sleep is often caused by excitement; the insomniac, while lying in bed, tends to emote hatred;[19] hate may enhance insomnia; and fatigue may produce irritability, excitement and rage—a vicious circle, or rather, a vicious spiral. Sound sleepers, by contrast, usually "abreact" their hostile emotions through sleep. Headaches also cause a morose, spiteful, suspicious disposition which interacts with insomnia and tension.

The apparent agoraphobia which became noticeable during his last illness may have troubled Lenin throughout his life; it would explain his contentment with living in dark, small, uncomfortable flats. Circumstances often placed him in good living quarters, but he was personally satisfied with little rooms overlooking sooty courtyards. Agoraphobia involves a tendency to withdraw from unbearable environmental tension and is a frequent reaction among psychopathic personalities, a manner of self-imposed incarceration.

[18]It has been suggested that he might have been suffering from colitis but the psychosomatic pattern of this illness does not fit Lenin. It is more probable that he had a gastritis or a gastric neurosis—a "diagnosis" which is not incompatible with the fact that the disorder was cured through very simple dietary measures and enforced rest in prison and exile. (Compare Alexander, p. 99f, 118-128). Nothing, incidentally, is known of his digestion, but his pattern suggests that he must occasionally have suffered from constipation.

[19]This was Bismarck's pattern.

It represents, in any event, a symptom of disturbance and regression toward infantilism. Perhaps persons who elect the career of revolutionaries-in-exile must, for several reasons, be of this nature to adhere to their vocation.

Lenin had the ability to relax, once he released himself from his environment; even in the midst of work he was artful enough to reduce tension by a distraction or some humor. Yet otherwise he was always tense, preoccupied, engaged in "struggle." The normal methods of relaxation—love, art, exercise—were rarely exercised by him. On the contrary, he rejected leisure precisely because it would have "untensed" him for long periods. He was sensitive enough to enjoy the arts and his own writing style was poignant and dramatic.[20] Yet his interest in literature was limited to a few favorite authors. Though he claimed to enjoy music and occasionally liked to sing, he more or less excluded it from his life. What is known of his tastes demonstrate that he was above the appreciation level which characterized the typical *petit bourgeois* of his time, but "great art" was closed to him. Perhaps there is some truth in the allegation that he liked one of Beethoven's Sonata's because a prominent passage reminded him of the Bund's revolutionary hymn. In any event, he did not attend concerts and hardly ever went to the theater. During the many years he spent in Paris, he did not even once visit the Louvre; but he did know a third-rate painter when he saw one. He recognized beauty at times, but he did not want to admire it lest he mellow and become soft. Lenin deliberately narrowed his personality.

It is said that he possessed a *joie de vivre,* but except for a few stories about banter with his friends and his capacity to laugh heartily at jokes, he did not practice this joy very often. Krupskaya denied that in his personal relations he was as expansive as he often is described. He even forsook chess, a game at which he excelled. (Yelizarov, with whom he often played, once checkmated Emmanuel Lasker who later became world champion.)

Similarly, Lenin's attitude towards nature was ambivalent. Like Nietzsche, he often craved fresh mountain air and undoubtedly enjoyed the scenery. But he always feared that he might lose himself. He worried that his dedication to destruction might be weakened by a realization that not everything should be destroyed but that some values ought to be preserved. He was extraordinarily careful to avoid personal attachments which might inhibit his ruthless actions. This addiction to a colossal self-discipline was in part culturally conditioned. Dimitri Pisarev, the foremost "nihilist" writer of an earlier generation, proclaimed that all thinking and activity must be devoted to solving the "problem of the naked and hungry." But such dedication always has its psychological roots. Bakunin in

[20]He edited Anna Yelizarova's translation of Gerhart Hauptmann's *Die Weber.*

1870, for example, anticipating the Lenin of 1917, preached that the entire state apparatus, from the Minister of War down to the last watchman, must be destroyed. He recognized in 1862 that bloody revolutions are "invariably an evil, a terrible evil and a great misfortune," yet they are "frequently necessary . . . owing to human stupidity." (Among other afflictions, Bakunin was impotent.) Lenin had no doubts. Unable or unwilling to enjoy objects of enduring value, he found no reason to limit revolution to its natural sphere of political organization.

Lenin was by no means the dreaded "man of one book." But he certainly was a man of a single idea, and that was a negative one. In connection with this idea he exuded "elementary fanaticism, elementary trickery, elementary intelligence, elementary recklessness," according to a close observer. Axelrod commented that there is no other person who devotes twenty-four hours daily to revolution, who thinks only of revolution, and who even dreams of revolution. "How can one get along with such a man?" Axelrod asked. Axelrod was himself a highly dedicated revolutionary.

Lenin was preoccupied, in fact, with *violent* revolution. The society of the future did not particularly interest him. He was infatuated with revolution as a purpose of struggle and conflict. Within this dedication, his chief interest centered on violence and the "black arts." Lenin was not a criminal; but he preferred criminal to non-criminal means and must have derived vicarious pleasure from illicit and unavowable activities perpetrated under his incitement or command. He was a coward who dreaded physical violence and several times in his life deserted his friends when a brawl was about to occur.

Though suspicious and prudent, at several stages of his career he surrounded himself with outlaws and thieves. Rather than being the leader of proletarians, he, with a staff of middle-class intellectuals, really commanded the *Lumpenproletariat;* or should we shun Marxian terminology and say that he commanded an organized troop of over-age juvenile delinquents? Malinowsky asserted that he told Lenin of his criminal past. Allegedly Lenin replied, "For Bosheviks, such things are of no importance." Later, when he was in power and friends complained about excesses committed by terrorists, he refused to listen. Throughout his life he appealed to the lowest of instincts, especially vengeance. This "complicated primitive" (as one observer called him) understood the mass but not the individuals of which it was composed.

When Lenin entered political life at twenty-three, he was characterized by a forceful intellect, a fairly broad education, a strong capacity for work, enormous will power, and a dominant power urge. These drives were superimposed on an initial timidity and were combined with caution and a predilection for methodical procedure. His work was disciplined and accurate; he paid careful attention to detail and clarity of expression. At the same time he was given to repetition and hair-splitting. From the start, his work was polemic in nature and his arguments were dogmatic, one-sided, and self-serving. Thus, in psychoanalytical terms, Lenin's character could be described as "fixated" at the "sadistic-anal" stage, with a strong component of intellectual narcissism. This character diagnosis is consistent with Lenin's orderliness, endurance, and perseverance, opposition to "property" and ownership, spitefulness and hostility, power drive, and also (because he did not reach the genital stage) his inability to achieve inner balance and enjoy affectionate inter-personal relationships.

Lenin was arrested when he was almost twenty-six. He remained in a house of detention for almost a year. Although the conditions of his arrest were not severe, he lived in almost complete isolation. During the first period of his Siberian exile, he had contacts with local peasants and with fellow exiles, but he was intellectually isolated. Krupskaya's arrival ended his solitude, but after he moved to Germany he was again lonely for about a year. Including the years spent on the farm, he lived for close to five of his first thirty-one years in varying degrees of isolation.

His personality changed after leaving Russia. Traits were strengthened and hardened which in a weak form had been observed earlier. His demeanor remained that of a loyal and harmless citizen: the revolutionary passion stayed well concealed from such superficial observers as the French and Swiss police agents.

But the urge to quarrel predominated in his mind and his power consciousness became manifest. He increasingly concentrated on a very limited number of themes and argued and functioned within a fixed frame of reference (more accurately described as a mental strait jacket). He possessed native self-confidence. Gradually his sturdy belief in himself evolved to a sublime conviction of being always right and this was coupled with distaste for skepticism and open-mindedness.

The evidence suggests that in his isolation he had suffered a paranoid reaction. Such a reaction is a common occurrence among prisoners. As is usual in such situations, Lenin's reaction developed slowly and never quite eliminated his self-effacing manners and his personal unobtrusiveness. The reaction was strengthened gradually by Krupskaya who psychologically was closely identified with Lenin and who stimulated him in his distrust, quarrels, and claims of infallibility. The Siberian "togetherness" and Lenin's and Krup-skaya's subsequent joint involvement in organizational tasks and in power struggles created the condition of a *folie à deux*.

The most significant result of this paranoid reaction was that Lenin fell under the spell of over-valued ideas.[21] He had been committed to *the* idea for seven or more years. Younger men, who often devote themselves initially to a single subject, usually broaden their horizons as they mature. The prison and exile-induced reaction prevented this balancing of interests in Lenin's case; or, perhaps more accurately, the broadening that did occur remained within the frame of reference of the initial intellectual commitment.

Over-valued ideas are frequently dealt with in psychiatric practice and should not be confused with obsession, compulsive thinking, delusions, or hallucinations. Over-valued ideas tend to be sound and often are entirely valid. Abnormality results from the emotional value given to an idea, not necessarily from error. A deficient sense of proportion, an unwillingness to balance thoughts against values, the propensity to push an idea to absurd limits, an urge to argue constantly, and an inability to consider or accept criticism: these are some of the characteristics of over-valued ideas.

Persons who suffer from over-valued ideas frequently make invalid observations. (Affected scientists have been known to falsify experiments.) Lenin conceded that he had read Hegel only to absorb what he wanted; he disregarded those points which may have raised doubts in his mind.

Victims of over-valued ideas secretly, and sometimes unconsciously, suffer grave doubts. By concerning themselves with ever smaller details, by professing radicalism, by simplifying, and by ignoring invalidating evidence, the idea is upheld against the strongest indications that it is wrong or exaggerated in importance.

If intellectual development is based on "selective" evidence, the mind inevitably becomes deformed. The idea which is taken for granted and removed from conscious doubt engenders misconceptions, misinterpretations, and false conclusions. Lenin's mind might have enabled him to become one of mankind's great thinkers. But he was interested neither in advancing knowledge nor discovering truth. He regarded the mind as a weapon and he wielded it with considerable skill to gain advantage in struggle. The incisiveness of his pen and tongue gave to this weapon a devastating effectiveness.

If the over-valued idea is of a practical or political nature, it almost invariably leads the person to misconstrue reality and to belittle restraints, especially moral restraints.[22] Attention focuses increasingly upon the means of execution. As the ends become fuzzy and ritualistic, increasingly radical means and techniques are chosen.

[21]Oswald Bumke, *Lehrbuch der Geisteskrankheiten*, 7th ed., (München, Bergmann, 1948), p. 60ff.

[22]Unless, that is, the over-valued idea is concerned with such restraints, in which case paralysis of action ensues.

The validity of arguments opposing extreme measures is not grasped, even if those measures are self-defeating. In the end, every obstacle, fancied or real, must be destroyed by either force or ruse. The most striking aspect of this mental affliction is that the person becomes "incorrigible."

As a frequent by-product, entirely pertinent and even moderate objections to over-valued ideas arouse considerable irritation. Irritability (which may be enhanced by fatigue and worry and by such external stimuli as noise) is by no means a minor complaint: irritation is easily recorded on an electroencephalogram. It creates restlessness and affects personal relations. Lenin's irritability has been noted. It is plain that he was caught in devastating psychosomatic mechanisms with numerous feedbacks between his ideas, his psyche, and his physiology.

A vast difference distinguishes the private person from the political or public figure: the private person lives within a close group of friends and family and, negatively, his personal enemies. His psychology and his power urges are projected into this immediate entourage. The political or public figure, by contrast, becomes an organization man. He maintains formalized relationships with persons oriented toward the same power goals, as well as relations of hostility with those who hinder his movement toward his goals. The political type may be a "participant" who derives gratification from being a member of a formal (and usually stratified) group; or he may be a "leader" whose gratification is derived from the exercise of command. There are many shadings between these extremes and there are degrees of the leadership urge; extremely few men are driven to insist on an absolute power monopoly.

Lenin was a paramount example of the autocratic-despotic individual who is unable to remain a "participant." Due to the nature of things he originally joined as a participant. He soon sought co-leadership. When he realized that he was psychologically unfit to share power, he set up his own organization. He remained formally within a larger party for some time only because it was expedient and because he desired to gain control of the larger organization.

Lenin's leadership was wedded to expediency as the supreme rule. Overemphasis on functional utility is typical of persons with "psychopathological" traits. Such individuals are disinclined to worry about either the past or the future. They live rigidly within the present and for an immediate material gain. Lenin does not entirely fit this type,[23] for he lacked the hedonistic interests of the "psychopath" and, in terms of bodily pleasures, was unconcerned about personal gains. Furthermore, his extreme opportunism was

[23]According to Stefano Stefani, "I dittatori: lo Stalin di Khrushev," *Minerva Medica,* Vol. XLIX, No. 12, 1958.

united with a sense of direction towards and permanency of his goals and, despite the corruption of his means, he always absolved himself in his conscience by the nobility of his purpose. Yet he almost completely identified his personal with his political goals and operated his organization as though it was an extension of his personality. For him, gratification was political, and perhaps, *only* political. Even his family relations were permeated with politics.

The concept of "psychopathological personality" has been criticized. The syndrome perhaps can be best described as an "opportunistic personality." In any event, Lenin, with some qualifications, displayed characteristics of this personality type as it is described in psychiatric literature. He had the ability to influence and persuade, and whenever he wanted, charm people or crush those who were weaker. Self-righteous, rude, demanding, ruthless, despotic, formalistic, bureaucratic, disciplined, cunning, intolerant, stubborn, one-sided, suspicious, distant, asocial, cold-blooded, ambitious, purposive, vindictive, spiteful, a grudge-holder, a coward who was able to face danger only when he deemed it unavoidable—Lenin was his complete law unto himself and he was entirely serene about it.24 His uninterrupted role as the sole group leader reinforced each of these traits.

The Greeks taught that knowledge must be combined with ethics and virtue. True knowledge is harmonious and respects proportions. Measure and moderation must be applied to all thoughts and all actions. Wisdom consists essentially of balance in judgment. Justice recognizes the rights of all, without over or understating any rights and obligations. Lenin lacked, above all, that supreme intellectual virtue which the Greeks called *sophrosyne* and which is perhaps best translated as "humane wisdom paired with intelligence and temperance."

Lenin appeared to be unpretentious and soft-spoken. His enormous willpower was hidden behind a façade of modesty. His personality was basically cold, yet he gave an impression of warmth. His human relationships were depersonalized but he was able to feign interest in people as human beings. There rarely was a person to whom the dictum "to understand everything means to forgive everything" was less applicable; yet he managed to impress his followers as a beneficent humane leader. Because he was not a showman, friends and foes often mistook him for a poor actor.

Personality structures of this type are denoted "schizoid." Lenin

---

24Solomon tells that he once observed a comrade who had just left the hospital and still was very weak carrying Lenin's luggage. *(op. cit.,* p. 33.) There is little evidence that he ever took much care of his people, except that he wrote in 1914 to Inessa that once he spent the night with a sick comrade *(delirium tremens)* and that another time he dissuaded a comrade from committing suicide. *(Werke,* Vol. 35, p. 119).

fits the type extremely well. (A schizoid structure is not to be confused with schizophrenia.)

But there was still another side to his personality: his cyclothymic tendency to mood swings. Later in life, personalities with cyclothymic dispositions often suffer from arteriosclerosis. Lenin's depressions, which sometimes were accompanied by hypochondriac symptoms, were not very deep, but they tended to exacerbate his emotions of hatred and vengeance. The friendliness, cordiality, and cheerfulness which are typical of cyclothymics were often repressed by the schizoid components of his character, but in his personal contacts they manifested themselves in sufficient strength so that his entourage could overlook his more negative traits. Even his opponents were impressed by his apparent sincerity and did not realize that this typical cyclothymic trait was counterbalanced by the schizoid components of his make-up.

Lenin's depressive phases followed career failures and sometimes resulted from excessive fatigue. But a physician who knew a great deal about Lenin reported that his mood fluctuations, as well as his rages and subsequent breakdowns, sometimes occurred spontaneously.[25] This suggests that his psychological crises were not always initiated by objective factors, but that some failures were brought about by prior psychological disturbance. Hence Lenin displayed genuine though comparatively light symptoms of manic-depression.

Apparently he began suffering from mood cycles when he was eighteen. He had many shallow depressions until he was thirty, when this disposition was hardened by his paranoid reaction. During the *Iskra* period, his mood swings became sharper. During the latter part of 1903 and through most of 1904 he suffered a relatively deep depression which was followed, in 1905 and 1906, by a hypomanic phase with frequent acute paranoid reactions. From 1907 to 1909 he was almost constantly depressed, though in a mild way, and for the following two or three years was relatively free of trouble. He became hypomanic in 1912. During the second half of 1914 he fell into a depression which, intermittently, lasted until his return to Russia in 1917. Numerous short-lived mood swings occurred within these broader phases.

A manic phase between April and July, 1917, was followed by a short but very deep depression. After he overcame this period, he shifted into a hypomanic phase with paranoid reaction. After he had attained power he was fatigued and exhausted but apparently not depressed.

During the first two and one-half years of Lenin's rule, his

---

[25]Both traffic accidents he suffered occurred in depressive periods of his life. It must be stressed, however, that there is no evidence that Lenin had suicidal tendencies; the evidence points in the other direction.

schizoid personality predominated, though cyclic periods were quite evident. Possibly there occurred a genuine depression after the attempt on his life in 1918; a hypomanic phase occurred during 1919 and a paranoid period during 1920. He entered into a depressive phase in the fall of the same year. At that time cerebral arteriosclerosis, though as yet undiagnosed, already was affecting him. Continuous tension, possibly essential hypertension, accelerated the sclerotic process, and was in turn affected by physical deterioration.[26] Some hypomanic episodes during 1921 were characterized by flights of ideas, but from late 1921 onward depression prevailed and presently physical disease predominated.

In view of the enormous psychological impact of cerebral arteriosclerosis it is quite important to date the onset of the disease with precision. A change of Lenin's behavior is reported from the period of Inessa's death late in 1920. This blow, together with the failure of the Polish war, the collapse of war communism, the party crisis and Kronstadt, put an enormous strain on Lenin's nervous system. Presumably this strain activated the illness.

By the end of December, 1920, Lenin acknowledged his health troubles publically,[27] which means that he must have been experiencing difficulties for some time. The first really strong indication of a change in thought pattern can be discovered in a letter of May 16, 1921, in which he wrote[28]: "You can chase away the Tsar, the landholders, the capitalists. That we did. But you don't 'chase away' . . . bureaucratism. . . . You can only reduce it by patient and steady work. To excise the 'bureaucratism', . . . this is posing the question wrongly. . . . For such a problem surgery is absurd . . . only slow healing [can help], everything else is charlatanism or naiveté." This "conservative formula" was a far cry from his former destructive ideas, and it went beyond the strictures against left infantilism and Communist stupidity which he had voiced before.

By July, 1921, evidence of strongly accentuated suspiciousness abounded.[29] On or before July 8, Dr. Guetier ordered a one-month vacation, allowing him, however, to participate, two or three times a week, in important sessions. Lenin wanted to keep his hand both in party and government affairs but the party restricted him to meetings

---

[26]No blood pressure data are available. Lenin's psychosomatic pattern would fit a diagnosis of essential hypertension only late in his life, if at all. (Compare Alexander, p. 147.) Essential hypertension is chronically high blood pressure without apparent organic cause. There would have been an organic cause from about 1920. Apparently no lastingly irregular blood pressure was found in August, 1918, after he was wounded or in April, 1922, when he was operated upon. Krupskaya reported that Lenin tended to become very pale when excited.

[27]*Werke*, Vol. 32, p. 1.

[28]*Werke*, Vol. 35, p. 467.

[29]Compare *Leninskii Sbornik*, Vol. XXXV, pp. 267 and 307.

of the Politbureau.[30] Lenin left by about July 14 but felt unwell throughout August.[31] In a letter of September 25, 1921, instructing the recipient to answer him in telegraphic style, he intimated that he was suffering from mental fatigue. There are many signs that Lenin was then unable to concentrate for prolonged work. Late in October, he disclosed that his memory was failing.[32] He found it difficult to remember figures, although he formerly excelled in statistical manipulation: memory lapses with respect to numbers occur frequently in cerebral arteriosclerosis. In December, 1921, he again was forced to take sick leave, and in February, 1922, he felt so sick that he interrupted the writing of an important letter for six days. He also displayed disinclination against analyzing difficult problems[33] and investigating new questions. In all this time—and this is another typical symptom—he was very much aware of the seriousness of his illness.

It is typical of cerebral arteriosclerosis that the pre-morbid personality remains intact for a relatively long time: the disease is clearly experienced by the sick person himself, but it is not necessarily visible to others.

Lenin's cerebral arteriosclerosis remained undiagnosed for such an extended period because typical early symptoms (headaches, vertigo, insomnia, irritability, depression, rage, occasional memory lapses, and doubtful ethical judgments) had been observed throughout his entire adult life. Lenin's symptoms were interpreted as "neurasthenia", but these same symptoms also are indicative of cerebral arteriosclerosis. This similarity of symptoms was, of course, well understood at that time,[34] but whether his illness could have been properly diagnosed is debatable. The psychological and mental symptoms, together with the unending exhaustion, seem clear enough but it is a safe bet that the doctors had no opportunity to analyze Lenin's intellectual behavior.

As to the physical symptoms, his handwriting, for example, remained unimpaired for a long while. We must assume that his blood pressure was checked. It also is probable that the other classical method, an examination of the eyes to determine possible sclerotic degeneration, was resorted to. We know that Prof. Mikhail I. Auerbach examined his eyes on April 1, 1922. He discovered that Lenin's right eye was farsighted and the left eye shortsighted but not blind, as Lenin had been supposing for many years.[35] Auerbach presumably

[30]*Leninskii Sbornik*, Vol. XXXVI, p. 272.

[31]*Werke*, Vol. 35, p. 493; *Leninskii Sbornik*, Vol. XXXV, p. 274.

[32]*Werke*, Vol. 35, pp. 500 and 504.

[33]*Werke*, Vol. 35, p. 527f.

[34]Giovanni Galli, "Le sindromi nervose dell'arteriosclerosi cerebrale," *Gazetta degli Ospedali e delle Cliniche*, July 26, 1925, p. 704-708.

[35]*Pravda*, March 1, 1924, p. 2f.

also looked for diagnostic signs. He certainly did so several weeks later when, presumably after the first stroke, he examined Lenin again and Lenin asked him whether he was suffering from progressive paresis.[36] Auerbach maintained that till the very end there were no visible pathological changes in Lenin's eyes.

In October, 1922, Foerster allowed Lenin to resume working. Foerster justified this medical decision by arguing that this work constituted the last satisfaction which Lenin had in his life. This was unquestionably true but this sort of argument seems justified only when the patient's activity affects himself alone and does not have an impact on an entire nation or perhaps the entire world.

In retrospect, then, it is obvious that Lenin was suffering from what the French call *cérébrosclérose progressive* since the second half of 1920. It must be added, however, that already in 1918, a narrowing though fluctuating span of interest is to be noted. His willpower lapsed temporarily in 1918-1919, declined strongly in 1920 but recovered briefly early in 1921, only to decline precipitously after his first stroke, at which time speech disturbances also were noticed.

Lenin's intellectual faculties were not impaired substantially before his third stroke, except that his work capacity and productivity had declined sharply and his thinking was becoming both more balanced and more general. His intellectual understanding constricted slowly, and despite his isolation he not only did not lose comprehension of reality but in some ways acquired a sharper perception. Defects in judgment are very characteristic of this disease. Paradoxically, in Lenin's case, intellectual judgment actually improved, even though it became more hesistant.

Yet Lenin made an enormous error in human judgment when, to lighten his own burdens, he advanced Stalin to a key "lever of power." This was the first and only time that Lenin, perhaps in spite of himself, trusted someone to this extent.[37] He was cruelly punished by the enormous psychological pressure which Stalin exerted on Lenin's weakened constitution, to accelerate his illness and perhaps cause his ultimate incapacitation.

The diagnosis of a "dualistic" schizoid and cyclothymic personality seems quite incontrovertible from the record *as it is available*. In the overwhelming majority of cases, these two personality types occur separately, but occasionally mixed types are found.[38] Lenin, it seems, was one of these rare specimens.

Very few people succeed in holding together such a multivalent psychological endowment. What was the basis on which Lenin's

[36] Walter, p. 471.

[37] Sverdlov was never given the scope of power Stalin acquired by 1922.

[38] W. Mayer-Gross, Eliot Slater, Martin Roth, *Clinical Psychiatry*, 2nd ed. (Baltimore, Williams and Wilkins, 1960), p. 271.

extraordinarily complex personality was integrated? Contrary to the accepted theory that Lenin centered himself around his "will to power," Lenin, in a very basic sense, was a cerebral being and over-valued ideas formed the core of his integration. He once commented on a profound passage by Ludwig Feuerbach, who had ridiculed politicians who believe "the Lord merely must say, 'Let there be freedom' . . . My teachings do not recognize any gods and conse-quently do not expect any miracles in politics." Lenin extracted this passage very inadequately and added, "Feuerbach does not under-stand the revolution of 1848." He completely ignored the point about miracles in politics, which would have invalidated his revolu-tionary mystique. The overvaluation of a simple myth—complete redemption through violent revolution—constricted his human existence.

Genuine paranoid personalities practically always have pro-nounced superiority complexes and, while suffering from intense feelings of inferiority, tend to overrate themselves. Despite his supreme confidence in himself, Lenin never overrated himself and there is no shred of evidence that suggests he suffered from inferiority complexes. But there was a transference of his paranoid attitude to ideas, which he either overvalued, despised, or ignored. It has been stated that he was strongly activated by hatred for tsarism. In 1923, when he vainly tried to speak again, practically the only long word anyone understood and which he attempted repeatedly to pronounce was "rre . . . rre . . . revolu . . ." After 1917 Lenin undoubtedly rectified to some extent his erstwhile over-evaluation of revolution. But it is typical of the later phases of cerebral arteriosclerosis that the patient remembers earlier phases of his life and forgets what has happened more recently.

Bakunin once said, "I believe in nothing, I read nothing, I think of but one thing: twist the neck, twist it yet further, screw off the head, let not a trace of it remain . . ." This could be Lenin's *leit-motiv*, except that Bakunin was a "nihilist" and Lenin a man intent on power and organization. Lenin's destructive urge was paired with an urge to reach for the pinnacle of power. He once asked a companion to remember that Pisarev had cried, "Break everything! Beat every-body! Beat and destroy! What goes under is old stuff which has no right to exist. What remains whole, be blessed."

Hearing the passage, Lenin began to laugh hysterically and proclaimed, "We shall pulverize the bourgeoisie." People objected that the purpose was not destruction for destruction's sake. Lenin replied that what existed was rotten. "Consider the bourgeoisie, or democracy, if you prefer. It is doomed. By destroying it, we only fulfill the inevitable historical process."[39]

[39]Solomon, p. 89.

But Lenin really did not destroy for destruction's sake. Lenin disorganized and destroyed in order *to seize power* and, in turn, used power to disorganize and destroy. This dialectic was rooted in his psyche and driven forward by his personal needs. It prevented him from recognizing the challenge of political *creation*. Only toward the end of his life when activity and success had extinguished much of his inner rage did he begin to suspect that there were limits to the usefulness of destruction. Construction requires more than clearing the ground, if indeed revolution is suitable even to perform this preliminary job.

Curzio Malaparte suggested that Lenin considered himself to be *lupus Dei qui tollit peccata mundi.* But Lenin did not think in these terms. His psychology may better be described by paraphrasing Louis XIV's remark, "La révolution, c'est moi." Lenin was successful precisely because revolution served as challenge and response to every part of his being: he was totally absorbed in being a revolutionary for revolution's sake. Revolution was for him more than a profession; it was his talent and vocation, his genius and his destiny—his *absolutum. This* was the key to his success and the reason why his revolution proved to be a historical catastrophe.

It was a pity that sickness felled him at the exact moment when he began to revaluate his ideas. Without ceasing to be a revolutionary socialist, he was abandoning over-valuation of "rre . . . rre . . . revolu. . . ." Had he remained healthy, he would not have succeeded in making communism "work," but he might have guided his state in a more positive direction than his successors were willing and able to do.

Lenin often was accused of treason. He was called a traitor to his friends, his party, and his country; and sometimes he was accused of being an "agent" of imperial Germany. The word "agent" has many meanings; obviously Lenin always was his own agent, never acting to further the fortunes of Germany, let alone to help Wilhelm II. In a technical and legalistic sense, Lenin was a traitor because he dealt with foreign and hostile powers. In a personal and political sense, he betrayed the Social Democratic party and behaved ruthlessly and treacherously toward many of his followers. But he never betrayed *his* own cause or the party which *he* led. He was always faithful to *himself.*

For this very reason, the accusation of treason constitutes a profound misinterpretation of Lenin's psychology. The traitor constantly seeks new fathers; his shifts from one to the next loyalty are painful and accompanied by intense guilt feelings. Traitors frequently show open or repressed homosexual inclinations and their infantile background often is devoid of motherly love. Lenin, by contrast, utterly lacked homosexual components, and was attached to his mother. He was not seeking fathers but rather sons and followers. Far from suffering guilt, he enjoyed switches, and derived pleasure from meting out punishment by abandoning followers whom he found objectionable. He also favored punishing his competitors by incapacitating them. The persons or institutions with whom he collaborated were "temporary allies" on whom he did not depend psychologically and who could be destroyed once they had served his purposes. The traitor needs attachments, if only temporary ones, but Lenin was strong in his self-reliant solitude. Psychologically, he could not have been an agent, but everybody else could have been his "agent," even a German emperor. Again psychologically speaking, Lenin could never betray: betrayals always were directed against him. Lenin met the supreme criterion of leadership: he was, entirely and always, his own master.

And what was his attitude toward his own life? On December 18, 1916, he summed it up: "This is my fate. One struggle after another. . . . Yet I would not change my destiny for 'peace' with the knuckle-heads."[40]

The psychology of his successors differed from that of Lenin. Convinced of the morality of his ends, Lenin felt free to use all techniques, regardless of their immorality. He despised the ruling classes that he wanted to overthrow and it never occurred to him that the humanistic endowment of the "proletarian class" (i.e., the Communist party) which he was bringing to power would be just as unsatisfactory as that of the human group he sought to "liquidate."

So long as immoral means are used for the attainment of moral ends, or at least ends believed to be moral, the ethical justification of such means can be *argued*. But, in the case of Stalin (whom Krupskaya termed an "Asiatic monster"),[41] the Machiavellian means were used almost exclusively to satisfy ego needs, and were impressed into the service of a mania to persecute. Inevitably the party struggle degenerated into purge, terror into mass murder, and social revolution into genocide. When the original motivation vanished, Lenin's monstrous policies could not but beget worse monstrosities. In retrospect, the best that can be said about V. I. Lenin is that, had he recovered, he would have been purged by J. V. Stalin.

[40]The Russian word is *poshlyak. Sochineniya*, 4th ed., Vol. 35, p. 209.

[41]Avtorkhanov, p. 84.

SELECTED BIBLIOGRAPHY

Adoratski, V. *Vospominaniya o Lenine.* Moscow: Partinoye Izdatelstvo, 1933.

Agafonov, V. K. *Zagranichnaya Okhranka s prilozheniyem ocherka "Yevno Azef" i spiska sekretnykh sotrudnikov zagranichnoi agentury.* Petrograd: Kniga, 1918.

Aldanov-Landau, M. A. *Lénine.* (4ème édition.) Paris: Jacques Povolotzky, 1920.

———— *Lenin und der Bolschewismus.* Berlin: Ullstein, 1920.

———— *Samoubiistvo.* New York: Literaturny Fond, 1958.

Aline. *Lénine à Paris, Souvenirs inédits.* (2ème édition.) Paris: La Librairie Matérialiste, n.d.

Allendy, René. *Treason Complex.* New York: Social Sciences Publisher, 1949.

Annenkov, Y. "Vospominaniya o Lenine," *Novyi Zhurnal* (New York) No. 65, 1961.

Antonow-Owsejenko, W. *Im Jahre Siebzehn.* Berlin: Dietz, 1958.

Anweiler, Oskar. *Die Rätebewegung in Russland 1905-1921.* Leiden: E. J. Brill, 1958.

Aronson, Grigorii. *Revolyutsionnaya Yunost, Vospominaniya 1903-1917.* (Inter-University Project on the History of the Menshevik Movement, Paper No. 6.) New York, August, 1961.

Badajew, A. E. *Die Bolschewiki in der Reichsduma.* Berlin: Mopr, 1932.

Balabanov, Angelica. *Lenin.* Hannover: Verlag für Literatur und Zeitgeschichte, 1961.

Billington, James H. *Mikhailovsky and Russian Populism.* Oxford: Clarendon Press, 1958.

Berdyayev, Nicolas. *The Origin of Russian Communism.* London: Geoffrey Bles, 1948.

Bonch-Bruyevich, Michael D. *Petrograd, Erinnerungen eines Generals.* Berlin: Verlag des Ministeriums für Nationale Verteidigung, 1959.

Bonch-Bruyevich, Vladimir D. *Na boyevykh postakh Fevralskoi i Oktyabrskoi revolyutsii.* Moscow: Federatsiya, 1931.

———— *Pokusheniye na V. I. Lenina v Moskve 30go avgusta 1918 goda.* Moscow: Zhizn i Znaniye, 1924.

———— *Tri pokusheniya na Lenina.* Moscow: Federatsiya, 1930.

401

————— *V. I. Lenin v Petrograde i Moskve (1917-1920)*. Moscow: Gospolitizdat, 1956.

Browder, Robert Paul and Kerensky, Alexander F. (eds.). *The Russian Provisional Government 1917, Documents*, 3 vols. Hoover Institution Publications, Stanford, Cal.: Stanford University Press, 1961.

Buat, E. A. L. *L'armée allemande pendant la guerre de 1914 1918*. Paris: Chapelot, 1920.

Bulygin, Paul. *The Murder of the Romanovs*. London: Hutchinson & Co., 1935.

Bumke, Oswald. *Erinnerungen und Betrachtungen*. München: Richard Pflaum, 1952.

Bunyan, James. *Intervention, Civil War, and Communism in Russia*, Baltimore: Johns Hopkins Press, 1936.

Bunyan, James & Fisher, H. H. *The Bolshevik Revolution 1917-1918*. Stanford: Stanford University Press, 1934.

Busch, Tristan. *Entlarvter Geheimdienst*. Zurich: Pegasus, 1946.

Carr, Edward Hallett. *Studies in Revolution*. London: Macmillan & Co., 1950.

Chekin, A. *Vvedeniye v izucheniye professionalnogo dvizheniya*. Moscow, 1925.

Churchill, Winston S. *The Unknown War*. New York: Charles Scribner's Sons, 1931.

Chuyev, V. V. *V. I. Lenin v Samare, (1889-1893 gg.)*. Moscow: Gospolitizdat, 1960.

Daniels, Robert Vincent. *The Conscience of the Revolution*. Cambridge: Harvard University Press, 1960.

————— *Der bolschewistische Parteitag vor der Machtergreifung, 6. Parteitag—August 1917*. Moscow: Verlagsgenossenschaft Auslaendischer Arbeiter in der USSR, 1933.

Donath, Friedrich. *Lenin in Leipzig*. Berlin: Dietz Verlag, 1958.

Dridzo, V. S. and Bogdanova, K. F. (ed.). "Otzyvy N.K. Krupskoi na khudozhestvenniye proizvedeniya o V. I. Lenine," *Istoricheskii Arkhiv*, No. 4, 1958.

Engelberg, Ernst. *Revolutionäre Politik und Rote Feldpost 1878-1890*. Berlin: Akademie, 1959.

Fedosseyev, Nikolai Yevgrafovich. *Stati i pisma*. Moscow: Gospolitizdat, 1958.

Filiya, M. "Iz davnikh vstrech," *O Lenine, Sbornik Vospominanii*. Moscow: Izdaniye Pravda, 1927.

Fisher, H. H. *The Famine in Soviet Russia 1919-1923*. New York: Macmillan, 1927.

Foerster, Otfried. "Vospominaniya o bolezni i smerti Lenina," *O Lenine, Vospominaniya*, Kniga IV. Moscow: Gosudarstvennoye Izdatelstvo, 1925.

Fofanova, M. V. "O Date vozvrashcheniya V. I. Lenina iz Finlyandii v Petrograd v 1917g.," *Istoricheskii Arkhiv*, No. 2, 1958.

Footman, David. *Red Prelude*. New Haven: Yale University Press, 1945.

Fotieva, Lidiya Alexandrovna. *Iz zhizni Lenina*. Moscow: Gosizdat, 1956 & 1959.

————— *Pages from Lenin's Life*. Moscow: Foreign Languages Publishing House, 1960.

————— *Kak rabotal Vladimir Ilyich Lenin*. Moscow: Znaniye, 1956.

Futrell, Michael. "Alexander Keskuela," *Soviet Affairs No. 3, St. Antony's Papers No. 12.* London: Chatto & Windus, 1962.

———— *Northern Underground, Episodes of Russian Revolutionary Transport and Communications through Scandinavia and Finland 1863-1917,* London, Faber and Faber, 1963.

Gankin, Olga Hess & Fisher, H. H. *The Bolsheviks and the World War.* Stanford: Stanford University Press, 1940.

Geyer, Dietrich. *Lenin in der russischen Sozialdemokratie.* Köln: Böhlau, 1962.

Gorbunov, N. P. *Lenin, Erinnerungen eines Sekretärs des Rats der Volkskommissare.* Moscow-Leningrad: Verlagsgenossenschaft Ausländischer Arbeiter, 1934.

Gorky, Maxim. *Erinnerungen an Zeitgenossen,* Berlin: Aufbau Verlag, 1953.

———— *Days with Lenin,* New York, International Publishers, 1932.

Gottlieb, W. W. *Studies in Secret Diplomacy during the First World War.* London: George Allen & Unwin Ltd., 1957.

Gourfinkel, Nina. *Lénine.* Paris: Editions du Seuil, n.p., 1959.

Grinischin, Oberst D. *Die Militärische Tätigkeit Wladimir Iljitsch Lenins.* Berlin: Ministerium für Nationale Verteidigung, 1958.

Groener, Wilhelm. *Lebenserinnerungen.* Göttingen: Vandenhoeck & Ruprecht, 1957.

Gronsky, Paul P. & Astrov, Nicholas J. *The War and the Russian Government.* New Haven: Yale University Press, 1929.

Gurko, V. I. *Features and Figures of the Past.* Stanford: Stanford University Press, 1939.

Hahlweg, Werner. *Der Diktatfrieden von Brest-Litowsk 1918 und die Bolschewistische Weltrevolution.* Münster-Westfalen: Aschendorff, 1960.

———— *Lenin's Rückkehr nach Russland 1917.* Leiden: Brill, 1957.

Haimson. Leopold H. *The Russian Marxists and the Origins of Bolshevism.* Cambridge: Harvard University Press, 1955.

Hill, Christopher. *Lenin and the Russian Revolution.* New York: Macmillan, 1950.

Hill, Elizabeth & Mudie, Doris (ed.). *Letters of Lenin.* London: Chapman and Hall, 1937.

Hoelzle, Erwin. *Lenin 1917, Die Geburt der Revolution aus dem Kriege.* München: R. Oldenbourg, 1957.

Institut für Marxismus-Leninismus beim ZK der SED (ed.). *Roter Oktober 1917.* Berlin: Dietz Verlag, 1957.

Institut Marxizma-Leninizma. *Lénine, tel qu'il fut. Souvenirs de contemporains.* (Editions en Langues Etrangères, 2 vols.) 1958 and 1959.

Istorik. "O Predkakh Lenina," *Novyi Zhurnal* (New York), No. 63, 1961.

Ivankov, A. G. *Lenin v sibirskoi ssylke, (1897-1900).* Moscow: Sotsekgiz, 1962.

Ivanski, A. I. (ed.). *Molodiye Gody V. I. Lenina, po vospominaniyam sovremennikov i dokumentam.* (2nd edition.) Moscow: Molodaya Gvardia, 1958.

Karpovich, Michael. "A Forerunner of Lenin: P.N. Tkachev," *Review of Politics,* Vol. VI, No. 3, 1944.

Katkov, George. "The Assassination of Count Mirbach," *Soviet Affairs No. 3, St. Antony's Papers No. 12.* London: Chatto & Windus, 1962.

———— "The Kronstadt Rising," *Soviet Affairs No. 2, St. Antony's Papers No. 6.* London: Chatto & Windus, 1959.

Kautsky, Karl. *Die Soziale Revolution, I, Sozialreform und Soziale Revolution.* Berlin: Vorwärts, 1902.

———— *Die Soziale Revolution. II. Am Tage nach der Sozialen Revolution.* Berlin: Vorwärts, 1902.

———— *Ein Leben für den Sozialismus, Erinnerungen an Karl Kautsky.* Hannover: Dietz, 1954.

Koenen, Wilhelm. *Meine Begegnungen mit Lenin.* Berlin: Dietz, 1957.

Korostowetz, V. K. *Neue Väter- Neue Söhne.* Berlin: Verlag für Kulturpolitik, 1926.

Krupskaya, Nadyezhda K. *Ma vie avec Lénine, 1893-1917.* Paris: Payot, 1933.

———— *Memories of Lenin.* London: Lawrence and Wishart Ltd., 1942.

———— *Reminiscences of Lenin.* Moscow: Foreign Languages Publishing House, 1959.

Krylenko, N. V. *Za pyat let, 1918-1922 g.g., Obvinitelniye rechi.* Moscow-Petrograd: Gosudarstvennoye Izdatelstvo, 1923.

Kucharzewski, Jan. *The Origins of Modern Russia.* New York: The Polish Institute of Arts and Sciences in America, 1948.

Kulczycki, Ludwik. *Geschichte der Russischen Revolution, 3 vols.* Gotha: F. A. Perthes, 1910-1914.

Laporte, Maurice. *Histoire de l'Okhrana.* Paris: Payot, 1935.

Lazitch, Branko. *Lénine et la IIIe Internationale.* Paris: Editions de la Baconnière, 1951.

Lenin, V. I. *Sochineniya* (3rd edition.) Moscow: Institut Marxisma-Leninizma, 1935-1937.

———— *Sochineniya.* (4th edition.) Moscow: Institut Marxizma-Leninizma, 1952-1957.

———— *Leninskii Sbornik, 36* vols. Moscow: Institut Marxizma-Leninizma, 1924-1959.

———— *Sämtliche Werke.* (incomplete.) Wien-Berlin-Zurich: Verlag für Literatur und Politik, 1928-1934.

———— *Werke.* 37 vols., Berlin: Dietz, 1959-1962.

———— *Selected Works.* New York: International Publishers, 1943.

———— *Aus dem Philosophischen Nachlass, Exzerpte und Randglossen.* Berlin: Dietz Verlag, 1958.

———— *Clausewitz' Werk "Vom Kriege", Auszüge und Randglossen,* Berlin: Ministerium für Verteidigung, 1957.

———— *O Literature i iskusstve.* Moscow: Gosizdat, 1957.

———— "The Right of Nations to Self-Determination," *Selected Writings.* New York: International Publishers, 1951.

———— *Ueber Krieg, Armee und Militärwissenschaft. 3* vols. Berlin: Ministerium für Nationale Verteidigung, 1958.

———— *Lenin wie wir ihn kannten, Erinnerungen alter Kampfgefährten,* Berlin: Dietz Verlag, 1956.

Lermolo, Elizabeth. *Face of a Victim.* New York: Harper, 1955.

Lopukhin, A. A. *Nastoyashcheye i budushcheye russkoi politsii.* Moscow: Sablin, 1907.

Lozgachev-Elizarov, Gregorii Y. *Nezabyvayemoye.* Saratov: Saratovskoye Knizhnoye Izdatelstvo, 1959.

Lunacharsky, A. V. *Vospominaniya o Lenine.* Moscow: Partinoye Izdatelstvo, 1933.

Luxemburg, Rosa. *The Russian Revolution* (with an introduction by Bertram D. Wolfe), New York: Workers Age Publishers, 1940.

Malkov, P. D. *Zapiski Komendanta Moskovskogo Kremlya.* Moscow: Molodaya Gvardiya, 1959.

Masaryk, Thomas Garrigue. *The Spirit of Russia,* 2 vols. London: George Allen & Unwin Ltd., 1955. (reprint)

Maximoff, G. P. *The Guillotine at Work, Twenty Years of Terror in Russia (Data and Documents).* Chicago: Alexander Berkman Fund, 1940.

Melgunov, S. P. *Legenda o separatnom mire, (kanun revolyutsii).* Paris: 1957.

———— *Zolotoi nemetskii klyuch bolshevikov.* Paris: La Maison du Livre Etranger, 1940.

Menshchikov, Leonid Petrovich. *Okhrana i revolyutsiya, k istorii tainykh politicheskikh organisatsii v Rossii.* 3 vols. Moscow: Katorga i Ssylka, 1925-1932.

Meshcheryakov, N. L. (ed.). *O Lenine, Vospominaniya,* 4 vols. Moscow: Gosizdat, 1925.

Mstislavski, S. "Zapiski o Lenine," *O Lenine,* Vol. 4. Moscow: Gosizdat, 1925.

Mushtukov, V. Y. and Nikitin, P. Y. *Zdes zhil i rabotal Lenin.* Leningrad: Lenizdat, 1961.

Neubauer, Helmut. *München und Moskau 1918/1919.* München: Isarverlag, 1958.

Nicolai, Oberst W. *Geheime Mächte.* Leipzig: Koehler, 1925.

Nikitine, B. V. *The Fatal Years, Fresh Revelations on a Chapter of Underground History.* London: William Hodge and Company, 1938.

Nikolayevsky, B. "Pismo v redaktsiyu," *Sotsialisticheskii Vestnik.* (New York), No. 5, May, 1961.

Oldenbourg, Serge. *Le coup d'état bolchéviste.* Paris: Payot, 1929.

———— *O Lenine, Sbornik Vospominanii.* Moscow: Izdaniye Gazety Pravda, 1927.

———— *O Lenine, Vospominaniya zarubezhnykh sovremennikov.* Moscow: Gospolitizdat, 1962.

Pianzola, Maurice. *Lénine en Suisse.* N. P. Librairie Nouvelle, n.d.

Piatnitsky, O. *Memoirs of a Bolshevik.* New York: International Publishers, n.d.

Pipes, Richard. *Social Democracy and the St. Petersburg Labor Movement, 1885-1897.* Cambridge: Mass., Harvard University Press, 1963.

———— *The Formation of the Soviet Union; Communism and Nationalism 1917-1923,* Cambridge, Harvard University Press, 1954.

Podvoisky, Nikolai I. *et al. Ueber Lenins militärische Tätigkeit 1917-1920.* Berlin: Verlag des Ministeriums für Nationale Verteidigung, 1957.

Pospelov, P. N. (ed.). *Vladimir Ilyich Lenin, Biografiya.* Moscow: Gospolitizdat, 1960.

Preobrazhenski, E. "Vozhd partii," *V. I. Lenin (Ulyanov), Biograficheskii Sbornik.* Kiev: Izdatelstvo "Bolshevik," 1923.

Pushkaryev, S. "Tainyi soyuz Lenina s Wilgelmom II," *Novoye Russkoye Slovo.* (New York. Jan. 21-24, 1962.)

Reichskriegsministerium. *Die Rückführung des Ostheeres.* Berlin: Mittler, 1936.

Rein, Gustav Adolf. *Die Revolution in der Politik Bismarcks.* Berlin: Muster-schmidt, 1957.

Reshetar, John S. *A Concise History of the Communist Party of the Soviet Union.* New York: Praeger, 1960.

Ronge, Max. *Kriegs- und Industrie-Spionage.* Wien: Amalthea, 1930.

Rozanov, V. "Iz vospominanii o Vladimire Iliche," *O Lenine, Vospominaniya,* Moscow: Gosudarstvennoye Izdatelstvo, 1925.

Rutych, N. *Le parti communiste au pouvoir en U.R.S.S. 1917-1960.* Paris: La Table Ronde, 1961.

Ryazanov D. (ed.). *Marx-Engels-Archiv.* Vol. I, Frankfurt am Main: 1927.

Schaginjan, Marietta S. *Die Familie Uljanow.* Berlin: Verlag Kultur und Fort-schritt, 1959.

Schapiro, Leonard. *The Origin of the Communist Autocracy, Political Opposi-tion in the Soviet State, First Phase 1917-1922.* London: G. Bell and Sons, 1955.

———— *The Communist Party of the Soviet Union.* New York: Randon House, 1959.

Scheibert, Peter. "Ueber Lenins Anfänge," *Historische Zeitschrift,* Vol. 182.

Scheidemann, Philipp. *Memoiren eines Sozialdemokraten,* 2 vols. Dresden: Carl Reissner, 1928.

Schilling, Victor. "Vor der einbalsamierten Leiche Lenins," *Die Umschau, Illustrierte Wochenschrift über die Fortschritte in Wissenschaft und Technik.* Frankfurt am Main: J. H. Bechthold, 1927.

Serebrov, Alexander (A. N. Tikhonov.) *Vremya i lyudi.* (1898-1905.) Moscow: Gosizdat, 1955.

Serge, Victor. *Memoires d'un Révolutionnaire.* Paris: Club des Editeurs, Edi-tions du Seuil, 1957.

Shcheprov, S. V. *Vydayushchiisya revolyutsioner, N.Y. Fedosseyev.* Moscow: Gos. Izdatelstvo Polit. Literatury, 1958.

Shebeko, Nikolai Ignatevich. *Chronique du mouvement socialiste en Russie 1878-1887.* St. Petersburg: Imprimerie officielle du ministère de l'intér-ieur, 1890.

Shotman, A. *Wie der Funke zur Flamme wurde, Aufzeichnungen eines alten Bolschewiken.* Moskau-Leningrad: Verlagsgenossenschaft Ausländischer Arbeiter in der UdSSR, 1935.

Shub, David. *Lenin,* Garden City, N.Y.: Doubleday, 1948.

———— "Lenin i Wilgelm II," *Novyi Zhurnal* (New York), No. 57, 1959.

———— 'O predkakh Lenina," *Novoye Russkoye Slovo* (New York, April 23, 1961.)

———— "Po povodu stati N. Valentinova i pisma v redaktsiyu 'Istorika'," *Novyi Zhurnal* (New York), No. 63, 1961.

Solomon, Georgii Alexandrovich. *Lenin i ego semya (Ulyanovy).* Paris: Imp. des Travailleurs Intellectuels, 1931.

Sorin, Vladimir. "Bolshoi Dom," *O Lenine, Sbornik Vospominanii.* Moscow: Izdaniye Gazety Pravda, 1927.

Spiridovich, Alexandre Ivanovich. *Histoire du terrorisme russe 1886-1917.* Paris: Payot, 1930.

_____ *Istoriya Bolshevizma v Rossii ot vozniknoveniya do zakhvata vlasti, 1883-1903-1917.* Paris: Franko-Russkaya Pechatj, 1922.

Spiro, George. *Marxism and the Bolshevik State.* New York: Red Star Press, 1951.

Stalin, J. V. *Sochineniya.* Moscow: Institut Marxizma-Leninizma, 1946-1949.

_____ *Works.* Moscow: Institut Marxizma-Leninizma, 1946-1952.

Stassova, Yelena Dmitriyevna. *Stranitsy zhizni i borby.* Moscow: Gos. Izdatelstvo Polit. Literatury, 1957.

Stassova, Y. D., Selikson-Bobrovskaya, Z. S., and Itkina, A. M. (ed.). *Frauen der Revolution, Portraits hervorragender Bolschewikinnen.* Berlin: Dietz, 1960.

Stern, Leo. *Der Einfluss der grossen sozialistischen Oktoberrevolution auf Deutschland und die deutsche Arbeiterbewegung.* Berlin: Rütten & Loening, 1958.

Streb, Xaver. *Lenin in Deutschland.* (2nd edition.) Berlin: Dietz, 1960.

Sukhanov, N. N. *The Russian Revolution 1917, A Personal Record.* New York: Oxford University Press, 1955.

Tarassov-Rodionov. *La Révolution de février 1917.* Paris: Gallimard, 1930.

Thun, Alphons. *Geschichte der revolutionären Bewegungen in Russland.* n.p., Duncker & Humblot, 1883.

Treadgold, Donald W. *Lenin and His Rivals.* New York: Praeger. 1955.

Trotsky, Leon. *Lenin.* New York: Blue Ribbon Books, 1925.

_____ *Stalin.* New York: Grosset & Dunlap, no date (copyright 1941).

_____ *Trotsky's Diary in Exile 1935.* Cambridge: Mass., Harvard University Press, 1958.

Tsiavlovsky, M. A. *Bolsheviki; dokumenty po istorii bolshevizma s 1903 po 1916 god byvsh. Moskovskogo Okhrannago Otdeleniya.* Moscow: Zadruga, 1918.

Tyusin, F. S. *Die militärische Tätigkeit der Bolschewiki in den Jahren 1905 bis 1907.* Berlin: Verlag des Ministeriums für Nationale Verteidigung, 1956.

U. S. Congress. Eighty-Sixth Congress, Second Session, House of Representatives, Committee on Un-American Activities. *Facts on Communism, The Soviet Union from Lenin to Khrushchev,* Vol. II. Washington, D.C.: United States Government Printing Office, 1960. (Most of this text was written by David Dallin.)

_____ *Unvergesslicher Lenin, Erinnerungen deutscher Genossen.* Berlin: Dietz. 1960.

Valentinov, N. (Volsky). "O predkakh Lenina i ego biografiyakh," *Novyi Zhurnal* (New York), No. 61, 1960.

_____ "Vstrecha Lenina s Marxizmom," *Novyi Zhurnal* (New York), No. 53, 1958.

_____ *Vstrecha s Leninym.* New York: Chekhov Publishing House, 1953.

Venturi, Franco. *Roots of Revolution.* New York: Knopf, 1960.

Vogt, Oskar. "Erster Bericht über die Arbeiten des Moskauer Staatsinstituts für Hirnforschung," *Journal für Psychologie und Neurologie,* Vol. 40, 1930, pp. 108-118.

Waldman, Eric. *The Spartacist Uprising.* Milwaukee: Marquette University Press, 1958.

Walter, Gérard. *Lénine*. Paris: Julliard, 1950.

Wetter, Gustav A. *Dialectical Materialism*. New York: Praeger, 1960.

Wolfe, Bertram D. *Three Who Made a Revolution*. New York: The Dial Press, 1948.

———— *Khrushchev and Stalin's Ghost, Text, Background and Meaning of Khrushchev's Secret Report to the Twentieth Congress on the Night of February 24-25, 1956*. New York: Praeger, 1957.

———— "Lenin and Inessa Armand," *Slavic Review*, Vol. XXII, No. 1, March 1963.

Zeman, Z. A. B. *Germany and the Revolution in Russia 1915-1918, Documents from the Archives of the German Foreign Ministry*. London: Oxford University Press, 1958.

Zetkin, Clara. *Erinnerungen an Lenin*. Berlin: Dietz Verlag, 1957.

INDEX

STEFAN T. POSSONY

Dr. Possony received his degree during study in Vienna and served with the psychological warfare section of the French Foreign Office during World War II. He came to the United States soon after the war and studied in the Institute for Advanced Study at Princeton University, becoming a professor of international relations at Georgetown University shortly thereafter. He has lectured at the National War College, the Naval War College and the Air University, and is an associate of the Foreign Policy Research Institute at the University of Pennsylvania. He is the author of numerous studies and books dealing with political warfare and semantics, including *Tomorrow's War, Strategic Air Power, Reflections on the Russian Revolution, A Century of Conflict,* and several government documents analyzing Communist programs and tactics. He is currently political studies director at the Hoover Institution on War, Revolution and Peace at Stanford University.